Fundamentals of CORPORATE FINANCE

Parrino • Kidwell

Volume 1

Selected Chapters

Customized for UMUC • MGMT 640

Financial Decision Making for Managers

To order books or for customer service, please call 1(800)-CALL-WILEY (225-5945).

Printed in the United States of America.

ISBN 978-0-470-46329-1

Printed and bound by Walsworth Publishing Company.
10 9 8 7 6 5 4 3 2 1

CONTENTS

Part 1 Introduction

CHAPTER 1 The Financial Manager and the Firm 1

Part 2 Foundations

CHAPTER 3 Financial Statements, Cash Flows, and Taxes 53

CHAPTER 4 Analyzing Financial Statements 85

Part 3 Valuation of Future Cash Flows and Risk

CHAPTER 5 The Time Value of Money 131

CHAPTER 6 Discounted Cash Flows and Valuation 167

CHAPTER 7 Risk and Return 209

Part 4 Capital Budgeting Decisions

CHAPTER 10 The Fundamentals of Capital Budgeting 312

Appendices A-B 727

Fundamentals of Corporate Finance

Robert Parrino

Lamar Savings Centennial Professor of Finance
University of Texas at Austin

David S. Kidwell

Professor of Finance and Dean Emeritus
University of Minnesota

WILEY
John Wiley & Sons, Inc.

ASSOCIATE PUBLISHER	Judith Joseph
SENIOR DEVELOPMENTAL EDITOR	Marian D. Provenzano
EXECUTIVE MARKETING MANAGER	Amy Scholz
SENIOR PRODUCTION EDITOR	William A. Murray
ASSOCIATE EDITOR	Brian Kamins
SENIOR ILLUSTRATION EDITOR	Sigmund Malinowski
ASSOCIATE PHOTO EDITOR	Sheena Goldstein
SENIOR MEDIA EDITOR	Allie K. Morris
SENIOR DESIGNER	Kevin Murphy
INTERIOR DESIGN	Nancy Field
COVER DESIGN	David Levy
COVER PHOTO	Bill Frymire/Masterfile

The CFA Institute Materials used in this book are reproduced and republished from the CFA Program Materials with permission from the CFA Institute. The authors and publisher are grateful for permission to use this material.

This book was set in Times Ten Roman by Aptara®, Inc. and printed and bound by R.R. Donnelley.

This book is printed on acid free paper. ∞

To order books or for customer service please call 1-800-CALL WILEY (225-5945).

ISBN 978-0-471-27056-0

Printed in the United States of America

10 9 8 7 6 5 4 3 2 1

THE FINANCIAL MANAGER AND THE FIRM

CHAPTER

1

LEARNING OBJECTIVES

1. Identify the key financial decisions facing the financial manager of any business firm.
2. Identify the basic forms of business organization used in the United States, and review their respective strengths and weaknesses.
3. Describe the typical organization of the financial function in a large corporation.
4. Explain why maximizing the current value of the firm's stock is the appropriate goal for management.
5. Discuss how agency conflicts affect the goal of maximizing stockholder value.
6. Explain why ethics is an appropriate topic in the study of corporate finance.

©AP/Wide World Photos

On February 25, 2007, TXU Corporation, a Texas-based electric utility company, announced that a group of investors had offered to acquire the company in a leveraged buyout—a transaction in which the purchaser uses a lot of debt. The investor group, led by the leveraged buyout firms Kohlberg Kravis Roberts & Co. (KKR) and Texas Pacific Group (TPG), was offering $69.25 per share for all of the outstanding shares of TXU. Only a month earlier, the stock had been trading at $54.30 per share. The price offered by KKR and TPG represented a 27.5 percent premium over this recent market price. With a total value of $46 billion, this was the largest leveraged buyout announced up to that point in time.

How did KKR and TPG arrive at this high offering price, and how could they justify it? Surely they did not make the offer planning to lose money. In fact, even though they were paying $69.25 per share, KKR and TPG still expected to earn more than 20 percent per year on their investment over the following five years. By focusing TXU's investment activities, increasing the efficiency of operations, and using a great deal of debt financing, the new owners planned to increase the value of the cash flows TXU would generate.

Investors in leveraged buyouts use many of the concepts covered in this chapter and elsewhere in this book to create the most possible value. They begin by structuring the compensation of firm managers to provide them with incentives to focus on value creation. Managers create value by investing only in projects whose benefits exceed their costs, managing the assets of the company as efficiently as possible, and financing the company with the least expensive combination of debt and equity. This chapter introduces you to the key financial aspects of these activities, and the remainder of the book fills in many of the details.

CHAPTER PREVIEW

This book provides an introduction to corporate finance. In it we focus on the responsibilities of the financial manager, who oversees the accounting and treasury functions and sets the overall financial strategy for the firm. We pay special attention to the financial manager's role as a decision maker. To that end, we emphasize the mastery of fundamental finance concepts and the use of a set of financial tools, which will result in sound financial decisions that create value for stockholders. These financial concepts and tools apply not only to business organizations but also to other venues, such as government entities, not-for-profit organizations, and sometimes even your own personal finances.

We open this chapter by discussing the three major types of decisions that a financial manager makes. We then describe common forms of business organization. After next discussing the major responsibilities of the financial manager, we explain why maximizing the price of the firm's stock is an appropriate goal for a financial manager. We go on to describe the conflicts of interest that can arise between stockholders and managers and the mechanisms that help align the interests of these two groups. Finally, we discuss the importance of ethical conduct in business.

1.1 The Role of the Financial Manager

The financial manager is responsible for making decisions that are in the best interests of the firm's owners, whether the firm is a start-up business with a single owner or a billion-dollar corporation owned by thousands of stockholders. The decisions made by the financial manager or owner should be one and the same. In most situations this means that the financial manager should make decisions that maximize the value of the owners' stock. This helps maximize the owners' **wealth**. Our underlying assumption in this book is that most people who invest in businesses do so because they want to increase their wealth. In the following discussion, we describe the responsibilities of the financial manager in a new business in order to illustrate the types of decisions that such a manager makes.

wealth
the economic value of the assets someone possesses

Stakeholders

Before we discuss the new business, you may want to look at Exhibit 1.1, which shows the cash flows between a firm and its owners (in a corporation, the stockholders) and various stakeholders. A **stakeholder** is someone other than an owner who has a claim on the cash flows of the firm: *managers,* who want to be paid salaries and performance bonuses; *creditors,* who want to be paid interest and principal; *employees,* who want to be paid wages; *suppliers,* who want to be paid for goods or services; and the *government,* which wants the firm to pay taxes. Stakeholders may have interests that differ from those of the owners. When this is the case, they may exert pressure on management to make decisions that benefit them. We will return to these types of conflict of interest later in the book. For now, though, we are primarily concerned with the overall flow of cash between the firm and its stockholders and stakeholders.

stakeholder
anyone other than an owner (stockholder) with a claim on the cash flows of a firm, including employees, suppliers, creditors, and the government

It's All about Cash Flows

To produce its products or services, a new firm needs to acquire a variety of assets. Most will be long-term assets or **productive assets**. Productive assets can be tangible assets, such as equipment, machinery, or a manufacturing facility, or intangible assets, such as patents, trademarks, technical expertise, or other types of intellectual capital.

productive assets
the tangible and intangible assets a firm uses to generate cash flows

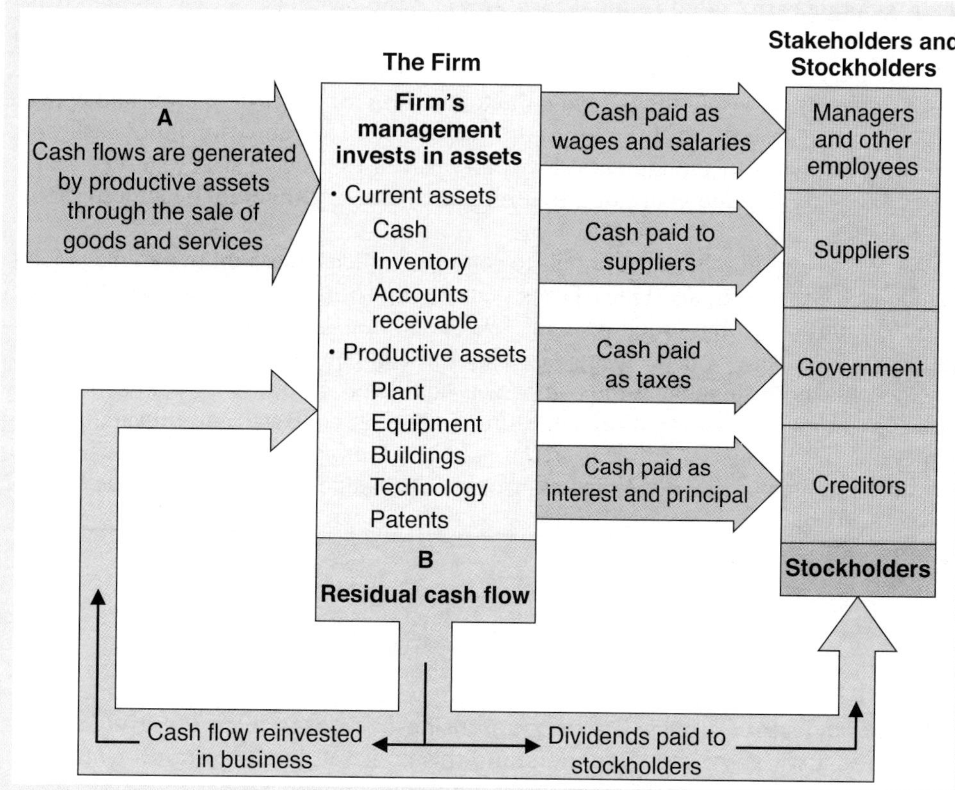

Exhibit 1.1
Cash Flows Between the Firm and Its Stakeholders and Owners
A. Making business decisions is all about cash flows, because only cash can be used to pay bills and buy new assets. Cash initially flows into the firm as a result of the sale of goods or services. The firm uses these cash inflows in a number of ways: to invest in assets, to pay wages and salaries, to buy supplies, to pay taxes, and to repay creditors.
B. Any cash that is left over (residual cash flows), can be reinvested in the business or paid as dividends to stockholders.

Regardless of the type of asset, the firm tries to select assets that will generate the greatest profits. The decision-making process through which the firm purchases long-term productive assets is called *capital budgeting,* and it is one of the most important decision processes in a firm.

Once the firm has selected its productive assets, it must raise money to pay for them. *Financing decisions* are concerned with the ways in which firms obtain and manage long-term financing to acquire and support their productive assets. There are two basic sources of funds: debt and equity. Every firm has some equity because equity represents ownership in the firm. It consists of capital contributions by the owners plus earnings that have been reinvested in the firm. In addition, most firms borrow from a bank or issue some type of long-term debt to finance productive assets.

After the productive assets have been purchased and the business is operating, the firm will try to produce products at the lowest possible cost while maintaining quality. This means buying raw materials at the lowest possible cost, holding production and labor costs down, keeping management and administrative costs to a minimum, and seeing that shipping and delivery costs are competitive. In addition, the firm must manage its day-to-day finances so that it will have sufficient cash on hand to pay salaries, purchase supplies, maintain inventories, pay taxes, and cover the myriad of other expenses necessary to run a business. The management of current assets, such as money owed by customers who purchase on credit, inventory, and current liabilities, such as money owed to suppliers, is called *working capital management.*[1]

A firm generates cash flows by selling the goods and services it produces. A firm is successful when these cash inflows exceed the cash outflows needed to pay operating expenses, creditors, and taxes. After meeting these obligations, the firm can pay

[1]From accounting, *current assets* are assets that will be converted into cash within a year; and *current liabilities* are liabilities that must be paid within one year.

residual cash flows
the cash remaining after a firm has paid operating expenses and what it owes creditors and in taxes; can be paid to the owners as a cash dividend or reinvested in the business

the remaining cash, called **residual cash flows**, to the owners as a cash dividend, or it can reinvest the cash in the business. The reinvestment of residual cash flows back into the business to buy more productive assets is a very important concept. If these funds are invested wisely, they provide the foundation for the firm to grow and provide larger residual cash flows in the future for the owners. The reinvestment of cash flows (earnings) is the most fundamental way that businesses grow in size. Exhibit 1.1 illustrates how the revenue generated by productive assets ultimately becomes residual cash flow.

bankruptcy
legally declared inability of an individual or a company to pay its creditors

A firm is unprofitable when it fails to generate sufficient cash inflows to pay operating expenses, creditors, and taxes. Firms that are unprofitable over time will be forced into **bankruptcy** by their creditors if the owners do not shut them down first. In bankruptcy the company will be reorganized or the company's assets will be liquidated, whichever is more valuable. If the company is liquidated, creditors are paid in a priority order according to the structure of the firm's financial contracts and prevailing bankruptcy law. If anything is left after all creditor and tax claims have been satisfied, which usually does not happen, the remaining cash, or residual value, is distributed to the owners.

BUILDING INTUITION

Cash Flows Matter Most to Investors

Cash is what investors ultimately care about when making an investment. The value of any asset—stocks, bonds, or a business—is determined by the future cash flows it will generate. To understand this concept, just consider how much you would pay for an asset from which you could never expect to obtain any cash flows. Buying such an asset would be like giving your money away. It would have a value of exactly zero. Conversely, as the expected cash flows from an investment increase, you would be willing to pay more and more for it.

Three Fundamental Decisions in Financial Management

Based on our discussion so far, we can see that financial managers are concerned with three fundamental decisions when running a business:

1. *Capital budgeting decisions:* Identifying the productive assets the firm should buy.
2. *Financing decisions:* Determining how the firm should finance or pay for assets.
3. *Working capital management decisions:* Determining how day-to-day financial matters should be managed so that the firm can pay its bills, and how surplus cash should be invested.

Exhibit 1.2 shows the impact of each decision on the firm's balance sheet. We briefly introduce each decision here and discuss them in greater detail in later chapters.

CAPITAL BUDGETING DECISIONS

A firm's capital budget is simply a list of the productive (capital) assets management wants to purchase over a budget cycle, typically one year. The capital budgeting decision process addresses which productive assets the firm should purchase and how much money the firm can afford to spend. As shown in Exhibit 1.2, capital budgeting decisions affect the asset side of the balance sheet and are concerned with a firm's long-term investments. Capital budgeting decisions, as we mentioned earlier, are

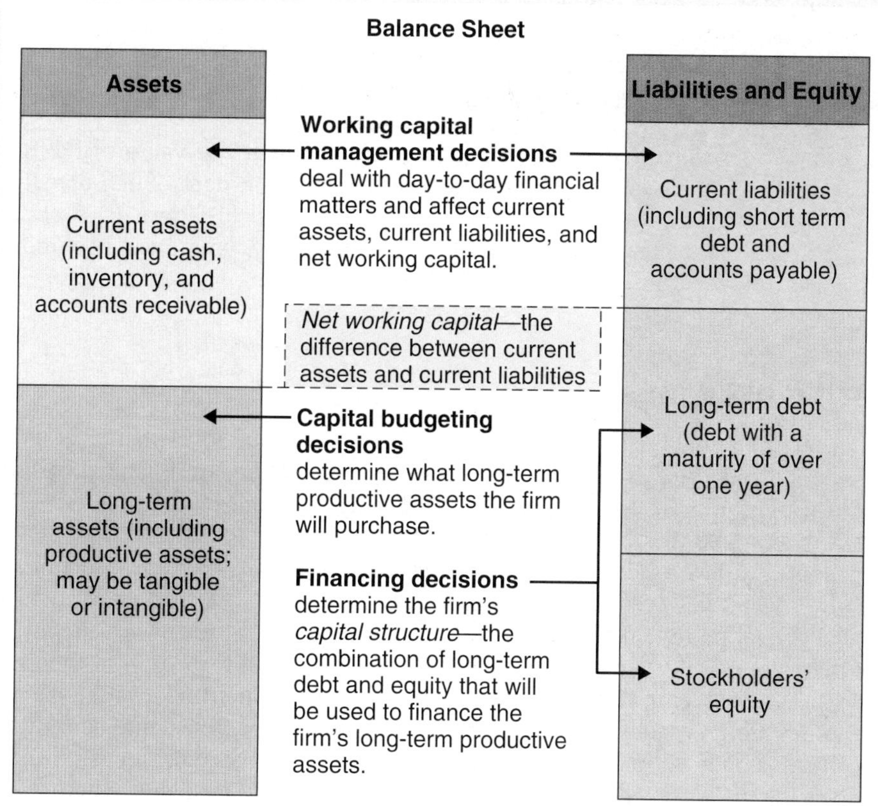

Exhibit 1.2
How the Financial Manager's Decisions Affect the Balance Sheet
Financial managers are concerned with three fundamental types of decisions: capital budgeting decisions, financing decisions, and working capital management decisions. Each type of decision has a direct and important effect on the firm's balance sheet—in other words, on the firm's profitability.

among management's most important decisions. Over the long run, they have a large impact on the firm's success or failure. The reason is twofold. First, capital assets generate most of the cash flows for the firm. Second, capital assets are long term in nature. Once they are purchased, the firm owns them for a long time, and they may be hard to sell without taking a financial loss.

The fundamental question in capital budgeting is this: Which productive assets should the firm purchase? A capital budgeting decision may be as simple as a movie theater's decision to buy a popcorn machine or as complicated as Boeing's decision to invest more than $6 billion to design and build the 7E7 *Dreamliner* passenger jet. Capital investments may also involve the purchase of an entire business, such as IBM's purchase of PricewaterhouseCoopers' (PwC) management consulting practice.

Regardless of the project, a good capital budgeting decision is one in which the benefits are worth more to the firm than the cost of the asset. For example, IBM paid around $3.5 billion for PwC's consulting practice. Presumably, IBM expects that the investment will produce a stream of cash flows worth more than that. Suppose IBM estimates that in terms of the current market value, the future cash flows from the PwC acquisition are worth $5 billion. Is the acquisition a good deal for IBM? The answer is yes because the value of the cash flow benefits from the acquisition exceeds the cost by $1.5 billion ($5.0 billion – $3.5 billion). If the PwC acquisition works out as planned, the value of IBM will be increased by $1.5 billion!

Not all investment decisions are successful. Just open the business section of any newspaper on any day, and you will find stories of bad decisions. For example, Walt Disney Studios' uninspiring movie *The Country Bear* turned out to be a dog. The film cost $40 million to make and took in about $5 million on its opening weekend. With a box office flop, it is unlikely that the movie's overall cash flow will be worth more than its $40 million cost. When, as in this case, the cost exceeds the value of the future cash flows, the project will decrease the value of the firm by that amount.

BUILDING INTUITION

Sound Investments Are Those Where the Value of the Benefits Exceeds Their Costs

Financial managers should invest in a capital project only if the value of its future cash flows exceeds the cost of the project (benefits > cost). Such investments increase the value of the firm and thus increase stockholders' (owners') wealth. This rule holds whether you're making the decision to purchase new machinery, build a new plant, or buy an entire business.

FINANCING DECISIONS

Financing decisions concern how firms raise cash to pay for their investments, as shown in Exhibit 1.2. Productive assets, which are long term in nature, are financed by long-term borrowing, equity investment, or both. Financing decisions involve trade-offs between advantages and disadvantages to the firm.

A major advantage of debt financing is that debt payments are tax deductible for many corporations. However, debt financing increases a firm's risk because it creates a contractual obligation to make periodic interest payments and, at maturity, to repay the amount that is borrowed. Contractual obligations must be paid regardless of the firm's operating cash flow, even if the firm suffers a financial loss. If the firm fails to make payments as promised, it defaults on its debt obligation and could be forced into bankruptcy.

capital structure
the mix of debt and equity that is used to finance a firm

capital markets
financial markets where equity and debt instruments with maturities greater than one year are traded

In contrast, equity has no maturity, and there are no guaranteed payments to equity investors. In a corporation, the board of directors has the right to decide whether dividends should be paid to stockholders. This means that if the board decides to omit or reduce a dividend payment, the firm will not be in default. Unlike interest payments, however, dividend payments to stockholders are not tax deductible.

The mix of debt and equity on the balance sheet is known as a firm's **capital structure**. The term *capital structure* is used because long-term funds are considered capital, and these funds are raised in **capital markets**—financial markets where equity and debt instruments with maturities greater than one year are traded.

BUILDING INTUITION

Financing Decisions Affect the Value of the Firm

How a firm is financed with debt and equity affects the value of the firm. The reason is that the mix between debt and equity affects the taxes the firm pays and the probability that the firm will go bankrupt. The financial manager's goal is to determine the combination of debt and equity that minimizes the cost of financing the firm.

WORKING CAPITAL MANAGEMENT DECISIONS

net working capital
the dollar difference between current assets and current liabilities

Management must also decide how to manage the firm's current assets, such as cash, inventory, and accounts receivable, and its current liabilities, such as trade credit and accounts payable. The dollar difference between current assets and current liabilities is called **net working capital**, as shown in Exhibit 1.2. As mentioned earlier, working capital management is the day-to-day management of the firm's short-term assets and liabilities. The goals of managing working capital are to ensure that the firm has enough money to pay its bills and to profitably invest any spare cash to earn interest.

The mismanagement of working capital can cause a firm to default on its debt and go into bankruptcy, even though, over the long term, the firm may be profitable. For example, a firm that makes sales to customers on credit but is not diligent about collecting the accounts receivable can quickly find itself without enough cash to pay its bills. If this condition becomes chronic, trade creditors can force the firm into bankruptcy if the firm cannot obtain alternative financing.

A firm's profitability can also be affected by its inventory level. If the firm has more inventory than it needs to meet customer demands, it has too much money tied up in nonearning assets. Conversely, if the firm holds too little inventory, it can lose sales because it does not have products to sell when customers want them. The firm must therefore determine the optimal inventory level.

Before You Go On

1. What are the three most basic types of financial decisions managers must make?
2. Why are capital budgeting decisions among the most important decisions in the life of a firm?
3. Explain why you would accept an investment project if the value of the expected cash flows exceeds the cost of the project.

1.2 Forms of Business Organization

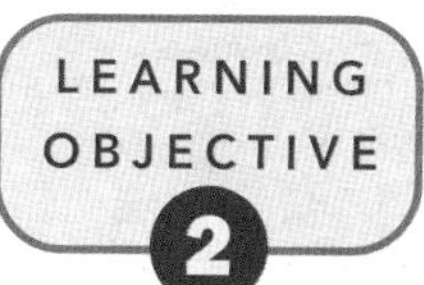

In this section we look at the way firms organize to conduct their business activities. The owners of a business usually choose the organizational form that will help management to maximize the value of the firm. Important considerations are the size of the business, the manner in which income from the business is taxed, the legal liability of the owners, and the ability to raise cash to finance the business.

Most start-ups and small businesses operate as either sole proprietorships or partnerships because of their small operating scale and capital requirements. Large businesses in the United States, such as Procter and Gamble, are most often organized as corporations. As a firm grows larger, the benefits to organizing as a corporation become greater and are more likely to outweigh any disadvantages.

Sole Proprietorships

A **sole proprietorship** is a business owned by one person. About 75 percent of all businesses in the United States are sole proprietorships, typically consisting of the proprietor and a handful of employees. A sole proprietorship offers several advantages. It is the simplest type of business to start, and it is the least regulated. In addition, sole proprietors keep all the profits from the business and do not have to share decision-making authority. Finally, profits from a sole proprietorship are subjected to lower income taxes than are those from the most common type of corporation.

sole proprietorship
a business owned by a single individual

On the downside, a sole proprietor is responsible for paying all the firm's bills and has unlimited liability for all business debts and other obligations of the firm. This means that creditors can look beyond the assets of the business to the proprietor's personal wealth for payment. Another disadvantage is that the amount of equity capital that can be invested in the business is limited to the owner's personal wealth, which may restrict the possibilities for growth. Finally, it is difficult to transfer ownership of a sole proprietorship because there is no stock or other such interest to sell. The owner must sell the company's assets, which can reduce the price that the owner receives for the business.

Partnerships

A **partnership** consists of two or more owners who have joined together legally to manage a business. Partnerships are typically larger than sole proprietorships, and about 10 percent of all businesses in the United States are organized in this manner. To form a

partnership
two or more owners who have joined together legally to manage a business and share in its profits

partnership, the owners enter into an agreement that details how much capital each partner will contribute to the partnership, what their management roles will be, how key management decisions will be made, how the profits will be divided, and how ownership will be transferred in case of specified events, such as the retirement or death of a partner.

A *general partnership* has the same basic advantages and disadvantages as a sole proprietorship. A key disadvantage of a general partnership is that all partners have unlimited liability for the partnership's debts and actions, regardless of what proportion of the business they own or how the debt or obligations were incurred. The problem of unlimited liability can be avoided in a *limited partnership,* which consists of *general* and *limited* partners. Here, one or more general partners have unlimited liability and actively manage the business, while each limited partner is liable for business obligations only up to the amount of capital he or she contributed to the partnership. In other words, the limited partners have **limited liability**. To qualify for limited partner status, a partner cannot be actively engaged in managing the business.

limited liability
the legal liability of a limited partner or stockholder in a business, which extends only to the capital contributed or the amount invested

Corporations

corporation
a legal entity formed and authorized under a state charter; in a legal sense, a corporation is a "person" distinct from its owners

Most large businesses are corporations. A **corporation** is a legal entity authorized under a state charter. In a legal sense, it is a "person" distinct from its owners. Corporations can sue and be sued, enter into contracts, issue debt, borrow money, and own assets, such as real estate. They can also be general or limited partners in partnerships, and they can own stock in other corporations. Although only 15 percent of all businesses are incorporated, corporations hold nearly 90 percent of all business assets, generate nearly 90 percent of revenues, and account for about 80 percent of all business profits in the United States. The owners of a corporation are its stockholders.

Starting a corporation is more costly than starting a sole proprietorship or partnership. Those starting the corporation, for example, must create articles of incorporation and bylaws that conform to the laws of the state of incorporation. These documents spell out the name of the corporation, its business purpose, its intended life span (it can be forever), the amount of stock to be issued, and the number of directors and their responsibilities.

Visit the Web sites of the NYSE and NASDAQ at www.nyse.com and www.nasdaq.com to get more information about market activity.

A major advantage of the corporate form of business organization is that stockholders have limited liability for debts and other obligations of the corporation. The "corporate veil" of limited liability exists because corporations are "legal persons" that borrow in their own names, not in the names of any individual owners. A major disadvantage of the most common corporate form of organization, compared with sole proprietorships and partnerships, is the way they are taxed. Because the corporation is a legal "person," it must pay taxes on the income it earns. If the corporation then pays a cash dividend, the stockholders pay taxes on that dividend as income. Thus, the owners of corporations are subject to double taxation—first at the corporate level and then at the personal level when they receive dividends.[2]

Corporations can be classified as public or private. Most large companies prefer to operate as public corporations, which can sell their debt or equity in the public markets, because large amounts of capital can be sold in these markets at a relatively low cost. **Public markets**, such as the New York Stock Exchange (NYSE) and NASDAQ, are regulated by the federal Securities and Exchange Commission (SEC). Although firms whose securities are publicly traded are technically called public corporations, they are generally referred to simply as corporations. We will follow that convention.

public markets
markets regulated by the Securities and Exchange Commission in which large amounts of debt and equity are publicly traded

In contrast, **privately held**, or **closely held**, corporations are typically owned by a small number of investors, and their shares are not traded publicly. When a corporation is first formed, the common stock is often held by a few investors, typically the founder, a small number of key managers, and financial backers. Over time, as the

privately held corporations
corporations whose stock is not traded in public markets; also called *closely held corporations*

[2]In recent years, businesses have increasingly been organizing as Subchapter S corporations. The key advantage of an S corporation is that stockholders receive all the organizational benefits of a corporation while escaping the double taxation. They are taxed like the partners in a partnership. A major limitation is that a Subchapter S corporation cannot have more than 75 shareholders.

[3]We examine the public and private markets in more detail in Chapters 2 and 15.

company grows in size and needs larger amounts of capital, management may decide that the company should "go public" in order to gain access to the public markets. Not all privately held corporations go public, however.

Hybrid Forms of Business Organization

Historically, law firms, accounting firms, investment banks, and other professional groups were organized as sole proprietorships or partnerships. For partners in these firms, all income was taxed as personal income, and general partners had unlimited liability for all debts and other financial obligations of the firm. It was widely believed that in professional partnerships, such as those of attorneys, accountants, or physicians, the partners should be liable individually and collectively for the professional conduct of each partner. This structure gave the partners an incentive to monitor each other's professional conduct and discipline poorly performing partners, resulting in a higher quality of service and greater professional integrity. Financially, however, misconduct by one partner could result in disaster for the entire firm. For example, a physician found guilty of malpractice exposes every partner in the medical practice to financial liability, even though the others never treated the patient in question.

In the early 1980s, because of sharp increases in the number of professional malpractice cases and large damages awards in the courts, professional groups began lobbying state legislators to create a hybrid form of business organization. These organizations, known as **limited liability partnerships (LLPs)**, are now permitted in most states. An LLP combines the limited liability of a corporation with the tax advantage of a partnership—there is no double taxation. In general, income to the partners of an LLP is taxed as personal income, the partners have limited liability for the business, and they are not personally liable for other partners' malpractice or professional misconduct. Other more recent organizational forms that are essentially equivalent to LLPs include limited liability companies (LLCs) and professional corporations (PCs).

limited liability partnerships (LLPs) hybrid business organizations that combine some of the advantages of corporations and partnerships; in general, income to the partners is taxed only as personal income, but the partners have limited liability

Before You Go On

1. Why are many businesses operated as sole proprietorships or partnerships?
2. What are some advantages and disadvantages of operating as a public corporation?
3. Explain why professional partnerships such as physicians' groups organize as limited liability partnerships.

1.3 Managing the Financial Function

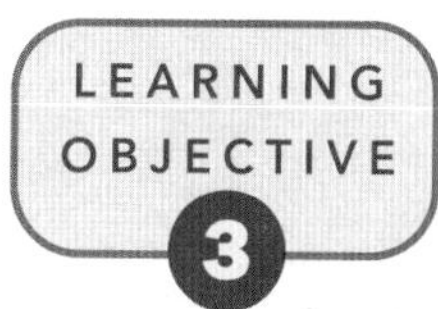

As we discussed earlier in the chapter, financial managers are concerned with a firm's investment, financing, and working capital management decisions. The senior financial manager holds one of the top executive positions in the firm. In a large corporation, the senior financial manager usually has the rank of vice president or senior vice president and goes by the title of **chief financial officer**, or **CFO**. In smaller firms, the job tends to focus more on the accounting function, and the top financial officer may be called the controller or chief accountant. In this section we focus on the financial function in a large corporation.

chief financial officer (CFO) the most senior financial manager in a company

Organization Structure

Exhibit 1.3 shows a typical organizational structure for a large corporation, with special attention to the financial function. As shown, the top management position in the firm is the chief executive officer (CEO), who has the final decision-making authority

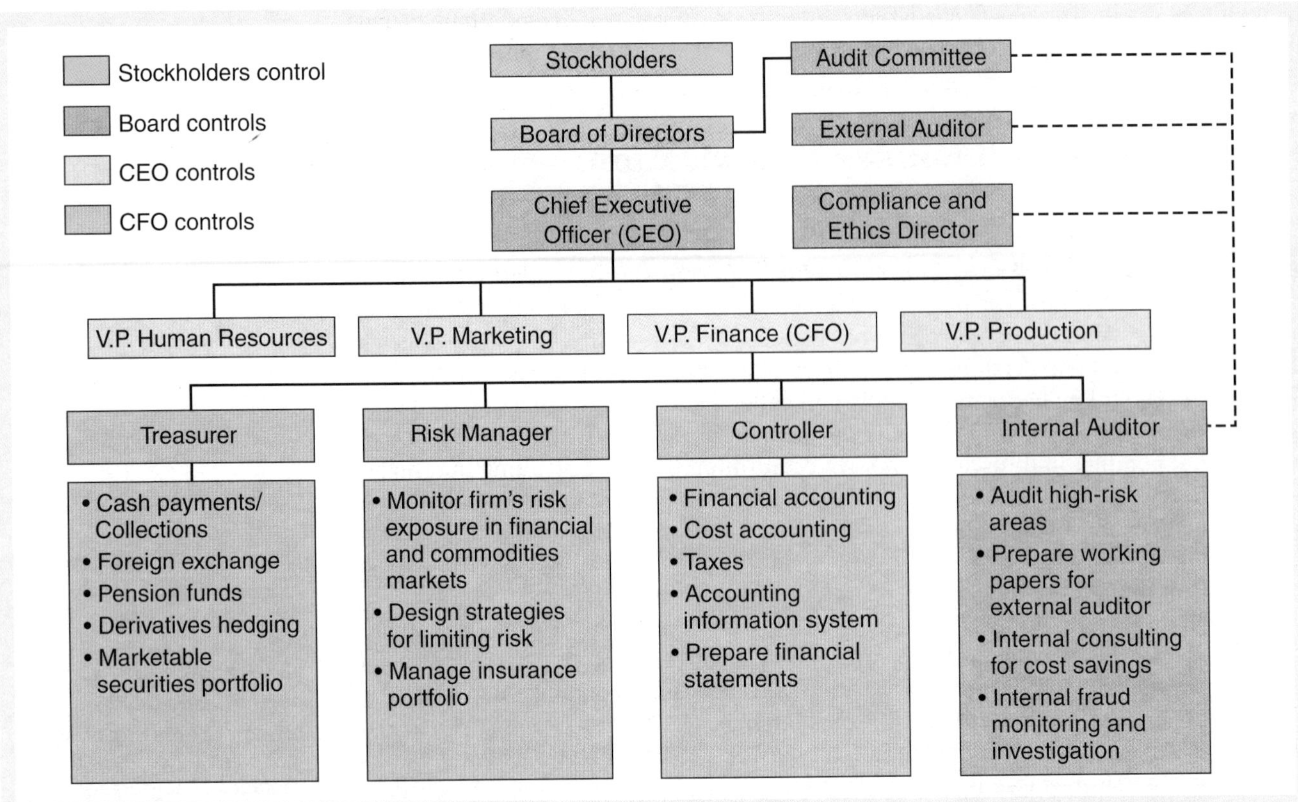

Exhibit 1.3
Simplified Corporate Organization Chart
The firm's top finance and accounting executive is the CFO, who reports directly to the CEO. Positions that report directly to the CFO include the treasurer, risk manager, and controller. The internal auditor reports both to the CFO and to the audit committee of the board of directors. The external auditor and the ethics director also are ultimately responsible to the audit committee.

Go to www.cfo.com to get a better idea of the responsibilities of a CFO.

among all the firm's executives. The CEO's most important responsibilities are to set the strategic direction of the firm and see that the management team executes the strategic plan. The CEO reports directly to the board of directors, which is accountable to the company's stockholders. The board's responsibility is to see that the top management makes decisions that are in the best interest of the stockholders.

The CFO reports directly to the CEO and focuses on managing all aspects of the firm's financial side, as well as working closely with the CEO on strategic issues. A number of positions report directly to the CFO. In addition, the CFO often interacts with people in other functional areas on a regular basis because all senior executives are involved in financial decisions that affect the firm and their areas of responsibility.

Positions Reporting to the CFO

Exhibit 1.3 also shows the positions that typically report to the CFO in a large corporation and the activities managed in each area.

- The *treasurer* looks after the collection and disbursement of cash, investing excess cash so that it earns interest, raising new capital, handling foreign exchange transactions, and overseeing the firm's pension fund managers. The treasurer also assists the CFO in handling important Wall Street relationships, such as those with investment bankers and credit rating agencies.

- The *risk manager* monitors and manages the firm's risk exposure in financial and commodity markets and the firm's relationships with insurance providers.
- The *controller* is really the firm's chief accounting officer. The controller's staff prepares the financial statements, maintains the firm's financial and cost accounting systems, prepares the taxes, and works closely with the firm's external auditors.
- The *internal auditor* is responsible for identifying and assessing major risks facing the firm and performing audits in areas where the firm might incur substantial losses. The internal auditor reports to the board of directors as well as the CFO.

External Auditors

Nearly every business hires a licensed certified public accounting (CPA) firm to provide an independent annual audit of the firm's financial statements. Through this audit the CPA comes to a conclusion as to whether the firm's financial statement presents fairly, in all material respects, the financial position of the firm and results of its activities. In other words, whether the financial numbers are reasonably accurate, accounting principles have been consistently applied year to year and do not significantly distort the firm's performance, and the accounting principles used conform to those generally accepted by the accounting profession. Creditors and investors require independent audits, and the SEC requires publicly traded firms to supply audited financial statements.

The Audit Committee

The audit committee, a powerful subcommittee of the board of directors, has the responsibility of overseeing the accounting function and the preparation of the firm's financial statements. In addition, the audit committee oversees or, if necessary, conducts investigations of significant fraud, theft, or malfeasance in the firm, especially if it is suspected that senior managers in the firm may be involved.

External auditors report directly to the audit committee to help ensure their independence from management. On a day-to-day basis, however, they work closely with the CFO staff. The internal auditor, too, reports to the audit committee so that the position more independent from management, and his or her ultimate responsibility is to the audit committee. On a day-to-day basis, however, the internal auditor, like the external auditors, works closely with the CFO staff.

The Compliance and Ethics Director

The SEC requires that all publicly traded companies have a compliance and ethics director who oversees three mandated programs: (1) a compliance program that ensures that the firm complies with federal and state laws and regulations, (2) an ethics program that promotes ethical conduct among executives and employees, and (3) a compliance hotline, which must include a whistleblower program. Like the internal auditor, the compliance director reports to the audit committee to ensure independence from management, though on a day-to-day basis the director typically reports to the firm's legal counsel.

Before You Go On

1. What are the major responsibilities of the CFO?
2. Identify three financial officers who typically report to the CFO and describe their duties.
3. Why does the internal auditor report to both the CFO and the board of directors?

1.4 The Goal of the Firm

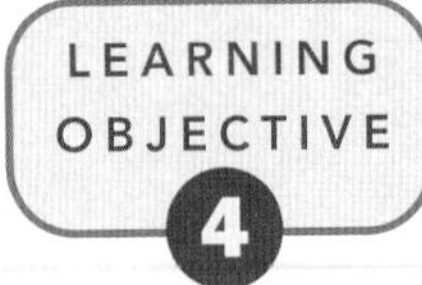

For business owners, it is important to determine the appropriate goal for financial management decisions. Should the goal be to try to keep costs as low as possible? or to maximize sales or market share? or to achieve steady growth and earnings? Let's look at this fundamental question more closely.

What Should Management Maximize?

Suppose you own and manage a pizza parlor. Depending on your preferences and tolerance for risk, you can set any goal for the business that you want. For example, you might have a fear of bankruptcy and losing money. To avoid the risk of bankruptcy, you could focus on keeping your costs as low as possible, paying low wages, avoiding borrowing, advertising minimally, and remaining reluctant to expand the business. In short, you will avoid any action that increases your firm's risk. You will sleep well at night, but you may eat poorly because of meager profits.

Conversely, you could focus on maximizing market share and becoming the largest pizza business in town. Your strategy might include cutting prices to increase sales, borrowing heavily to open new pizza parlors, spending lavishly on advertising, and developing exotic menu items such as *pizza de foie gras*. In the short run, your high-risk, high-growth strategy will have you both eating poorly and sleeping poorly as you push the firm to the edge. In the long run, you will either become very rich or go bankrupt! There must be a better operational goal than either of these extremes.

Why Not Maximize Profits?

One goal for financial decision making that seems reasonable is *profit maximization*. After all, don't stockholders and business owners want their companies to be profitable? Although profit maximization seems a logical goal for a business, it has some serious drawbacks.

One problem with profit maximization is that it is hard to pin down what is meant by "profit." To the average businessperson, profits are just revenues minus expenses. To an accountant, however, a decision that increases profits under one set of accounting rules can reduce it under another. This is the origin of the term *creative accounting*. A second problem is that accounting profits are not necessarily the same as cash flows. For example, many firms recognize revenues at the time a sale is made, which is typically before the cash payment for the sale is received. Ultimately, the owners of a business want cash because only cash can be used to make investments or to buy goods and services.

Yet another problem with profit maximization as a goal is that it does not distinguish between getting a dollar today and getting a dollar some time in the future. In finance, the timing of cash flows is extremely important. For example, the longer you go without paying your credit card balance, the more interest you must pay the bank for the use of the money. The interest accrues because of the *time value of money;* the longer you have access to money, the more you have to pay for it. The time value of money is one of the most important concepts in finance and is the focus of Chapters 5 and 6.

BUILDING INTUITION

The Timing of Cash Flows Affects Their Value

A dollar today is worth more than a dollar in the future because if you have a dollar today, you can invest it and earn interest. For businesses, cash flows can involve large sums of money, and receiving money one day late can cost a great deal. For example, if a bank has $100 billion of consumer loans outstanding and the average annual interest payment is 5 percent, it would cost the bank $13.7 million if every consumer decided to make an interest payment one day later.

Finally, profit maximization ignores the uncertainty, or risk, associated with cash flows. A basic principle of finance is that there is a trade-off between expected return and risk. When given a choice between two investments that have the same expected returns but different risk, most people choose the less risky one. This makes sense because most people do not like bearing risk and, as a result, must be compensated for taking it. The profit maximization goal ignores differences in value caused by differences in risk. We return to the important topics of risk, its measurement, and the trade-off between risk and return in Chapter 7. What is important at this time is that you understand that investors do not like risk and must be compensated for bearing it.

BUILDING INTUITION

The Riskiness of Cash Flows Affects Their Value

A risky dollar is worth less than a safe dollar. The reason is that investors do not like risk and must be compensated for bearing it. For example, if two investments have the same return—say 5 percent—most people will prefer the investment with the lower risk. Thus, the more risky an investment's cash flows, the less it is worth.

In sum, it appears that profit maximization is not an appropriate goal for a firm because the concept is difficult to define and does not directly account for the firm's cash flows. What we need is a goal that looks at a firm's cash flows and considers both their timing and their riskiness. Fortunately, we have just such a measure: the market value of the firm's stock.

Maximize the Value of the Firm's Stock

The underlying value of any asset is determined by the future cash flows generated by that asset. This principle holds whether we are buying a bank certificate of deposit, a corporate bond, or an office building. Furthermore, as we will discuss in Chapter 9, when security analysts and investors on Wall Street determine the value of a firm's stock, they consider (1) the size of the expected cash flows, (2) the timing of the cash flows, and (3) the riskiness of the cash flows. Notice that the mechanism for determining stock values overcomes all the cash flow objections we raised with regard to profit maximization as a goal.

Thus, an appropriate goal for financial management is to maximize the current value of the firm's stock. By maximizing the current stock price, the financial manager will be maximizing the value of the stockholders' shares. Notice that maximizing share value is an unambiguous objective, and it is easy to measure. We simply look at the market value of the stock in the newspaper on a given day to determine the value of the stockholders' shares and whether it went up or down. Publicly traded securities are ideally suited for this task because public markets are wholesale markets with large numbers of buyers and sellers where securities trade near their true value.

What about firms whose equity is not publicly traded, such as private corporations and partnerships? The total value of the stock in such a company is equal to the value of the stockholders' equity. *Thus, our goal can be restated for these firms as this: maximize the current value of owner's equity.* The only other restriction is that the entities must be for-profit businesses.

BUILDING INTUITION

The Financial Manager's Goal Is to Maximize the Value of the Firm's Stock

The goal for financial managers is to make decisions that maximize the firm's stock price. By maximizing stock price, management will help maximize stockholders' wealth. To do this, managers must make investment and financing decisions so that the total value of cash inflows exceeds the total value of cash outflows by the greatest possible amount (benefits > costs). Notice that the focus is on maximizing the value of cash flows, not profits.

Can Management Decisions Affect Stock Prices?

An important question is whether management decisions actually affect the firm's stock price. Fortunately, the answer is yes. As noted earlier, a basic principle in finance is that the value of an asset is determined by the future cash flows it is expected to generate. As shown in Exhibit 1.4, a firm's management makes numerous decisions that affect its cash flows. For example, management decides what type of products or services to produce and what productive assets to purchase. Managers also make decisions concerning the mix of debt to equity, debt collection policies, and policies for paying suppliers, to mention a few. In addition, cash flows are affected by how efficient management is in making products, the quality of the products, management's sales and marketing skills, and the firm's investment in research and development for new products. Some of these decisions affect cash flows over the long term, such as the decision to build a new plant, and other decisions have a short-term impact on cash flows, such as launching an advertising campaign.

Of course, the firm also must deal with a number of external factors over which it has little or no control, such as economic conditions (recession or expansion), war or

Exhibit 1.4
Major Factors Affecting Stock Prices

The firm's stock price is affected by a number of factors, and management can control only some of them. Managers exercise little control over external conditions (blue boxes), such as the general economy, although they can closely observe these conditions and make appropriate changes in strategy. Also, managers make many other decisions that directly affect the firm's expected cash flows (green boxes)—and hence the price of the firm's stock.

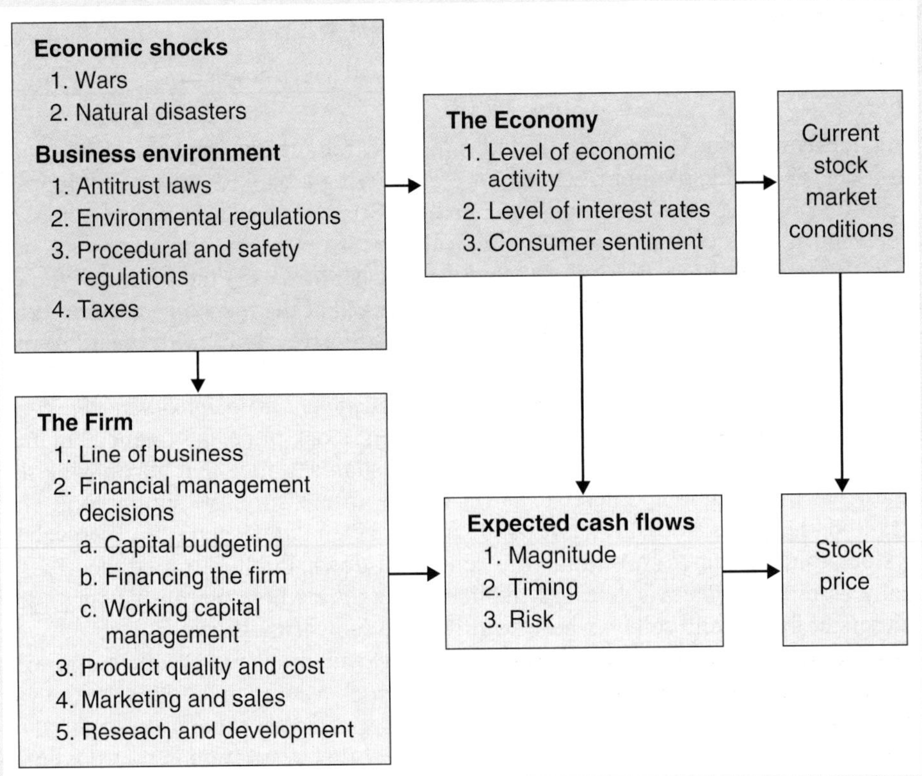

peace, and new government regulations. External factors are constantly changing, and management must weigh the impact of these changes and adjust its strategy and decisions accordingly.

The important point here is that, over time, management makes a series of decisions when executing the firm's strategy that affect the firm's cash flows and, hence, the price of the firm's stock. Firms that have a better business strategy, are more nimble, make better business decisions, and can execute their plans well will have a higher stock price than similar firms that just can't get it right.

Before You Go On

1. Why is profit maximization an unsatisfactory goal for managing a firm?
2. Explain why maximizing the current market price of a firm's stock is an appropriate goal for the firm's management.
3. What is the fundamental determinant of an asset's value?

1.5 Agency Conflicts: Separation of Ownership and Control

LEARNING OBJECTIVE 5

We turn next to an important issue facing stockholders of large corporations: the separation of ownership and control of the firm. In a large corporation, ownership is often spread over a large number of stockholders who may effectively have little control over management. Management may therefore make decisions that benefit their own interests rather than those of the stockholders. In contrast, in smaller firms owners and managers are usually one and the same, and there is no conflict of interest between owners and managers. As you will see, this self-interested behavior may affect the value of the firm.

Ownership and Control

To illustrate, let's continue with our pizza parlor example. As the owner of a pizza parlor, you have decided your goal is to maximize the value of the business, and thereby your ownership interest. There is no conflict of interest in your dual roles as owner and manager because your personal and economic self-interest is tied to the success of the pizza parlor. The restaurant has succeeded because you have worked hard and have focused on customer satisfaction.

Now suppose you decide to hire a college student to manage the restaurant. Will the new manager always act in your interest? Or could the new manager be tempted to give free pizza to friends now and then or, after an exhausting day, leave early rather than spend time cleaning and preparing for the next day? From this example, you can see that once ownership and management are separated, managers may be tempted to pursue goals that are in their own self-interest rather than the interests of the owners.

Agency Relationships

The relationship we have just described between the pizza parlor owner and the student manager is an example of an agency relationship. An agency relationship arises whenever one party, called the *principal,* hires another party, called the *agent,* to perform some service on behalf of the principal. The relationship between stockholders and management is an agency relationship. Legally, managers (who are the agents) have a fiduciary duty to the stockholders (the principals), which means managers are obligated to put the interests of the stockholders above their own. However, in these and all other agency relationships, the potential exists for a conflict of interest between the principal and the agent. These conflicts are called **agency conflicts**.

agency conflicts
conflicts of interest between a principal and an agent

Do Managers Really Want to Maximize Stock Price?

It is not difficult to see how conflicts of interest between managers and stockholders can arise in the corporate setting. In most large corporations, especially those that are publicly traded, there is a significant degree of separation between ownership and management. For example, General Motors Corporation (GMC) has more than two million stockholders. As a practical matter, it is not possible for all of the stockholders to be active in the management of the firm or to individually bear the high cost of monitoring management. The bottom line is that stockholders own the corporation, but managers control the money and have the opportunity to use it for their own benefit.

How might management be tempted to indulge itself and pursue its own self-interest? We need not look far for an answer to this question. Corporate excesses are legion, but high on the list are palatial office buildings, corporate hunting and fishing lodges in exotic places, expensive corporate jets, extravagant expense-account dinners kicked off with bottles of Dom Perignon and washed down with 1953 Margaux—and, of course, a king's compensation package.[4] Besides economic nest feathering, corporate managers may focus on maximizing market share and their industry prestige, job security, and so forth.

Needless to say, these types of activities and spending conflict with the goal of maximizing a firm's stock price. The costs of these activities are called *agency costs.* **Agency costs** are the costs incurred because of conflicts of interest between a principal and an agent. Examples are the cost of the lavish dinner mentioned earlier and the cost of a corporate jet for executives. However, not all agency costs are frivolous. The cost of hiring an external auditor to certify financial statements is also an agency cost.

agency costs
the costs arising from conflicts of interest between a principal and an agent; for example, between a firm's owners and its management

Aligning the Interests of Management and Stockholders

If the linkage between stockholder and management goals is weak, a number of mechanisms can help to better align the behavior of managers with the goals of corporate stockholders. These include (1) management compensation, (2) managerial labor markets, (3) board of directors, (4) other managers, (5) large stockholders, (6) the takeover market, and (7) the legal and regulatory environment.

MANAGEMENT COMPENSATION

The most effective means of aligning the interests of managers with those of stockholders is a well-designed compensation (pay) package that rewards managers when they do what stockholders want them to do and penalizes them when they do not. This type of plan is effective because a manager will quickly internalize the benefits and costs of making good and bad decisions and, thus, will be more likely to make the decisions that stockholders want. Therefore, there is no need for some outside monitor, such as the board of directors, to try to figure out whether the managers are making the right decisions. The information that outside monitors have is not as good as the managers' information, so these outside monitors are always at a disadvantage in trying to determine whether a manager is acting in the interest of stockholders.

Most corporations have management compensation plans that tie compensation to the performance of the firm. The idea behind these plans is that if compensation is

[4]A favorite premeal "quaffing" champagne of young investment bankers on Wall Street is Dom Perignon, known as the "Domer," which is priced in the range of $250 a bottle. Senior partners who are more genteel are reported to favor a 1953 Margaux, a French Bordeaux wine from Château Margaux; 1953 is considered a stellar vintage year, and Margaux 1953 is an excellent but very pricey (about $1,300 per bottle wholesale in 2006) choice.

sensitive to the performance of the firm, managers will have greater incentives to make decisions that increase the stockholders' wealth. Although these incentive plans vary widely, they usually include (1) a base salary, (2) a bonus based on the accounting performance, and (3) some compensation that is tied to the firm's stock price.[5] The base salary assures the executive of some minimum compensation as long as he or she remains with the firm, and the bonus and stock price–based compensation are designed to align the manager's incentives with those of the stockholders. The trick in designing such a program is to choose the right mix of these three components so that the manager has the right incentives and the overall package is sufficiently appealing to attract and retain high-quality managers at the lowest possible cost.

MANAGERIAL LABOR MARKET

The managerial labor market also provides managers with incentives to act in the interests of stockholders. Firms that have a history of poor performance or a reputation for "shady operations" or unethical behavior have difficulty hiring top managerial talent. Individuals who are top performers have better alternatives than to work for such firms. Therefore, to the extent that managers want to attract high-quality people, the labor market provides incentives to run a good company.

Furthermore, studies show that executives who "manage" firms into bankruptcy or are convicted of white-collar crimes can rarely secure equivalent positions after being fired for poor performance or convicted for criminal behavior. Thus, the penalty for extremely poor performance or a criminal conviction is a significant reduction in the manager's lifetime earnings potential. Managers know this, and the fear of such consequences helps keep them working hard and honestly.[6]

BOARD OF DIRECTORS

A corporation's board of directors has a legal responsibility to represent stockholders' interests. The board's duties include hiring and firing the CEO, setting his or her compensation, and monitoring his or her performance. The board also approves major decisions concerning the firm, such as the firm's annual capital budget or the acquisition of another business. These responsibilities make the board a key mechanism for ensuring that managers' decisions are aligned with those of stockholders.

How well boards actually perform in this role has been questioned in recent years. As an example, critics point out that some boards are unwilling to make hard decisions such as firing the CEO when a firm performs poorly. Other people believe that a lack of independence is a reason that boards are not as effective as they might be. For example, the CEO typically chairs the board of directors. This dual position can give the CEO undue influence over the board, as the chairperson sets the agenda for and chairs board meetings, appoints committees, and controls the flow of information to the board. Also inhibiting board independence in the past was the practice that allowed any number of the companies' own executives to serve on the board. Before passage of the Sarbanes-Oxley Act, discussed later in this chapter, these *inside directors* could actually outnumber *outside directors*, who were not employees of the firm.

OTHER MANAGERS

Competition among managers within firms also helps provide incentives for management to act in the interests of stockholders. Managers compete to attain the CEO position and in doing so try to attract the board of directors' attention by acting in the stockholders' interests. Furthermore, even when a manager becomes CEO, he or she is always looking over his or her shoulder because other managers covet that job.

---

[5]This component, which may include stock options, will increase and decrease with the stock price.

[6]Nonquantifiable costs of convictions for crimes are the perpetrators' personal embarrassment and the embarrassment of their families and the effect it may have on their lives. On average, the overall cost of such convictions is higher than even that suggested by the labor market argument.

LARGE STOCKHOLDERS

All stockholders obviously have a strong interest in providing managers with incentives to maximize stockholder value. After all, that is what stockholders want, and it is an appropriate goal for management. We single out stockholders who own a lot of shares because they have enough money at stake—and enough power—to make it worthwhile to actively monitor managers and try to influence their decisions.

THE TAKEOVER MARKET

The market for takeovers provides incentives for managers to act in the interests of stockholders. When a firm performs poorly because management is doing a poor job, an opportunity arises for astute investors, so-called corporate raiders, to make money by buying the company at a price that reflects its poor performance and replacing the current managers with a top-flight management team. If the investors have evaluated the situation correctly, the firm will soon be transformed into a strong performer, its stock price will increase, and investors can sell their stock for a significant profit. The possibility that a firm might be discovered by corporate raiders provides incentives for management to perform.

THE LEGAL AND REGULATORY ENVIRONMENT

Finally, the laws and regulations that firms must adhere to limit the ability of managers to make decisions that harm the interests of stockholders. An example is federal and state statutes that make it illegal for managers to steal corporate assets. Similarly, regulatory reforms such as the Sarbanes-Oxley Act, discussed next, limit the ability of managers to mislead stockholders.

Sarbanes-Oxley and Other Regulatory Reforms

A series of accounting scandals and ethical lapses by corporate officers shocked the nation in the early years of the twenty-first century. A case in point was WorldCom's bankruptcy filing in 2002 and the admission that its officers had "cooked the books" by misstating \$7.2 billion of expenses, which allowed WorldCom to report "profits" when the firm had actually lost money. The accounting fraud at WorldCom followed similar scandals at Enron, Global Crossing, Tyco, and elsewhere. These scandals—and the resulting losses to stockholders—resulted in a set of far-reaching regulatory reforms passed by Congress in 2002.[7] Relevant to our discussion is the Sarbanes-Oxley Act of 2002, which focuses on (1) reducing agency costs in corporations, (2) restoring ethical conduct within the business sector, and (3) improving the integrity of accounting reporting system within firms.

To find out more about current ethics issues in corporate America, visit www.sarbanes-oxley.com.

Overall, the new regulations require all public corporations to implement five overarching strategies. (Private corporations and partnerships are not required to implement these measures.)

1. **Ensure greater board independence.** Firms must restructure their boards so that the majority of the members are outside directors. Furthermore, it is recommended that the positions of chair and CEO be separated. Finally, Sarbanes-Oxley makes it clear that board members have a fiduciary responsibility to represent and act in the interest of stockholders, and board members who fail to meet their fiduciary duty can be fined and receive jail sentences.

2. **Establish internal accounting controls.** Firms must establish internal accounting control systems to protect the integrity of the accounting systems and safeguard the firms' assets. The internal controls are intended to improve the reliability of accounting data and the quality of financial reports and to reduce the likelihood that individuals within the firm engage in accounting fraud.

---

[7]The major laws passed by Congress in this area in 2002 were the Public Accounting Reform and Investor Protection Act and the Sarbanes-Oxley Act.

3. **Establish compliance programs.** Firms must establish corporate compliance programs that ensure that the firms comply with important federal and state regulations. For example, a compliance program would document whether a firm's truck drivers complied with all federal and state truck and driver safety regulations, such as the number of hours one can drive during the day and the gross highway weight of the truck.

4. **Establish an ethics program.** Firms must establish ethics programs that monitor the ethical conduct of employees and executives through a compliance hotline, which must include a whistleblower protection provision. The intent is to create an ethical work environment so that employees will know what is expected of them and their relationships with customers, suppliers, and other stakeholders. If fraud is detected, the programs should provide an established procedure to follow.

5. **Expand the audit committee's oversight powers.** The external auditor, the internal auditor, and the compliance/ethics officer owe their ultimate legal responsibilities to the audit committee, not to the firm. These reporting lines give the audit committee deep tentacles into the firm to discover financial improprieties. In addition, the audit committee has the unconditional power to probe and question any person in the firm, including the CEO, regarding any matter that might materially impact the firm or its financial statements.

Exhibit 1.5 summarizes some of the recent regulatory changes that significantly expand the board of directors' powers.

Exhibit 1.5 Corporate Governance Regulations That Reduce Agency Costs

Board of Directors

- Board has a fiduciary responsibility to represent the best interest of the firm's owners.
- Majority of the board must be outside independent directors.
- Firm is required to have code of ethics, which has to be approved by the board.
- Firm must establish an ethics program that has a complaint hotline and a whistleblower protection provision which is approved by the board of directors.
- Separation of chairman and CEO positions is recommended.
- Board memebers can be fined or receive jail sentences if they fail to fulfill their fiduciary responsibilities.

Audit Committee

- External auditor, internal auditor, and compliance officer's fiduciary (legal) responsibilities are to the audit committee.
- Audit committee approves the hiring, firing, and fees paid to external auditors.
- CEO and CFO must certify financial statements.
- All audit committee members must be outside independent directors.
- One member must be a financial expert.

External Auditors

- Lead partner must change every five years.
- There are limits on consulting (nonaudit) services that external auditors can provide.

Source: Sarbanes-Oxley Act, the Public Accounting Reform and Investor Protection Act, and NYSE and NASDAQ new listing requirements.

Recent regulatory changes have significantly expanded the powers of corporate boards of directors. The most important changes resulted from the Sarbanes-Oxley Act, passed by Congress in 2002. The act was aimed at reducing agency costs, promoting ethical conduct, and improving the integrity of accounting reporting systems.

It is too early to tell how effective the new regulations will be. Indications are, however, that a noticeable shift has occurred in the behavior of board members and management. Boards appear much more serious about monitoring firms' performance and ratifying important decisions by management. Audit committees, with their new independence and investigative powers, are providing greater oversight in the preparation of financial statements. Stronger internal accounting controls systems, compliance programs, and ethics programs are improving the integrity of the accounting systems and reducing the likelihood of fraud and other illegal activities. Thus, the Sarbanes-Oxley Act does appear to be having an effect. The major complaint from business has been the cost of compliance, which averaged $5 million to $8 million per firm in 2004 but declined to $4.7 million in 2006.

Before You Go On

1. What are agency conflicts?
2. What are corporate raiders?
3. List the three main objectives of the Sarbanes-Oxley Act.

1.6 The Importance of Ethics in Business

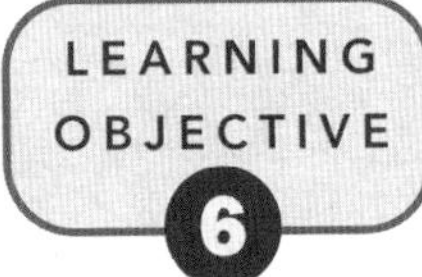

We have just seen that Congress included ethics program requirements in the Sarbanes-Oxley Act. Why are ethics important to business?

Business Ethics

The site www.web-miner.com/busethics.htm offers a wide range of articles on the role of ethics in business today.

The term *ethics* describes a society's ideas about what actions are right and wrong. Ethical values are not moral absolutes, and they can and do vary across societies. Regardless of cultural differences, however, if we think about it, all of us would probably prefer to live in a world where people behave ethically—where people try to do what is right.

In our society, ethical rules include considering the impact of our actions on others, being willing to sometimes put the interests of others ahead of our own interests, and realizing that we must follow the same rules we expect others to follow. The golden rule—"Do unto others as you would have done unto you"—is an example of a widely accepted ethical norm.[8]

Are Business Ethics Different from Everyday Ethics?

Perhaps business is a dog-eat-dog world where ethics do not matter. People who take this point of view link business ethics to the "ethics of the poker game" and not to the ethics of everyday morality. Poker players, they suggest, must practice cunning deception and must conceal their strengths and their intentions. After all, they are playing the game to win. How far does one go to win?

In 2002, investors learned the hard way about a number of firms that had been behaving according to the ethics of the poker game: cunning deception and concealment of information were the order of the day at WorldCom, Enron, Global Crossing, Tyco, and a host of other firms. The market's reaction to their concealment and deception was to wipe out $2.3 trillion of stockholder value.

[8] The golden rule can be stated in a number of ways. One version, in the Gospel of Matthew, states, "In everything do to others as you would have them do to you." A less noble version you occasionally hear in business is "He who has the gold makes the rules."

We believe that those who argue that ethics do not matter in business are mistaken. Indeed, most academic studies on the topic suggest that traditions of morality are very relevant to business and to financial markets in particular. The reasons are practical as well as ethical. Corruption in business creates inefficiencies in an economy, inhibits the growth of capital markets, and slows a country's rate of economic growth.

For example, as Russia made the transition to a market economy, it had a difficult time establishing a stock market and attracting foreign investment. The reason was a simple one. Corruption was rampant in local government and in business. Contractual agreements were not enforceable, and there was no reliable financial information about Russian companies. Not until the mid-1990s did some Russian companies begin to display enough honesty and financial transparency to attract investment capital.[9]

Types of Ethical Conflicts in Business

We turn next to a consideration of the ethical problems that arise in business dealings. Most problems involve three related areas: agency costs, conflicts of interest, and informational asymmetry.

AGENCY COSTS

As we discussed earlier in this chapter, many relationships in business are agency relationships. Agents can be bound both legally and ethically to act in the interest of the principal. Financial managers have agency obligations to act honestly and to see that subordinates act honestly with respect to financial transactions. Of all the corporate officers, financial managers, when they are guilty of misconduct, present among the most serious danger to stockholder wealth. A product recall or environmental offense may cause temporary declines in stock prices. However, revelations of dishonesty, deception, and fraud in financial matters have a huge impact on the stock price. If the dishonesty is flagrant, the firm may go bankrupt, as we saw with the bankruptcies of Enron and WorldCom.

CONFLICTS OF INTEREST

Conflicts of interest often arise in agency relationships. A conflict of interest in such a situation can arise when the agent's interests are different from those of the principal. For example, suppose you're interested in buying a house and a local real estate agent is helping you find the home of your dreams. As it turns out, the dream house is one for which your agent is also the listing agent. Your agent has a conflict of interest because her professional obligation to help you find the right house at a fair price conflicts with her professional obligation to get the highest price possible for the client whose house she has listed.

Organizations can be either principals or agents and, hence, can be parties to conflicts of interest. In the past, for example, many large accounting firms provided both consulting services and audits for corporations. This dual function may compromise the independence and objectivity of the audit opinion, even though the work is done by different parts of the firm. For example, if consulting fees from an audit client become a large source of income, is the auditing firm less likely to render an adverse audit opinion and thereby risk losing the consulting business?

Conflicts of interest are typically resolved in one of two ways. Sometimes complete disclosure is sufficient. Thus, in real estate transactions, it is not unusual for the same lawyer or realtor to represent both the buyer and the seller. This practice is not considered unethical as long as both sides are aware of the fact and give their consent. Alternatively, the conflicted party can withdraw from serving the interests of one of the parties. Sometimes the law mandates this solution. For example, recent legislation requires that public accounting firms stop providing certain consulting services to their audit clients.

---

[9]In economics, *transparency* refers to openness and access to information.

INFORMATION ASYMMETRY

information asymmetry the situation in which one party in a business transaction has information that is unavailable to the other parties in the transaction

Information asymmetry occurs when one party in a business transaction has information that is unavailable to the other parties in the transaction. The existence of information asymmetry in business relationships is commonplace. For example, suppose you decide to sell your 10-year-old car. You know much more about the real condition of the car than does the prospective buyer. The moral issue is this: How much should you tell the prospective buyer? In other words, to what extent is the party with the information advantage obligated to reduce the amount of information asymmetry?

Decisions in this area often center on issues of fairness. Consider the insider trading of stocks based on confidential information not available to the public. Using insider information is considered morally wrong and, as a result, has been made illegal. The rationale for the notion is ethical fairness. The central idea is that investment decisions should be made on a "level playing field."

What counts as fair and as unfair is somewhat controversial, but there are a few ways to determine fairness. One relates to the golden rule and the notion of impartiality that underlies it. You treat another fairly when you "do unto others as you want them to do unto you." Another test of fairness is whether you are willing to publicly advocate the principle behind your decision. Actions based on principles that do not pass the golden rule test or that cannot be publicly advocated are not likely to be fair.

The Importance of an Ethical Business Culture

Some economists have noted that the legal system and market forces impose substantial costs on individuals and institutions that engage in unethical behavior. As a result, these forces provide important incentives that foster ethical behavior in the business community. The incentives include financial losses, legal fines, jail time, and destruction of companies (bankruptcy). Ethicists argue, however, that laws and market forces are not enough. For example, the financial sector is one of the most heavily regulated areas of the U.S. economy. Yet despite heavy regulation, the sector has a long and rich history of financial scandals.

In addition to laws and market forces, then, it is important to create an ethical culture in the firm. Why is this important? An ethical business culture means that people have a set of principles—a moral compass, so to speak—that help them identify moral issues and make ethical judgments without being told what to do. The culture has a powerful influence on the way people behave and the way they make decisions.

The people at the top of a company determine whether or not the culture of that company is ethical. At Enron, for example, top officers promoted a culture of aggressive risk taking and willingness, at times, to cross over ethical and even legal lines. Once this type of culture is established at the top, people in the organization think it is acceptable to step over legal and ethical boundaries themselves.

More than likely, you will be confronted with ethical issues during your professional career. Knowing how to identify and deal with ethical issues is thus an important part of your professional "survival kit." Exhibit 1.6 presents a framework for making ethical judgments.

Serious Consequences

In recent years the "rules" have changed, and the cost of ethical mistakes can be extremely high. In the past, the business community and legal authorities often dismissed corporate scandals as a "few rotten apples" in an otherwise sound barrel. This is no longer true today. In 2005, for instance, Bernard J. Ebbers, the 63-year-old CEO of WorldCom, was found guilty of fraud and theft and was sentenced to 25 years in prison. Judge Barbara S. Jones, acknowledging that Ebbers would probably serve the rest of his days in jail, said "I find a sentence of anything less would not reflect the seriousness of the crime." In the past, sentences for white-collar crimes were minimal; even for serious crimes, there often was no jail time at all. Clearly, business ethics is a topic of high interest and increasing importance in the business community, and it is a topic that will be discussed throughout the book.

Exhibit 1.6 A Framework for the Analysis of Ethical Conflicts

The first step toward ethical behavior is to recognize that you face a moral issue. In general, if your actions or decisions will cause harm to others, you are facing a moral issue. When you find yourself in this position, you might ask yourself the following questions:

1. What does the law require? When in doubt, consult the legal department.
2. What do your role-related obligations require? What is your station, and what are its duties? If you are a member of a profession, what does the code of conduct of your profession say you should do in these circumstances?
3. Are you an agent employed on behalf of another in these circumstances? If so, what are the interests and desires of the employing party?
4. Are the interests of the stockholders materially affected? Your obligation is to represent the best interests of the firm's owners.
5. Do you have a confilict of interest? Will full diclosure of the conflict be sufficient? If not, you must determine what interest has priority.
6. Are you abusing information asymmetry? Is your use of the information asymmetry fair? It probably is fair if you would make the same decision if the roles of the parties were reversed or if you would publicly advocated the principle behind your decision.
7. Would you be willing to have your action and all the reasons that motivated it reported in the *Wall Street Journal?*

Dealing with ethical conflicts is an inescapable part of professional life for most people. An analytical framework can be helpful in understanding and resolving such conflicts.

Before You Go On

1. What is a conflict of interest in a business setting?
2. How would you define an ethical business culture?

Summary of Learning Objectives

1. **Identify the key financial decisions facing the financial manager of any business firm.**

   In running a business, the financial manager faces three basic decisions: (1) which productive assets the firm should buy (capital budgeting), (2) how the firm should finance the productive assets purchased (financing decision), and (3) how the firm should manage its day-to-day financial activities (working capital decisions). The financial manager should make these decisions in a way that maximizes the current value of the firm's stock.

2. **Identify the basic forms of business organization used in the United States, and review their respective strengths and weaknesses.**

   A business can organize in three basic ways: as a sole proprietorship, a partnership, or a corporation (public or private). The owners of a firm select the form of organization that they believe will best allow management to maximize the value of the firm. Most large firms elect to organize as public corporations because of the ease of raising money; the major disadvantage is double taxation. Smaller companies tend to organize as sole proprietorships or partnerships. The advantages of these forms of organization include ease of formation and taxation at the personal income tax rate. The major disadvantage is the owners' unlimited personal liability.

3. **Describe the typical organization of the financial function in a large corporation.**

   In a large corporation, the financial manager generally has the rank of vice president and goes by the title of chief financial officer. The CFO reports directly to the firm's CEO. Positions reporting directly to the CFO generally include the treasurer, the risk manager, the controller, and the internal auditor. The audit committee of the board of directors is also important in the financial function. The committee hires the external auditor for the firm, and the internal auditor, external auditor, and compliance officer all report to the audit committee.

4. **Explain why maximizing the current value of the firm's stock is the appropriate goal for management.**

   The goal of the financial manager is to maximize the current value of the firm's stock. Maximizing stock value is an appropriate goal because it forces management to focus on decisions that will generate the greatest amount of wealth for stockholders. Since the value of a share of stock (or any asset) is determined by its cash flows, management's decisions must consider the size of the cash flow (larger is better), the timing of the cash flow (sooner is better), and the riskiness of the cash flow (given equal returns, lower risk is better).

5. **Discuss how agency conflicts affect the goal of maximizing stockholder value.**

   In most large corporations, there is a significant degree of separation between management and ownership. As a result, stockholders have little control over corporate managers, and management may thus be tempted to pursue its own self-interest rather than maximizing the wealth of the owners. The resulting conflicts give rise to agency costs. Ways of reducing agency costs include developing compensation agreements that link employee compensation to the firm's performance and having independent boards of directors monitor management.

6. **Explain why ethics is an appropriate topic in the study of managerial finance.**

   If we lived in a world without ethical norms, we would soon discover that it would be difficult to do business. As a practical matter, the law and market forces provide important incentives that foster ethical behavior in the business community, but they are not enough to ensure ethical behavior. An ethical culture is also needed. In an ethical culture, people have a set of moral principles—a moral compass—that helps them identify ethical issues and make ethical judgments without being told what to do.

Self-Study Problems

1.1 Give an example of a financing decision and a capital budgeting decision.

1.2 What is the decision criterion for financial managers when selecting a capital project?

1.3 What are some ways to manage working capital?

1.4 Which one of the following characteristics does not pertain to corporations?
- **a.** can enter into contracts
- **b.** can borrow money
- **c.** are the easiest type of business to form
- **d.** can be sued
- **e.** can own stock in other companies

1.5 What are typically the main components of an executive compensation package?

Solutions to Self-Study Problems

1.1 Financing decisions determine how a firm will raise capital. Examples of financing decisions would be securing a bank loan or selling debt in the public capital markets. Capital budgeting involves deciding which productive assets the firm invests in, such as buying a new plant or investing in a renovation of an existing facility.

1.2 Financial managers should select a capital project only if the value of the project's future cash flows exceeds the cost of the project. In other words, firms should only take on investments that will increase their value and thus increase the stockholders' wealth.

1.3 Working capital is the day-to-day management of a firm's short-term assets and liabilities. It can be managed through maintaining the optimal level of inventory, keeping track of all the receivables and payables, deciding to whom the firm should extend credit, and making appropriate investments with excess cash.

1.4 The answer that does *not* pertain to corporations is (c) are the easiest type of business to form.

1.5 The three main components of an executive compensation package are: base salary, bonus based on accounting performance, and some compensation tied to the firm's stock price.

Critical Thinking Questions

1.1 Describe the cash flows between a firm and its stakeholders.

1.2 What are the three fundamental decisions the financial management team is concerned with, and how do they affect the firm's balance sheet?

1.3 What is the difference between stockholders and stakeholders?

1.4 Suppose that a group of accountants wants to start their own accounting company. What organizational form of business would they choose, and why?

1.5 What does double taxation in the corporate setting mean?

1.6 Explain why profit maximization is not the best goal for a company. What is an appropriate goal?

1.7 In determining the price of a firm's stock, what are some of the external and internal factors that affect price? What is the difference between these two types of variables?

1.8 Identify the sources of agency costs. What are some ways a company can control these factors?

1.9 What is the Sarbanes-Oxley Act, and what are its main goals that affect the board of directors?

1.10 Give an example of a conflict of interest in a business setting other than the one involving the real estate agent discussed in the text.

Questions and Problems

1.1 **Capital:** What are the two basic sources of funds for all businesses?

1.2 **Management role:** What is working capital management?

1.3 **Cash flows:** Explain the difference between profitable and unprofitable firms.

1.4 **Management role:** What three major decisions are of most concern to financial managers?

1.5 **Cash flows:** What is the general decision rule for a firm considering undertaking a project? Give a real-life example.

1.6 **Management role:** What is capital structure, and why is it important to a company?

1.7 **Management role:** What are some of the working capital decisions that a financial manager faces?

1.8 **Organizational form:** What are the three basic forms of business organization discussed in this chapter?

1.9 **Organizational form:** What are the advantages and disadvantages of a sole proprietorship?

1.10 **Organizational form:** What is a partnership, and what is the biggest disadvantage of this form of business organization? How can this disadvantage be avoided?

1.11 **Organizational form:** Who are the owners of a corporation, and how is their ownership represented?

1.12 **Organizational form:** Explain what is meant by stockholders' limited liability.

1.13 **Organizational form:** What is double taxation?

1.14 **Organizational form:** What is the business organization form preferred by most physicians, lawyers, and accountants, and why?

1.15 **Finance function:** What is the most important governing body within a business organization? What responsibilities does it have?

1.16 **Finance function:** Almost all public companies hire a certified public accounting firm to perform an independent audit of the financial statements. What exactly does an audit mean?

1.17 **Firm's goal:** What are some of the drawbacks to setting profit maximization as the main goal of a company?

1.18 **Firm's goal:** What is the appropriate goal of financial managers? Can managers' decisions affect this goal in any way? If so, how?

1.19 **Firm's goal:** What are the major factors affecting stock price?

1.20 **Agency conflicts:** What is an agency relationship, and what is an agency conflict? How can agency conflicts be reduced in a corporation?

1.21 **Firm's goal:** What can happen if a firm is poorly managed and its stock price falls substantially below its maximum?

1.22 **Agency conflicts:** What are some of the regulations that pertain to boards of directors that were put in place to reduce agency conflicts?

1.23 **Business ethics:** How could business dishonesty and low integrity cause an economic downfall? Give an example.

1.24 **Agency conflicts:** What are some possible ways to resolve a conflict of interest?

1.25 **Business ethics:** What ethical conflict does insider trading present?

Sample Test Problems

1.1 Why is value maximization superior to profit maximization as a goal for the firm?

1.2 The major advantage of debt financing is
a. it allows a firm to use creditors' money.
b. interest payments are more predictable than dividend payments.
c. interest payments are not required when a firm is not doing well.
d. interest payments are tax deductible.

1.3 Identify three fundamental decisions that a financial manager has to make in running a firm.

1.4 What are agency costs? Explain.

1.5 Identify four of the seven mechanisms that align the goals of managers with those of stockholders.

FINANCIAL STATEMENTS, CASH FLOWS, AND TAXES

CHAPTER 3

Suzi Altman/NewsCom

LEARNING OBJECTIVES

1. Discuss generally accepted accounting principles (GAAP) and their importance to the economy.
2. Know the balance sheet identity, and explain why a balance sheet must balance.
3. Describe how market-value balance sheets differ from book-value balance sheets.
4. Identify the basic equation for the income statement and the information it provides.
5. Explain the difference between cash flows and accounting income.
6. Explain how the four major financial statements discussed in this chapter are related.
7. Discuss the difference between average and marginal tax rates.

The new millennium has been a difficult period for the accounting profession. A case in point is the bankruptcy filing of WorldCom, whose officers had misstated $7.2 billion of expenses in the firm's financial statements. As accounting misconduct cases mounted in the early 2000s, investors and creditors became more and more concerned about the reliability and integrity of the financial statements of U.S.-based firms. To restore investor confidence and protect U.S. financial markets, Congress and federal regulators tightened accounting standards and oversight of the accounting profession. Passage of the Sarbanes-Oxley Act, discussed in Chapter 1, is an example of these steps.

There are many reasons for the accounting scandals that plagued the U.S. economy in the early years of this century. Many observers, however, place some of the blame on Wall Street's obsession with the earnings estimates set by financial analysts. Analysts estimate how much firms should earn in a particular reporting period, and firms that fail to meet these estimates can be severely punished by falling stock prices—and their CEOs can find themselves out of a job. These intense pressures led some firms to engage in a questionable practice called "backing in." It works as follows: Instead of starting by calculating sales and subtracting expenses and taxes to get profits, they work backward—that is, they start with the profits that analysts are expecting and then manipulate sales and expenses to make sure the numbers work out.

Clearly, the correct preparation of financial statements is crucial. In this chapter and the next, we focus on the preparation, interpretation, and limitations of financial statements. As you will see, the preparation of financial statements is not a cut-and-dried affair but involves considerable professional judgment, which can and does lead to variations in financial statements.

CHAPTER PREVIEW

In Chapter 1 we noted that all businesses have stakeholders—managers, creditors, suppliers, and the government, among others—who have some claim on the firms' cash flows. The stakeholders in a firm, along with the stockholders, need to monitor the firm's progress and evaluate its performance. Financial statements enable them to do these things. The accounting system is the framework that gathers information about the firm's business activities and translates the information into objective numerical financial reports.

Most firms prepare financial statements on a regular basis and have independent auditors certify that the financial statements have been prepared in accordance with generally accepted accounting principles and contain no material misstatements. The audit increases the confidence of the stakeholders that the financial statements prepared by management present a "fair and accurate" picture of the firm's financial condition at a particular point in time. In fact, it is difficult to get any type of legitimate business loan without audited financial statements.

This chapter reviews the basic structure of a firm's financial statements and explains how the various statements fit together. We examine the preparation of the balance sheet, the income statement, the statement of retained earnings, and the statement of cash flows. As you read through this part of the chapter, pay particular attention to the differences between (1) cash flows and accounting income and (2) book value and market value. Understanding the differences between these two sets of concepts is necessary to avoid serious analytical and decision-making errors. The last part of the chapter discusses essential features of the federal tax code for corporations. In finance we make most decisions on an after-tax basis, so understanding the tax code is very important.

3.1 Financial Statements and Accounting Principles

Before we can meaningfully interpret and analyze financial statements, we need to understand some accounting principles that guide their preparation. Thus, we begin the chapter with a discussion of generally accepted accounting principles, which guide firms in the preparation of financial statements. First, however, we briefly discuss the annual report.

Annual Reports

To see samples of annual reports from a variety of companies, visit http://www.zpub.com/sf/arl.

The *annual report* is the most important report that firms issue to their stockholders and make available to the general public. Historically, annual reports were dull, black-and-white publications that presented the firm's audited financial statements. Today some annual reports, especially those of large public companies, are slick, picture-laden, glossy "magazines" in full color with orchestrated media messages exalting the deeds of top management.

Annual reports typically are divided into three distinct sections. First are the financial tables, which contain financial information about the firm and its operations for the year, and an accompanying summary explaining the firm's performance over the past year. For example, the summary might explain that sales and profits were down because of lost sales in the Gulf States due to Hurricane Katrina in 2005. Often, there is a letter from the chairman or CEO that provides some insights into the reasons for the firm's performance, a discussion of new developments, and a high-level view of the firm's strategy and future direction. It is important to note that the financial tables are historical records reflecting past performance of the firm and do not necessarily indicate what the firm will do in the future.

The second part of the report is often a corporate public relations piece discussing the firm's product lines, its services to its customers, and its contributions to the communities in which it operates.

The third part of the annual report presents the audited financial statements: the balance sheet, the income statement, the statement of retained earnings, and the statement of cash flows. Overall, the annual report provides a good overview of the firm's operating and financial performance and states why, in management's judgment, things turned out the way they did.

Generally Accepted Accounting Principles

In the United States, accounting statements are prepared in accordance with **generally accepted accounting principles (GAAP)**, a set of widely agreed-upon rules and procedures that define how companies are to maintain financial records and prepare financial reports. These principles are important because without them, financial statements would be less standardized. Accounting standards such as GAAP make it easier for analysts and management to make meaningful comparisons of a company's performance against that of other companies.

generally accepted accounting principles (GAAP)
a set of rules that defines how companies are to prepare financial statements

Accounting principles and reporting practices for U.S. firms are promulgated by the Financial Accounting Standards Board (FASB), a not-for-profit body that operates in the public interest. FASB derives its authority from the Securities and Exchange Commission (SEC). GAAP and reporting practices are published in the form of FASB statements, and certified public accountants are required to follow these statements in their auditing and accounting practices.

You can find more information about FASB at www.fasb.org.

Fundamental Accounting Principles

To better understand financial statements, it is helpful to look at some fundamental accounting principles embodied in GAAP. These principles determine the manner of recording, measuring, and reporting company transactions. As you will see, the practical application of these principles requires professional judgment, which can result in considerable differences in financial statements.

THE ASSUMPTION OF ARM'S-LENGTH TRANSACTIONS

Accounting is based on the recording of economic transactions that can be quantified in dollar amounts. It assumes that the parties to a transaction are economically rational and are free to act *independently* of each other. To illustrate, let's assume that you are preparing a personal balance sheet for a bank loan on which you must list all your assets. You are including your BMW 325 as an asset. You bought the car a few months ago from your father for $3,000 when the retail price of the car was $15,000. You got a good deal. However, the price you paid, which would be the number recorded on your balance sheet, was not the market price. Since you did not purchase the BMW in an arm's-length transaction, your balance sheet would not reflect the true value of the asset.

THE COST PRINCIPLE

Generally, the value of an asset that is recorded on a company's "books" reflects its historical cost. The historical cost is assumed to represent the fair market value of the item at the time it was acquired and is recorded as the **book value**. Over time, it is unlikely that an asset's book value will be equal to its market value because market values tend to change over time. The major exception to this principle is marketable securities, such as the stock of another company, which are recorded at their current market value.

book value
the net value of an asset or liability recorded on the financial statements—normally reflects historical cost

It is important to note that accounting statements are records of past performance; they are based on historical costs, not on current market prices or values. Accounting statements translate the business's past performance into dollars and cents, which helps management and investors better understand how the business has performed in the past.

THE REALIZATION PRINCIPLE

Under the realization principle, revenue is recognized only when the sale is virtually completed and the exchange value for the goods or services can be reliably determined. As a practical matter, this means that most revenues are recognized at the time of sale whether or not cash is actually received. At this time, if a firm sells to its customers on credit, an account receivable is recorded. The firm receives the cash only when the customer actually makes the payment. Although the realization principle concept seems straightforward, there can be considerable ambiguity in its interpretation. For example, should revenues be recognized when goods are ordered, when they are shipped, or when payment is received from the customer?

THE MATCHING PRINCIPLE

Accounting tries to match revenue on the income statement with the expenses used to generate the revenue. In practice, this principle means that revenue is first recognized (according to the realization principle) and then is matched with the costs associated with producing the revenue. For example, if we manufacture a product and sell it on credit (accounts receivable), the revenue is recognized at the time of sale. The expenses associated with manufacturing the product—expenditures for raw materials, labor, equipment, and facilities—will be recognized at the same time. Notice that the actual cash outflows for expenses may not occur at the same time the expenses are recognized. It should be clear that the figures on the income statement more than likely will not correspond to the actual cash inflows and outflows during the period.

THE GOING CONCERN ASSUMPTION

The going concern assumption is the assumption that a business will remain in operation for the foreseeable future. This assumption underlies much of what is done in accounting. For example, suppose that Kmart has $4.6 billion of inventory on its balance sheet, representing what the firm actually paid for the inventory in arm's-length transactions. If we assume that Kmart is a going concern, the balance sheet figure is a reasonable number because in the normal course of business we expect Kmart to be able to sell the goods for its cost plus some reasonable markup.

However, suppose Kmart declares bankruptcy and is forced by its creditors to liquidate its assets. If this happens, Kmart is no longer a going concern. What will the inventory be worth then? We cannot be certain, but 50 cents on the dollar might be a high figure. The going concern assumption allows the accountant to record assets at cost rather than their value in a liquidation sale, which is usually much less.

You can see that the fundamental accounting principles just discussed leave considerable professional discretion to accountants in the preparation of financial statements. As a result, financial statements can and do differ because of honest differences in professional judgments. Of course, there are limits on "honest professional differences," and at some point, an accountant's choices can cross a line and result in "cooking the books."

International GAAP

Accounting is often called the language of business. Just as there are different dialects within languages, there are different international "dialects" in accounting. For example, the set of generally accepted accounting principles in the United Kingdom is called

U.K. GAAP. With the emergence of the European Union (EU), member countries are moving toward a "European GAAP." In other parts of the world, the accounting system used often depends on a country's history. For example, Hong Kong and India, which were once colonies of England, use a variant of the British accounting system.

The good news is that it is not difficult for accountants to adjust financial statements so that meaningful comparisons can be made between statements based on differing accounting principles. At the same time, these adjustments represent an economic inefficiency that adds a cost to international business transactions.

As more businesses operate internationally and world economies become more integrated, maintaining and translating between different accounting systems makes less and less economic sense. Economic and political pressures are thus building in both the United States and Europe to develop a unified accounting system. As of now, the adoption of a common accounting standard by the United States and Europe is not around the corner. How soon it will occur depends on the political climate between the two economic powers and the continued globalization of commerce.

Illustrative Company: Diaz Manufacturing

In the next part of the chapter, we turn to a discussion of four fundamental financial statements: the balance sheet, the income statement, the statement of retained earnings, and the statement of cash flows. To more clearly illustrate these financial statements, we use data from Diaz Manufacturing Company, a fictional Houston-based provider of petroleum and industrial equipment and services worldwide.[1] Diaz Manufacturing was formed in 2003 as a spin-off of several divisions of Cooper Industries. The firm specializes in the design and manufacturing of systems used in petroleum production and has two divisions: (1) Diaz Energy Services, which sells oil and gas compression equipment, and (2) Diaz Manufacturing, which makes valves and related parts for energy production.

In 2008 Diaz Manufacturing's sales increased to $1.56 billion, an increase of 12.8 percent from the previous year. A letter to stockholders in the 2008 annual report stated that management did not expect earnings in 2009 to exceed the 2008 earnings. The reason for caution was that Diaz's earnings are very susceptible to changes in the political and economic environment in the world's energy-producing regions, and in 2008 the environment in the Middle East was highly unstable. Management reassured investors, however, that Diaz had the financial strength and the management team needed to weather any economic adversity.

Before You Go On

1. What types of information does a firm's annual report contain?
2. What is the realization principle, and why may it lead to a difference in the timing of when revenues are recognized on the books and cash is collected?

3.2 The Balance Sheet

LEARNING OBJECTIVE 2

The **balance sheet** reports the firm's financial position at a particular point in time. Exhibit 3.1 shows the balance sheets for Diaz Manufacturing on December 31, 2007 and December 31, 2008. The left-hand side of the balance sheet identifies the firm's assets, most of which are listed at book value. These assets are owned by the firm and

[1]Although Diaz Manufacturing Company is not a real firm, the financial statements and situations presented are based on a composite of actual firms.

Exhibit 3.1 Diaz Manufacturing Balance Sheets as of December 31 ($ millions)

Assets	2008	2007	Liabilities and Stockholders' Equity	2008	2007
Cash[a]	$ 288.5	$ 16.6	Accounts payable and accruals	$ 349.3	$ 325.0
Accounts receivable	306.2	268.8	Notes payable	10.5	4.2
Inventories	423.8	372.7	Accrued taxes	18.0	16.8
Other current assets	21.3	29.9	Total current liabilities	$ 377.8	$ 346.0
Total current assets	$1,039.8	$ 688.0	Long-term debt	574.0	305.6
Plant and equipment	911.6	823.3	Total liabilities	$ 951.8	$ 651.6
Less: Accumulated depreciation	512.2	429.1	Preferred stock[b]	—	—
Net plant and equipment	$ 399.4	$ 394.2	Common stock (54,566,054 shares)[c]	50.0	50.0
Goodwill and other assets	450.0	411.6	Additional paid-in capital	842.9	842.9
			Retained earnings	67.8	(50.7)
			Treasury stock (571,320 shares)	(23.3)	—
			Total stockholders' equity	$ 937.4	$ 842.2
Total assets	$1,889.2	$1,493.8	Total liabilities and equity	$1,889.2	$1,493.8

[a]Cash includes marketable securities.
[b]10,000,000 preferred stock shares authorized.
[c]150,000,000 common stock shares authorized.

The left-hand side of the balance sheet lists the assets that the firm has at a particular point in time, while the right-hand side shows how the firm has financed those assets.

balance sheet
financial statement that shows a firm's financial position (assets, liabilities, and equity) at a point in time

Go to the EDGAR database at www.sec.gov, the Web site of the SEC, to see the financial statements of any publicly traded company.

are used to generate income. The right-hand side of the balance sheet includes liabilities and stockholders' equity, which tell us how the firm has financed its assets. Liabilities are obligations of the firm that represent claims against its assets. These claims arise from debts and other obligations to pay creditors, employees, or the government. In contrast, stockholders' equity represents the residual claim of the owners on the remaining assets of the firm after all liabilities have been paid.[2] The basic balance sheet identity can thus be stated as follows:[3]

$$\text{Total assets} = \text{Total liabilities} + \text{Total stockholders' equity} \tag{3.1}$$

Since stockholders' equity is the residual claim, stockholders would receive the residual value if the firm decided to sell off all of its assets and use the money to pay its creditors. That is why the balance sheet always balances. Simply put, if you total what the firm owns and what it owes, then the difference between the two is the total stockholders' equity:

$$\text{Total stockholders' equity} = \text{Total assets} - \text{Total liabilities}$$

Notice that total stockholders' equity can be positive, negative, or equal to zero.

Next, we examine some important balance sheet accounts of Diaz Manufacturing as of December 31, 2008 (see Exhibit 3.1). As a matter of convention, accountants divide assets and liabilities into short-term (or current) and long-term parts. We will start by looking at current assets and liabilities.

---

[2]The terms *owners' equity, stockholders' equity, shareholders' equity, net worth,* and *equity* are used interchangeably to refer to the ownership of a corporation's stock.

[3]An *identity* is an equation that is true by definition; thus, a balance sheet must balance.

Current Assets and Liabilities

Current assets are assets that can reasonably be expected to be converted into cash within one year. Besides cash, which includes marketable securities, other current assets are accounts receivable, which are typically payable within 30 to 45 days, and inventory, which is money invested in raw materials, work-in-process inventory, and finished goods. Diaz's current assets total $1,039.8 million.

Current liabilities are obligations payable within one year. Typical current liabilities are accounts payable, which arise in the purchases of goods and services from vendors and are normally paid within 30 to 60 days; notes payable, which are formal borrowing agreements with a bank or some other lender that have a stated maturity; and accrued taxes from federal, state, and local governments, which are taxes Diaz owes but has not yet paid. Diaz's total current liabilities equal $377.8 million.

NET WORKING CAPITAL

Recall from Chapter 1 that the dollar difference between total current assets and total current liabilities is the firm's net working capital:

$$\text{Net working capital} = \text{Total current assets} - \text{Total current liabilities} \quad (3.2)$$

Net working capital is a measure of a firm's liquidity, which is the ability of the firm to meet its obligations as they come due. One way that firms maintain their liquidity is by holding assets that are highly liquid. Recall that the liquidity of an asset is how quickly it can be converted into cash without loss of value. Thus, an asset's liquidity has two dimensions: (1) the speed and ease with which the asset can be sold and (2) whether the asset can be sold without loss of value. Of course, any asset can be sold easily and quickly if the price is low enough.

For Diaz Manufacturing, total current assets are $1,039.8 million, and total current liabilities are $377.8 million. The firm's net working capital is thus:

$$\begin{aligned}\text{Net working capital} &= \text{Total current assets} - \text{Total current liabilities}\\ &= \$1{,}039.8 \text{ million} - \$377.8 \text{ million}\\ &= \$662.0 \text{ million}\end{aligned}$$

To interpret this number, if Diaz Manufacturing took its current stock of cash and liquidated its marketable securities, accounts receivables, and inventory at book value, it would have $1,039.8 million with which to pay off its short-term liabilities of $377.8 million, leaving $662.0 million of "cushion." As a short-term creditor, such as a bank, you would view the net working capital position as positive because Diaz's current assets exceed current liabilities by almost three times ($1,039.8/$377.8 = 2.75).

ACCOUNTING FOR INVENTORY

Inventory, as noted earlier, is a current asset on the balance sheet, but it is usually the least liquid of the current assets. The reason is that it can take a long time for a firm to convert inventory into cash. For a manufacturing firm, the inventory cycle begins with raw materials, continues with goods in process, proceeds with finished goods, and finally concludes with selling the asset for cash or an account receivable. For a firm such as The Boeing Company, for example, the inventory cycle in manufacturing an aircraft can be nearly a year.

An important decision for management is the selection of an inventory valuation method. The most common methods are FIFO (first in, first out) and LIFO (last in, first out). During periods of changing price levels, how a firm values its inventory affects both its balance sheet and its income statement. For example, suppose that prices have been rising (inflation). If a company values its inventory using the FIFO method, when the firm makes a sale, it assumes the sale is from the oldest, lowest-cost inventory—first in, first out. Thus, during rising prices, firms using FIFO will have the lowest cost of goods sold, the highest net income, and the highest inventory value. In contrast, a company using the LIFO method assumes the sale is from the newest, highest-cost inventory—last in, first out. During a period of inflation, firms using LIFO will have the highest cost of goods sold, the lowest net income, and the lowest inventory value.

Because inventory valuation methods can have a significant impact on both the income statement and the balance sheet, when financial analysts compare different companies, they make adjustments to the financial statements for differences in inventory valuation methods. Although firms can switch from one inventory valuation method to another, this type of change is an extraordinary event and cannot be done frequently.

Diaz Manufacturing reports inventory values in the United States using the LIFO method. The remaining inventories, which are located outside the United States and Canada, are calculated using the FIFO method. Diaz's total inventory is $423.8 million.

Long-Term Assets and Liabilities

The remaining assets on the balance sheet are classified as long-term assets. Typically, these assets are financed by long-term liabilities and stockholders' equity.

LONG-TERM ASSETS

Long-term or productive assets are the assets that the firm uses to generate most of its income. Long-term assets may be tangible or intangible. Tangible assets are balance sheet items such as land, mineral resources, buildings, equipment, machinery, and vehicles that are used over an extended period of time. In addition, tangible assets can include other businesses that a firm wholly or partially owns, such as foreign subsidiaries. Intangible assets are items such as patents, copyrights, licensing agreements, technology, and other intellectual capital the firm owns.

Goodwill is an intangible asset that arises only when a firm purchases another firm. Conceptually, goodwill is a measure of how much the value of the acquired firm exceeds the sum of the values of its individual assets. This additional value is created by the way in which those assets are being used. For example, if Diaz Manufacturing paid $2.0 million for a company that had individual assets with a total fair market value of $1.9 million, the goodwill premium paid would be $100,000 ($2.0 million − $1.9 million).

Diaz Manufacturing's long-term assets comprise net plant and equipment of $399.4 million and intangible and other assets of $450.0 million, as shown in Exhibit 3.1. The term *net plant and equipment* indicates that accumulated depreciation has been subtracted to arrive at the net value. That is, net plant and equipment equals total plant and equipment less accumulated depreciation; accumulated depreciation is the total amount of depreciation expense taken on plant and equipment up to the balance sheet date. For Diaz Manufacturing, the above method yields the following result:

$$\begin{aligned}\text{Net plant and equipment} &= \text{Total plant and equipment} - \text{Accumulated depreciation}\\ &= \$911.6 \text{ million} - \$512.2 \text{ million}\\ &= \$399.4 \text{ million}\end{aligned}$$

ACCUMULATED DEPRECIATION

depreciation
allocation of the cost of an asset over its estimated life to reflect the wear and tear on the asset as it is used to produce the firm's goods and services

When a firm acquires a tangible asset that deteriorates with use and wears out, accountants try to allocate the asset's cost over its useful life. The matching principle requires that the cost be expensed against the period in which the firm benefited from use of the asset. Thus, **depreciation** allocates the cost of a limited-life asset to the periods in which the firm is assumed to benefit from the asset. Tangible assets with an unlimited life, such as land, are not depreciated. Depreciation affects the balance sheet through the accumulated depreciation account; we discuss its effect on the income statement in Section 3.4.

A company can elect whether to depreciate its assets using straight-line depreciation or one of the approved accelerated depreciation methods. Accelerated depreciation methods allow for more depreciation expense in the early years of an asset's life than straight-line depreciation.

Diaz Manufacturing uses the straight-line method of depreciation. Had Diaz elected to use accelerated depreciation, the value of its depreciable assets would have been written off to the income statement more quickly (higher depreciation expense), resulting in a lower "net plant and equipment" account on its balance sheet and a lower net income for the period.

LONG-TERM LIABILITIES

Long-term liabilities include debt instruments due and payable beyond one year as well as other long-term obligations of the firm. They include bonds, bank term loans, mortgages, and other types of liabilities, such as pension obligations and deferred compensation. Typically, firms finance long-term assets with long-term liabilities. Diaz Manufacturing has a single long-term liability of $574.0 million, which is a long-term debt.

Equity

We have summarized the types of assets and liabilities that appear on the balance sheet. Now we look at the equity accounts. Diaz Manufacturing's total stockholders' equity at the end of 2008 is $937.4 million and is made up of four accounts—common stock, additional paid-in capital, retained earnings, and treasury stock—which we discuss next. We conclude with a discussion of preferred stock. Although preferred stock appears on Diaz Manufacturing's balance sheets, the company has no shares of preferred stock outstanding.

THE COMMON STOCK ACCOUNTS

The most important equity accounts are those related to the common stock, which represent the true ownership of the firm. Certain basic rights of ownership typically come with common stock; those rights are as follows:

1. The right to vote on corporate matters such as the election of the board of directors or important actions such as the purchase of another company.

2. The preemptive right, which allows stockholders to purchase any additional shares of stock issued by the corporation in proportion to the number of shares they currently own. This allows common stockholders to retain the same percentage of ownership in the firm, if they choose to do so.

3. The right to receive cash dividends if they are paid.

4. If the firm is liquidated, the right to all remaining corporate assets after all creditors and preferred stockholders have been paid.

A common source of confusion is the number of different common stock accounts, each of which identifies a source of the firm's equity. The *common stock account* identifies the initial funding from investors that was used to start the business and is priced at a par value. The par value is an arbitrary number set by management, usually a nominal amount such as $1.

Clearly, par value has little to do with the market value of the stock. The *additional paid-in capital account* is the amount of capital received for the common stock in excess of par value. Thus, if the new business is started with $40,000 in cash and the firm decides to issue 1,000 shares of common stock with a par value of $1, the owners' equity account looks as follows:

Common stock (1,000 shares @ $1 par value)	$ 1,000
Additional paid-in capital	39,000
Total paid-in capital	$ 40,000

Note the money put up by the initial investors: $1,000 in total par value (1,000 shares of common stock with a par value of $1) and $39,000 additional paid-in capital, for a total of $40,000.

As you can see in Exhibit 3.1, Diaz manufacturing has 54,566,054 shares of common stock with a par value of 91.63 cents, for a total value of $50.0 million (54,566,054 shares × 91.63 cents). The additional paid-in capital is $842.9 million. Thus, Diaz's total paid-in capital is $892.9 million ($50.0 + $842.9).

RETAINED EARNINGS

The retained earnings account represents earnings that have been retained and reinvested in the business over time rather than being paid out as cash dividends. Diaz Manufacturing's retained earnings account is only $67.8 million, compared with the total paid-in capital of $892.9 million. Reading the annual report, we learn that in the recent past the company "wrote down" a substantial amount of assets. This transaction, which will be discussed later in the chapter, reduced the size of the retained earnings account.

Note that retained earnings are not the same as cash. In fact, a company can have a very large retained earnings account and no cash. Conversely, it can have lots of cash and a very small retained earnings account. Because retained earnings appear on the liability side of the balance sheet, they do not represent an asset, as cash and marketable securities do.

TREASURY STOCK

treasury stock
stock that the firm has repurchased from investors

The **treasury stock** account represents stock that the firm has purchased back from investors. Publicly traded companies can simply buy shares of stock from stockholders on the market at the prevailing price. Typically, repurchased stock is held as "treasury stock," and the firm can reissue it in the future if it desires. Diaz Manufacturing has spent a total of $23.3 million to repurchase the 571,320 shares of common stock it currently holds as treasury stock. The company has had a policy of repurchasing common stock, which has been subsequently reissued to senior executives under the firm's stock-option plan.

You may wonder why a firm's management would repurchase its own stock. This is a classic finance question, and it has no simple answer. The conventional wisdom is that when a company has excess cash and management believes its stock price is undervalued, it makes sense to purchase stock with the cash.

However, it is not obvious that management can beat the market over the long term when buying and selling company stock. A case in point is Hewlett-Packard (HP), the computer equipment giant, which spent $6.4 billion to purchase its own shares from November 1998 to July 2000 at an average price per share of $53.60. At the time, HP's public relations department said the shares were a "bargain." But as of March 15, 2007, about seven years later, the "bargain" shares traded for about $40.22 per share. Furthermore, bear in mind that the company could have used those funds to pay down debt, finance new products and development, or finance strategic acquisitions or could simply have kept the cash for a rainy day.

PREFERRED STOCK

Preferred stock is a cross between common stock and long-term debt. Preferred stock pays dividends at a specified fixed rate, which means that the firm cannot increase or decrease the dividend rate, regardless of whether the firm's earnings increase or decrease. However, like common stock dividends, preferred stock dividends are declared by the board of directors, and in the event of financial distress, the board can elect not to pay a preferred stock dividend. If preferred stock dividends are missed, the firm is typically required to pay dividends that have been skipped in the past before they can pay dividends to common stockholders. In the event of bankruptcy, preferred stockholders are paid before common stockholders but after bondholders and other creditors. As shown in Exhibit 3.1, Diaz Manufacturing has no preferred stock outstanding, but the company is authorized to issue up to 10 million shares of preferred stock.

Before You Go On

1. What is net working capital? Why might a low value for this number be considered undesirable?
2. Explain the accounting concept behind depreciation.
3. What is treasury stock?

3.3 Market Value versus Book Value

Although accounting statements are helpful to analysts and managers, they have a number of limitations. One of these limitations, mentioned earlier, is that accounting statements are historical—they are based on data such as the cost of a building that was built years ago. Thus, the value of assets on the balance sheet is what the firm paid for them and not their current **market value**—the amount they are worth today.

market value
the price at which an item can be sold

Investors and management, however, care about how the company will do in the future. The best information concerning how much a company's assets can earn in the future, as well as how much of a burden its liabilities are, comes from the current market value of those assets and liabilities. Accounting statements would therefore be more valuable if they measured current value. The process of recording assets at their current market value is often called *marking to market.*

In theory, everyone agrees that it is better to base financial statements on current information. Marking to market provides decision makers with financial statements that more closely reflect a company's true financial condition; thus, they have a better chance of making the correct economic decision, given the information available. For example, providing current market values means that managers can no longer conceal a failing business or hide unrealized gains on assets.

An article in *Business Week Online* offers a perspective on market-value accounting; go to www.businessweek.com/magazine/content/02_10/b3773103.htm.

On the downside, the current value of some assets can be hard to estimate, and accountants are reluctant to make estimates. Critics also point out that some of the valuation models used to estimate market values are complicated to apply and the resulting numbers are potentially open to abuse. For example, Enron manipulated its forecasts of energy prices to maximize the value of long-term gas and electric contracts on its books.

A More Informative Balance Sheet

To illustrate why market value provides better economic information than book value, let's revisit the balance sheet components discussed earlier. Our discussion will also help you understand why there can be such large differences between some book-value and market-value balance sheet accounts.

ASSETS

For current assets, market value and book value may be reasonably close. The reason is that current assets have a short life cycle and typically are converted into cash quickly. Then, as new current assets are added to the balance sheet, they are entered at their current market price.

In contrast, fixed assets have a long life cycle, and their market value and book value are not likely to be equal. In addition, if an asset is depreciable, the amount of depreciation shown on the balance sheet does not necessarily reflect actual loss of economic value. As a general rule, the longer the time that has passed since an asset was acquired, the more likely it is that the current market value will differ from the book value.

For example, suppose a firm purchased land for a trucking depot in Atlanta, Georgia, 30 years ago for $100,000. Today the land is nestled in an expensive suburban area and is worth around $5.5 million. The difference between the book value of $100,000 and the market value is $5.4 million. In another example, say an airline company decided to replace its aging fleet of aircraft with new fuel-efficient jets in the late 1990s. Following the September 11, 2001, terrorist attack, airline travel declined dramatically; and during 2003 nearly one-third of all commercial jets were "mothballed." In 2003 the current market value of the replacement commercial jets was about two-thirds their original cost. Why the decline? Because the expected cash flows from owning a commercial aircraft had declined a great deal.

LIABILITIES

The market value of liabilities can also differ from their book value, though typically by smaller amounts than is the case with assets. For liabilities, the balance sheet shows the amount of money that the company has promised to pay. This figure is generally close to the actual market value for short-term liabilities.

For long-term debt, however, book value and market value can differ substantially. The market value of debt with fixed interest payments is affected by the level of interest rates in the economy. More specifically, after long-term debt is issued, if the market rate of interest increases, the market price of the debt will decline. Conversely, if interest rates decline, the value of the debt will increase. For example, assume that a firm has $1 million of 20-year bonds outstanding. If the market rate of interest increases from 5 to 8 percent, the price of the bonds will decline to around $700,000.[4] Thus, changes in interest rates can have an important effect on the market values of long-term liabilities, such as corporate bonds. Even if interest rates do not change, the market value of long-term liabilities can change if the performance of the firm declines and the probability of default increases.

STOCKHOLDERS' EQUITY

The book value of the firm's equity is one of the least informative items on the balance sheet. The book value of equity, as suggested earlier, is simply a historical record. As a result, it says very little about the market value of the stockholders' stake in the firm.

In contrast, on a balance sheet where both assets and liabilities are marked to market, the firm's equity is more informative to management and investors. *The difference between the market values of the assets and liabilities provides a better estimate of the market value of stockholders' equity than the difference in the book values.* Intuitively, this makes sense because if you know the "true" market value of the firm's assets and liabilities, the difference must equal the market value of the stockholders' equity.

You should be aware, however, that the difference between the sum of the market values of the individual assets and total liabilities will not give us an exact estimate of the market value of stockholders' equity. The reason is that the true total value of a firm's assets depends on how these assets are utilized. By utilizing the assets efficiently, management can make the total value greater than the simple sum of parts. We will discuss this concept in more detail in Chapter 18.

Finally, if you know the market value of the stockholders' equity and the number of shares of stock outstanding, it is easy to compute the stock price. Specifically, the price of a share of stock is the market value of the firm's stockholders' equity divided by the number of shares outstanding.

---

[4]We will discuss precisely how changes in interest rates affect the market price of debt in Chapter 8, so for now, don't worry about the numerical calculation.

A Market-Value Balance Sheet

Let's look at an example of how a market-value balance sheet can differ from a book-value balance sheet. Marvel Airline is a small regional carrier that has been serving the Northeast for five years. The airline has a fleet of short-haul jet aircrafts, most of which were purchased over the past two years. The fleet has a book value of $600 million. Recently, the airline industry has suffered substantial losses in revenue due to price competition, and most carriers are projecting operating losses for the foreseeable future. As a result, the market value of Marvel's aircraft fleet is only $400 million. The book value of Marvel's long-term debt is $300 million, which is near its current market value. The firm has 100 million shares outstanding. Using these data, we can construct two balance sheets, one based on historical book values and the other based on market values:

Marvel Airlines
Market-Value versus Book-Value Balance Sheets ($ millions)

Assets	Book	Market	Liabilities and Stockholders' Equity	Book	Market
Aircraft	$ 600	$ 400	Long-term debt	$ 300	$ 300
			Stockholders' equity	300	100
Total	$ 600	$ 400		$ 600	$ 400

Based on the book-value balance sheet, the firm's financial condition looks fine; the book value of Marvel's aircraft at $600 million is near what the firm paid, and the stockholders' equity account is $300 million. But when we look at the market-value balance sheet, a different story emerges. We immediately see that the value of the aircraft has declined by $200 million and the stockholders' equity has declined by $200 million!

Why the decline in stockholders' equity? Recall that in Chapter 1 we argued that the value of any asset—stocks, bonds, or a firm—is determined by the future cash flows the asset will generate. At the time the aircraft were purchased, it was expected that they would generate a certain amount of cash flows over time. Now that hard times plague the industry, the cash flow expectations have been lowered, and hence the decline in the value of stockholders' equity.

The Market-Value Balance Sheet

LEARNING BY DOING APPLICATION 3.1

Problem: Grady Means and his four partners in Menlo Park Consulting (MPC) have developed a revolutionary new continuous audit program that can monitor high-risk areas within a firm and identify abnormalities so that corrective actions can be taken. The partners have spent about $300,000 developing the program. The firm's bookkeeper carries the audit program as an asset valued at cost, which is $300,000. To launch the product, the four partners recently invested an additional $1 million, and the money is currently in the firm's bank account. At a recent trade show, a number of accounting and financial consulting firms tried to buy the new continuous product—the highest offer being $15 million. Assuming these are MPC's only assets and liabilities, prepare the firm's book-value and market-value balance sheet and explain the difference between the two.

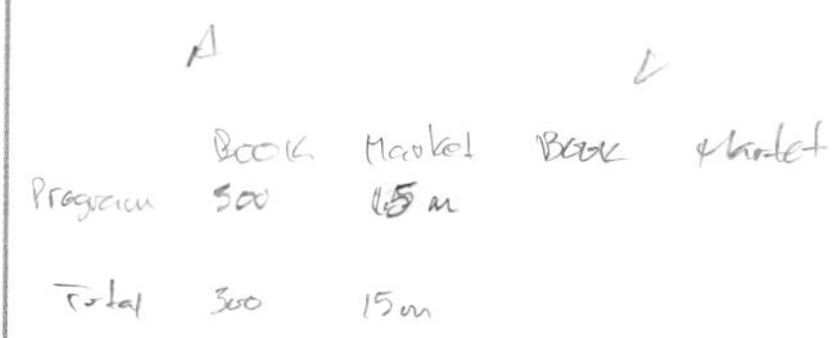

Approach: The main differences between the two balance sheets will be the treatment of the $300,000 already spent to develop the program and the $15 million offer. The book-value balance sheet is a historical document, which means all assets are valued at what it cost to put them in service, while the market-value balance sheet reflects the value of the assets if they were sold under current market conditions. The differences between the two approaches can be considerable.

(continued)

Solution: The two balance sheets are as follows:

Menlo Park Consulting
Market-Value versus Book-Value Balance Sheets ($ thousands)

Assets	Book	Market	Liabilities and Stockholder's Equity	Book	Market
Cash in bank	$ 1,000	$ 1,000	Long-term debt	$ —	$ —
Intangible assets	300	15,000	Stockholders' equity	1,300	16,000
Total	$ 1,300	$ 16,000		$ 1,300	$ 16,000

The book-value balance sheet provides little useful information. The book value of the firm's total assets is $1.3 million, which consists of cash in the bank and the cost of developing the audit program. Since the firm has no debt, total assets must equal the book value of stockholders' equity. The market value tells a dramatically different story. The market value of the audit program is estimated to be $15.0 million; thus, the market value of stockholders' equity is $16.0 million and not $1.3 million as reported in the book-value balance sheet.

Before You Go On

1. What is the difference between book value and market value?
2. What are some objections to the preparation of marked-to-market balance sheets?

3.4 The Income Statement and the Statement of Retained Earnings

In the previous sections, we examined a firm's balance sheet, which is like a financial snapshot of the firm at a point in time. In contrast, the income statement is like a video clip showing how profitable a firm is between two points in time.

The Income Statement

income statement
a financial statement that reports a firm's revenues, expenses, and profits or losses over a period of time

The **income statement** summarizes the revenues, expenses, and the profitability (or losses) of the firm over some period of time, usually a month, a quarter, or a year. The basic equation for the income statement can be expressed as follows:

$$\text{Net income} = \text{Revenues} - \text{Expenses} \quad (3.3)$$

Let's look more closely at each element in this equation.

REVENUES

A firm's revenues arise from the products and services it creates through its business operations. For manufacturing and merchandising companies, revenues come from the sale of merchandise. Service companies, such as consulting firms, generate fees for the services they perform. Other kinds of businesses earn revenues by charging interest or collecting rent. Regardless of how they earn revenues, most firms either receive cash or create an account receivable for each transaction, which increases their total assets.

EXPENSES

Expenses are the various costs that the firm incurs to generate revenues. Broadly speaking, expenses are (1) the value of long-term assets consumed through business operations, such as depreciation expense; and (2) the costs incurred in conducting business, such as labor, utilities, materials, and taxes.

NET INCOME

The firm's net income reflects its accomplishments (revenues) relative to its efforts (expenses) during a time period. If revenues exceed expenses, the firm generates net income for the period. If expenses exceed revenues, the firm has a net loss. Net income is often referred to as profits, as income, or simply as the "bottom line," since it is the last item on the income statement. Net income is often reported on a per-share basis and is then called **earnings per share (EPS)**, where EPS equals net income divided by the number of common shares outstanding. A firm's earnings per share tell a stockholder how much the firm has earned (or lost) for each share of stock outstanding.

earnings per share (EPS) net income divided by the number of common shares outstanding

Income statements for Diaz Manufacturing for 2007 and 2008 are shown in Exhibit 3.2. You can see that in 2008 total revenues from all sources (sales) were $1,563.7 million. Total expenses for producing and selling those goods were $1,445.2 million—the total of the amounts for cost of goods sold, selling and administrative expenses, depreciation, interest expense, and taxes.[5]

Exhibit 3.2 **Diaz Manufacturing Income Statements for Year Ending December 31 ($ millions)**

	2008	2007
Net sales[a]	$1,563.7	$1,386.7
Cost of goods sold	1,081.1	974.8
Selling and administrative expenses	231.1	197.4
Earnings before Interest, taxes, depreciation, and amortization (EBITDA)	$ 251.5	$ 214.5
Depreciation and amortization	83.1	75.3
Earnings before interest and taxes (EBIT)	$ 168.4	$ 139.2
Interest expense	5.6	18.0
Earnings before taxes (EBT)	$ 162.8	$ 121.2
Taxes	44.3	16.1
Net income	$ 118.5	$ 105.1
Common stock dividend	—	—
Addition to retained earnings	$ 118.5	$ 105.1
Per-share data:		
Common stock price		
Earnings per share (EPS)	$ 2.17	$ 1.93
Dividends per share (DPS)	—	—
Book value per share (BVPS)	—	—
Cash flow per share (CFPS)	$ 3.69	$ 3.31

[a]Net sales is defined as total sales less all sales discounts and sales returns and allowances.

The income statement shows the sales, expenses, and profits earned by the firm over a specific period of time.

[5]Looking at Exhibit 3.2, we find that the total expenses (in millions) are as follows: $1,081.1 + $231.1 + $83.1 + $5.6 + $44.3 = $1,445.2.

Using Equation 3.3, we can use these numbers to calculate Diaz Manufacturing's net income for the year:

$$\begin{aligned}\text{Net income} &= \text{Revenues} - \text{Expenses}\\ &= \$1{,}563.7\text{ million} - \$1{,}445.2\text{ million} = \$118.5\text{ million}\end{aligned}$$

Since Diaz Manufacturing had 54,566,054 common shares outstanding at year's end, its EPS was $2.17 per share ($118.5 million/54.566 million).

A CLOSER LOOK AT SOME EXPENSE CATEGORIES

Next, we take a closer look at some of the expense items on the income statement. We discussed depreciation earlier in relation to the balance sheet, and we now look at the role of depreciation in the income statement.

Depreciation Expense. An interesting feature of financial reporting is that companies are allowed to prepare two sets of financial statements: one for tax purposes and one for managing the company and for financial reporting to the SEC and investors. For tax purposes, most firms elect to accelerate depreciation as quickly as is permitted under the tax code. The reason is that accelerated depreciation results in a higher depreciation expense to the income statement, which in turn results in a lower net income and a lower tax liability in the first few years after the asset is acquired. The good news about accelerating depreciation for tax purposes is that the firm pays lower taxes but does not actually write a bigger check for depreciation expense. The depreciation method does not affect the cost of the asset. In contrast, straight-line depreciation results in lower depreciation expenses to the income statement, which results in higher net income and higher tax payments. Firms generally use straight-line depreciation in the financial statements they report to the SEC and investors because it makes their earnings look better.

It is important to understand that the company does not take more total depreciation under accelerated depreciation methods than under the straight-line method; the total amount of depreciation expensed to the income statement over the life of an asset is the same. Total depreciation cannot exceed the price paid for the asset. Accelerating depreciation only alters the timing of when the depreciation is expensed.

Amortization Expense. Amortization is the process of writing off expenses for intangible assets—such as patents, licenses, copyrights, and trademarks—over their useful life. Since depreciation and amortization are very similar, they are often lumped together on the income statement. Both are noncash expenses, which means that an expense is recorded on the income statement, but the associated cash does not necessarily leave the firm in that period. For Diaz Manufacturing, the depreciation and amortization expense for 2008 was $83.1 million.

At one time, goodwill was one of the intangible assets subject to amortization. As of June 2001, however, goodwill could no longer be amortized. The value of the goodwill on a firm's balance sheet is now subject to an annual *impairment test.* This test requires that the company annually value the businesses that were acquired in the past to see if the value of the goodwill associated with those businesses has declined below the value at which it is being carried on the balance sheet. If the value of the goodwill has declined (been impaired), management must write off the amount of the impairment. This write-off reduces the firm's reported net income.

Extraordinary Items. Other items reported separately in the income statement are extraordinary items, which are reserved for nonoperating gains or losses. Extraordinary items are unusual and infrequent occurrences, such as gains or losses from floods, fires, or earthquakes. For example, in 1980 the volcano Mount St. Helens erupted in Washington state, and Weyerhaeuser Company reported an extraordinary loss of $67 million to cover the damage to its standing timber, buildings, and equipment. Diaz Manufacturing has no extraordinary expense item during 2008.

STEP BY STEP TO THE BOTTOM LINE

You probably noticed in Exhibit 3.2 that Diaz Manufacturing's income statement showed income at several intermediate steps before reaching net income, the so-called bottom line. These intermediate income figures, which are typically included on a firm's income statement, provide important information about the firm's performance and help identify what factors are driving the firm's income or losses.

EBITDA. The first intermediate income figure is EBITDA, or earnings before interest, taxes, depreciation, and amortization. The importance of EBITDA is that it shows what is earned purely from operations and reflects how efficiently the firm can manufacture and sell its products without taking into account the cost of the productive asset base (plant and equipment and intangible assets). For Diaz Manufacturing, EBITDA was $251.5 million in 2008.

EBIT. Subtracting depreciation and amortization from EBITDA yields the next intermediate figure, EBIT, or earnings before interest and taxes. EBIT for Diaz Manufacturing was $168.4 million.

EBT. When interest expense is subtracted from EBIT, the result is EBT, or earnings before taxes. Diaz Manufacturing had an EBT of $162.8 million in 2008.

Net Income. Finally, taxes are subtracted from EBT to arrive at net income. For Diaz Manufacturing, as we have already seen, net income in 2008 was $118.5 million.

In Chapter 4 you will see how to use these intermediate income figures to evaluate the firm's financial condition. Next, we look at the statement of retained earnings, which provides detailed information about how management allocated the $118.5 million of net income earned during the period.

The Statement of Retained Earnings

Corporations often prepare a statement of retained earnings, which identifies the changes in the retained earnings account from one accounting period to the next. During any accounting period, two events can affect the retained earnings account balance:

1. When the firm reports net income or loss
2. When the board of directors declares and pays a cash dividend

Exhibit 3.3 shows the activity in the retained earnings account for 2008 for Diaz Manufacturing. The beginning balance is a negative $50.7 million. The firm's annual report explains that the retained earnings deficit resulted from a $441 million write-down of assets that occurred when Diaz Manufacturing became a stand-alone business in June 2003. As reported in the 2008 income statement (Exhibit 3.2), the firm earned $118.5 million that year, and the board of directors elected not to declare any dividends. Retained earnings consequently went from a negative $50.7 million to a positive balance of $67.8 million, an increase of $118.5 million.

Exhibit 3.3 **Diaz Manufacturing Statement of Retained Earnings for the Year Ending December 31, 2008 ($ millions)**

Balance of retained earnings, December 31, 2007	$ (50.7)
Add: Net income, 2008	118.5
Less: Dividends to common stockholders	—
Balance of retained earnings, December 31, 2008	$ 67.8

The statement of retained earnings accompanies the balance sheet and shows the beginning balance of retained earnings, the adjustments made to retained earnings during the year, and the ending balance.

Before You Go On

1. How do you compute net income?
2. What is EBITDA, and what does it measure?
3. What accounting events trigger changes to the retained earnings account?

3.5 Cash Flows

As we discussed in Chapter 1, the concept of cash flows is an important one in financial management. Financial managers are concerned with maximizing the value of stockholders' shares, which means making decisions that will maximize the value of the firm's future cash flows. It is important to recognize that the revenues, expenses, and net income reported in a firm's income statement do not necessarily reflect cash flows. We must therefore distinguish between a company's net income and the cash flows it generates.

Net Income versus Cash Flows

net cash flow
a firm's actual cash receipts less cash payments in a given period

As we explained earlier, net income is equal to revenues minus expenses. **Net cash flow** is the cash that a firm generates in a given period (cash receipts less cash payments). Why is net income different from net cash flow? The reason is that when accountants prepare financial statements, they do not count the cash coming in and the cash going out. Under GAAP, they recognize revenues at the time a sale is substantially completed, not when the customer pays. In addition, because of the matching principle, accountants match revenues with the costs of producing the revenues. Finally, capital expenditures are paid for at the time of purchase, but the expense for the use of the capital asset is spread out over the asset's useful life through depreciation and amortization. As a result of these accounting rules, typically a significant lag in time exists between when revenues and expenses are recorded and when the cash is actually collected (in the case of revenue) or paid (in the case of expenses).[6]

Though neither method is precise, two "rough and ready" ways can be used to convert accounting profits into net cash flows from operating activities. The first method adjusts the firm's net income for all noncash revenue and noncash expenses. Net cash flow from operating activities (NCFOA) is:

$$\text{NCFOA} = \text{Net income} - \text{Noncash revenues} + \text{Noncash expenses} \qquad (3.4)$$

For most businesses, the largest noncash expenses are depreciation and amortization. These two items are deducted from revenues on the income statement, but no cash is paid out. The cash outflows took place when the assets were purchased. Other noncash items include the following:

- Depletion charges, which are like depreciation but which apply to extractive natural resources, such as crude oil, natural gas, timber, and mineral deposits (noncash expense)
- Deferred taxes, which are the portion of a firm's income tax expense that is postponed because of differences in the accounting policies adopted for management financial reporting and for tax reporting (noncash expense)
- Prepaid expenses that are paid in advance, such as for rent and insurance (noncash expense)
- Deferred revenues, which are revenues received as cash but not yet earned. An example of deferred revenue would be prepaid magazine subscriptions to a publishing company (noncash revenue)

The second method simply recognizes the fact that depreciation and amortization are usually the largest noncash charges and assumes that the remaining noncash revenues or charges cancel one another. The result is a simplified version of Equation 3.4:

$$\text{NCFOA} = \text{Net income} + \text{Depreciation and amortization} \qquad (3.5)$$

[6]The accounting practice of recognizing revenues and expenses as they are earned and incurred, and not when cash is received or paid, is called accrual accounting.

Equation 3.5 provides satisfactory estimates of NCFOA for many finance problems, unless there are significant noncash items beyond depreciation and amortization. To illustrate, we can use the data from Diaz Manufacturing's 2008 income statement (Exhibit 3.2):

$$\text{NCFOA} = \$118.5 + \$83.1 = \$201.6 \text{ million}$$

Diaz Manufacturing's net cash flow is much larger than its net income, illustrating the point that profits and net cash flow are not the same. However, as a cautionary warning, note that neither Equation 3.4 nor Equation 3.5 adjusts for changes in the working capital accounts, such as inventory levels and accounts payable, and if changes in these accounts are significant, the equations cannot be used. We consider these adjustments next.

The Statement of Cash Flows

There are times when the financial manager wants to know in detail all the cash flows that have taken place during the year and reconcile the beginning-of-year and end-of-year cash balances. The reason for the focus on cash flows is very practical. There is ample evidence from practice that business firms can post significant earnings (net income) but still have inadequate cash to pay wages, suppliers, and other creditors. On occasion, these firms have had to file for bankruptcy. The problem, of course, lies in the fact that profits (net income) are not the same as cash flows.

SOURCES AND USES OF CASH

The **statement of cash flows** shows the company's cash inflows (receipts) and cash outflows (payments) for a period of time. We derive these cash flows by looking at changes in balance sheet accounts from the end of one accounting period to the end of next and at the firm's net income for the period. In analyzing the cash flow statement, it is important to understand that changes in the balance sheet accounts reflect cash flows. More specifically, increases in assets or decreases in liabilities and equity are uses of cash, while decreases in assets or increases in liabilities and equity are sources of cash, as explained in the following:

statement of cash flows
a financial statement that shows a firm's cash receipts and cash payments for a period of time

- *Working capital.* An increase in current assets (such as accounts receivable and inventory) is a use of cash. For example, if a firm increases its inventory, it must use cash to purchase the additional inventory. Conversely, the sale of inventory increases a firm's cash position. An increase in current liabilities (such as accounts and notes payable) is a source of cash. For example, if during the year a firm increases its accounts payable, it has effectively "borrowed" money from suppliers and increased its cash position.
- *Fixed assets.* An increase in fixed assets is a use of cash. If a company purchases fixed assets during the year, it decreases cash because it must use cash to pay for the purchase. If the firm sells a fixed asset during the year, the firm's cash position will increase.
- *Long-term liabilities and equity.* An increase in long-term debt (bonds or private placement) or equity (common and preferred stock) is a source of cash. The retirement of debt or the purchase of treasury stock requires the firm to pay out cash, reducing cash balances.
- *Dividends.* Any cash dividend payment decreases a firm's cash balance.

ORGANIZATION OF THE STATEMENT OF CASH FLOWS

The statement of cash flows is organized around three business activities—operating activities, investing activities, and financing activities—and the reconciliation of the cash account. We discuss each of these elements next and illustrate them with reference to the statement of cash flows for Diaz Manufacturing, which is shown in Exhibit 3.4.

Exhibit 3.4 **Diaz Manufacturing Statement of Cash Flows for the Year Ending December 31, 2008 ($ millions)**

Operating Activities	
Net income	$118.5
Additions (sources of cash)	
Depreciation and amortization	83.1
Increase in accounts payable	24.3
Decrease in other current assets	8.6
Increase in accrued income taxes	1.2
Subtractions (uses of cash)	
Increase in accounts receivable	(37.4)
Increase in inventories	(51.1)
Net cash provided by operating activities	$147.2
Long-Term Investing Activities	
Property, equipment, and other assets	$ (88.3)
Increase in goodwill and other assets	(38.4)
Net cash used in investing activities	($126.7)
Financing Activities	
Increase in long-term debt	$268.4
Purchase of treasury stock	(23.3)
Increase in notes payable	6.3
Net cash provided by financing activities	$251.4
Cash Reconciliation[a]	
Net increase in cash and marketable securities	$271.9
Cash and securities at beginning of year	16.6
Cash and securities at end of year	$288.5

[a]Cash includes marketable securities.

The statement of cash flows shows the sources of the cash that has come into the firm during a period of time and the ways in which this cash has been used.

Operating Activities. Cash flows from operations are the net cash flows that are related to a firm's principal business activities. The most important items are the firm's net income, depreciation expense, and working capital accounts (other than cash and short-term debt obligations, which are classified elsewhere).

In Exhibit 3.4, the first section of the statement of cash flows for Diaz Manufacturing shows the cash flow from operations. The section starts with the firm's net income of $118.5 million for the year ending December 31, 2008. Depreciation expense ($83.1 million) is added because it is a noncash expense on the income statement.

Next come changes in the firm's working capital accounts that affect operating activities. Note that working capital accounts that involve financing (bank loans and notes payable) and cash reconciliation (cash and marketable securities) will be classified separately. For Diaz, the working capital accounts that are *sources* of cash are: (1) increase in accounts payable of $24.3 million ($349.3 – $325.0), (2) decrease in other current assets of $8.6 million ($29.9 – $21.3), and (3) increase in accrued income taxes of $1.2 million ($18.0 – $16.8). Changes in working capital items that are *uses* of cash are: (1) increase in accounts receivable of $37.4 million ($306.2 – $268.8) and (2) increase in inventory of $51.1 million ($423.8 – $372.7). The total cash provided to the firm from operations is $147.2 million.

To clarify why changes in working capital accounts affect the statement of cash flows, let's look at some of the changes. Diaz had a $37.4 million increase in accounts receivable, which is subtracted from net income as a use of cash. The increase in accounts receivable is a use of cash because the number represents sales that were included in the income statement but for which no cash has been collected. Diaz provided financing for these sales to its customers. The $24.3 million increase in accounts payable represents a source of cash because goods and services the company purchased were received but no cash was paid out.

Investing Activities. Cash flows from investment activities relate to the buying and selling of long-term assets. The primary investment activities for manufacturing and service firms are the purchase or sale of land, buildings, and plant and equipment.

In Exhibit 3.4, the second section shows the cash flows from long-term investing activities. Diaz Manufacturing made long-term investments in two areas, which resulted in a cash outflow of $126.7 million. They were as follows: (1) the purchase of plant and equipment, totaling $88.3 million ($911.6 − $823.3) and (2) an increase in goodwill and other assets of $38.4 ($450.0 − $411.6). Diaz's investments in property, equipment, and other assets resulted in a cash outflow of $126.7 million.

Financing Activities. Cash flows from financing come from activities in which cash is obtained from or repaid to creditors or owners (stockholders). Typical financing activities involve cash received from owners as they invest in the firm by buying common stock or preferred stock, as well as cash from bank loans, notes payable, and long-term debt. Cash payments of dividends to stockholders and cash purchases of treasury stock reduce a company's cash position.

Diaz Manufacturing's financing activities include the sale of bonds for $268.4 million ($574.0 − $305.6), which is a source of cash and the purchase of treasury stock for $23.3 million, which is a use of cash. The firm's notes payable position was also increased by $6.3 million ($10.5 − $4.2). Overall, Diaz had a net cash inflow from financing activities of $251.4 million.

Cash Reconciliation. The final part of the statement of cash flows is a reconciliation of the firm's beginning and ending cash positions. For Diaz Manufacturing, these cash positions are as shown on the 2007 and 2008 balance sheets. The first step in reconciling the company's beginning and ending cash positions is to add together the amounts from the first three sections of the statement of cash flows: (1) the net cash inflows from operations of $147.2 million, (2) the net cash outflow from long-term investment activities of − $126.7 million, (3) and the net cash inflow from financing activities of $251.4 million. Together, these three items represent a total net increase in cash to the firm of $271.9 million ($147.2 − $126.7 + $251.4). Finally, we add this amount ($271.9 million) to the beginning cash balance of $16.6 million to obtain the ending cash balance for 2008 of $288.5 million ($271.9 + $16.6).

Additional Cash Flow Calculations

This section has introduced cash flow calculations. We will return to the topic of cash flows in Chapters 11 and 18. In those chapters we will develop more precise measures of cash flows that will allow us to determine (1) the incremental cash flows necessary to estimate the value of a capital project and (2) the free cash flows needed to estimate the value of a firm.

Before You Go On

1. What is the difference between accounting profits and net cash flows?
2. Should a firm consider only depreciation and amortization expenses when calculating the net cash flow? Explain.
3. Explain the difference between financing and investing activities.

3.6 Tying the Financial Statements Together

LEARNING OBJECTIVE 6

Up to this point, we have treated a firm's financial statements as if they were independent of one another. As you might suspect, though, the four financial statements presented in this chapter are related. Let's see how.

Recall that the balance sheet summarizes what assets the firm has at a particular point in time and how the firm has financed those assets with debt and equity. From

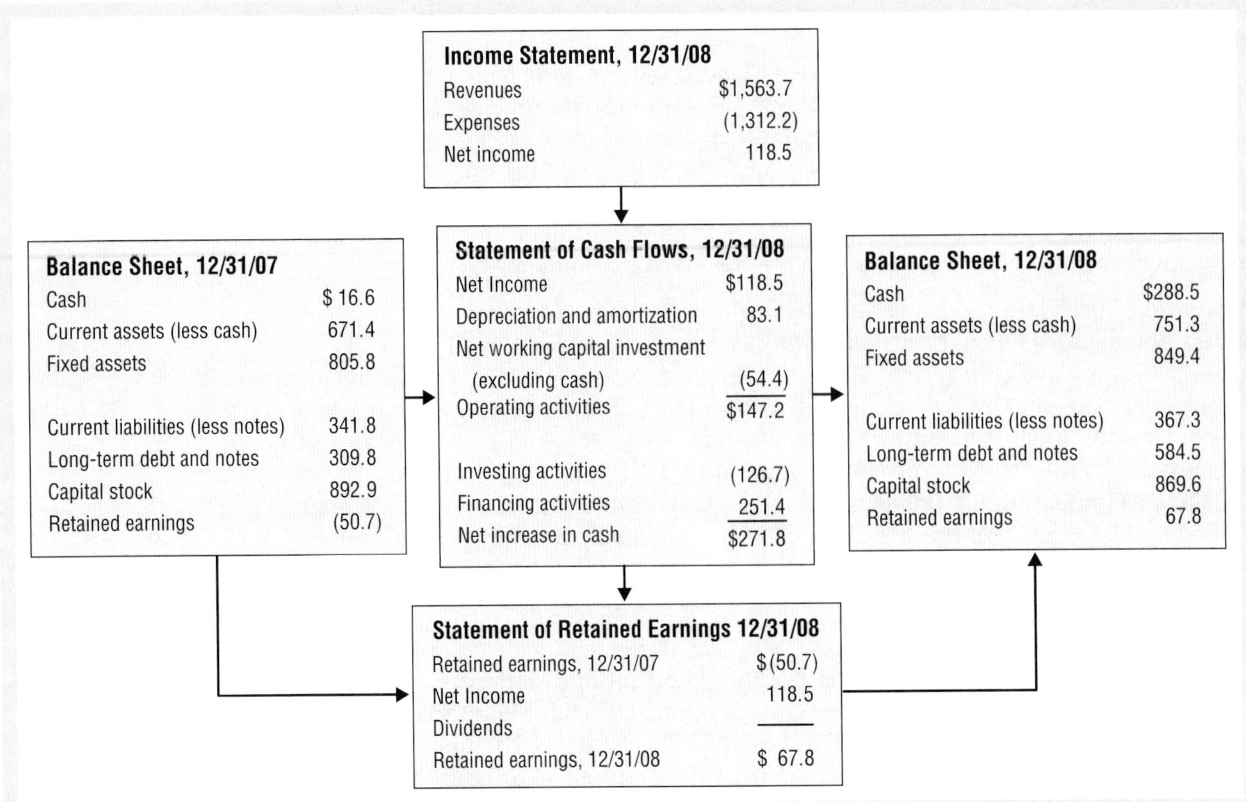

Exhibit 3.5
The Interrelations among the Financial Statements: Illustrated Using Diaz Manufacturing Financial Results
The statement of cash flows ties together the income statement with the balance sheets from the beginning and the end of the period. The statement of retained earnings shows how the retained earnings account has changed from the beginning to the end of the period.

one year to the next, the firm's balance sheet will change because the firm will buy or sell assets and the dollar value of the debt and equity financing will change. These changes are exactly the ones presented in the statement of cash flows. In other words, the statement of cash flows presents a summary of the changes in a firm's balance sheet from the beginning of a period to the end of that period.

This concept is illustrated in Exhibit 3.5, which presents summaries of the four financial statements for Diaz Manufacturing for the year 2008. The exhibit also presents the balance sheet for the beginning of that year, which is dated December 31, 2007. If you compare the changes in the balance sheet numbers from the beginning of the year to the end of the year, you can see that these changes are in fact summarized in the statement of cash flows. For example, the change in the cash balance of \$271.8 (\$288.5 − \$16.6) appears at the bottom of the statement of cash flows. Similarly, excluding cash, the change in net working capital from the beginning to the end of 2008 is \$54.4, which is calculated as follows: [(\$751.3 − \$367.3) − (\$671.4 − \$341.8)] = (\$384.0 − \$329.6) = \$54.4.[7] This number is equal to the net working capital investment reflected in the statement of cash flows. Note, too, that the net working capital investment in Diaz's statement of cash flows is just the total change in the firm's investment in the working capital accounts—accounts payable, other current assets, accrued income taxes, accounts receivable, and inventories. You can also see in Exhibit 3.5 that the change in fixed assets, which includes net property plant and equipment, goodwill, and other assets, is \$43.6 (\$849.4 − \$805.8). This number is equal to the sum of the cash flows from invest-

[7]From the 2008 balance sheet: (1) working capital less cash = \$1,039.8 − \$288.5 = \$751.3, and (2) current liabilities − notes payable = \$377.8 − \$10.5 = \$367.3. The calculations are similar for the 2007 balance

depreciation and amortization, − $126.7 + $83.1 = − $43.6, in the statement of cash flows. We add depreciation to investing activities in the latter calculation because the fixed asset accounts in the balance sheet are net of depreciation.

Turning to the liability and equity side of the balance sheet, notice the change in the amount of debt plus equity that the firm has sold in 2008, which is represented by the sum of the long-term liabilities and notes and capital stock in the balance sheet. This sum equals the value of the financing activities in the statement of cash flows. The change in the balance sheet values is calculated as follows: [($584.5 + $869.6) − ($309.8 + $892.9)] = ($1,454.1 − $1,202.7) = 251.4.[8] Finally, since Diaz did not pay a dividend in 2008, the change in retained earnings of $118.5, which equals $67.8 − (−$50.7), exactly equals the company's net income, which appears on the top line of the statement of cash flows.

Again, the important point here is that the statement of cash flows summarizes the changes in the balance sheet. How do the other financial statements fit into the picture? Well, the income statement calculates the firm's net income, which is used to calculate the retained earnings at the end of the year and is included as the first line in the statement of cash flows. The income statement provides an input that is used in the balance sheet and the statement of cash flows. The statement of retained earnings just summarizes the changes to the retained earnings account a little differently than the statement of cash flows. This different format makes it simpler for managers and investors to see why retained earnings changed as it did.

Before You Go On

1. Explain how the four financial statements are related.

3.7 Federal Income Tax

We conclude the chapter with a discussion of corporate income taxes. Taxes take a big bite out of the income of most businesses and represent one of their largest cash outflows. For example, as shown in the income statement (Exhibit 3.2) for Diaz Manufacturing, the firm's earnings before interest and taxes (EBIT) in 2008 amounted to $168.4 million, and its tax bill was $44.3 million, or 26.3 percent of EBIT ($44.3/168.4)—not a trivial amount by any standard. Because of their magnitude, taxes play a critical role in most business financial decisions.

As you might suspect, corporations spend a considerable amount of effort and money deploying tax specialists to find legal ways to minimize their tax burdens. The tax laws are complicated, continually changing, and at times seemingly bizarre—in part because the tax code is not an economically rational document, but reflects the political and social values of Congress and the President.

If you work in the finance or accounting area, a tax specialist will advise you on the tax implications of most decisions in which you will be involved as a businessperson. Consequently, we will not try to make you a tax expert, but we will present a high-level view of the major portions of the federal tax code that have a significant impact on the operations of corporations and their business decision making.

Corporate Income Tax Rates

Exhibit 3.6 shows the 2007 federal income tax schedule for corporations. As you can see, the marginal tax rate varies from 15 percent to 39 percent. In general, smaller companies with lower taxable incomes have lower tax rates than larger companies with

[8]From the 2008 balance sheet, note the following: debt = $574.0 (long-term debt) + $10.5 (notes payable) = $584.5 and equity = $50.0 (common stock) + $842.9 (additional paid-in capital) − $23.3 (treasury stock) = $869.6. The calculations for 2007 are made in a similar manner.

Exhibit 3.6 Corporate Tax Rates for 2007

(1) Corporations' Taxable Income	(2) Pay This Amount on the Base of the Bracket	(3) Marginal Tax Rate: Tax Rate on the Excess over the Base	(4) Average Tax Rate at Top of Bracket
\$0–\$50,000	\$ 0	15%	15.0%
50,001–75,000	7,500	25	18.3
75,001–100,000	13,750	34	22.3
100,001–335,000	22,250	39	34.0
335,001–10,000,000	113,900	34	34.0
10,000,001–15,000,000	3,400,000	35	34.3
15,000,001–18,333,333	5,150,000	38	35.0
More than 18,333,333	6,416,667	35	35.0

The federal corporate marginal tax rate varies from 15 to 39 percent. Generally speaking, smaller companies with lower taxable income have lower tax rates than larger companies with higher taxable incomes. Smaller businesses are given preferential treatment to encourage new business formation.

The U.S. Department of the Treasury provides a comprehensive tax information site at www.irs.gov.

higher taxable incomes. Historically, the federal income tax code has given preferential treatment to small businesses and start-up companies as a means of stimulating new business formation. In addition, the federal system is a progressive income tax system; that is, as the level of income rises, the tax rate rises. Under the current tax code, which has its origins in the Tax Reform Act of 1986, marginal tax rates do not increase continuously through the income brackets, however. As you can see in Exhibit 3.6, marginal tax rates rise from 15 percent to 39 percent for incomes up to \$335,000; they decrease to 34 percent, then increase to 38 percent for incomes up to \$18.3 million; and they ultimately rest at 35 percent for all taxable income above \$18.3 million.

Average versus Marginal Tax Rates

average tax rate
total taxes paid divided by taxable income

marginal tax rate
the tax rate paid on the last dollar of income earned

The difference between the average tax rate and the marginal tax rate is an important consideration in financial decision making. The **average tax rate** is simply the total taxes paid divided by taxable income. In contrast, the **marginal tax rate** is the tax rate that is paid on the last dollar of income earned. Exhibit 3.6 shows the marginal tax rates (column 3) and average tax rates (column 4) for corporations.

A simple example will clarify the difference between the average and marginal tax rates. Suppose a corporation has a taxable income of \$150,000. Using the data in Exhibit 3.6, we can determine the firm's federal income tax bill, its marginal tax rate, and its average tax rate. The firm's total tax bill is computed as follows:

$$\begin{aligned}
0.15 \times \$50{,}000 &= \$\ 7{,}500 \\
0.25 \times (\$75{,}000 - \$50{,}000) &= \quad 6{,}250 \\
0.34 \times (\$100{,}000 - \$75{,}000) &= \quad 8{,}500 \\
0.39 \times (\$150{,}000 - \$100{,}000) &= \underline{\quad 19{,}500} \\
&\quad \$41{,}750
\end{aligned}$$

The firm's average tax rate is equal to the total taxes divided by the firm's total taxable income; thus, the average tax rate is \$41,750/\$150,000 = 0.278, or 27.8 percent. The firm's marginal tax rate is the rate paid on the last dollar earned, which is 39 percent.

LEARNING BY DOING APPLICATION 3.2

The Difference between Average and Marginal Tax Rates

Problem: Taxland Corporation has taxable corporate income of \$90,000. What is the firm's federal corporate income tax liability? What are the firm's average and marginal tax rates?

Approach: Use Exhibit 3.6 to calculate the firm's tax bill. To calculate the average tax rate, divide the total amount of taxes paid by the \$90,000 of taxable income. The marginal tax rate is the tax rate paid on the last dollar of taxable income.

Solution:

$$\begin{aligned} \text{Tax bill} &= (0.15 \times \$50{,}000) + [0.25 \times (\$75{,}000 - \$50{,}000)] \\ &\quad + [0.34 \times (\$90{,}000 - \$75{,}000)] \\ &= \$7{,}500 + \$6{,}250 + \$5{,}100 \\ &= \$18{,}850 \\ \text{Average tax rate} &= \$18{,}850/\$90{,}000 = 0.209, \text{ or } 20.9\% \\ \text{Marginal tax rate} &= 34\% \end{aligned}$$

When you are making investment decisions for a firm, the relevant tax rate to use is usually the marginal tax rate. The reason is that new investments (projects) are expected to generate new cash flows, which will be taxed at the firm's marginal tax rate. Thus, the marginal tax rate is used to compute the project's tax bill.

To simplify calculations throughout the book, we will generally specify a single tax rate for a corporation, such as 40 percent. The rate may include some payment for state and local taxes, which will add an upward adjustment to the total tax rate firms pay. We use different corporate tax rates to emphasize that taxes change over time and may differ from one location to another.

Unequal Treatment of Dividends and Interest Payments

An interesting anomaly in the tax code is the unequal treatment of interest expense and dividend payments. For the most common type of corporation, interest paid on debt obligations is a tax-deductible business expense. Dividends paid to common or preferred stockholders are not deductible, however. Because of this difference, a firm must generate more earnings to support a \$100 payment of dividends than a \$100 payment of interest. For example, if a firm pays \$100 in interest, it must generate \$100 of earnings before interest and taxes (EBIT) to support this payment. However, for the \$100 of dividends, the firm will need more than \$100 of EBIT because the dividends are not tax deductible. More specifically, if the average tax rate is 40 percent, the firm will need to generate \$166.70 to cover the cash dividend.[9]

The unequal treatment of interest expense and dividend payments is not without consequences. In effect, it lowers the cost of debt financing compared with the cost of an equal amount of common or preferred stock financing. Thus, there is a tax-induced bias toward the use of debt financing, which we discuss more thoroughly in later chapters.

---

[9]To find the amount of EBIT necessary to support the cash dividend, simply divide the amount by 1 minus the average tax rate $(1 - t)$. If the average tax rate (t) is 40 percent, the necessary EBIT to support \$100 of cash dividends is as follows: EBIT necessary = \$100/(1 − 0.40) = \$100/0.60 = \$166.70.

Before You Go On

1. Why is it important to consider the consequences of taxes when financing a new project?
2. Which type of tax rate, marginal or average, should be used in analyzing the expansion of a product line, and why?
3. What are the tax implications of a decision to finance a project using debt rather than new equity?

Summary of Learning Objectives

1. **Discuss generally accepted accounting principles (GAAP) and their importance to the economy.**

   GAAP are a set of authoritative guidelines that define accounting practices at a particular point in time. The principles determine the rules for how a company maintains its accounting system and how it prepares financial statements. Accounting standards are important because without them, each firm could develop its own unique accounting practices, which would make it difficult for anyone to monitor the firm's true performance or compare the performance of different firms. The result would be a loss of confidence in the accounting system and the financial reports it produces. Fundamental accounting principles include that transactions are arms-length, the cost principle, the realization principle, the matching principle, and the going concern assumption.

2. **Know the balance sheet identity, and explain why a balance sheet must balance.**

   A balance sheet provides a summary of a firm's financial position at a particular point in time. The balance sheet identifies the productive resources (assets) that a firm uses to generate income, as well as the sources of funding from creditors (liabilities) and owners (stockholders' equity) that were used to buy the assets. The balance sheet identity is: Total assets = Total liabilities + Total stockholders' equity. Stockholders' equity represents ownership in the firm and is the residual claim of the owners after all other obligations to creditors, employees, and vendors have been paid. The balance sheet must always balance because the owners get what is left over after all creditors have been paid—that is Total stockholders' equity = Total assets − Total liabilities.

3. **Describe how market-value balance sheets differ from book-value balance sheets.**

   Book value is the amount a firm paid for its assets at the time of purchase. The current market value of an asset is the amount that a firm would receive for the asset if it were sold on the open market (not in a forced liquidation). Most managers and investors are more concerned about what a firm's assets can earn in the future than in what the assets cost in the past. Thus, balance sheets marked to market are more helpful in showing a company's true financial condition than balance sheets based on historical costs. Of course, the problem with marked-to-market balance sheets is that it is difficult to estimate market values for some assets and liabilities.

4. **Identify the basic equation for the income statement and the information it provides.**

   An income statement is a video clip of the firm's profit or loss for a period of time, usually a month, quarter, or year. The income statement identifies the major sources of revenues generated by the firm and the corresponding expenses needed to generate those revenues. The equation for the income statement is Net income = Revenues − Expenses. If revenues exceed expenses, the firm generates a net profit for the period. If expenses exceed revenues, the firm generates a net loss. Net profit or income is the most comprehensive accounting measure of a firm's performance.

5. **Explain the difference between cash flows and accounting income.**

   Cash flows represent the movement of cash within the firm. Cash flows are important in finance because the value of any asset—stocks, bonds, or a business—is determined by the future cash flows generated by the asset. Accounting profits, in contrast, are calculated according to GAAP to determine taxes and to report to stakeholders in a consistent manner. Accounting profits include noncash revenues (such as revenue booked by a manufacturer when products are shipped on credit) and noncash expenses (such depreciation), whereas cash flows do not include these items.

6. **Explain how the four major financial statements discussed in this chapter are related.**

   The four financial statements discussed in the chapter are the balance sheet, the income statement, the statement of cash flows, and the statement of retained earnings. The key financial statement that ties the other three statements together is the statement of cash flows, which summarizes changes in the balance sheet from the beginning of the year to the end. These changes reflect the information in the income statement and in the statement of retained earnings.

7. **Discuss the difference between average and marginal tax rates.**

   The average tax rate is computed by dividing the total taxes by taxable income. It takes into account the taxes paid at all levels of income and will normally be lower than the marginal tax rate, which is the rate that is paid on the last dollar of income earned. However, for very high income earners, these two rates can be equal. When companies are making financial investment decisions, they use the marginal tax rate because new projects are expected to generate additional cash flows, which will be taxed at the firm's marginal tax rate.

Summary of Key Equations

Equation	Description	Formula
3.1	Balance sheet identity	Total assets = Total liabilities + Total stockholders' equity
3.2	Net working capital	Net working capital = Total current assets − Total current liabilities
3.3	Income Statement identity	Net income = Revenues − Expenses
3.4	Net cash flow from operating activities	NCFOA = Net income − Noncash revenues + Noncash expenses
3.5	Net cash flow from operating activities	NCFOA = Net income + Depreciation and amortization

Self-Study Problems

3.1 The *going concern assumption* of GAAP implies that the firm:
a. is going under and needs to be liquidated at historical cost.
b. will continue to operate and its assets should be recorded at historical cost.
c. will continue to operate and that all assets should be recorded at their cost rather than at their liquidation value.
d. is going under and needs to be liquidated at liquidation value.

3.2 The Ellicott City Ice Cream Company management has just completed an assessment of its assets and liabilities and has come up with the following information. It has total current assets worth $625,000 at book value and $519,000 at market value. In addition, its long-term assets include plant and equipment valued at market for $695,000, while their book value is $940,000. The company's total current liabilities are valued at market for $543,000, while their book value is $495,000. Both the book value and the market value of its long-term debt is $350,000. If the company's total assets are equal to a market value of $1,214,000 (book value of $1,565,000), what are the book value and market value of its stockholders' equity?

3.3 Depreciation and amortization expenses are:
a. part of current assets on the balance sheet.
b. after-tax expenses that reduce a firm's cash flows.
c. long-term liabilities that reduce a firm's net worth.
d. noncash expenses that cause a firm's after-tax cash flows to exceed its net income.

3.4 You are given the following information about Clarkesville Plumbing Company. The company's annual report on December 31, 2008, showed that during the year its revenues totaled $896, current assets $121, current liabilities $107, depreciation expenses $75, costs of goods sold $365, and interest expenses $54. The company is in the 34 percent tax bracket. Calculate its net income by setting up an income statement.

3.5 The Huntington Rain Gear Company had $633,125 in taxable income in the year ending September 30, 2007. Calculate the company's tax using the tax schedule in Exhibit 3.6.

Solutions to Self-Study Problems

3.1 One of the key assumptions under GAAP is the *going concern assumption*, which states that the firm (c) will continue to operate and that all assets should be recorded at their cost rather than at their liquidation value.

3.2 The book value and market value are as follows (in thousands of dollars):

Assets	Book Value	Market Value	Liabilities	Book Value	Market Value
Total current assets	$ 625	$ 519	Total current liabilities	$ 495	$ 543
Fixed assets	940	695	Long-term debt	350	350
			Stockholders' equity	720	321
Total assets	$1,565	$1,214	Total liabilities and equity	$1,565	$1,214

3.3 Depreciation and amortization expenses are (d) noncash expenses that cause a firm's after-tax cash flows to exceed its net income.

3.4 Clarkesville's income statement and net income are as follows:

Clarkesville Plumbing Company
Income Statement for Year Ending December 31, 2008

	Amount
Revenues	$ 896.00
Costs	365.00
EBITDA	$ 531.00
Depreciation	75.00
EBIT	$ 456.00
Interest	54.00
EBT	$ 402.00
Taxes (34%)	136.68
Net income	$ 265.32

3.5 Huntington's tax bill is calculated as follows:

Tax rate	Income	Tax
15%	$50,000	$ 7,500
25	(75,000 − 50,000)	6,250
34	(100,000 − 75,000)	8,500
39	(335,000 − 100,000)	91,650
34	(633,125 − 335,000)	101,363
	Total taxes payable	$ 215,263

Critical Thinking Questions

3.1 What is a major reason for the accounting scandals in recent years? How do firms sometimes attempt to meet Wall Street analysts' projection of earnings?

3.2 Why are taxes and the tax code important for managerial decision making?

3.3 Identify the five fundamental principles of GAAP, and explain briefly their importance.

3.4 Explain why firms prefer to use accelerated depreciation methods over the straight-line method for tax purposes.

3.5 What is treasury stock? Why do firms have treasury stock?

3.6 Define book-value accounting and market-value accounting.

3.7 Compare and contrast depreciation expense and amortization expense.

3.8 Why are retained earnings not considered an asset of the firm?

3.9 How does net cash flow differ from net income, and why?

3.10 What is the statement of cash flows, and what is its role?

Questions and Problems

BASIC

3.1 **Balance sheet:** Given the following information about Elkridge Sporting Goods, Inc., construct a balance sheet for the period ending June 30, 2008. The firm had cash and marketable securities of $25,135, accounts receivable of $43,758, inventory of $167,112, net fixed assets of $325,422, and other assets of $13,125. It had accounts payables of $67,855, notes payables of $36,454, long-term debt of $223,125, and common stock of $150,000. How much retained earnings does the firm have?

3.2 **Inventory accounting:** Differentiate between FIFO and LIFO.

3.3 **Inventory accounting:** Explain how the choice of FIFO versus LIFO can affect a firm's balance sheet and income statement.

3.4 **Market-value accounting:** How does the use of market-value accounting help managers?

3.5 **Working capital:** Laurel Electronics reported the following information at its annual meetings: The company had cash and marketable securities worth $1,235,455, accounts payables worth $4,159,357, inventory of $7,121,599, accounts receivables of $3,488,121, short-term notes payable worth $1,151,663, and other current assets of $121,455. What is the company's net working capital?

3.6 **Working capital:** The financial information for Laurel Electronics referred to in Problem 3.5 is all book value. Suppose marking to market reveals that the market value of the firm's inventory is 20 percent below its book value and its receivables are 25 percent below its book value. The market value of its current liabilities is identical to the book value. What is the firm's net working capital using market values? What is the percentage change in net working capital?

3.7 **Income statement:** The Oakland Mills Company has disclosed the following financial information in its annual reports for the period ending March 31, 2008: sales of $1.45 million, costs of goods sold to the tune of $812,500, depreciation expenses of $175,000, and interest expenses of $89,575. Assume that the firm has a tax rate of 35 percent. What is the company's net income? Set up an income statement to answer the question.

3.8 **Cash flows:** Describe the organization of the statement of cash flows.

3.9 **Cash flows:** During 2008 Towson Recording Company increased its investment in marketable securities by $36,845, funded fixed-assets acquisitions of $109,455, and had marketable securities of $14,215 mature. What is the net cash used in investing activities?

3.10 **Cash flows:** Caustic Chemicals identified the following cash flows as significant in its meeting with analysts: During the year it had repaid existing debt of $312,080 and raised additional debt capital of $650,000. It also repurchased stock in the open market for a total of $45,250. What is the net cash provided by financing activities?

3.11 **Cash flows:** Identify and explain the noncash expenses that a firm may incur.

3.12 **Tax:** Define average tax rate and marginal tax rate.

3.13 **Tax:** What is the relevant tax rate to use when making financial decisions? Explain why.

3.14 **Tax:** Manz Property Management Company announced that in the year ended June 30, 2008, its earnings before taxes amounted to $1,478,936. Calculate its taxes using Exhibit 3.6.

INTERMEDIATE

EXCEL®

3.15 Balance sheet: Tim Dye, the CFO of Blackwell Automotive, Inc., is putting together this year's financial statements. He has gathered the following information: The firm had a cash balance of $23,015, accounts payable of $163,257, common stock of $313,299, retained earnings of $512,159, inventory of $212,444, goodwill and other assets equal to $78,656, net plant and equipment of $711,256, and short-term notes payable of $21,115. It also had accounts receivable of $141,258 and other current assets of $11,223. What amount of long-term debt does Blackwell Automotive have?

3.16 Balance sheet: Refer to the information for Blackwell Automotive in Problem 3.15. What level of net working capital does Blackwell Automotive have?

3.17 Working capital: Mukhopadhya Network Associates has a current ratio of 1.60, where the current ratio is defined as follows: current ratio = current assets/current liabilities. The firm's current assets are equal to $1,233,265, its accounts payables are $419,357, and its notes payables are $351,663. Its inventory is currently at $721,599. The company plans to raise funds in the short-term debt market and invest the entire amount in additional inventory. How much can their notes payable increase without lowering their current ratio below 1.50?

3.18 Market value: Reservoir Bottling Company reported to stockholders the following information: total current assets worth $237,513 at book value and $219,344 at market value. In addition, its long-term assets include plant and equipment valued at market for $343,222, while their book value is $362,145. The company's total current liabilities are valued at market for $134,889, while their book value is $129,175. Both the book value and the market value of its long-term debt is $144,000. If the company's total assets are equal to a market value of $562,566 (book value of $599,658), what is the difference in the book value and market value of its stockholders' equity?

3.19 Income statement: Nimitz Rental Company provided the following information to its auditors: for the year ended March 31, 2009, the company had revenues of $878,412, general and administrative expenses of $352,666, depreciation expenses of $131,455, leasing expenses of $108,195, and interest expenses equal to $78,122. If the company's tax rate is 34 percent, what is its net income after taxes?

3.20 Income statement: Sosa Corporation recently reported an EBITDA of $31.3 million and net income of $9.7 million. The company has $6.8 million interest expense, and the corporate tax rate is 35 percent. What was its depreciation and amortization expense?

3.21 Income statement: Fraser Corporation has announced that its net income for the year ended June 30, 2008, is $1,353,412. The company had an EBITDA of $4,967,855, and its depreciation and amortization expense was equal to $1,112,685. The company's tax rate is 34 percent. What is the amount of interest expense for Fraser Corporation?

EXCEL®

3.22 Income statement: Carmichael Hobby Shop has an EBITDA of $512,725.20, EBIT of $362,450.20, and a cash flow of $348,461.25. What is this firm's net income after taxes?

3.23 Retained earnings: Columbia Construction Company earned $451,888 during the year ended June 30, 2008. After paying out $225,794 in dividends, the balance went into retained earnings. If the firm's total retained earnings were $846,972, what was the level of retained earnings on its balance sheet on July 1, 2007?

3.24 Cash flows: Refer to the information given in Problem 3.19. What is the cash flow for Nimitz Rental?

3.25 Tax: Mount Hebron Electrical Company's financial statements indicated that the company had earnings before interest and taxes of $718,323. Its interest rate on debt of $850,000 was 8.95 percent. Calculate the amount of taxes the company is likely to owe. What are the marginal and average tax rates for this company?

ADVANCED

EXCEL®

3.26 The Centennial Chemical Corporation announced that for the period ending March 31, 2008, it had earned income after taxes worth $5,330,275 on revenues of $13,144,680. The company's costs (excluding depreciation and amortization) amounted to 61 percent of sales, and it had interest expenses of $392,168. What is the firm's depreciation and amortization expense if its tax rate is 34 percent?

3.27 Eau Claire Paper Mill, Inc., had, at the beginning of the fiscal year, April 1, 2007, retained earnings of $323,325. During the year ended March 31, 2008, the company produced net income after taxes of $713,445 and paid out 45 percent of its net income as dividends. Construct a statement of retained earnings and compute the year-end balance of retained earnings.

3.28 Menomonie Casino Company earned $23,458,933 before interest and taxes for the fiscal year ending March 31, 2008. If the casino had interest expenses of $1,645,123, calculate its tax burden using Exhibit 3.6. What are the marginal tax rate and the average tax rate for this company?

3.29 Vanderheiden Hog Products Corp. provided the following financial information for the quarter ending June 30, 2008: EXCEL®

Net income: $189,425
Depreciation and amortization: $63,114
Increase in receivables: $62,154
Increase in inventory: $57,338
Increase in accounts payable: $37,655
Decrease in other current assets: $27,450
What is this firm's cash flow from operating activities during this quarter?

3.30 Cash flows: Analysts following the Tomkovick Golf Company were given the following information for the year ended June 30, 2008: EXCEL®

Assets	2008	2007
Cash and marketable securities	$ 33,411	$ 16,566
Accounts receivable	260,205	318,768
Inventory	423,819	352,740
Other current assets	41,251	29,912
Total current assets	$ 758,686	$ 717,986
Plant and equipment	1,931,719	1,609,898
Less: Accumulated depreciation	(419,044)	(206,678)
Net plant and equipment	$ 1,512,675	$ 1,403,220
Goodwill and other assets	382,145	412,565
Total assets	$ 2,653,506	$ 2,533,771

Liabilities and Equity	2008	2007
Accounts payable and accruals	$ 378,236	$ 332,004
Notes payable	14,487	7,862
Accrued income taxes	21,125	16,815
Total current liabilities	$ 413,848	$ 356,681
Long-term debt	679,981	793,515
Total liabilities	$ 1,093,829	$ 1,150,196
Preferred stock	—	—
Common stock (10,000 shares)	10,000	10,000
Additional paid-in capital	975,465	975,465
Retained earnings	587,546	398,110
Less: Treasury stock	13,334	—
Total common equity	$ 1,559,677	$ 1,383,575
Total liabilities and equity	$ 2,653,506	$ 2,533,771

In addition, it was reported that the company had a net income of $3,155,848 and that depreciation expenses were equal to $212,366.

a. Construct a cash flow statement for this firm.
b. Calculate the net cash provided by operating activities.
c. What is the net cash used in investing activities?
d. Compute the net cash provided by financing activities.

Sample Test Problems

3.1 Drayton, Inc., has current assets of $256,312 and total assets of $861,889. It also has current liabilities of $141,097, common equity of $200,000, and retained earnings of $133,667. How much long-term debt does the firm have?

3.2 Ellicott Testing Company produced revenues of $745,000 in 2008. It has expenses (excluding depreciation) of $312,640, depreciation of $65,000, and interest expense of $41,823. It pays a marginal tax rate of 34 percent. What is the firm's net income after taxes?

3.3 Tejada Enterprises reported an EBITDA of $7,300,125 and $3,328,950 of net income for the fiscal year ended September 30, 2008. The company has $1,155,378 interest expense, and the corporate tax rate is 35 percent. What was the company's depreciation and amortization expense?

3.4 In the year ended June 30, 2008, Tri King Company increased its investment in marketable securities by $234,375, funded fixed-assets acquisition by $1,324,766, and sold $77,215 of long-term debt. In addition, the firm had a net inflow of $365,778 from selling certain assets. What is the net cash used in investing activities?

3.5 Triumph Soccer Club has the following cash flows during this year: It repaid existing debt of $875,430, while raising additional debt capital of $1,213,455. It also repurchased stock in the open markets for a total of $71,112. What is the net cash provided by financing activities?

ANALYZING FINANCIAL STATEMENTS

CHAPTER

4

REUTERS/Peter Jones

LEARNING OBJECTIVES

1. **Explain the three perspectives from which financial statements can be viewed.**
2. **Describe common-size financial statements, explain why they are used, and be able to prepare and use them to analyze the historical performance of a firm.**
3. **Discuss how financial ratios facilitate financial analysis, and be able to compute and use them to analyze a firm's performance.**
4. **Describe the DuPont system of analysis, and be able to use it to evaluate a firm's performance and identify corrective actions that may be necessary.**
5. **Explain what benchmarks are, describe how they are prepared, and discuss why they are important in financial statement analysis.**
6. **Identify the major limitations in using financial statement analysis.**

Today the largest U.S. airlines are struggling to compete against smaller, more nimble carriers that feature low-cost fares with no-frills service. As a result, several large airlines have been forced into bankruptcy, while a number of smaller carriers, such as Southwest Airlines and AirTran, have achieved rapid growth and profitability.

Just how do analysts compare the performance of companies like those named above? One approach is to compare the accounting data from the financial statements that the companies file with the SEC. Below are selected accounting data for Southwest Airlines (SWA), a successful low-cost carrier, and American Airlines (AA), the largest U.S. airline, for the fiscal year ending in December 2006:

	SWA ($ millions)	AA ($ millions)
Total sales	$ 9,086	$ 22,563
Net income	499	231

The accounting numbers by themselves do not provide much insight, and they are difficult to analyze because of the size difference between the two firms. However, if we compute one of the profitability ratios discussed in this chapter, the net profit margin, we see a dramatic difference in performance between the two airlines. The net profit margins (Net income/Total sales) for SWA and AA are 5.49 percent and 1.02 percent, respectively. This means that for every $100 in revenues, SWA is able to generate $5.49 of profit, whereas AA can only squeeze out $1.02. As this example illustrates, one advantage of using ratios is that they make direct comparisons possible by adjusting for size differences.

This chapter focuses on financial ratio analysis (or financial statement analysis), which involves the calculation and comparison of ratios derived from financial statements. These ratios can be used to draw useful conclusions about a company's financial condition, its operating efficiency, and the attractiveness of its securities as investments.

CHAPTER PREVIEW

In Chapter 3 we reviewed the basic structure of financial statements. This chapter explains how financial statements are used to evaluate a company's overall performance and assess its strengths and shortcomings. The basic tool used to do this is financial ratio analysis. Financial ratios are computed by dividing one number from a firm's financial statements by another such number in order to allow for meaningful comparisons between firms or areas within a firm.

Management can use the information from this type of analysis to help maximize the firm's value by identifying areas where performance improvements are needed. For example, the analysis of data from financial statements can help determine why a firm's cash flows are increasing or decreasing, why a firm's profitability is changing, and whether a firm will be able to pay its bills next month.

We begin the chapter by discussing some general guidelines for financial statement analysis, along with three different perspectives on financial analysis: those of the stockholder, manager, and creditor. Next, we describe how to prepare common-size financial statements, which allow us to compare firms that differ in size and to analyze a firm's financial performance over time. We then explain how to calculate and interpret key financial ratios and discuss the DuPont system, a diagnostic tool that uses financial ratios. After a discussion of benchmarks, we conclude with a description of the limitations of financial statement analysis.

4.1 Background for Financial Statement Analysis

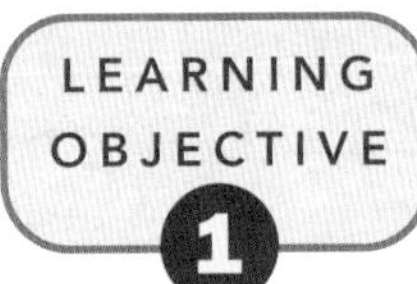

This chapter will guide you through a typical **financial statement analysis**, which involves the use of financial ratios to analyze a firm's performance. We start with some general background. First, we look at the different perspectives we can take when analyzing financial statements; then we present some helpful guidelines for financial statement analysis.

financial statement analysis the use of financial statements to evaluate a company's overall performance and assess its strengths and shortcomings

Perspectives on Financial Statement Analysis

Stockholders and stakeholders may differ in the information they want to gain when analyzing financial statements. In this section, we discuss three perspectives from which we can view financial statement analysis: those of (1) stockholders, (2) managers, and (3) creditors. Although members of each of these groups view financial statements from their own point of view, the perspectives are not mutually exclusive.

STOCKHOLDERS' PERSPECTIVE

Stockholders are primarily concerned with the value of their stock and with how much cash they can expect to receive from dividends and/or capital appreciation. Therefore, stockholders want financial statements to tell them how profitable the firm is, what the return on their investment is, whether the firm can pay a dividend and, if so, how much, and how much cash is available for stockholders, both in total and on a per-share basis. Ultimately, stockholders are interested in how much a share of stock is worth in the market and whether the market is pricing the stock correctly. We address pricing issues in detail in Chapter 9, but financial analysis is a key step in valuing a company's stock.

MANAGERS' PERSPECTIVE

Broadly speaking, management's perspective of financial statement analysis is similar to that of stockholders. The reason is that stockholders own the firm and managers have a fiduciary responsibility to make decisions that are in the owners' best interests. Thus, managers are interested in the same performance measures as stockholders; profitability, dividends, capital appreciation, return on investment, and the like.

Managers, however, are also responsible for running the business on a daily basis and must make decisions that will maximize stockholder wealth in the long run. Maximizing stockholder wealth is not a single "big decision," but a series of day-to-day decisions. Thus, managers need feedback on the short-term impact these decisions have on the firm's financial statements and the current stock price. For example, managers can track trends in sales and can determine how well they are controlling expenses and how much of each sales dollar goes to the bottom line. In addition, managers can see the impact of their investment, financing, and working capital decisions reflected in the financial statements. Keep in mind that managers, as insiders, have access to much more detailed financial information than those outside the firm. Generally, outsiders have access to only published financial statements for publicly traded firms.

CREDITORS' PERSPECTIVE

The primary concern of creditors is whether and when they will receive the interest payments they are entitled to and when they will be repaid the money they loaned to the firm. Thus, a firm's creditors, including long-term bondholders, closely monitor how much debt the firm is currently using, whether the firm is generating enough cash to pay its day-to-day bills, and whether the firm will have sufficient cash in the future to make interest and principal payments on long-term debt *after* satisfying obligations that have a higher legal priority, such as paying employees' wages. Of course, the firm's ability to pay ultimately depends on cash flows and profitability; hence, creditors—like stockholders and managers—are interested in those aspects of the firm's financial performance. When millions or billions of dollars are at stake, you can bet that banks, insurance companies, and other creditors will examine the financial statements closely to uncover potential future problems.

Guidelines for Financial Statement Analysis

We turn now to some general guidelines that will help you when analyzing a firm's financial statements. First, make sure you understand which perspective you are adopting to conduct your analysis: stockholder, manager, or creditor. The perspective will dictate the type of information you need for the analysis and may affect the actions you take based on the results.

Second, always use audited financial statements, if they are available. As we discussed in Chapter 1, an audit means that an independent accountant has attested that the financial statements were correctly prepared and fairly represent the firm's financial condition at a point in time. If the statements are unaudited, you may need to make an extra effort. For example, if you are a creditor considering making a loan, you will need to make an especially diligent examination of the company's books before closing the deal. It would also be a good idea to make sure you know the company's management team and accountant very well. This will provide additional insight into the credit worthiness of the firm.

Third, use financial statements that cover three to five years, or more, to conduct your analysis. This enables you to perform a **trend analysis**, which involves looking at historical financial statements to see how various ratios are increasing, decreasing, or staying constant over time.

trend analysis
analysis of trends in financial data

Fourth, when possible, it is always best to compare a firm's financial statements with those of competitors that are roughly the same size and that offer similar products and services. If you compare firms of disparate size, the results may be meaningless because the two firms may have very different infrastructures, sources of financing, production capabilities, product mixes, and distribution channels. For example, comparing The Boeing Company's financial statements with those of Piper Aircraft, a firm that manufactures small aircraft, makes no sense whatsoever, although both firms manufacture aircraft. You will have to use your judgment as to whether relevant comparisons can be made between firms with large size differences. In general, the greater the size disparity, the less likely the comparisons between firms in the same business will be relevant.

benchmark
a standard against which performance is measured

In business it is common to **benchmark** a firm's performance, as discussed in the previous paragraph. The most common type of benchmarking involves comparing a firm's performance with the performance of similar firms that are relevant competitors. For example, Ford Motor Company may want to benchmark itself against General Motors and Toyota, its major competitors in the North American market. Firms can also benchmark against themselves—comparing this year's performance with last year's, for example—or compare against a goal, such as a 10 percent growth in sales. We discuss benchmarking in more detail later in the chapter.

Before You Go On

1. Why is it important to look at a firm's historical financial statements?
2. What is the primary concern of a firm's creditors?

4.2 Common-Size Financial Statements

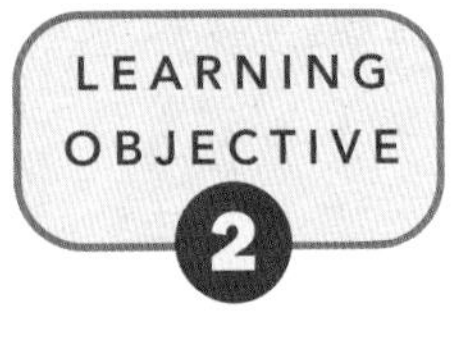

common-size financial statement
a financial statement in which each number is expressed as a percent of a base number, such as total assets or total revenues

Common-size financial statement analysis is one of the most basic forms of financial statement analysis. A **common-size financial statement** is one in which each number is expressed as a percentage of some base number, such as total assets or total revenues. For example, each number on a balance sheet may be divided by total assets. Dividing numbers by a common base to form a ratio is called *scaling.* It is an important concept, and you will read more about it later in the chapter, in the discussion of financial ratios. Financial statements scaled in this manner are also called *standardized financial statements.*

Common-size financial statements allow you to make meaningful comparisons between the financial statements of two firms that are different in size. For example, in the oil and gas field equipment market, Schlumberger Limited is the major competitor of Diaz Manufacturing, the illustrative firm introduced in Chapter 3. However, Schlumberger has $19.4 billion in total assets while Diaz Manufacturing's assets are only $1.9 billion. Without common-size financial statements, comparisons of these two firms would be difficult to interpret. Common-size financial statements are also useful for analyzing trends within a single firm over time, as you will see.

Common-Size Balance Sheets

To create a *common-size balance sheet,* we divide each of the asset accounts by total assets. We also divide each of the liability and equity accounts by total assets since Total assets = Total liabilities + Total equity. You can see the common-size balance sheet for Diaz Manufacturing in Exhibit 4.1. Assets are shown in the top portion of the exhibit, and liabilities and equity in the lower portion. The calculations are simple. For example,

Exhibit 4.1 **Common-Size Balance Sheets for Diaz Manufacturing on December 31 ($ millions)**

	2008		2007		2006	
		% of Total		% of Total		% of Total
Assets:						
Cash and marketable securities	$ 288.5	15.3	$ 16.6	1.1	$ 8.2	0.6
Accounts receivable	306.2	16.2	268.8	18.0	271.5	19.4
Inventories	423.8	22.4	372.7	24.9	400.0	28.6
Other current assets	21.3	1.1	29.9	2.0	24.8	1.8
Total current assets	$1,039.8	55.0	$ 688.0	46.1	$ 704.5	50.4
Plant and equipment (net)	399.4	21.1	394.2	26.4	419.6	30.0
Goodwill and other assets	450.0	23.8	411.6	27.6	273.9	19.6
Total assets	$1,889.2	100.0	$1,493.8	100.0	$1,398.0	100.0
Liabilities and Stockholders' Equity:						
Accounts payable and accruals	$ 349.3	18.5	$ 325.0	21.8	$ 395.0	28.3
Notes payable	10.5	0.6	4.2	0.3	14.5	1.0
Accrued income taxes	18.0	1.0	16.8	1.1	12.4	0.9
Total current liabilities	$ 377.8	20.0	$ 346.0	23.2	$ 421.9	30.2
Long-term debt	574.0	30.4	305.6	20.5	295.6	21.1
Total liabilities	$ 951.8	50.4	$ 651.6	43.6	$ 717.5	51.3
Common stock (54,566,054 shares)	0.5	0.0	0.5	0.0	0.5	0.0
Additional paid in capital	892.4	47.2	892.4	59.7	892.4	63.8
Retained earnings	67.8	3.6	(50.7)	(3.4)	(155.8)	(11.1)
Less: treasury stock	(23.3)	(1.2)	—	—	(56.6)	(4.0)
Total stockholders' equity	$ 937.4	49.6	$ 842.2	56.4	$ 680.5	48.7
Total liabilities and equity	$1,889.2	100.0	$1,493.8	100.0	$1,398.0	100.0

In common-size balance sheets, such as those in this exhibit, each asset account and each liability and equity account is expressed as a percentage of total assets. Common-size statements allow financial analysts to compare firms that are different in size and to identify trends within a single firm over time.

on the asset side in 2008, cash and marketable securities were 15.3 percent of total assets ($288.5/$1,889.2), and inventory was 22.4 percent of total assets ($423.8/$1,889.2). Notice that the percentages of total assets add up to 100 percent. On the liability side, accounts payable are 18.5 percent of total assets ($349.3/$1,889.2), and long-term debt is 30.4 percent ($574.0/$1,889.2). To test yourself, see if you can re-create the percentages in Exhibit 4.1 using your calculator. Make sure the percentages add up to 100, but realize that you may obtain slight variations from 100 because of rounding.

A good source for financial statements is http://finance.yahoo.com.

What kind of information can Exhibit 4.1 tell us about Diaz Manufacturing's operations? Here are some examples. Notice that in 2008, inventories accounted for 22.4 percent of total assets, down from 24.9 percent in 2007 and 28.6 percent in 2006. In other words, Diaz Manufacturing has been steadily reducing the proportion of its money tied up in inventory. This is probably good news because it is usually a sign of more efficient inventory management.

Now look at liabilities and equity, and notice that in 2008 total liabilities represent 50.4 percent of Diaz Manufacturing's total liabilities and equity. This means that common stockholders have provided 49.6 percent of the firm's total financing and that creditors have provided 50.4 percent of the financing. In addition, you can see that from 2006 to 2008, Diaz Manufacturing substantially increased the proportion of financing from long-term debt holders. Long-term debt provided 21.1 percent ($295.6/$1.398.0) of the financing in 2006 and 30.4 percent ($574.0/$1,889.2) in 2008.

Overall, we can identify the following trends in Diaz Manufacturing's common-size balance sheet. First, Diaz Manufacturing is a growing company. Its assets increased from $1,398.0 million in 2006 to $1,889.2 million in 2008. Second, the percentage of total assets held in current assets grew from 2006 to 2008, a sign of increasing liquidity. Recall from Chapter 2 that assets are liquid if they can be sold easily and quickly for cash without a loss of value. Third, the percentage of total assets in plant and equipment declined from 2006 to 2008, a sign that Diaz Manufacturing is becoming more efficient because it is using fewer long-term assets in producing sales (below you will see that sales have increased over the same period). Finally, as mentioned, Diaz Manufacturing has significantly increased the percentage of its financing from long-term debt. Generally, these are considered signs of a solidly performing company, but we have a long way to go before we can confidently reach that conclusion. We will now turn to Diaz Manufacturing's common-size income statement.

Common-Size Income Statements

The most useful way to prepare a *common-size income statement* is to express each account as a percentage of net sales, as shown for Diaz Manufacturing in Exhibit 4.2. *Net sales* are defined as total sales less all sales discounts and sales returns and allowances. You should note that when looking at accounting information and "sales" numbers as reported, they almost always mean net sales, unless otherwise stated. We will follow this convention in the book. Again, the percent calculations are simple. For example, in 2008 selling and administrative expenses are 14.8 percent of sales ($231.1/$1,563.7), and net income is 7.6 percent of sales ($118.5 /$1,563.7). Before proceeding, make sure that you can verify each percentage in Exhibit 4.2 with your calculator.

Interpreting the common-size income statement is also straightforward. As you move down the income statement, you will find out exactly what happens to each dollar of sales that the firm generates. For example, in 2008 it cost Diaz Manufacturing 69.1 cents in cost of goods sold to generate one dollar of sales. Similarly, it cost 14.8 cents in selling and administrative expenses to generate a dollar of sales. The government takes 2.8 percent of sales in the form of taxes.

Exhibit 4.2 **Common-Size Income Statements for Diaz Manufacturing for Fiscal Years Ending December 31 ($ millions)**

	2008		2007		2006	
		% of Total		% of Total		% of Total
Net sales	$1,563.7	100.0	$1,386.7	100.0	$1,475.1	100.0
Cost of goods sold	1,081.1	69.1	974.8	70.3	1,076.3	73.0
Selling and administrative expenses	231.1	14.8	197.4	14.2	205.7	13.9
Earnings before interest, taxes, depreciation, and amortization (EBITDA)	$ 251.5	16.1	$ 214.5	15.5	$ 193.1	13.1
Depreciation	83.1	5.3	75.3	5.4	71.2	4.8
Earnings before interest and taxes (EBIT)	$ 168.4	10.8	$ 139.2	10.0	$ 121.9	8.3
Interest expense	5.6	0.4	18.0	1.3	27.8	1.9
Earnings before taxes (EBT)	$ 162.8	10.4	$ 121.2	8.7	$ 94.1	6.4
Taxes	44.3	2.8	16.1	1.2	27.9	1.9
Net income	$ 118.5	7.6	$ 105.1	7.6	$ 66.2	4.5
Dividends	—		—		—	
Addition to retained earnings	$ 118.5		$ 105.1		$ 66.2	

Common-size income statements express each account as a percentage of net sales. These statements allow financial analysts to better compare firms of different sizes and to analyze trends in a single firm's income statement accounts over time.

The common-size income statement can tell us a lot about a firm's efficiency and profitability. For example, in 2006, Diaz Manufacturing's cost of goods sold and selling and administrative expenses totaled 86.9 percent of sales (73.0 + 13.9). By 2008, these expenses declined to 83.9 percent of sales (69.1 + 14.8). This might mean that Diaz Manufacturing is negotiating lower prices from its suppliers or is more efficient in its use of materials and labor. Or it could mean that the company is getting higher net prices for its products, perhaps by offering fewer discounts or rebates. The important point, however, is that more of each sales dollar is contributing to net income.

Examination of the trends in the income statement and balance sheet suggests that Diaz Manufacturing is improving along a number of dimensions. The real question, however, is whether Diaz Manufacturing is performing well, as compared with other firms in the same industry. For example, the fact that 7.6 cents of every sales dollar reaches the bottom line may not be a good sign if we find out that Diaz Manufacturing's competitors average 10 cents of net income for every sales dollar.

This CNBC Web site offers lots of financial information, including ratios of firms of your choice: moneycentral .msn.com/investor/research/ welcome.asp.

Before You Go On

1. Why does it make sense to standardize financial statements?
2. What are common-size, or standardized, financial statements, and how are they prepared?

4.3 Financial Statement Analysis

In addition to the common-size ratios we have just discussed, other specialized financial ratios help analysts interpret the myriad of numbers in financial statements. In this section we examine financial ratios that measure a firm's liquidity, efficiency, leverage, profitability, and market value, using Diaz Manufacturing as an example. Keep in mind that for ratio analysis to be most useful, it should also include trend and benchmark analysis, which we discuss in more detail later in the chapter.

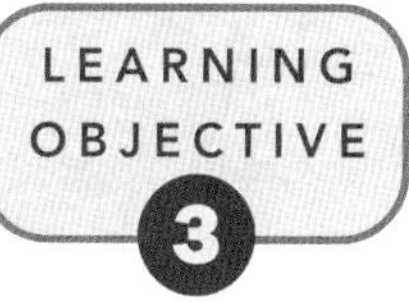

Another source of financial statements for publicly held firms is the U.S. Securities and Exchange Commission at www.sec.gov.

Why Ratios Are Better Measures

A **financial ratio** is simply one number from a financial statement that has been divided by another financial number. Like the percentages in common-size financial statements, ratios eliminate problems arising from differences in size because size is effectively "divided out"; more precisely, the denominator of the ratio adjusts, or scales, the numerator to a common base.

financial ratio
A number from a financial statement that has been scaled by dividing by another financial number

Here's an example. Suppose you want to assess the profitability of two firms. Firm A's net income is $5, and firm B's is $50. Which firm had the best performance? You really cannot tell because you have no idea what asset base was used to generate the income. In this case, a relevant measure of financial performance might be net income scaled by the firm's stockholders' equity—that is, the return on equity (ROE):

$$\text{ROE} = \frac{\text{Net income}}{\text{Stockholders' equity}}$$

If firm A's total stockholders' equity is $25 and firm B's stockholders' equity is $5,000, the ROE for each firm is as follows:

Company	ROE Calculation	ROE Ratio	ROE
Firm A	$5/$25	0.20	20%
Firm B	$50/$5,000	0.01	1%

As you can see, the ROE for firm A is 20 percent—much larger than the ROE for firm B at 1 percent. Even though firm B had the higher net income in absolute terms ($50 versus $5), its stockholders had invested more money in the firm ($5,000 versus

$25), and it generated less income per dollar of invested equity than firm A. Clearly, firm A's performance is better than firm B's, given its smaller equity investment.

The bottom line is that accounting numbers are more easily compared and interpreted when they are scaled. This is why, for example, consumer groups pressured grocery stores to provide unit pricing. When comparing a bottle of Mel's Picante Sauce with four other brands, all in different-sized bottles, you need to know the cost per ounce, not the cost per bottle. The same is true in business. Common-size financial statements, for example, allow us to compare the financial data of large and small firms with the effect of size held constant.

CHOICE OF SCALE IS IMPORTANT

An important decision is your choice of the "size factor" for scaling. The size factor you select must be relevant and make economic sense. For example, suppose you want a measure that will enable you to compare the productivity of employees at a particular plant with the productivity of employees at other plants that make similar products. Your assistant makes a suggestion: divide net income by the number of parking spaces available at the plant. Will this ratio tell you how productive labor is at a plant? Clearly, the answer is no.

Your assistant comes up with another idea: divide net income by the number of employees. This ratio makes sense as a measure of employee productivity. A higher ratio indicates that employees are more productive because, on average, each employee is generating more income. In business, the type of variable most commonly used for scaling is a measure of size, such as total assets or total net sales. Other scaling variables are used in specific industries where they are especially informative. For example, in the airline industry, a key measure of performance is revenue per available seat mile; in the steel industry, it is sales or cost per ton; and in the automobile industry, it is cost per car.

OTHER COMMENTS ON RATIOS

The ratios we present in this chapter are widely accepted and are almost always included in any financial workup. However, you will find that different analysts will compute many of these standard ratios slightly differently. Modest variations in how ratios are computed are not a problem as long as the analyst carefully documents the work done and discloses the ratio formula. These differences are particularly important when you are comparing data from different sources.

Short-Term Liquidity Ratios

Liquid assets have active secondary markets and can be sold quickly for cash without a loss of value. Some assets are more liquid than others. For example, short-term marketable securities are very liquid because they can be easily sold in the secondary market at or near the original purchase price. In contrast, plant and equipment can take months or years to sell and often must be sold substantially below the cost of building or acquiring them.

When we examine a company's *liquidity position,* we want to know whether the firm can pay its bills when cash from operations is insufficient to pay short-term obligations, such as payroll, invoices from vendors, and maturing bank loans. As the name implies, *short-term liquidity ratios* focus on whether the firm has the ability to convert current assets into cash quickly without loss of value. As we have noted before, even a profitable business can fail if it cannot pay its current bills on time. The inability to pay debts when they are due is known as **insolvency**. Thus, liquidity ratios are also known as *short-term solvency ratios.* The two most important liquidity ratios are the current ratio and the quick ratio.

insolvency
the inability to pay debts when they are due

THE CURRENT RATIO

To calculate the current ratio, we divide current assets by current liabilities.[1] The formula appears in the following, along with a calculation of the current ratio for Diaz Manufacturing for 2008 based on balance sheet account data from Exhibit 4.1:

[1]This calculation involves dividing total current assets by total current liabilities. We drop the word "total" in the interest of brevity.

$$\begin{aligned}\text{Current ratio} &= \frac{\text{Current assets}}{\text{Current liabilities}} \quad (4.1)\\ &= \frac{\$1{,}039.8}{\$377.8}\\ &= 2.75\end{aligned}$$

Diaz Manufacturing's current ratio is 2.75, which should be read as "2.75 times." What does this number mean? If Diaz Manufacturing were to take its current supply of cash and add to it the proceeds of liquidating its other current assets—such as marketable securities, accounts receivable, and inventory—it would have $1,039.8 million. This $1,039.8 million would cover the firm's short-term obligations of $377.8 million approximately 2.75 times, leaving a "cushion" of $662.0 million ($1,039.8 − $377.8).

Now turn to Exhibit 4.3, which shows the ratios discussed in this chapter for Diaz Manufacturing for the three-year period 2006–2008. The exhibit will allow us to identify important trends in the company's financial statements. Note that Diaz Manufacturing's current ratio has been steadily increasing over time. What does this trend mean? From the perspective of a potential creditor, it is a positive sign. To a potential creditor, more liquidity is better because it means that the firm will have the ability, at least in the short term, to make payments. From a stockholder's perspective, however, too much liquidity is not necessarily a good thing. If we were to discover that Diaz Manufacturing has a much higher current ratio than its competitors, it could mean that management is being too conservative by keeping too much money tied up in low-risk and low-yield assets, such as marketable securities. Generally, more liquidity is better and is a sign of a healthy firm. Only a benchmark analysis can tell us the complete story, however.

THE QUICK RATIO

The quick ratio is similar to the current ratio except that inventory is subtracted from current assets in the numerator. This change reflects the fact that inventory is often much less liquid than other current assets. Inventory is the most difficult current asset to convert to cash without loss of value. Of course, the liquidity of inventory varies with the industry. For example, inventory of a raw material commodity, such as gold or crude oil, is more likely to be sold with little loss in value than inventory consisting of perishables, such as fruit, or fashion items, such as basketball shoes. Another reason for excluding inventory in the quick ratio calculation is that the book value of inventory may be significantly more than its market value because it may be obsolete, partially completed, spoiled, out of fashion, or out of season.

To calculate the quick ratio—or *acid-test ratio,* as it is sometimes called—we divide current assets, less inventory, by current liabilities. The calculation for Diaz Manufacturing for 2008 is as follows, based on balance sheet data from Exhibit 4.1:

$$\begin{aligned}\text{Quick ratio} &= \frac{\text{Current assets} - \text{Inventory}}{\text{Current liabilities}} \quad (4.2)\\ &= \frac{\$1{,}039.8 - \$423.8}{\$377.8}\\ &= 1.63\end{aligned}$$

The quick ratio of 1.63 times means that if we exclude inventory, Diaz Manufacturing had $1.63 of current assets for each dollar of current liabilities. You can see from Exhibit 4.3 that Diaz Manufacturing's liquidity position, as measured by its quick ratio, has been improving over time; this is generally a sign of good financial health.

Note that the quick ratio is almost always less than the current ratio, as it was for Diaz Manufacturing in 2008.[2] The quick ratio is a very conservative measure of liquidity because the calculation assumes that the inventory is valued at zero, which in most cases is not a realistic assumption. Even in a bankruptcy "fire sale," the inventory can be sold for some small percentage of its book value, generating at least some cash.

[2]The quick ratio will always be less than the current ratio for any firm that has inventory.

Exhibit 4.3 Ratios for Time-Trend Analysis for Diaz Manufacturing for Fiscal Years Ending December 31

Financial Ratio	2008	2007	2006
Liquidity Ratios:			
Current ratio	2.75	1.99	1.67
Quick ratio	1.63	0.91	0.72
Efficiency Ratios:			
Inventory turnover	2.55	2.62	2.69
Day's sales in inventory	143.14	139.31	135.69
Accounts receivable turnover	5.11	5.16	5.43
Day's sales outstanding	71.43	70.74	67.22
Total asset turnover	0.83	0.93	1.06
Fixed asset turnover	3.92	3.52	3.52
Leverage Ratios:			
Total debt ratio	0.50	0.44	0.51
Debt-to-equity ratio	1.02	0.77	1.05
Equity multiplier	2.02	1.77	2.05
Times interest earned	30.07	7.73	4.38
Cash coverage	44.91	11.92	6.95
Profitability Ratios:			
Gross profit margin	30.86 %	29.70 %	27.04 %
Operating profit margin	10.77 %	10.04 %	8.26 %
Net profit margin	7.58 %	7.58 %	4.49 %
EBIT return on assets	8.91 %	9.32 %	8.72 %
Return on assets	6.27 %	7.04 %	4.74 %
Return on equity	12.64 %	12.48 %	9.73 %
Market-Value Indicators:			
Price-earnings ratio	22.40	18.43	14.29
Earnings per share	$ 2.17	$ 1.93	$ 1.21

Note: Numbers may not add up because of rounding.

Comparing how financial ratios, such as these ratios for Diaz Manufacturing, change over time enables financial analysts to identify trends in company performance.

DECISION-MAKING EXAMPLE 4.1

The Liquidity Paradox

Situation: You are asked by your boss whether Wal-Mart or H&R Block is more liquid. You have the following information:

	Wal-Mart	H&R Block
Current ratio	0.92	1.20
Quick ratio	0.21	1.20

You also know that Wal-Mart carries a large inventory and that H&R Block is a service firm that specializes in income-tax preparation. Which firm is the most liquid? Your boss asks you to explain the reasons for your answers, and also to explain why H&R Block's current and quick ratios are the same.

Decision: H&R Block is much more liquid than Wal-Mart. Looking at the difference between the quick ratios—0.21 versus 1.20—pretty much tells the story. Inventory is the least liquid of all the current assets. Because H&R Block does not manufacture or sell goods, it has no inventory; hence, the current and quick ratios are equal. Wal-Mart has a lot of inventory relative to the rest of its current assets, and that explains the large numerical drop between the current and quick ratios.

Efficiency Ratios

Now we turn to a group of ratios, called *efficiency ratios* or *asset turnover ratios,* that measure how efficiently a firm uses its assets to generate sales. These ratios are most useful to managers, who use them to identify inefficiencies in operations, and to creditors, who use them to find out how quickly inventory can be turned into receivables and ultimately into cash that can be used to satisfy debt obligations.

INVENTORY TURNOVER AND DAYS' SALES IN INVENTORY

We measure inventory turnover by dividing the cost of goods sold from the income statement by inventory from the balance sheet (see Exhibits 4.1 and 4.2). The formula for inventory turnover and its value for Diaz Manufacturing in 2008 are:

$$\begin{aligned}\text{Inventory turnover} &= \frac{\text{Cost of goods sold}}{\text{Inventory}} \qquad (4.3)\\ &= \frac{\$1{,}081.1}{\$423.8}\\ &= 2.55\end{aligned}$$

The firm "turned over" its inventory 2.55 times during the year. Looking back at Exhibit 4.3, you can see that this ratio remained about the same over the period covered.

What exactly does "turning over" inventory mean? Consider a simple example. Assume that a firm starts the year with an inventory worth $100 and replaces the inventory when it is all sold; that is, the inventory goes to zero. Over the course of the year, the firm sells the inventory and replaces it three times. For the year, the firm has an inventory turnover of three times.

As a general rule, turning over inventory faster is a good thing because it means that the firm is doing a good job of minimizing its investment in inventory. Nevertheless, like all ratios, inventory turnover can be either too high or too low. Too high an inventory turnover ratio may signal that the firm has too little inventory and could be losing sales as a result. If the firm's inventory turnover level is too low, it could mean that management is not managing the firm's inventory efficiently or that an unusually large portion of the inventory is obsolete or out of date and has not yet been written off. In sum, inventory turnover that is significantly lower or significantly higher than that of competitors calls for further investigation.[3]

Based on the inventory turnover figure, and using a 365-day year, we can also calculate the *days' sales in inventory,* which tells us how long it takes a firm to turn over its inventory on average. The formula for days' sales in inventory, along with a calculation for Diaz Manufacturing, is as follows:

[3]Some financial analysts compute inventory turnover using sales rather than cost of goods sold in the numerator. On the one hand, this alternative calculation (Inventory turnover = Sales/Inventory) makes sense if the analyst wants to know the amount of sales generated per dollar of inventory. On the other hand, the calculation can be misleading if the firm generates a significant amount of revenues from activities that are not associated with inventory, such as providing services.

$$\text{Day's sales in inventory} = \frac{365 \text{ days}}{\text{Inventory turnover}} \quad (4.4)$$
$$= \frac{365 \text{ days}}{2.55}$$
$$= 143.14 \text{ days}$$

Note that inventory turnover in the formula is computed from Equation 4.3. On average, Diaz Manufacturing takes about 140 days to turn over its inventory. Generally speaking, the smaller the number, the more efficient the firm is at moving its inventory.

ALTERNATIVE CALCULATION FOR INVENTORY TURNOVER

Normally, we determine inventory turnover by dividing cost of goods sold by the inventory level at the end of the period. However, if a firm's inventory fluctuates widely or is growing (or decreasing) over time, some analysts prefer to compute inventory turnover using the average inventory value for the time period. In this case, the inventory turnover is calculated in two steps:

1. We first calculate average inventory by adding beginning and ending inventory and dividing by 2:

$$\text{Average inventory} = \frac{\text{Beginning inventory} + \text{Ending inventory}}{2}$$

2. We then divide the cost of goods sold by average inventory to find inventory turnover:

$$\text{Inventory turnover} = \frac{\text{Cost of goods sold}}{\text{Average inventory}}$$

LEARNING BY DOING APPLICATION 4.1

Alternative Calculations for Efficiency Ratios

Problem: For Diaz Manufacturing, compute the inventory turnover based on the average inventory. Then compare that value with 2.55, the turnover ratio based on Equation 4.3. Why do you think the two values differ?

Approach: Use the alternative calculation described above. In comparing the two values, you want to consider fluctuations in inventory over time.

Solution:

1. Average inventory

$$\text{Average inventory} = \frac{\text{Beginning inventory} + \text{Ending inventory}}{2}$$
$$= \frac{\$372.7 + \$423.8}{2}$$
$$= \$398.3$$

2. Inventory turnover

$$\text{Inventory turnover} = \frac{\text{Cost of goods sold}}{\text{Average inventory}}$$
$$= \frac{\$1{,}081.1}{\$398.3}$$
$$= 2.71$$

The inventory turnover computed with average inventory, 2.71 times, is slightly higher than 2.55 because the inventory increased during the year.

Note that all six efficiency ratios presented in the chapter (Equations 4.3 through 4.8) can be computed using an average asset value. For much work that financial analysts do, the adjustment will have little effect on either the analysis or the decision reached. For simplicity, we will generally use the ending of the period asset value in our calculations.

ACCOUNTS RECEIVABLE TURNOVER AND DAYS' SALES OUTSTANDING

Many firms make sales to their customers on credit, which creates an account receivable on the balance sheet. It does not do the firm much good to ship products or provide the services on credit if it cannot ultimately collect the cash from its customers. A firm that collects its receivables faster is generating cash faster. We can measure the speed at which a firm converts its receivables into cash with a ratio called accounts receivable turnover; the formula and calculated values for Diaz Manufacturing in 2008 are as follows:

$$\begin{aligned}\text{Accounts receivable turnover} &= \frac{\text{Net sales}}{\text{Accounts receivable}} \\ &= \frac{\$1{,}563.7}{\$306.2} \\ &= 5.11\end{aligned} \tag{4.5}$$

The data to compute this ratio is from Diaz's balance sheet and income statement (Exhibits 4.1 and 4.2). Roughly, this ratio means that Diaz Manufacturing loans out and collects an amount equal to its outstanding accounts receivable 5.11 times over the course of a year.

In most circumstances, higher accounts receivable turnover is a good thing—it means that the firm is collecting cash payments from its credit customers faster. As shown in Exhibit 4.3, Diaz's collection speed slowed down slightly from 2006 to 2008. This may be a cause for management concern, for at least three reasons. First, Diaz's system for collecting accounts receivable may be inefficient. Second, the firm's customers may not be paying on time because their businesses are slowing down due to industry or general economic conditions. Finally, Diaz may be extending credit to customers that are poor credit risks. Making a determination of the cause would require us to compare Diaz's accounts receivable turnover with corresponding figures from its competitors.

You may find it easier to evaluate a firm's credit and collection policies by using days' sales outstanding, often referred to as DSO, which is calculated as follows:

$$\begin{aligned}\text{Days' sales outstanding} &= \frac{\text{365 days}}{\text{Accounts receivable turnover}} \\ &= \frac{\text{365 days}}{5.11} \\ &= 71.43 \text{ days}\end{aligned} \tag{4.6}$$

Note that accounts receivable turnover is computed from Equation 4.5. The DSO for Diaz Manufacturing means that, on average, the company converts its credit sales into cash in 71.43 days. DSO is commonly called the *average collection period.*

Generally, faster collection is better. Whether 71.43 days is fast enough really depends on industry norms and on the credit terms Diaz Manufacturing extends to its customers. For example, if the industry average DSO is 77 days and Diaz Manufacturing gives customers 90 days to pay, then a DSO of 71.43 days is an indication of good management. If, in contrast, Diaz gives customers 60 days to pay, the company has a problem, and management needs to determine why customers are not paying on time.

ASSET TURNOVER RATIOS

We turn next to a discussion of some broader efficiency ratios. In this section we discuss two ratios that measure how efficiently management is using the firm's assets to generate sales.

Total asset turnover measures the dollar amount of sales generated with each dollar of total assets. Generally, the higher the total asset turnover, the more efficiently management is using total assets. Thus, if a firm increases its asset turnover, management is squeezing more sales out of a constant asset base. When a firm's asset turnover ratio is high for its industry, the firm may be approaching full capacity. In such a situation, if management wants to increase sales, it will need to make an investment in additional fixed assets.

The formula for total asset turnover and the calculation for Diaz Manufacturing's turnover value in 2008 (based on data from Exhibits 4.1 and 4.2) are as follows:

$$\text{Total asset turnover} = \frac{\text{Net sales}}{\text{Total assets}} \qquad (4.7)$$

$$= \frac{\$1{,}563.7}{\$1{,}889.2}$$

$$= 0.83$$

Total asset turnover for Diaz Manufacturing is 0.83 times. In other words, in 2008, Diaz Manufacturing generated $0.83 in sales for every dollar in assets. In Exhibit 4.3 you can see that Diaz Manufacturing's total asset turnover has declined slightly since 2006. This does not necessarily mean that the company's management team is performing poorly. The decline could be part of a typical industry sales cycle, or it could be due to a slowdown in the business of Diaz Manufacturing's customers. As always, getting a better fix on potential problems requires comparing Diaz Manufacturing's total asset turnover with comparable figures for its close competitors.

The turnover of total assets is a "big picture" measure. In addition, management may want to see how particular types of assets are being put to use. A common asset turnover ratio measures sales per dollar invested in fixed assets (plant and equipment). The fixed asset turnover formula and the 2008 calculation for Diaz are:

$$\text{Fixed asset turnover} = \frac{\text{Net sales}}{\text{Net fixed assets}} \qquad (4.8)$$

$$= \frac{\$1{,}563.7}{\$399.4}$$

$$= 3.92$$

Diaz Manufacturing generates $3.92 of sales for each dollar of fixed assets in 2008, which is an increase over the 2007 value of $3.52. This means that the firm is generating more sales for every dollar in fixed assets. In a manufacturing firm that relies heavily on plant and equipment to generate output, the fixed asset turnover number is an important ratio. In contrast, in a service-industry firm with little plant and equipment, *total* asset turnover is more relevant.

DECISION-MAKING EXAMPLE 4.2

Ranking Firms by Fixed Asset Turnover

Situation: Different industries use different amounts of fixed assets to generate their revenues. For example, the airline industry is capital intensive, with large investments in airplanes, whereas firms in service industries use more human capital (people) and have very little invested in fixed assets. As a financial analyst, you are given the following fixed asset turnover ratios: 0.79, 4.42, and 15.10. You must decide which ratios match up with three firms: Delta Air Lines, H&R Block, and Wal-Mart. Make this decision, and explain your reasoning.

Decision: At the extremes, Delta is a capital-intensive firm, and H&R Block is a service firm. We would expect firms with large investments in fixed assets (Delta) to have lower asset turnover than service-industry firms, which have few fixed assets. Wal-Mart is the middle-ground firm, with fixed asset holdings primarily in stores and land. Thus, the firms and their respective fixed asset turnovers are: Delta = 0.79, Wal-Mart = 4.42, and H&R Block = 15.10.

Leverage Ratios

Leverage ratios measure the extent to which a firm uses debt rather than equity financing and indicate the firm's ability to meet its long-term financial obligations, such as interest payments on debt and lease payments. The ratios are also called *long-term solvency ratios*. They are of interest to the firm's creditors, stockholders, and managers. Many different leverage ratios are used in industry; in this chapter we present some of the most widely used.

FINANCIAL LEVERAGE

financial leverage
the use of debt in a firm's capital structure; the more debt, the higher the financial leverage

The term **financial leverage** refers to the use of debt in a firm's capital structure. When a firm uses debt financing, rather than only equity financing, the returns to stockholders may be magnified. This so-called leveraging effect occurs because the interest payments associated with debt are fixed, regardless of the level of the firm's operating profits. On the one hand, if the firm's operating profits increase from one year to the next, debt holders continue to receive only their fixed-interest payments, and all of the increase goes to the stockholders. On the other hand, if the firm falls on hard times and suffers an operating loss, debt holders receive the same fixed-interest payment (assuming that the firm does not go bankrupt), and the loss is charged against the stockholders' equity. Thus, debt increases the returns to stockholders during good times and reduces the returns during bad times. In Chapter 16 we discuss financial leverage in greater depth and present a detailed example of how debt financing creates the leveraging effect.

default risk
the risk that a firm will not be able to pay its debt obligations as they come due

The use of debt in a company's capital structure increases the firm's **default risk**—the risk that it will not be able to pay its debt as it comes due. The explanation is, of course, that debt payments are a fixed obligation and debt holders must be paid the interest and principal payments they are owed, regardless of whether the company earns a profit or suffers a loss. If a company fails to make an interest payment on the prescribed date, the company defaults on its debt and could be forced into bankruptcy by creditors.

DEBT RATIOS

We next look at three leverage ratios that focus on how much debt, rather than equity, the firm employs in its capital structure. The more debt a firm uses, the higher its financial leverage, the more volatile its earnings, and the greater its risk of default.

Total Debt Ratio. The total debt ratio measures the extent to which the firm finances its assets from sources other than the stockholders. The higher the total debt ratio, the more debt the firm has in its capital structure. The total debt ratio and a calculation for Diaz Manufacturing for 2008 based on data from Exhibit 4.1 appear as follows:

$$\begin{aligned}\text{Total debt ratio} &= \frac{\text{Total debt}}{\text{Total assets}} \qquad (4.9)\\ &= \frac{\$951.8}{\$1{,}889.2}\\ &= 0.50\end{aligned}$$

How do we determine the figure to use for total debt? Many variations are used, but perhaps the easiest is to subtract total equity from total assets. In other words, total debt is equal to total liabilities. Using Exhibit 4.1, we can calculate total debt for Diaz Manufacturing in 2008 as follows:

$$\text{Total debt} = \$1{,}889.2 - \$937.4 = \$951.8$$

As you can see from Equation 4.9, the total debt ratio for Diaz Manufacturing is 0.50, which means that 50 percent of the company's assets are financed with debt.

Looking back at Exhibit 4.3, we find that Diaz Manufacturing increased its use of debt from 2007 to 2008. The current total debt ratio of 50 percent appears relatively high, raising questions about the company's financing strategy. Whether a high or low value for the total debt ratio is good or bad, however, depends on how the firm's capital structure affects the value of the firm. We explore this topic in greater detail in Chapter 16.

We turn next to two common variations of the total debt ratio: the debt-to-equity ratio and the equity multiplier.

Debt-to-Equity Ratio. The *total debt ratio* tells us the amount of debt for each dollar of total assets. The *debt-to-equity ratio* tells us the amount of debt for each dollar of equity. Based on data from Exhibit 4.1, Diaz Manufacturing's debt-to-equity ratio for 2008 is 1.02:

$$\begin{aligned}\text{Debt-to-equity ratio} &= \frac{\text{Total debt}}{\text{Total equity}} \qquad (4.10)\\ &= \frac{\$951.8}{\$937.4}\\ &= 1.02\end{aligned}$$

The total debt ratio and the debt-to-equity ratio are directly related by the following formula, shown with a calculation for Diaz Manufacturing:

$$\begin{aligned}\text{Total debt ratio} &= \frac{\text{Debt-to-equity ratio}}{1 + \text{Debt-to-equity ratio}}\\ &= \frac{1.02}{1 + 1.02}\\ &= 0.50\end{aligned}$$

As you can see, once you know one of these ratios, you can compute the other. Which of the two ratios you use is really a matter of personal preference.

Equity Multiplier. The equity multiplier tells us the amount of assets that the firm has for every dollar of equity. Diaz Manufacturing's equity multiplier ratio is 2.02, as shown here:

$$\begin{aligned}\text{Equity multiplier} &= \frac{\text{Total assets}}{\text{Total equity}} \qquad (4.11)\\ &= \frac{\$1{,}889.2}{\$937.4}\\ &= 2.02\end{aligned}$$

Notice that the equity multiplier is directly related to the debt-to-equity ratio:

$$\text{Equity multiplier} = 1 + \text{Debt-to-equity ratio}$$

This is no accident. Recall the balance sheet identity: Total assets = Total liabilities (debt) + Total stockholders' equity. This identity can be substituted into the numerator of the equity multiplier formula (Equation 4.11):

$$\begin{aligned}\text{Equity multiplier} &= \frac{\text{Total assets}}{\text{Total equity}}\\ &= \frac{\text{Total equity} + \text{Total debt}}{\text{Total equity}}\\ &= \frac{\text{Total equity}}{\text{Total equity}} + \frac{\text{Total debt}}{\text{Total equity}}\\ &= 1 + \frac{\text{Total debt}}{\text{Total equity}}\end{aligned}$$

$$= 1 + \frac{\$951.8}{937.4}$$
$$= 1 + 1.02$$
$$= 2.02$$

Therefore, all three of these leverage ratios (Equations 4.9–4.11) are related by the balance sheet identity, and once you know one of the three ratios, you can compute the other two ratios. All three ratios provide the same information.

LEARNING BY DOING APPLICATION **4.2**

Finding a Leverage Ratio

Problem: A firm's debt-to-equity ratio is 0.5. What is the firm's total debt ratio?

Approach: Use the equation that relates the total debt ratio to the debt-to-equity ratio.

Solution:

$$\text{Total debt ratio} = \frac{\text{Debt-to-equity ratio}}{1 + \text{Debt-to-equity ratio}}$$
$$= \frac{0.5}{1 + 0.5}$$
$$= 0.33$$

LEARNING BY DOING APPLICATION **4.3**

Solving for an Unknown Using the Debt-to-Equity Ratio

Problem: You are given the follow information about H&R Block's year-end balance sheet. The firm's debt-to-equity ratio is 1.83, and its total equity is \$1.90 billion. Determine the book (accounting) values for H&R Block's total debt and total assets.

Approach: We know that the debt-to-equity ratio is 1.83 and that total equity is \$1.90 billion. We also know that the debt-to-equity ratio (Equation 4.10) is equal to total debt divided by total equity, and we can use this information to solve for total debt. Once we have a figure for total debt, we can use the basic accounting identity to solve for total assets.

Solution:

$$\text{Total debt} = \text{Debt-to-equity ratio} \times \text{Total equity}$$
$$= 1.83 \times \$1.90$$
$$= \$3.48 \text{ billion}$$

$$\text{Total assets} = \text{Total debt} + \text{Total equity}$$
$$= \$3.48 + \$1.90$$
$$= \$5.38 \text{ billion}$$

COVERAGE RATIOS

A second type of leverage ratio measures the firm's ability to service its debts, or how easily the firm can "cover" debt payments out of earnings or cash flow. What does "coverage" mean? If your monthly take-home pay from your part-time job is \$400 and the rent on your apartment is \$450, you are going to be in some financial distress because your income does not "cover" your \$450 fixed obligation to pay the rent. If, on the other hand, your take-home pay is $900, your monthly coverage ratio with respect to rent is $900/$450 = 2 times. This means that for every dollar of rent you must pay, you earn two dollars of revenue. The higher your coverage ratio, the less likely you will default on your rent payments.

Times Interest Earned. Our first coverage ratio is times interest earned, which measures the extent to which operating profits (earnings before interest and taxes, or EBIT) cover the firm's interest expenses. Creditors prefer to lend to firms whose EBIT is far in excess of their interest payments. The equation for the times-interest-earned ratio and a calculation for Diaz Manufacturing from its income statement (Exhibit 4.2) for 2008 are:

$$\begin{aligned}\text{Times interest earned} &= \frac{\text{EBIT}}{\text{Interest expense}} \qquad (4.12)\\ &= \frac{\$168.4}{\$5.6}\\ &= 30.07\end{aligned}$$

Diaz Manufacturing can cover its interest charges about 30 times with its operating income. This is an extremely large figure, which appears to point to a good margin of safety for creditors. In general, the larger the times interest earned figure, the more likely the firm is to meet its interest payments.

Cash Coverage. As we have discussed before, depreciation is a noncash expense, and as a result, no cash goes out the door when depreciation is deducted on the income statement. Thus, rather than asking whether operating profits (EBIT) are sufficient to cover interest payments, we might ask how much cash is available to cover interest payments. The cash a firm has available from operations to meet interest payments are better measured by EBIT plus depreciation and amortization (EBITDA).[4] Thus, the cash coverage ratio for Diaz Manufacturing in 2008 is:

$$\begin{aligned}\text{Cash coverage} &= \frac{\text{EBITDA}}{\text{Interest expense}} \qquad (4.13)\\ &= \frac{\$251.5}{\$5.6}\\ &= 44.91\end{aligned}$$

For a firm with depreciation or amortization expenses, which includes virtually all firms, EBITDA coverage will be larger than times interest earned coverage.

Profitability Ratios

Profitability ratios measure management's ability to efficiently use the firm's assets to generate sales and manage the firm's operations. These measurements are of interest to stockholders, creditors, and managers because they focus on the firm's earnings. The profitability ratios presented in this chapter are among a handful of ratios used by virtually all stakeholders when analyzing a firm's performance. In general, the higher the profitability ratios, the better the firm is performing.

GROSS PROFIT MARGIN

The gross profit margin measures the percentage of net sales remaining after the cost of goods sold is paid. It captures the firm's ability to manage the expenses directly

[4]EBITDA can differ from actual cash flows because of the accounting accruals discussed in Chapter 3.

associated with producing the firm's products or services. Next we show the gross profit margin formula, along with a calculation for Diaz Manufacturing in 2008, using data from Exhibit 4.2:

$$\begin{aligned}\text{Gross profit margin} &= \frac{\text{Net sales} - \text{Cost of goods sold}}{\text{Net sales}} \\ &= \frac{\$1{,}563.7 - \$1{,}081.1}{\$1{,}563.7} \\ &= 30.86\%\end{aligned} \tag{4.14}$$

Thus, after paying the cost of goods sold, Diaz Manufacturing has 30.86 percent of the sales amount remaining to pay other expenses. From Exhibit 4.3, you can see that Diaz Manufacturing's gross profit margin has been increasing over the past several years, which is good news.

OPERATING PROFIT MARGIN AND EBITDA MARGIN

Moving farther down the income statement, you can measure the percentage of sales that remains after payment of cost of goods sold and all other expenses, except for interest and taxes. Operating profit is typically measured as EBIT. The operating profit margin, therefore, gives an indication of the profitability of the firm's operations, independent of its financing policies or tax management strategies. The operating profit margin formula, along with Diaz Manufacturing's 2008 operating profit margin calculated from Exhibit 4.2, is as follows:

$$\begin{aligned}\text{Operating profit margin} &= \frac{\text{EBIT}}{\text{Net sales}} \\ &= \frac{\$168.4}{\$1{,}563.7} \\ &= 10.77\%\end{aligned} \tag{4.15}$$

Many Wall Street stock analysts are concerned with cash flows generated by operations rather than operating earnings and will use EBITDA in the numerator instead of EBIT. Calculated in this way, the operating profit margin is known as the EBITDA margin.

NET PROFIT MARGIN

The net profit margin indicates the percentage of sales remaining after all of the firm's expenses, including interest and taxes, have been paid. The net profit margin formula is shown here, along with the calculated value for Diaz Manufacturing in 2008, using data from the firm's income statement (Exhibit 4.2):

$$\begin{aligned}\text{Net profit margin} &= \frac{\text{Net income}}{\text{Net sales}} \\ &= \frac{\$118.5}{\$1{,}563.7} \\ &= 7.58\%\end{aligned} \tag{4.16}$$

As you can see from Exhibit 4.3, Diaz Manufacturing's net profit margin improved dramatically from 2006 to 2008. This is good news. The question remains, however, whether 7.58 percent is a good profit margin in an absolute sense. Answering this question requires that we compare Diaz Manufacturing's performance to the performance of its competitors, which we will do later in this chapter. What qualifies as a good profit margin varies significantly across industries. Generally speaking, the higher a company's profit margin, the better the company's performance.

RETURN ON ASSETS

So far, we have examined profitability as a percentage of sales. It is also important that we analyze profitability as a percentage of investment, either in assets or in equity. First, let's look at return on assets. In practice, return on assets is calculated in two different ways.

One approach provides a measure of operating profit (EBIT) per dollar of assets. This is a powerful measure of return because it tells us how efficiently management utilized the assets under their command, independent of financing decisions and taxes. It can be thought of as a measure of the pre-tax return on the total net investment in the firm from operations. The formula for this version of return on assets, which we call EBIT return on assets (EROA), is shown next, together with the calculated value for Diaz Manufacturing in 2008, using data from Exhibits 4.1 and 4.2:

$$\begin{aligned} \text{EROA} &= \frac{\text{EBIT}}{\text{Total assets}} \\ &= \frac{\$168.4}{\$1{,}889.2} \\ &= 8.91\% \end{aligned} \tag{4.17}$$

Exhibit 4.3 shows us that, unlike the other profitability ratios, Diaz Manufacturing's EROA did not really improve from 2006 to 2008. The very similar EROA values for 2006 and 2008 indicate that assets increased at approximately the same rate as operating profits.

Some analysts calculate return on assets (ROA) as:

$$\begin{aligned} \text{Return on assets} &= \frac{\text{Net income}}{\text{Total assets}} \\ &= \frac{\$118.5}{\$1{,}889.2} \\ &= 6.27\% \end{aligned} \tag{4.18}$$

Although it is a common calculation, we advise against using the calculation in Equation 4.18 unless you are using the DuPont system, which we discuss shortly. The ROA calculation divides a measure of earnings available to stockholders (net income) by total assets (debt plus equity), which is a measure of the investment in the firm by both stockholders and creditors. Constructing a ratio of those two numbers is like mixing apples and oranges. The information that this ratio provides about the efficiency of asset utilization is obscured by the financing decisions the firm has made and the taxes it pays. You can see this in Exhibit 4.3, which shows that, in contrast to the very small change in EROA, ROA increases substantially for 2006 to 2008. This increase in ROA is due not to improved efficiency but rather to a large decrease in interest expense (see Exhibit 4.2).

The key point is that EROA surpasses ROA as a measure of how efficiently assets are utilized in operations. Dividing a measure of earnings to both debt holders and stockholders by a measure of how much both debt holders and stockholders have invested gives us a clearer view of what we are trying to measure.

In general, when you calculate a financial ratio, if you have a measure of income to stockholders in the numerator, you want to make sure that you have only investments by stockholders in the denominator. Similarly, if you have a measure of total profits from operations in the numerator, you want to divide it by a measure of total investments by both debt holders and stockholders.

RETURN ON EQUITY

Return on equity (ROE) measures net income as a percentage of the stockholders' investment in the firm. The return on equity formula and the calculation for Diaz Manufacturing in 2008 based on data from Exhibits 4.1 and 4.2 are as follows:

$$\text{Return on equity} = \frac{\text{Net income}}{\text{Total equity}} \qquad (4.19)$$
$$= \frac{\$118.5}{\$937.4}$$
$$= 12.64\%$$

ALTERNATIVE CALCULATION OF ROA AND ROE

As with efficiency ratios, the calculation of ROA and ROE involves dividing an income statement value, which relates to a period of time, by a balance sheet value from the end of the time period. Some analysts prefer to calculate ROA and ROE using the average asset value or equity value, where the average value is determined as follows:

$$\text{Average asset or equity value} = \frac{\text{Beginning value} + \text{Ending value}}{2}$$

LEARNING BY DOING APPLICATION **4.4**

Alternative Calculations for EROA and ROE Ratios

Problem: Calculate the EROA and ROE for Diaz Manufacturing using average balance sheet values, compare the results with the calculations based on Equations 4.17 and 4.19, and explain why some analysts might prefer the alternative calculation.

Approach: To make the calculations, first find average values for the asset and equity accounts using data in Exhibit 4.1. Then use these values to calculate the EROA and ROE. In explaining why some analysts might prefer the alternative calculation, consider possible fluctuations of assets or equity over time.

Solution:

$$\text{Average asset or equity value} = \frac{\text{Beginning value} + \text{Ending value}}{2}$$

$$\text{Average asset value} = \frac{\$1{,}493.8 + \$1{,}889.2}{2}$$
$$= \$1{,}691.5$$

$$\text{Average equity value} = \frac{\$842.2 + \$937.4}{2}$$
$$= \$889.8$$

$$\text{EROA} = \frac{\text{EBIT}}{\text{Total assets}} = \frac{\$168.4}{\$1{,}691.5}$$
$$= 9.96\%$$

$$\text{ROE} = \frac{\text{Net income}}{\text{Total equity}} = \frac{\$118.5}{\$889.8}$$
$$= 13.32\%$$

Both EROA (9.96 percent versus 8.91 percent) and ROE (13.32 percent versus 12.64 percent) are higher when the average values are used. The reason is that Diaz's total assets grew from \$1,493.8 million in 2007 to \$1,889.2 million in 2008 and its equity grew from \$842.2 million to \$937.4 million during the same period. We could argue in favor of using the average asset or equity value by pointing out that the earnings for the one-year period are earned with the average value of assets or equity over the period.

Market-Value Indicators

The ratios we have discussed so far rely solely on the firm's financial statements, and we know that much of the data in those statements are historical and do not represent current market value. Also, as we discussed in Chapter 1, the appropriate objective for the firm's management is to maximize stockholder value, and the market value of the stockholders' claims is the value of the *cash flows* that they are entitled to receive, which is not necessarily the same as accounting income. To find out how the stock market evaluates a firm's liquidity, efficiency, leverage, and profitability, we need ratios based on market values.

Over the years, financial analysts have developed a number of ratios, called *market-value ratios,* which combine market-value data with data from a firm's financial statements. Here we examine the most commonly used market-value ratios: earnings per share and the price-earnings ratio.

EARNINGS PER SHARE

Dividing a firm's net income by the number of shares outstanding yields earnings per share (EPS). At the end of 2008, Diaz Manufacturing had 54,566,054 shares outstanding (see Exhibit 3.1 in Chapter 3) and net income of \$118.5 million (Exhibit 4.2). Its EPS at that point is thus calculated as follows:

$$\begin{aligned}\text{Earning per share} &= \frac{\text{Net income}}{\text{Shares outstanding}} \qquad (4.20)\\ &= \frac{\$118{,}500{,}000}{54{,}566{,}054} = \$2.17 \text{ per share}\end{aligned}$$

PRICE-EARNINGS RATIO

The price-earnings (P/E) ratio relates earnings per share to price per share. The formula, with a calculation for Diaz Manufacturing for the end of 2008, is as follows:

$$\begin{aligned}\text{Price-earnings ratio} &= \frac{\text{Price per share}}{\text{Earnings per share}} \qquad (4.21)\\ &= \frac{\$48.61}{\$2.17} = 22.4\end{aligned}$$

Price per share on a given date can be obtained from listings in the *Wall Street Journal* or from an online source, such as Yahoo! Finance.

What does it mean for a firm to have a price-earnings ratio of 22.4? It means that the stock market places a value of \$22.40 on every \$1 of net income. Why are investors willing to pay \$22.40 for a claim on \$1 of earnings? The answer is that the stock price does not only reflect the earnings this year. It reflects all future cash flows from earnings, and the especially high P/E ratio can indicate that investors expect the firm's earnings to grow in the future. Alternatively, a high P/E ratio might be due to unusually low earnings in a particular year and investors might expect earnings to recover to a normal level soon. We will discuss how expected growth affects P/E ratios in detail in later chapters. As with other measures, to understand whether the P/E ratio is too high or too low, we must compare the firm's P/E ratio with those of competitors and also look at movements in the firm's P/E ratio relative to market trends.

Concluding Comments on Ratios

We could have covered many more ratios, but that is enough for now; we will introduce additional ratios as we need them in future chapters. However, the group of ratios presented in this chapter is a fair representation of the ratios needed to analyze the performance of a business. When using ratios, it is important that you consider each ratio and ask yourself, "What does this ratio mean, or what is it measuring?" rather than trying to memorize a definition. Good ratios make good economic sense when you look at them.

Before You Go On

1. What are the efficiency ratios, and what do they measure? Why, for some firms, is the total asset turnover more important than the fixed asset turnover?
2. List the leverage ratios discussed in this section, and explain how they are related.
3. List the profitability ratios discussed in this section, and explain how they differ from each other.

4.4 The DuPont System: A Diagnostic Tool

By now, your mind may be swimming with ratios. Fortunately, some enterprising financial managers at the DuPont Company developed a system in the 1960s that ties together some of the most important financial ratios and provides a systematic approach to financial ratio analysis.

An Overview of the DuPont System

The DuPont system of analysis is a diagnostic tool that uses financial ratios to evaluate a company's financial health. The process has three steps. First, management assesses the company's financial health using the DuPont ratios. Second, if any problems are identified, management corrects them. Finally, management monitors the firm's financial performance over time, looking for differences from ratios established as benchmarks by management.

Under the DuPont system, management is charged with making decisions that maximize the firm's return on equity (ROE) as opposed to maximizing the value of the stockholders' shares. The system is primarily designed to be used by management as a diagnostic and corrective tool, though investors and other stakeholders have found its diagnostic powers of interest.

The DuPont system is derived from two equations that link the firm's return on assets (ROA) and return on equity (ROE). The system identifies three areas where management should focus its efforts in order to maximize the firm's ROE: (1) how much profit management can earn on sales, (2) how efficient management is in using the firm's assets, and (3) how much financial leverage management is using. Each of these areas is monitored by a single ratio, and together the ratios comprise the *DuPont equation*. We now develop the DuPont equation and discuss its managerial implications. We start by looking at the equation for ROA.

The ROA Equation

The ROA equation links the firm's return on assets with its total asset turnover and net profit margin. We derive this relationship from the ROA equation as follows:

$$\text{ROA} = \frac{\text{Net income}}{\text{Total assets}}$$

$$= \frac{\text{Net income}}{\text{Total assets}} \times \frac{\text{Net sales}}{\text{Net sales}}$$
$$= \frac{\text{Net income}}{\text{Net sales}} \times \frac{\text{Net sales}}{\text{Total assets}}$$
$$= \text{Net profit margin} \times \text{Total asset turnover}$$

As you can see, we start with the ROA formula presented earlier as Equation 4.18. Then we multiply ROA by net sales divided by net sales. In the third line, we rearrange the terms, coming up with the expression ROA = (Net income/Net sales) × (Net sales/Total assets). You may recognize the first ratio in the third line as the firm's net profit margin (Equation 4.16) and the second ratio as the firm's total asset turnover (Equation 4.7). Thus, we end up with the final equation for ROA, which is restated as Equation 4.22:

$$\text{ROA} = \text{Net profit margin} \times \text{Total asset turnover} \quad (4.22)$$

Equation 4.22 says that a firm's ROA is determined by two factors: (1) the firm's net profit margin and (2) the firm's total asset turnover. Let's look at the managerial implications of each of these terms.

Net Profit Margin. The net profit margin ratio can be written as follows:

$$\text{Net profit margin} = \frac{\text{Net income}}{\text{Net sales}} = \frac{\text{EBIT}}{\text{Net sales}} \times \frac{\text{EBT}}{\text{EBIT}} \times \frac{\text{Net income}}{\text{EBT}}$$

As you can see, the net profit margin can be viewed as the product of three ratios: (1) the operating profit margin (EBIT/Net sales), which is Equation 4.15, (2) a ratio that measures the impact of interest expenses on profits (EBT/EBIT), and (3) a ratio that measures the impact of taxes on profits (Net income/EBT). Thus, the profit margin focuses on management's ability to generate profits from sales by efficiently managing the firm's (1) operating expenses, (2) interest expenses, and (3) tax expenses.

Total Asset Turnover. Total asset turnover, which is defined as Net sales/Total assets, measures how efficiently management uses the assets under its command—that is, how much output management can generate with a given asset base. Thus, total asset turnover is a measure of *asset use efficiency.*

PROFIT MARGINS VERSUS ASSET TURNOVER

The ROA equation provides some very interesting managerial insights. It says that if management wants to increase the firm's ROA, it can increase the net profit margin, total asset turnover, or both. Of course, every firm would like to make both terms as large as possible so as to earn the highest possible ROA. Though every industry is different, competition, marketing considerations, technology, and manufacturing capabilities, to name a few, place upper limits on asset turnover and net profit margins and, thus, ROA. However, Equation 4.22 suggests that management can follow two distinct strategies to maximize ROA. Deciding between the strategies involves a trade-off between asset turnover and profit margin.

The first management strategy emphasizes high profit margin and low asset turnover. Examples of companies that use this strategy are luxury stores, such as jewelry stores, high-end department stores, and upscale specialty boutiques. Such stores carry expensive merchandise that has a high profit margin but tends to sell slowly. The second management strategy depends on low profit margins and high turnover. Typical examples of firms that use this strategy are discount stores and grocery stores, which have very low profit margins but make up for it by turning over their inventory very quickly. A typical chain grocery store, for example, turns over its inventory more than 12 times per year.

Exhibit 4.4 illustrates both strategies. The exhibit shows asset turnover, profit margin, and ROA for four retailing firms in 2006. Nordstrom is a department store that sells expensive merchandise, and Polo Ralph Lauren stores are upscale boutiques that

Exhibit 4.4 Two Basic Strategies to Earn a Higher ROA[a]

Company	Asset Turnover	×	Profit Margin (%)	=	ROA (%)
High Profit Margin:					
Polo Ralph Lauren	1.21		8.22		9.95
Nordstrom	1.57		7.13		11.19
High Turnover:					
Whole Foods Market	2.74		3.63		9.95
Wal-Mart Stores	2.28		3.56		8.12

[a]Ratios are calculated using financial results for 2006.

To maximize a firm's ROA, management can focus more on achieving high profit margins or on achieving high asset turnover. High-end retailers like Polo Ralph Lauren and Nordstrom focus more on achieving high profit margins, while grocery and discount stores like Whole Foods Market and Wal-Mart tend to focus more on achieving high asset turnover because competition limits their ability to achieve very high profit margins.

carry expensive casual wear for men and women. At the other end of the spectrum are Wal-Mart, which is famous for its low-price, high-volume strategy, and Whole Foods Markets, a successful grocery chain based in Austin, Texas.

Notice that the two luxury-item stores (Nordstrom and Polo Ralph Lauren) have lower asset turnover and higher profit margins, while the discount and grocery stores have lower profit margins and much higher asset turnover. Whole Foods and Wal-Mart are strong financial performers in their industry sectors. Whole Foods' ROA of 9.95 percent is quite remarkable for the grocery business. Both Polo Ralph Lauren and Nordstrom are top performers in their sectors of the economy, and their high ROAs (9.95 and 11.19 percent, respectively) corroborate that fact, as well as reflecting the strength of the U.S. economy during 2006.

The ROE Equation

To derive the ROE equation, we start with the formula from Equation 4.19:

$$\begin{aligned}
\text{ROE} &= \frac{\text{Net income}}{\text{Total equity}} \\
&= \frac{\text{Net income}}{\text{Total equity}} \times \frac{\text{Total assets}}{\text{Total assets}} \\
&= \frac{\text{Net income}}{\text{Total assets}} \times \frac{\text{Total assets}}{\text{Total equity}} \\
&= \text{ROA} \times \text{Equity multiplier}
\end{aligned}$$

Next, we multiply by total assets divided by total assets, and then we rearrange the terms so that ROE = (Net income/Total assets) × (Total assets/Total equity), as shown in the third line. By this definition, ROE is the product of two ratios already familiar to us: ROA (Equation 4.18) and the equity multiplier (Equation 4.11). The equation for ROE is shown as Equation 4.23:

$$\text{ROE} = \text{ROA} \times \text{Equity multiplier} \tag{4.23}$$

Interesting here is the fact that ROE is determined by the firm's ROA and its use of leverage. The greater the use of debt in the firm's capital structure, the greater the

ROE. Thus, increasing the use of leverage is one way management can increase the firm's ROE—but at a price. That is, the greater the use of financial leverage, the more risky the firm. How aggressively a company uses this strategy depends on management's preferences for risk and the willingness of creditors to lend money and bear the risk.

The DuPont Equation

Now we can combine our two equations into a single equation. From Equation 4.23, we know that ROE = ROA × Equity multiplier; and from Equation 4.22, we know that ROA = Net profit margin × Total asset turnover. Substituting Equation 4.22 into Equation 4.23 yields an expression formally called the DuPont equation, as follows:

$$\text{ROE} = \text{Net profit margin} \times \text{Total asset turnover} \times \text{Equity multiplier} \quad (4.24)$$

We can also express the DuPont equation in ratio form:

$$\text{ROE} = \frac{\text{Net income}}{\text{Net sales}} \times \frac{\text{Net sales}}{\text{Total assets}} \times \frac{\text{Total assets}}{\text{Total equity}} \quad (4.25)$$

To check the DuPont relationship, we will use some values from Exhibit 4.3, which lists financial ratios for Diaz Manufacturing. For 2008, Diaz's net profit margin is 7.58 percent, total asset turnover is 0.83, and the equity multiplier is 2.02. Substituting these values into Equation 4.24 yields:

$$\begin{aligned} \text{ROE} &= \text{Net profit margin} \times \text{Total asset turnover} \times \text{Equity multiplier} \\ &= 7.58 \times 0.83 \times 2.02 \\ &= 12.71 \text{ percent} \end{aligned}$$

With rounding error, this agrees with the value computed for ROE in Exhibit 4.3.

Applying the DuPont System

In summary, the DuPont equation tells us that a firm's ROE is determined by three factors: (1) net profit margin, which measures the firm's operating efficiency and how it manages its interest expense and taxes; (2) total asset turnover, which measures the efficiency with which the firm's assets are utilized; and (3) the equity multiplier, which measures the firm's use of financial leverage. The ROA is the product of the firm's net profit margin and total asset turnover. The schematic diagram in Exhibit 4.5 shows how the three key DuPont ratios are linked together and how they relate to the balance sheet and income statement for Diaz Manufacturing.

The DuPont system of analysis is a useful tool to help identify problem areas within a firm. For example, suppose that North Sails Group, a sailboat manufacturer located in San Diego, California, is having financial difficulty. The firm hires you to help apply the DuPont system of analysis to find out why the ship is financially sinking. The firm's CFO has you calculate the DuPont ratio values for the firm and obtain some industry averages to use as benchmarks, as shown.

DuPont Ratios	Firm	Industry
ROE	8%	16%
ROA	4%	8%
Equity multiplier	2	2
Net profit margin	8%	16%
Asset turnover	0.5	0.5

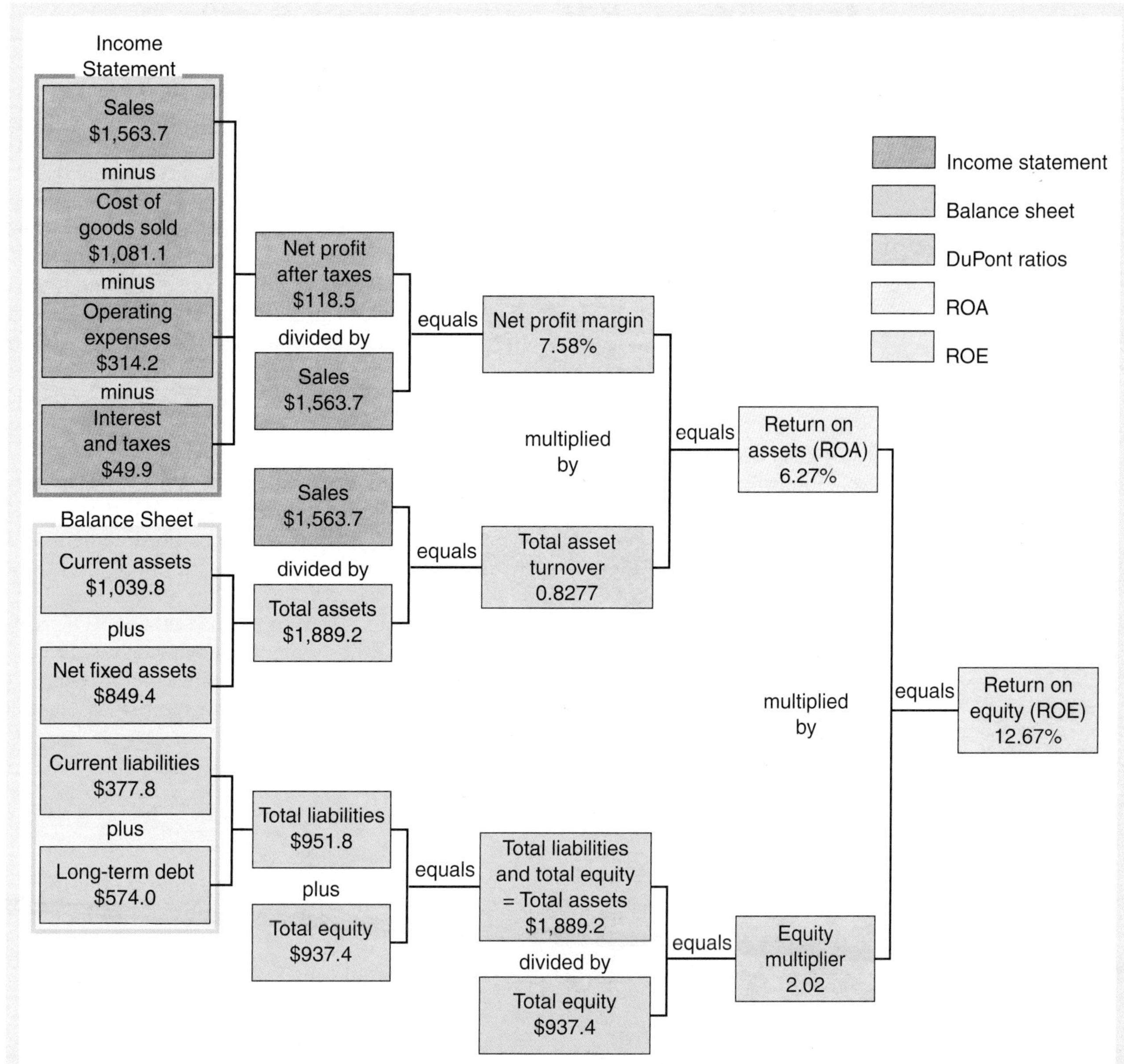

Exhibit 4.5

Relations in the DuPont System of Analysis for Diaz Manufacturing in 2008 ($ millions)

The diagram shows how the three key DuPont ratios are linked together and to the firm's balance sheet and income statement. Numbers in the exhibit are in millions of dollars and represent 2008 data from Diaz Manufacturing. The ROE of 12.67 percent differs from the 12.64 percent in Exhibit 4.3 due to rounding.

Clearly, the firm's ROE is quite low compared with the benchmark data (8 percent versus 16 percent), so without question the firm has problems. Next, you examine the values for the firm's ROA and equity multiplier and find that the firm's use of financial leverage is equal to the industry standard of 2 times but that its ROA is half that of the industry (4 percent versus 8 percent). Because ROA is the product of net profit margin and total asset turnover, you next examine these two ratios. Asset turnover does not appear to be a problem because the firm's ratio is equal to the industry standard of 0.5 times. However, the firm's net profit margin is substantially below the benchmark standard (8 percent versus 16 percent). Thus, the firm's performance problem stems from a low profit margin.

Identifying the low profit margin as an area of concern is only a first step, of course. Further investigation will be necessary to determine the underlying problem and its causes. The point to remember is that financial analysis identifies areas of concern within the firm, but rarely does such analysis tell us all we need to know.

Is Maximizing ROE an Appropriate Goal?

Throughout the book we have stressed the notion that management should make decisions that maximize the current value of the company stock. An important question is whether maximizing the value of ROE, as suggested by the DuPont system, is equivalent to wealth maximization. The short answer is that the two goals are not equivalent, but some discussion is warranted.

A major shortcoming of ROE is that it does not directly consider cash flow. ROE considers earnings, but earnings are not the same as future cash flows. Second, ROE does not consider risk. As discussed in Chapter 1, management and stockholders are very concerned about the degree of risk they face. Third, ROE does not consider the size of the initial investment or the size of future cash payments. As we stressed in Chapter 1, the essence of any business or investment decision is this: What is the size of the cash flows to be received, when do you expect to receive the cash flows, and how likely are you to receive them? More succinctly, what are the size, timing, and risk of the cash flows to be received?

In spite of these shortcomings, ROE analysis is widely used in business as a measure of operating performance. Proponents of ROE analysis argue that it provides a systematic way for management to work through the income statement and balance sheet and to identify problem areas within the firm. Furthermore, they note that ROE and stockholder value are often highly correlated. Thus, they argue, ROE is a legitimate diagnostic tool for management and focusing on maximizing ROE is an appropriate goal. We agree that ROE analysis can be a helpful diagnostic tool to help identify and correct problems within the firm. However, any investment decision should involve the analysis of current and future cash flows and the risk associated with them.

Before You Go On

1. What is the purpose of the DuPont system of analysis?
2. What is the equation for ROA in the DuPont system, and how do the factors in that equation influence the ratio?
3. What are the three major shortcomings of ROE?

4.5 Selecting a Benchmark

How do you judge whether a ratio value is too high or too low? Is the value good or bad? We touched on these questions several times earlier in the chapter. As we suggested, the starting point for making these judgments is selecting an appropriate benchmark—a standard that will be the basis for meaningful comparisons. Financial managers can gather appropriate benchmark data in three ways: through trend, industry, and peer group analysis.

Trend Analysis

Visit the Web site of the Risk Management Association for benchmark information: www.rmahq.org/RMA/ProductsandServices/RMABookstore/StatementStudies.

Trend analysis uses history as its standard by evaluating a single firm's performance over time. This sort of analysis allows management to determine whether a given ratio value has increased or decreased over time and whether there has been an abrupt shift in a ratio value. An increase or decrease in a ratio value is in itself neither good nor bad. However, a ratio value that is changing typically prompts the financial manager to sort out the issues surrounding the change and to take any action that is warranted. Exhibit 4.3 shows the trends in Diaz Manufacturing's ratios. For example, the exhibit shows that Diaz's current ratio has improved, suggesting that the company is not having a problem with liquidity at the present time.

Industry Analysis

A second way to establish a benchmark is to conduct an industry group analysis. To do that, we identify a group of firms that have the same product line, compete in the same market, and are about the same size. The average ratio values for these firms will be our benchmarks. Obviously, no two firms are identical, and deciding which firms to include in the analysis is always a judgment call. If we can construct a sample of reasonable size, however, the average values provide defensible benchmarks.

Financial ratios and other financial data for industry groups are published by a number of sources—the U.S. Department of Commerce, Dun & Bradstreet, the Risk Management Association, and Standard & Poor's (S&P), to name a few. One widely used system for identifying industry groups is the **Standard Industrial Classification (SIC) System**. The SIC codes are four-digit numbers established by the federal government for statistical reporting purposes. The first two digits describe the type of business in a broad sense (for example, firms engaged in building construction, mining of metals, manufacturing of machinery, food stores, or banking). Shown in the following list are the two-digit SIC codes for some manufacturing industries. Diaz's two-digit code is 35, "Industrial and commercial machinery and computer equipment":

Standard Industrial Classification (SIC) System
a numerical system developed by the U.S. Government to classify businesses according to the type of activity they perform

- 20 Food and kindred products
- 22 Textile mill products
- 28 Chemicals and allied products
- 29 Petroleum refining and related industries
- 31 Leather and leather products
- 35 Industrial and commercial machinery and computer equipment
- 37 Transportation equipment

More than 400 companies fall into the "Industrial and commercial machinery and computer equipment" code category. To narrow the group, we use more digits. Diaz Manufacturing's four-digit code is 3533 ("oil and gas field machinery and equipment"), and there are only 35 firms in this category. Among firm's within an SIC code, financial ratio data can be further categorized by asset size or by sales, which allows for more meaningful comparisons.

In 1977, the **North American Industry Classification System (NAICS)** was introduced as a new classification system. It was intended to refine and replace the older SIC codes, but it has been slow to catch on. Industry databases still allow you to sort data by either SIC or NAICS classifications.

North American Industry Classification System (NAICS)
a classification system for businesses introduced to refine and replace the older SIC codes

Although industry databases are readily available and easy to use, they are far from perfect. When trying to find a sample of firms that are "similar" to your company, you may find the classifications too broad. For example, Wal-Mart and Nordstrom have the same SIC code, but as our brief discussion in this chapter reveals, they are very different firms. Another problem is that different industrial databases may compute ratios differently. Thus, when making benchmark comparisons, you must be careful that your calculations match those in the database, or there could be some distortions in your findings.

You can find information about SIC and NAICS at www.census.gov/epcd/www/naicstab.htm.

Peer Group Analysis

The third way to establish benchmark information is to identify a group of firms that compete with the company we are analyzing. Ideally, the firms are in similar lines of business, are about the same size, and are direct competitors of the target firm. These firms form a *peer group*. Once a peer group has been identified, management can obtain their annual reports and compute average ratio values against which the firm can compare its performance.

Exhibit 4.6 Peer Group Ratios for Diaz Manufacturing

	2008	2007	2006
Liquidity Ratios:			
Current ratio	2.10	2.20	2.10
Quick ratio	1.50	1.60	1.50
Efficiency Ratios:			
Inventory turnover	5.40	5.30	5.20
Day's sales in inventory	67.59	68.87	70.19
Accounts receivable turnover	4.90	4.20	4.10
Days' sales outstanding	76.70	89.80	90.00
Total asset turnover	0.87	0.90	0.80
Fixed asset turnover	3.50	3.30	2.40
Leverage Ratios:			
Total debt ratio	0.18	0.11	0.21
Debt-to-equity ratio	0.40	0.20	0.50
Equity multiplier	2.02	1.77	2.05
Times interest earned	7.00	5.60	1.60
Cash coverage	7.50	8.20	1.30
Profitability Ratios:			
Gross profit margin	26.80%	24.10%	19.20%
Operating profit margin	12.00%	6.90%	2.70%
Net profit margin	10.74%	3.30%	0.10%
Return on assets	9.34%	3.30%	0.80%
Return on equity	13.07%	7.00%	1.00%
Market-Value Indicators:			
Price-to-earnings ratio	18.10	38.40	44.60
Earnings per share	$1.65	$3.85	$3.78

Peer group analysis is one way to establish benchmarks for a firm. Ideally, a firm's peer group is made up of firms that are its direct competitors and are of about the same size. Diaz Manufacturing's peer group is made up of FMC Technologies, Halliburton, Hydril, Varco, and Weatherford International. The exhibit shows the average financial ratios for these companies for 2006, 2007, and 2008.

How do we determine which firms should be in the peer group? The senior management team within a company will know its competitors. If you're working outside the firm, you can look at the firm's annual report and at financial analysts' reports. Both of these sources usually identify key competitors. Exhibit 4.6 shows ratios for a five-firm peer group constructed for Diaz Manufacturing for 2006 through 2008.

We consider the peer group methodology the best way to establish a benchmark if financial data for peer firms are publicly available. We should note, however, that comparison against a single firm is acceptable when there is a clear market leader and we want to compare a firm's performance and other characteristics against those of a firm considered the best. For example, Ford Motor Company may want to compare itself directly against Toyota, which is the "best in breed" in manufacturing productivity and quality. It is worthwhile to compare a firm with the market leader to identify areas of weakness as well of possible strength.

Before You Go On

1. In what three ways can a financial manager choose a benchmark?
2. Explain what the SIC codes are, and discuss the pros and cons of using them in financial analysis.

4.6 Using Financial Ratios

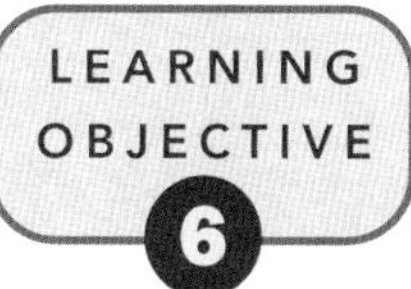

So far, our focus has been on the calculation of financial ratios. As you may already have concluded, however, the most important tasks are to *correctly interpret* the ratio values and to *make appropriate decisions* based on this interpretation. In this section we discuss using financial ratios in performance analysis.

Performance Analysis of Diaz Manufacturing

Let's examine Diaz Manufacturing's performance during 2008 using the DuPont system of analysis as our diagnostic tool and the peer group sample in Exhibit 4.6 as our benchmark. For ease of discussion, Diaz's financial ratios and the benchmark data are assembled in Exhibit 4.7.

We start our analysis by looking at the big picture—the three key DuPont ratios for the firm and a peer group of firms (see Exhibit 4.7). We see that Diaz Manufacturing's ROE of 12.64 percent is below the benchmark value of 13.07 percent, a difference of 0.43 percent, which is not good news. More dramatically, Diaz's ROA is 3.07 percent below the peer group benchmark, which is a serious difference. Clearly, Diaz Manufacturing has some performance problems that need to be investigated.

Exhibit 4.7 Peer Group Analysis for Diaz Manufacturing

	(1) Diaz Ratio	(2) Peer Group Ratio	(3) Difference (Column 1 − Column 2)
DuPont Ratios:			
Return on equity (%)	12.64	13.07	(0.43)
Return on assets (%)	6.27	9.34	(3.07)
Equity multiplier (%)	2.02	1.40	0.62
Net profit margin (%)	7.58	10.74	(3.16)
Total asset turnover	0.83	0.87	(0.04)
Profit Margins:			
Gross profit margin (%)	30.86	26.80	4.06
Operating margin (%)	10.77	12.00	(1.23)
Net profit margin (%)	7.58	10.74	(3.16)
Asset Ratios:			
Current ratio	2.75	2.10	0.65
Fixed asset turnover	3.92	3.50	0.42
Inventory turnover	2.55	5.40	(2.85)
Accounts receivable turnover	5.11	4.90	0.21

Examining the differences between the ratios of a firm and its peer group is a good way to spot areas that require further analysis.

To determine the problems, we examine the firm's equity multiplier and ROA results in more detail. The equity multiplier value of 2.02, versus the benchmark value of 1.40, suggests that Diaz Manufacturing is using more leverage than the average firm in the benchmark sample. Management is comfortable with the higher-than-average leverage. Conversations with the firm's investment banker, however, indicate that although the current use of leverage is not a problem, the company's debt could become a problem if the economy deteriorated and went into a recession.

Without the higher equity multiplier and management's willingness to bear additional risk, Diaz Manufacturing's ROE would be much lower. To illustrate this point, suppose management reduced the company's leverage to the peer group average of 1.40 (see Exhibit 4.7). With an equity multiplier of 1.40, the firm's ROE would be only 8.78 percent (0.0627×1.40); this is 3.86 percent below the firm's current ROE of 12.64 percent and 4.29 percent below the peer group benchmark. Thus, the use of higher leverage has, to some extent, masked the severity of the firm's problem with ROA.

Recall that ROA equals the product of the net profit margin and total asset turnover. Diaz's net profit margin is 3.16 percent lower than the benchmark value ($7.58 - 10.74$), and its total asset turnover ratio is slightly below the benchmark value (0.83 versus 0.87). Thus, both ratios that comprise ROA are below the peer group benchmark standard, but the net profit margin appears to be the larger problem.

Turning to the detailed asset turnover ratios shown in Exhibit 4.7, we find that the ratios for Diaz are generally similar to the corresponding peer group ratios. An exception is inventory turnover ratio, which is substantially below the benchmark: 2.55 for Diaz versus 5.40 for the benchmark. Diaz's management needs to investigate why the inventory turnover ratio is off the mark.

Because Diaz Manufacturing's net profit margin is low, we next look at the various profit margins shown in Exhibit 4.7 to gain insight into this situation. Diaz Manufacturing's gross profit margin is 4.06 percentage points above the benchmark value ($30.86 - 26.80$), which is good news. Since gross profit margin is a factor of sales and the cost of goods sold, we can conclude that there is no problem with the price the firm is charging for its products or with its cost of goods sold.

Diaz's problems begin with its operating margin of 10.77 percent, which is 1.23 percentage points below the peer group benchmark of 12.00 percent ($10.77 - 12.00$). The major controllable expense here is selling and administrative costs, and management needs to investigate why these expenses appear to be out of line.

In sum, the DuPont analysis of Diaz Manufacturing has identified two areas that warrant detailed investigation by management: (1) the larger-than-average inventory (slow inventory turnover) and (2) the above-average selling and administrative expenses. Management must now investigate each of these areas and come up with a course of action. Management may want to give careful consideration to the firm's high degree of financial leverage and whether it represents a prudent degree of risk.

LEARNING BY DOING APPLICATION 4.5

Ron's Jewelry Store and the Missing Data

Problem: Ron Roberts has owned and managed a profitable jewelry business in San Diego County for the past five years. He believes his jewelry store is one of the best managed in the county, and he is considering opening several new stores.

When Ron started the store, he supplied all the equity financing himself and financed the rest with personal loans from friends and family members. To open more stores, Ron needs a bank loan. The bank will want to examine his financial statements and know something about the competition he faces.

Ron has asked his brother-in-law, Dennis O'Neil, a CPA, to analyze the financials. Ron has also gathered some financial information about a company he considers the chief competition in the San Diego County market. The company has been in business for 25 years, has a number of stores, and is widely admired for its owners' management skills. Dennis organizes the available information in the following table:

Financial Ratio/Data	Ron's Store	Competitor
Sales	\$240	\$300
Net income	\$ 6	—
ROE	13.13%	—
Net profit margin	—	5.84%
Asset turnover	1.5	1.5
Equity multiplier	—	1.5
Debt-to-equity ratio	2.5	—

Calculate the missing values for the financial data above.

Approach: Use the ratio equations discussed in the text to calculate the missing financial ratios for both Ron's store and the competitor.

Solution:

Ron's jewelry store:

1. $\text{Net profit margin} = \dfrac{\text{Net income}}{\text{Sales}} = \dfrac{\$6}{\$240} = 0.025, \text{ or } 2.5\%$
2. $\text{Equity multiplier} = 1 + \text{Debt-to-equity ratio} = 1 + 2.5 = 3.5$

Competitor:

1. $\text{ROE} = \text{Net profit margin} \times \text{Asset turnover} \times \text{Equity multiplier}$
   $= 0.0584 \times 1.5 \times 1.5 = 0.1314, \text{ or } 13.14\%$
2. $\text{Net profit} = \text{Net profit margin} \times \text{Net sales} = 0.0584 \times \$300 = \$17.52$
3. $\text{Debt-to-equity ratio} = \dfrac{\text{Debt}}{\text{Equity}} = \dfrac{\$66.82}{\$133.1} = 0.50$
   (a) $\text{Equity} = \dfrac{\text{NI}}{\text{ROE}} = \dfrac{\$17.5}{0.1314} = \$133.18$
   (b) $\text{Assets} = \dfrac{\text{Net sales}}{\text{Asset turnover}} = \dfrac{\$300}{1.5} = \$200.0$
   (c) $\text{Debt} = \text{Assets} - \text{Equity} = \$200.0 - \$133.18 = \$66.82$

DECISION-MAKING EXAMPLE 4.3

Ron's Jewelry Store and the DuPont Analysis

Situation: Let's continue with our analysis of Ron's jewelry store, introduced in Learning by Doing Application 4.5. Brother-in-law Dennis has been asked to analyze the company's financials. He decides to use the DuPont system of analysis as a framework. He arranges the critical information as follows:

Financial Ratios	Ron's Store	Competitor
ROE	13.13%	13.14%
ROA	3.75%	8.76%
Net profit margin	2.50%	5.84%
Asset turnover	1.5	1.5
Equity multiplier	3.5	1.5
Debt-to-equity ratio	2.5	0.5
Net sales	\$240	\$300
Net income	\$ 6.0	\$ 17.5

Given the above financial ratios, what recommendations should Dennis make regarding Ron's jewelry store and its management?

(continued)

Decision: The good news is that Ron is able to earn about the same ROE as his major competitor. Unfortunately for Ron, it's pretty much downhill from there. Turning to the first two DuPont system ratios, we can see that Ron's ROA of 3.75 percent is much lower than his major competitor's ROA of 8.76 percent. Ron's business is also very highly leveraged, with an equity multiplier of 3.5 times, compared with 1.5 times for the competitor. In fact, the only reason Ron's ROE is comparable to the competitor's is the high leverage.

Breaking the ROA into its components, we find that Ron's asset turnover ratio is the same as the competitor's, 1.5. However, the profitability of Ron's store is extremely poor as measured by the firm's net profit margin of 2.50 percent, compared with the competitor's margin of 5.84 percent. One possible explanation is that to stimulate sales and maintain asset turnover, Ron has been selling his merchandise at too low a price.

As mentioned, Ron is employing a very high degree of financial leverage. Ron's debt-to-equity ratio is 2.5, while the competitor's is only 0.5. To illustrate how big the difference is, suppose both firms have $100 in equity financing. For $100 of equity, the competitor would hold $50 in debt, and Ron would hold $250.

In summary, Ron's jewelry store is not well managed. Ron needs to either increase his net profit margin or increase his inventory turnover to bring his ROA into line with that of his major competitor. Ron also needs to reduce his dependence on financial leverage. If San Diego County were to suffer a significant economic downturn, Ron's business would be a likely candidate for failure.

Financial ratio analysis is an excellent diagnostic tool. It helps management identify the problem areas in the firm—the symptoms. However, it does not tell management what the causes of the problems are or what course of action should be taken. Management must drill down into the accounting data, talk with managers in the field, and if appropriate, talk with people outside the firm, such as suppliers, to understand what is causing the problems.

Limitations of Financial Statement Analysis

Financial statement and ratio analysis as discussed in this chapter presents two major problems. First, it depends on accounting data based on historical costs. As we discussed in Chapter 3, knowledgeable financial managers would prefer to use financial statements in which all of the firm's assets and liabilities are valued at market. Financial statements based on current market values more closely reflect a firm's true economic conditions than do statements based on historical cost.

Second, there is little theory to guide us in making judgments based on financial statement and ratio analysis. That is why it is difficult to say a current ratio of 2.0 is good or bad or to say whether ROE or ROA is a more important ratio. The lack of theory explains, in part, why rules of thumb are often used as decision rules in financial statement analysis. The problem with decision rules based on experience and "common sense" rather than theory is that they may work fine in a stable economic environment but may fail when a significant shift takes place. For example, if you were in an economic environment with low inflation, you could develop a set of decision rules to help manage your business. However, if the economy became inflationary, more than likely many of your decision rules would fail.

Despite the limitations, we know that financial managers and analysts routinely use financial statements and ratio analysis to evaluate a firm's performance and to make a variety of decisions about the firm. These financial statements and the resulting analysis are the primary means by which financial information is communicated both inside and outside firms. At this time, the availability of market value data is limited for public corporations and not available for privately held firms and other entities such as government units.

Thus, we conclude that, practically speaking, historical accounting information represents the best available information. However, times are changing. As the accounting profession becomes more comfortable with the use of market data and as technology increases its availability and reliability and lowers its cost, we expect to see an increase in the use of market-based financial statements.

Before You Go On

1. Explain how the DuPont identity allows us to evaluate a firm's performance.
2. What are the limitations on traditional financial statement analysis?
3. List some of the problems that financial analysts confront when analyzing financial statements.

Summary of Learning Objectives

1. **Explain the three perspectives from which financial statements can be viewed.**

   Financial statements can be viewed from the owners', managers', or creditors' perspective. All three groups are ultimately interested in a firm's profitability, but each group takes a different view. Stockholders want to know how much cash they can expect to receive for their stock, what their return on investment will be, and/or how much their stock is worth in the market. Managers are concerned with maximizing the firm's long-term value through a series of day-to-day management decisions; thus, they need to see the impact of their decisions on the financial statements to confirm that things are going as planned. Creditors monitor the firm's use of debt and are concerned with how much debt the firm is using and whether the firm will have enough cash to meet its obligations.

2. **Describe common-size financial statements, explain why they are used, and be able to prepare and use them to analyze the historical performance of a firm.**

   Common-size financial statements are financial statements in which each number has been scaled by a common measure of firm size: balance sheets are expressed as a percentage of total assets, and income statements are expressed as a percentage of net sales. Common-size financial statements are necessary when comparing firms that are significantly different in size. The preparation of common-size financial statements and their use are illustrated for Diaz Manufacturing in Section 4.2.

3. **Discuss how financial ratios facilitate financial analysis, and be able to compute and use them to analyze a firm's performance.**

   Financial ratios are used in financial analysis because they eliminate problems caused by comparing two or more companies of different size or when looking at the same company over time as the size changes. Financial ratios can be divided into five categories: (1) Liquidity ratios measure the ability of a company to cover its current bills. (2) Efficiency ratios tell how efficiently the firm uses its assets. (3) Leverage ratios tell how much debt a firm has in its capital structure and whether the firm can meet its long-term financial obligations. (4) Profitability ratios focus on the firm's earnings. Finally, (5) market value indicators look at a company based on market data as opposed to historical data used in financial statements. The computation and analysis of major financial ratios are presented in Section 4.3 (also see the Summary of Key Equations that follows the Summary of Learning Objectives).

4. **Describe the DuPont system of analysis and be able to use it to evaluate a firm's performance and identify corrective actions that may be necessary.**

   The DuPont system of analysis is a diagnostic tool that uses financial ratios to assess a firm's financial strength. Once the financial ratios are calculated and the assessment is complete, management focuses on correcting the problems within the context of maximizing the firm's ROE. For analysis, the DuPont system breaks ROE into three components: net profit margin, which measures operating efficiency; total asset turnover, which measures how efficiently the firm deploys its assets; and the equity multiplier, which measures financial leverage. A diagnostic analysis of a firm's performance using the DuPont system is illustrated in Section 4.4.

5. **Explain what benchmarks are, describe how they are prepared, and discuss why they are important in financial statement analysis.**

   Once we have calculated financial ratios, we need some way to evaluate them. A benchmark provides a standard for comparison. In financial statement analysis, a number of benchmarks are used. Most often, benchmark comparisons involve competitors that are roughly the same size and that offer a similar range of products. Another form of benchmarking is time-trend analysis, which compares a firm's current financial ratios against the same ratios from past years. Time-trend analysis tells us whether a ratio is increasing or decreasing over time. The preparation and use of peer group benchmark data are illustrated in Section 4.6.

6. **Identify the major limitations in using financial statement analysis.**

   The major limitations to financial statement and ratio analysis are the use of historical accounting data and the lack of theory to guide the decision maker. The lack of theory explains, in part, why there are so many rules of thumb. Though rules of thumb are useful, and they may work under certain conditions, they may lead to poor decisions if circumstances or the economic environment have changed.

Summary of Key Equations

Equation	Description	Formula
4.1		$\text{Current ratio} = \dfrac{\text{Current assets}}{\text{Current liabilities}}$
4.2	Liquidity Ratios	$\text{Quick ratio} = \dfrac{\text{Current assets} - \text{Inventory}}{\text{Current liabilities}}$
4.3		$\text{Inventory turnover} = \dfrac{\text{Cost of goods sold}}{\text{Inventory}}$
4.4		$\text{Day's sales in inventory} = \dfrac{\text{365 Days}}{\text{Inventory turnover}}$
4.5		$\text{Accounts receivable turnover} = \dfrac{\text{Net sales}}{\text{Accounts receivable}}$
4.6	Efficiency Ratios	$\text{Day's sales outstanding} = \dfrac{\text{365 days}}{\text{Accounts receivable turnover}}$
4.7		$\text{Total asset turnover} = \dfrac{\text{Net sales}}{\text{Total assets}}$
4.8		$\text{Fixed asset turnover} = \dfrac{\text{Net sales}}{\text{Net fixed assets}}$
4.9		$\text{Total debt ratio} = \dfrac{\text{Total debt}}{\text{Total assets}}$
4.10		$\text{Debt-to-equity ratio} = \dfrac{\text{Total debt}}{\text{Total equity}}$
4.11	Leverage Ratios	$\text{Equity multiplier} = \dfrac{\text{Total assets}}{\text{Total equity}}$
4.12		$\text{Times interest earned} = \dfrac{\text{EBIT}}{\text{Interest expense}}$
4.13		$\text{Cash coverage} = \dfrac{\text{EBITDA}}{\text{Interest expense}}$
4.14		$\text{Gross profit margin} = \dfrac{\text{Net sales} - \text{Cost of goods sold}}{\text{Net sales}}$
4.15		$\text{Operating profit margin} = \dfrac{\text{EBIT}}{\text{Net sales}}$
4.16		$\text{Net profit margin} = \dfrac{\text{Net income}}{\text{Net sales}}$
4.17	Profitability Ratios	$\text{EBIT return on assets (EROA)} = \dfrac{\text{EBIT}}{\text{Total assets}}$
4.18		$\text{Return on assets (ROA)} = \dfrac{\text{Net income}}{\text{Total assets}}$
4.19		$\text{Return on equity (ROE)} = \dfrac{\text{Net income}}{\text{Total equity}}$
4.20	Market Value Indicators	$\text{Earning per share} = \dfrac{\text{Net income}}{\text{Shares outstanding}}$
4.21		$\text{Price-earnings ratio} = \dfrac{\text{Price per share}}{\text{Earnings per share}}$

4.22		$ROA = \text{Net profit margin} \times \text{Total asset turnover}$
4.23		$ROE = ROA \times \text{Equity multiplier}$
4.24	DuPont Equation	$ROE = \text{Net profit margin} \times \text{Total asset turnover} \times \text{Equity multiplier}$
4.25		$ROE = \dfrac{\text{Net income}}{\text{Net sales}} \times \dfrac{\text{Net sales}}{\text{Total assets}} \times \dfrac{\text{Total assets}}{\text{Total equity}}$

Self-Study Problems

4.1 The Abercrombie Supply Company reported the following information for the year ended June 30, 2008. Prepare a common-size income statement for the year ended June 30, 2008.

Abercrombie Supply Company
Income Statement ($ thousands)

	2008
Net sales	$ 2,110,965
Cost of goods sold	1,459,455
Selling and administrative expenses	312,044
Nonrecurring expenses	27,215
Earnings before interest, taxes, depreciation, and amortization (EBITDA)	$ 312,251
Depreciation	112,178
Earnings before interest and taxes (EBIT)	$ 200,073
Interest expense	117,587
Earnings before taxes (EBT)	$ 82,486
Taxes (35%)	28,870
Net income	$ 53,616

4.2 Prepare a common-size balance sheet from the following information for Abercrombie Supply Company.

Abercrombie Supply Company
Balance Sheet as of June 30, 2008 ($ thousands)

Assets:		Liabilities and Equity:	
Cash and marketable securities	$ 396,494	Accounts payable	$ 817,845
Accounts receivable	708,275	Notes payable	101,229
Inventories	1,152,398	Accrued income taxes	41,322
Other current assets	42,115		
Total current assets	$ 2,299,282	Total current liabilities	$ 960,396
Net plant and equipment	1,978,455	Long-term debt	1,149,520
		Total liabilities	$ 2,109,916
		Common stock	1,312,137
		Retained earnings	855,684
		Total common equity	$ 2,167,821
Total assets	$ 4,277,737	Total liabilities and equity	$ 4,277,737

4.3 Using the 2008 data for the Abercrombie Supply Company, calculate the following liquidity ratios:

a. Current ratio

b. Quick ratio

4.4 Refer to the balance sheet and income statement for Abercrombie Supply Company for the year ended June 30, 2008. Calculate the following ratios:

- **a.** Inventory turnover ratio
- **b.** Days' sales outstanding
- **c.** Total asset turnover
- **d.** Fixed asset turnover
- **e.** Total debt ratio
- **f.** Debt-to-equity ratio
- **g.** Times-interest-earned ratio
- **h.** Cash coverage ratio

4.5 Refer to the balance sheet and income statement for Abercrombie Supply Company for the year ended June 30, 2008. Use the DuPont equation to calculate the return on equity (ROE). In the process, calculate the following ratios: profit margin, total asset turnover, equity multiplier, EBIT return on assets, and return on assets.

Solutions to Self-Study Problems

4.1 The standardized income statement for Abercrombie Supply Company should look like the following one:

Abercrombie Supply Company
Income Statement ($ thousands)

	2008	Percent of Sales
Net sales	$ 2,110,965	100.0%
Cost of goods sold	1,459,455	69.1
Selling and administrative expenses	312,044	14.8
Nonrecurring expenses	27,215	1.3
Earnings before interest, taxes, depreciation and amortization (EBITDA)	$ 312,251	14.8%
Depreciation	112,178	5.3
Earnings before interest and taxes (EBIT)	$ 200,073	9.5%
Interest expense	117,587	5.6
Earnings before taxes (EBT)	$ 82,486	3.9%
Taxes (35%)	28,870	1.4
Net income	$ 53,616	2.5%

4.2 Abercrombie Supply's common-size balance sheet is as follows:

Assets:	2008	Percent of Total Assets	Liabilities and Equity:	2008	Percent of Total Assets
Cash and marketable sec.	$ 396,494	9.3%	Accounts payable and accruals	$ 817,845	19.1%
Accounts receivable	708,275	16.5%	Notes payable	101,229	2.4
Inventories	1,152,398	26.9%	Accrued income taxes	41,322	1.0
Other current assets	42,115	1.0%			
Total current assets	$ 2,299,282	53.7%	Total current liabilities	$ 960,396	22.4%
Net plant and equipment	1,978,455	46.2%	Long-term debt	1,149,520	26.9
			Total liabilities	$ 2,109,916	49.3%
			Common stock	1,312,137	30.7
			Retained earnings	855,684	20.0
			Total common equity	$ 2,167,821	50.7%
Total asssets	$ 4,277,737	100.0%	Total liabilities and equity	$ 4,277,737	100.0%

4.3 Abercrombie Supply's current ratio and quick ratio are calculated as follows:

a. Current ratio $= \frac{\$2{,}299{,}282}{\$960{,}396} = 2.39$

b. Quick ratio $= \frac{\$2{,}299{,}282 - \$1{,}152{,}375}{\$960{,}396} = 1.19$

4.4 The ratios are calculated as shown in the following table:

Ratio	Calculation	Value
Inventory turnover ratio	$1,459,455 / 1,152,398	1.27
Days' sales outstanding	$708,275 / ($2,110,965/365)	122.5 days
Total asset turnover	$2,110,965 / $4,277,737	0.49
Fixed asset turnover	$2,110,965 / $1,978,455	1.07
Total debt ratio	$2,109,916 / $4,277,737	0.493
Debt-to-equity ratio	$2,109,916 / $2,167,821	0.974
Times-interest-earned ratio	$200,073 / $117,587	1.7
Cash coverage ratio	$312,251 / $117,587	2.66

4.5 Following are the calculations for the ROE and associated ratios:

$$\text{Profit margin} = \frac{\text{Net income}}{\text{Net sales}} = \frac{\$53{,}616}{\$2{,}110{,}965} = 2.54\%$$

$$\text{EBIT ROA} = \frac{\text{EBIT}}{\text{Total assets}} = \frac{\$200{,}073}{\$4{,}277{,}737} = 4.68\%$$

$$\text{Return on assets} = \frac{\text{Net income}}{\text{Total assets}} = \frac{\$53{,}616}{\$4{,}277{,}737} = 1.25\%$$

$$\text{Equity multiplier} = \frac{\text{Total assets}}{\text{Total equity}} = \frac{\$4{,}277{,}737}{\$2{,}167{,}821} = 1.97$$

$$\text{Total asset turnover} = \frac{\text{Net sales}}{\text{Total assets}} = \frac{\$2{,}110{,}965}{\$4{,}277{,}737} = 0.49$$

DuPont identity:

$$\begin{aligned}\text{ROE} &= \text{ROA} \times \text{EM}\\ &= \text{Profit margin} \times \text{Total assets turnover ratio} \times \text{EM}\\ &= \frac{\text{Net income}}{\text{Net sales}} \times \frac{\text{Net sales}}{\text{Total assets}} \times \frac{\text{Total assets}}{\text{Total equity}}\\ &= 0.0254 \times 0.49 \times 1.97\\ &= 2.45\%\end{aligned}$$

Critical Thinking Questions

4.1 What does it mean when a company's return on assets (ROA) is equal to its return on equity (ROE)?

4.2 Why is too much liquidity not a good thing?

4.3 Inventory is excluded when the quick ratio or acid-test ratio is calculated because inventory is the most difficult current asset to convert to cash without loss of value. What types of inventory are likely to be most easily converted to cash?

4.4 What does a very high inventory turnover ratio signify?

4.5 How would one explain a low receivables turnover ratio?

4.6 What additional information does the fixed assets turnover ratio provide over the total assets turnover ratio? For which industries does it carry greater significance?

4.7 How does financial leverage help shareholders?

4.8 Why do banks have a low ROA (relative to other industries) but a high ROE?

4.9 Why is the ROE a more appropriate proxy of wealth maximization for smaller firms rather than for larger ones?

4.10 Why is it not enough for an analyst to look at just the short-term and long-term debt on a firm's balance sheet?

Questions and Problems

BASIC

4.1 Liquidity ratios: Explain why the quick ratio or acid-test ratio is a better measure of a firm's liquidity than the current ratio.

4.2 Liquidity ratios: Flying Penguins Corp. has total current assets of $11,845,175, current liabilities of $5,311,020, and a quick ratio of 0.89. What is its level of inventory?

4.3 Efficiency ratio: If Newton Manufacturers has an accounts receivable turnover of 4.8 times and net sales of $7,812,379, what is its level of receivables?

4.4 Efficiency ratio: Bummel and Strand Corp. has a gross profit margin of 33.7 percent, sales of $47,112,365, and inventories of $14,595,435. What is its inventory turnover ratio?

4.5 Efficiency ratio: Sorenson Inc. has sales of $3,112,489, a gross profit margin of 23.1 percent, and inventory of $833,145. What are the company's inventory turnover ratio and days' sales in inventory?

4.6 Leverage ratios: Breckenridge Ski Company has total assets of $422,235,811 and a debt ratio of 29.5 percent. Calculate the company's debt-to-equity ratio and the equity multiplier.

4.7 Leverage ratios: Norton Company has a debt-to-equity ratio of 1.65, ROA of 11.3 percent, and total equity of $1,322,796. What are the company's equity multiplier, debt ratio, and ROE?

4.8 DuPont equation: The Rangoon Timber Company has the following relationships:

Sales/Total assets = 2.23; ROA = 9.69%; ROE = 16.4%

What are Rangoon's profit margin and debt ratio?

4.9 Benchmark analysis: List the ways a company's financial manager can benchmark the company's own performance.

4.10 Benchmark analysis: Trademark Corp.'s financial manager collected the following information for its peer group so that it can compare its own performance against that of its peers.

Ratios	Trademark	Peer Group
DSO	33.5 days	27.9 days
Total assets turnover	2.3	3.7
Inventory turnover	1.8	2.8
Quick ratio	0.6	1.3

a. Explain how Trademark is doing relative to its peers.
b. How do the industry ratios help Trademark's management?

4.11 Market-value ratios: Rockwell Jewelers has announced net earnings of $6,481,778 for this year. The company has 2,543,800 shares outstanding, and the year-end stock price is $54.21. What are the company's earnings per share and P/E ratio?

INTERMEDIATE

4.12 Liquidity ratios: Laurel Electronics has a quick ratio of 1.15, current liabilities of $5,311,020, and inventories of $7,121,599. What is the firm's current ratio?

4.13 Efficiency ratio: Payton Corp. has total sales of $31,115,964, inventories of $4,412,933, cash and equivalents of $2,469,050, and days' sales outstanding of 39 days. If the firm's management wanted its DSO to be 30 days, by how much will the accounts receivable have to change?

4.14 Efficiency ratio: Norwood Corp. currently has accounts receivable of $1,223,675 on net sales of $6,216,900. What are its accounts receivable turnover ratio and days' sales outstanding?

4.15 Efficiency ratio: If Norwood Corp.'s management wants to reduce the DSO from that calculated in the above problem to an industry average of 56.3 days and its net sales are expected to decline by about 12 percent, what would be the new level of receivables?

4.16 Coverage ratios: Nimitz Rental Company had depreciation expenses of $108,905, interest expenses of $78,112, and an EBIT of $1,254,338 for the year ended June 30, 2008. What are the times-interest-earned and cash coverage ratios for this company?

4.17 **Leverage ratios:** Conseco, Inc., has a debt ratio of 0.56. What are the company's debt-to-equity ratio and equity multiplier?

4.18 **Profitability ratios:** Cisco Systems has total assets of $35.594 billion, total debt of $9.678 billion, and net sales of $22.045 billion. Their net profit margin for the year is 20 percent, while the operating profit margin was 30 percent. What are Cisco's net income, EBIT ROA, ROA, and ROE?

4.19 **Profitability ratios:** Procter & Gamble reported the following information for year-end 2008: On net sales of $51.407 billion, the company earned a net income after taxes of $6.481 billion. It had a cost of goods sold of $25.076 billion and an EBIT of $9.827 billion. What is the company's (a) gross profit margin, (b) operating profit margin, and (c) net profit margin?

4.20 **Profitability ratios:** Wal-Mart, Inc., has net income of $9,054,000 on net sales of $256,329,812. The company has total assets of $104,912,112 and shareholders' equity of $43,623,445. Use the extended DuPont identity to find the return on assets and return on equity for the firm.

4.21 **Profitability ratios:** Xtreme Sports Innovations has disclosed the following information:

EBIT = $25,664,300	Net income = $13,054,000	Net sales = $83,125,336
Total debt = $20,885,753	Total assets = $71,244,863	

Compute the following ratios for this firm using the DuPont identity: debt-to-equity ratio, EBIT ROA, ROA, and ROE.

4.22 **Market-value ratios:** Cisco Systems had net income of $4.401 billion and, at year end, 6.735 billion shares outstanding. Calculate the earnings per share for the company.

4.23 **Market-value ratios:** Use the information for Cisco Systems in the last problem. In addition, the company's EBITDA was $6.834 billion and its share price was $22.36. Compute the firm's price-earnings ratio and the price-EBITDA ratio.

4.24 **DuPont equation:** Carter, Inc., a manufacturer of electrical supplies, has an ROE of 23.1 percent, a profit margin of 4.9 percent, and a total asset turnover ratio of 2.6 times. Its peer group also has an ROE of 23.1 percent but has outperformed Carter with a profit margin of 5.3 percent and a total assets turnover ratio of 3.0 times. Explain how Carter managed to achieve the same level of profitability as reflected by the ROE.

4.25 **DuPont equation:** Grossman Enterprises has an equity multiplier of 2.6 times, total assets of $2,312,000, an ROE of 14.8 percent, and a total assets turnover of 2.8 times. Calculate the firm's sales and ROA.

ADVANCED

4.26 Complete the balance sheet of Flying Roos Corp., given the following information:

Flying Roos Corp. Balance Sheet as of 12/31/2008

Assets:		Liabilities and Equity:	
Cash and marketable securities		Accounts payable and accruals	
Accounts receivable		Notes payable	$ 300,000
Inventories			
Total current assets		Total current liabilities	
		Long-term debt	$2,000,000
Net plant and equipment		Common stock	
		Retained earnings	$1,250,000
Total assets	$8,000,000	Total liabilities and equity	

You are also given the following information:

Debt ratio = 40%	DSO = 39 days
Current ratio = 1.5	Inventory turnover ratio = 3.375
Sales = $2.25 million	Cost of goods sold = $1.6875 million

4.27 For the year ended June 30, 2008, Northern Clothing Company has total assets of $87,631,181, ROA of 11.67 percent, ROE of 21.19 percent, and a profit margin of 11.59 percent. What are the company's net income and net sales? Calculate the firm's debt-to-equity ratio.

4.28 Blackwell Automotive's balance sheet at year-end 2007–2008 shows the following information:

Blackwell Automotive Balance Sheet as of 3/31/2008

Assets:		Liabilities and Equity:	
Cash and marketable sec.	$ 23,015	Accounts payable and accruals	$ 163,257
Accounts receivable	141,258	Notes payable	21,115
Inventories	212,444		
Total current assets	$ 376,717	Total current liabilities	$ 184,372
		Long-term debt	168,022
Net plant and equipment	711,256	Total liabilities	$ 352,394
Goodwill and other assets	89,899	Common stock	313,299
		Retained earnings	512,159
Total assets	$1,177,852	Total liabilities and equity	$1,177,852

In addition, it was reported that the firm had a net income of $156,042 on sales of $4,063,589.

a. What are the firm's current ratio and quick ratio?

b. Calculate the firm's days' sales outstanding, total asset turnover ratio, and fixed asset turnover ratio.

4.29 The following are the financial statements for Nederland Consumer Products Company for the fiscal year ended September 30, 2008.

As Reported on Annual Income Statement	9/30/08
Net sales	$51,407
Cost of products sold	25,076
Gross margin	$26,331
Marketing, research, administrative exp.	15,746
Depreciation	758
Operating income (loss)	$ 9,827
Interest expense	477
Earnings (loss) before income taxes	$ 9,350
Income taxes	2,869
Net earnings (loss)	$ 6,481

Balance Sheet as of 9/30/2008

Assets:		Liabilities and Equity:	
Cash and marketable securities	$ 5,469	Accounts payable	$ 3,617
Investment securities	423	Accrued and other liabilities	7,689
Accounts receivable	4,062	Taxes payable	2,554
Total inventories	4,400	Debt due within one year	8,287
Deferred income taxes	958		
Prepaid expenses and other receivables	1,803		
Total current assets	$17,115	Total current liabilities	$22,147
Property, plant, and equipment, at cost	25,304	Long-term debt	12,554
Less: Accumulated depreciation	11,196	Deferred income taxes	2,261
Net property, plant, and equipment	$14,108	Other noncurrent liabilities	2,808
Net goodwill and other intangible assets	23,900	Total liabilities	$39,770
Other noncurrent assets	1,925	Convertible class A preferred stock	1,526
		Common stock	2,141
		Retained earnings	13,611
		Total stockholders' equity (deficit)	$17,278
Total assets	$57,048	Total liabilites and share-holders' equity	$57,048

Calculate all the ratios (for which industry figures are available) for Nederland and compare the firm's ratios with the industry ratios.

Ratio	Industry Average
Current ratio	2.05
Quick ratio	0.78
Gross margin	23.9%
Net profit margin	12.3%
Debt ratio	0.23
Long-term debt to equity	0.98
Interest coverage	5.62
ROA	5.3%
ROE	18.8%

4.30 Refer to the preceding information for Nederland Consumer Products Company. Compute the firm's ratios for the following categories and briefly evaluate the company's performance from these numbers.

a. Efficiency ratios
b. Asset turnover ratios
c. Leverage ratios
d. Coverage ratios

4.31 Refer to the earlier information for Nederland Consumer Products Company. Using the DuPont identity, calculate the return on equity for Nederland, after calculating the ratios that make up the DuPont identity.

4.32 Nugent, Inc., has a gross profit margin of 31.7 percent on sales of $9,865,214 and total assets of $7,125,852. The company has a current ratio of 2.7 times, accounts receivable of $1,715,363, cash and marketable securities of $315,488, and current liabilities of $870,938.

a. What is Nugent's level of current assets?
b. How much inventory does the firm have? What is the inventory turnover ratio?
c. What is Nugent's days' sales outstanding?
d. If management wants to set a target DSO of 30 days, what should Nugent's accounts receivable be?

4.33 Recreational Supplies Co. has net sales of $11,655,000, an ROE of 17.64 percent, and a total asset turnover of 2.89 times. If the firm has a debt-to-equity ratio of 1.43, what is the company's net income?

4.34 Nutmeg Houseware Inc. has an operating profit margin of 10.3 percent on revenues of $24,547,125 and total assets of $8,652,352.

a. Find the company's total asset turnover ratio and its operating profit (EBIT).
b. If the company's management has set a target for the total asset turnover ratio to be 3.25 next year without any change in the total assets of the company, what will have to be the new sales level for the next year? Calculate change in sales necessary and the percentage sales necessary.
c. If the operating profit margin now shrinks to 10 percent, what will be the EBIT at the new level of sales?

4.35 Modern Appliances Corporation has reported its financial results for the year ended December 31, 2008.

Income Statement for the Fiscal Year Ended December 31, 2008

Net sales	$5,398,412,000
Cost of goods sold	3,432,925,255
Gross profit	$1,965,486,745
Selling, general, and administrative expenses	1,036,311,231
Depreciation	299,928,155
Operating income	$ 629,247,359
Interest expense	35,826,000
EBT	$ 593,421,359
Income taxes	163,104,554
Net earnings	$ 430,316,805

Consolidated Balance Sheet
Modern Appliances Corporation
December 31, 2008

Assets:		Liabilities and Equity:	
Cash and cash equivalents	$ 514,412,159	Short-term borrowings	$ 117,109,865
Accounts receivables	1,046,612,233	Trade accounts payable	466,937,985
Inventories	981,870,990	Other current liabilities	994,289,383
Other current assets	313,621,610		
Total current assets	$2,856,516,992	Total current liabilities	$1,578,337,233
Net fixed assets	754,660,275	Long-term debt	1,200,691,565
Goodwill	118,407,710	Common stock	397,407,352
Other assets	665,058,761	Retained earnings	1,218,207,588
Total asssets	$4,394,643,738	Total liabilities and equity	$4,394,643,738

Using the information from the financial statements, complete a comprehensive ratio analysis for Modern Appliances Corporation.

a. Calculate these liquidity ratios: current and quick ratios.
b. Calculate these efficiency ratios: inventory turnover, accounts receivable turnover, DSO.
c. Calculate these asset turnover ratios: total asset turnover, fixed asset turnover.
d. Calculate these leverage ratios: total debt ratio, debt-to-equity ratio, equity multiplier.
e. Calculate these coverage ratios: times interest earned, cash coverage.
f. Calculate these profitability ratios: gross profit margin, net profit margin, ROA, ROE.
g. Use the DuPont identity, and after calculating the component ratios, compute the ROE for this firm.

CFA PROBLEMS

4.36 Common-size analysis is used in financial analysis to
a. evaluate changes in a company's operating cycle over time.
b. predict changes in a company's capital structure using regression analysis.
c. compare companies of different sizes or compare a company with itself over time.
d. restate each element in a company's financial statement as a proportion of the similar account for another company in the same industry.

4.37 The TBI Company has a number of days of inventory of 50. Therefore, the TBI Company's inventory turnover is closest to
a. 4.8 times.
b. 7.3 times.
c. 8.4 times.
d. 9.6 times.

4.38 DuPont analysis involves breaking return-on-assets ratios into their
a. profit components.
b. marginal and average components.
c. operating and financing components.
d. profit margin and turnover components.

4.39 If a company's net profit margin is −5 percent, its total asset turnover is 1.5 times, and its financial leverage ratio is 1.2 times, its return on equity is closest to
a. −9.0 percent.
b. −7.5 percent.
c. −3.2 percent.
d. 1.8 percent.

Sample Test Problems

4.1 Morgan Sports Equipment Company has accounts payable of $1,221,669, cash of $677,423, inventory of $2,312,478, accounts receivable of $845,113, and net working capital of $2,297,945. What are the company's current ratio and quick ratio?

4.2 Southwest Airlines, Inc., has total operating revenues of $6.53 million on total assets of $11.337 million. Their property, plant, and equipment, including their ground equipment and other assets, are listed at a historical cost of $11.921 million, while the accumulated depreciation and amortization amount to $3.198 million. What are the airline's total asset turnover and fixed asset turnover ratios?

4.3 Haugen Enterprises has an equity multiplier of 2.5. What is the firm's debt ratio?

4.4 Centennial Chemical Corp. has a gross profit margin of 31.4 percent on revenues of $13,144,680 and EBIT of $2,586,150. What are the company's cost of goods sold and operating profit margin?

4.5 National City Bank has 646,749,650 shares of common stock outstanding, and they are currently priced at $37.55. If its net income is $2,780,955,000, what are its earnings per share and price-earnings ratio?

A Sad Tale: The Demise of Arthur Andersen

ETHICS CASE

In January 2002, there were five major public accounting firms: Arthur Andersen, Deloitte Touche, KPMG, Pricewaterhouse-Coopers, and Ernst & Young. By late fall of that year, the number had been reduced to four. Arthur Andersen became the first major public accounting firm to be found guilty of a felony (a conviction later overturned), and as a result it virtually ceased to exist.

That such a fate could befall Andersen is especially sad given its early history. When Andersen and Company was established in 1918, it was led by Arthur Andersen, an acknowledged man of principle, and the company had a credo that became firmly embedded in the culture: "Think Straight and Talk Straight." Andersen became an industry leader partly on the basis of high ethical principles and integrity.

How did a one-time industry leader find itself in a position where it received a corporate death penalty over ethical issues? First, the market changed. During the 1980s, a boom in mergers and acquisitions and the emergence of information technology fueled the growth of an extremely profitable consulting practice at Andersen. The profits from consulting contracts soon exceeded the profits from auditing, Andersen's core business. Many of the consulting clients were also audit clients, and the firm found that the audit relationship was an ideal bridge for selling consulting services. Soon the audit fees became "loss leaders" to win audits, which allowed the consultants to sell more lucrative consulting contracts.

Tension between Audit and Consulting

At Andersen, tension between audit and consulting partners broke into open and sometimes public warfare. At the heart of the problem was how to divide up the earnings from the consulting practice among the two groups. The resulting conflict ended in divorce, with the consultants leaving to form their own firm. The firm, Accenture, continues to thrive today.

Once the firm split in two, Andersen began to rebuild a consulting practice as part of the accounting practice. Consulting continued to be a highly profitable business, and audit partners were now asked to sell consulting services to other clients, a role that many auditors found uncomfortable.

Although the accountants were firmly in charge, the role of partners as salespersons compounded an already existing ethical issue—that of conflict of interest. It is legally well established that the fiduciary responsibility of a certified public accounting (CPA) firm is to the investors and creditors of the firm being audited. CPA firms are supposed to render an opinion as to whether a firm's financial statements are reasonably accurate and whether the firm has applied generally accepted accounting principles in a consistent manner over time so as not to distort the financial statements. To meet their fiduciary responsibilities, auditors must maintain independence from the firms they audit.

What might interfere with the objective judgment of the public accounting firms? One problem arises because it is the audited companies themselves that pay the auditors' fees. Auditors might not be completely objective when auditing a firm because they fear losing consulting business. This is an issue that regulators and auditors have not yet solved. But another problem arises in situations where accounting firms provide consulting services to the companies they audit. Although all of the major accounting firms were involved in this practice to some extent, Andersen had developed an aggressive culture for engaging partners to sell consulting services to audit clients.

Andersen's Problems Mount

The unraveling of Andersen began in the 1990s with a series of accounting scandals at Sunbeam, Waste Management, and Colonial Realty—all firms that Andersen had audited. But scandals involving the energy giant Enron proved to be the firm's undoing. The account was huge. In 2000 alone, Andersen received $52 million in fees from Enron, approximately 50 percent for auditing and 50 percent for other consulting services, especially tax services. The partner in charge of the account and his entire 100-person team worked out of Enron's Houston office. Approximately 300 of Enron's senior and middle managers had been Andersen employees.

Enron went bankrupt in December 2001 after large-scale accounting irregularities came to light, prompting an investigation by the Securities and Exchange Commission (SEC). It soon became clear that Enron's financial statements for some time had been largely the products of accounting fraud, showing the company to be in far better financial condition than was actually the case. The inevitable question was asked: Why hadn't the auditors called attention to Enron's questionable accounting practices? The answer was a simple one. Andersen had major conflicts of interest. Indeed, when one member of Andersen's Professional Standards Group objected to some of Enron's accounting practices, Andersen removed him from auditing responsibilities at Enron—in response to a request from Enron management.

Playing Hardball and Losing

The SEC was determined to make an example of Andersen. The Justice Department began a criminal investigation, but investigators were willing to explore some "settlement options" in return for Andersen's cooperation. However, Andersen's senior management appeared arrogant and failed to grasp the political mood in Congress and in the country after a series of business scandals that had brought more than one large company to bankruptcy.

After several months of sparring with the Andersen senior management team, the Justice Department charged Andersen with a felony offense—obstruction of justice. Andersen was found guilty in 2002 of illegally instructing its employees to destroy documents relating to Enron, even as the government was conducting inquiries into Enron's finances. During the trial, government lawyers argued that by instructing its staff to "undertake an unprecedented campaign of document destruction," Andersen had obstructed the government's investigation.

Since a firm convicted of a felony cannot audit a publicly held company, the conviction spelled the end for Andersen. But even before the guilty verdict, there had been a massive defection of Andersen clients to other accounting firms. The evidence presented at trial showed a breakdown in Andersen's internal controls, a lack of leadership, and an environment in Andersen's Houston office that fostered recklessness and unethical behavior by some partners.

In 2005, the United States Supreme Court unanimously overturned the Andersen conviction on the grounds that the jury was given overly broad instructions by the federal judge who presided over the case. But by then it was too late. Most of the Andersen partners had either retired or gone to work for former competitors, and the company had all but ceased to exist.

Discussion Questions

1. To what extent do market pressures encourage unethical behavior? Can the demise of Andersen be blamed on the fact that the market began rewarding consulting services of the kind Andersen could provide?
2. How serious are the kinds of conflicts of interest discussed in this case? Did Sarbanes-Oxley eliminate the most serious conflicts?
3. Was it fair for the government to destroy an entire company because of the misdeeds of some of its members, or had Andersen become such a serious offender that such an action on the part of the government was justified?

THE TIME VALUE OF MONEY

CHAPTER

5

Alamy

LEARNING OBJECTIVES

1. **Explain what the time value of money is and why it is so important in the field of finance.**
2. **Explain the concept of future value, including the meaning of *principal amount, simple interest,* and *compound interest,* and be able to use the future value formula to make business decisions.**
3. **Explain the concept of present value and how it relates to future value, and be able use the present value formula to make business decisions.**
4. **Discuss why the concept of compounding is not restricted to money, and be able to use the future value formula to calculate growth rates.**

When you purchase an automobile from a dealer, the decision of whether to pay cash or finance your purchase can affect the price you pay. For example, when market conditions are tough, automobile manufacturers often offer customers a choice between a cash rebate and low-cost financing. Both of these alternatives affect the cost of purchasing an automobile, but one alternative can be worth more than the other.

To see why, consider the following. In September 2007, the automobile manufacturer Chrysler wanted to increase sales of its Sebring model. The company offered consumers a choice between (1) receiving $1,500 off the base price of $25,840 if they paid cash and (2) receiving 0 percent financing on a three-year loan if they paid the base price. For someone who had enough cash to buy the car outright and did not need the cash for some other use, the decision of whether to pay cash or finance the purchase of a Sebring depended on the rate of return that they could earn by investing the cash. On the one hand, if it was possible to earn only a 3 percent interest rate by investing in a certificate of deposit at a bank, the buyer was better off paying cash. On the other hand, if it was possible to earn 5 percent, the buyer was better off taking the financing. With a 4 percent rate of return, the buyer would have been largely indifferent between the two alternatives.

As with most business transactions, a crucial element in the analysis of the alternatives offered by Chrysler is the value of the expected cash flows. Because the cash flows for the two alternatives take place in different time periods, they must be adjusted to account for the time value of money before they can be compared. A car buyer wants to select the alternative with the cash flows that have the lowest value (price). This chapter and the next provide the knowledge and tools you need to make the correct decision. You will learn that at the bank, in the boardroom, or in the showroom, money has a time value—dollars today are worth more than dollars in the future—and you must account for this when making financial decisions.

CHAPTER PREVIEW

Business firms routinely make decisions to invest in productive assets to earn income. Some assets, such as plant and equipment, are tangible, and other assets, such as patents and trademarks, are intangible. Regardless of the type of investment, a firm pays out money now in the hope that the value of the future benefits (cash inflows) will exceed the cost of the asset. This process is what *value creation* is all about—buying capital assets that are worth more than they cost.

The valuation models presented in this book will require you to compute the present and future values of cash flows. This chapter and the next one provide the fundamental tools for making these calculations. Chapter 5 explains how to value a single cash flow in different time periods, and Chapter 6 covers valuation of multiple cash flows. These two chapters are critical for your understanding of corporate finance.

We begin this chapter with a discussion of the time value of money. We then look at future value, which tells us how funds will grow if they are invested at a particular interest rate. Next, we discuss present value, which answers the question "What is the value today of cash payments received in the future?" We conclude the chapter with a discussion of several additional topics related to time value calculations.

5.1 The Time Value of Money

LEARNING OBJECTIVE 1

In financial decision making, one basic problem managers face is determining the value of (or price to pay for) cash flows expected in the future. Why is this a problem? Consider as an example the popular Mega Millions™ lottery game, which is played in 12 states across the U.S. In Mega Millions, the jackpot continues to build up until some lucky person buys a winning ticket—the payouts for a number of jackpot winning tickets have exceeded \$100 million.[1]

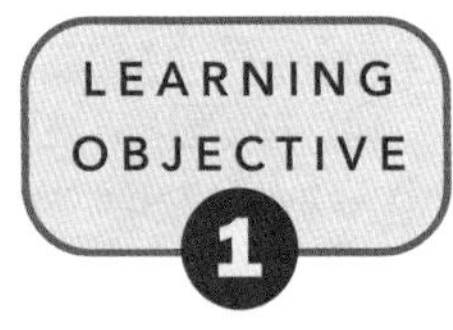

Take an online lesson on the time value of money from TeachMeFinance.com at http://teachmefinance.com/timevalueofmoney.html.

If you won \$100 million, headlines would read "Lucky Student Wins \$100 Million Jackpot!" Does this mean that your ticket is worth \$100 million on the day you win? The answer is no. A Mega Millions jackpot is paid either as a series of 26 payments over 25 years or as a cash lump sum. If you win "\$100 million" and choose to receive the series of payments, the 26 payments will total \$100 million. If you choose the lump sum option, Mega Millions will pay you less than the stated value of \$100 million. This amount was about \$60 million in February 2008. Thus, the value, or market price, of a "\$100 million" winning Mega Millions ticket is really about \$60 million because of the time value of money and the timing of the 26 cash payments. An appropriate question to ask now is, "What is the time value of money?"

Consuming Today or Tomorrow

time value of money
the difference in value between a dollar in hand today and a dollar promised in the future; a dollar today is worth more than a dollar in the future

The **time value of money** is based on the belief that people have a positive time preference for consumption. That is, people prefer to consume goods today rather than wait to consume similar goods in the future. Most people would prefer to have a

[1]As of February 3, 2008, the largest Mega Million jackpot was \$370 million, won in March 2007. Mega Millions is operated by a consortium of the state lottery commissions in California, Georgia, Illinois, Maryland, Massachusetts, Michigan, New Jersey, New York, Ohio, Texas, Virginia, and Washington. To play the game, a player pays one dollar and picks five numbers from 1 to 56 and one additional number from 1 to 46 (the Mega Ball number). Twice a week, a machine mixes numbered balls and randomly selects six balls (five white balls and one Mega Ball), which determines the winning combination for that drawing. There are various winning combinations, but a ticket that matches all six numbers, including the Mega Ball number, is the jackpot winner.

large-screen TV today than to have one a year from now, for example. Money has a time value because a dollar in hand today is worth more than a dollar to be received in the future. This makes sense because if you had the dollar today, you could buy something with it—or, instead, you could invest it and earn interest. For example, if you had \$100,000, you could buy a one-year bank certificate of deposit paying 5 percent interest and earn \$5,000 interest for the year. At the end of the year, you would have \$105,000 (\$100,000 + \$5,000). The \$100,000 today is worth \$105,000 a year from today. If the interest rate was higher, you would have even more money at the end of the year.

Based on this example, we can make several generalizations. First, the value of a dollar invested at a positive interest rate grows over time. Thus, the further in the future you receive a dollar, the less it is worth today. Second, the trade-off between money today and money at some future date depends in part on the rate of interest you can earn by investing. The higher the rate of interest, the more likely you will elect to invest your funds and forgo current consumption. Why? At the higher interest rate, your investment will earn more money.

BUILDING INTUITION

The Value of Money Changes with Time

The term *time value of money* reflects the notion that people prefer to consume things today rather than at some time in the future. For this reason, people require compensation for deferring consumption. The effect is to make a dollar in the future worth less than a dollar today.

In the remainder of this section, we look at two views of time value—future value and present value. First, however, we describe time lines, which are pictorial aids to help solve future and present value problems.

Time Lines as Aids to Problem Solving

Time lines are an important tool for analyzing problems that involve cash flows over time. They provide an easy way to visualize the cash flows associated with investment decisions. A time line is a horizontal line that starts at time zero (today) and shows cash flows as they occur over time. For example, Exhibit 5.1 shows the time line for a five-year investment opportunity and its cash flows. Here, as in most finance problems, cash flows are assumed to occur at the end of the period. The project involves a \$10,000 initial investment (cash outflow), such as the purchase of a new machine, that is expected to generate cash inflows over a five-year period: \$5,000 at the end of year 1, \$4,000 at the end of year 2, \$3,000 at the end of year 3, \$2,000 at the end of year 4, and \$1,000 at the end of year 5. Because of the time value of money, it is critical that you identify not only the size of the cash flows, but also the timing.

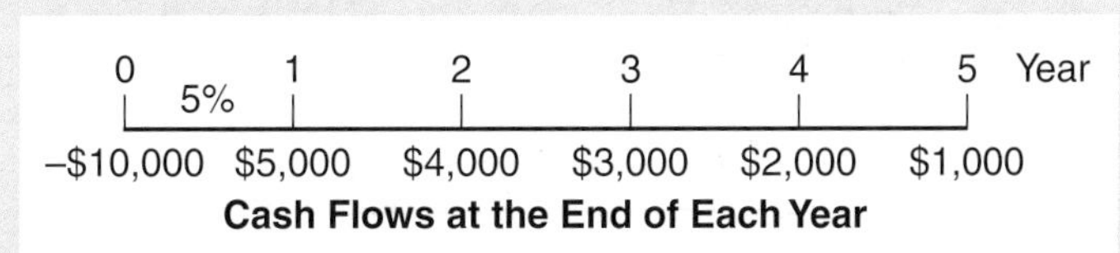

Exhibit 5.1
Five-year Time Line for a \$10,000 Investment
Time lines help us to correctly identify the size and timing of cash flows—critical tasks in solving time value problems. This time line shows the cash flows generated over five years by a \$10,000 investment in a situation where the relevant interest rate is 5 percent.

If it is appropriate, the time line will also show the relevant interest rate for the problem. In Exhibit 5.1 this is shown as 5 percent. Also, note in Exhibit 5.1 that the initial cash flow of $10,000 is represented by a negative number. It is conventional that cash outflows from the firm, such as for the purchase of a new machine, are treated as negative values on a time line and that cash inflows to the firm, such as revenues earned, are treated as positive values. The −$10,000 therefore means that there is a cash outflow of $10,000 at time zero. As you will see, it makes no difference how you label cash inflows and outflows as long as you are consistent. That is, if *all* cash outflows are given a negative value, then *all* cash inflows must have a positive value. If the signs get "mixed up"—if some cash inflows are negative and some positive—you will get the wrong answer to any problem you are trying to solve.

Future Value versus Present Value

We can analyze financial decisions using either future value or present value techniques. Although the two techniques approach the decision differently, both yield the same result. Both techniques focus on the valuation of cash flows received over time. In corporate finance, future value problems typically measure the value of cash flows at the end of a project, whereas present value measures the value of cash flows at the start of a project (time zero).

Exhibit 5.2 compares the $10,000 investment decision shown in Exhibit 5.1 in terms of future value and present value. When managers are making a decision about whether to accept a project, they must look at all of the cash flows associated with that project with reference to the same point in time. As Exhibit 5.2 shows, for most business decisions, that point is either the start (time zero) or the end of the project (in this example, year 5). The present value technique uses *discounting* to find the present value of each cash flow at the beginning of the project. Alternatively, the future value technique uses *compounding* to find the future value of each cash flow at the end of the project's life. We will look more closely at compounding and discounting later in the chapter.

For a discussion of simple versus compound interest, go to www.financeprofessor.com/introcorpfinnotes/simplevscompound.htm.

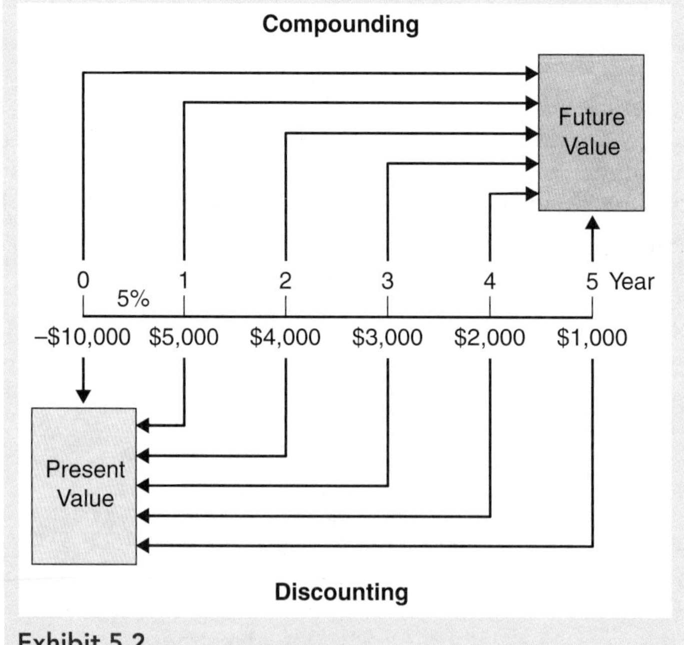

Exhibit 5.2
Future Value and Present Value Compared
Compounding converts a present value into its future value, taking into account the time value of money. Discounting is just the reverse—it converts future cash flows into their present value.

Financial Calculator

We recommend that students purchase a financial calculator for this course. A financial calculator will provide the computational tools—financial and algebraic—to solve most problems in the book. A financial calculator is just an ordinary calculator that has preprogrammed future value and present value algorithms. Thus, all the variables you need to make financial calculations exist on the calculator keys. To solve problems, all you have to do is press the proper keys. The instructions in this book are generally meant for Texas Instruments calculators, such as the TI BAII Plus. If you are using an HP or Sharp calculator, consult the user's manual for instructions.

It may sound as if the financial calculator will solve problems for you. It won't. To get the correct answer to textbook or real-world problems, you must first analyze the problem correctly and then identify the cash flows (size and timing), placing them correctly on a time line. Only then will you enter the correct inputs into the financial calculator. The calculator will, however, eliminate computation errors, save you a great deal of time, and eliminate an enormous source of frustration in your life.

To help you master your financial calculator, throughout this chapter, we provide helpful hints on how to best use the calculator. We also recognize that some professors or students may want to solve problems using one of the popular spreadsheet programs. In this chapter and a number of other chapters, we provide solutions to several problems that lend themselves to spreadsheet analysis. In solving these problems, we used Microsoft Excel™ for those using other types of spreadsheets, the analysis and basic commands are similar. We also provide spreadsheet solutions for additional problems on the book's Web site.

Before You Go On

1. Why is a dollar today worth more than a dollar one year from now?
2. What is a time line, and why is it important in financial analysis?

5.2 Future Value and Compounding

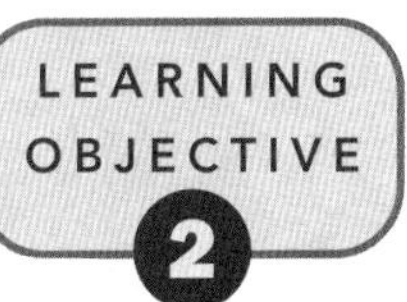

The **future value (FV)** of an investment is what the investment will be worth after earning interest for one or more time periods. The process of converting the initial amount into future value is called *compounding*. We will define this term more precisely later. First, though, we illustrate the concepts of future value and compounding with a simple example.

future value (FV) the value of an investment after it earns interest for one or more periods

Single-Period Investment

Suppose you place \$100 in a bank savings account that pays interest at 10 percent a year. How much money will you have in one year? Go ahead and make the calculation. Most people can intuitively arrive at the correct answer, \$110, without the aid of a formula. Your calculation could have looked something like this:

$$\begin{aligned}
\text{Future value at the end of year 1} &= \text{Principal} + \text{Interest earned} \\
&= \$100 + (\$100 \times 0.10) \\
&= \$100 \times (1 + 0.10) \\
&= \$100 \times (1.10) \\
&= \$110
\end{aligned}$$

This approach computes the amount of interest earned ($100 × 0.10) and then adds it to the initial, or *principal,* amount ($100). Notice that when we solve the equation, we factor out the $100. Recall from algebra that if you have the equation $y = c + (c \times x)$, you can factor out the common term c as follows:

$$\begin{aligned} y &= c + (c \times x) \\ &= c \times (1 + x) \end{aligned}$$

By doing this in our future value calculation, we arrived at the term (1 + 0.10). This term can be stated more generally as $(1 + i)$, where i is the interest rate. As you will see, this is a pivotal term in both future value and present value calculations.

Let's use our intuitive calculation to generate a more general formula. First, we need to define the variables used to calculate the answer. In our example $100 is the principal amount (P_0), which is the amount of money at the beginning of the transaction (time zero); the 10 percent is the simple interest rate (i); and the $110 is the future value (FV_1) of the deposit after one year, which is one year in the future. We can write the formula for a single-period investment as follows:

$$\begin{aligned} FV_1 &= P_0 + (P_0 \times i) \\ &= P_0 \times (1 + i) \end{aligned}$$

Looking at the formula, we more easily see mathematically what is happening in our intuitive calculation. P_0 is the principal amount invested at time zero. If you invest for one period at an interest rate of i, your investment, or principal, will grow by $(1 + i)$ per dollar invested. The term $(1 + i)$ is the *future value interest factor*—often called simply the *future value factor*—for a single period, such as one year. To test the equation, we plug in our values:

$$\begin{aligned} FV_1 &= \$100 \times (1 + 0.10) \\ &= \$100 \times 1.10 \\ &= \$110 \end{aligned}$$

Good, it works!

Two-Period Investment

We have determined that at the end of one year (one period), your $100 investment has grown to $110. Now let's say you decide to leave this new principal amount (FV_1) of $110 in the bank for another year earning 10 percent interest. How much money would you have at the end of the second year (FV_2)? To arrive at the value for FV_2, we multiply the new principal amount by the future value factor $(1 + i)$. That is, $FV_2 = FV_1 \times (1 + i)$. We then substitute the value of FV_1 (the single-period investment value) into the equation and algebraically rearrange terms, which yields $FV_2 = P_0 \times (1 + i)^2$. The mathematical steps to arrive at the equation for FV_2 are shown in the following; recall that $FV_1 = P_0 \times (1 + i)$:

$$\begin{aligned} FV_2 &= FV_1 \times (1 + i) \\ &= [P_0 \times (1 + i)] \times (1 + i) \\ &= P_0 \times (1 + i)^2 \end{aligned}$$

The future value of your $110 at the end of the second year (FV_2) is as follows:

$$\begin{aligned} FV_2 &= P_0 \times (1 + i)^2 \\ &= \$100 \times (1 + 0.10)^2 \\ &= 100 \times (1.10)^2 \\ &= \$100 \times 1.21 \\ &= \$121 \end{aligned}$$

Exhibit 5.3 Future Value of $100 at 10 Percent

(1)	(2)	(3)		(4)		(5)	(6)
		Interest Earned					
Year	Value at Beginning of Year	Simple Interest		Interest on Interest		Total (Compound) Interest	Value at End of Year
1	$100.00	$10.00	+	$ 0.00	=	$10.00	$110.00
2	110.00	10.00	+	1.00	=	11.00	121.00
3	121.00	10.00	+	2.10	=	12.10	133.10
4	133.10	10.00	+	3.31	=	13.31	146.41
5	146.41	10.00	+	4.64	=	14.64	161.05
Five-year total	$100.00	$50.00	+	$11.05	=	$61.05	$161.05

With compounding, interest earned on an investment is reinvested so that in future periods, interest is earned on interest as well as on the principal amount. Here, interest on interest begins accruing in year 2.

Another way of thinking of a two-period investment is that it is two single-period investments back-to-back. From that perspective, based on the preceding equations, we can represent the future value of the deposit held in the bank for two years as follows:

$$FV_2 = P_0 \times (1 + i)^2$$

Turning to Exhibit 5.3, we can see what is happening to your $100 investment over the two years we have already discussed and beyond. The future value of $121 at year 2 consists of three parts. First is the initial *principal* of $100 (column 2). Second is the $20 ($10 + $10) of *simple interest* earned at 10 percent for the first and second years (column 3). Third is the $1 interest earned during the second year (column 4) on the $10 of interest from the first year ($10 × 0.10 = $1.00). This is called *interest on interest.* The total amount of interest earned is $21 ($10 + $11), which is shown in column 5 and is called *compound interest.*

We are now in a position to formally define some important terms already mentioned in our discussion. The **principal** is the amount of money on which interest is paid. In our example, the principal amount is $100. **Simple interest** is the amount of interest paid on the original principal amount. With simple interest, the interest earned each period is paid only on the original principal. In our example, the simple interest is $10 per year or $20 for the two years. **Interest on interest** is the interest earned on the reinvestment of previous interest payments. In our example, the interest on interest is $1. **Compounding** is the process by which interest earned on an investment is reinvested so that in future periods, interest is earned on the interest previously earned as well as the principal. In other words, with compounding, you are able to earn **compound interest**, which consists of both simple interest and interest on interest. In our example, the compound interest is $21.

principal
the amount of money on which interest is paid

simple interest
interest earned on the original principal amount only

interest on interest
interest earned on interest that is earned in previous periods

compounding
the process by which interest earned on an investment is reinvested, so in future periods interest is earned on the interest as well as the principal

compound interest
interest earned both on the original principal amount and on interest previously earned

The Future Value Equation

Let's continue our bank example. Suppose you decide to leave your money in the bank for three years. Looking back at equations for a single-period and two-period investment, you can probably guess that the equation for the future value of money invested for three years would be:

$$FV_3 = P_0 \times (1 + i)^3$$

CNNMoney's Web site has a savings calculator at cgi.money.cnn.com/tools/savingscalc/savingscalc.html.

With this pattern clearly established, we can see that the general equation to find the future value after any number of periods is as follows:

$$FV_n = PV \times (1 + i)^n \tag{5.1}$$

where:

FV_n = future value of investment at the end of period n
PV = original principal (P_0) or the present value
i = the rate of interest per period, which is often a year
n = the number of periods; a period is typically a year but can be a quarter, a month, a day, or some other unit of time
$(1 + i)^n$ = the future value factor

Let's test our general equation. Say you leave your $100 invested in the bank savings account at 10 percent interest for five years. How much would you have in the bank at the end of five years? Applying Equation 5.1 yields the following:

$$\begin{aligned} FV_5 &= \$100 \times (1 + 0.10)^5 \\ &= \$100 \times (1.10)^5 \\ &= \$100 \times 1.6105 \\ &= \$161.05 \end{aligned}$$

Exhibit 5.3 shows how the interest is earned on a year-by-year basis. Notice that the total compound interest earned over the five-year period is $61.05 (column 5) and that it is made up of two parts: (1) $50.00 of simple interest (column 3) and (2) $11.05 of interest on interest (column 4). Thus, the total interest can be expressed as follows:

$$\begin{aligned} \text{Total compound interest} &= \text{Total simple interest} + \text{Total interest on interest} \\ &= \$50.00 + \$11.05 \\ &= \$61.05 \end{aligned}$$

The simple interest earned is ($100 × 0.10) = $10.00 per year, and thus, the total simple interest for the five-year period is $50.00 (5 years × $10.00). The remaining balance of $11.05 ($61.05 − $50.00) comes from earning interest on interest.

A helpful equation for calculating the simple interest can be derived by using the equation for a single-period investment and solving for the term $FV_1 - P_0$, which is equal to the simple interest.[2] The equation for the simple interest earned (SI) is:

$$SI = P_0 \times i$$

where:

i = the simple interest rate for the period, usually one year
P_0 = the initial or beginning principal amount

Thus, the calculation for simple interest is:[3]

$$SI = P_0 \times i = \$100 \times 0.10 = \$10.00$$

Exhibit 5.4 shows graphically how the compound interest in Exhibit 5.3 grows. Notice that the simple interest earned each year remains constant at $10 per year but that the amount of interest on interest increases every year. The reason, of course, is

---

[2]The formula for a single-period investment is $FV_1 = P_0 + (P_0 \times i)$. Solving the equation for $FV_1 - P_0$ yields the simple interest, SI.

[3]Another helpful equation is the one which computes the total simple interest over several periods (TSI): TSI = Number of periods × SI = Number of periods × ($P_0 \times i$).

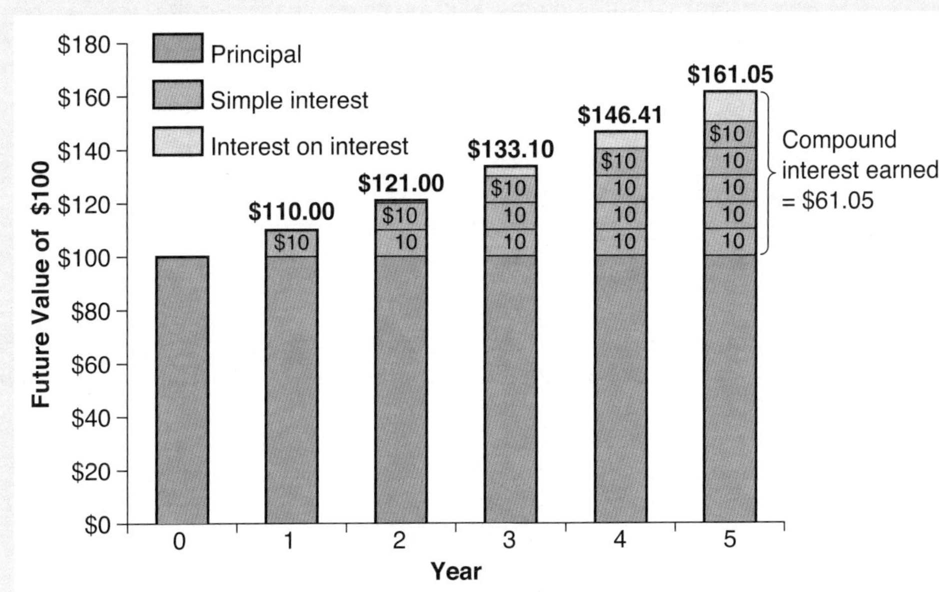

Exhibit 5.4
How Compound Interest Grows on $100 at 10 Percent
The amount of simple interest earned on $100 invested at 10 percent remains constant at $10 per year, but the amount of interest earned on interest increases each year. As more and more interest builds, the effect of compounding accelerates the growth of the total interest earned.

that interest on interest begins to build every time you compound. As more and more interest builds, the effect of compounding accelerates the growth of the total interest earned.

An interesting observation about Equation 5.1 is that the higher the interest rate, the faster the investment will grow. This fact can be seen in Exhibit 5.5, which shows the growth in the future value of $1.00 at different interest rates and for different time periods into the future. First, notice that the growth in the future value over time is not linear, but exponential. In other words, the growth of the invested funds is accelerated by the compounding of interest. Second, the higher the interest rate, the more money accumulated for any time period. Looking at the right-hand side of the exhibit, you can

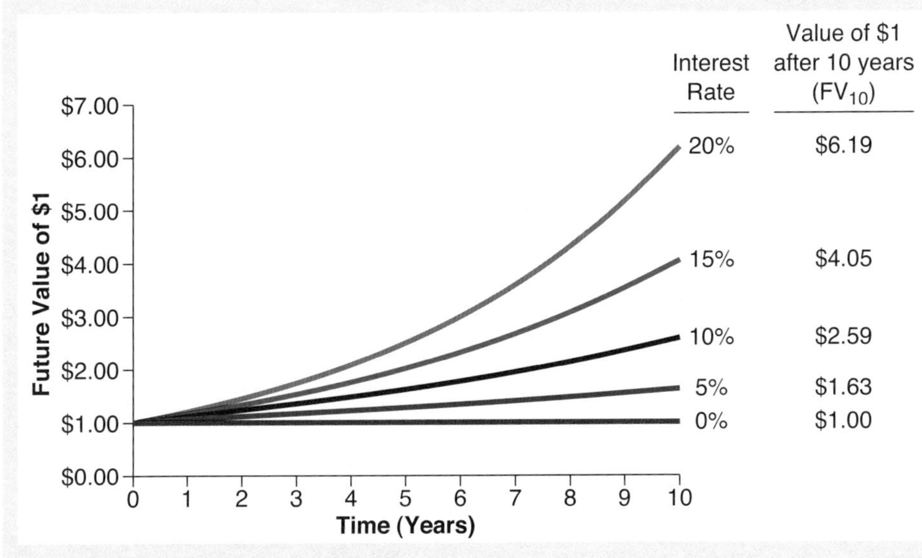

Exhibit 5.5
Future Value of $1 for Different Periods and Interest Rates
The higher the interest rate, the faster the value of an investment will grow, and the larger the amount of money that will accumulate over time. Because of compounding, the growth over time is not linear but exponential—the dollar increase in the future value is greater in each subsequent period.

see the difference in total dollars accumulated if you invest a dollar for 10 years: At 5 percent, you will have \$1.63; at 10 percent, you will have \$2.59; at 15 percent, you will have \$4.05; and at 20 percent, you will have \$6.19. Finally, as you should expect, if you invest a dollar at 0 percent for 10 years, you will only have a dollar at the end of the period.

The Future Value Factor

To solve a future value problem, we need to know the future value factor, $(1 + i)^n$. Fortunately, almost any calculator suitable for college-level work has a power key (the y^x key) that we can use to make this computation. For example, to compute $(1.08)^{10}$, we enter 1.08, press the y^x key and enter 10, and press the "=" key. The number 2.159 should emerge.[4] Give it a try with your calculator.

Alternatively, we can use future value tables to find the future value factor at different interest rates and maturity periods. Exhibit 5.6 is an example of a future value table. For example, to find the future value factor $(1.08)^{10}$, we first go to the row corresponding to 10 years and then move along the row until we reach the 8 percent interest column. The entry is 2.159, which is identical to what we found when we used a calculator. This comes as no surprise, but we sometimes find small differences between calculator solutions and future value tables due to rounding differences. Exhibit A.1 at the end of the book provides a more comprehensive version of Exhibit 5.6.

Future value tables (and the corresponding present value tables) are rarely used today, partly because they are tedious to work with. In addition, the tables show values for only a limited number of interest rates and time periods. For example, what if the interest rate on your \$100 investment was not a nice round number such as 10 percent but was 10.236 percent? You would not find that number in the future value table. In spite of their shortcomings, tables were very commonly used in the days before financial calculators and spreadsheet programs were readily available. You can still use them—for example, to check the answers from your computations of future value factors.

SmartMoney's personal finance Web site provides a lot of useful information for day-to-day finance dealings at www.smartmoney.com/pf/?nav=dropTab.

Applying the Future Value Formula

Next, we will review a number of examples of future value problems to illustrate the typical types of problems you will encounter in business and in your personal life.

Exhibit 5.6 Future Value Factors

Number of Years	Interest Rate per Year: 1%	5%	6%	7%	8%	9%	10%
1	\$1.010	\$1.050	\$1.060	\$1.070	\$1.080	\$1.090	\$1.100
2	1.020	1.103	1.124	1.145	1.166	1.188	1.210
3	1.030	1.158	1.191	1.225	1.260	1.295	1.331
4	1.041	1.216	1.262	1.311	1.360	1.412	1.464
5	1.051	1.276	1.338	1.403	1.469	1.539	1.611
10	1.105	1.629	1.791	1.967	2.159	2.367	2.594
20	1.220	2.653	3.207	3.870	4.661	5.604	6.727
30	1.348	4.322	5.743	7.612	10.063	13.268	17.449

To find a future value factor, simply locate the row with the appropriate number of periods and the column with the desired interest rate. The future value factor for 10 years at 8 percent is 2.159.

[4]An alternative way to perform the calculation is to multiply 1.08 by itself 10 times. However, we do not recommend this procedure.

THE POWER OF COMPOUNDING

Our first example illustrates the effects of compounding. Suppose you have an opportunity to make a $5,000 investment that pays 15 percent per year. How much money will you have at the end of 10 years? The time line for the investment opportunity is:

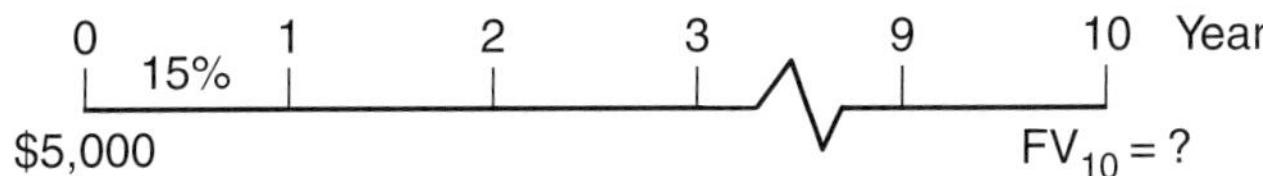

We can apply Equation 5.1 to find the future value of $5,000 invested for 10 years at 15 percent interest. We want to multiply the principal amount (PV) times the appropriate future value factor for 10 years at 15 percent, which is $(1 + 0.15)^{10}$; thus:

$$\begin{aligned} FV_n &= PV \times (1 + i)^n \\ FV_{10} &= \$5{,}000 \times (1 + 0.15)^{10} \\ &= \$5{,}000 \times 4.045558 \\ &= \$20{,}227.79 \end{aligned}$$

Now let's determine how much of the interest is from simple interest and how much is from interest on interest. The total compound interest earned is $15,227.79 ($20,227.79 − $5,000.00). The simple interest is the amount of interest paid on the original principal amount: $SI = P_0 \times i = \$5{,}000 \times 0.15 = \$750$ per year, which over 10 years is $\$750 \times 10 = \$7{,}500$. The interest on interest must be the difference between the total compound interest earned and the simple interest: $15,227.79 − $7,500 = $7,727.79. Notice how quickly the value of an investment increases and how the reinvestment of interest earned—interest on interest—impacts that total compound interest when the interest rates are high.

You can find a compound interest calculator at SmartMoney.com: www.smartmoney.com/compoundcalc.

LEARNING BY DOING APPLICATION 5.1

The Power of Compounding

Problem: Your wealthy uncle passed away, and one of the assets he left to you was a savings account that your great-grandfather had set up 100 years ago. The account had a single deposit of $1,000 and paid 10 percent interest. How much money have you inherited, what is the total compound interest, and how much of the interest earned came from interest on interest?

Approach: We first need to determine the value of the inheritance, which is the future value of $1,000 retained in a savings account for 100 years at 10 percent interest. Our time line for the problem is:

0	1	2	3	99	100 Year
10%					
$1,000					FV_{100} = ?

To calculate FV_{100}, we begin by computing the future value factor. We then plug this number into the future value formula (Equation 5.1) and solve for the total inheritance. Finally, we calculate the total compound interest and the total simple interest and find the difference between these two numbers, which will give us the interest earned on interest.

Solution:

First, we find the future value factor:

$$(1 + i)^n = (1 + 0.10)^{100} = (1.10)^{100} = 13{,}780.612$$

(continued)

Then we find the future value:

$$\begin{aligned} FV_n &= PV \times (1 + i)^n \\ FV_{100} &= \$1{,}000 \times (1.10)^{100} \\ &= \$1{,}000 \times 13{,}780.612 \\ &= \$13{,}780{,}612 \end{aligned}$$

Your total inheritance is $13,780,612. The total compound interest earned is this amount less the original $1,000 investment, or $13,779,612:

$$\$13{,}780{,}612 - \$1{,}000 = \$13{,}779{,}612$$

The total simple interest earned is calculated as follows:

$$\begin{aligned} P_0 \times i = \$1{,}000 \times 0.10 &= \$100 \text{ per year} \\ \$100 \times 100 \text{ years} &= \$10{,}000 \end{aligned}$$

The interest earned on interest is the difference between the total compound interest earned and the simple interest:

$$\$13{,}779{,}612 - \$10{,}000 = \$13{,}769{,}612$$

That's quite a difference!

The following table shows the exponential growth of interest on interest in the savings account described in Learning by Doing Application 5.1. In the first year, simple interest equals compound interest. By year 10, total interest on interest, at $594, is still less than total simple interest, at $1,000. But after 20 years, interest on interest is $3,727—almost double the simple interest of $2,000. After 60 years, interest on interest is nearly 50 times the size of the simple interest—$297,482 versus $6,000. After 80 years, the difference is 255 times ($2,039,400 versus $8,000); and after 100 years, the difference is staggering ($13.78 million versus a mere $10,000). This example illustrates the power of compounding and explains why the future value curves in Exhibit 5.5 increase so sharply for longer time periods at higher interest rates.

Investment Period (years)	Total Compound Interest	Total Simple Interest	Total Interest on Interest
1	$100	$100	$0
10	$1,594	$1,000	$594
20	$5,727	$2,000	$3,727
40	$44,259	$4,000	$40,259
60	$303,482	$6,000	$297,482
80	$2,047,400	$8,000	$2,039,400
100	$13,779,612	$10,000	$13,769,612

BUILDING INTUITION

Compounding Drives Much of the Earnings on Long-Term Investments

The earnings from compounding drive much of the return earned on a long-term investment. The reason is that the longer the investment period, the greater the proportion of total earnings from interest earned on interest. Interest earned on interest grows exponentially as the investment period increases.

COMPOUNDING MORE FREQUENTLY THAN ONCE A YEAR

Interest can, of course, be compounded more frequently than once a year. In Equation 5.1, the term n represents the number of periods and can describe annual, semiannual, quarterly, monthly, or daily payments. The more frequently interest payments are compounded, the larger the future value of $1 for a given time period. Equation 5.1 can be rewritten to explicitly recognize different compounding periods:

$$FV_n = PV \times (1 + i/m)^{m \times n} \tag{5.2}$$

where m is the number of times per year that interest is compounded and n is the number of periods specified in years.

Let's say you invest $100 in a bank account that pays a 5 percent interest rate semiannually (2.5 percent twice a year) for two years. In that case, the amount of interest you would have at the end of the period would be:

$$\begin{aligned} FV_2 &= \$100 \times (1 + 0.05/2)^{2\times2} \\ &= \$100 \times (1 + 0.025)^4 \\ &= \$100 \times 1.1038 \\ &= \$110.38 \end{aligned}$$

Moneychimp.com provides a compound interest calculator at www.moneychimp.com/calculator/compound_interest_calculator.htm.

It is not necessary to "memorize" Equation 5.2; using Equation 5.1 will do fine. All you have to do is determine the interest paid per compounding period (i/m) and calculate the total number of compounding periods ($m \times n$) as the exponent for the future value factor. For example, if the bank compounds interest quarterly, then both the interest rate and compounding periods must be expressed in quarterly terms: ($i/4$) and ($4 \times n$).

During the late 1960s, the effects of compounding periods became an issue in banking. At that time, the interest rates that banks and thrift institutions could pay on consumer savings accounts were limited by regulation. However, financial institutions discovered they could keep their rates within the legal limit and pay their customers additional interest by increasing the compounding frequency. Prior to this, banks and thrifts had paid interest on savings accounts quarterly. You can see the difference between quarterly and daily compounding in Learning by Doing Application 5.2.

LEARNING BY DOING APPLICATION 5.2

Changing the Compounding Period

Problem: Your grandmother has $10,000 she wants to put into a bank savings account for five years. The bank she is considering is within walking distance, pays 5 percent annual interest compounded quarterly (5/4 = 1.25 percent each quarter), and provides free coffee and doughnuts in the morning. Another bank in town pays 5 percent interest compounded daily. Getting to this bank requires a bus trip, but your grandmother can ride free as a senior citizen. More important, though, this bank does not serve coffee and doughnuts. Which bank should your grandmother select?

Approach: We need to calculate the difference between the two banks' interest payments. Bank A, which compounds quarterly, will pay one-fourth of the annual interest per quarter (0.05/4) = 0.0125, and there will be 20 compounding periods over the five-year investment horizon (5 years × 4). The time line for quarterly compounding is as follows:

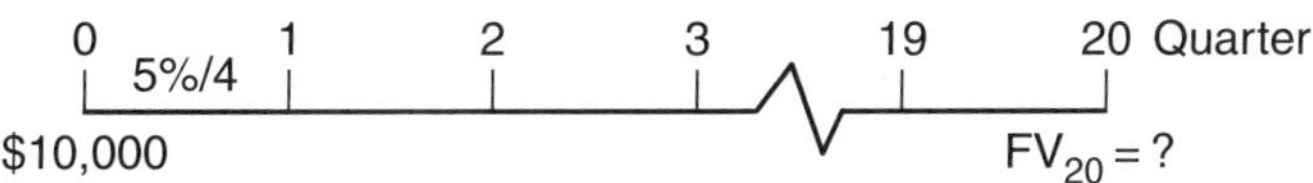

(continued)

Bank B, which compounds daily, has 365 compounding periods per year. Thus, the daily interest rate is 0.000137 (0.05/365), and there are 1,825 (5 years × 365) compounding periods. The time line for daily compounding is:

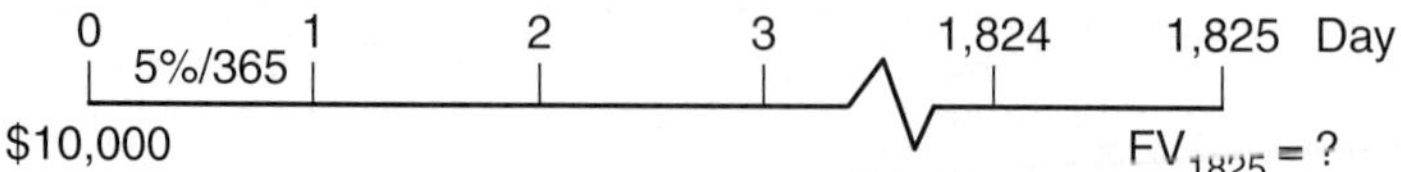

We use Equation 5.2 to solve for the future values the investment would generate at each bank. We then compare the two.

Solution:

Bank A:

$$\begin{aligned} FV_n &= PV \times (1 + i/m)^{m \times n} \\ FV_{qtrly} &= \$10{,}000 \times (1 + 0.05/4)^{4 \times 5} \\ &= \$10{,}000 \times (1 + 0.0125)^{20} \\ &= \$12{,}820.37 \end{aligned}$$

Bank B:

$$\begin{aligned} FV_n &= PV \times (1 + i/m)^{m \times n} \\ FV_{daily} &= \$10{,}000 \times (1 + 0.05/365)^{365 \times 5} \\ &= \$10{,}000 \times (1 + 0.000137)^{1{,}825} \\ &= \$12{,}840.03 \end{aligned}$$

With daily compounding, the additional interest earned by your grandmother is $19.66:

$$\$12{,}840.03 - \$12{,}820.37 = \$19.66$$

Given that the interest gained by daily compounding is less than $20, your grandmother should probably select her local bank and enjoy the daily coffee and doughnuts. (If she is on a diet, of course, she should take the higher interest payment and walk to the other bank).

CONTINUOUS COMPOUNDING

We can continue to divide the compounding interval into smaller and smaller time periods, such as minutes and seconds, until, at the extreme, we would compound continuously. In this case, m in Equation 5.2 would approach infinity (∞). The formula to compute the future value for continuous compounding (FV_∞) is stated as follows:

$$FV_\infty = PV \times e^{i \times n} \tag{5.3}$$

where e is the exponential function, which has a known mathematical value of about 2.71828, n is the number of periods specified in years, and i is the annual interest rate. Although the formula may look a little intimidating, it is really quite easy to apply. Look for a key on your calculator labeled e^x. If you don't have the key, you still can work the problem.

Let's go back to the example in Learning by Doing Application 5.2, in which your grandmother wants to put $10,000 in a savings account at a bank. How much money would she have at the end of five years if the bank paid 5 percent annual interest compounded continuously? To find out, we enter these values into Equation 5.3:

$$\begin{aligned} FV_\infty &= PV \times e^{i \times n} \\ &= \$10{,}000 \times e^{0.05 \times 5} \\ &= \$10{,}000 \times e^{0.25} \\ &= \$10{,}000 \times 2.71828^{0.25} \\ &= \$10{,}000 \times 1.284025 \\ &= \$12{,}840.25 \end{aligned}$$

If your calculator has an exponent key, all you have to do to calculate $e^{0.25}$ is enter the number 0.25, then hit the e^x key, and the number 1.28403 should appear (depending on your calculator, you may have to press the equal [=] key for the answer to appear). Then multiply 1.284025 by $10,000, and you're done! If your calculator does not have an exponent key, then you can calculate $e^{0.25}$ by inputting the value of e (2.71828) and raising it to the 0.25 power using the y^x key, as described earlier in the chapter.

Let's look at your grandmother's $10,000 bank balance at the end of five years with several different compounding periods: yearly, quarterly, daily, and continuous:[5]

(1) Compounding Period	(2) Total Earnings	(3) Compound Interest	(4) Additional Interest
Yearly	$12,762.82	$2,762.82	—
Quarterly	$12,820.37	$2,820.37	$57.55 more than yearly compounding
Daily	$12,840.03	$2,840.03	$19.66 more than quarterly compounding
Continuous	$12,840.25	$2,840.25	$0.22 more than daily compounding

Notice that your grandmother's total earnings get larger as the frequency of compounding increases, as shown in column 2, but the earnings increase at a decreasing rate, as shown in column 4. The biggest gain comes when the compounding period goes from an annual interest payment to quarterly interest payments. The gain from daily compounding to continuous compounding is small on a modest savings balance such as your grandmother's. Twenty-two cents over five years will not buy grandmother a cup of coffee, let alone a doughnut. However, for businesses and governments with mega-dollar balances at financial institutions, the difference in compounding periods can be substantial.

DECISION-MAKING EXAMPLE 5.1

Which Bank Offers Depositors the Best Deal?

Situation: You have just received a bonus of $10,000 and are looking to deposit the money in a bank account for five years. You investigate the annual deposit rates of several banks and collect the following information:

Bank	Compounding Frequency	Annual Rate
A	Annually	5.00%
B	Quarterly	5.00%
C	Monthly	4.80%
D	Daily	4.85%

You understand that the more frequently interest is earned in each year, the more you will have at the end of your investment horizon. To determine which bank you should deposit your money in, you calculate how much money you will earn at the end of five years at each bank. You apply Equation 5.2 and come up with these results. Which bank should you choose?

Bank	Investment Amount	Compounding Frequency	Rate	Value after 5 Years
A	$10,000	Annually	5.00%	$12,762.82
B	$10,000	Quarterly	5.00%	$12,820.37
C	$10,000	Monthly	4.80%	$12,706.41
D	$10,000	Daily	4.85%	$12,744.11

(continued)

[5]The future value calculation for annual compounding is: $FV_{yearly} = \$10,000 \times (1.05)^5 = \$12,762.82$.

Decision: Even though you might expect Bank D's daily compounding to result in the highest value, the calculations reveal that Bank B provides the highest value at the end of five years. Thus, you should deposit the amount in Bank B because its higher rate offsets the more frequent compounding at Banks C and D.

USING EXCEL

Time Value of Money

Spreadsheet computer programs are a popular method for setting up and solving finance and accounting problems. Throughout this book, we will show you how to structure and calculate some problems using Microsoft Excel, a widely used spreadsheet program. Spreadsheet programs are like your financial calculator but are especially efficient at doing repetitive calculations. For example, once the spreadsheet program is set up, it will allow you to make computations using preprogrammed formulas. Thus, you can simply change any of the input cells, and the preset formula will automatically recalculate the answer based on the new input values. For this reason, we recommend that you use formulas whenever possible.

We begin our spreadsheet applications with time value of money calculations. As with the financial calculator approach, there are five variables used in these calculations, and knowing any four of them will let you calculate the fifth one. Excel has already preset formulas for you to use. These are as follows:

Solving for	Formula
PV	= PV(RATE, NPER, PMT, FV)
FV	= FV(RATE, NPER, PMT, PV)
Discount Rate	= RATE(NPER, PMT, PV, FV)
Payment	= PMT(RATE, NPER, PV, FV)
Number of Periods	= NPER(RATE, PMT, PV, FV)

To enter a formula, all you have to do is type in the equal sign, the abbreviated name of the variable you want to compute, and an open parenthesis, and Excel will automatically prompt you to enter the rest of the variables. Here is an example of what you would type to compute the future value:

1. =
2. FV
3. (

	A	B	C	D	E	F
1						
2	Time Value of Money Calculations					
3						
4	Your grandmother wants to put $10,000 into a bank savings account for five years. Bank A pays 5 percent					
5	interest compounded quarterly, while Bank B offers 5 percent compounded daily. Which bank should your					
6	grandmother choose?					
7						
8	To answer the question, we need to solve for the future value.					
9						
10	**Problem set-up and solution:**					
11						
12		**Bank A**	**Bank B**		**Comment**	
13	Present value	($10,000)	($10,000)		Value given	
14	Interest rate	0.01250	0.00014		Interest rate/# compounding periods per year	
15	Number of periods	20	1825		# years × # compounding periods per year	
16	**Future value**	**$12,820.37**	**$12,840.03**		See note below	
17						
18–22	The formula entered to calculate the future value for Bank A in cell B16 is =FV(B14, B15, 0, B13). Similarly, the formula to calculate the future value for Bank B in cell C16 is =FV(C14, C15, 0, C13). Since there are no payments, we enter PMT as zero. Also, notice that to be consistent with what we have said about cash inflows and outflows so far, the present value is entered as a negative number.					
23						

Here are a few important things to note when entering the formulas: (1) be consistent with signs for cash inflows and outflows; (2) enter the rate of return as a decimal number, not a percentage; and (3) enter the amount of an unknown payment as zero.

To see how a problem is set up and how the calculations are made using a spreadsheet, return to Learning by Doing Application 5.2.

Calculator Tips for Future Value Problems

As we have mentioned, all types of future value calculations can be done easily on a financial calculator. Here we discuss how to solve these problems, and we identify some potential problem areas to avoid.

A financial calculator includes the following five basic keys for solving future value and present value problems:

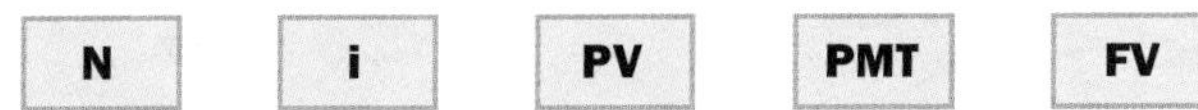

The keys represent the following inputs:

- **N** is the number of periods. The periods can be days, months, quarters, or years.
- **i** is the interest rate per period, expressed as a percentage.
- **PV** is the present value or the original principal (P_0).
- **PMT** is the amount of any recurring payment.
- **FV** is the future value.

Given any four of these inputs, the financial calculator will solve for the fifth. Note that the interest rate key i differs with different calculator brands: Texas Instruments uses the I/Y key, Hewlett-Packard an i, %i or I/Y key, and Sharp the i key.

For future value problems, we need to use only four of the five keys: N for the number of periods, i for the interest rate (or growth rate), PV for the present value (at time zero), and FV for the future value in n periods. The PMT key is not used at this time, but, when doing a problem, always enter a zero to effectively clear the register.[6]

To solve a future value problem, enter the known data into your calculator. For example, if you know that the number of periods is five, key in 5 and press the N key. Repeat the process for the remaining known values. Once you have entered *all* of the values you know, then press the key for the unknown quantity, and you have your answer. Note that with some calculators, including the TI BAII Plus, you get the answer by first pressing the key labeled CPT (compute).

Let's try a problem to see how this works. Suppose we invest $5,000 at 15 percent for 10 years. How much money will we have in 10 years? To solve the problem, we enter data on the keys as displayed in the following calculation and solve for FV. Note that the initial investment of $5,000 is a negative number because it represents a cash outflow. Use the +/− key to make a number negative.

Enter 10 15 −5,000 0

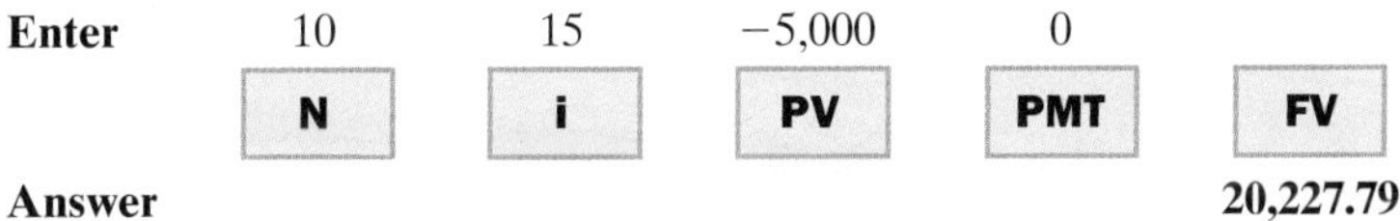

Answer **20,227.79**

If you did not get the correct answer of $20,227.79, you may need to consult the instruction manual that came with your financial calculator. However, before you do that, you may want to look through Exhibit 5.7, which lists the most common problems with using financial calculators. Also, note again that the PMT is entered as zero, which effectively clears the register.

One advantage of using a financial calculator is that if you have values for any three of the four variables in Equation 5.1, you can solve for the remaining variable at the press of a button. Suppose that you have an opportunity to invest $5,000 in a bank and that the bank will pay you $20,227.79 at the end of 10 years. What interest rate does the bank pay? The time line for our situation is as follows:

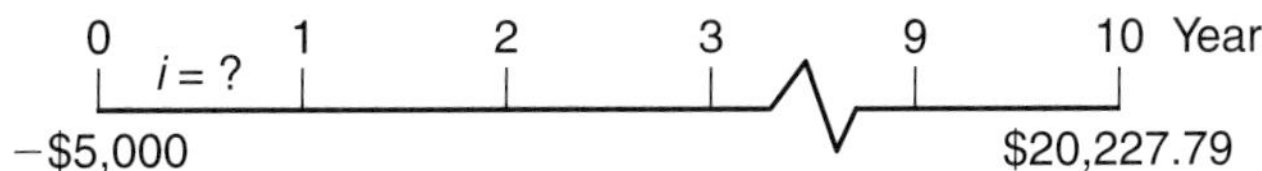

We know the values for N (10 years), PV ($5,000), and FV ($20,227.79), so we can enter these values into our financial calculator:

Enter 10 −5,000 0 20,227.79

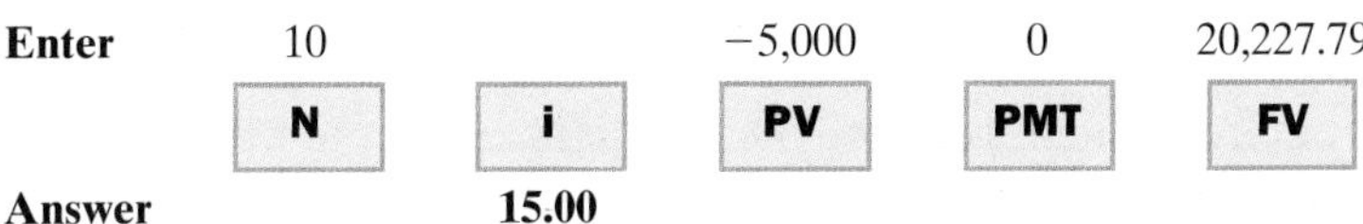

Answer **15.00**

---

[6]The PMT key is used for annuity calculations, which we will discuss in Chapter 6.

Exhibit 5.7 **Tips for Using Financial Calculators**

Use the Correct Compounding Period. Make sure that your calculator is set to compound one payment per period or per year. Because financial calculators are often used to compute monthly payments, some will default to monthly payments unless you indicate otherwise. You will need to consult your calculator's instruction manual because procedures for changing settings vary by manufacturer. Most of the problems you will work in other chapters of the book will compound annually.

Clear the Calculator Before Starting. Be sure you clear the data out of the financial register before starting to work a problem because most calculators retain information between calculations. Since the information may be retained even when the calculator is turned off, turning the calculator off and on will not solve this problem. Check your instruction manual for the correct procedure for clearing the financial register of your calculator.

Negative Signs on Cash Outflows. For certain types of calculations, it is critical that you input a negative sign for all cash outflows and a positive sign for all cash inflows. Otherwise, the calculator cannot make the computation, and the answer screen will display some type of error message.

Putting a Negative Sign on a Number. To create a number with a negative sign, enter the number first and then press the "change of sign key." These keys are typically labeled "CHS" or "+/−".

Interest Rate as a Percentage. Most financial calculators require that interest rate data be entered in percentage form, not in decimal form. For example, enter 7.125 percent as 7.125 and not 0.07125. Unlike nonfinancial calculators, financial calculators assume that rates are stated as percentages.

Rounding off Numbers. Never round off any numbers until all your calculations are complete. If you round off numbers along the way, you can generate significant rounding errors.

Adjust Decimal Setting. Most calculators are set to display two decimal places. You will find it convenient at times to display four or more decimal places when making financial calculations, especially when working with interest rates or present value factors. Again, consult your instruction manual.

Have Correct BEG or END mode. In finance, most problems that you solve will involve cash payments that occur at the end of each time period, such as with the ordinary annuities discussed in Chapter 6. Most calculators normally operate in this mode, which is usually designated as "END" mode. However, for annuities due, which are also discussed in Chapter 6, the cash payments occur at the beginning of each period. This setting is designated as the "BEG" mode. Most leases and rent payments fall into this category. When you bought your financial calculator, it was set in the END mode. Financial calculators allow you to switch between the END and BEG modes.

Following these tips will help you avoid problems that sometimes arise in solving time value of money problems with a financial calculator.

Press the interest rate (i) key, and 15.00 percent appears as the answer. Notice that the cash outflow ($5,000) was entered as a negative value and the cash inflow ($20,227.79) as a positive value. If both values were entered with the same sign, your financial calculator algorithm could not compute the equation, yielding an error message. Go ahead and try it.

Before You Go On

1. What is compounding, and how does it affect the future value of an investment?
2. What is the difference between simple interest and compound interest?
3. How does changing the compounding period affect the amount of interest earned on an investment?

5.3 PRESENT VALUE AND DISCOUNTING

In our discussion of future value, we asked the question "If you put $100 in a bank savings account that paid 10 percent annual interest, how much money would accumulate in one year?" Another type of question that arises frequently in finance concerns present value. This question asks, "What is the value today of a cash flow promised in the future?" We'll illustrate the present value concept with a simple example.

Single-Period Investment

Suppose that a rich uncle gives you a bank certificate of deposit (CD) that matures in one year and pays \$110. The CD pays 10 percent interest annually and cannot be redeemed until maturity. Being a student, you need the money and would like to sell the asset. What would be a fair price if you sold the CD today?

From our earlier discussion, we know that if we invest \$100 in a bank at 10 percent for one year, it will grow to a future value of \$110 = \$100 × (1 + 0.10). It seems reasonable to conclude that if a CD has an interest rate of 10 percent and will have a value of \$110 a year from now, it is worth \$100 today.

More formally, to find the present value of a future cash flow, or its value today, we "reverse" the compounding process and divide the future value (\$110) by the future value factor (1 + 0.10). The result is \$100 = \$110/(1 + 0.10), which is the same answer we derived from our intuitive calculation. If we write the calculations above as a formula, we have a one-period model for calculating the present value of a future cash flow:

$$\text{PV} = \frac{\text{FV}_1}{1 + i}$$

The numerical calculation for the present value (PV) from our one-period model follows:

$$\begin{aligned} \text{PV} &= \frac{\text{FV}_1}{1 + i} \\ &= \frac{\$110}{1 + 0.10} \\ &= \frac{\$110}{1.10} \\ &= \$100 \end{aligned}$$

We have noted that while future value calculations involve *compounding* an amount forward into the future, *present value* calculations involve the reverse. That is, present value calculations involve determining the current value (or present value) of a future cash flow. The process of calculating the present value is called **discounting**, and the interest rate i is known as the **discount rate**. Accordingly, the **present value (PV)** can be thought of as the *discounted value of a future amount*. The present value is simply the current value of a future cash flow that has been discounted at the appropriate discount rate.

Just as we have a future value factor, $(1 + i)$, we also have a *present value factor*, which is more commonly called the *discount factor*. The discount factor, which is $1/(1 + i)$, is the reciprocal of the future value factor. This expression may not be obvious in the equation above, but note that we can write that equation in two ways:

1. $\text{PV} = \dfrac{\text{FV}}{1 + i}$
2. $\text{PV} = \text{FV}_1 \times \dfrac{1}{1 + i}$

These equations amount to the same thing; the discount factor is explicit in the second one.

discounting
the process by which the present value of future cash flows is obtained

discount rate
the interest rate used in the discounting process to find the present value of future cash flows

present value (PV)
the current value of future cash flows discounted at the appropriate discount rate

Multiple-Period Investment

Now suppose your uncle gives you another 10 percent CD, but this CD matures in two years and pays \$121 at maturity. Like the other CD, it cannot be redeemed until maturity. From the previous section, we know that if we invest \$100 in a bank at 10 percent for two years, it will grow to a future value of $121 = $100 × (1 + 0.10)²$. To calculate the present value, or today's price, we divide the future value ($121) by the future value factor $(1 + 0.10)^2$. The result is $\$100 = \$121/(1 + 0.10)^2$.

If we capture the calculations we made as an equation, the result is a two-period model for computing the present value of a future cash flow:

$$PV = \frac{FV_2}{(1 + i)^2}$$

Plugging the data from our example into the equation yields no surprises:

$$\begin{aligned} PV &= \frac{FV_2}{(1 + i)^2} \\ &= \frac{\$121}{(1 + 0.10)^2} \\ &= \frac{\$121}{1.21} \\ &= \$100 \end{aligned}$$

By now, you know the drill. We can extend the equation to a third year, a fourth year, and so on until we reach n years:

Year	Equation
1	$PV = \frac{FV_1}{1 + i}$
2	$PV = \frac{FV_2}{(1 + i)^2}$
3	$PV = \frac{FV_3}{(1 + i)^3}$
4	$PV = \frac{FV_4}{(1 + i)^4}$
...	
n	$PV = \frac{FV_n}{(1 + i)^n}$

The Present Value Equation

Given the pattern shown in the foregoing, we can see that the general formula for the present value is:[7]

$$PV = \frac{FV_n}{(1 + i)^n} \tag{5.4}$$

where:

PV = the value today ($t = 0$) of a cash flow or series of cash flows
FV_n = the future value at the end of period n
i = the discount rate, which is the interest rate per period
n = the number of periods, which could be years, month, days, or some other unit of time

[7]Equation 5.4 can also be written as $PV = FV_n \times (1+i)^{-n}$.

Note that Equation 5.4 is sometimes written in a slightly different way, which we will use sometimes in the book. The first form, introduced earlier, separates out the discount factor, $1/(1 + i)$:

$$PV = FV_n \times \frac{1}{(1 + i)^n}$$

In the second form, DF_n is the discount factor for the nth period: $DF_n = 1/(1 + i)^n$:

$$PV = FV_n \times DF_n$$

Future and Present Value Equations Are the Same

By now, you may have recognized that the present value equation, Equation 5.4, is just a restatement of the future value equation, Equation 5.1. That is, to get the future value (FV_n) of funds invested for n years, we multiply the original investment by $(1 + i)^n$. To find the present value of a future payment (FV_n), we divide FV_n by $(1 + i)^n$. Stated another way, we can start with the future value equation (Equation 5.1), $FV_n = PV \times (1 + i)^n$ and then solve it for PV; the resulting equation is the present value equation (Equation 5.4), $PV = FV_n/(1 + i)^n$.

Exhibit 5.8 illustrates the relationship between the future value and present value calculations for $100 invested at 10 percent interest. You can see from the exhibit that present value and future value are just two sides of the same coin. The formula used to calculate the present value is really the same as the formula for future value, just rearranged.

Applying the Present Value Formula

Let's work through some examples to see how the present value equation is used. Suppose you are interested in buying a new BMW 330 Sports Coupe a year from now. You estimate that the car will cost $40,000. If your local bank pays 5 percent interest on savings deposits, how much money will you need to save in order to buy the car as planned? The time line for the car purchase problem is as follows:

```
0                                   1 Year
|        5%                         |
PV = ?                              $40,000
```

The problem is a direct application of Equation 5.4. What we want to know is how much money you have to put in the bank today to have $40,000 a year from now to buy

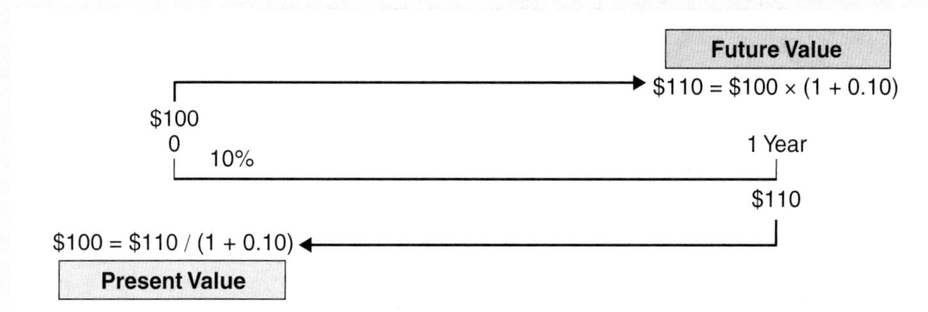

Exhibit 5.8
Comparing Future Value and Present Value Calculations
The future value and present value formulas are one and the same; the present value factor, $1/(1 + i)^n$, is just the reciprocal of the future value factor, $(1 + i)^n$.

your BMW. To find out, we compute the present value of \$40,000 using a 5 percent discount rate:

$$\begin{aligned} PV &= \frac{FV_1}{1 + i} \\ &= \frac{\$40{,}000}{1 + 0.05} \\ &= \frac{\$40{,}000}{1.05} \\ &= \$38{,}095.24 \end{aligned}$$

If you put \$38,095.24 in a bank savings account at 5 percent today, you will have the \$40,000 to buy the car in one year.

Since that's a lot of money to come up with, your mother suggests that you leave the money in the bank for two years instead of one year. If you follow her advice, how much money do you need to invest? The time line is as follows:

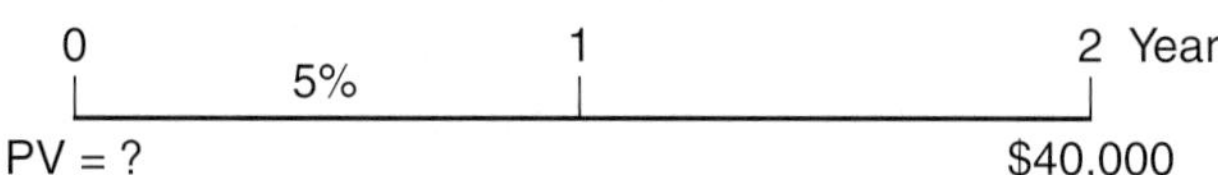

For a two-year waiting period, assuming the car price will stay the same, the calculation is:

$$\begin{aligned} PV &= \frac{FV_2}{(1 + i)^2} \\ &= \frac{\$40{,}000}{(1 + 0.05)^2} \\ &= \frac{\$40{,}000}{1.1025} \\ &= \$36{,}281.18 \end{aligned}$$

Given the time value of money, the result is exactly what we would expect. The present value of \$40,000 two years out is lower than the present value of \$40,000 one year out—\$36,281.18 compared with \$38,095.24. Thus, if you are willing to leave your money in the bank for two years instead of one, you can make a smaller initial investment to reach your goal.

Now suppose your rich neighbor says that if you invest your money with him for one year, he will pay you 15 percent interest. The time line is:

0   15%   1 Year

PV = ?   \$40,000

The calculation for the initial investment at this new rate is as follows:

$$\begin{aligned} PV &= \frac{FV_1}{1 + i} \\ &= \frac{\$40{,}000}{1 + 0.15} \\ &= \frac{\$40{,}000}{1.15} \\ &= \$34{,}782.61 \end{aligned}$$

Thus, when the interest rate, or discount rate, is 15 percent, the present value of \$40,000 to be received in a year's time is \$34,782.61, compared with \$38,095.24 at a rate of

5 percent and a time of one year. Holding maturity constant, an increase in the discount rate decreases the present value of the future cash flow. This makes sense because when interest rates are higher, it is more valuable to have dollars in hand today to invest; thus, dollars in the future are worth less.

LEARNING BY DOING APPLICATION 5.3

European Graduation Fling

Problem: Suppose you plan to take a "graduation vacation" to Europe when you finish college in two years. If your savings account at the bank pays 6 percent, how much money do you need to set aside today to have \$8,000 when you leave for Europe?

Approach: The money you need today is the present value of the amount you will need for your trip in two years. Thus, the value of FV_2 is \$8,000. The interest rate is 6 percent. Using these values and the present value equation, we can calculate how much money you need to put in the bank at 6 percent to generate \$8,000. The time line is:

0	6%	1		2	Year
PV = ?				\$8,000	

Solution:

$$
\begin{aligned}
PV &= FV_n \times \frac{1}{(1+i)^n} \\
&= FV_2 \times \frac{1}{(1+i)^2} \\
&= \$8{,}000 \times \frac{1}{(1.06)^2} \\
&= \$8{,}000 \times 0.889996 \\
&= \$7{,}119.97
\end{aligned}
$$

Thus, if you invest \$7,119.97 in your savings account today, at the end of two years you will have exactly \$8,000.

The Relations among Time, the Discount Rate, and Present Value

From our discussion so far, we can see that (1) the farther in the future a dollar will be received, the less it is worth today, and (2) the higher the discount rate, the lower the present value of a dollar. Let's look a bit more closely at these relations.

Recall from Exhibit 5.5 that future value factors grow exponentially over time because of compounding. Similarly, present value factors become smaller the longer the time horizon. The reason is because the present value factor $1/(1 + i)^n$ is the reciprocal of the future value factor $(1 + i)^n$. Thus, the present value of \$1 must become smaller as the time to payment becomes longer. You can see this relation in Exhibit 5.9, which shows the present value of \$1 for various interest rates and time periods. For example, at 10 percent, the present value of \$1 one year in the future is 90.9 cents (\$1/1.10); at two years in the future, 82.6 cents [$\$1/(1.10)^2$]; at five years in the future, 62.1 cents [$\$1/(1.10)^5$]; and at thirty years in the future, 5.7 cents [$\$1/(1.10)^{30}$]. The relation is consistent with our view of the time value of money. That is, the longer you have to wait for money, the less it is worth today. Exhibit A.2, at the end of the book, provides present value factors for a wider range of years and interest rates.

Exhibit 5.9 **Present Value Factors**

Number of Years	Interest Rate per Year						
	1%	5%	6%	7%	8%	9%	10%
1	$0.990	$0.952	$0.943	$0.935	$0.926	$0.917	$0.909
2	0.980	0.907	0.890	0.873	0.857	0.842	0.826
3	0.971	0.864	0.840	0.816	0.794	0.772	0.751
4	0.961	0.823	0.792	0.763	0.735	0.708	0.683
5	0.951	0.784	0.747	0.713	0.681	0.650	0.621
10	0.905	0.614	0.558	0.508	0.463	0.422	0.386
20	0.820	0.377	0.312	0.258	0.215	0.178	0.149
30	0.742	0.231	0.174	0.131	0.099	0.075	0.057

To locate a present value factor, find the row for the number of periods and the column for the proper discount rate. Notice that whereas future value factors grow larger over time and with increasing interest rates, present value factors become smaller. This pattern reflects the fact that the present value factor is the reciprocal of the future value factor.

Exhibit 5.10 shows the present values of $1 for different time periods and discount rates. For example, at 10 years, the present value of $1 discounted at 5 percent is 61 cents, at 10 percent it is 39 cents, and at 20 percent, 16 cents. Thus, the higher the discount rate, the lower the present value of $1 for a given time period. Exhibit 5.10 also shows that, just as with future value, the relation between the present value of $1 and time is not

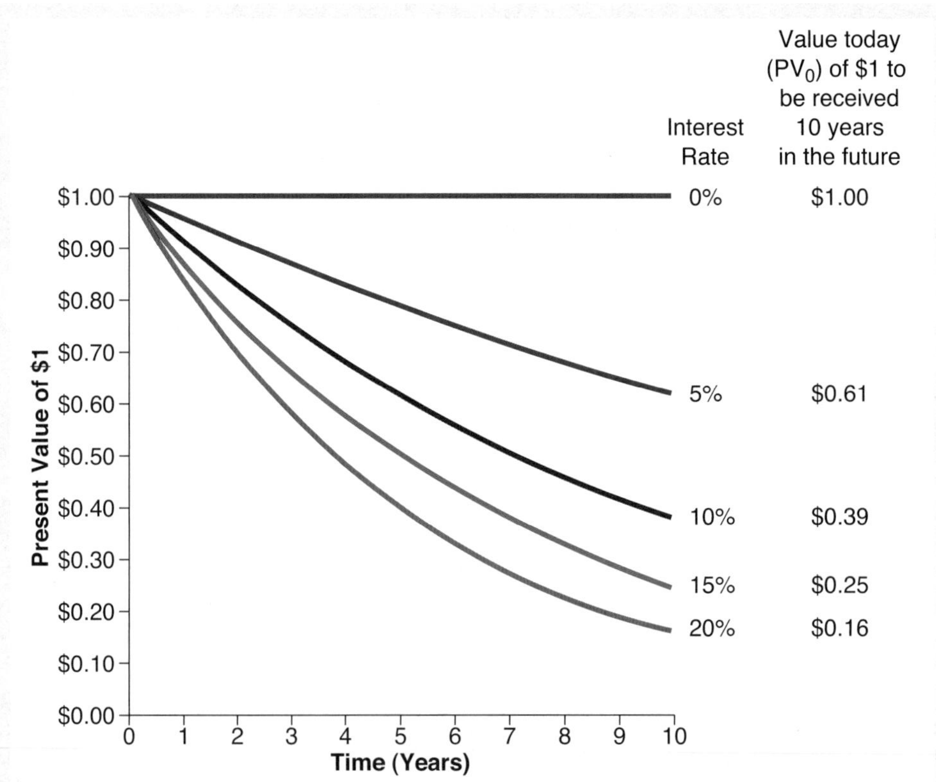

Exhibit 5.10
Present Value of $1 for Different Time Periods and Discount Rates
The higher the discount rate, the lower the present value of $1 for a given time period. Just as with future value, the relation between the present value and time is not linear but exponential.

linear but exponential. Finally, it is interesting to note that if interest rates are zero, the present value of $1 is $1; that is, there is no time value of money. In this situation, $1,000 today has the same value as $1,000 a year from now or, for that matter, 10 years from now.

DECISION-MAKING EXAMPLE 5.2

Picking the Best Lottery Payoff Option

Situation: Congratulations! You have won the $1 million lottery grand prize. You have been presented with several payout alternatives, and you have to decide which one to accept. The alternatives are as follows:

- $1 million today
- $1.2 million lump sum in two years
- $1.5 million lump sum in five years
- $2 million lump sum in eight years

You are intrigued by the choice of collecting the prize money today or receiving double the amount of money in the future. Which payout option should you choose?

Your cousin, a stockbroker, advises you that over the long term you should be able to earn 10 percent on an investment portfolio. Based on that rate of return, you make the following calculations:

Alternative	Nominal Value	Present Value
Today	$1 million	$1 million
2 years	$1.2 million	$991,736
5 years	$1.5 million	$931,382
8 years	$2 million	$933,015

Decision: As appealing as the higher amounts may sound, waiting for the big payout is not worthwhile in this case. Applying the present value formula has enabled you to convert future dollars into present, or current, dollars. Now the decision is simple—you can directly compare the present values. Given the above choices, you should take the $1 million today.

Calculator Tips for Present Value Problems

Calculating the discount factor (present value factor) on a calculator is similar to calculating the future value factor but requires an additional keystroke on most advanced-level calculators. The discount factor, $1/(1 + i)^n$, is the reciprocal of the future value factor, $(1 + i)^n$. The additional keystroke involves the use of the reciprocal key ($1/x$) to find the discount factor. For example, to compute $1/(1.08)^{10}$, first enter 1.08, press the y^x key and enter 10, then press the equal (=) key. The number on the screen should be 2.159. This is the future value factor. It is a calculation you have made before. Now press the $1/x$ key, then the equal key, and you have the present value factor, 0.463!

Calculating present value (PV) on a financial calculator is the same as calculating the future value (FV_n) except that you solve for PV rather than FV_n. For example, what is the present value of $1,000 received 10 years from now at a 9 percent discount rate? To find the answer on your financial calculator, enter the following keystrokes:

Enter	10	9		0	1,000
	N	**i**	**PV**	**PMT**	**FV**
Answer			**−422.41**		

Then solve for the present value (PV), which is −$422.41. Notice that the answer has a negative sign. As we discussed previously, the $1,000 represents an inflow, and the $442.41 represents an outflow.

Before You Go On

1. What is the present value and when is it used?
2. What is the discount rate? How does the discount rate differ from the interest rate in the future value equation?
3. What is the relation between the present value factor and the future value factor?
4. Explain why you would expect the discount factor to become smaller the longer the time to payment.

5.4 Additional Concepts and Applications

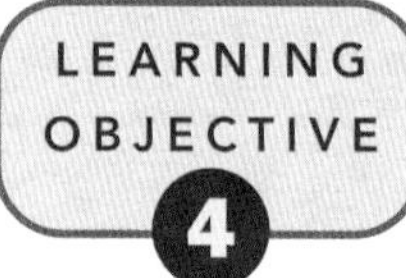

In this final section, we discuss several additional issues concerning present and future value, including how to find an unknown discount rate, how to estimate the length of time it will take to "double your money," and how to find the growth rates of various kinds of investments.

Finding the Interest Rate

In finance, some situations require you to determine the interest rate (or discount rate) for a given future cash flow. These situations typically arise when you want to determine the return on an investment. For example, an interesting Wall Street innovation is the *zero coupon bond.* These bonds pay no periodic interest; instead, at maturity the issuer (the firm that borrows the money) makes a payment that includes repayment of the amount borrowed plus interest. Needless to say, the issuer must prepare in advance to have the cash to pay off bondholders.

Suppose a firm is planning to issue $10 million worth of zero coupon bonds with 20 years to maturity. The bonds are issued in denominations of $1,000 and are sold for $90 each. In other words, you buy the bond today for $90, and 20 years from now, the firm pays you $1,000. If you bought one of these bonds, what would be your return on investment?

Year	0	1	2	3	19	20
	$i = ?$					
	−$90					$1,000

To find the return, we need to solve Equation 5.4, the present value equation, for i, the interest, or discount, rate. The $90 you pay today is the PV (present value), the $1,000 you get in 20 years is the FV (future value), and 20 years is n (the compounding period). The resulting calculation is as follows:

$$\text{PV} = \frac{\text{FV}_n}{(1 + i)^n}$$

$$\$90 = \frac{\$1{,}000}{(1 + i)^{20}}$$

$$(1 + i)^{20} = \frac{\$1{,}000}{\$90}$$

$$1 + i = \left(\frac{\$1{,}000}{\$90}\right)^{1/20}$$

$$i = (11.1111)^{1/20} - 1$$
$$= 1.1279 - 1$$
$$= 0.1279, \text{ or } 12.79\%$$

The rate of return on your investment, compounded annually, is 12.79 percent. Using a financial calculator, we arrive at the following solution:

	N	i	PV	PMT	FV
Enter	20		−90	0	1,000
Answer		**12.79**			

LEARNING BY DOING APPLICATION 5.4

Interest Rate on a Loan

Problem: Greg and Joan Hubbard are getting ready to buy their first house. To help make the down payment, Greg's aunt offers to loan them $15,000, which can be repaid in 10 years. If Greg and Joan borrow the money, they will have to repay Greg's aunt the amount of $23,750. What rate of interest would Greg and Joan be paying on the 10-year loan?

Approach: In this case, the present value is the value of the loan ($15,000), and the future value is the amount due at the end of 10 years ($23,750). To solve for the rate of interest on the loan, we can use the present value equation, Equation 5.4. Alternatively, we can use a financial calculator to compute the interest rate. The time line for the loan is as follows:

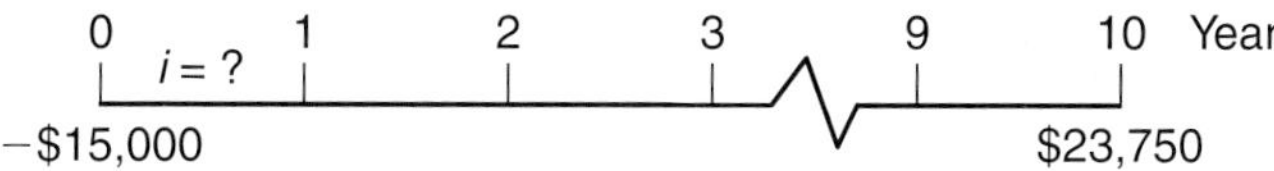

Solution:

Using Equation 5.4:

$$\begin{aligned}
PV &= \frac{FV_n}{(1+i)^n} \\
\$15{,}000 &= \frac{\$23{,}750}{(1+i)^{10}} \\
(1+i)^{10} &= \frac{\$23{,}750}{\$15{,}000} \\
1+i &= \left(\frac{\$23{,}750}{\$15{,}000}\right)^{1/10} \\
i &= (1.58333)^{1/10} - 1 \\
&= 1.04703 - 1 \\
&= 0.04703, \text{ or } 4.703\%
\end{aligned}$$

Financial calculator steps:

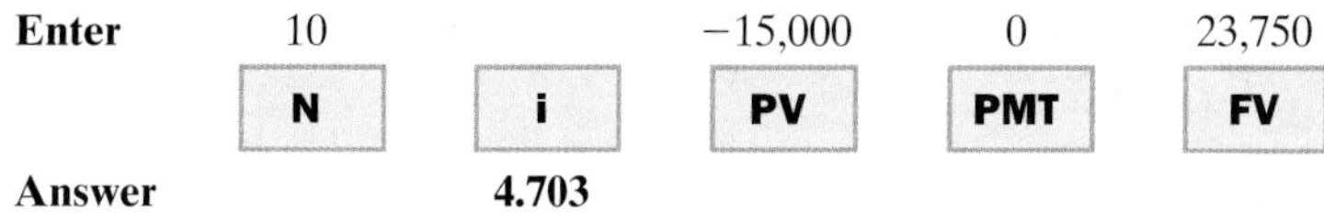

	N	i	PV	PMT	FV
Enter	10		−15,000	0	23,750
Answer		**4.703**			

The Rule of 72

People are fascinated by the possibility of doubling their money. Infomercials on television tout speculative land investments, claiming that "some investors have doubled their money in four years." Before there were financial calculators, people used rules of thumb to approximate difficult present value calculations. One such rule is the Rule of 72, which was used to determine the amount of time it takes to double an investment.

Rule of 72
a rule proposing that the time required to double money invested (TDM) approximately equals $72/i$, where i is expressed as a percentage

The **Rule of 72** says that the time to double your money (TDM) approximately equals $72/i$, where i is expressed as a percentage. Thus,

$$\text{TDM} = \frac{72}{i} \tag{5.5}$$

Applying the Rule of 72 to our land investment example suggests that if you double your money in four years, your annual rate of return will be 18 percent ($i = 72/4 = 18$).

Let's check the rule's accuracy by applying the present value formula to the land example. We are assuming that you will double our money in four years, so $n = 4$. We did not specify a present value or future value amount; however, doubling our money means that we will get back \$2 (FV) for every \$1 invested (PV). Using Equation 5.4 and solving for the interest rate (i), we find that $i = 0.1892$, or 18.92 percent.[8]

That's not bad for a simple rule of thumb: 18.92 percent versus 18 percent. Within limits, the Rule of 72 provides a quick "back of the envelope" method for determining the amount of time it will take to double an investment for a particular rate of return. The Rule of 72 is a linear approximation of a nonlinear function, and as such, the rule is fairly accurate for interest rates between 5 and 20 percent. Outside these limits, the rule is not very accurate.

Compound Growth Rates

The concept of compounding is not restricted to money. Any number that changes over time, such as the population of a city, changes at some compound growth rate. Compound growth occurs when the initial value of a number increases or decreases each period by the factor (1 + growth rate). As we go through the course, we will discuss many different types of interest rates, such as the discount rate on capital budgeting projects, the yield on a bond, and the internal rate of return on an investment. All of these "interest rates" can be thought of as growth rates (g) that relate future values to present values.

When we refer to the compounding effect, we are really talking about what happens when the value of a number increases or decreases by $(1 + \text{growth rate})^n$. That is, the future value of a number after n periods will equal the initial value times $(1 + \text{growth rate})^n$. Does this sound familiar? If we want, we can rewrite Equation 5.1 in a more general form as a compound growth rate formula, substituting g, the growth rate, for i, the interest rate:

$$\text{FV}_n = \text{PV} \times (1 + g)^n \tag{5.6}$$

where:

FV_n = future value of the economic factor, such as sales or population, at the end of period n
PV = original amount or present value of economic factor
g = growth rate per period
n = number of periods: a period may be a year but can also be a quarter, month, week, day, minute, or any other length of time

Suppose, for example, that because of an advertising campaign, a firm's sales increased from \$20 million in 2007 to more than \$35 million three years later. What has been the average annual growth rate in sales? Here, the future value is \$35 million, the present value is \$20 million, and n is 3 since we are interested in the annual growth rate over three years.

[8]Solve Equation 5.4 for i: $\text{PV} = \text{FV}_n/(1+i)^n$, where PV = \$1, FV = \$2, and $n = 4$.

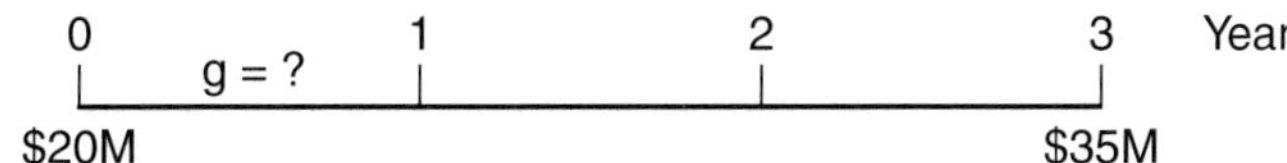

Applying Equation 5.6 and solving for the growth factor (g) yields:

$$\begin{aligned} FV_3 &= PV \times (1+g)^3 \\ 35 &= 20 \times (1+g)^3 \\ 1.75 &= (1+g)^3 \\ g &= (1.75)^{1/3} - 1 \\ &= 1.2051 - 1 \\ &= 0.2051, \text{ or } 20.51\% \end{aligned}$$

Thus, sales grew nearly 21 percent per year. More precisely, we could say that sales grew at a **compound annual growth rate (CAGR)** of nearly 21 percent. If we use our financial calculator, we find the same answer:

compound annual growth rate (CAGR)
the average annual growth rate over a specified period of time

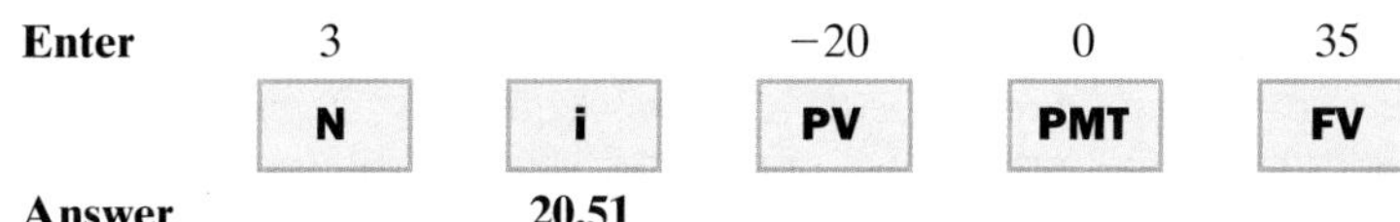

LEARNING BY DOING APPLICATION 5.5

The Growth Rate of the World's Population

Problem: Hannah, an industrial relations major, is writing a term paper and needs an estimate of how fast the world population is growing. In her almanac, she finds that the world's population was an estimated 6 billion people in 2000. The United Nations estimates that the population will reach 9 billion people in 2054. Calculate the annual population growth rate implied by these numbers. At that growth rate, what will be the world's population in 2010?

Approach: We first find the annual rate of growth through 2054 by applying Equation 5.6 for the 54-year period 2054–2000. For the purpose of this calculation, we can use the estimated population of 6 billion people in 2000 as the present value, the estimated future population of 9 million people as the future value, and 54 years as the number of compounding periods (n). We want to solve for g, which is the annual compound growth rate over the 54-year period. We can then plug the 54-year population growth rate in Equation 5.6 and solve for the world's population in 2010 (FV_{10}). Alternatively, we can get the answer by using a financial calculator.

Solution:

Using Equation 5.6, we find the growth rate as follows:

$$\begin{aligned} FV_n &= PV \times (1+g)^n \\ 9 &= 6 \times (1+g)^{54} \\ 1.5 &= (1+g)^{54} \\ (1.5)^{1/54} &= 1 + g \\ g &= (1.5)^{1/54} - 1 \\ &= 1.0075 - 1 \\ &= 0.0075, \text{ or } 0.75\% \end{aligned}$$

The world's population in 2010 is therefore estimated to be:

$$\begin{aligned} FV_{10} &= 6 \times (1 + 0.0075)^{10} \\ &= 6 \times 1.0776 \\ &= 6.47 \text{ billion people} \end{aligned}$$

(continued)

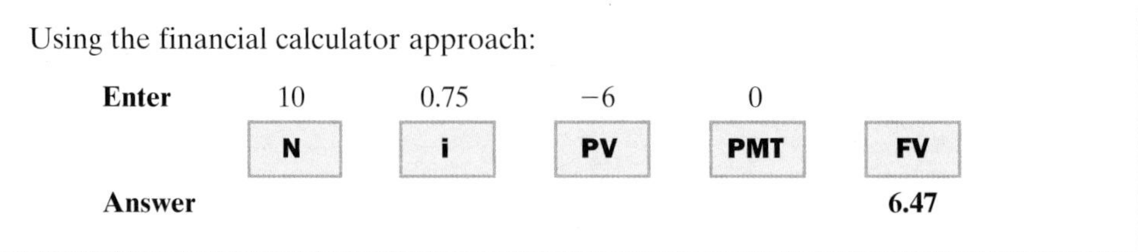

Using the financial calculator approach:

Enter	10	0.75	−6	0	
	N	i	PV	PMT	FV
Answer					**6.47**

LEARNING BY DOING APPLICATION 5.6

Calculating Projected Earnings

Problem: IBM's current earnings are $3.19 million. Wall Street analysts expect earnings to increase by 6 percent per year over the next three years. Using your financial calculator, determine what IBM's earnings should be in three years.

Approach: This problem involves the growth rate (g) of IBM's earnings. We already know the value of g, which is 6 percent, and we need to find the future value. Since the general compound growth rate formula, Equation 5.6, is the same as Equation 5.1, the future value formula, we can use the same calculator procedure we used earlier to find the future value. We enter the data on the calculator keys as shown below, using the growth rate value for the interest rate. Then we solve for the future value:

Solution:

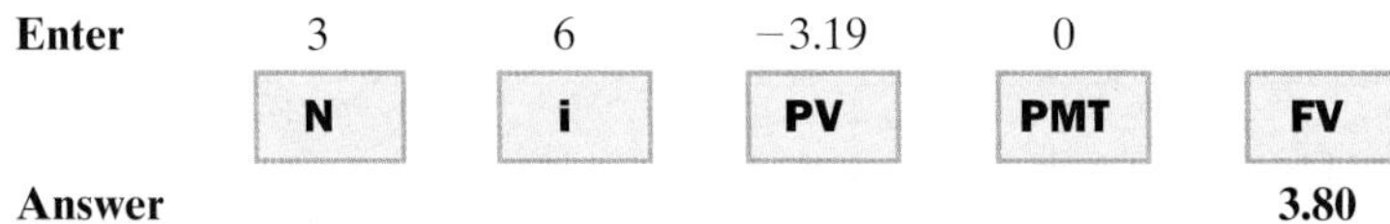

Enter	3	6	−3.19	0	
	N	i	PV	PMT	FV
Answer					**3.80**

Note that we enter $3.19 million as a negative number. This is because one cash flow must be negative—both cash flows cannot have the same sign. It makes no difference which cash flow number is negative and which is positive.

Concluding Comments

This chapter has introduced the basic principles of present value and future value. The table at the end of the chapter summarizes the key equations developed in the chapter. The basic equations for present value (Equation 5.4) and future value (Equation 5.1) are two of the most fundamental relations in finance and will be applied throughout the balance of the textbook.

Before You Go On

1. What is the difference between the interest rate (i) and the growth rate (g) in the future value equation?

Summary of Learning Objectives

1. Explain what the time value of money is and why it is so important in the field of finance.

The idea that money has a time value is one of the most fundamental concepts in the field of finance. The concept is based on the idea that most people prefer to have goods today rather than wait to have similar goods in the future. Since money buys goods, they would rather have money today than in the future. Thus, *a dollar today is worth more than a dollar received in the future.* Another way of viewing the time value of money is that your money is worth more today than at some point in the future because, if you had the money now, you could invest it and earn interest. Thus, the time value of money is the opportunity cost of forgoing consumption today.

Applications of the time value of money focus on the trade-off between current dollars and dollars received at some future date. This is an important element in financial decisions because most investment decisions require the comparison of cash invested today with the value of expected future cash inflows. Investment opportunities are undertaken only when the value of future cash inflows exceeds the cost of the investment (the initial cash outflow).

2. Explain the concept of future value, including the meaning of *principal amount, simple interest,* and *compound interest,* and be able to use the future value formula to make business decisions.

The future value is the sum to which an investment will grow after earning interest. The principal amount is the amount of the investment. Simple interest is the interest paid on the original investment; the amount of money earned on simple interest remains constant from period to period. Compound interest includes not only simple interest, but also interest earned on the reinvestment of previously earned interest, the so-called interest on interest. For future value calculations, the higher the interest rate, the faster the investment will grow. The application of the future value formula in business decisions is presented in Section 5.4.

3. Explain the concept of present value and how it relates to future value, and be able to use the present value formula to make business decisions.

The present value is the value today of a future cash flow. Computing the present value involves discounting future cash flows back to the present at an appropriate discount rate. The process of discounting cash flows adjusts the cash flows for the time value of money. Computationally, the present value factor is the reciprocal of the future value factor, or $1/(1 + i)$. The computation and application of the present value formula in business decisions is presented in Section 5.3.

4. Discuss why the concept of compounding is not restricted to money, and be able to use the future value formula to calculate growth rates.

Any number of changes that are observed over time in the physical and social sciences follow a compound growth rate pattern. The future value formula can be used in calculating these growth rates.

Summary of Key Equations

Equation	Description	Formula
5.1	Future value of an *n*-period investment with annual compounding	$FV_n = PV \times (1 + i)^n$
5.2	Future value with compounding more than annually	$FV_n = PV \times (1 + i/m)^{m \times n}$
5.3	Future value with continuous compounding	$FV_\infty = PV \times e^{i \times n}$
5.4	Present value	$PV = \frac{FV_n}{(1 + i)^n}$
5.5	Rule of 72	$TDM = \frac{72}{i}$
5.6	Future value with general growth rate	$FV_n = PV \times (1 + g)^n$

Self-Study Problems

5.1 Amit Patel is planning to invest $10,000 in a bank certificate of deposit (CD) for five years. The CD will pay interest of 9 percent. What is the future value of Amit's investment?

5.2 Megan Gaumer expects to need $50,000 as a down payment on a house in six years. How much does she need to invest today in an account paying 7.25 percent?

5.3 Kelly Martin has $10,000 that she can deposit into a savings account for five years. Bank A pays compounds interest annually, Bank B twice a year, and Bank C quarterly. Each bank has a stated interest rate of 4 percent. What amount would Kelly have at the end of the fifth year if she left all the interest paid on the deposit in each bank?

5.4 You have an opportunity to invest $2,500 today and receive $3,000 in three years. What will be the return on your investment?

5.5 Emily Smith deposits $1,200 in her bank today. If the bank pays 4 percent simple interest, how much money will she have at the end of five years? What if the bank pays compound interest? How much of the earnings will be interest on interest?

Solutions to Self-Study Problems

5.1 Present value of Amit's investment = PV = $10,000
Interest rate on CD = i = 9%
Number of years = n = 5

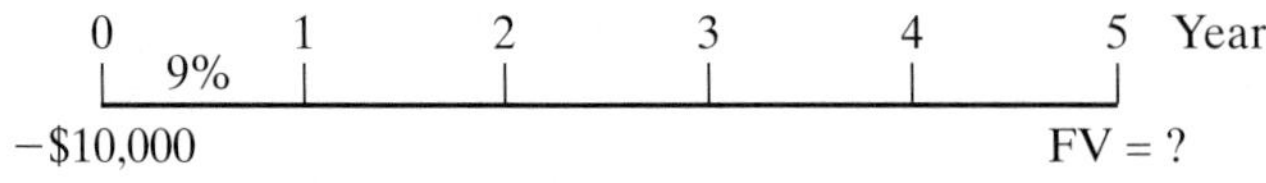

$$\begin{aligned} FV_n &= PV \times (1 + i)^n \\ &= \$10{,}000 \times (1 + 0.09)^5 \\ &= \$15{,}386.24 \end{aligned}$$

5.2 Amount Megan will need in six years = FV_6 = $50,000
Number of years = n = 6
Interest rate on investment = i = 7.25%
Amount needed to be invested now = PV = ?

0 — 1 — 2 — 3 — 4 — 5 — 6 Year (7.25%)
PV = ? FV = $50,000

$$\begin{aligned} PV &= \frac{FV_n}{(1 + i)^n} \\ &= \frac{\$50{,}000}{(1 + 0.0725)^6} \\ &= \$32{,}853.84 \end{aligned}$$

5.3 Present value of Kelly's deposit = PV = $10,000
Number of years = n = 5
Interest rate = i = 4%
Compound period (m):

A = 1
B = 2
C = 4

Amount at the end of five years = FV_5 = ?

0 — 1 — 2 — 3 — 4 — 5 Year (4%)
−$10,000 FV = ?

Bank A: $FV_n = PV \times (1 + i/m)^{m \times n}$
$FV_5 = 10{,}000 \times (1 + 0.04/1)^{1 \times 5}$
$FV_5 = \$12{,}166.53$

Bank B: $FV_5 = 10{,}000 \times (1 + 0.04/2)^{2 \times 5}$
$FV_5 = \$12{,}189.94$

Bank C: $FV_5 = 10{,}000\ (1 + 0.04/4)^{4 \times 5}$
$FV_5 = \$12{,}201.90$

5.4 Your investment today = PV = $2,500
Amount to be received = FV_3 = $3,000
Time of investment = n = 3
Return on the investment = i = ?

$FV_n = PV \times (1 + i)^n$
$\$3{,}000 = \$2{,}500 \times (1 + i)^3$
$\frac{\$3{,}000}{\$2{,}500} = (1 + i)^3$
$i = 6.27\%$

5.5 Emily's deposit today = PV = \$1,200
Interest rate = i = 4%
Number of years = n = 5
Amount to be received back = FV_5 = ?

a. Future value with simple interest
Simple interest per year = \$1,200 × 0.04 = \$48.00
Simple interest for 5 years = \$48 × 5 = \$240.00
FV_5 = \$1,200 + \$240 = \$1,440.00

b. Future value with compound interest
$FV_5 = \$1{,}200 \times (1 + 0.04)^5$
FV_5 = \$1,459.98
Simple interest = (\$1,440 − \$1,200) = \$240
Interest on interest = \$1,459.98 − \$1,200 − \$240 = \$19.98

Critical Thinking Questions

5.1 Explain the phrase "a dollar today is worth more than a dollar tomorrow."

5.2 Explain the importance of a time line.

5.3 Differentiate future value from present value.

5.4 What are the two factors to be considered in time value of money?

5.5 Differentiate between compounding and discounting.

5.6 Explain how compound interest differs from simple interest.

5.7 If you were given a choice of investing in an account that paid quarterly interest and one that paid monthly interest, which one should you choose and why?

5.8 Growth rates are exponential over time. Explain.

5.9 What is the Rule of 72?

5.10 You are planning to take a spring break trip to Cancun your senior year. The trip is exactly two years away, but you want to be prepared and have enough money when the time comes. Explain how you would determine the amount of money you will have to save in order to pay for the trip.

Questions and Problems

BASIC

5.1 Future value: Chuck Tomkovick is planning to invest \$25,000 today in a mutual fund that will provide a return of 8 percent each year. What will be the value of the investment in 10 years?

5.2 Future value: Ted Rogers is investing \$7,500 in a bank CD that pays a 6 percent annual interest. How much will the CD be worth at the end of five years?

5.3 Future value: Your aunt is planning to invest in a bank deposit that will pay 7.5 percent interest semiannually. If she has \$5,000 to invest, how much will she have at the end of four years?

5.4 Future value: Kate Eden received a graduation present of \$2,000 that she is planning on investing in a mutual fund that earns 8.5 percent each year. How much money can she collect in three years?

5.5 Future value: Your bank pays 5 percent interest semiannually on your savings account. You don't expect the current balance of \$2,700 to change over the next four years. How much money can you expect to have at the end of this period?

5.6 Future value: Your birthday is coming up and instead of any presents, your parents promised to give you $1,000 in cash. Since you have a part-time job and, thus, don't need the cash immediately, you decide to invest the money in a bank CD that pays 5.2 percent quarterly for the next two years. How much money can you expect to gain in this period of time?

5.7 Multiple compounding periods: Find the future value of an investment of $100,000 made today for five years and paying 8.75 percent for the following compounding periods:

a. Quarterly
b. Monthly
c. Daily
d. Continuous

5.8 Growth rates: Matt Murton, an outfielder for the Chicago Cubs, is expected to hit 25 home runs in 2008. If his home-run-hitting ability is expected to grow by 12 percent every year for the next five years, how many home runs is he expected to hit in 2013?

5.9 Present value: Roy Gross is considering an investment that pays 7.6 percent. How much will he have to invest today so that the investment will be worth $25,000 in six years?

5.10 Present value: Maria Addai has been offered a future payment of $750 two years from now. If her opportunity cost is 6.5 percent compounded annually, what should she pay for this investment today?

5.11 Present value: You brother has asked you for a loan and has promised to pay back $7,750 at the end of three years. If you normally invest to earn 6 percent, how much will you be willing to lend to your brother?

5.12 Present value: Tracy Chapman is saving to buy a house in five years. She plans to put 20 percent down at that time, and she believes that she will need $35,000 for the down payment. If Tracy can invest in a fund that pays 9.25 percent annually, how much will she need to invest today?

5.13 Present value: You want to buy some deep-discount bonds that have a value of $1,000 at the end of seven years. The bonds are said to pay 4.5 percent interest. How much should you pay for them today?

5.14 Present value: Elizabeth Sweeney wants to accumulate $12,000 by the end of 12 years. If the interest rate is 7 percent, how much will she have to invest today to achieve her goal?

5.15 Interest rate: You are in desperate need of cash and turn to your uncle, who has offered to lend you some money. You decide to borrow $1,300 and agree to pay back $1,500 in two years. Alternatively, you could borrow from your bank that is charging 6.5 percent interest. Should you go with your uncle or the bank?

5.16 Time to attain goal: You invest $150 in a mutual fund today that pays 9 percent interest. How long will it take to double your money?

INTERMEDIATE

5.17 Growth rate: Your finance textbook sold 53,250 copies in its first year. The publishing company expects the sales to grow at a rate of 20 percent for the next three years and by 10 percent in the fourth year. Calculate the total number of copies that the publisher expects to sell in years 3 and 4. Draw a time line to show the sales level for each of the next four years.

5.18 Growth rate: CelebNav, Inc., had sales last year of $700,000, and the analysts are predicting a good year for the start-up, with sales growing 20 percent a year for the next three years. After that, the sales should grow 11 percent per year for two years, at which time the owners are planning to sell the company. What are the projected sales for the last year of the company's operation?

5.19 Growth rate: You decide to take advantage of the current online dating craze and start your own Web site. You know that you have 450 people who will sign up immediately and, through a careful marketing research and analysis, determine that membership can grow by 27 percent in the first two years, 22 percent in year 3, and 18 percent in year 4. How many members do you expect to have at the end of four years?

5.20 Multiple compounding periods: Find the future value of an investment of $2,500 made today for the following rates and periods:

a. 6.25 percent compounded semiannually for 12 years
b. 7.63 percent compounded quarterly for 6 years
c. 8.9 percent compounded monthly for 10 years
d. 10 percent compounded daily for 3 years
e. 8 percent compounded continuously for 2 years

5.21 Growth rates: Xenix Corp had sales of $353,866 in 2008. If it expects its sales to be at $476,450 in three years, what is the rate at which the company's sales are expected to grow?

5.22 Growth rate: Infosys Technologies, Inc., an Indian technology company, reported a net income of $419 million this year. Analysts expect the company's earnings to be $1.468 billion in five years. What is the company's earnings expected growth rate?

5.23 Time to attain goal: Zephyr Sales Company has currently reported sales of $1.125 million. If the company expects its sales to grow at 6.5 percent annually, how long will it be before the company can double its sales? Use a financial calculator to solve this problem.

5.24 Time to attain goal: You are able to deposit $850 in a bank CD today, and you will withdraw the money only once the balance is $1,000. If the bank pays 5 percent interest, how long will it take you to attain your goal?

5.25 Time to attain goal: Neon Lights Company is a private company with sales of $1.3 million a year. They want to go public but have to wait until the sales reach $2 million. Providing that they are expected to grow at a steady 12 percent annually, when is the earliest that Neon Lights can start selling their shares?

5.26 Present value: Caroline Weslin needs to decide whether to accept a bonus of $1,900 today or wait two years and receive $2,100 then. She can invest at 6 percent. What should she do?

5.27 Multiple compounding periods: Find the present value of $3,500 under each of the following rates and periods:

a. 8.9 percent compounded monthly for five years.
b. 6.6 percent compounded quarterly for eight years.
c. 4.3 percent compounded daily for four years.
d. 5.7 percent compounded continuously for three years.

5.28 Multiple compounding periods: Samantha is looking to invest some money, so she can collect $5,500 at the end of three years. Which investment should she make given the following choices:

a. 4.2 percent compounded daily
b. 4.9 percent compounded monthly
c. 5.2 percent compounded quarterly
d. 5.4 percent compounded annually

ADVANCED

5.29 You have $2,500 you want to invest in your classmate's start-up business. You believe the business idea to be great and hope to get $3,700 back at the end of three years. If all goes according to plan, what will be your return on investment?

5.30 Patrick Seeley has $2,400 that he is looking to invest. His brother approached him with an investment opportunity that could double his money in four years. What interest rate would the investment have to yield in order for Patrick's brother to deliver on his promise?

5.31 You have $12,000 in cash. You can deposit it today in a mutual fund earning 8.2 percent semiannually, or you can wait, enjoy some of it, and invest $11,000 in your brother's business in two years. Your brother is promising you a return of at least 10 percent on your investment. Whichever alternative you choose, you will need to cash in at the end of 10 years. Assume your brother is trustworthy and both investments carry the same risk. Which one will you choose? **EXCEL®**

5.32 When you were born your parents set up a bank account in your name with an initial investment of $5,000. You are turning 21 in a few days and will have access to all your funds. The account was earning 7.3 percent for the first seven years, but then the rates went down to 5.5 percent for six years. The economy was doing well at the end of the 1990s, and your account was earning 8.2 percent for three years in a row. Unfortunately, the next two years you earned only 4.6 percent. Finally, as the economy recovered, your return jumped to 7.6 percent for the last three years. **EXCEL®**

a. How much money was in your account before the rates went down drastically (end of year 16)?
b. How much money is in your account now (end of year 21)?
c. What would be the balance now if your parents made another deposit of $1,200 at the end of year 7?

5.33 Cedric Benson, a top-five draft pick of the Chicago Bears, and his agent are evaluating three contract options. Each option offers a signing bonus and a series of payments over the **EXCEL®**

life of the contract. Benson uses a 10.25 percent rate of return to evaluate the contracts. Given the cash flows for each option, which one should he choose?

Year	Cash Flow Type	Option A	Option B	Option C
0	Signing Bonus	$3,100,000	$4,000,000	$4,250,000
1	Annual Salary	$ 650,000	$ 825,000	$ 550,000
2	Annual Salary	$ 715,000	$ 850,000	$ 625,000
3	Annual Salary	$ 822,250	$ 925,000	$ 800,000
4	Annual Salary	$ 975,000	$1,250,000	$ 900,000
5	Annual Salary	$1,100,000		$1,000,000
6	Annual Salary	$1,250,000		

EXCEL®

5.34 Surmec, Inc., reported earnings of $2.1 million last year. The company's primary business line is manufacturing of nuts and bolts. Since this is a mature industry, the analysts are certain that the sales will grow at a steady rate of 7 percent a year for as far as they can tell. The company reports net income that represents 23 percent of sales. The management would like to buy a new fleet of trucks but can only do so once the profit reaches $620,000 a year. At the end of what year will Surmec be able to buy the new fleet of trucks? What will the sales and profit be that year?

EXCEL®

5.35 You are graduating in two years, and you start thinking about your future. You know that you will want to buy a house five years after you graduate and that you will want to put down $60,000. As of right now, you have $8,000 in your savings account. You are also fairly certain that once you graduate, you can work in the family business and earn $32,000 a year, with a 5 percent raise every year. You plan to live with your parents for the first two years after graduation, which will enable you to minimize your expenses and put away $10,000 each year. The next three years, you will have to live on your own as your younger sister will be graduating from college and has already announced her plan to move back into the family house. Thus, you will be able to save only 13 percent of your annual salary. Assume that you will be able to invest savings from your salary at 7.2 percent. At what interest rate will you need to invest the current savings account balance in order to achieve your goal? *Hint:* Draw a time line that shows all the cash flows for years 0 through 7. Remember, you want to buy a house seven years from now and your first salary will be in year 3.

Sample Test Problems

5.1 Santiago Hernandez is planning to invest $25,000 in a money market account for two years. The account pays interest of 5.75 percent compounded on a monthly basis. How much will Santiago Hernandez have at the end of two years?

5.2 Michael Carter is expecting an inheritance of $1.25 million in four years. If he had the money today, he could earn interest at an annual rate of 7.35 percent. What is the present value of this inheritance?

5.3 What is the future value of an investment of $3,000 for three years compounded at the following rates and frequencies:

a. 8.75 percent compounded monthly
b. 8.625 percent compounded daily
c. 8.5 percent compounded continuously

5.4 Twenty-five years ago, Amanda Cortez invested $10,000 in an account paying an annual interest rate of 5.75 percent. What is the value of the investment today? What is the interest on interest earned on this investment?

5.5 You just bought a corporate bond at $863.75 today. In five years the bond will mature and you will receive $1,000. What is the rate of return on this bond?

DISCOUNTED CASH FLOWS AND VALUATION

CHAPTER

6

Landov LLC

LEARNING OBJECTIVES

1. Explain why cash flows occurring at different times must be adjusted to reflect their value as of a common date before they can be compared, and be able to compute the present value and future value for multiple cash flows.
2. Describe how to calculate the present value of an ordinary annuity and how an ordinary annuity differs from an annuity due.
3. Explain what a perpetuity is and how it is used in business, and be able to calculate the value of a perpetuity.
4. Discuss growing annuities and perpetuities, as well as their application in business, and be able to calculate their value.
5. Discuss why the effective annual interest rate (EAR) is the appropriate way to annualize interest rates, and be able to calculate EAR.

Guidant Corporation ended one of the biggest takeover battles in the history of the medical-device industry when it announced that it had turned down a takeover bid from Johnson & Johnson (J & J) in favor of an offer from Boston Scientific. The acquisition price for Guidant, a top company in the market for implantable heart devices, was $27.2 billion. The deal was completed in April 2006.

Guidant's decision was remarkable in that it had agreed to merge with J & J as far back as December 2004 at an offer price of $25.4 billion. But then several costly product recalls and liability trials began to surface, which analysts believed could cost Guidant more than $2 billion in damages. As a result, J & J reduced its offer by nearly $4 billion. Soon after, Boston Scientific mounted a surprise takeover effort. After that, the two bidders made a series of offers interspersed with behind-the-scenes attacks on one another.

J & J appeared to be the winner when, in January 2006, its negotiators persuaded Guidant to back out of a previously announced merger with Boston Scientific at an offering price of $24.9 billion and to accept J & J's lower offer of $24.2 billion. Boston Scientific responded by raising its offer to $27.2 billion, and J & J withdrew.

In the excitement of a bidding war like this one, it is important not to lose sight of the central question: What is the firm really worth? A company invests in an asset—a business or a capital project—because it expects the asset to be worth more than it costs. That's how value is created. The value of a business is the sum of its discounted future cash flows. Thus, the task for both J & J and Boston Scientific was to estimate the value of the future cash flows that Guidant could generate under there ownership. This chapter, which discusses the discounting of future cash flows, provides the tools that help answer the key question in the Guidant bidding war: What is the firm worth?

CHAPTER PREVIEW

In the previous chapter, we introduced the concept of the time value of money: Dollars today are more valuable than dollars to be received in the future. Starting with that concept, we developed the basics of simple interest, compound interest, and future value calculations. We then went on to discuss present value and discounted cash flow analysis. This was all done in the context of a single cash flow.

In this chapter, we consider the value of multiple cash flows. Most business decisions, after all, involve cash flows over time. For example, if Mrs. Smith's, an Atlanta-based firm that makes frozen pies, wants to consider adding a production line, the decision will require an analysis of the project's expected cash flows over a number of periods. Initially, there will be large cash outlays to build and get the new line operational. Thereafter, the project should produce cash inflows for many years. Because the cash flows occur over time, the analysis must consider the time value of money, discounting each of the cash flows by using the present value formula.

We begin the chapter by describing calculations of future and present values for multiple cash flows. We then examine some situations in which future cash flows are level over time: These involve annuities, in which the cash flow stream goes on for a finite period, and perpetuities, in which the stream goes on forever. Next, we examine annuities and perpetuities in which the cash flows grow at a constant rate over time. These cash flows resemble common cash flow patterns encountered in business. Finally, we describe the effective annual interest rate and compare it with the annual percentage rate (APR), which is a rate that is used to describe the interest rate in consumer loans.

6.1 Multiple Cash Flows

We begin our discussion of the time value of multiple cash flows by calculating the future value and then the present value of multiple cash flows. These calculations, as you will see, are nothing more than applications of the techniques you learned in Chapter 5.

Future Value of Multiple Cash Flows

In Chapter 5, we worked through several examples that involved the future value of a lump sum of money invested in a savings account that paid 10 percent interest per year. But suppose you are investing more than one lump sum. Let's say you put $1,000 in your bank savings account today and another $1,000 a year from now. If the bank continues to pay 10 percent interest per year, how much money will you have at the end of two years?

To solve this future value problem, we can use Equation 5.1: $\text{FV}_n = \text{PV} \times (1 + i)^n$. First, however, we construct a time line so that we can see the magnitude and timing of the cash flows. As Exhibit 6.1 shows, there are two cash flows into the savings plan. The first cash flow is invested for two years and compounds to a value that is computed as follows:

$$\begin{aligned}\text{FV}_2 &= \text{PV} \times (1 + i)^2 \\ &= \$1{,}000 \times (1 + 0.10)^2 \\ &= \$1{,}000 \times 1.21 \\ &= \$1{,}210\end{aligned}$$

The second cash flow earns simple interest for a single period only and grows to:

$$\begin{aligned}\text{FV}_1 &= \text{PV} \times (1 + i) \\ &= \$1{,}000 \times (1 + 0.10) \\ &= \$1{,}000 \times 1.10 \\ &= \$1{,}100\end{aligned}$$

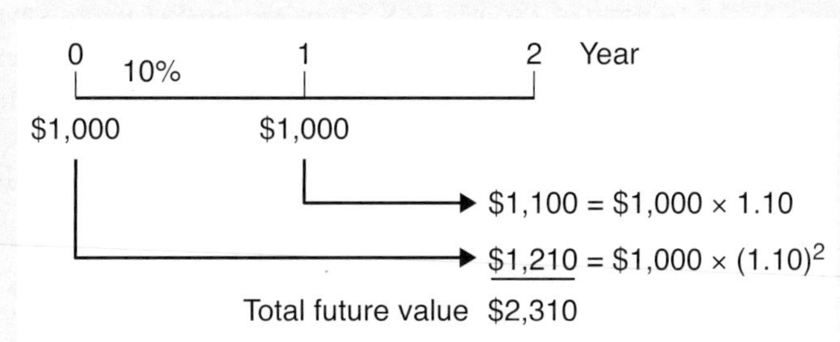

Exhibit 6.1
Future Value of Two Cash Flows
This exhibit shows a time line for two cash flows invested in a savings account that pays 10 percent interest annually. The total amount in the savings account after two years is $2,310, which is the sum of the future values of the two cash flows.

As Exhibit 6.1 shows, the total amount of money in the savings account after two years is the sum of these two amounts, which is $2,310 ($1,100 + $1,210).

Now suppose that you expand your investment horizon to three years and invest $1,000 today, $1,000 a year from now, and $1,000 at the end of two years. How much money will you have at the end of three years? First, we draw a time line to be sure that we have correctly identified the time period for each cash flow. This is shown in Exhibit 6.2. Then we compute the future value of each of the individual cash flows using Equation 5.1. Finally, we add up the future values. The total future value is $3,641. The calculations are as follows:

$$
\begin{aligned}
FV_1 &= PV \times (1 + i) &&= \$1{,}000 \times (1 + 0.10) &&= \$1{,}000 \times 1.100 = \$1{,}100 \\
FV_2 &= PV \times (1 + i)^2 &&= \$1{,}000 \times (1 + 0.10)^2 &&= \$1{,}000 \times 1.210 = \$1{,}210 \\
FV_3 &= PV \times (1 + i)^3 &&= \$1{,}000 \times (1 + 0.10)^3 &&= \$1{,}000 \times 1.331 = \underline{\$1{,}331} \\
& && &&\text{Total future value} \quad \$3{,}641
\end{aligned}
$$

To summarize, solving future value problems with multiple cash flows involves a simple process. First, draw a time line to make sure that each cash flow is placed in the correct time period. Second, calculate the future value of each cash flow for its time period. Third, add up the future values. It's that simple!

Let's use this process to solve a practical problem. Suppose you want to buy a condominium in three years and estimate that you will need $20,000 for a down payment.

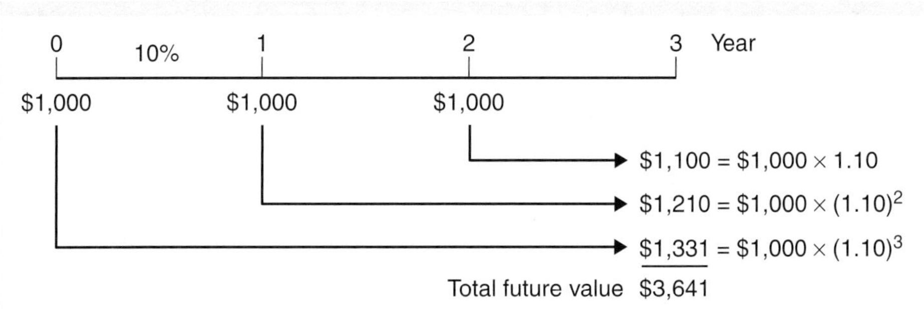

Exhibit 6.2
Future Value of Three Cash Flows
The exhibit shows a time line for an investment program with a three-year horizon. The value of the investment at the end of three years is $3,641, the sum of the future values of the three separate cash flows.

If the interest rate you can earn at the bank is 8 percent and you can save \$3,000 now, \$4,000 at the end of the first year, and \$5,000 at the end of the second year, how much money will you have to come up with at the end of the third year to have a \$20,000 down payment?

The time line for the future value calculation in this problem looks like this:

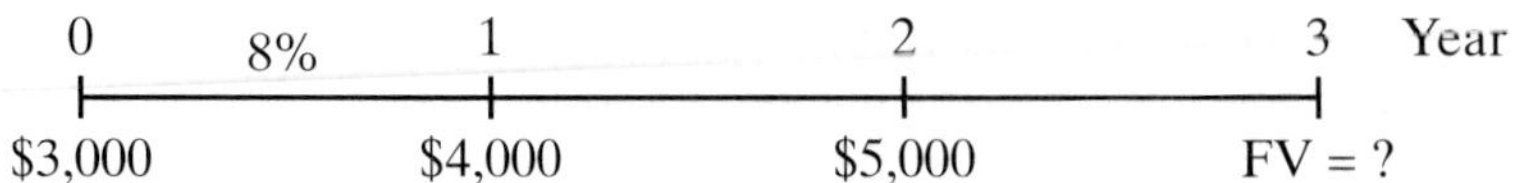

To solve the problem, we need to calculate the future value for each of the expected cash flows, add up these values, and find the difference between this amount and the \$20,000 needed for the down payment. Using Equation 5.1, we find that the future values of the cash flows at the end of the third year are:

$$
\begin{aligned}
FV_1 &= PV \times (1 + i) &&= \$5{,}000 \times 1.08 &&= \$5{,}000 \times 1.0800 = \$\ 5{,}400.00 \\
FV_2 &= PV \times (1 + i)^2 &&= \$4{,}000 \times (1.08)^2 &&= \$4{,}000 \times 1.1664 = \$\ 4{,}665.60 \\
FV_3 &= PV \times (1 + i)^3 &&= \$3{,}000 \times (1.08)^3 &&= \$3{,}000 \times 1.2597 = \underline{\$\ 3{,}779.14} \\
& && &&\text{Total future value} \quad \$13{,}844.74
\end{aligned}
$$

At the end of the third year, you will have \$13,844.74, so you will need an additional \$6,155.26 (\$20,000 − \$13,844.74).

CALCULATOR TIP: CALCULATING THE FUTURE VALUE OF MULTIPLE CASH FLOWS

To calculate the future value of multiple cash flows with a financial calculator, we can use exactly the same process we used in Chapter 5. We simply calculate the future value of each of the individual cash flows, write down each computed future value, and add them up.

Alternatively, we can generally use a shortcut. More than likely, your financial calculator has a memory where you can store numbers; refer to your calculator's instruction manual for the keys to use. For the preceding example, you would use your financial calculator's memory (M) as follows: Calculate the future value of the first number, then store the value in the memory (M1); compute the second value, and store it in the memory (M2); compute the third value, and store it in the memory (M3). Finally, retrieve the three numbers from the memory and add them up (M1 + M2 + M3). The advantage of using the calculator's memory is that you eliminate two potential sources of error: (1) writing down a number incorrectly and (2) making a mistake when adding up the numbers.

LEARNING BY DOING APPLICATION 6.1

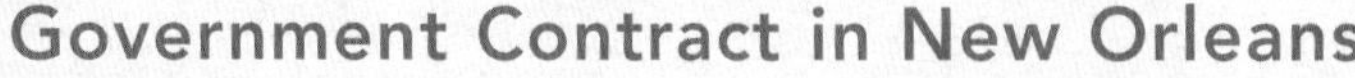

Government Contract in New Orleans

Problem: The firm you work for is considering bidding on a government contract to rebuild a power station in New Orleans that was damaged during Hurricane Katrina in 2005. The two-year contract will pay the firm \$9,000 at the end of the second year. The firm's estimator believes that the project will require an initial expenditure of \$5,000 for equipment. The expenses for years 1 and 2 are estimated at \$1,000 per year. Because the cash inflow of \$9,000 at the end of the contract exceeds the total cash outflows of \$7,000 (\$5,000 + \$1,000 + \$1,000), the estimator believes that the firm should accept the job. Drawing on your knowledge of finance from college, you point out that the estimator's decision process ignores the time value of money. Not fully understanding what you mean, the estimator asks you how the time value of money should be incorporated into the decision process. Assume that the appropriate interest rate is 18 percent.

Approach: First, construct the time line for the costs in this problem, as shown here:

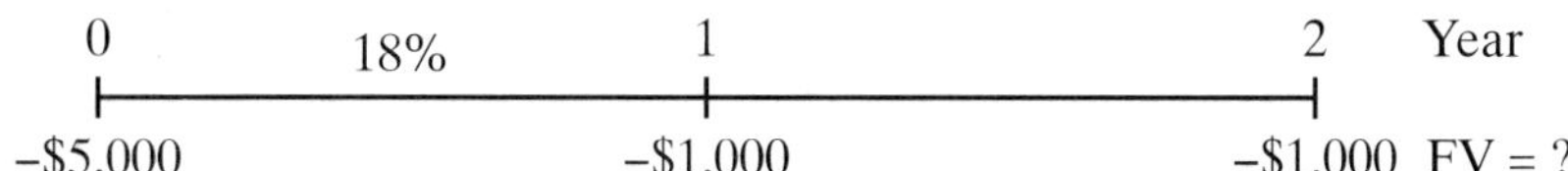

Second, use Equation 5.1 to convert all of the cash outflows into period-two dollars. This will make all the cash flows comparable because they will,represent the same amount of purchasing power—period-two dollars. Finally, compare the sum of the cash outflows, stated in period-two dollars, to the $9,000 that you would receive under the contract.

Solution:

$$
\begin{aligned}
FV_2 &= PV \times (1 + i)^2 = -\$5{,}000 \times (1.18)^2 = -\$5{,}000 \times 1.3924 = -\$6{,}962 \\
FV_1 &= PV \times (1 + i) = -\$1{,}000 \times 1.18 = -\$1{,}000 \times 1.1800 = -\$1{,}180 \\
FV_0 &= PV \times (1 + i)^0 = -\$1{,}000 \times (1.18)^0 = -\$1{,}000 \times 1.0000 = \underline{-\$1{,}000} \\
& \qquad\qquad\qquad\qquad \text{Total net future value} \quad -\$9{,}142
\end{aligned}
$$

Once the future value calculations have been made, the decision is self-evident. With all the dollars stated as period-two dollars, the cash inflow (benefits) is $9,000 and the cash outflow (costs) is $9,142. Thus, the costs exceed the benefits, and the firm's management should reject the contract. If management accepts the contract, the value of the firm will be decreased.

Present Value of Multiple Cash Flows

You can find plenty of problems to work out at StudyFinance.com, www.studyfinance.com/lectures/timevalue/index.mv.

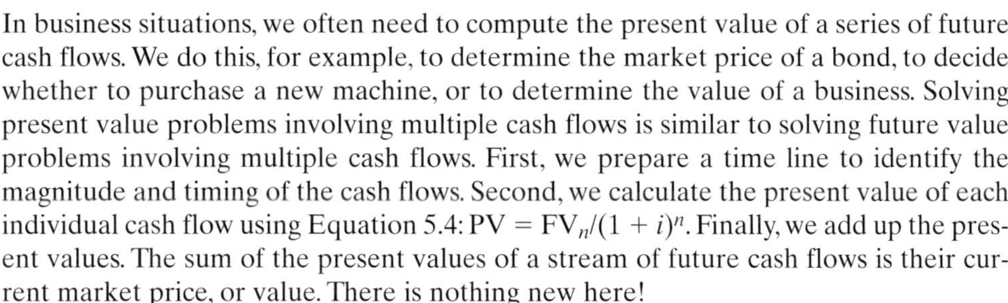

In business situations, we often need to compute the present value of a series of future cash flows. We do this, for example, to determine the market price of a bond, to decide whether to purchase a new machine, or to determine the value of a business. Solving present value problems involving multiple cash flows is similar to solving future value problems involving multiple cash flows. First, we prepare a time line to identify the magnitude and timing of the cash flows. Second, we calculate the present value of each individual cash flow using Equation 5.4: $PV = FV_n/(1 + i)^n$. Finally, we add up the present values. The sum of the present values of a stream of future cash flows is their current market price, or value. There is nothing new here!

USING THE PRESENT VALUE EQUATION

Next, we will work through some examples to see how we can use Equation 5.4 to find the present value of multiple cash flows. Suppose that your best friend needs cash and offers to pay you $1,000 at the end of each of the next three years if you will give him $3,000 cash today. You realize, of course, that because of the time value of money, the cash flows he has promised to pay are worth less than $3,000. If the interest rate on similar loans is 7 percent, how much should you pay for the cash flows your friend is offering?

To solve the problem, we first construct a time line, as shown in Exhibit 6.3. Then, using Equation 5.4, we calculate the present value for each of the three cash flows, as follows:

$$
\begin{aligned}
PV &= FV_1 \times 1/(1 + i) = FV_1 \times 1/1.07 = \$1{,}000 \times 0.9346 = \$\ 934.58 \\
PV &= FV_2 \times 1/(1 + i)^2 = FV_2 \times 1/(1.07)^2 = \$1{,}000 \times 0.8734 = \$\ 873.44 \\
PV &= FV_3 \times 1/(1 + i)^3 = FV_3 \times 1/(1.07)^3 = \$1{,}000 \times 0.8163 = \underline{\$\ 816.30} \\
& \qquad\qquad\qquad\qquad \text{Total present value} \quad \$2{,}624.32
\end{aligned}
$$

If you view this transaction from a purely business perspective, you should not give your friend more than $2,624.32, which is the sum of the individual discounted cash flows.

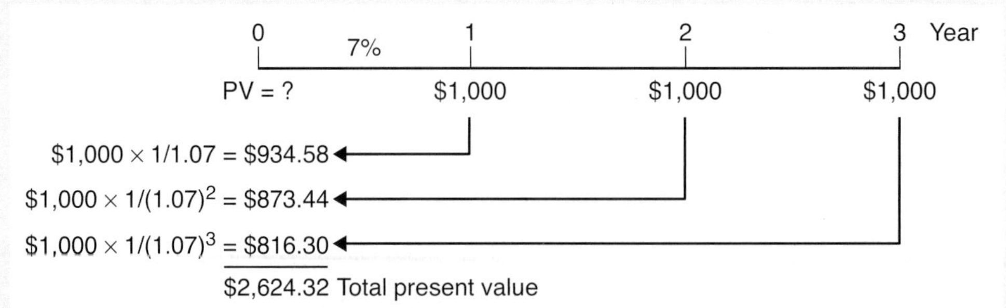

Exhibit 6.3
Present Value of Three Cash Flows
The exhibit shows the time line for a three-year loan with a payment of $1,000 at the end of each year and an annual interest rate of 7 percent. To calculate the value of the loan today, we compute the present value of each of the three cash flows and then add them up. The present value of the loan is $2,624.32.

LEARNING BY DOING APPLICATION 6.2

The Value of a Gift to the University

Problem: Suppose that you made a gift to your university, pledging $1,000 per year for four years and $3,000 for the fifth year, for a total of $7,000. After making the first three payments, you decide to pay off the final two payments of your pledge because your financial situation has improved. How much should you pay to the university if the interest rate is 6 percent?

Approach: The key to understanding this problem, of course, is recognizing the need for a present value calculation. Because your pledge to the university is for future cash payments, the value of the amount you will pay for the remaining two years is worth less than the $4,000 ($1,000 + $3,000) you promised. If the appropriate discount rate is 6 percent, the time line for the cash payments for the remaining two years of the pledge is as follows:

0 (6%)	1	2 Year
PV = ?	$1,000	$3,000

We now need only calculate the present value of the last two payments.

Solution: The present value calculation for the last two payments is:

$$\begin{aligned} PV &= FV_1 \times 1/(1 + i) &&= \$1{,}000 \times 1/1.06 &&= \$\ \ 943.40 \\ PV &= FV_2 \times 1/(1 + i)^2 &&= \$3{,}000 \times 1/(1.06)^2 &&= \$2{,}669.99 \\ & && \text{Total present value} && \ \ \ \$3{,}613.39 \end{aligned}$$

The payment of $3,613.39 to the university today (the end of year 3) is a fair payment because at a 6 percent interest rate, it has precisely the same value as paying the university $1,000 at the end of year 4 and $3,000 at the end of year 5.

Now let's consider another example. Suppose you have the opportunity to buy a small business while you are in school. The business involves selling sandwiches, soft drinks, and snack foods to students from a truck that you drive around campus. The annual cash flows from the business have been predictable. You believe you can expand the business, and you estimate that cash flows will be as follows: $2,000 the first year, $3,000 the second and third years, and $4,000 the fourth year. At the end of the fourth year, the business will be closed down because the truck and other equipment will need to be replaced. The total of the estimated cash flows is $12,000. You did some research at school and found that a 10 percent discount rate would be appropriate. How much should you pay for the business?

To value the business, we compute the present value of the expected cash flows, discounted at 10 percent. The time line for the investment is:

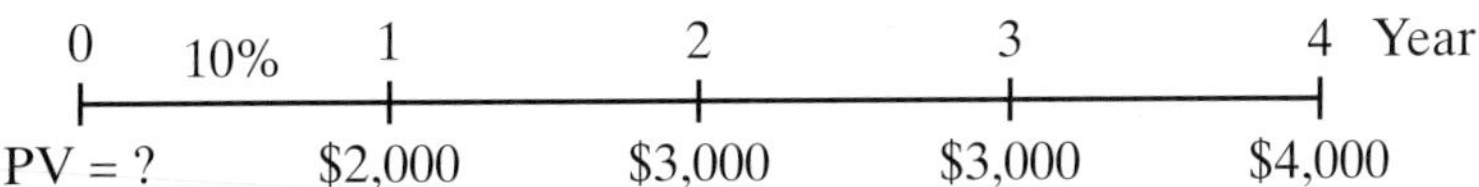

We compute the present value of each cash flow and then add them up:

$$\begin{aligned}
PV &= FV_1 \times 1/(1+i) = \$2{,}000 \times 1/1.10 = \$2{,}000 \times 0.9091 = \$1{,}818.18 \\
PV &= FV_2 \times 1/(1+i)^2 = \$3{,}000 \times 1/(1.10)^2 = \$3{,}000 \times 0.8264 = \$2{,}479.34 \\
PV &= FV_3 \times 1/(1+i)^3 = \$3{,}000 \times 1/(1.10)^3 = \$3{,}000 \times 0.7513 = \$2{,}253.94 \\
PV &= FV_4 \times 1/(1+i)^4 = \$4{,}000 \times 1/(1.10)^4 = \$4{,}000 \times 0.6830 = \$2{,}732.05 \\
&\text{Total present value} \quad \$9{,}283.51
\end{aligned}$$

This computation tells us that the value of the business is $9,283.51. Of course, you should buy the business for the lowest price possible. If the price goes above $9,283.51, however, you should walk away from the deal. You should never pay more for an investment than it is worth.

CALCULATOR TIP: CALCULATING THE PRESENT VALUE OF MULTIPLE CASH FLOWS

To calculate the present value of future cash flows with a financial calculator, we use exactly the same process we used in finding the future value, except that we solve for the present value instead of the future value. We can compute the present values of the individual cash flows, save them in the calculator's memory, and then add them up to obtain the total present value.

LEARNING BY DOING APPLICATION 6.3

Buying a Used Car—Help!

Problem: For a student—or anyone else—buying a used car can be a harrowing experience. Once you find the car you want, the next difficult decision is how to pay for it—cash or a loan. Suppose the cash price you have negotiated for the car is $5,600, but that amount will stretch your budget for the year. The dealer says, "No problem. The car is yours for $4,000 down and payments of $1,000 per year for the next two years. Or you can put $2,000 down and pay $2,000 per year for two years. The choice is yours." Which offer is the best deal? The interest rate you can earn on your money is 8 percent.

Approach: In this problem, we have three alternative cash flows. We need to convert all of the cash flows (CF_n) into today's dollars (present value) and select the alternative with the lowest present value or price.[1] The time line for the three alternatives, along with the cash flows for each alternative, is as follows. (The cash flows at time zero represent the cash price of the car in the case of alternative A and the down payment in the case of alternatives B and C.)

0	8%	1	2 Year
Cash price or down payment		CF_1	CF_2

	Cash Price or Down Payment	CF_1	CF_2	Total
Alternative A	$5,600	-	-	$5,600
Alternative B	$4,000	$1,000	$1,000	$6,000
Alternative C	$2,000	$2,000	$2,000	$6,000

Now we use Equation 5.4 to find the present value of each alternative.

(continued)

[1]Up to this point, we have used the notation FV_n to represent a cash flow in period n. We have done this to stress that, for $n > 0$, we were referring to a future value. From this point on, we will use the notation CF_n, instead of FV_n, because the CF_n notation is more commonly used by financial analysts.

Solution:

Alternative A:

$$\$5{,}600 \times 1/(1.08)^0 = \$5{,}600.00$$

Alternative B:

$$\begin{aligned} \$4{,}000 \times 1/(1.08)^0 &= \$4{,}000.00 \\ \$1{,}000 \times 1/1.08 &= \$925.93 \\ \$1{,}000 \times 1/(1.08)^2 &= \underline{\$857.34} \\ \text{Total} &\quad \$5{,}783.27 \end{aligned}$$

Alternative C:

$$\begin{aligned} \$2{,}000 \times 1/(1.08)^0 &= \$2{,}000.00 \\ \$2{,}000 \times 1/1.08 &= \$1{,}851.85 \\ \$2{,}000 \times 1/(1.08)^2 &= \underline{\$1{,}714.68} \\ \text{Total} &\quad \$5{,}566.53 \end{aligned}$$

Once we have converted the three cash flow streams to present dollars, the answer is clear. Alternative C has the lowest present value, so it has the lowest price and is the alternative you should choose.

DECISION-MAKING EXAMPLE 6.1

The Investment Decision

Problem: You are thinking of buying a business, and your investment adviser presents you with two possibilities. Both businesses are priced at $60,000, and you have only $60,000 to invest. She has provided you with the cash flows for each business, along with the present value of the cash flows discounted at 10 percent, as follows:

	Cash flow per year ($ thousands)				
Business	1	2	3	Total	PV at 10%
A	$50	$30	$ 20	$100	$85.27
B	$ 5	$ 5	$100	$110	$83.81

Which business should you acquire?

Decision: At first glance, business B may look to be the best choice because its undiscounted cash flows for the three years total $110,000, versus $100,000 for A. However, to make the decision on the basis of the undiscounted cash flows ignores the time value of money. By discounting the cash flows, we eliminate the time value of money effect by converting all cash flows to current dollars. The present value of business A is $85,270 and that of B is $83,810. Thus, you should acquire business A.

Before You Go On

1. Explain how to calculate the future value of a stream of cash flows.
2. Explain how to calculate the present value of a stream of cash flows.
3. Why is it important to adjust all cash flows to a common date?

6.2 Level Cash Flows: Annuities and Perpetuities

In finance we commonly encounter contracts that call for the payment of equal amounts of cash over several time periods. For example, most business term loans and insurance policies require the holder to make a series of equal payments, usually monthly. Similarly, nearly all consumer loans, such as auto, personal, and home mortgage loans, call for equal monthly payments. Any financial contract that calls for equally spaced and level cash flows over a finite number of periods is called an **annuity**. If the cash flow payments continue forever, the contract is called a **perpetuity**. Most annuities are structured so that cash payments are received at the end of each period. Because this is the most common structure, these annuities are often called **ordinary annuities**.

Visit New York Life Insurance Company's Web site to learn more about investment products that pay out annuities: https://www.newyorklife.com/cda/0,3254,10468,00.html.

Present Value of an Annuity

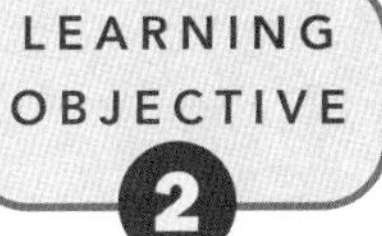

We frequently need to find the **present value of an annuity (PVA)**. Suppose, for example, that a financial contract pays $2,000 at the end of each year for three years and the appropriate discount rate is 8 percent. The time line for the situation is:

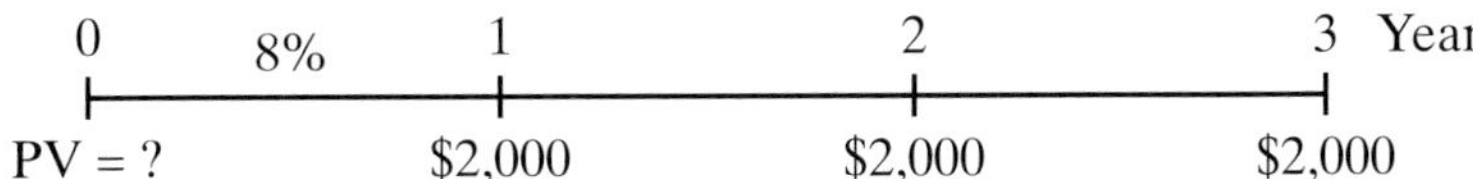

annuity
a series of equally spaced and level cash flows extending over a finite number of periods

What is the most we should pay for this annuity? Of course, we have worked problems like this one before. All we need to do is calculate the present value of each individual cash flow (CF_n) and add them up. Using Equation 5.4, we find that the present value of the three year annuity (PVA_3) at 8 percent interest is:

perpetuity
a series of level cash flows that continue forever

$$
\begin{aligned}
PVA_3 &= CF_1 \times \frac{1}{1+i} + CF_2 \times \frac{1}{(1+i)^2} + CF_3 \times \frac{1}{(1+i)^3} \\
&= \$2{,}000 \times \frac{1}{1.08} + \$2{,}000 \times \frac{1}{(1.08)^2} + \$2{,}000 \times \frac{1}{(1.08)^3} \\
&= \$1{,}851.85 + \$1{,}714.68 + \$1{,}587.66 \\
&= \$5{,}154.19
\end{aligned}
$$

ordinary annuity
an annuity in which payments are made at the ends of the periods

This approach to computing the present value of an annuity works as long as the number of cash flows is relatively small. In many situations that involve annuities, however, the number of cash flows is large, and doing the calculations by hand would be tedious. For example, a typical 30-year home mortgage has 360 (12 months × 30 years) monthly payments.

present value of an annuity (PVA)
the present value of the cash flows from an annuity, discounted at the appropriate discount rate

Fortunately, our problem can be simplified because the cash flows (CF) for an annuity are all the same ($CF_1 = CF_2 = \ldots CF_n = CF$). Thus, the present value of an annuity (PVA_n) with n equal cash flows (CF) at interest rate i is the sum of the individual present value calculations:

$$
PVA_n = CF \times \frac{1}{1+i} + CF \times \frac{1}{(1+i)^2} + \cdots + CF \times \frac{1}{(1+i)^n}
$$

With some mathematical manipulations that are beyond the scope of this discussion, we can simplify this equation to yield a useful formula for the present value of an annuity:

$$
\begin{aligned}
PVA_n &= \frac{CF}{i} \times \left[1 - \frac{1}{(1+i)^n}\right] \\
&= CF \times \frac{1 - 1/(1+i)^n}{i}
\end{aligned}
\qquad (6.1)
$$

where:

PVA_n = present value of an n period annuity
CF = level and equally spaced cash flow
i = discount rate, or interest rate
n = number of periods (often called the annuity's maturity)

Notice in Equation 6.1 that $1/(1 + i)^n$ is a term you have already encountered: It is the present value factor. Thus, we can also write Equation 6.1 as follows:

$$PVA_n = CF \times \frac{1 - \text{Present value factor}}{i}$$

where the term on the right is what we call the PV annuity factor:

$$\text{PV annuity factor} = \frac{1 - \text{Present value factor}}{i}$$

It follows that yet another way to state Equation 6.1 is:

$$PVA_n = CF \times \text{PV annuity factor}$$

Let's apply Equation 6.1 to the example involving a three-year annuity with a \$2,000 annual cash flow. To solve for PVA_n, we first compute the PV annuity factor for three years at 8 percent. The calculation is made in two steps:

1. Calculate the present value factor for three years at 8 percent:

$$\begin{aligned}\text{Present value factor} &= \frac{1}{(1+i)^n} \\ &= \frac{1}{(1+0.08)^3} \\ &= \frac{1}{(1.08)^3} \\ &= \frac{1}{1.2597} \\ &= 0.7938\end{aligned}$$

2. Calculate the PV annuity factor for three years at 8 percent, using the present value factor calculated in step 1:

$$\begin{aligned}\text{PV annuity factor} &= \frac{1 - \text{Present value factor}}{i} \\ &= \frac{1 - 0.7938}{0.08} \\ &= \frac{0.2062}{0.08} \\ &= 2.577\end{aligned}$$

Investopedia is a great Web site for a variety of finance topics. For example, you can find a discussion of annuities at www.investopedia.com/articles/03/101503.asp.

We now can calculate PVA_3 by plugging our values into the equation:

$$\begin{aligned}PVA_3 &= CF \times \text{PV annuity factor} \\ &= \$2{,}000 \times 2.577 \\ &= \$5{,}154.00\end{aligned}$$

The calculation nearly agrees with our earlier hand calculation. The difference is due to rounding.

ANNUITY TABLES: PRESENT VALUE FACTORS

Instead of calculating the PV annuity factor by hand, we can use tables that list selected annuity factors. Exhibit 6.4 contains some entries from such a table, and a more complete set of tables can be found in Appendix A. The annuity table shows the present value of a stream of cash flows that equals $1 a year for n years at different interest rates. Looking at the exhibit, we find that the value for a three-year annuity factor at 8 percent is 2.577, which agrees with our previous calculations.

Exhibit 6.4 Present Value Annuity Factors

Number of Years	Interest Rate per Year 1%	5%	6%	7%	8%	9%	10%
1	$0.990	$0.952	$0.943	$0.935	$0.926	$0.917	$0.909
2	1.970	1.859	1.833	1.808	1.783	1.759	1.736
3	2.941	2.723	2.673	2.624	2.577	2.531	2.487
4	3.902	3.546	3.465	3.387	3.312	3.240	3.170
5	4.853	4.329	4.212	4.100	3.993	3.890	3.791
10	9.471	7.722	7.360	7.024	6.710	6.418	6.145
20	18.046	12.462	11.470	10.594	9.818	9.129	8.514
30	25.808	15.372	13.765	12.409	11.258	10.274	9.427

The table of present value annuity factors shows the present value of $1 for different numbers of years and different interest rates. To locate the desired PV annuity factor, find the row for the appropriate number of years and the column for the proper interest rate.

Computing a PV Annuity Factor

LEARNING BY DOING APPLICATION 6.4

Problem: Compute the PV annuity factor for 30 years at a 10 percent interest rate.

Approach: First, we calculate the present value factor at 10 percent for 30 years. Then, using this value, we calculate the PV annuity factor.

Solution:

$$\begin{aligned}\text{Present value factor} &= \frac{1}{(1+i)^n}\\ &= \frac{1}{(1.10)^{30}}\\ &= \frac{1}{17.4494}\\ &= 0.0573\end{aligned}$$

Then, using this value, we calculate the PV annuity factor:

$$\begin{aligned}\text{PV annuity factor} &= \frac{1 - \text{Present value factor}}{i}\\ &= \frac{1 - 0.0573}{0.10}\\ &= \frac{0.9427}{0.10}\\ &= 9.427\end{aligned}$$

The answer matches the number in Exhibit 6.4.

(continued)

Fortunately, no one in business today calculates the present value of an annuity by hand or uses annuity tables. We worked through the tedious calculations to show where the numbers come from and how the calculations are made. Generally, analysts use financial calculators or spreadsheet programs.

CALCULATOR TIP: FINDING THE PRESENT VALUE OF AN ANNUITY

There are four variables in a present value of an annuity equation (PVA_n, CF, n, and i), and if you know three of them, you can solve for the fourth in a few seconds with a financial calculator. The calculator key that you have not used so far is the PMT (payment) key, which is the key for level cash flows over the life of an annuity.

To illustrate problem solving with a financial calculator, we will revisit the financial contract that paid $2,000 per year for three years, discounted at 8 percent. To find the present value of the contract, we enter 8 percent for the interest rate (i), $2,000 for the payment (PMT), and 3 for the number of periods (N). The key for FV is not relevant for this calculation, so we enter zero into this register to clear it. The key entries and the answer are as follows:

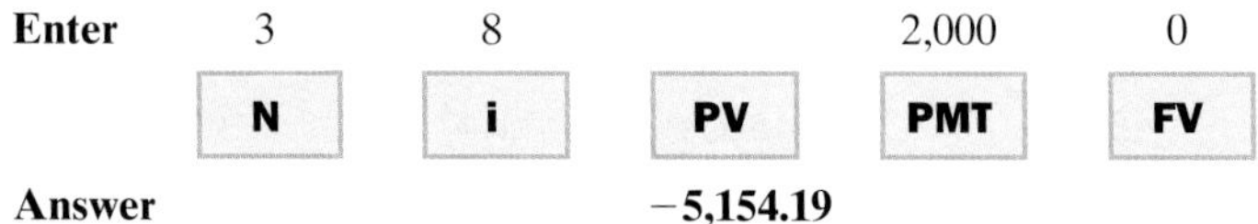

The price of the contract is $5,154.19, which agrees with our other calculations. As discussed in Chapter 5, the negative sign on the financial calculator box indicates that $5,154.19 is a cash outflow.[2]

FINDING MONTHLY OR YEARLY PAYMENTS

A very common problem in finance is determining the payment schedule for a loan on a consumer asset, such as a car or a home that was purchased on credit. Nearly all consumer credit loans call for equal monthly payments. Suppose, for example, that you have just purchased a $450,000 condominium in Miami's South Beach district. You were able to put $50,000 down and obtain a 30-year fixed rate mortgage at 6.125 percent for the balance. What are your monthly payments?

In this problem we know the present value of the annuity. It is $400,000, the price of the condominium less the down payment ($450,000 − $50,000). We also know the number of payments; since the payments will be made monthly for 30 years, you will make 360 payments (12 months × 30 years). Because the payments are monthly, both the interest rate and maturity must be expressed in monthly terms. For consumer loans, to get the monthly interest rate, we divide the annual interest rate by 12. Thus, the monthly interest rate equals 0.51042 percent (6.125 percent/12 months). What we need to calculate is the monthly cash payments (CF) over the loan period. The time line looks like the following:

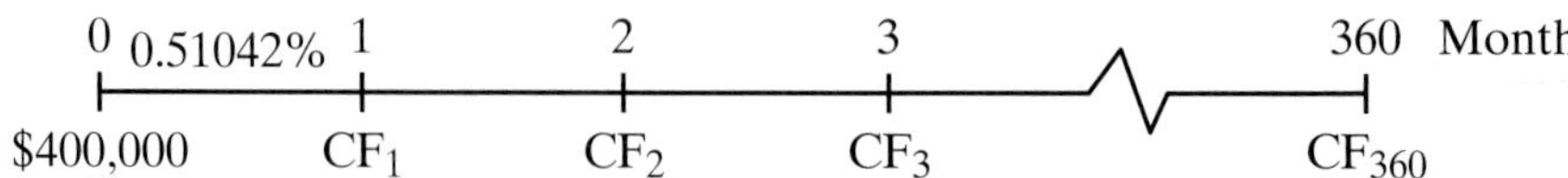

To find CF (remember that $CF_1 = CF_2 = \ldots CF_{360} = CF$), we use Equation 6.1. We need to make two preliminary calculations:

[2]Recall that, when using a financial calculator, it is common practice to enter cash outflows as negative numbers and cash inflows as positive numbers. See Chapter 5 for a complete discussion the importance of assigning the proper sign (+ or −) to cash flows when using a financial calculator.

1. First, we calculate the present value factor for 360 months at 0.51042 percent per month (or, in decimal form, 0.0051042):

$$\text{Present value factor} = \frac{1}{(1+i)^n} = \frac{1}{(1.0051042)^{360}} = \frac{1}{6.25160595} = 0.1599589$$

2. Next, we solve for the PV annuity factor:

$$\text{PV annuity factor} = \frac{1 - \text{Present value factor}}{i} = \frac{1 - 0.1599589}{0.0051042} = \frac{0.8400411}{0.0051042} = 164.578406$$

We can now plug all the data into Equation 6.1 and solve it for CF:

$$\begin{aligned} \text{PVA}_n &= \text{CF} \times \text{PV annuity factor} \\ \$400{,}000 &= \text{CF} \times 164.578406 \\ \text{CF} &= \frac{\$400{,}000}{164.578406} \\ \text{CF} &= \$2{,}430.45 \end{aligned}$$

Your mortgage payments will be about $2,430.45 per month.

To solve the problem on a financial calculator takes only a few seconds once the time line is prepared. The most common error students make when using financial calculators is failing to convert all contract variables to be consistent with the compounding period. Thus, if the contract calls for monthly payments, the interest rate and contract duration must be stated in monthly terms.

Having converted our data to monthly terms, we enter into the calculator: N = 360 (30 years × 12 months/year) months, i = 0.51042 (6.125 percent/12 months), PV = $400,000, and FV = 0 (to clear the register). Then, pressing the payment button (PMT), we find the answer, which is −$2,430.44. The necessary keystrokes are:

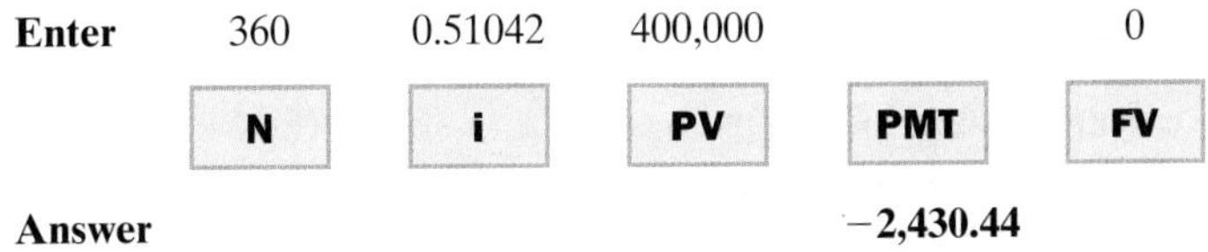

Notice that the hand and financial calculator answers differ by only 1 cent ($2,430.45 − $2,430.44). The answers are so close because when doing the hand calculation, we carried six to eight decimal places through the entire set of calculations. Had we rounded off each number as the calculations were made, the errors between the two calculation methods would have been about $2.00. The moral of the story is to round as few numbers as possible when making a series of hand calculations. The more numbers that are rounded during the calculations, the greater the possible rounding error.

LEARNING BY DOING APPLICATION 6.5

What Are Your Monthly Car Payments?

NEED MORE HELP? WILEY PLUS www.wileyplus.com

Problem: You have decided to buy a new car, and the dealer's best price is \$16,000. The dealer agrees to provide financing with a five-year auto loan at 12 percent interest. Using a financial calculator, calculate your monthly payments.

Approach: All the problem data must be converted to monthly terms. The number of periods is 60 months (5 years × 12 months per year), and the monthly interest charge is 1 percent (12 percent/12 months). The time line for the car purchase is as follows:

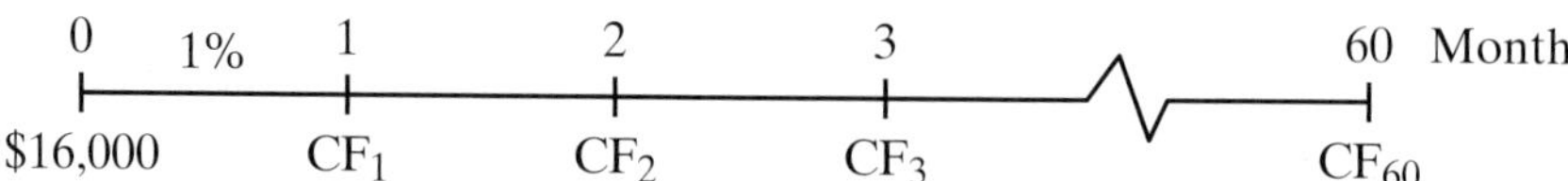

Having converted our data to monthly terms, we enter the following values into the calculator: N = 60 months, i = 1, PV = \$16,000, and FV = 0 (to clear the register). Pressing the payment key (PMT) will give us the answer.

Solution:

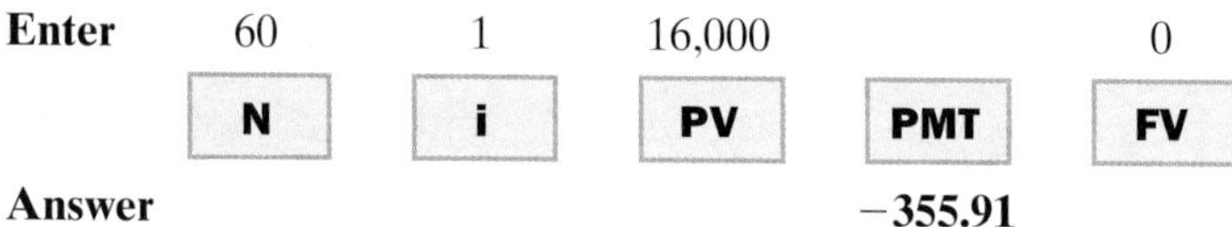

Note that since we entered \$16,000 as a positive number, the monthly payment of \$355.91 is a negative number.

PREPARING A LOAN AMORTIZATION SCHEDULE

Once you understand how to calculate a monthly or yearly loan payment, you have all of the tools that you need to prepare a loan amortization schedule. The term *amortization* describes the way in which the principal (the amount borrowed) is repaid over the life of a loan. With an amortizing loan, some portion of each month's loan payment goes to paying down the principal. When the final loan payment is made, the unpaid principal is reduced to zero and the loan is paid off. The other portion of each loan payment is interest, which is payment for the use of outstanding principal (the amount of money still owed). Thus, with an **amortizing loan**, each loan payment contains some repayment of principal and an interest payment. Nearly all loans to consumers are amortizing loans.

amortizing loan
a loan for which each loan payment contains repayment of some principal and a payment of interest that is based on the remaining principal to be repaid

A loan **amortization schedule** is just a table that shows the loan balance at the beginning and end of each period, the payment made during that period, and how much of that payment represents interest and how much represents repayment of principal. To see how an amortization schedule is prepared, consider an example. Suppose that you have just borrowed \$10,000 at a 5 percent interest rate from a bank to purchase a car. Typically, you would make monthly payments on such a loan. For simplicity, however, we will assume that the bank allows you to make annual payments and that the loan will be repaid over five years. Exhibit 6.5 shows the amortization schedule for this loan.

amortization schedule
with regard to a loan, a table that shows the loan balance at the beginning and end of each period, the payment made during that period, and how much of that payment represents interest and how much represents repayment of principal

To prepare a loan amortization schedule, we must first compute the loan payment. Since, for consumer loans, the amount of the loan payment is fixed, all the payments are identical in amount. Applying Equation 6.1 and noting from Exhibit

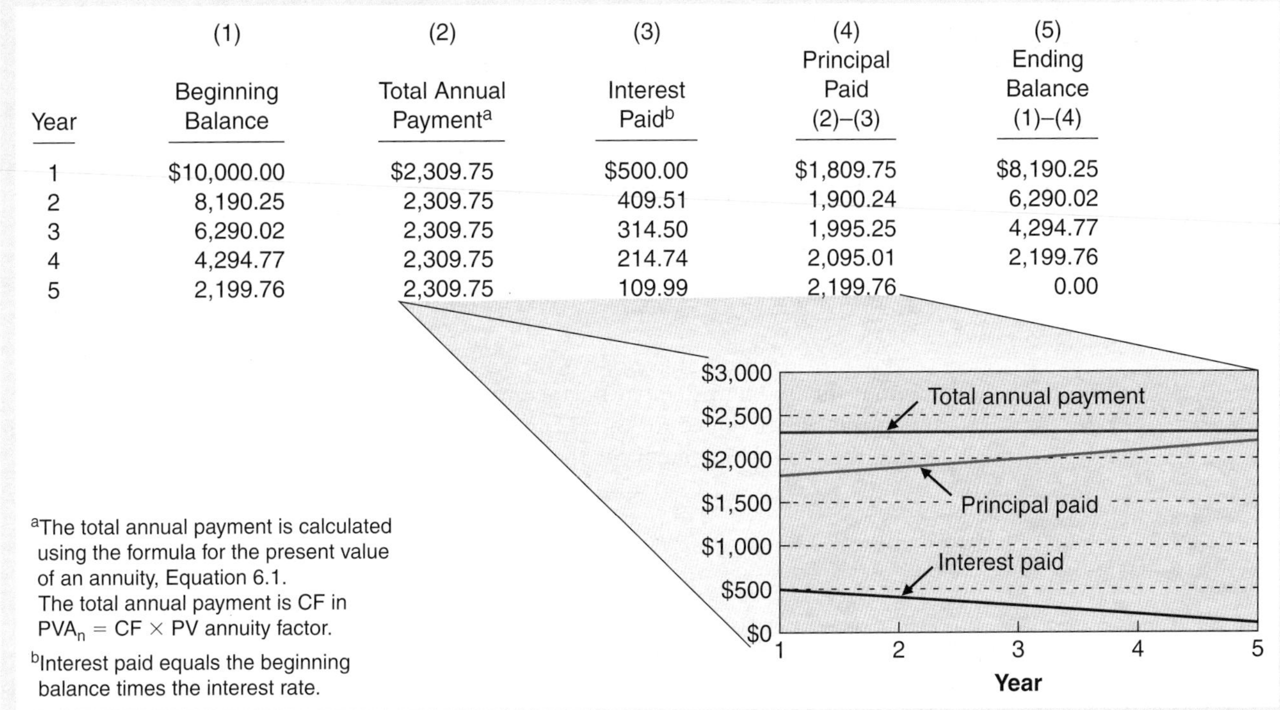

Year	(1) Beginning Balance	(2) Total Annual Payment[a]	(3) Interest Paid[b]	(4) Principal Paid (2)–(3)	(5) Ending Balance (1)–(4)
1	$10,000.00	$2,309.75	$500.00	$1,809.75	$8,190.25
2	8,190.25	2,309.75	409.51	1,900.24	6,290.02
3	6,290.02	2,309.75	314.50	1,995.25	4,294.77
4	4,294.77	2,309.75	214.74	2,095.01	2,199.76
5	2,199.76	2,309.75	109.99	2,199.76	0.00

[a]The total annual payment is calculated using the formula for the present value of an annuity, Equation 6.1. The total annual payment is CF in $\text{PVA}_n = \text{CF} \times \text{PV annuity factor}$.

[b]Interest paid equals the beginning balance times the interest rate.

Exhibit 6.5
Amortization Table for a Five-Year, $10,000 Loan at 5 Percent Interest
A loan amortization table shows how regular payments of principal and interest are applied to repay a loan. The exhibit is an amortization table for a five-year, $10,000 loan with an interest rate of 5 percent and annual payments of $2,309.75. Notice that the interest paid declines with each payment, while the principal paid increases. These relations are illustrated in the pullout graphic in the exhibit.

6.4 that the PV annuity factor for five years at 5 percent is 4.329, we calculate as follows:

$$\begin{aligned} \text{PVA}_n &= \text{CF} \times \text{PV annuity factor} \\ \$10{,}000 &= \text{CF} \times 4.329 \\ \text{CF} &= \frac{\$10{,}000}{4{,}329} \\ \text{CF} &= \$2{,}310.00 \text{ per year} \end{aligned}$$

Alternatively, we enter the values N = 5 years, i = 5 percent, and PV = $10,000 in a financial calculator and then press the PMT key to solve for the loan payment amount. The answer is −$2,309.75 per year. The difference between the two answers results from rounding. For the amortization table calculation, we will use the more precise answer from the financial calculator.

Turning to Exhibit 6.5, we can work through the amortization schedule to see how the table is prepared. For the first year, the values are determined as follows:

1. The amount borrowed, or the beginning principal balance, is $10,000.
2. The annual loan payment, as calculated earlier, is $2,309.75.
3. The interest payment for the first year is $500 and is calculated as follows:

$$\begin{aligned} \text{Interest payment} &= i \times P_0 \\ &= 0.05 \times \$10{,}000 \\ &= \$500 \end{aligned}$$

4. The principal paid for the year is \$1,809.75, calculated as follows:

$$\begin{aligned} \text{Principal paid} &= \text{Loan payment} - \text{Interest payment} \\ &= \$2{,}309.75 - \$500 \\ &= \$1{,}809.75 \end{aligned}$$

5. The ending principal balance is \$8,190.25, computed as follows:

$$\begin{aligned} \text{Ending principal balance} &= \text{Beginning principal balance} - \text{Principal paid} \\ &= \$10{,}000 - \$1{,}809.75 \\ &= 8{,}190.25 \end{aligned}$$

Note that the ending principal balance for the first year (\$8,190.25) becomes the beginning principal balance for the second year (\$8,190.25), which in turn is used in calculating the interest payment for the second year:

$$\begin{aligned} \text{Interest payment} &= i \times P_0 \\ &= 0.05 \times \$8{,}190.25 \\ &= \$409.51 \end{aligned}$$

This calculation makes sense because each loan payment includes some principal repayment. This is why the interest in column 3 declines each year. We repeat the calculations until the loan is fully amortized, at which point the principal balance goes to zero and the loan is paid off.

If you are preparing an amortization table for monthly payments, of course, all of your principal balances, loan payments, and interest rates must be adjusted to a monthly basis. For example, to calculate monthly payments for our auto loan, we would make the following adjustments: $n = 60$ payments (12 months per year × 5 years), $i = 0.4167$ percent (5 percent/12 months per year), and monthly payment = \$188.71.

An interesting characteristic of amortized loans is the breakdown between the payment of interest and the repayment of principal in each loan payment. In the early years of a loan, interest payments are at their peak because very little principal has been repaid (see column 1). Near the end of the loan contract, when most of the principal has been paid off, payments to principal are at their peak, and interest payments have become smaller. Thus, as a loan is gradually paid off, the proportion of a monthly payment devoted to interest steadily declines, while the proportion used to reduce the principal steadily increases. The final loan payment repays just enough principal to pay off the loan in full.

Finally, the separation between interest and principal payments is also important for tax purposes. Individual taxpayers can deduct interest on a home mortgage for their principal residence and, within limits, on a second residence. For corporations, interest expense is tax deductible.

USING EXCEL

Loan Amortization Table

Loan amortization tables are most easily constructed using a spreadsheet program. Here, we have reconstructed the loan amortization table shown in Exhibit 6.5 using Excel.

Notice that all the values in the amortization table are obtained by using formulas. Once you have built an amortization table like this one, you can change any of the input variables, such as the loan amount, and all of the other numbers will automatically be updated.

	A	B	D	F	H	J	L
1							
2				Loan Amortization Table			
3							
4		Loan amount	$10,000				
5		Interest rate	0.05				
6		Loan period	5				
7		**PMT**	**$2,309.75**				
8							
9		**Year**	**Beginning Balance**	**Total Annual Payment**	**Simple Interest Paid**	**Principal Paid**	**Ending Balance**
10		1	$10,000.00	$2,309.75	$500.00	$1,809.75	$8,190.25
11		2	8,190.25	2,309.75	409.51	1,900.24	6,290.02
12		3	6,290.02	2,309.75	314.50	1,995.25	4,294.77
13		4	4,294.77	2,309.75	214.74	2,095.01	2,199.76
14		5	2,199.76	2,309.75	109.99	2,199.76	0.00
15							
16	**Corresponding formulas:**						
17							
18		**Payment:**	=PMT(D5, D6, -D4)				
19							
20		**Year**	**Beginning Balance**	**Total Annual Payment**	**Simple Interest Paid**	**Principal Paid**	**Ending Balance**
21		1	=D4	=$D$7	=D10*$D$5	=F10-H10	=D10-J10
22		2	=L10	=$D$7	=D11*$D$5	=F11-H11	=D11-J11
23		3	=L11	=$D$7	=D12*$D$5	=F12-H12	=D12-J12
24		4	=L12	=$D$7	=D13*$D$5	=F13-H13	=D13-J13
25		5	=L13	=$D$7	=D14*$D$5	=F14-H14	=D14-J14
26							

FINDING THE INTEREST RATE

Another important calculation in finance is determining the interest, or discount, rate for an annuity. The interest rate tells us the rate of return on an annuity contract. For example, suppose your parents are getting ready to retire and decide to convert some of their retirement portfolio, which is invested in the stock market, into an annuity that guarantees them a fixed annual income. Their insurance agent asks for $350,000 for an annuity that guarantees to pay them $50,000 a year for 10 years. What is the rate of return on the annuity?

As we did when we found the payment amount, we can insert these values into Equation 6.1:

$$\text{PVA}_n = \text{CF} \times \frac{1 - 1/(1 + i)^n}{i}$$

$$\$350{,}000 = \$50{,}000 \times \frac{1 - 1/(1 + i)^{10}}{i}$$

To determine the rate of return for the annuity, we need to solve the equation for the unknown value i. Unfortunately, it is not possible to solve the resulting equation for i algebraically. The only way to solve the problem is by trial and error. We normally solve this kind of problem using a financial calculator or computer spreadsheet program that finds the solution for us. However, it is important to understand how the solution is arrived at by trial and error, so let's work this problem without such aids.

To start the process, we must select an initial value for i, plug it into the right-hand side of the equation, and solve the equation to see if the present value of the annuity stream equals $350,000, which is the left-hand side of the equation. If the present value of the annuity is too large (PVA > $350,000), we need to select a higher value for i. If the present value of the annuity stream is too small (PVA < $350,000), we need to select a smaller value. We continue the trial-and-error process until we find the value for i at which PVA = $350,000.

The key to getting started is to make the best guess we can as to the possible value of the interest rate given the information and data available to us. We will assume that the current bank savings rate is 4 percent. Since the annuity rate of return should exceed the bank rate, we will start our calculations with a 5 percent discount rate. The present value of the annuity is:

$$\begin{aligned} PVA_{5\%} &= \$50{,}000 \times \frac{1 - 1/(1 + 0.05)^{10}}{0.05} \\ &= \$50{,}000 \times 7.722 \\ &= \$386{,}100 \end{aligned}$$

That's a pretty good first guess, but our present value is greater than $350,000, so we need to try a higher discount rate.[4] Let's try 7 percent:

$$\begin{aligned} PVA_{7\%} &= \$50{,}000 \times \frac{1 - 1/(1 + 0.07)^{10}}{0.07} \\ &= \$50{,}000 \times 7.024 \\ &= \$351{,}200 \end{aligned}$$

The present value of the annuity is still slightly higher than $350,000, so we still need a larger value of i. How about 7.10 percent:

$$\begin{aligned} PVA_{7.1\%} &= \$50{,}000 \times \frac{1 - 1/(1 + 0.071)^{10}}{0.071} \\ &= \$50{,}000 \times 6.991 \\ &= \$349{,}550 \end{aligned}$$

The value is too small, but we now know that i is between 7.00 and 7.10 percent. On the next try, we need to use a slightly smaller value of i—say, 7.07 percent:

$$\begin{aligned} PVA_{7.07\%} &= \$50{,}000 \times \frac{1 - 1/(1 + 0.0707)^{10}}{0.0707} \\ &= \$50{,}000 \times 7.001 \\ &= \$350{,}050 \end{aligned}$$

Since this value is slightly too high, we should try a number for i that is only slightly greater than 7.07 percent. We'll try 7.073 percent:

$$\begin{aligned} PVA_{7.073\%} &= \$50{,}000 \times \frac{1 - 1/(1 + 0.07073)^{10}}{0.07073} \\ &= \$50{,}000 \times 7.000 \\ &= \$350{,}000 \end{aligned}$$

The cost of the annuity, $350,000, is now exactly the same as the present value of the annuity stream ($350,000); thus, 7.073 percent is the rate of return earned by the annuity.

It typically takes many more guesses to solve for the interest rate than it did in this example. Our "guesses" were good because we knew the answer before we started guessing! Clearly, solving for i by trial and error can be a long and tedious process. Fortunately, as mentioned, these types of problems are easily solved with a financial calculator or computer spreadsheet program. Next, we describe how to compute the interest rate or rate of return on an annuity on a financial calculator.

CALCULATOR TIP: FINDING THE INTEREST RATE

To illustrate how to find the interest rate for an annuity on a financial calculator, we will enter the information from the previous example. We know the number of periods

---

[4]Notice that we have rounded the PV annuity factor to three decimal places (7.722). If we use a financial calculator and do not round, we get a more precise answer of $386,086.75.

(N = 10), the payment amount (PMT = $50,000), and the present value (PV = −$350,000), and we want to solve for the interest rate (i):

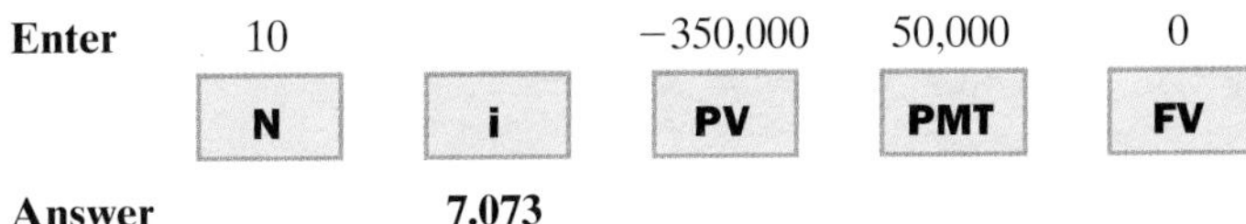

The interest rate is 7.073 percent. Notice that we have used a negative sign for the present value of the annuity contract, representing a cash outflow, and a positive sign for the annuity payments, representing cash inflows. Using the present value formula, you must always have at least one inflow and one outflow. If we had entered both the PV and PMT amounts as positive values (or both as negative values), the calculator would have reported an error since the equation cannot be solved. As we have mentioned before, we could have reversed *all* of the signs—that is, made cash outflows positive and cash inflows negative—and still gotten the correct answer. Finally, the FV was entered as zero to make sure that the register was cleared.

LEARNING BY DOING APPLICATION 6.6

Return on Investments: Good Deal or Bad?

Problem: With some business opportunities you know the price of a financial contract and the promised cash flows, and you want to calculate the interest rate or rate of return on the investment. For example, suppose you have a chance to invest in a small business. The owner wants to borrow $200,000 from you for five years and will make yearly payments of $60,000 at the end of each year. Similar types of investment opportunities will pay 5 percent. Is this a good investment opportunity?

Approach: First, we draw a time line for this situation:

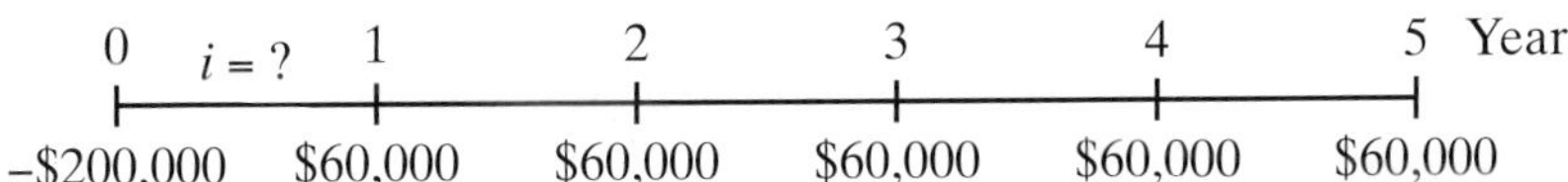

To compute the rate of return on the investment, we need to compute the interest rate that equates the initial investment of $200,000 to the present value of the promised cash flows of $60,000 per year. We can use the trial-and-error approach with Equation 6.1, a financial calculator, or a spreadsheet program to solve this problem. Here we will use a financial calculator.

Solution: The financial calculator steps are:

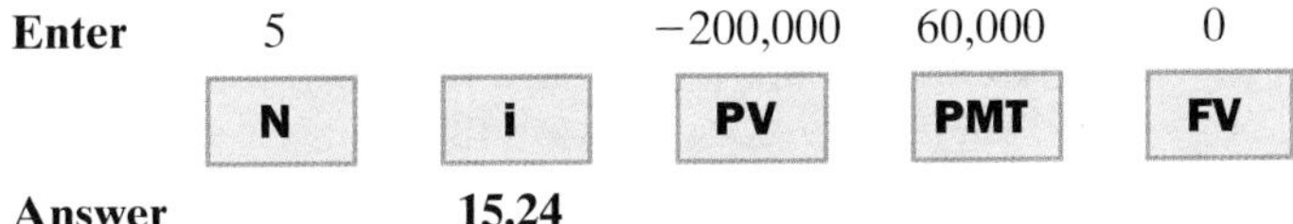

The return on this investment is 15.24 percent, well above the market interest rate of 5 percent. It is a good investment opportunity.

DECISION-MAKING EXAMPLE 6.2

The Pizza Dough Machine

Problem: As the owner of a pizza parlor, you are considering whether to buy a fully automated pizza dough preparation machine. Your staff is wildly supportive of

(continued)

the purchase because it would eliminate a tedious part of their work. Your accountant provides you with the following information:

- The cost, including shipping, for the Italian Pizza Dough Machine is \$25,000.
- Cash savings, including labor, raw materials, and tax savings due to depreciation, are \$3,500 per year for 10 years.
- Present value of cash savings is \$21,506 at a 10 percent discount rate.[5]

Given the above data, what should you do?

Decision: As you arrive at the pizza parlor in the morning, the staff is in a festive mood because word has leaked out that the new machine will save the shop \$35,000 and only cost \$25,000.

With a heavy heart, you explain that the analysis done at the water cooler by some of the staff is incorrect. To make economic decisions involving cash flows, even for a small business such as your pizza parlor, you cannot compare cash values from different time periods unless they are adjusted for the time value of money. The present value formula takes into account the time value of money and converts the future cash flows into current or present dollars. The cost of the machine is already in current dollars.

The correct analysis is as follows: the machine costs \$25,000, and the present value of the cost savings is \$21,506. Thus, the cost of the machine exceeds the benefits; the correct decision is not to buy the new dough preparation machine.

Future Value of an Annuity

future value of an annuity (FVA)
the value of an annuity at some point in the future

Generally, when we are working with annuities, we are interested in computing their present value. On occasion, though, we need to compute the **future value of an annuity (FVA)**. Such computations typically involve some type of saving activity, such as a monthly savings plan. Another application is computing terminal values for retirement or pension plans with constant contributions.

We will start with a simple example. Suppose that you plan to save \$1,000 at the end of every year for four years with the goal of buying a racing bicycle. The bike you want is an Orbea Orca, a top-of-the-line Spanish racing bike that costs around \$4,500. The bike has a carbon frame and forks, is fitted with Shimano Dura Ace components, and weighs 15 pounds, 7 ounces. If your bank pays 8 percent interest a year, will you have enough money to buy the bike at the end of four years?

To solve this problem, we can first lay out the cash flows on a time line, as we discussed earlier in this chapter. We can then calculate the future value for each cash flow using Equation 5.1, which is $FV_n = PV \times (1 + i)^n$. Finally, we can add up all the cash flows. The time line and calculations are shown in Exhibit 6.6. Given that the total future value of the four payments is \$4,506.11, as shown in the exhibit, you should have enough money to buy the bike.

FUTURE VALUE OF ANNUITY EQUATIONS

Of course, most business applications involve longer periods of time than the Orbea bike example. One way to solve more complex problems involving the future value of an annuity is first to calculate the present value of the annuity, PVA, using Equation 6.1 and then to use Equation 5.1 to calculate the future value of the PVA. In practice, many

[5]The annuity present value factor for 10 years at 10 percent is 6.1446. Thus, $PV_{10} = CF \times \text{Annuity factor} = \$3,500 \times 6.1446 = \$21,506.10$. Using a financial calculator, $PV_{10} = \$21,505.98$. The difference is due to rounding errors.

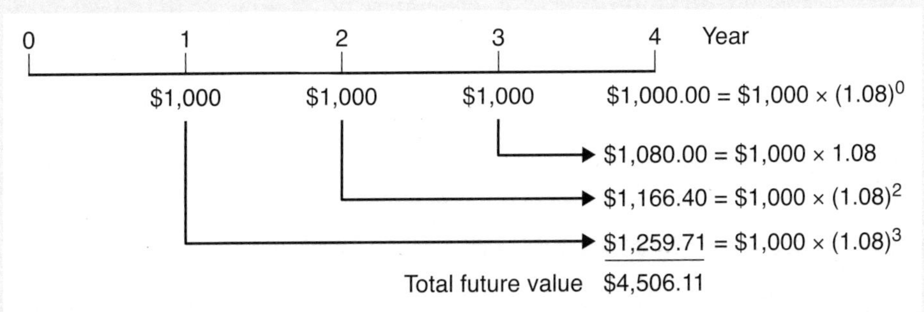

Exhibit 6.6
Future Value of a Four-Year Annuity: Orbea Orca Bicycle
The exhibit shows a time line for a savings plan to buy an Orbea bicycle. Under this savings plan, $1,000 is invested at the end of each year for four years at an annual interest rate of 8 percent. We find the value at the end of the four-year period by adding the future values of the separate cash flows, just as in Exhibits 6.1 and 6.2.

analyses condense this calculation into a single step by using the future value of annuity (FVA) formula, which we obtain by substituting PVA for PV in Equation 5.1.

$$\begin{aligned} \text{FVA}_n &= \text{PVA}_n \times (1+i)^n \\ &= \frac{\text{CF}}{i} \times \left[1 - \frac{1}{(1+i)^n}\right] \times (1+i)^n \\ &= \frac{\text{CF}}{i} \times [(1+i)^n - 1] \\ &= \text{CF} \times \frac{(1+i)^n - 1}{i} \end{aligned} \tag{6.2}$$

where:

FVA_n = future value of an annuity at the end of n periods
PVA_n = present value of an n period annuity
CF = level and equally spaced cash flow
i = discount rate, or interest rate
n = number of periods

We can rearrange Equation 6.2 to write it in terms of the Future value factor and the FV annuity factor:

$$\begin{aligned} \text{FVA}_n &= \text{CF} \times \frac{(1+i)^n - 1}{i} \\ &= \text{CF} \times \frac{\text{Future value factor} - 1}{i} \\ &= \text{CF} \times \text{FV annuity factor} \end{aligned}$$

As you would expect, there are tables listing FV annuity factors. Appendix A includes a table that shows the value of a $1 annuity for various interest rates and maturities.

Using Equation 6.2 to compute FVA for the Orbea bike problem is straightforward. The calculation and process are similar to those we developed for PVA problems. That is, we first calculate the FV annuity factor for four years at 8 percent:

$$\text{Future value factor} = (1+i)^n = (1.08)^4 = 1.36049$$

$$\text{FV annuity factor} = \frac{\text{Future value factor} - 1}{i} = \frac{1.36049 - 1}{0.08} = 4.5061$$

Now we can compute the future value of the annuity by multiplying the constant cash flow (CF) by the FV annuity factor. We plug our computed values into the equation:

$$FVA_n = CF \times \text{FV annuity factor} = \$1{,}000 \times 4.5061 = \$4{,}506.10$$

This value differs slightly from the one we calculated in Exhibit 6.6 because of rounding.

CALCULATOR TIP: FINDING THE FUTURE VALUE OF AN ANNUITY

The procedure for calculating the future value of an annuity on a financial calculator is precisely the same as the procedure for calculating the present value of an annuity discussed earlier. The only difference is that we use the FV (future value) key instead of the PV (present value) key. The PV key is entered as a zero to clear the register.

Let's work the Orbea bicycle problem on a calculator. Recall that we decided to put $1,000 in the bank at the end of each year for four years. The bank pays 8 percent interest. Clear the financial register and make the following entries:

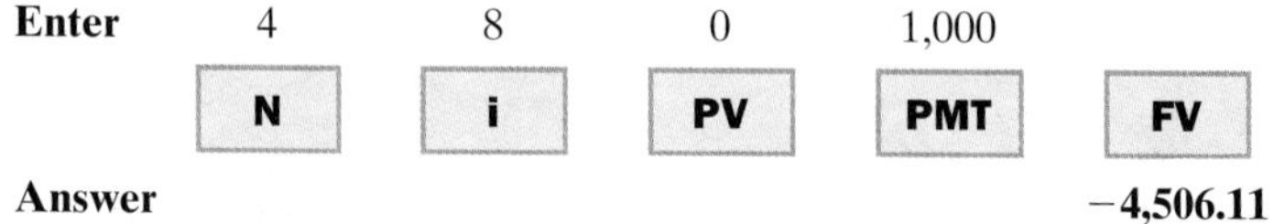

Enter	4	8	0	1,000	
	N	i	PV	PMT	FV
Answer					−4,506.11

The calculated value of $4,506.11 is the same as in Exhibit 6.6.

Perpetuities

A perpetuity is a constant stream of cash flows that goes on forever. Perpetuities in the form of bonds were used by the British Treasury Department to pay off the debt incurred by the government to finance the Napoleonic wars. These perpetual bonds, called *consols*, have no maturity date and are still traded in the international bond markets today.

The most important perpetuities in the securities markets today are preferred stock issues. The issuer of preferred stock promises to pay investors a fixed dividend forever unless a retirement date for the perferred stock has been set. If preferred stock dividends are not paid, all previous unpaid dividends must be repaid before any dividends are paid to common stockholders. This preferential treatment is one source of the term *preferred* stock.

From Equation 6.1, we can calculate the present value of a perpetuity by setting n, which is the number of periods, equal to infinity (∞).[6] When that is done, the value of the term $1/(1 + i)^{\infty}$ approaches 0, and thus:

$$\begin{aligned} PVA_{\infty} &= \frac{CF}{i} \times \left[1 - \frac{1}{(1+i)^{\infty}}\right] \\ &= \frac{CF}{i} \times [1 - 0] \\ &= \frac{CF}{i} \end{aligned} \tag{6.3}$$

As you can see, the present value of a perpetuity is the promised constant cash payment (CF) divided by the interest rate (i). A nice feature of the final equation ($PVA_{\infty} = CF/i$) is that it is algebraically very simple to work with, since it allows us to solve for i directly rather than by trial and error, as is required with Equations 6.1 and 6.2.

[6]Conversely, we can derive the formula for the present value of an ordinary annuity, Equation 6.1, from the formula for a perpetuity, as explained in the appendix at the end of this chapter.

For example, suppose you had a great experience during college at the school of business and decided to endow a chair in finance. Endowed chairs provide salary and research support for top faculty.[7] The goal of the chair is to provide the chair holder with \$100,000 of additional financial support per year forever. If the rate of interest is 8 percent, how much money will you have to give the university foundation to provide the desired level of support? Using Equation 6.3, we find that the present value of the perpetuity is:

$$PVA_{\infty} = \frac{CF}{i} = \frac{\$100{,}000}{0.08} = \$1{,}250{,}000$$

Thus, a gift of \$1.25 million will provide a constant annual payment of \$100,000 to the chair holder forever.

There are two subtleties here that you should note. First, as mentioned earlier, the present value formula assumes that cash flows are paid at the end of the year. If our worthy chair holder needs to be paid when the chair is awarded, the donor would have to provide the university with an additional \$100,000. Thus, the total gift would be \$1.35 million. Note that the \$100,000 is already in present value terms, so it can be added to the \$1.25 million, which has been converted into present value terms. Second, in our problem, no adjustment was made for inflation. If the economy is expected to experience inflation, which is generally the case, the chair holder's purchasing power will decline each year.

LEARNING BY DOING APPLICATION 6.7

Preferred Stock Dividends

Problem: Suppose that you are the CEO of a public company and your investment banker recommends that you issue some preferred stock at \$50 per share. Similar preferred stock issues are yielding 6 percent. What annual cash dividend does the firm need to offer to be competitive in the marketplace? In other words, what cash dividend paid annually forever would be worth \$50 with a 6 percent discount rate?

Approach: As we have already mentioned, preferred stock is a type of perpetuity; thus, we can solve this problem by applying Equation 6.3. As usual, we begin by laying out the time line for the cash flows:

0	6%	1	2	3	4	5	6	∞	Year
PVA_{∞}		CF	CF	CF	CF	CF	CF	CF	

For preferred stock, PVA_{∞} is the value of a share of stock, which is \$50 per share. The discount rate is 6 percent. CF is the fixed-rate cash dividend, which is the unknown value. Knowing all this information, we can use Equation 6.3 and solve for CF.

Solution:

$$\begin{aligned} PVA_{\infty} &= \frac{CF}{i} \\ CF &= PVA_{\infty} \times i \\ &= \$50 \times 0.06 \\ &= \$3 \end{aligned}$$

The annual dividend on the preferred stock would be \$3 per share.

[7]The market for top research and teaching faculty is very competitive. Endowed chairs are a means that universities use to attract and retain their best faculty. The typical chair is endowed for \$1 million or more and is usually named after the donor.

Annuities Due

annuity due
an annuity in which payments are made at the beginning of each period

So far we have discussed only annuities whose cash flow payments occur at the end of the period, so-called ordinary annuities. Another type of annuity that is fairly common in business is known as an **annuity due.** Here, cash payments start immediately, at the beginning of the first period. For example, when you rent an apartment, the first rent payment is typically due immediately. The second rent payment is due the first of the second month, and so on. In this kind of payment pattern, you are effectively prepaying for the service.

More examples concerning topics discussed in this chapter can be found at Modlin.org: www.modlin.org/L1ModVidDemo.htm.

Exhibit 6.7 compares the cash flows for an ordinary annuity and an annuity due. Note that both annuities are made up of four $1,000 cash flows and carry an 8 percent interest rate. Part A shows an ordinary annuity, in which the cash flows take place at the end of the period, and part B shows an annuity due, in which the cash flows take place at the beginning of the period. There are several ways to calculate the present and future values of an annuity due, and we discuss them next.

A. Ordinary Annuity (present value: four years at 8 percent)

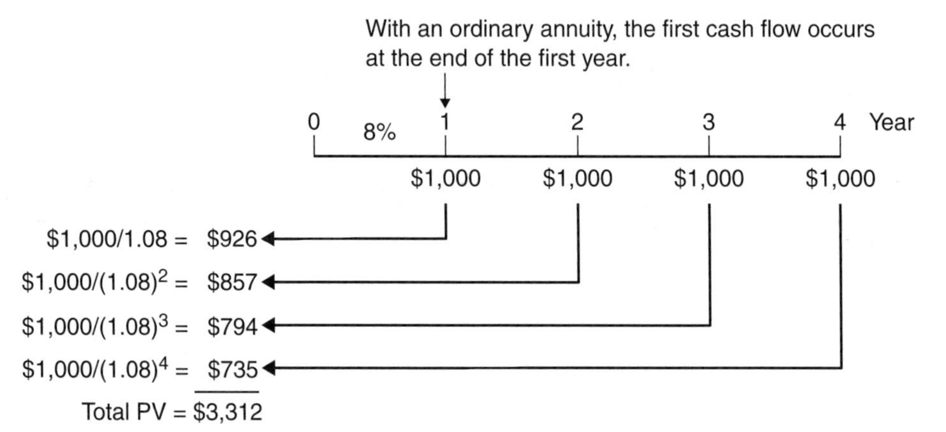

B. Annuity Due (present value: four years at 8 percent)

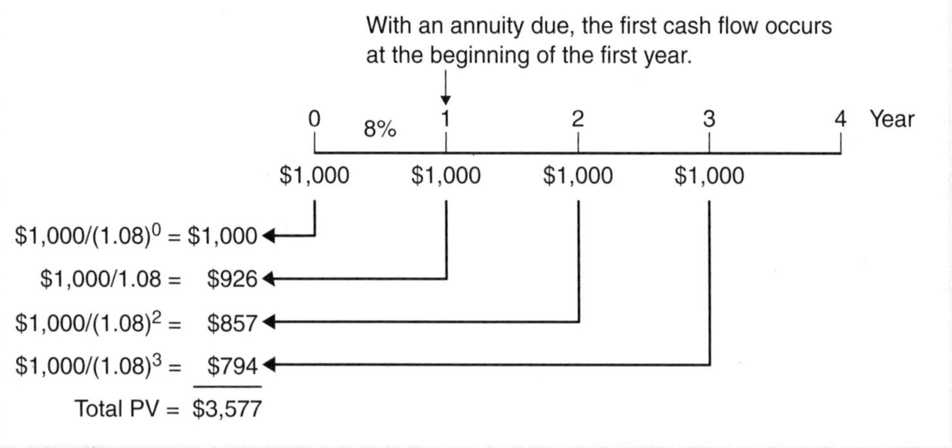

Exhibit 6.7
Ordinary Annuity versus Annuity Due
The difference between an ordinary annuity (part A) and an annuity due (part B) is that with an ordinary annuity, the cash flows take place at the end of each period, while with an annuity due, the cash flows take place at the beginning of each period. As you can see in this example, the PV of the annuity due is larger than the PV of the ordinary annuity. The reason is that the cash flows of the annuity due are shifted forward one year and thus are discounted less.

PRESENT VALUE METHOD

One way to compute the present value of an annuity due is to discount each individual cash flow to the present, as shown in Exhibit 6.7B. Note that since the first $1,000 cash flow takes place at the current time ($t = 0$), the cash flow is already in present value terms. The present value of the cash flows is $3,577.

Compare this present value with the present value of the ordinary annuity, $3,312, as calculated in Exhibit 6.7A. It should be no surprise that the present value of the annuity due is larger than the present value of the ordinary annuity ($3,577 > $3,312), even though both annuities have four $1,000 cash flows. The reason is that the cash flows of the annuity due are shifted forward one year and, thus, are discounted less.

ANNUITY TRANSFORMATION METHOD

An easier way to work annuity due problems is to transform our formula for the present value of an annuity (Equation 6.1) so that it will work for annuity due problems. To do this, we pretend that each cash flow occurs at the end of the period (although it actually occurs at the beginning of the period) and use Equation 6.1. Since Equation 6.1 discounts each cash flow by one period too many, we then correct for the extra discounting by multiplying our answer by $(1 + i)$, where i is the discount rate or interest rate.

The relation between an ordinary annuity and an annuity due can be formally expressed as:

$$\text{Annuity due value} = \text{Ordinary annuity value} \times (1 + i) \qquad (6.4)$$

This relation is especially helpful because it works for both present value and future value calculations. Calculating the value of an annuity due using Equation 6.4 involves three steps:

1. Adjust the problem time line as if the cash flows were an ordinary annuity.
2. Calculate the present or future value as though the cash flows were an ordinary annuity.
3. Finally, multiply the answer by $(1 + i)$.

Let's calculate the value of the annuity due shown in Exhibit 6.7B using Equation 6.4, the transformation technique. First, we restate the time line as if the problem were an ordinary annuity; the revised time line looks like the one in Exhibit 6.7A. Second, we calculate the present value of the annuity as if the problem involved an ordinary annuity. The value of the ordinary annuity is $3,312, as shown in part A of the exhibit. Finally, we use Equation 6.4 to make the adjustment to an annuity due:

$$\begin{aligned}\text{Annuity due value} &= \text{Ordinary annuity value} \times (1 + i)\\ &= \$3{,}312 \times 1.08\\ &= \$3{,}577\end{aligned}$$

As they should, the answers for the two methods of calculation agree.[8]

Before You Go On

1. How do an ordinary annuity, an annuity due, and a perpetuity differ?
2. Give two examples of perpetuities.
3. What is the annuity transformation method?

[8]The easy way to calculate the present value or future value of an annuity due is by using the BEG/END switch in your financial calculator. All financial calculators have a key that switches the cash flow from the end of each period to the beginning of each period. The keys are typically labeled "BEG" for cash flows at the beginning of the period and "END" for the cash flows at the end of the period. To calculate the PV of an annuity due: (1) switch the calculator to the BEG mode, (2) enter the data, and (3) press the PV key for the answer. As an example, work the problem from Exhibit 6.7B using your financial calculator.

6.3 Cash Flows That Grow at a Constant Rate

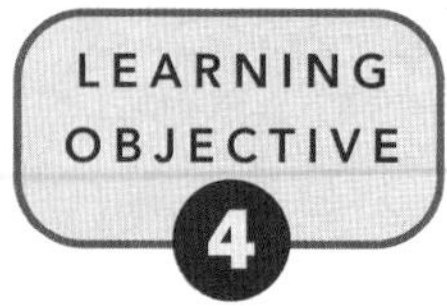

LEARNING OBJECTIVE 4

So far, we have been examining level cash flow streams. Often, though, management needs to value a cash flow stream that increases at a constant rate over time. These cash flow streams are called growing annuities or growing perpetuities.

Growing Annuity

growing annuity an annuity in which the cash flows increase at a constant rate

Financial managers often need to compute the value of multiyear product or service contracts with cash flows that increase each year at a constant rate. These are called **growing annuities.** For example, you may want to value the cost of a 25-year lease that adjusts annually for the expected rate of inflation over the life of the contract. Equation 6.5 can be used to compute the present value of an annuity growing at a constant rate for a finite time period:

$$\text{PVA}_n = \frac{\text{CF}_1}{i - g} \times \left[1 - \left(\frac{1 + g}{1 + i}\right)^n\right] \tag{6.5}$$

where:

PVA_n = present value of a growing annuity with n periods
CF_1 = cash flow one period in the future ($t = 1$)
i = interest rate, or discount rate
g = constant growth rate per period

You should be aware of several important points when applying Equation 6.5. First, the cash flow (CF_1) used is not the cash flow for the current period (CF_0), but is the cash flow to be received in the next period ($t = 1$). The relation between these two cash flows is $\text{CF}_1 = \text{CF}_0 \times (1 + g)$. Second, a necessary condition for using Equation 6.5 is that $i > g$. If this condition is not met ($i \leq g$), the calculations from the equation will be meaningless, as you will get a negative value for positive cash flows. A negative value essentially says that someone would have to pay you money to get you to accept a positive cash flow.

As an example of how Equation 6.5 is applied, suppose you work for a company that owns a number of coffee shops in the New York City area. One coffee shop is located in the Empire State Building, and your boss wants to know how much it is worth. The coffee shop has a 50-year lease, so we will assume that it will be in business for 50 years.[9] It produced cash flows of \$300,000 after all expenses this year, and the discount rate used by similar businesses is 15 percent. You estimate that, over the long term, cash flows will grow at 2.5 percent per year because of inflation. Thus, you calculate that the coffee shop's cash flow next year (CF_1) will be \$307,500, or \$300,000 × (1 + 0.025).

Plugging the values from the coffee shop example into Equation 6.5 yields the following result:

$$\begin{aligned}\text{PVA}_n &= \frac{\$307{,}500}{0.15 - 0.025} \times \left[1 - \left(\frac{1.025}{1.15}\right)^{50}\right] \\ &= \$2{,}460{,}000 \times 0.9968 \\ &= \$2{,}452{,}128\end{aligned}$$

The estimated value of the coffee shop is \$2,452,128.

[9]For those interested, the Empire State Building has three coffee shops.

Growing Perpetuity

Sometimes cash flows are expected to grow at a constant rate indefinitely. In this case the cash flow stream is called a **growing perpetuity**. The formula to compute the present value for a growing perpetuity (PVA_∞) is as follows:

growing perpetuity
a cash flow stream that grows at a constant rate forever

$$PVA_\infty = \frac{CF_1}{i - g} \tag{6.6}$$

As before, CF_1 is the cash flow occurring at the end of the first period, i is the discount rate, and g is the constant rate of growth of the cash flow (CF). Equation 6.6 is an easy equation to work with, and it is used widely in the valuation of common stock for firms that have a policy and history of paying dividends that grow at a constant rate. It is also widely used in the valuation of entire companies, as we will discuss in Chapter 18.

Notice that we can easily derive Equation 6.6 from Equation 6.5 by setting n equal to ∞. If i is greater than g, as we said it must be, the term $[(1 + g)/(1 + i)]^\infty$ is equal to 0, leading to the following result:

$$\begin{aligned} PVA_\infty &= \frac{CF_1}{i - g} \times \left[1 - \left(\frac{1 + g}{1 + i}\right)^\infty\right] \\ &= \frac{CF_1}{i - g} \times [1 - 0] \\ &= \frac{CF_1}{i - g} \end{aligned}$$

This makes sense, of course, since Equation 6.5 describes a growing annuity and Equation 6.6 describes a growing cash flow stream that goes on forever. Notice that Equations 6.5 and 6.6 are exactly the same as Equations 6.1 and 6.3 when g equals zero.

To illustrate a growing perpetuity, we will consider an example. Suppose that you and a partner, after graduating from college, started a health and athletic club. Your concept included not only providing workout facilities, such as weights, treadmills, and elliptical trainers, but also promoting a healthy lifestyle through a focus on cooking and nutrition. The concept has proved popular, and after only five years, you have seven clubs in operation. Your accountant reports that the firm's cash flow last year was \$450,000, and the appropriate discount rate for the club is 18 percent. You expect the firm's cash flows to increase by 5 percent per year, which includes 2 percent for expected inflation. The business has no fixed life, so you can assume it will continue operating indefinitely into the future. What is the value of the firm?

We can use Equation 6.6 to solve this problem. Although the equation is very easy to use, a common mistake is using the current period's cash flow (CF_0) and not the *next* period's cash flow (CF_1). Since the cash flow is growing at a constant growth rate, g, we simply multiply CF_0 by $(1 + g)$ to get the value of CF_1. Thus,

$$CF_1 = CF_0 \times (1 + g)$$

We can then substitute the result into Equation 6.6, which yields a helpful variant of this equation:

$$PVA_\infty = \frac{CF_1}{i - g} = \frac{CF_0 \times (1 + g)}{i - g}$$

Now we can insert the values for the health club into the equation and solve for PVA_∞:

$$\begin{aligned} PVA_\infty &= \frac{CF_0 \times (1 + g)}{i - g} \\ &= \frac{\$450{,}000 \times (1 + 0.05)}{0.18 - 0.05} \\ &= \$3{,}634{,}615 \end{aligned}$$

The business is worth $3,634,615.

The growing annuity and perpetuity formulas are useful, and we will be applying them later on in the book. Unfortunately, even though advanced financial calculators have special programs for annuities and perpetuities with constant cash flows, typical financial calculators do not include programs for growing annuities and perpetuities.

Before You Go On

1. What is the difference between a growing annuity and a growing perpetuity?

6.4 The Effective Annual Interest Rate

In this chapter and the preceding one, there has been little question about which interest rate to use in a particular computation. In most cases, a single interest rate was supplied. When working with real market data, however, the situation is not so clear-cut. We often encounter interest rates that can be computed in different ways. In this final section, we try to untangle some of the issues that can cause problems.

Why the Confusion?

annual percentage rate (APR)
the simple interest rate charged per period multiplied by the number of periods per year

To better understand why interest rates can be so confusing, consider a familiar situation. Suppose you borrow $100 on your bank credit card and plan to keep the balance outstanding for one year. The credit card's stated interest rate is 1 percent per month. The federal Truth-in-Lending Act requires the bank and other financial institutions to disclose to consumers the **annual percentage rate (APR)** charged on a loan. The APR is the annualized interest rate using *simple interest*. Thus, the APR is defined as the simple interest charged per period multiplied by the number of periods per year. For the bank credit card loan, the APR is 12 percent (1 percent per month × 12 months).

At the end of the year, you go to pay off the credit card balance as planned. It seems reasonable to assume that with an APR of 12 percent, your credit card balance at the end of one year would be $112 (1.12 × $100). Wrong! The bank's *actual* interest rate is 1 percent per month, meaning that the bank will compound your credit card balance monthly, 12 times over the year. The bank's calculation for the balance due is $112.68 [$\$100 \times (1.01)^{12}$].[10] The bank is actually charging you 12.68 percent per year, and the total interest paid for the one-year loan is $12.68 rather than $12.00. This example raises a question: What is the correct way to annualize an interest rate?

Calculating the Effective Annual Interest Rate

effective annual interest rate (EAR)
the annual interest rate that reflects compounding within a year

In making financial decisions, the correct way to annualize an interest rate is to compute the effective annual interest rate. The **effective annual interest rate (EAR)** is defined as

[10]If you have any doubt about the total credit card debt at the end of one year, make the calculation 12 times on your calculator: the first month is $100 × 1.01 = 101.00; the second month is $101.00 × 1.01 = $102.01; the third month is $102.01 × 1.01 = $103.03; and so on for 12 months.

the annual growth rate that takes compounding into account. Mathematically, the EAR can be stated as follows:

$$1 + \text{EAR} = \left(1 + \frac{\text{Quoted interest rate}}{m}\right)^m \tag{6.7}$$

$$\text{EAR} = \left(1 + \frac{\text{Quoted interest rate}}{m}\right)^m - 1$$

where m is the number of compounding periods during a year. The **quoted interest rate** is by definition a *simple* annual interest rate, like the APR. That means that the quoted interest rate has been annualized by multiplying the rate per period by the number of periods per year. The EAR conversion formula accounts for the number of compounding periods and, thus, effectively adjusts the annualized quoted interest rate for the time value of money. Because the EAR is the true cost of borrowing and lending, it is the rate that should be used for making all finance decisions.

quoted interest rate
a simple annual interest rate, such as the APR

Many useful financial calculators, including an APR calculator, can be found at Efunda.com. Go to www.efunda.com/formulae/finance/apr_calculator.cfm.

We will use our bank credit card example to illustrate the use of Equation 6.7. Recall that the credit card has an APR of 12 percent (1 percent per month). The APR is the quoted interest rate, and the number of compounding periods (m) is 12. Applying Equation 6.7, we find that the effective annual interest rate is:

$$\begin{aligned}\text{EAR} &= \left(1 + \frac{\text{Quoted interest rate}}{m}\right)^m - 1\\ &= \left(1 + \frac{0.12}{12}\right)^{12} - 1\\ &= (1.01)^{12} - 1\\ &= 1.1268 - 1\\ &= 0.1286, \text{ or } 12.68\%\end{aligned}$$

The EAR value of 12.68 percent is the true cost of borrowing the \$100 on the bank credit card for one year. The EAR calculation adjusts for the effects of compounding and, hence, the time value of money.

Finally, notice that interest rates are quoted in the marketplace in three ways:

1. *The quoted interest rate.* This is an interest rate that has been annualized by multiplying the rate per period by the number of compounding periods. The APR is an example. All consumer borrowing and lending rates are annualized in this manner.
2. *The interest rate per period.* The bank credit card rate of 1 percent per month is an example of this kind of rate. You can find the interest rate per period by dividing the quoted interest rate by the number of compounding periods.
3. *The effective annual interest rate (EAR).* This is the interest rate actually paid (or earned), which takes compounding into account. Sometimes it is difficult to distinguish a quoted rate from an EAR. Generally, however, an annualized consumer rate is an APR rather than an EAR.

Comparing Interest Rates

When borrowing or lending money, it is sometimes necessary to compare and select among interest rate alternatives. Quoted interest rates are comparable when they cover the same overall time period, such as one year, and have the same number of compounding periods. If quoted interest rates are *not* comparable, we must adjust them to a common time period. The easiest way, and the correct way, to make interest rates comparable for making finance decisions is to convert them to effective annual interest rates. Consider an example.

Suppose you are the chief financial officer of a manufacturing company. The company is planning a \$1 billion plant expansion and will finance it by borrowing money for five years. Three financial institutions have submitted interest rate quotes; all are APRs:

Lender A: 10.40 percent compound monthly
Lender B: 10.90 percent compounded annually
Lender C: 10.50 percent compounded quarterly

Although all the loans have the same maturity, the loans are not comparable because the APRs have different compounding periods. To make the adjustments for the different time periods, we apply Equation 6.7 to convert each of the APR quotes into an EAR:

$$\begin{aligned}\text{Lender A: EAR} &= \left(1 + \frac{0.1040}{12}\right)^{12} - 1\\ &= (1.0087)^{12} - 1\\ &= 1.1091 - 1\\ &= 0.1091, \text{ or } 10.91\%\end{aligned}$$

$$\begin{aligned}\text{Lender B: EAR} &= \left(1 + \frac{0.1090}{1}\right)^{1} - 1\\ &= 1.1090 - 1\\ &= 0.1090, \text{ or } 10.90\%\end{aligned}$$

$$\begin{aligned}\text{Lender C: EAR} &= \left(1 + \frac{0.1050}{4}\right)^{4} - 1\\ &= (1.0263)^{4} - 1\\ &= 1.1092 - 1\\ &= 0.1092, \text{ or } 10.92\%\end{aligned}$$

As shown, Lender B offers the lowest interest cost at 10.90 percent.

Notice the shift in rankings that takes place as a result of the EAR calculations. When we initially looked at the APR quotes, it appeared that Lender A offered the lowest rate and Lender B had the highest. After computing the EAR, we find that when we account for the effect of compounding, Lender B actually offers the lowest interest rate.

Another important point is that if all the interest rates are quoted as APRs with the same annualizing period, such as monthly, the interest rates are comparable and you can select the correct rate by simply comparing the quotes. That is, the lowest APR corresponds with the lowest cost of funds. Thus, it is correct for borrowers or lenders to make economic decisions with APR data as long as interest rates have the same maturity and the same compounding period. To find the true cost of the loan, however, it is still necessary to compute the EAR.

LEARNING BY DOING APPLICATION 6.8

What Is the True Cost of a Loan?

Problem: During a period of economic expansion, Frank Smith became financially overextended and was forced to consolidate his debt with a loan from a consumer finance company. The consolidated debt provided Frank with a single loan and lower monthly payments than he had previously been making. The loan agreement quotes an APR of 20 percent, and Frank must make monthly payments. What is the true cost of the loan?

Approach: The true cost of the loan is the EAR, not the APR. Thus, we must convert the quoted rate into the EAR, using Equation 6.7, to get the true cost of the loan.

Solution:

$$
\begin{aligned}
\text{EAR} &= \left(1 + \frac{\text{Quoted interest rate}}{m}\right)^m - 1 \\
&= \left(1 + \frac{0.20}{12}\right)^{12} - 1 \\
&= (1 + 0.0167)^{12} - 1 \\
&= (1.0167)^{12} - 1 \\
&= 1.2194 - 1 \\
&= 0.2194, \text{ or } 21.94\%
\end{aligned}
$$

The true cost of the loan is 21.94 percent, not the 20 percent APR.

Consumer Protection Acts and Interest Rate Disclosure

In 1968 Congress passed the **Truth-in-Lending Act** to ensure that all borrowers receive meaningful information about the cost of credit so that they can make intelligent economic decisions.[11] The act applies to all lenders that extend credit to consumers, and it covers credit card loans, auto loans, home mortgage loans, home equity loans, home improvement loans, and some small-business loans. Similar legislation, the so-called **Truth-in-Savings Act,** applies to consumer savings vehicles such as certificates of deposit (CDs). These two pieces of legislation require by law that the APR be disclosed on all consumer loans and savings plans and that it be prominently displayed on advertising and contractual documents.

Truth-in-Lending Act
a federal law requiring lenders to fully inform borrowers of important information related to loans, including the annual percentage rate charged

Truth-in-Savings Act
a federal law requiring institutions offering consumer savings vehicles, such as certificates of deposit (CDs), to fully inform consumers of important information about the savings vehicles, including the annual percentage rate paid

We know that the EAR, not the APR, represents the true economic interest rate. So why did the Truth-in-Lending and Truth-in-Savings Acts specify that the APR must be the disclosed rate? The APR was selected because it's easy to calculate and easy to understand. When the legislation was passed in 1969, computers were still using punch cards, and PCs and handheld calculators did not exist.[12] Down at the auto showroom, salespeople needed an easy way to explain and annualize the monthly interest charge, and the APR provided just such a method. And most important, if all the auto lenders quoted monthly APR, consumers could select the loan with the lowest economic interest cost.

Today, although lenders and borrowers are legally required to quote the APR, they run their businesses using interest rate calculations based on the present value and future value formulas. Consumers are bombarded with both APR and EAR rates, and confusion reigns. At the car dealership, for example, you may find that your auto loan's APR is 5 percent but the "actual borrowing rate" is 5.12 percent. And at the bank where your grandmother gets free coffee and doughnuts, she may be told that the bank's one-year CD has an APR of 3 percent, but it really pays 3.04 percent. Because of confusion arising from conflicting interest rates in the marketplace, some observers believe that the APR calculation has outlived its usefulness and should be abandoned by regulators and replaced by the EAR.

The Appropriate Interest Rate Factor

Here is a final question to consider: What is the appropriate interest rate to use when making future or present value calculations? The answer is simple: use the EAR. Under no circumstance should the APR or any other quoted rate be used as the interest rate

[11]The Truth-in-Lending Act is Title I of the Consumer Credit Protection Act.

[12]The first handheld calculator was the Bomar Brain, which was first sold in 1971.

in present or future value calculations. Consider an example of using the EAR in such a calculation.

Petra, an MBA student at Georgetown University, has purchased a $100 savings note with a two-year maturity from a small consumer finance company. The contract states that the note has a 20 percent APR and pays interest quarterly. The quarterly interest rate is thus 5 percent (20 percent/4). Petra has several questions about the note: (1) What is the note's actual interest rate (EAR)? (2) How much money will she have at the end of two years? (3) When making the future value calculation, should she use the quarterly interest rate or the annual EAR?

To answer Petra's questions, we first compute the EAR, which is the actual interest earned on the note:

$$\begin{aligned}\text{EAR} &= \left(1 + \frac{\text{APR}}{m}\right)^m - 1\\ &= \left(1 + \frac{0.20}{4}\right)^4 - 1\\ &= (1 + 0.05)^4 - 1\\ &= 1.21551 - 1\\ &= 0.21551, \text{ or } 21.551\%\end{aligned}$$

Next, we calculate the future value of the note using the EAR. Because the EAR is an annual rate, for this problem we use a total of two compounding periods. The calculation is as follows:

$$\begin{aligned}\text{FV}_2 &= \text{PV} \times (1 + i)^n\\ &= \$100 \times (1 + 0.21551)^2\\ &= \$100 \times 1.4775\\ &= \$147.75\end{aligned}$$

We can also calculate the future value using the quarterly rate of interest of 5 percent with a total of eight compounding periods. In this case, the calculation is as follows:

$$\begin{aligned}\text{FV}_2 &= \$100 \times (1 + 0.050)^8\\ &= \$100 \times 1.4775\\ &= \$147.75\end{aligned}$$

The two calculation methods yield the same answer, $147.75.

In sum, any time you do a future value or present value calculation, you must use either the interest rate per period (quoted rate/m) or the EAR as the interest rate factor. It does not matter which of these you use. Both will properly account for the impact of compounding on the value of cash flows. Interest rate proxies such as the APR should never be used as interest rate factors for calculating future or present values. Because they do not properly account for the number of compounding periods, their use can lead to answers that are economically incorrect.

Before You Go On

1. What is the APR, and why are lending institutions required to disclose this rate?
2. What is the correct way to annualize an interest rate in financial decision making?
3. Distinguish between quoted interest rate, interest rate per period, and effective annual interest rate.

Summary of Learning Objectives

1. **Explain why cash flows occurring at different times must be adjusted to reflect their value as of a common date before they can be compared, and be able to compute the present value and future value for multiple cash flows.**

   When making decisions involving cash flows over time, we should first identify the magnitude and timing of the cash flows and then adjust each individual cash flow to reflect its value as of a common date. For example, the process of discounting (compounding) the cash flows adjusts them for the time value of money because today's dollars are not equal in value to dollars in the future. Once all of the cash flows are in present (future) value terms, they can be compared to make decisions. Section 6.1 discusses the computation of present values and future values of multiple cash flows.

2. **Describe how to calculate the present value of an ordinary annuity and how an ordinary annuity differs from an annuity due.**

   An ordinary annuity is a series of equally spaced, level cash flows over time. The cash flows for an ordinary annuity are assumed to take place at the end of each period. To find the present value of an ordinary annuity, we multiply the present value of an annuity factor, which is equal to (1 − present value factor)/i, by the amount of the constant cash flow. An annuity due is an annuity in which the cash flows occur at the beginning of each period. A lease is an example of an annuity due. In this case, we are effectively prepaying for the service. To calculate the value of an annuity due, we calculate the present value (or future value) as though the cash flows were an ordinary annuity. We then multiply the ordinary annuity value times $(1 + i)$. Section 6.2 discusses the calculation of the present value of an ordinary annuity and annuity due.

3. **Explain what a perpetuity is and how it is used in business, and be able to calculate the value of a perpetuity.**

   A perpetuity is like an annuity except that the cash flows are perpetual—they never end. British Treasury Department bonds, called consols, were the first widely used securities of this kind. The most common example of a perpetuity today is preferred stock. The issuer of preferred stock promises to pay fixed-rate dividends forever. To calculate the present value of a perpetuity, we simply divide the promised constant payment (CF) by the interest rate (i).

4. **Discuss growing annuities and perpetuities, as well as their application in business, and be able to calculate their value.**

   Financial managers often need to value cash flow streams that increase at a constant rate over time. These cash flow streams are called growing annuities or growing perpetuities. An example of a growing annuity is a 10-year lease contract with an annual adjustment for the expected rate of inflation over the life of the contract. If the cash flows continue to grow at a constant rate indefinitely, this cash flow stream is called a growing perpetuity. Application and calculation of cash flows that grow at a constant rate are discussed in Section 6.3.

5. **Discuss why the effective annual interest rate (EAR) is the appropriate way to annualize interest rates, and be able to calculate EAR.**

   The EAR is the annual growth rate that takes compounding into account. Thus, the EAR is the true cost of borrowing or lending money. When we need to compare interest rates, we must make sure that the rates to be compared have the same time and compounding periods. If interest rates are not comparable, they must be converted into common terms. The easiest way to convert rates to common terms is to calculate the EAR for each interest rate. The use and calculations of EAR are discussed in Section 6.4.

Summary of Key Equations

Equation	Description	Formula
6.1	Present value of an ordinary annuity	$\text{PVA}_n = \frac{\text{CF}}{i} \times \left[1 - \frac{1}{(1+i)^n}\right]$ $= \text{CF} \times \frac{1 - 1/(1+i)^n}{i}$ $= \text{CF} \times \frac{1 - \text{Present value factor}}{i}$ $= \text{CF} \times \text{PV annuity factor}$
6.2	Future value of an ordinary annuity	$\text{FVA}_n = \frac{\text{CF}}{i} \times [(1+i)^n - 1]$ $= \text{CF} \times \frac{(1+i)^n - 1}{i}$

		$= \text{CF} \times \dfrac{\text{Future value factor} - 1}{i}$ $= \text{CF} \times \text{FV annuity factor}$
6.3	Present value of a perpetuity	$\text{PVA}_\infty = \dfrac{\text{CF}}{i}$
6.4	Value of an annuity due	$\text{Annuity due value} = \text{Ordinary annuity value} \times (1 + i)$
6.5	Present value of a growing annuity	$\text{PVA}_n = \dfrac{\text{CF}_1}{i - g} \times \left[1 - \left(\dfrac{1 + g}{1 + i}\right)^n\right]$
6.6	Present value of a growing perpetuity	$\text{PVA}_\infty = \dfrac{\text{CF}_1}{i - g}$
6.7	Effective annual interest rate	$\text{EAR} = \left(1 + \dfrac{\text{Quoted interest rate}}{m}\right)^m - 1$

Self-Study Problems

6.1 Kronka, Inc., is expecting cash flows of $13,000, $11,500, $12,750, and $9,635 over the next four years. What is the present value of these cash flows if the appropriate discount rate is 8 percent?

6.2 Your grandfather has agreed to deposit a certain amount of money each year into an account paying 7.25 percent annually to help you go to graduate school. Starting next year, and for the following four years, he plans to deposit $2,250, $8,150, $7,675, $6,125, and $12,345 into the account. How much will you have at the end of the five years?

6.3 Mike White is planning to save up for a trip to Europe in three years. He will need $7,500 when he is ready to make the trip. He plans to invest the same amount at the end of each of the next three years in an account paying 6 percent. What is the amount that he will have to save every year to reach his goal of $7,500 in three years?

6.4 Becky Scholes has $150,000 to invest. She wants to be able to withdraw $12,500 every year forever without using up any of her principal. What interest rate would her investment have to earn in order for her to be able to do so?

6.5 Dynamo Corp. is expecting annual payments of $34,225 for the next seven years from a customer. What is the present value of this annuity if the discount rate is 8.5 percent?

Solutions to Self-Study Problems

6.1 The time line for Kronka's cash flows and their present value is as follows:

Year	0	1	2	3	4
8%		$13,000	$11,500	$12,750	$9,635

$$\text{PV}_4 = \frac{\$13{,}000}{1.08} + \frac{\$11{,}500}{(1.08)^2} + \frac{\$12{,}750}{(1.08)^3} + \frac{\$9{,}635}{(1.08)^4}$$
$$= \$12{,}037.03 + \$9{,}859.40 + \$10{,}121.36 + \$7{,}082.01$$
$$= \$39{,}099.80$$

6.2 The time line for your cash flows and their future value is as follows:

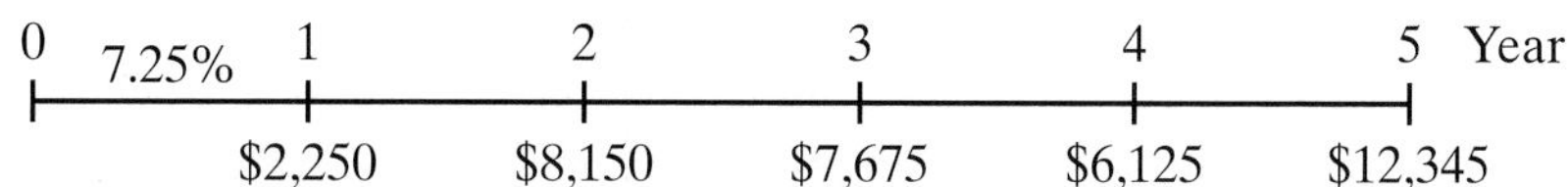

$$\begin{aligned} FV_5 &= \$2{,}250 \times (1.0725)^4 + \$8{,}150 \times (1.0725)^3 + \$7{,}675 \times (1.0725)^2 + \$6{,}125 \times 1.0725 + \$12,345 \\ &= \$2{,}976.95 + \$10{,}054.25 + \$8{,}828.22 + \$6{,}569.06 + \$12{,}345.00 \\ &= \$40{,}773.48 \end{aligned}$$

6.3 Amount Mike White will need in three years = FVA_3 = $7,500
Number of years = $n = 3$
Interest rate on investment = $i = 6.0\%$
Amount that Mike needs to invest every year = PMT = ?

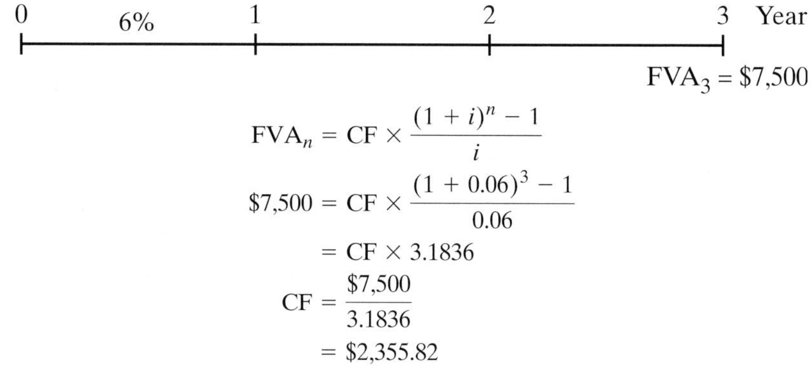

$$FVA_n = CF \times \frac{(1+i)^n - 1}{i}$$

$$\begin{aligned} \$7{,}500 &= CF \times \frac{(1+0.06)^3 - 1}{0.06} \\ &= CF \times 3.1836 \\ CF &= \frac{\$7{,}500}{3.1836} \\ &= \$2{,}355.82 \end{aligned}$$

Mike will have to invest $2,355.82 every year for the next three years.

6.4 Present value of Becky Scholes's investment = $150,000
Amount needed annually = $12,500
This is a perpetuity!

$$PVA_\infty = \frac{CF}{i}$$

$$i = \frac{CF}{PVA_\infty} = \frac{\$12{,}500}{\$150{,}000}$$

$$i = 8.33\%$$

6.5 The time line for Dynamo's cash flows and their present value is as follows:

0	1	2	3	4	5	6	7 Year
8.5%							
PVA = ?	$34,225	$34,225	$34,225	$34,225	$34,225	$34,225	$34,225

$$PVA_7 = CF \times \frac{1 - 1/(1+i)^n}{i}$$

$$\begin{aligned} &= \$34{,}225 \times \frac{1 - 1/(1+0.085)^7}{0.085} \\ &= \$34{,}225 \times 5.118514 \\ &= \$175{,}181.14 \end{aligned}$$

Critical Thinking Questions

6.1 Identify the steps involved in computing the future value when you have multiple cash flows.

6.2 What is the key economic principle involved in calculating the present value and future value of multiple cash flows?

6.3 What is the difference between a perpetuity and an annuity?

6.4 Define *annuity due.* Would an investment be worth more if it were an ordinary annuity or an annuity due? Explain.

6.5 Raymond Bartz is trying to choose between two equally risky annuities, each paying $5,000 per year for five years. One is an ordinary annuity, the other is an annuity due. Which of the following statements is most correct?

a. The present value of the ordinary annuity must exceed the present value of the annuity due, but the future value of an ordinary annuity may be less than the future value of the annuity due.

b. The present value of the annuity due exceeds the present value of the ordinary annuity, while the future value of the annuity due is less than the future value of the ordinary annuity.

c. The present value of the annuity due exceeds the present value of the ordinary annuity, and the future value of the annuity due also exceeds the future value of the ordinary annuity.

d. If interest rates increase, the difference between the present value of the ordinary annuity and the present value of the annuity due remains the same.

6.6 Which of the following investments will have the highest future value at the end of three years? Assume that the effective annual rate for all investments is the same.

a. You earn $3,000 at the end of three years (a total of one payment).

b. You earn $1,000 at the end of every year for the next three years (a total of three payments).

c. You earn $1,000 at the beginning of every year for the next three years (a total of three payments).

6.7 Explain whether or not each of the following statements is correct.

a. A 15-year mortgage will have larger monthly payments than a 30-year mortgage of the same amount and same interest rate.

b. If an investment pays 10 percent interest compounded annually, its effective rate will also be 10 percent.

6.8 When will the annual percentage rate (APR) be the same as the effective annual rate (EAR)?

6.9 Why is the EAR superior to the APR in measuring the true economic cost or return?

6.10 Suppose two investments have equal lives and multiple cash flows. A high discount rate tends to favor

a. the investment with large cash flows early.

b. the investment with large cash flows late.

c. the investment with even cash flows.

d. neither investment since they have equal lives.

Questions and Problems

BASIC

6.1 **Future value with multiple cash flows:** Konerko, Inc., expects to earn cash flows of $13,227, $15,611, $18,970, and $19,114 over the next four years. If the company uses an 8 percent discount rate, what is the future value of these cash flows at the end of year 4?

6.2 **Future value with multiple cash flows:** Ben Woolmer has an investment that will pay him the following cash flows over the next five years: $2,350, $2,725, $3,128, $3,366, and $3,695. If his investments typically earn 7.65 percent, what is the future value of the investment's cash flows at the end of five years?

6.3 **Future value with multiple cash flows:** You are a freshman in college and are planning a trip to Europe when you graduate from college at the end of four years. You plan to save the following amounts annually, starting today: $625, $700, $700, and $750. If the account pays 5.75 percent annually, how much will you have at the end of four years?

6.4 **Present value with multiple cash flows:** Saul Cervantes has just purchased some equipment for his landscaping business. He plans to pay the following amounts at the end of each of the next five years: $10,450, $8,500, $9,675, $12,500, and $11,635. If he uses a discount rate of 10.875 percent, what is the cost of the equipment he purchased today?

6.5 **Present value with multiple cash flows:** Jeremy Fenloch borrowed a certain amount from his friend and promised to repay him the amounts of $1,225, $1,350, $1,500, $1,600, and

$1,600 over the next five years. If the friend normally discounts investments at 8 percent annually, how much did Jeremy borrow?

6.6 **Present value with multiple cash flows:** Biogenesis Inc. expects the following cash flow stream over the next five years. The company discounts all cash flows at a 23 percent discount rate. What is the present value of this cash flow stream?

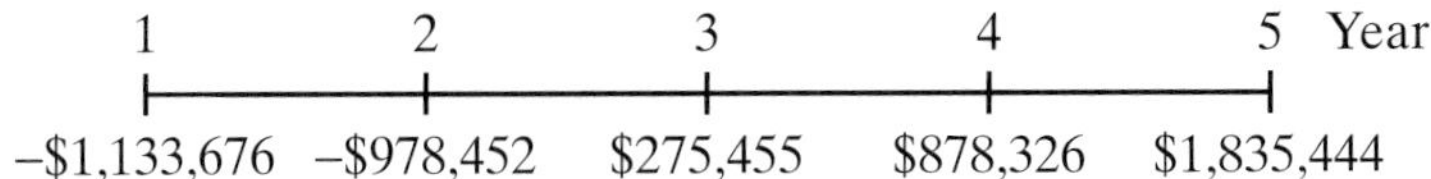

6.7 **Present value of an ordinary annuity:** An investment opportunity requires a payment of $750 for 12 years, starting a year from today. If your required rate of return is 8 percent, what is the value of the investment today?

6.8 **Present value of an ordinary annuity:** Dynamics Telecommunications Corp. has made an investment in another company that will guarantee it a cash flow of $22,500 each year for the next five years. If the company uses a discount rate of 15 percent on its investments, what is the present value of this investment?

6.9 **Future value of an ordinary annuity:** Robert Hobbes plans to invest $25,000 a year at the end of each year for the next seven years in an investment that will pay him a rate of return of 11.4 percent. How much money will Hobbes have at the end of seven years?

6.10 **Future value of an ordinary annuity:** Cecelia Thomas is a sales executive at a Baltimore firm. She is 25 years old and plans to invest $3,000 every year in an IRA account, beginning at the end of this year until she turns 65 years old. If the IRA investment will earn 9.75 percent annually, how much will she have in 40 years, when she turns 65 years old?

6.11 **Future value of an annuity due:** Refer to Problem 6.10. If Cecelia Thomas invests at the beginning of each year, how much will she have at age 65?

6.12 **Computing annuity payment:** Kevin Winthrop is saving for an Australian vacation in three years. He estimates that he will need $5,000 to cover his airfare and all other expenses for a week-long holiday in Australia. If he can invest his money in an S&P 500 equity index fund that is expected to earn an average return of 10.3 percent over the next three years, how much will he have to save every year if he starts saving at the end of this year?

6.13 **Computing annuity payment:** The Elkridge Bar & Grill has a seven-year loan of $23,500 with Bank of America. It plans to repay the loan in seven equal installments starting today. If the rate of interest is 8.4 percent, how much will each payment be worth?

6.14 **Perpetuity:** Your grandfather is retiring at the end of next year. He would like to ensure that he, and after he dies, his heirs receive payments of $10,000 a year forever, starting when he retires. If he can invest at 6.5 percent, how much does your grandfather need to invest to receive the desired cash flow?

6.15 **Perpetuity:** Calculate the perpetuity payments for each of the following cases:
a. $250,000 invested at 6 percent.
b. $50,000 invested at 12 percent.
c. $100,000 invested at 10 percent.

6.16 **Effective annual interest rate:** Raj Krishnan bought a Honda Accord for a price of $17,345. He put down $6,000 and financed the rest through the dealer at an APR of 4.9 percent for four years. What is the effective annual interest rate (EAR) if payments are made monthly?

6.17 **Effective annual interest rate:** Cyclone Rentals borrowed $15,550 from a bank for three years. If the quoted rate (APR) is 6.75 percent, and the compounding is daily, what is the effective annual interest rate (EAR)?

6.18 **Growing perpetuity:** You are evaluating a growing perpetuity product from a large financial services firm. The product promises an initial payment of $20,000 at the end of this year and subsequent payments will thereafter grow at a rate of 3.4 percent annually. If you use a 9 percent discount rate for investment products, what is the present value of this growing perpetuity?

6.19 **Future value with multiple cash flows:** Trigen Corp. is expecting to invest cash flows of $331,000, $616,450, $212,775, $818,400, $1,239,644, and $1,617,848 in research and development over the next six years. If the appropriate interest rate is 6.75 percent, what is the future value of these investment cash flows? **INTERMEDIATE**

6.20 Future value with multiple cash flows: Stephanie Watson plans to adopt the following investment pattern beginning next year. She will invest $3,125 in each of the next three years and will then make investments of $3,650, $3,725, $3,875, and $4,000 over the following four years. If the investments are expected to earn 11.5 percent annually, how much will she have at the end of the seven years?

6.21 Present value with multiple cash flows: Carol Jenkins, a lottery winner, will receive the following payments over the next seven years. If she can invest her cash flows in a fund that will earn 10.5 percent annually, what is the present value of her winnings?

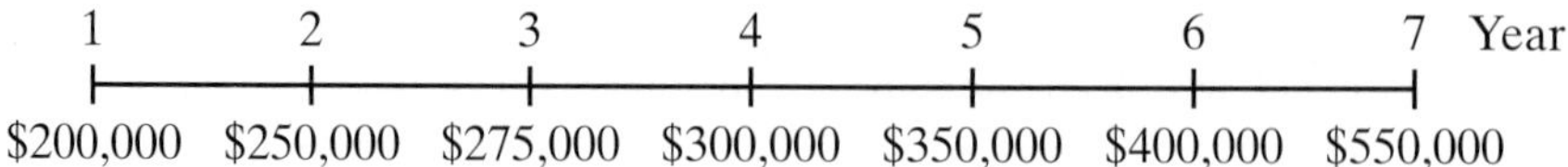

6.22 Computing annuity payment: Gary Whitmore is a high school sophomore. He currently has $7,500 in a savings account that pays 5.65 percent annually. Gary plans to use his current savings plus what he can save over the next four years to buy a car. He estimates that the car will cost $12,000 in four years. How much money should Gary save each year if he wants to buy the car?

6.23 Growing annuity: Modern Energy Company owns several gas stations. Management is looking to open a new station in the western suburbs of Baltimore. One possibility they are evaluating is to take over a station located at a site that has been leased from the county. The lease, originally for 99 years, currently has 73 years before expiration. The gas station generated a net cash flow of $92,500 last year, and the current owners expect an annual growth rate of 6.3 percent. If Modern Energy uses a discount rate of 14.5 percent to evaluate such businesses, what is the present value of this growing annuity?

6.24 Future value of annuity due: Jeremy Denham plans to save $5,000 every year for the next eight years, starting today. At the end of eight years, Jeremy will turn 30 years old and plans to use his savings toward the down payment on a house. If his investment in a mutual fund will earn him 10.3 percent annually, how much will he have saved in eight years when he will need the money to buy a house?

6.25 Present value of an annuity due: Grant Productions has borrowed a huge sum from the California Finance Company at a rate of 17.5 percent for a seven-year period. The loan calls for a payment of $1,540,862.19 each year beginning today. What is the amount borrowed by this company? Round to the nearest dollar.

6.26 Present value of an annuity due: Sharon Kabana has won a state lottery and will receive a payment of $89,729.45 every year, starting today, for the next 20 years. If she invests the proceeds at a rate of 7.25 percent, what is the present value of the cash flows that she will receive? Round to the nearest dollar.

6.27 Perpetuity: Calculate the present value of the following perpetuities:
a. $1,250 discounted to the present at 7 percent.
b. $7,250 discounted to the present at 6.33 percent.
c. $850 discounted to the present at 20 percent.

6.28 Effective annual interest rate: Find the effective annual interest rate (EAR) on each of the following:
a. 6 percent compounded quarterly.
b. 4.99 percent compounded monthly.
c. 7.25 percent compounded semiannually.
d. 5.6 percent compounded daily.

6.29 Effective annual interest rate: Which of the following investments has the highest effective annual interest rate (EAR)?
a. A bank CD that pays 8.25 percent compounded quarterly.
b. A bank CD that pays 8.25 percent compounded monthly.
c. A bank CD that pays 8.45 percent compounded annually.
d. A bank CD that pays 8.25 percent compounded semiannually.
e. A bank CD that pays 8 percent compounded daily (on a 365-day basis).

6.30 Effective annual interest rate: You are considering three alternative investments: (1) a three-year bank CD paying 7.5 percent compounded quarterly; (2) a three-year bank CD paying 7.3 percent compounded monthly; and (3) a three-year bank CD paying 7.75 percent compounded annually. Which investment has the highest effective annual interest rate?

ADVANCED

6.31 Tirade Owens, a professional athlete, currently has a contract that will pay him a large amount in the first year of his contract and smaller amounts thereafter. He and his agent have asked the team to restructure the contract. The team, though reluctant, obliged. Tirade and his agent came up with a counter offer. What are the present values of each of the contracts using a 14 percent discount rate? Which of the three contacts has the highest present value?

Year	Current Contract	Team's Offer	Counter Offer
1	$8,125,000	$4,000,000	$5,250,000
2	$3,650,000	$3,825,000	$7,550,000
3	$2,715,000	$3,850,000	$3,625,000
4	$1,822,250	$3,925,000	$2,800,000

6.32 Gary Kornig will be 30 years old next year and wants to retire when he is 65. So far he has saved (1) $6,950 in an IRA account in which his money is earning 8.3 percent annually and (2) $5,000 in a money market account in which he is earning 5.25 percent annually. Gary wants to have $1 million when he retires. Starting next year, he plans to invest a fixed amount of money every year until he retires in a mutual fund in which he expects to earn 9 percent annually. How much will Gary have to invest every year to achieve his savings goal? EXCEL®

6.33 Babu Baradwaj is saving for his son's college tuition. His son is currently 11 years old and will begin college in seven years. Babu has an index fund investment worth $7,500 that is earning 9.5 percent annually. Total expenses at the University of Maryland, where his son says he plans to go, currently total $15,000 per year, but are expected to grow at roughly 6 percent each year. Babu plans to invest in a mutual fund that will earn 11 percent annually to make up the difference between the college expenses and his current savings. In total, Babu will make seven equal investments with the first starting today and with the last being made a year before his son begins college. EXCEL®

a. What will be the present value of the four years of college expenses at the time that Babu's son starts college? Assume a discount rate of 5.5 percent.

b. What will be the value of the index mutual fund when his son just starts college?

c. What is the amount that Babu will have to have saved when his son turns 18 if Babu plans to cover all of his son's college expenses?

d. How much will Babu have to invest every year in order to have enough funds to cover all his son's expenses?

6.34 You are now 50 years old and plan to retire at age 65. You currently have a stock portfolio worth $150,000, a 401(k) retirement plan worth $250,000, and a money market account worth $50,000. Your stock portfolio is expected to provide you annual returns of 12 percent, your 401(k) investment will earn you 9.5 percent annually, and the money market account earns 5.25 percent, compounded monthly. EXCEL®

a. If you do not save another penny, what will be the total value of your investments when you retire at age 65?

b. Assume you plan to invest $12,000 every year in your 401(k) plan for the next 15 years (starting one year from now). How much will your investments be worth when you retire at 65?

c. Assume that you expect to live 25 years after you retire (until age 90). Today, at age 50, you take all of your investments and place them in an account that pays 8 percent (use the scenario from part b in which you continue saving). If you start withdrawing funds starting at age 66, how much can you withdraw every year (e.g., an ordinary annuity) and leave nothing in your account after a 25th and final withdrawal at age 90?

d. You want your current investments, which are described in the problem statement, to support a perpetuity that starts a year from now. How much can you withdraw each year without touching your principal?

6.35 Trevor Diaz is looking to purchase a Mercedes Benz SL600 Roadster, which has an invoice price of $121,737 and a total cost of $129,482. Trevor plans to put down $20,000 and will pay the rest by taking on a 5.75 percent five-year bank loan. What is the monthly payment on this auto loan? Prepare an amortization table using Excel. EXCEL®

6.36 The Sundarams are buying a new 3,500-square-foot house in Muncie, Indiana, and will borrow $237,000 from Bank One at a rate of 6.375 percent for 15 years. What is their monthly loan payment? Prepare an amortization schedule using Excel. EXCEL®

6.37 Assume you will start on a job as soon as you graduate. You plan to start saving for your retirement when you turn 25 years old. Assume you are 21 years of age at the time of EXCEL®

graduation. Everybody needs a break! Currently, you plan to retire when you turn 65 years old. After retirement, you expect to live at least until you are 85. You wish to be able to withdraw $40,000 (in today's dollars) every year from the time of your retirement until you are 85 years old (i.e., for 20 years). You can invest, starting when you turn 25 years old, in a portfolio fund. The average inflation rate is likely to be 5 percent.

a. Calculate the lump sum you need to have accumulated at age 65 to be able to draw the desired income. Assume that your return on the portfolio investment is likely to be 10 percent.
b. What is the dollar amount you need to invest every year, starting at age 26 and ending at age 65 (i.e., for 40 years) to reach the target lump sum at age 65?
c. Now answer questions a and b assuming your rate of return to be 8 percent per year, then again at 15 percent per year.
d. Now assume you start investing for your retirement when you turn 30 years old and analyze the situation under rate of return assumptions of (i) 8 percent, (ii) 10 percent, and (iii) 15 percent.
e. Repeat the analysis by assuming that you start investing when you are 35 years old.

Sample Test Problems

6.1 Groves Corp. is expecting annual cash flows of $225,000, $278,000, $312,500, and $410,000 over the next four years. If it uses a discount rate of 6.25 percent, what will be the present value of this cash flow stream?

6.2 Freisinger, Inc., is expecting a new project to start paying off, beginning at the end of next year. It expects cash flows to be as follows:

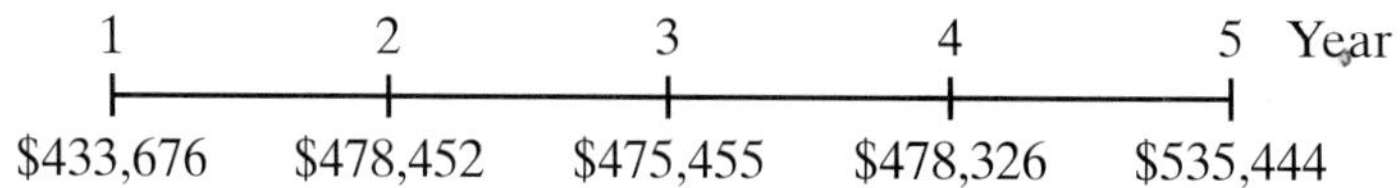

If Freisinger can reinvest these cash flows to earn a return of 7.8 percent, what is the future value of this cash flow stream at the end of five years?

6.3 Vancouver, Canada is the site of the next Winter Olympics in 2010. City officials plan to build a new multipurpose stadium. The projected cost of the stadium in 2010 dollars is $7.5 million. Assume that it is 2007 and city officials intend to put away a certain amount at the end of each of the next three years in an account that will pay 8.75 percent. What is the annual payment necessary to meet the projected cost of the stadium?

6.4 You have just won a lottery that promises an annual payment of $118,312 beginning immediately. You will receive a total of 10 payments. If you can invest the cash flows in an investment paying 7.65 percent annually, what is the present value of this annuity?

6.5 Which of the following investments has the highest effective annual interest rate (EAR)?
a. A bank CD that pays 5.50 percent compounded quarterly.
b. A bank CD that pays 5.45 percent compounded monthly.
c. A bank CD that pays 5.65 percent compounded annually.
d. A bank CD that pays 5.55 percent compounded semiannually.
e. A bank CD that pays 5.35 percent compounded daily (on a 365-day basis).

Appendix: Deriving the Formula for the Present Value of an Ordinary Annuity

In this chapter we showed that the formula for a perpetuity can be obtained from the formula for the present value of an ordinary annuity if n is set equal to ∞. It is also possible to go the other way. In other words, the present value of an ordinary annuity formula can be derived from the formula for a perpetuity. In fact, this is how the annuity formula was originally obtained. To see how this was done, assume that someone has offered to pay you $1 per year forever, beginning next year, but that, in return, you will have to pay that person $1 per year forever, beginning in year $n + 1$.

The cash flows you will receive and the cash flows you will pay are represented in the following time line:

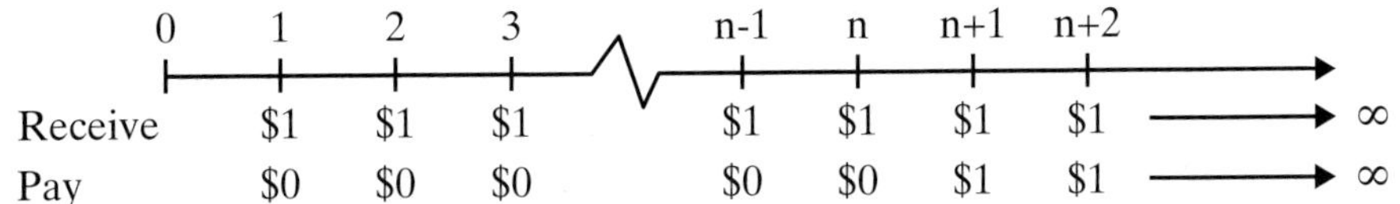

The first row of dollar values shows the cash flows for the perpetuity that you will receive. This perpetuity is worth:

$$\text{PVA}_{\infty,Receive} = \frac{\$1}{i} = \frac{\text{CF}}{i}$$

The second row shows the cash flows for the perpetuity that you will pay. The present value of what you owe is the value of a $1 perpetuity that is discounted for n years.

$$\text{PVA}_{\infty,Pay} = \frac{\$1/i}{(1+i)^n} = \frac{\text{CF}/i}{(1+i)^n}$$

Notice that if you subtract, year by year, the cash flows you would pay from the cash flows you would receive, you get the cash flows for an n-year annuity.

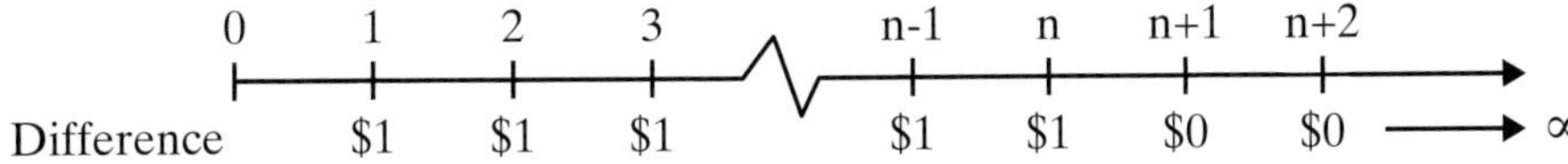

Therefore, the value of the offer equals the value of an n-year annuity. Solving for the difference between $\text{PVA}_{\infty,Receive}$ from $\text{PVA}_{\infty,Pay}$ we see that this is the same as Equation 6.1.

$$\begin{aligned}\text{PVA}_n &= \text{PVA}_{\infty,Receive} - \text{PVA}_{\infty,Pay}\\ &= \frac{\text{CF}}{i} - \frac{\text{CF}/i}{(1+i)^n}\\ &= \frac{\text{CF}}{i} \times \left[1 - \frac{1}{(1+i)^n}\right]\end{aligned}$$

Problem

6A.1 In the chapter text, you saw that the formula for a growing perpetuity can be obtained from the formula for the present value of a growing annuity if n is set equal to ∞. It is also possible to go the other way. In other words, the present value of a growing annuity formula can be derived from the formula for a growing perpetuity. In fact, this is how Equation 6.5 was actually derived. Show how Equation 6.5 can be derived from Equation 6.6.

Buy It on Credit and Be True to Your School[13]

ETHICS CASE

At the start of every school year, representatives from major banks come to campus to give students "free" credit cards. There are good reasons for banks to solicit students' business even though most students have neither steady jobs nor credit histories. First, students have a better record of paying their bills than the general public, because if they can't pay, usually their parents will. Second, students turn into loyal customers. Studies have shown that students keep their first credit card for an average of

[13]*Sources:* "Big Cards on Campus," *Business Week*, September 20, 1999, pp. 136–137; Marilyn Gardner, "A Generation Weighed Down by Debt," *Christian Science Monitor,* November 24, 2004; "Survey Reveals Aggressive Marketing of Credit Cards Continues on Many Maryland College Campuses," U.S. PIRG press release, February 19, 2004; and "Golden Eggs," *Boston Globe,* June 25, 2006.

15 years. That enables banks to sell them services over time, such as car loans, first mortgages, and (somewhat ironically) debt consolidation loans. Third and perhaps most importantly, students are ideal customers because they do not tend to pay off their credit balances each month, instead paying just the interest charges. One study in the 1990s revealed that 70 percent of students at four-year colleges had $2,000 or more of revolving debt. A more recent study in 2004 showed that 56 percent of college seniors have four or more cards and an average outstanding debt of $2,864.

Concern over Growing Student Debt

Concern has been growing that students cannot handle the debt they are taking on. According to a Consumer Federation study, college student debt almost tripled just in the 10 years between 1990 and 1999. This trend continues today. Many students fail to realize that when they apply for a car loan or a mortgage, the total ratio of debt to income is usually the most important factor determining whether they get the loan. Student educational loans are added to credit card debt, and that, in turn, is added to the requested loan amount to determine eligibility. When all the debt is summed up, many do not qualify for the loan they want. In many cases, people are forced to postpone marriage or purchase of a house because of their outstanding student loans and credit card debt.

To understand how students get into this kind of situation, consider the following hypothetical case. Suppose a student has a balance of $2,000 on a credit card. She makes the minimum payment every month but does not make any other purchases. Assuming a typical rate of interest, it would take six and one half years to pay off the credit card debt, and the student would have incurred interest charges of $2,500. As one observer noted, students like this one "will still be paying for all that pizza they bought in college when they are 30 years old."

A book published in 2000, *Credit Card Nation: The Consequences of America's Addiction to Credit*, was particularly critical of marketing credit cards to college students. The author, Robert Manning, identified a wide range of concerns, such as lowering of the age at which students can obtain credit cards, increasing credit limits on credit cards, students financing their education with credit card debt, and students using credit cards to conceal activities their parents might not approve of. Critics also point out that some of the advertising and marketing practices of the credit card companies are deceptive. In one case, for example, a credit card was touted as having no interest. That was true for the first month, but the annual percentage rate (APR) soared to 21 percent in the second month. Finally, many—including the students themselves—say that students do not receive sufficient education about how to manage credit card debt.

Supporters of credit card programs counter that most students do not "max out" their credit limits and that the three most common reasons for taking out a credit card are the establishment of a credit history, convenience, and emergency protection—all laudable goals.

Affinity Credit Cards

The marketing of credit cards to students has taken a new twist in relatively recent years. Banks compete fiercely to sign up students for their credit cards, and some banks are entering into exclusive arrangements with universities for the right to issue an affinity card—a credit card that features the university's name and logo. The card issuer may be willing to support the university to the tune of several million dollars in order to gain the exclusive right to issue the affinity card and to keep other banks off campus.

Georgetown University, for example, received $2 million from MBNA for a career counseling center; Michigan State received $5.5 million from MBNA for athletic and academic scholarship programs; and the University of Tennessee received $16 million from First USA primarily for athletics and scholarships. Universities gain other perks as well: They usually receive a half percent of the purchase value when the card is used. Often, they receive a fee for each new account, and sometimes they receive a small percentage of the loans outstanding. Every time a student uses the credit card, the university benefits.

Universities have been facing difficult financial times, and it is easy to understand why they enter into these arrangements. However, the price the university pays is that it becomes ensnared in the ethical issue of contributing to the rising level of student credit card debt. Moreover, universities with affinity credit cards cannot escape a conflict of interest: the higher student credit card debt climbs, the greater the revenues the university earns from the bank. As a result of these issues, some universities have increased the amount of information they provide to students about handling credit card debt, both through counseling and formal courses.

Certainly, learning to responsibly manage credit card purchases and any resulting debt is a necessary part of the passage to adulthood. We can applaud the fact that universities educate students about the dangers of excessive credit card debt. However, if universities make money on that debt, we must question whether they have less incentive to educate students about the associated problems.

Discussion Questions

1. Should universities enter into agreements to offer affinity credit cards to students?
2. Whether or not a university has an affinity credit card, does it have an obligation to educate students about credit card misuse and debt management?
3. Does the existence of an affinity credit card create a conflict of interest for a university if and when it adopts an education program on credit card misuse and debt management?
4. To what extent are students themselves responsible for their predicament?

RISK AND RETURN

CHAPTER

7

Zuma Press

LEARNING OBJECTIVES

1. **Explain the relation between risk and return.**
2. **Describe the two components of a total holding period return, and calculate this return for an asset.**
3. **Explain what an expected return is, and calculate the expected return for an asset.**
4. **Explain what the standard deviation of returns is, explain why it is especially useful in finance, and be able to calculate it.**
5. **Explain the concept of diversification.**
6. **Discuss which type of risk matters to investors and why.**
7. **Describe what the Capital Asset Pricing Model (CAPM) tells us and how to use it to evaluate whether the expected return of an asset is sufficient to compensate an investor for the risks associated with that asset.**

As the home mortgage market went into a tailspin in mid-2007, Countrywide Financial Corporation's stock price plummeted 63.7 percent, from a high of $41.91 per share on May 8 to $15.23 on October 19. Countrywide was one of the most prominent participants in the home mortgage market. Its stock price dropped in response to a rapid increase in defaults by mortgage borrowers as interest rates on adjustable-rate mortgages began to increase in response to an overall rise in interest rates.

The decline in the value of Countrywide's shares was compounded by the fact that it occurred at a time when the stock market as a whole was rising. Countrywide stockholders who did not hold diversified investment portfolios were much worse off after the 2007 stock price decline than they would have been if they had held diversified portfolios. They suffered large losses because they had not diversified their risk by investing in a variety of stocks and other types of assets. They bet on one company, and when that company's share price collapsed, so did the value of their investment portfolios.

Diversified Countrywide stockholders were better off in 2007, but they did not benefit as much when the home mortgage market took off and Countrywide's stock price rose 129 percent between July 2003 and July 2004. The accompanying exhibit shows how Countrywide's stock price and the S&P 500 index changed between the beginning of 2003 and October 2007.

The undiversified Countrywide stockholders took a lot of risk in anticipation of earning high returns. They did well when business was booming and paid a steep price when it was not. The concepts discussed in this chapter would have helped them better understand whether the expected returns on their stock justified the risks.

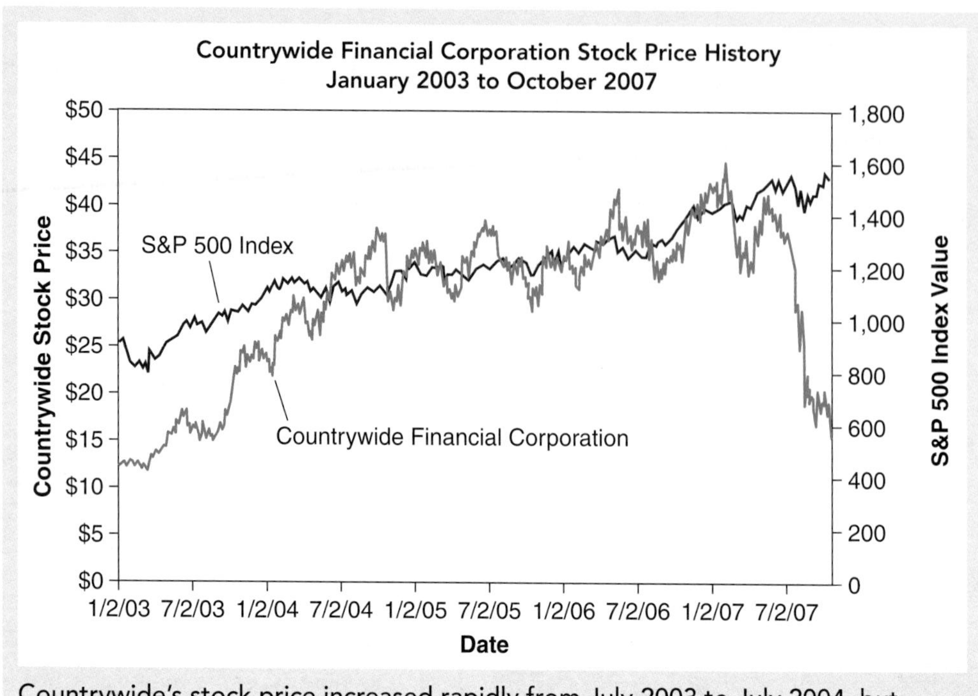

Countrywide's stock price increased rapidly from July 2003 to July 2004, but declined even faster in mid-2007. In contrast, the S&P 500 Index increased steadily during this period.

CHAPTER PREVIEW

Up to this point, we have often mentioned the rate of return that we use to discount cash flows, but we have not explained how that rate is determined. We have now reached the point where it is time to examine key concepts underlying the discount rate. This chapter introduces a quantitative framework for measuring risk and return. This framework will help you develop an intuitive understanding of how risk and return are related and what risks matter to investors. The relation between risk and return has implications for the rate we use to discount cash flows because the time value of money that we discussed in Chapters 5 and 6 is directly related to the returns that investors require. We must understand these concepts in order to determine the correct present value for a series of cash flows and to be able to make investment decisions that create value for stockholders.

We begin this chapter with a discussion of the general relation between risk and return to introduce the idea that investors require a higher rate of return from riskier assets. This is one of the most fundamental relations in finance. We next develop the statistical concepts required to quantify holding period returns, expected returns, and risk. We then apply these concepts to portfolios with a single asset, two assets, and more than two assets to illustrate the benefit of diversification. From this discussion, you will see how investing in more than one asset enables an investor to reduce the total risk associated with his or her investment portfolio, and you will learn how to quantify this benefit.

Once we have discussed the concept of diversification, we examine what it means for the relation between risk and return. We find that the total risk associated with an investment consists of two components: (1) unsystematic risk and (2) systematic risk. Diversification enables investors to eliminate the *unsystematic risk,* or unique risk, associated with an individual asset. Investors do not require higher returns for the *unsystematic risk* that they can eliminate through diversification. Only *systematic risk*—risk that cannot be diversified away—affects expected returns on an investment. The distinction between unsystematic and systematic risk and the recognition that unsystematic risk can be diversified away are extremely important in finance. After reading this chapter, you will understand precisely what the term *risk* means in finance and how it is related to the rates of return that investors require.

7.1 Risk and Return

LEARNING OBJECTIVE 1

The rate of return that investors require for an investment depends on the risk associated with that investment. The greater the risk, the larger the return investors require as compensation for bearing that risk. This is one of the most fundamental relations in finance. The *rate of return* is what you earn on an investment, stated in percentage terms. We will be more specific later, but for now you might think of *risk* as a measure of how certain you are that you will receive a particular return. Higher risk means you are less certain.

To get a better understanding of how risk and return are related, consider an example. You are trying to select the best investment from among the following three stocks:

Stock	Expected Return (%)	Risk Level (%)
A	12	12
B	12	16
C	16	16

Which would you choose? If you were comparing only Stocks A and B, you should choose Stock A. Both stocks have the same expected return, but Stock A has less risk. It does not make sense to invest in the riskier stock if the expected return is the same. Similarly, you can see that Stock C is clearly superior to Stock B. Stocks B and C have the same level of risk, but Stock C has a higher expected return. It would not make sense to accept a lower return for taking on the same level of risk.

But what about the choice between Stocks A and C? This choice is less obvious. Making it requires understanding the concepts that we discuss in the rest of this chapter.

BUILDING INTUITION

More Risk Means a Higher Expected Return

The greater the risk associated with an investment, the greater the return investors expect from it. A corollary to this idea is that investors want the highest return for a given level of risk or the lowest risk for a given level of return. When choosing between two investments that have the same level of risk, investors prefer the investment with the higher return. Alternatively, if two investments have the same expected return, investors prefer the less risky alternative.

7.2 Quantitative Measures of Return

Before we begin a detailed discussion of the relation between risk and return, we should define more precisely what these terms mean. We begin with measures of return.

Holding Period Returns

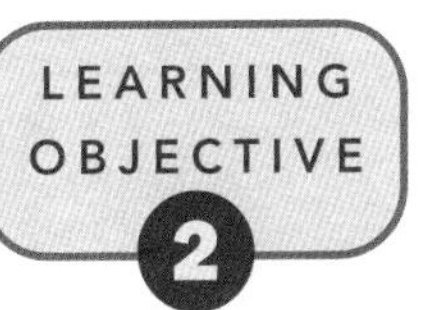

When people refer to the return from an investment, they are generally referring to the total return over some *investment period,* or *holding period.* The **total holding period return** consists of two components: (1) capital appreciation and (2) income. The capital appreciation component of a return, R_{CA}, arises from a change in the price of the asset over the investment or holding period and is calculated as follows:

total holding period return
the total return on an asset over a specific period of time or holding period

$$R_{CA} = \frac{\text{Capital appreciation}}{\text{Initial price}} = \frac{P_1 - P_0}{P_0} = \frac{\Delta P}{P_0}$$

where P_0 is the price paid for the asset at time zero and P_1 is the price at a later point in time.

The income component of a return arises from income that an investor receives from the asset while he or she owns it. For example, when a firm pays a cash dividend on its stock, the income component of the return on that stock, R_I, is calculated as follows:

$$R_I = \frac{\text{Cash flow}}{\text{Initial price}} = \frac{CF_1}{P_0}$$

where CF_1 is the cash flow from the dividend.

The total holding period return is simply the sum of the capital appreciation and income components of return:

$$R_T = R_{CA} + R_I = \frac{\Delta P}{P_0} + \frac{CF_1}{P_0} = \frac{\Delta P + CF_1}{P_0} \quad (7.1)$$

Let's consider an example of calculating the total holding period return on an investment. One year ago today, you purchased a share of Dell Inc. stock for \$26.50. Today it is worth \$29.00. Dell paid no dividend on its stock. What total return did you earn on this stock over the past year?

If Dell paid no dividend and you received no other income from holding the stock, the total return for the year equals the return from the capital appreciation, calculated as follows:

$$\begin{aligned} R_T = R_{CA} + R_I &= \frac{P_1 - P_0 + CF_1}{P_0} \\ &= \frac{\$29.00 - \$26.50 + \$0.00}{\$26.50} \\ &= 0.0943, \text{ or } 9.43\% \end{aligned}$$

What return would you have earned if Dell had paid a \$1 dividend and today's price was \$28.00? With the \$1 dividend and a correspondingly lower price, the total return is the same:

$$R_T = R_{CA} + R_I = \frac{P_1 - P_0 + CF_1}{P_0} = \frac{\$28.00 - \$26.50 + \$1.00}{\$26.50} = 0.0943, \text{ or } 9.43\%$$

You can see from this example that a dollar of capital appreciation is worth the same as a dollar of income.

> You can download actual realized investment returns for a large number of stock market indexes at the Callan Associates Web site, www.callan.com/resource/periodic_table/pertbl.pdf.

LEARNING BY DOING APPLICATION 7.1

Calculating the Return on an Investment

NEED MORE HELP? WILEY PLUS www.wileyplus.com

Problem: You purchased a beat-up 1974 Datsun 240Z sports car a year ago for \$1,500. Datsun is what Nissan, the Japanese car company, was called in the 1970s. The 240Z was the first in a series of cars that led to the Nissan 350Z that is being sold today. Recognizing that a mint-condition 240Z is a much sought-after car, you invested \$7,000 and a lot of your time fixing up the car. Last week, you sold it to a collector for \$18,000. Not counting the value of the time you spent restoring the car, what is the total return you earned on this investment over the one-year holding period?

Approach: Use Equation 7.1 to calculate the total holding period return. To calculate R_T using Equation 7.1, you must know P_0, P_1, and CF_1. In this problem, you can assume that the \$7,000 was spent at the time you bought the car to purchase parts and materials. Therefore, your initial investment, P_0, was \$1,500 + \$7,000 = \$8,500. Since there were no other cash inflows or outflows between the time that you bought the car and the time that you sold it, CF_1 equals \$0.

Solution: The total holding period return is:

$$R_T = R_{CA} + R_I = \frac{P_1 - P_0 + CF_1}{P_0} = \frac{\$18{,}000 - \$8{,}500 + \$0}{\$8{,}500} = 1.118, \text{ or } 111.8\%$$

Expected Returns

Suppose that you are a senior who plays college baseball and that your team is in the College World Series. Furthermore, suppose that you have been drafted by the Washington Nationals and are coming up for what you expect to be your last at-bat as a college player. The fact that you expect this to be your last at-bat is important because you just signed a very unusual contract with the Nationals. Your signing bonus will be determined solely by whether you get a hit in your final collegiate at-bat. If you get a hit, then your signing bonus will be \$800,000. Otherwise, it will be \$400,000. This past season, you got a hit 32.5 percent of the times you were at bat (you did not get a hit 67.5 percent of the time), and you believe this reflects the likelihood that you will get a hit in your last collegiate at-bat.[1]

What is the expected value of your bonus? If you have taken a statistics course, you might recall that an expected value represents the sum of the products of the possible outcomes and the probabilities that those outcomes will be realized. In our example the expected value of the bonus can be calculated using the following formula:

$$\text{E(Bonus)} = (p_\text{H} \times \text{B}_\text{H}) + (p_\text{NH} \times \text{B}_\text{NH})$$

where E(Bonus) is your expected bonus, p_H is the probability of a hit, p_NH is the probability of no hit, B_H is the bonus you receive if you get a hit, and B_NH is the bonus you receive if you get no hit. Since p_H equals 0.325, p_NH equals 0.675, B_H equals \$800,000, and B_NH equals \$400,000, the expected value of your bonus is:

$$\begin{aligned}\text{E(Bonus)} &= (p_\text{H} \times \text{B}_\text{H}) + (p_\text{NH} \times \text{B}_\text{NH})\\ &= (0.325 \times \$800{,}000) + (0.675 \times \$400{,}000) = \$530{,}000\end{aligned}$$

Notice that the expected bonus of \$530,000 is not equal to either of the two possible payoffs. Neither is it equal to the simple average of the two possible payoffs. This is because the expected bonus takes into account the probability of each event occurring. If the probability of each event had been 50 percent, then the expected bonus would have equaled the simple average of the two payoffs:

$$\text{E(Bonus)} = (0.5 \times \$800{,}000) + (0.5 \times \$400{,}000) = \$600{,}000$$

However, since it is more likely that you will not get a hit (a 67.5 percent chance) than that you will get a hit (a 32.5 percent chance), and the payoff is lower if you do not get a hit, the expected bonus is less than the simple average.

What would your expected payoff be if you got a hit 99 percent of the time? We intuitively know that the expected bonus should be much closer to \$800,000 in this case. In fact, it is:

$$\text{E(Bonus)} = (0.99 \times \$800{,}000) + (0.01 \times \$400{,}000) = \$796{,}000$$

The key point here is that the expected value reflects the relative likelihoods of the possible outcomes.

We calculate an **expected return** in finance in the same way that we calculate any expected value. The expected return is a weighted average of the possible returns from an investment, where each of these returns is weighted by the probability that it will occur. In general terms, the expected return on an asset, $\text{E(R}_\text{Asset})$, is calculated as follows:

expected return
an average of the possible returns from an investment, where each return is weighted by the probability that it will occur

$$\text{E(R}_\text{Asset}) = \sum_{i=1}^{n} (p_i \times \text{R}_i) = (p_1 \times \text{R}_1) + (p_2 \times \text{R}_2) + \cdots + (p_n \times \text{R}_n) \quad (7.2)$$

where R_i is possible return i and p_i is the probability that you will actually earn return R_i. The summation symbol in this equation

$$\sum_{i=1}^{n}$$

[1]For simplicity, let's ignore the possibility of your hitting a sacrifice fly and other such outcomes.

is mathematical shorthand indicating that n values are added together. In Equation 7.2, each of the n possible returns is multiplied by the probability that it will be realized, and these products are then added together to calculate the expected return.

It is important to make sure that the sum of the n individual probabilities, the p_i's, always equals 1, or 100 percent, when you calculate an expected value. The sum of the probabilities cannot be less than 100 percent because you must account for all possible outcomes in the calculation. On the other hand, as you may recall from statistics, the sum of the probabilities of all possible outcomes cannot exceed 100 percent. For example, notice that the sum of the p_i's equals 1 in each of the expected bonus calculations that we discussed earlier (0.325 + 0.625 in the first calculation, 0.5 + 0.5 in the second, and 0.99 + 0.01 in the third).

The expected return on an asset reflects the return that you can expect to receive from investing in that asset over the period that you plan to own it. It is your best estimate of this return, given the possible outcomes and their associated probabilities.

Note that if each of the possible outcomes is equally likely (that is, $p_1 = p_2 = p_3 = \ldots = p_n = p = 1/n$), this formula reduces to the formula for a simple (equally weighted) average of the possible returns:

$$E(R_{\text{Asset}}) = \frac{\sum_{i=1}^{n}(R_i)}{n} = \frac{R_1 + R_2 + \cdots + R_n}{n}$$

To see how we calculate the expected return on an asset, suppose you are considering purchasing Dell, Inc., stock for \$29.00 per share. You plan to sell the stock in one year. You estimate that there is a 30 percent chance that Dell stock will sell for \$28.00 at the end of one year, a 30 percent chance that it will sell for \$30.50, a 30 percent that it will sell for \$32.50, and a 10 percent chance that it will sell for \$36.00. If Dell pays no dividends on its shares, what is the return that you expect from this stock in the next year?

Since Dell pays no dividends, the total return on its stock equals the return from capital appreciation:

$$R_T = R_{CA} = \frac{P_1 - P_0}{P_0}$$

Therefore, we can calculate the return from owning Dell stock under each of the four possible outcomes using the approach we used for the similar Dell problem we solved earlier in the chapter. These returns are calculated as follows:

Dell Stock Price in One Year	Total Return
(1) \$28.00	$\frac{\$28.00 - \$29.00}{\$29.00} = -0.0345$
(2) \$30.50	$\frac{\$30.50 - \$29.00}{\$29.00} = 0.0517$
(3) \$32.50	$\frac{\$32.50 - \$29.00}{\$29.00} = 0.1207$
(4) \$36.00	$\frac{\$36.00 - \$29.00}{\$29.00} = 0.2414$

Applying Equation 7.2, the expected return on Dell stock over the next year is therefore 6.55 percent, calculated as follows:

$$\begin{aligned} E(R_{\text{Dell}}) &= \sum_{i=1}^{n}(p_i \times R_i) = (p_1 \times R_1) + (p_2 \times R_2) + \cdots + (p_n \times R_n) \\ E(R_{\text{Dell}}) &= (0.3 \times -0.0345) + (0.3 \times 0.0517) + (0.3 \times 0.1207) + (0.1 \times 0.2414) \\ &= -0.01035 + 0.01551 + 0.03621 + 0.02414 = 0.0655, \text{ or } 6.55\% \end{aligned}$$

Notice that the negative return is entered into the formula just like any other. Also notice that the sum of the p_i's equals 1.

LEARNING BY DOING APPLICATION 7.2

Calculating Expected Returns

Problem: You have just purchased 100 railroad cars that you plan to lease to a large railroad company. Demand for shipping goods by rail has recently increased dramatically due to the rising price of oil. You expect oil prices, which are currently at $115.00 per barrel, to reach $130.00 per barrel in the next year. If this happens, railroad shipping prices will increase, thereby driving up the value of your railroad cars as increases in demand outpace the rate at which new cars are being produced.

Given your oil price prediction, you estimate that there is a 30 percent chance that the value of your railroad cars will increase by 15 percent, a 40 percent chance that their value will increase by 25 percent, and a 30 percent chance that their value will increase by 30 percent in the next year. In addition to appreciation in the value of your cars, you expect to earn 10 percent on your investment over the next year (after expenses) from leasing the railroad cars. What total return do you expect to earn on your railroad car investment over the next year?

Approach: Use Equation 7.1 first to calculate the total return that you would earn under each of the three possible outcomes. Next use these total return values, along with the associated probabilities, in Equation 7.2 to calculate the expected total return.

Solution: To calculate the total returns using Equation 7.1,

$$R_T = R_{CA} + R_I = \frac{\Delta P}{P_0} + \frac{CF_1}{P_0}$$

you must recognize that $\Delta P/P_0$ is the capital appreciation under each outcome and that CF_1/P_0 equals the 10 percent that you expect to receive from leasing the rail cars. The expected returns for the three outcomes are:

Increase in Value of Rail Cars in One Year	Return from Leases	Total Return
15%	10%	$R_T = \frac{\Delta P}{P_0} + \frac{CF_1}{P_0} = 0.15 + 0.10 = 0.25$, or 25%
25%	10%	$R_T = \frac{\Delta P}{P_0} + \frac{CF_1}{P_0} = 0.25 + 0.10 = 0.35$, or 35%
30%	10%	$R_T = \frac{\Delta P}{P_0} + \frac{CF_1}{P_0} = 0.30 + 0.10 = 0.40$, or 40%

You can then use Equation 7.2 to calculate the expected return for your rail car investment:

$$\begin{aligned} E(R_{\text{Rail cars}}) &= \sum_{i=1}^{3} (p_i \times R_i) = (p_1 \times R_1) + (p_2 \times R_2) + (p_3 \times R_3) \\ E(R_{\text{Rail cars}}) &= (0.3 \times 0.25) + (0.4 \times 0.35) + (0.3 \times 0.40) \\ &= 0.335, \text{ or } 33.5\% \end{aligned}$$

Alternatively, since there is a 100 percent probability that the return from leasing the railroad cars is 10 percent, you could have simply calculated the expected increase in value of the railroad cars:

$$\begin{aligned} E\left(\frac{\Delta P}{P_0}\right) &= (0.3 \times 0.15) + (0.4 \times 0.25) + (0.3 \times 0.30) \\ &= 0.235, \text{ or } 23.5\% \end{aligned}$$

and added the 10 percent to arrive at the answer of 33.5 percent. Of course, this simpler approach only works if the return from leasing is known with certainty.

DECISION-MAKING EXAMPLE 7.1

Using Expected Values in Decision Making

Situation: You are deciding whether you should advertise your pizza business on the radio or on billboards placed on local taxicabs. For \$1,000 per month, you can either buy 20 one-minute ads on the radio or place your ad on 40 taxicabs.

There is some uncertainty regarding how many new customers will visit your restaurant after hearing one of your radio ads. You estimate that there is a 30 percent chance that 35 people will visit, a 45 percent chance that 50 people will visit, and a 25 percent chance that 60 people will visit. Therefore, you expect the following number of new customers to visit your restaurant in a month in response to each radio ad:

$$\text{E(New customers per ad}_{\text{Radio}}) = (0.30 \times 35) + (0.45 \times 50) + (0.25 \times 60) = 48$$

This means that you expect 20 one-minute ads to bring in $20 \times 48 = 960$ new customers.

Similarly, you estimate that there is a 20 percent chance you will get 20 new customers in response to an ad placed on a taxi, a 30 percent chance you will get 30 new customers, a 30 percent chance that you will get 40 new customers, and a 20 percent chance that you will get 50 new customers. Therefore, you expect the following number of new customers in response to each ad that you place on a taxi:

$$\begin{aligned}\text{E(New customers per ad}_{\text{Taxi}}) &= (0.2 \times 20) + (0.3 \times 30) + (0.3 \times 40) + (0.2 \times 50)\\ &= 35\end{aligned}$$

Placing ads on 40 taxicabs is therefore expected to bring in $40 \times 35 = 1{,}400$ new customers.

Which of these two advertising options is more attractive? Is it cost effective?

Decision: You should advertise on taxicabs. For a monthly cost of \$1,000, you expect to attract 1,400 new customers with taxicab advertisements but only 960 new customers if you advertise on the radio.

The answer to the question of whether advertising on taxicabs is cost effective depends on how much gross profits (profits after variable costs) are increased by those 1,400 customers. Gross profits will have to increase by \$1,000, or average 72 cents per new customer (\$1,000/1,400) to cover the cost of the advertising campaign.

Before You Go On

1. What are the two components of a total holding period return?
2. How is the expected return on an investment calculated?

7.3 The Variance and Standard Deviation as Measures of Risk

We turn next to a discussion of the two most basic measures of risk used in finance—the variance and the standard deviation. These are the same variance and standard deviation measures that you have studied if you have taken a course in statistics.

Calculating the Variance and Standard Deviation

Let's begin by returning to our College World Series example. Recall that you will receive a bonus of \$800,000 if you get a hit in your final collegiate at-bat and a bonus of $400,000 if you do not. The expected value of your bonus is $530,000. Suppose you want to measure the risk, or uncertainty, associated with the payoff. How can you do this? One approach would be to compute a measure of how much, on average, the bonus payoffs deviate from the expected value. The underlying intuition here is that the greater the difference between the actual payoff and the expected value, the greater the risk. For example, you might calculate the difference between each individual bonus payment and the expected value and sum these differences. If you do this, you will get the following result:

$$\begin{aligned}\text{Risk} &= (\$800{,}000 - \$530{,}000) + (\$400{,}000 - \$530{,}000)\\ &= \$270{,}000 + (-130{,}000)\\ &= \$140{,}000\end{aligned}$$

Unfortunately, using this calculation to obtain a measure of risk presents two problems. First, since one difference is positive and the other difference is negative, one difference partially cancels the other. As a result, you are not getting an accurate measure of total risk. Second, this calculation does not take into account the number of potential outcomes or the probability of each outcome.

A better approach would be to square the differences (squaring the differences makes all the numbers positive) and multiply each difference by its associated probability before summing them up. This calculation yields the **variance (σ^2)** of the possible outcomes. The variance does not suffer from the two problems mentioned earlier and provides a measure of risk that has a consistent interpretation across different situations or assets. For the original bonus arrangement, the variance is:

variance (σ^2)
a measure of the uncertainty surrounding an outcome

$$\begin{aligned}\text{Var(Bonus)} = \sigma^2_{\text{(Bonus)}} &= \{p_{\text{H}} \times [\text{B}_{\text{H}} - \text{E(Bonus)}]^2\}\\ &\quad + \{p_{\text{NH}} \times [\text{B}_{\text{NH}} - \text{E(Bonus)}]^2\}\\ &= [0.325 \times (\$800{,}000 - \$530{,}000)^2]\\ &\quad + [0.675 \times (\$400{,}000 - \$530{,}000)^2]\\ &= 35{,}100{,}000{,}000 \text{ dollars}^2\end{aligned}$$

Note that the square of the Greek symbol sigma, σ^2, is generally used to represent the variance.

Because it is somewhat awkward to work with units of squared dollars, in a calculation such as this we would typically take the square root of the variance. The square root gives us the **standard deviation (σ)** of the possible outcomes. For our example, the standard deviation is:

standard deviation (σ)
the square root of the variance

$$\sigma_{\text{(Bonus)}} = (\sigma^2_{\text{(Bonus)}})^{1/2} = (35{,}100{,}000{,}000 \text{ dollars}^2)^{1/2} = \$187{,}349.94$$

As you will see when we discuss the normal distribution, the standard deviation has a natural interpretation that is very useful for assessing investment risks.

The general formula for calculating the variance of returns can be written as follows:

$$\text{Var(R)} = \sigma^2_{\text{R}} = \sum_{i=1}^{n} \{p_i \times [\text{R}_i - \text{E(R)}]^2\} \tag{7.3}$$

Equation 7.3 simply extends the calculation illustrated above to the situation where there are n possible outcomes. Like the expected return calculation (Equation 7.2), Equation 7.3 can be simplified if all of the possible outcomes are equally likely. In this case it becomes:

$$\sigma^2_{\text{R}} = \frac{\sum_{i=1}^{n} [\text{R}_i - \text{E(R)}]^2}{n}$$

In both the general case and the case where all possible outcomes are equally likely, the standard deviation is simply the square root of the variance $\sigma_{\text{R}} = (\sigma^2_{\text{R}})^{\frac{1}{2}}$.

Interpreting the Variance and Standard Deviation

normal distribution
a symmetric frequency distribution that is completely described by its mean and standard deviation; also known as a bell curve due to its shape

The variance and standard deviation are especially useful measures of risk for variables that are normally distributed—those that can be represented by a normal distribution. The **normal distribution** is a symmetric frequency distribution that is completely described by its mean (average) and standard deviation. Exhibit 7.1 illustrates what this distribution looks like. Even if you have never taken a statistics course, you have already encountered the normal distribution. It is the "bell curve" on which instructors often base their grade distributions. SAT scores and IQ scores are also based on normal distributions.

This distribution is very useful in finance because the returns for many assets tend to be approximately normally distributed. This makes the variance and standard deviation practical measures of the uncertainty associated with investment returns. Since the standard deviation is more easily interpreted than the variance, we will focus on the standard deviation as we discuss the normal distribution and its application in finance.

In Exhibit 7.1, you can see that the normal distribution is symmetric: the left and right sides are mirror images of each other. The mean falls directly in the center of the distribution, and the probability that an outcome is less than or greater than a particular distance from the mean is the same whether the outcome is on the left or the right side of the distribution. For example, if the mean is 0, the probability that a particular outcome is −3 or less is the same as the probability that it is +3 or more (both are 3 or more units from the mean). This enables us to use a single measure of risk for the normal distribution. That measure is the standard deviation.

The standard deviation tells us everything we need to know about the width of the normal distribution or, in other words, the variation in the individual values. This variation is what we mean when we talk about risk in finance. In general terms, risk is a measure of the range of potential outcomes. The standard deviation is an especially useful measure of risk because it tells us the probability that an outcome will fall a particular distance from the mean, or within a particular range. You

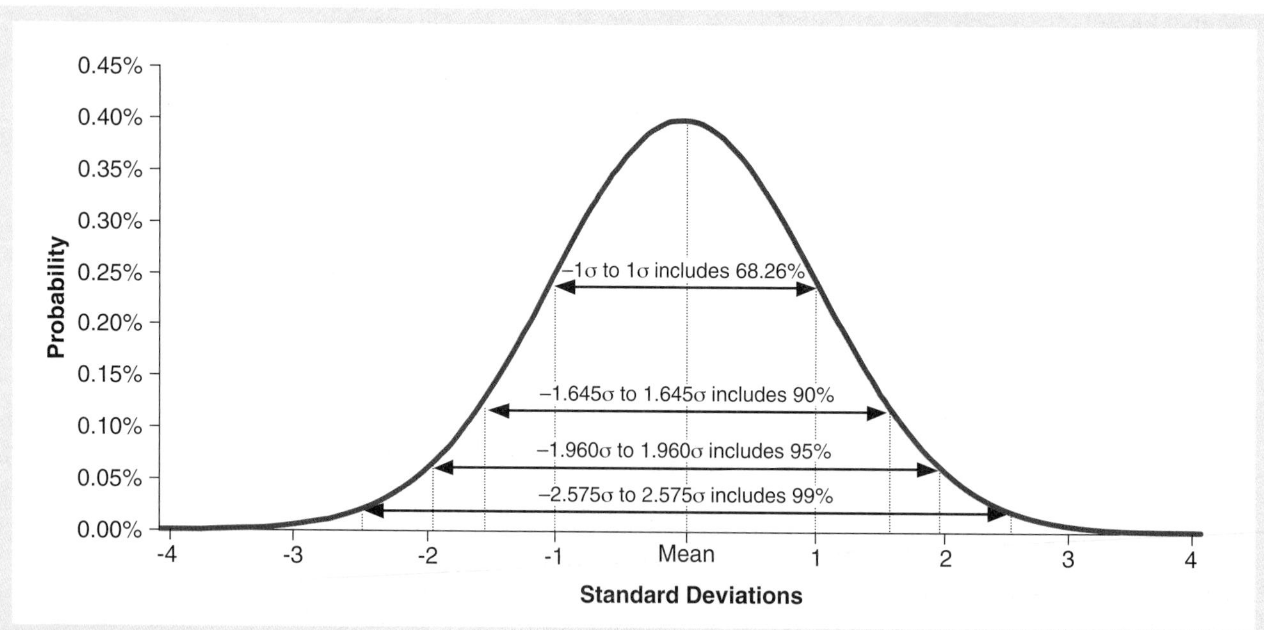

Exhibit 7.1
Normal Distribution
The normal distribution is a symmetric distribution that is described by its mean and standard deviation. The mean is the value that defines the center of the distribution, and the standard deviation, σ, describes the dispersion of the values centered around the mean.

can see this in the following table, which shows the fraction of all observations in a normal distribution that are within the indicated number of standard deviations from the mean.

Number of Standard Deviations from the Mean	Fraction of Total Observations
1.000	68.26%
1.645	90%
1.960	95%
2.575	99%

Since the returns on many assets are approximately normally distributed, the standard deviation provides a convenient way of computing the probability that the return on an asset will fall within a particular range. In these applications, the expected return on an asset equals the mean of the distribution, and the standard deviation is a measure of the uncertainty associated with the return.

For example, if the expected return for a real estate investment in Reno, Nevada, is 10 percent with a standard deviation of 2 percent, there is a 90 percent chance that the actual return will be within 3.29 percent of 10 percent. How do we know this? As shown in the table, 90 percent of all outcomes in a normal distribution have a value that is within 1.645 standard deviations of the mean value, and 1.645 × 2 percent = 3.29 percent. This tells us that there is a 90 percent chance that the realized return on the investment in Reno will be between 6.71 percent (10 percent − 3.29 percent) and 13.29 percent (10 percent + 3.29 percent), a range of 6.58 percent (13.29 percent − 6.71 percent).

You may be wondering what is *standard* about the standard deviation. The answer is that this statistic is standard in the sense that it can be used to directly compare the uncertainties (risks) associated with the returns on different investments. For instance, suppose you are comparing the real estate investment in Reno with a real estate investment in Las Cruces, New Mexico. Assume that the expected return on the Las Cruces investment is also 10 percent. If the standard deviation for the returns on the Las Cruces investment is 3 percent, there is a 90 percent chance that the actual return is within 4.935 percent (1.645 × 3 percent = 4.935 percent) of 10 percent. In other words, 90 percent of the time, the return will be between 5.065 percent (10 percent − 4.935 percent) and 14.935 percent (10 percent + 4.935 percent), a range of 9.87 percent (14.935 percent − 5.065 percent).

This range is exactly 9.87 percent/6.58 percent = 1.5 times as large as the range for the Reno investment opportunity. Notice that the ratio of the two standard deviations also equals 1.5 (3 percent/2 percent = 1.5). This is not a coincidence. We could have used the standard deviations to directly compute the relative uncertainty associated with the Las Cruces and Reno investment returns. The relation between the standard deviation of returns and the width of a normal distribution (the uncertainty) is illustrated in Exhibit 7.2.

Let's consider another example of how the standard deviation is interpreted. Suppose customers at your pizza restaurant have complained that there is no consistency in the number of slices of pepperoni that your cooks are putting on large pepperoni pizzas. One night you decide to work in the area where the pizzas are made so that you can count the number of pepperoni slices on the large pizzas to get a better idea of just how much variation there is. After counting the slices of pepperoni on 50 pizzas, you estimate that, on average, your pies have 18 slices of pepperoni and that the standard deviation is 3 slices.

With this information, you estimate that 95 percent of the large pepperoni pizzas sold in your restaurant have between 12.12 and 23.88 slices. You are able to estimate this range because you know that 95 percent of the observations in a normal distribution fall within 1.96 standard deviations of the mean. With a standard deviation of three slices, this implies that the number of pepperoni slices on 95 percent of your pizzas is within 5.88 slices of the mean (3 slices × 1.96). This, in turn, indicates a range of 12.12 (18 − 5.88) to 23.88 (18 + 5.88) slices.

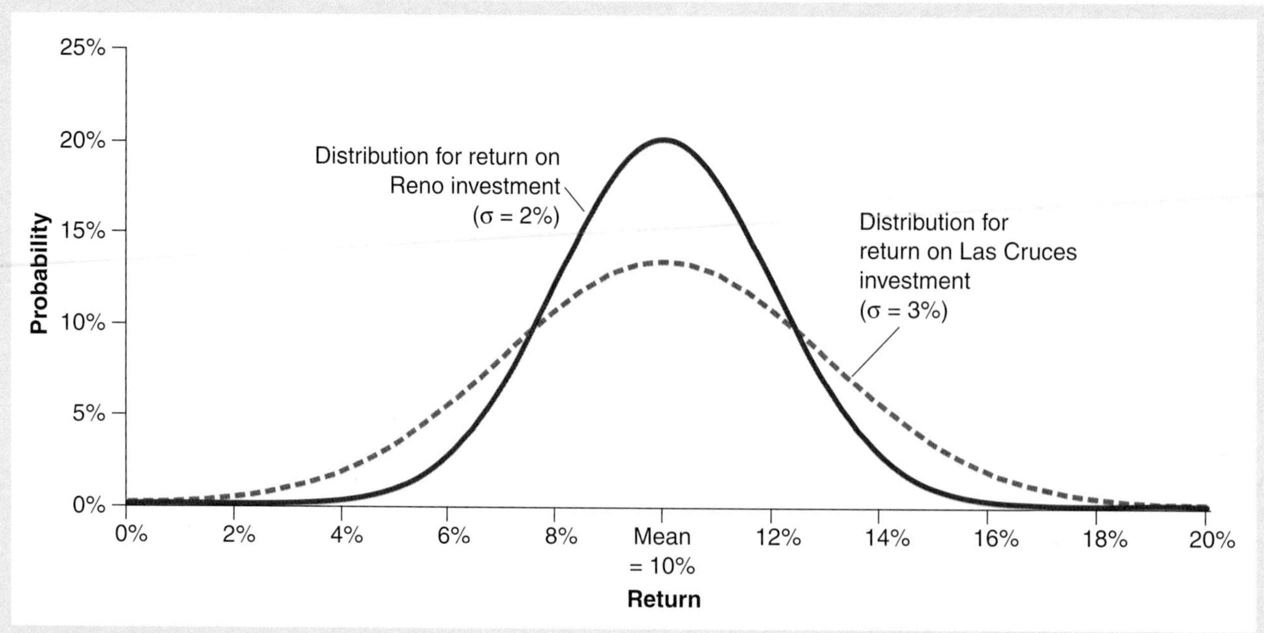

Exhibit 7.2
Standard Deviation and Width of the Normal Distribution
The larger standard deviation for the return on the Las Cruces investment means that the Las Cruces investment is riskier than the Reno investment. The actual return for the Las Cruces investment is more likely to be further from its expected return.

Since you put only whole slices of pepperoni on your pizzas, 95 percent of the time the number of slices is somewhere between 12 and 24. No wonder your customers are up in arms! In response to this information, you decide to implement a standard policy regarding the number of pepperoni slices that go on each type of pizza.

LEARNING BY DOING APPLICATION 7.3

Understanding the Standard Deviation

Problem: You are considering investing in a share of Dell, Inc., stock and want to evaluate how risky this potential investment is. You know that stock returns tend to be normally distributed, and you have calculated the expected return on Dell stock to be 4.67 percent and the standard deviation of the annual return to be 23 percent. Based on these statistics, within what range would you expect the return on this stock to fall during the next year? Calculate this range for a 90 percent level of confidence (that is, 90 percent of the time, the returns will fall within the specified range).

Approach: Use the values in the previous table or Exhibit 7.1 to compute the range within which Dell's stock return will fall 90 percent of the time. First, find the number of standard deviations associated with a 90 percent level of confidence in the table or Exhibit 7.1 and then multiply this number by the standard deviation of the annual return for Dell's stock. Then subtract the resulting value from the expected return (mean) to obtain the lower end of the range and add it to the expected return to obtain the upper end.

Solution: From the table, you can see that we would expect the return over the next year to be within 1.645 standard deviations of the mean 90 percent of the time. Multiplying this value by the standard deviation of Dell's stock (23 percent) yields 23 percent $\times$ 1.645 = 37.835 percent. This means that there is a 90 percent chance that the return will be between −33.165 percent (4.67 percent − 37.835 percent) and 42.505 percent (4.67 percent + 37.835 percent).

While the expected return of 4.67 percent is relatively low, the returns on Dell stock vary considerably, and there is a reasonable chance that the stock return in the next year could be quite high or quite low (even negative). As you will see shortly, this wide range of possible returns is similar to the range we observe for typical shares in the U.S. stock market.

Historical Market Performance

Now that we have discussed how returns and risks can be measured, we are ready to examine the characteristics of the historical returns earned by securities such as stocks and bonds. Exhibit 7.3 illustrates the distributions of historical returns for some securities in the United States and shows the average and standard deviations of these annual returns for the period from 1926 to 2006.

Note that the statistics reported in Exhibit 7.3 are for indexes that represent total *average* returns for the indicated types of securities, not total returns on individual securities. We generally use indexes to represent the performance of the stock or bond markets. For instance, when news services report on the performance of the stock market, they often report that the Dow Jones Industrial Average (DJIA), or the S&P 500 Index, or the NASDAQ Composite Index went up or down on a particular day. These and other indexes were discussed in Chapter 2.

The plots in Exhibit 7.3 are arranged in order of decreasing risk, which is indicated by the decreasing standard deviation of the annual returns. The top plot shows returns for a small-stock index that represents the 10 percent of U.S. firms that have the lowest total equity value (number of shares multiplied by price per share). The second plot shows returns for the S&P 500 Index, representing large U.S. stocks. The remaining plots show three different types of government debt. Long-term government bonds are bonds sold by the U.S. government that mature in 20 years, intermediate-term government bonds are bonds that mature in five years, and U.S. Treasury bills are short-term debts of the U.S. government that mature in from 30 days to one year.

The key point to note in Exhibit 7.3 is that, on average, annual returns have been higher for riskier securities. Small stocks, which have the largest standard deviation of total returns, at 32.74 percent, also have the largest average return, 17.36 percent. On the other end of the spectrum, Treasury bills have the smallest standard deviation, 3.10 percent, and the smallest average annual return, 3.77 percent. Returns for small stocks in any particular year may have been higher or lower than returns for the other types of securities, but on average, they were higher. This is evidence that investors require higher returns for investments with greater risks.

The statistics in Exhibit 7.3 describe actual investment returns, as opposed to expected returns. In other words, they represent what has happened in the past. Financial analysts often use historical numbers such as these to estimate the returns that might be expected in the future. That is exactly what we did in the baseball example earlier in this chapter. We used the percentage of at-bats in which you got a hit this past season to estimate the likelihood that you would get a hit in your last collegiate at-bat. We assumed that your past performance was a reasonable indicator of your future performance.

To see how historical numbers are used in finance, let's suppose that you are considering investing in a fund that mimics the S&P 500 Index (this is what we call an *index fund*) and that you want to estimate what the returns on the S&P 500 Index are likely to be in the future. If you believe that the 1926 to 2006 period provides a reasonable indication of what we can expect in the future, then the average historical return on the S&P 500 Index of 12.30 percent provides a perfectly reasonable estimate of the return you can expect from your investment in the S&P 500 Index fund. In Chapter 13 we will explore in detail how historical data can be used in this way to estimate the discount rate used to evaluate projects in the capital budgeting process.

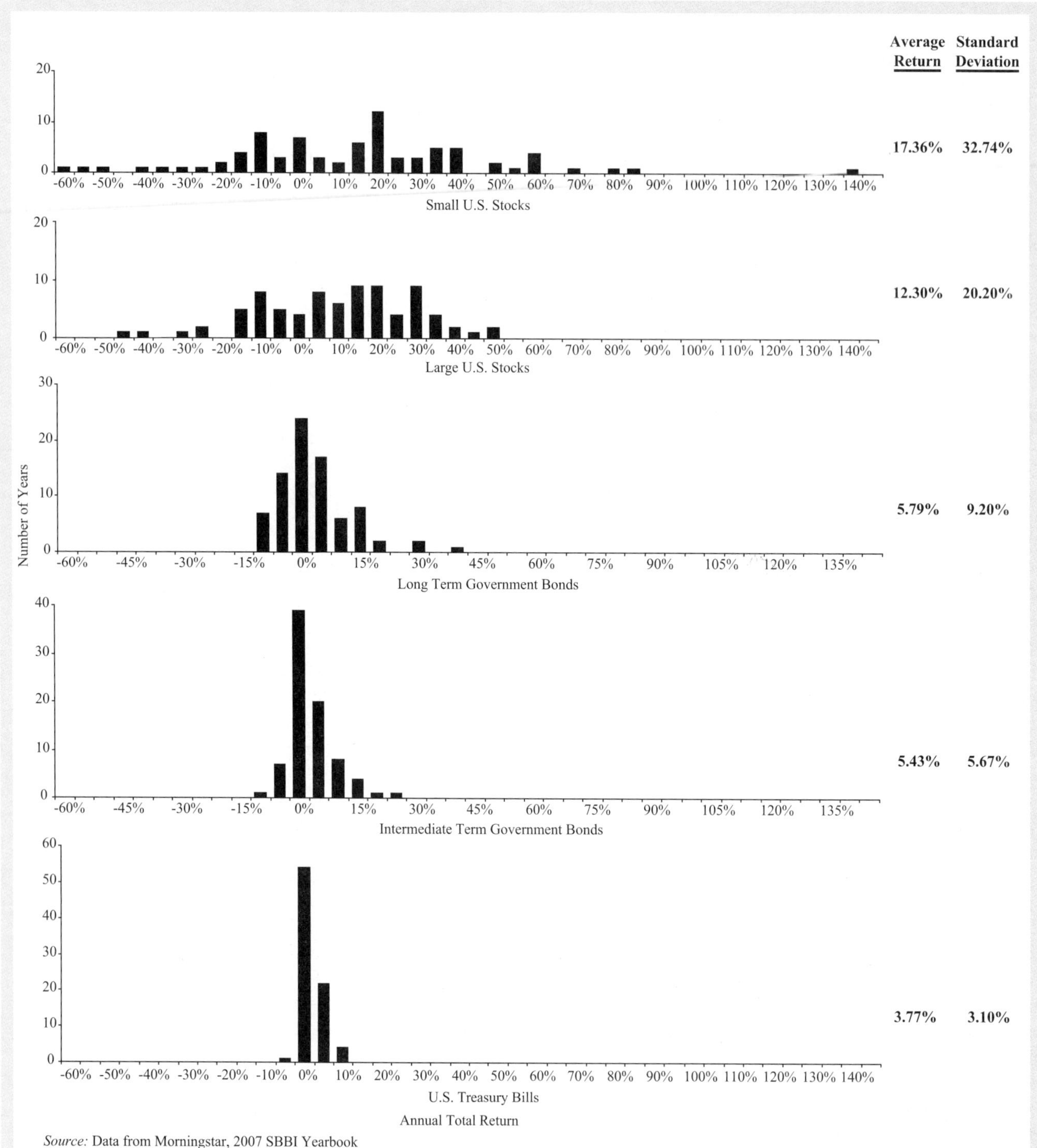

Source: Data from Morningstar, 2007 SBBI Yearbook

Exhibit 7.3

Distributions of Annual Total Returns for U.S. Stocks and Bonds from 1926 to 2006

Higher standard deviations of return have historically been associated with higher returns. For example, between 1926 and 2006, the standard deviation of the annual returns for small stocks was higher than the standard deviations of the returns earned by other types of securities, and the average return that investors earned from small stocks was also higher. At the other end of the spectrum, the returns on Treasury bills had the smallest standard deviation, and Treasury bills earned the smallest average return.

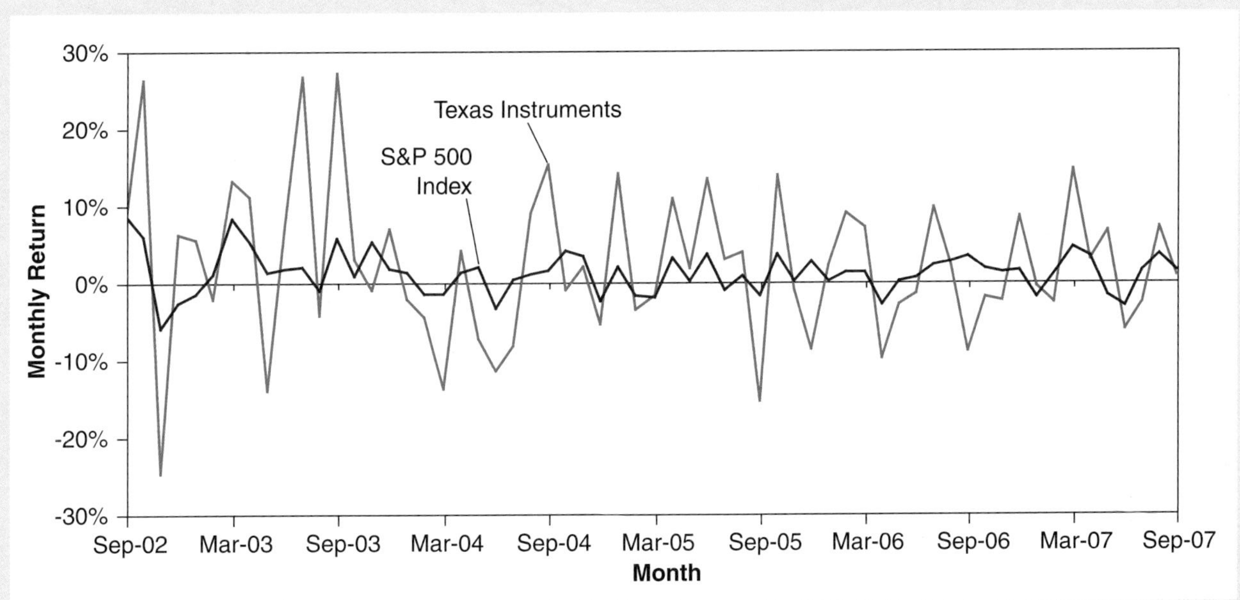

Exhibit 7.4

Monthly Returns for Texas Instruments and the S&P 500 Index from September 2002 through September 2007

The returns on shares of individual stocks tend to be much more volatile than the returns on portfolios of stocks, such as the S&P 500.

Comparing the historical returns for an individual stock with the historical returns for an index can also be instructive. Exhibit 7.4 shows such a comparison for Texas Instruments and the S&P 500 Index using monthly returns for the period from September 2002 to September 2007. Notice in the exhibit that the returns on Texas Instruments stock are much more volatile than the average returns on the firms represented in the S&P 500 Index. In other words, the standard deviation of returns for Texas Instruments stock is higher than that for the S&P 500 Index. This is not a coincidence; we will discuss shortly why returns on individual stocks tend to be riskier than returns on indexes.

One last point is worth noting while we are examining historical returns: the value of a $1.00 investment in 1926 would have varied greatly by 2006, depending on where that dollar was invested. Exhibit 7.5 shows that $1.00 invested in U.S. Treasury bills in 1926 would have been worth $19.29 by 2006. In contrast, that same $1.00 invested in small stocks would have been worth $15,922.43 by 2006![2] Over a long period of time, earning higher rates of return can have a dramatic impact on the value of an investment. This huge difference reflects the impact of compounding of returns (returns earned on returns), much like the compounding of interest we discussed in Chapter 5.

Before You Go On

1. What is the relation between the variance and the standard deviation?
2. What relation do we generally observe between risk and return when we examine historical returns?
3. How would we expect the standard deviation of the return on an individual stock to compare with the standard deviation of the return on a stock index?

[2]From a practical standpoint, it would not really have been possible to grow $1.00 to $15,922.43 by investing in small U.S. stocks because this increase assumes that an investor is able to rebalance the stock portfolio by buying and selling shares as necessary at no cost. Since buying and selling shares is costly, the final wealth would have been lower. Nevertheless, even after transaction costs, it would have been much more profitable to invest in small stocks than in U.S. Treasury bills.

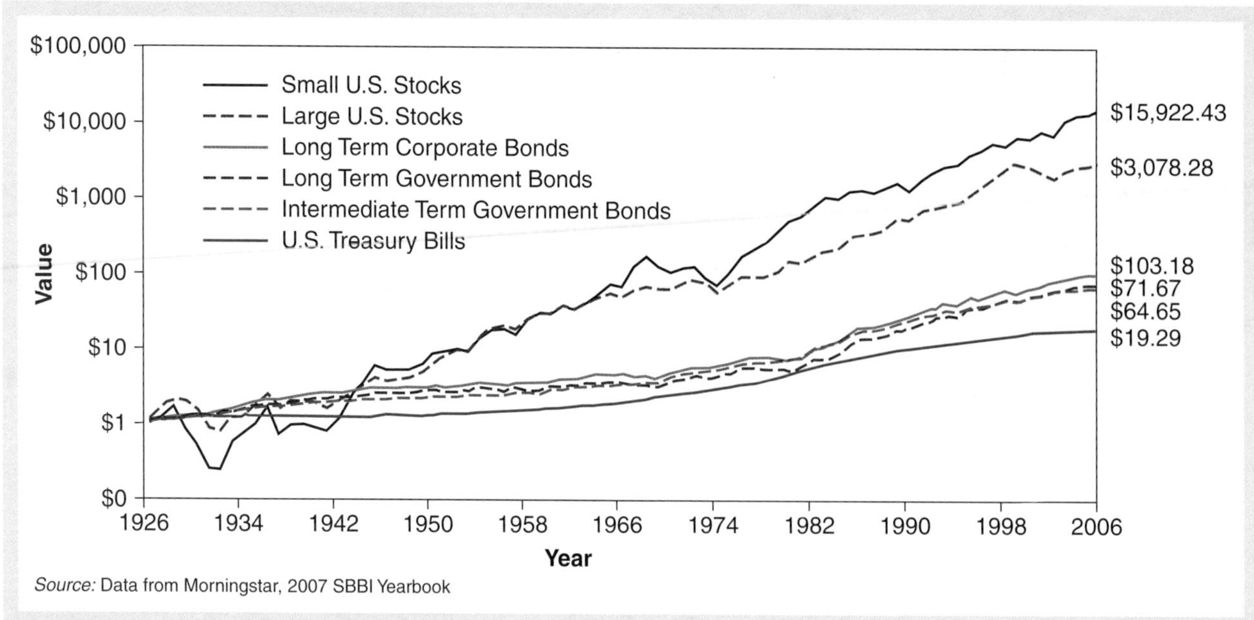

Source: Data from Morningstar, 2007 SBBI Yearbook

Exhibit 7.5
Cumulative Value of $1 Invested in 1926

The value of a $1 investment in stocks, small or large, grew much more rapidly than the value of a $1 investment in bonds or Treasury bills over the 1926 to 2006 period. This graph illustrates how earning a higher rate of return over a long period of time can affect the value of an investment portfolio. Although annual stock returns were less certain between 1926 and 2006, the returns on stock investments were much greater.

7.4 Risk and Diversification

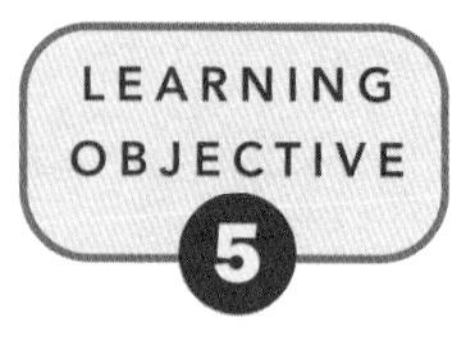

portfolio
the collection of assets an investor owns

diversification
a strategy of reducing risk by investing in two or more assets whose values do not always move in the same direction at the same time

It does not generally make sense to invest all of your money in a single asset. The reason is directly related to the fact that returns on individual stocks tend to be riskier than returns on indexes. By investing in two or more assets whose values do not always move in the same direction at the same time, an investor can reduce the risk of his or her collection of investments, or **portfolio**. This is the idea behind the concept of **diversification**.

This section develops the tools necessary to evaluate the benefits of diversification. We begin with a discussion of how to quantify risk and return for a single-asset portfolio, and then we discuss more realistic and complicated portfolios that have two or more assets. Although our discussion focuses on stock portfolios, it is important to recognize that the concepts discussed apply equally well to portfolios that include a range of assets, including stocks, bonds, and real estate, among others.

Single-Asset Portfolios

Returns for individual stocks from one day to the next have been found to be largely independent of each other and approximately normally distributed. In other words, the return for a stock on one day is largely independent of the return on that same stock the next day, two days later, three days later, and so on. Each daily return can be viewed as having been randomly drawn from a normal distribution where the probability associated with the return depends on how far it is from the expected value. If we know what the expected value and standard deviation are for the distribution of returns for a stock, it is possible to quantify the risks and expected returns that an investment in the stock might yield in the future.

To see how we might do this, assume that you are considering investing in one of two stocks for the next year: AMD or Intel. Also, to keep things simple, assume that there are only three possible economic conditions (outcomes) a year from now and that the returns on AMD and Intel under each of these outcomes are as follows:

Economic Outcome	Probability	AMD Return	Intel Return
Poor	0.2	−0.13	−0.10
Neutral	0.5	0.10	0.07
Good	0.3	0.25	0.22

With this information, we can calculate the expected returns for AMD and Intel by using Equation 7.2:

$$\begin{aligned} E(R_{AMD}) &= (p_{Poor} \times R_{Poor}) + (p_{Neutral} \times R_{Neutral}) + (p_{Good} \times R_{Good}) \\ &= (0.2 \times -0.13) + (0.5 \times 0.10) + (0.3 \times 0.25) \\ &= 0.099, \text{ or } 9.9\% \end{aligned}$$

and

$$\begin{aligned} E(R_{Intel}) &= (p_{Poor} \times R_{Poor}) + (p_{Neutral} \times R_{Neutral}) + (p_{Good} \times R_{Good}) \\ &= (0.2 \times -0.10) + (0.5 \times 0.07) + (0.3 \times 0.22) \\ &= 0.081, \text{ or } 8.1\% \end{aligned}$$

Similarly, we can calculate the standard deviations of the returns for AMD and Intel in the same way that we calculated the standard deviation for our baseball bonus example in Section 7.2:

$$\begin{aligned} \sigma^2_{R_{AMD}} &= \{p_{Poor} \times [R_{Poor} - E(R_{AMD})]^2\} + \{p_{Neutral} \times [R_{Neutral} - E(R_{AMD})]^2\} \\ &\quad + \{p_{Good} \times [R_{Good} - E(R_{AMD})]^2\} \\ &= [0.2 \times (-0.13 - 0.099)^2] + [0.5 \times (0.10 - 0.099)^2] + [0.3 \times (0.25 - 0.099)^2] \\ &= 0.01733 \\ \sigma_{R_{AMD}} &= (\sigma^2_{R_{AMD}})^{1/2} = (0.01733)^{1/2} = 0.13164, \text{ or } 13.164\% \end{aligned}$$

and

$$\begin{aligned} \sigma^2_{R_{Intel}} &= \{p_{Poor} \times [R_{Poor} - E(R_{Intel})]^2\} + \{p_{Neutral} \times [R_{Neutral} - E(R_{Intel})]^2\} \\ &\quad + \{p_{Good} \times [R_{Good} - E(R_{Intel})]^2\} \\ &= [0.2 \times (-0.10 - 0.081)^2] + [0.5 \times (0.07 - 0.081)^2] + [0.3 \times (0.22 - 0.081)^2] \\ &= 0.01241 \\ \sigma_{R_{Intel}} &= (\sigma^2_{R_{Intel}})^{1/2} = (0.01241)^{1/2} = 0.11140, \text{ or } 11.140\% \end{aligned}$$

Having calculated the expected returns and standard deviations for the expected returns on AMD and Intel stock, the natural question to ask is which provides the highest risk-adjusted return. Before we answer this question, let's return to the example at the beginning of Section 7.1. Recall that, in this example, we proposed choosing among three stocks: A, B, and C. We stated that investors would prefer the investment that provides the highest expected return for a given level of risk or the lowest risk for a given expected return. This made it fairly easy to choose between Stocks A and B, which had the same return but different risk levels, and between Stocks B and C, which had the same risk but different returns. We were stuck when trying to choose between Stocks A and C, however, because they differed in both risk and return. Now, armed with tools for quantifying expected returns and risk, we can at least take a first pass at comparing stocks such as these.

The **coefficient of variation (CV)** is a measure that can help us in making comparisons such as that between Stocks A and C. The coefficient of variation for stock *i* is calculated as follows:

coefficient of variation (CV)
a measure of the risk associated with an investment for each one percent of expected return

$$CV_i = \frac{\sigma_{R_i}}{E(R_i)} \qquad (7.4)$$

In this equation, CV is a measure of the risk associated with an investment for each one percent of expected return.

Recall that Stock A has an expected return of 12 percent and a risk level of 12 percent, while Stock C has an expected return of 16 percent and a risk level of 16 percent. If we assume that the risk level given for each stock is equal to the standard deviation of its return, we can find the coefficients of variation for the stocks as follows:

$$CV(R_A) = \frac{0.12}{0.12} = 1.00 \quad \text{and} \quad CV(R_C) = \frac{0.16}{0.16} = 1.00$$

Since these values are equal, the coefficient of variation measure suggests that these two investments are equally attractive on a risk-adjusted basis.

Now returning to our AMD and Intel example, we find that the coefficients of variation for those shares are:

$$CV_{AMD} = \frac{\sigma R_{AMD}}{E(R_{AMD})} = \frac{0.13164}{0.099} = 1.330$$

and

$$CV_{Intel} = \frac{\sigma R_{Intel}}{E(R_{Intel})} = \frac{0.11140}{0.081} = 1.375$$

We can see that while AMD stock has a higher expected return (9.9 percent versus 8.1 percent) and a higher standard deviation of returns (13.154 percent versus 11.140 percent), it has a lower coefficient of variation than Intel stock. This tells us that the amount of risk for each one percent of expected return is lower for AMD shares than for Intel shares. On a risk-adjusted basis, then, the expected returns from AMD stock are more attractive.

LEARNING BY DOING APPLICATION 7.4

Calculating and Using the Coefficient of Variation

Problem: You are trying to choose between two investments. The first investment, a painting by Picasso, has an expected return of 14 percent with a standard deviation of 30 percent over the next year. The second investment, a pair of blue suede shoes once worn by Elvis, has an expected return of 20 percent with a standard deviation of return of 40 percent. What is the coefficient of variation for each of these investments, and what do these coefficients tell us?

Approach: Use Equation 7.4 to compute the coefficients of variation for the two investments.

Solution: The coefficients of variation are:

$$CV(R_{Painting}) = \frac{0.3}{0.14} = 2.14 \quad \text{and} \quad CV(R_{Shoes}) = \frac{0.4}{0.2} = 2.00$$

The coefficient of variation for the painting is slightly higher than that for Elvis's blue suede shoes. This indicates that the risk for each one percent of expected return is higher for the painting than for Elvis's shoes.

You can read about other ratios that are used to measure risk-adjusted returns for investments at the following Web site: www.andreassteiner.net/performanceanalysis/?External_Analysis:Risk-Adjusted_Performance_Measures.

Portfolios with More Than One Asset

It may seem like a good idea to evaluate investments by calculating a measure of risk for each one percent of expected return. However, the coefficient of variation has a critical shortcoming that is not quite evident when we are considering only a single asset. In order to explain this shortcoming, we must discuss the more realistic setting in which an investor has constructed a two-asset portfolio.

EXPECTED RETURN ON A PORTFOLIO WITH MORE THAN ONE ASSET

Suppose that you own a portfolio that consists of \$500 of AMD stock and \$500 of Intel stock and that over the next year you expect to earn returns on the AMD and Intel shares of 9.9 percent and 8.1 percent, respectively. How would you calculate the expected return for the overall portfolio?

Let's try to answer this question using our intuition. If half of your funds are invested in each stock, it would seem reasonable that the expected return for this portfolio should be a 50-50 mixture of the expected returns from the two stocks, or:

$$E(R_{\text{Portfolio}}) = (0.5 \times 0.099) + (0.5 \times 0.081) = 0.09, \text{ or } 9.0\%$$

Notice that this formula is just like the expected return formula for an individual stock. However, in this case, instead of multiplying outcomes by their associated probabilities, we are multiplying expected returns for individual stocks by the fraction of the total portfolio value that each of these stocks represents. In other words, the formula for the expected return for a two-stock portfolio is:

$$E(R_{\text{Portfolio}}) = x_1E(R_1) + x_2E(R_2)$$

where x_i represents the fraction of the portfolio invested in asset i. The corresponding equation for a portfolio with n assets is:

$$\begin{aligned} E(R_{\text{Portfolio}}) &= \sum_{i=1}^{n} [x_i \times E(R_i)] \\ &= [x_1 \times E(R_1)] + [x_2 \times E(R_2)] + \cdots + [x_n \times E(R_n)] \end{aligned} \tag{7.5}$$

This equation is just like Equation 7.2, except that (1) the returns are expected returns for individual assets and (2) instead of multiplying by the probability of an outcome, we are multiplying by the fraction of the portfolio invested in each asset. Note that this equation can be used only if you have already calculated the expected return for each stock.

To see how Equation 7.5 is used to calculate the expected return on a portfolio with more than two assets, consider an example. Suppose that you were recently awarded a \$500,000 grant from a national foundation to pursue your interest in advancing the art of noodling—a popular pastime in some parts of the country in which people catch 40- to 50-pound catfish by putting their hands into catfish holes and wiggling their fingers like noodles to attract the fish.[3] Since your grant is intended to support your activities for five years, you kept \$100,000 to cover your expenses for the next year and invested the remaining \$400,000 in U.S. Treasury bills and stocks. Specifically, you invested \$100,000 in Treasury bills (TB) that yield 4.5 percent; \$150,000 in Procter & Gamble stock (P&G), which has an expected return of 7.5 percent; and \$150,000 in Exxon Mobil Corporation stock (EMC), which has an expected return of 9.0 percent. What is the expected return on this \$400,000 portfolio?

In order to use Equation 7.5, we must first calculate x_i, the fraction of the portfolio invested in asset i, for each investment. These fractions are as follows:

$$x_{\text{TB}} = \frac{\$100{,}000}{\$400{,}000} = 0.25$$

$$x_{\text{P\&G}} = x_{\text{EMC}} = \frac{\$150{,}000}{\$400{,}000} = 0.375$$

Therefore, the expected return on the portfolio is:

$$\begin{aligned} E(R_{\text{Portfolio}}) &= [x_{\text{TB}} \times E(R_{\text{TB}})] + [x_{\text{P\&G}} \times E(R_{\text{P\&G}})] + [x_{\text{EMC}} \times E(R_{\text{EMC}})] \\ &= (0.25 \times 0.045) + (0.375 \times 0.075) + (0.375 \times 0.090) \\ &= 0.0731, \text{ or } 7.31\% \end{aligned}$$

[3]For more information on noodling, see the April 21, 2006, *New York Times* article titled "In the Jaws of a Catfish," by Ethan Todras-Whitehill.

LEARNING BY DOING APPLICATION 7.5

Calculating the Expected Return on a Portfolio

Problem: You have become concerned that you have too much of your money invested in your pizza restaurant and have decided to diversify your personal portfolio. Right now the pizza restaurant is your only investment. To diversify, you plan to sell 45 percent of your restaurant and invest the proceeds from the sale, in equal proportions, into a stock market index fund and a bond market index fund. Over the next year, you expect to earn a return of 15 percent on your remaining investment in the pizza restaurant, 12 percent on your investment in the stock market index fund, and 8 percent on your investment in the bond market index fund. What return will you expect from your diversified portfolio over the next year?

Approach: First, calculate the fraction of your portfolio that will be invested in each type of asset after you have diversified. Then use Equation 7.5 to calculate the expected return on the portfolio.

Solution: After you have diversified, 55 percent (100 percent − 45 percent) of your portfolio will be invested in your restaurant, 22.5 percent (45 percent × 0.50) will be invested in the stock market index fund, and 22.5 percent (45 percent × 0.50) will be invested in the bond market index fund. Therefore, from Equation 7.5, we know that the expected return for your portfolio is:

$$\begin{aligned} E(R_{\text{Portfolio}}) &= [x_{\text{Rest}} \times E(R_{\text{Rest}})] + [x_{\text{Stock}} \times E(R_{\text{Stock}})] + [x_{\text{Bond}} \times E(R_{\text{Bond}})] \\ &= (0.550 \times 0.15) + (0.225 \times 0.12) + (0.225 \times 0.08) \\ &= 0.1275, \text{ or } 12.75\% \end{aligned}$$

At 12.75 percent, the expected return is an average of the returns on the individual assets in your portfolio, weighted by the fraction of your portfolio that is invested in each.

RISK OF A PORTFOLIO WITH MORE THAN ONE ASSET

Now that we have calculated the expected return on a portfolio with more than one asset, the next question is how to quantify the risk of such a portfolio. Before we discuss the mechanics of how to do this, it is important to have some intuitive understanding of how volatility in the returns for different assets interact to determine the volatility of the overall portfolio.

The prices of two stocks in a portfolio will rarely, if ever, change by the same amount and in the same direction at the same time. Normally, the price of one stock will change by more than the price of the other. In fact, the prices of two stocks will frequently move in different directions. These differences in price movements affect the total volatility in the returns for a portfolio.

Exhibit 7.6 shows monthly returns for the stock of CSX (a railroad company) and Wal-Mart (the big retailer) over the period from September 2002 through September 2007. Notice that the returns on these shares are generally different and that the prices of the shares can move in different directions in a given month (one stock has a positive return when the other has a negative return). When the stock prices move in opposite directions, the change in the price of one stock offsets at least some of the change in the price of the other stock. As a result, the level of risk for a portfolio of the two stocks is less than the average of the risks associated with the individual shares.

This means that we *cannot* calculate the variance of a portfolio containing two assets simply by calculating the average of the variances of the individual stocks using a formula such as:

$$\sigma^2_{R_{2\text{ Asset portfolio}}} = x_1^2\sigma^2_{R_1} + x_2^2\sigma^2_{R_2}$$

where x_i represents the fraction of the portfolio invested in stock i and $\sigma^2_{R_i}$ is the variance of the return on stock i. We have to account for the fact that the returns on

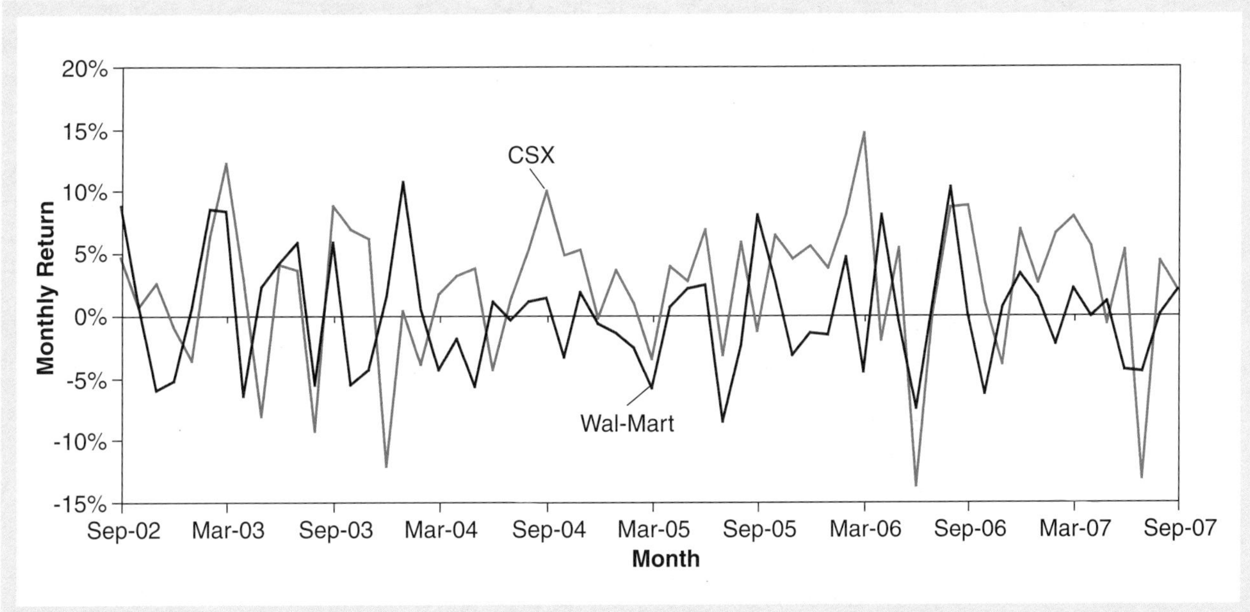

Exhibit 7.6
Monthly Returns for CSX and Wal-Mart Stock from September 2002 through September 2007
The returns on two stocks are generally different. In some periods, the return on one stock is positive, while the return on the other is negative. Even when the returns on both are positive or negative, they are rarely exactly the same.

different shares in a portfolio tend to partially offset each other. We do this by adding a third term to the formula. For a two-asset portfolio, we calculate the variance of the returns using the following formula:

$$\sigma^2_{\text{R}_2\text{ Asset portfolio}} = x_1^2\sigma^2_{\text{R}_1} + x_2^2\sigma^2_{\text{R}_2} + 2x_1x_2\sigma_{\text{R}_{1,2}} \quad (7.6)$$

where $\sigma_{\text{R}_{1,2}}$ is the **covariance** between stocks 1 and 2. The covariance is a measure of how the returns on two assets covary, or move together. The third term in Equation 7.6 accounts for the fact that returns from the two assets will offset each other to some extent. The covariance is calculated using the following formula:

covariance
a measure of how the returns on two assets covary, or move together

$$\text{Cov}(\text{R}_1, \text{R}_2) = \sigma_{\text{R}_{1,2}} = \sum_{i=1}^{n}\{p_i \times [(\text{R}_{1,i} - \text{E}(\text{R}_1)] \times [(\text{R}_{2,i} - \text{E}(\text{R}_2)]\} \quad (7.7)$$

where i represents outcomes rather than assets. Compare this equation with Equation 7.3, reproduced here:

$$\text{Var}(\text{R}) = \sigma^2_{\text{R}} = \sum_{i=1}^{n}\{p_i \times [\text{R}_i - \text{E}(\text{R})]^2\}$$

You can see that the covariance calculation is very similar to the variance calculation. The difference is that, instead of squaring the difference between the value from each outcome and the expected value for an individual asset, we calculate the product of this difference for two different assets.

Just as it is difficult to directly interpret the variance of the returns for an asset—recall that the variance is in units of squared dollars—it is difficult to directly interpret the covariance of returns between two assets. We get around this problem by dividing the covariance by the product of the standard deviations of the returns for the two assets. This gives us the correlation, ρ, between the returns on those assets:

$$\rho = \frac{\sigma_{\text{R}_{1,2}}}{\sigma_{\text{R}_1}\sigma_{\text{R}_2}} \quad (7.8)$$

The correlation between the returns on two assets will always have a value between -1 and $+1$. This makes the interpretation of this variable straightforward. A *negative correlation* means that the returns tend to have opposite signs. For example, when the return on one asset is positive, the return on the other asset tends to be negative. If the correlation is exactly -1, the returns on the two assets are perfectly negatively correlated. In other words, when the return on one asset is positive, the return on the other asset will always be negative. A *positive correlation* means that when the return on one asset is positive, the return on the other asset also tends to be positive. If the correlation is exactly equal to $+1$, then the returns of the two assets are said to be perfectly positively correlated. The return on one asset will always be positive when the return on the other asset is positive. Finally, a *correlation of 0* means that the returns on the assets are not correlated. In this case, the fact that the return on one asset is positive or negative tells you nothing about how likely it is that the return on the other asset will be positive or negative.

Let's work an example to see how Equation 7.6 is used to calculate the variance of a portfolio that consists of 50 percent CSX and 50 percent Wal-Mart stock. Using the data plotted in Exhibit 7.6, we can calculate the variance of the annual returns for CSX and Wal-Mart stock, σ^2_R, to be 0.03949 and 0.02584, respectively. The covariance between the annual returns on these two stocks is 0.00782. We do not show the calculations for the variances and the covariance because each of these numbers was calculated using 60 different monthly returns. These calculations are too cumbersome to illustrate. Rest assured, however, that they were calculated using Equations 7.3 and 7.7.[4] With these values, we can calculate the variance of a portfolio that consists of 50 percent CSX stock and 50 percent Wal-Mart stock as:

$$\begin{aligned}\sigma^2_{R_{\text{Portfolio of CSX and Wal-Mart}}} &= x^2_{\text{CSX}}\sigma^2_{R_{\text{CSX}}} + x^2_{\text{Wal-Mart}}\sigma^2_{R_{\text{Wal-Mart}}} + 2x_{\text{CSX}}x_{\text{Wal-Mart}}\sigma_{R_{\text{CSX, Wal-Mart}}}\\ &= (0.5)^2(0.03949) + (0.5)^2(0.02584) + 2(0.5)(0.5)(0.00782)\\ &= 0.02024\end{aligned}$$

You can see that this portfolio variance is smaller than the variance of either CSX or Wal-Mart stock on its own.

If we calculate the standard deviations by taking the square roots of the variances, we find that the standard deviations for CSX, Wal-Mart, and the portfolio consisting of those two stocks are 0.199 (19.9 percent), 0.161 (16.1 percent), and 0.142 (14.2 percent), respectively.

Exhibit 7.7 illustrates the monthly returns for the portfolio of CSX and Wal-Mart stock, along with the monthly returns for the individual stocks. You can see in this exhibit that, while the returns on the portfolio vary quite a bit, this variation is slightly less than that for the individual company shares.

Using Equation 7.8, we can calculate the correlation of the returns between CSX and Wal-Mart stock as:

$$\rho = \frac{\sigma_{R_{1,2}}}{\sigma_{R_1}\sigma_{R_2}} = \frac{0.00782}{0.199 \times 0.161} = 0.244$$

The positive correlation tells us that the prices on CSX and Wal-Mart stock tend to move in the same direction. However, the correlation of less than one tells us that they do not always do so. The fact that the prices of these two shares do not always move together is the reason that the returns on a portfolio of the two stocks have less variation than the returns on the individual company shares. This example illustrates the benefit of *diversification*—how holding more than one asset with different risk characteristics can reduce the risk of a portfolio. Note that if the correlation of the returns between CSX and Wal-Mart stock equaled one, holding these two stocks would not reduce risk because their prices would always move up or down together.

As we add more and more stocks to a portfolio, calculating the variance using the approach illustrated in Equation 7.6 becomes increasingly complex. The reason for this is that we have to account for the covariance between each pair of assets. These more

[4]The only adjustment that we had to make was to account for the fact that our calculations used monthly returns rather than annual returns. This adjustment simply required us to multiply each number we calculated by 12 because there are 12 months in a year.

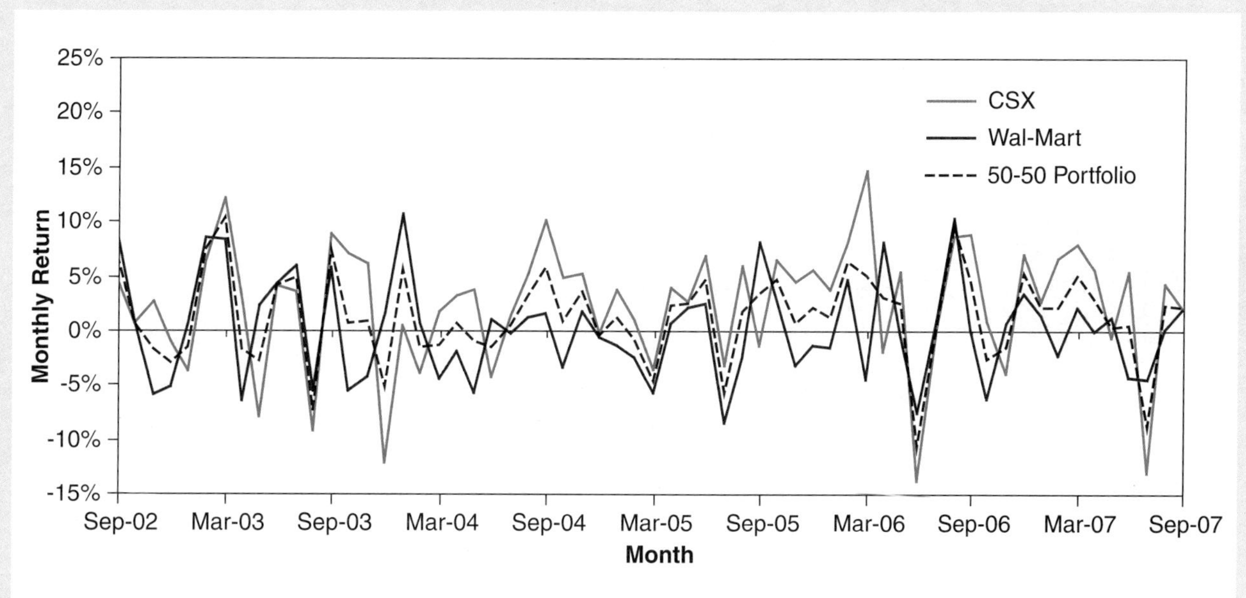

Exhibit 7.7
Monthly Returns for CSX and Wal-Mart Stock and for a Portfolio with 50 Percent of the Value in Each of these Two Stocks from September 2002 through September 2007
The variation in the returns from a portfolio that consists of CSX and Wal-Mart stock in equal proportions is less than the variation in the returns from either of those stocks alone.

extensive calculations are beyond the scope of this book, but they are conceptually the same as those for a portfolio with two assets.

Calculating the Variance of a Two-Asset Portfolio

LEARNING BY DOING APPLICATION 7.6

Problem: You are still planning to sell 45 percent of your pizza restaurant in order to diversify your personal portfolio. However, you have now decided to invest all of the proceeds in the stock market index fund. After you diversify, you will have 55 percent of your wealth invested in the restaurant and 45 percent invested in the stock market index fund. You have estimated the variances of the returns for these two investments and the covariance between their returns to be as follows:

$\sigma^2_{R_{\text{Restaurant}}}$	0.0625
$\sigma^2_{R_{\text{Stock market index}}}$	0.0400
$\sigma_{R_{\text{Restaurant, Stock market index}}}$	0.0250

What will be the variance and standard deviation of your portfolio after you have sold the ownership interest in your restaurant and invested in the stock market index fund?

Approach: Use Equation 7.6 to calculate the variance of the portfolio and then take the square root of this value to obtain the standard deviation.

Solution:

The variance of the portfolio is:

$$\begin{aligned}\sigma^2_{R_{\text{Portfolio}}} &= x^2_{R_{\text{Restaurant}}}\sigma^2_{R_{\text{Restaurant}}} + x^2_{R_{\text{Stock market index}}}\sigma^2_{R_{\text{Stock market index}}} \\ &\quad + 2x_{\text{Restaurant}}x_{\text{Stock market index}}\sigma_{R_{\text{Restaurant, Stock market index}}} \\ &= [(0.55)^2 \times 0.0625] + [(0.45)^2 \times 0.0400] + (2 \times 0.55 \times 0.45 \times 0.0250) \\ &= 0.0394\end{aligned}$$

and the standard deviation is $(0.0394)^{1/2} = 0.1985$, or 19.85 percent.

(continued)

Comparing the portfolio variance of 0.0394 with the variances of the restaurant, 0.0625, and the stock market index fund, 0.0400, shows once again that a portfolio with two or more assets can have a smaller variance (and thus a smaller standard deviation) than any of the individual assets in the portfolio.

BUILDING INTUITION

Diversified Portfolios are Less Risky

Diversified portfolios generally have less risk for a given level of return than the individual risky assets in the portfolio. This is because the prices of individual assets rarely change by the same amount and in the same direction at the same time. As a result, some of the variation in an asset's price can be diversified away by owning another asset at the same time. This is important because it tells us that investors can eliminate some of the risk associated with individual investments by holding them in a diversified portfolio.

The Limits of Diversification

In the sample calculations for the portfolio containing CSX and Wal-Mart stock, we saw that the standard deviation of the returns for a portfolio consisting of equal investments in those two stocks was 14.2 percent from September 2002 through September 2007 and that this figure was lower than the standard deviation for either of the individual stocks (19.9 percent and 16.1 percent). You might wonder how the standard deviation for the portfolio is likely to change if we increase the number of assets in the portfolio. The answer is simple. If the returns on the individual stocks added to our portfolio do not all change in the same way, then increasing the number of stocks in the portfolio will reduce the standard deviation of the portfolio returns even further.

Let's consider a simple example to illustrate this point. Suppose that all assets have a standard deviation of returns that is equal to 40 percent and that the covariance between the returns for each pair of assets is 0.048. If we form a portfolio in which we have an equal investment in two assets, the standard deviation of returns for the portfolio will be 32.25 percent. If we add a third asset, the portfolio standard deviation of returns will decrease to 29.21 percent. It will be even lower, at 27.57 percent, for a four-asset portfolio. Exhibit 7.8 illustrates how the standard deviation for the portfolio declines as more stocks are added.

In addition to showing how increasing the number of assets decreases the overall risk of a portfolio, Exhibit 7.8 illustrates three other very important points. First, the decrease in the standard deviation for the portfolio gets smaller and smaller as more assets are added. You can see this effect by looking at the distance between the straight horizontal line and the plot of the standard deviation of the portfolio returns.

The second important point is that, as the number of assets becomes very large, the portfolio standard deviation does not approach zero. It decreases only so far. In the example in Exhibit 7.8, it approaches 21.9 percent. The standard deviation does not approach zero because we are assuming that the variations in the asset returns do not completely cancel each other out. This is a realistic assumption because in practice investors can rarely diversify away all risk. They can diversify away risk that is unique to the individual assets, but they cannot diversify away risk that is common to all assets. The risk that can be diversified away is called **diversifiable**, **unsystematic**, or **unique risk**, and the risk that cannot be diversified away is called **nondiversifiable** or **systematic risk**. In the next section, we will discuss systematic risk in detail.

diversifiable, unsystematic, or unique risk
risk that can be eliminated through diversification

nondiversifiable or systematic risk
risk that cannot be eliminated through diversification

The third key point illustrated in Exhibit 7.8 is that most of the risk-reduction benefits from diversification can be achieved in a portfolio with 15 to 20 assets. Of course, the number of assets required to achieve a high level of diversification depends on the covariances between the assets in the portfolio. However, in general, it is not necessary to invest in a very large number of different assets.

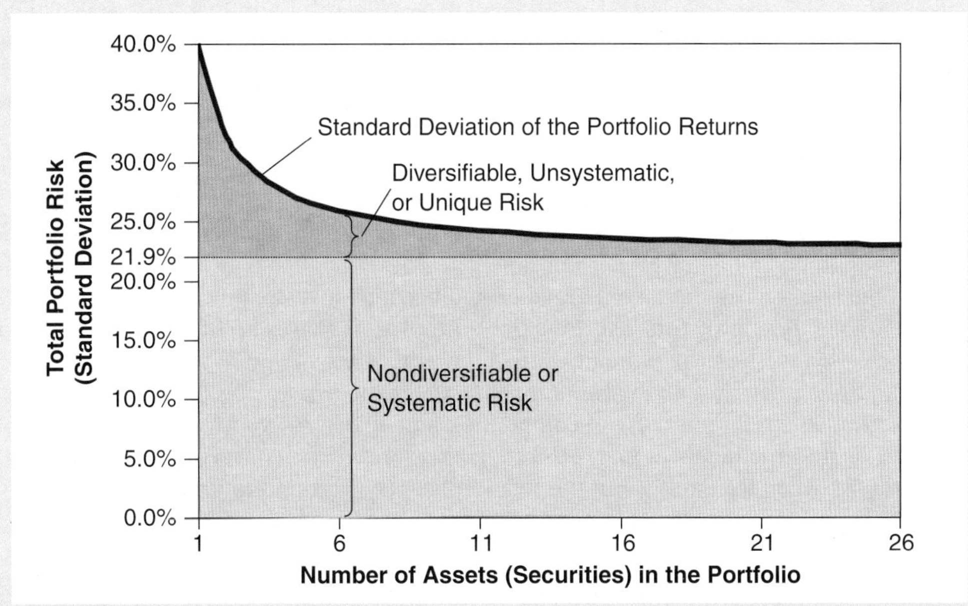

Exhibit 7.8
Unique and Systematic Risk in a Portfolio as the Number of Assets Increases
The total risk of a portfolio decreases as the number of assets increases. This is because the amount of unsystematic or unique risk in the portfolio decreases. The diversification benefit from adding another asset declines as the total number of assets in the portfolio increases and the unsystematic or unique risk approaches zero. Most of the diversification benefit can often be achieved with as few as 15 or 20 assets.

Before You Go On

1. What does the coefficient of variation tell us?
2. What are the two components of total risk?
3. Why does the total risk of a portfolio not approach zero as the number of assets in a portfolio becomes very large?

7.5 Systematic Risk

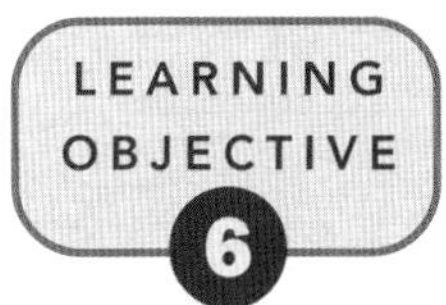

The objective of diversification is to eliminate variations in returns that are unique to individual assets. We diversify our investments across a number of different assets in the hope that these unique variations will cancel each other out. With complete diversification, all of the unique risk is eliminated from the portfolio. An investor with a diversified portfolio still faces systematic risk, however, and we now turn our attention to that form of risk.

Why Systematic Risk Is All That Matters

The idea that unique, or unsystematic, risk can be diversified away has direct implications for the relation between risk and return. If the transaction costs associated with constructing a diversified portfolio are relatively low, then rational, informed investors, such as the students who are taking this class, will prefer to hold diversified portfolios.

Diversified investors face only systematic risk, whereas investors whose portfolios are not well diversified face systematic risk plus unsystematic risk. Because they face less risk, the diversified investors will be willing to pay higher prices for individual assets than the other investors. Therefore, expected returns on individual assets will be lower than the total risk (systematic plus unsystematic risk) of those assets suggests they should be.

To illustrate, consider two individual investors, Emily and Jane. Each of them is trying to decide if she should purchase stock in your pizza restaurant. Emily holds a diversified portfolio and Jane does not. Assume your restaurant's stock has five units of systematic risk and nine units of total risk. You can see that Emily faces less risk than Jane and will require a lower expected rate of return. Consequently, Emily will be willing to pay a higher price than Jane.

If the market includes a large number of diversified investors such as Emily, competition among these investors will drive the price of your shares up further. Competition among these investors will ultimately drive the price up to the point where the expected return just compensates all investors for the systematic risk associated with your stock. The bottom line is that because of competition among diversified investors only systematic risk is rewarded in asset markets. For this reason, we are concerned only about systematic risk when we think about the relation between risk and return in finance.

BUILDING INTUITION

Systematic Risk Is the Risk That Matters

The required rate of return on an asset depends only on the systematic risk associated with that asset. Because unique (unsystematic) risk can be diversified away, investors can and will eliminate their exposure to this risk. Competition among diversified investors will drive the prices of assets to the point where the expected returns will compensate investors for only the systematic risk that they bear.

Measuring Systematic Risk

If systematic risk is all that matters when we think about expected returns, then we cannot use the standard deviation as a measure of risk.[5] The standard deviation is a measure of total risk. We need a way of quantifying the systematic risk of individual assets.

A natural starting point for doing this is to recognize that the most diversified portfolio possible will come closest to eliminating all unique risk. Such a portfolio provides a natural benchmark against which we can measure the systematic risk of an individual asset. What is the most diversified portfolio possible? The answer is simple. It is the portfolio that consists of all assets, including stocks, bonds, real estate, precious metals, commodities, art, baseball cards, and so forth from all over the world. In finance, we call this the **market portfolio**.

market portfolio
the portfolio of all assets

Unfortunately, we do not have very good data for most of these assets for most of the world, so we use the next best thing: the U.S. public stock market. A large number of stocks from a broad range of industries trade in this market. The companies that issue these stocks own a wide range of assets all over the world. These characteristics, combined with the facts that the U.S. market has been operating for a very long time and that we have very reliable and detailed information on prices for U.S. stocks, make the U.S. stock market a natural benchmark for estimating systematic risk.

market risk
a term commonly used to refer to nondiversifiable, or systematic, risk

Since systematic risk is, by definition, risk that cannot be diversified away, the systematic risk of an individual asset is really just a measure of the relation between the returns on the individual asset and the returns on the market. In fact, systematic risk is often referred to as **market risk**. To see how we might use data from the U.S. public

[5]This statement is true in the context of how expected returns are determined. However, the standard deviation is still a very useful measure of the risk faced by an individual investor who does not hold a diversified portfolio. For example, the owners of most small businesses have much of their personal wealth tied up in their businesses. They are certainly concerned about the total risk because it is directly related to the probability that they will go out of business and lose much of their wealth.

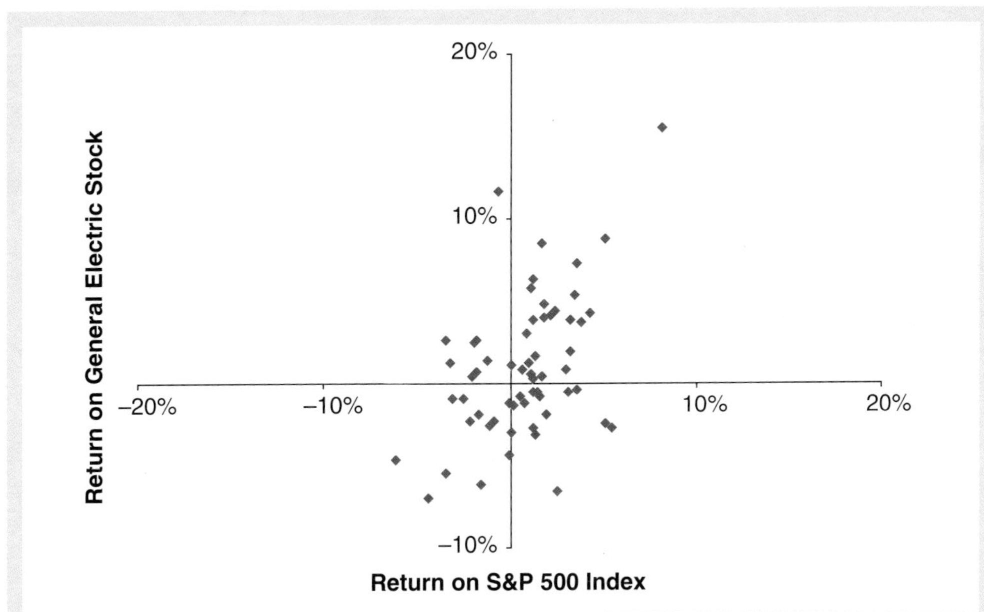

Exhibit 7.9
Plot of Monthly General Electric Company Stock and S&P 500 Index Returns: April 2003 to March 2008
The monthly returns on General Electric stock are positively related to the returns on the S&P 500 index. In other words, the return on General Electric's stock tends to be higher when the return on the S&P 500 index is higher and lower when the return on the S&P 500 index is lower.

stock market to estimate the systematic risk of an individual asset, look at Exhibit 7.9, which plots 60 historical monthly returns for General Electric Company (GE) against the corresponding monthly returns for the S&P 500 index (A proxy for the U.S. stock market). In this plot, you can see that returns on GE stock tend to be higher when returns on the S&P 500 tend to be higher. The measure of systematic risk that we use in finance is a statistical measure of this relation.

We quantify the relation between the returns on GE stock and the general market by finding the slope of the line that best represents the relation illustrated in Exhibit 7.9. Specifically, we estimate the slope of the *line of best fit.* We do this using the statistical technique called regression analysis. If you are not familiar with regression analysis, don't worry; the details are beyond the scope of this course. All you have to know is that this technique gives us the line that fits the data best.

Exhibit 7.10 illustrates the line that was estimated for the data in Exhibit 7.9 using regression analysis. Note that the slope of this line is 0.76. Recall from your math classes that the slope of a line equals the ratio of the rise (vertical distance) divided by the corresponding run (horizontal distance). In this case, the slope is the change in the return on GE stock divided by the change in the return on the U.S. stock market. A slope of 0.76 therefore means that, on average, the change in the return on GE stock was 0.76 times as large as the change in the return on the S&P 500 index. Thus, if the S&P 500 index goes up 1 percent, the average increase in GE's stock is 0.76 percent. This is a measure of systematic risk because it tells us that the volatility of the returns on GE stock is 0.76 times as large as that for the S&P 500 as a whole.

To explore this idea more completely, let's consider another, simpler example. Suppose that you have data for Nike stock and for the U.S. stock market for each of the past two years. In the first year, the return on the market was 10 percent, and the return on Nike stock was 15 percent. In the second year, the return on the market was 12 percent, and the return on Nike stock was 19 percent. From this information, we know that the return on Nike stock increased by 4 percent while the return on the market increased 2 percent. If we plotted the returns for Nike stock and for the market for each of the last two periods, as we did for GE stock and the market in Exhibits 7.9 and 7.10, and estimated

Exhibit 7.10
Slope of Relation Between General Electric Company Monthly Stock Returns and S&P 500 Index Returns: April 2003 to March 2008
The line shown in the exhibit best represents the relation between the monthly returns on General Electric stock and the returns on the S&P 500 index. The slope of this line, which equals 0.76, indicates that the return on General Electric stock tends to equal about 0.76 times the return on the S&P 500 index.

the line that best fit the data, it would be a line that connected the dots for the two periods. The slope of this line would equal 2, calculated as follows:

$$\text{Slope} = \frac{\text{Rise}}{\text{Run}} = \frac{\text{Change in Nike return}}{\text{Change in market return}} = \frac{19\% - 15\%}{12\% - 10\%} = \frac{4\%}{2\%} = 2$$

Although we have to be careful about drawing conclusions when we have only two data points, we might interpret the slope of 2 to indicate that new information that causes the market return to increase by 1 percent will tend to cause the return on Nike stock to increase by 2 percent. Of course, the reverse might also be true. That is, new information that causes the market return to decrease by 1 percent may also cause the return on Nike stock to go down by 2 percent. To the extent that the same information is driving the changes in returns on Nike stock and on the market, it would not be possible for an investor in Nike stock to diversify this risk away. It is nondiversifiable, or systematic, risk.

beta (β)
a measure of nondiversifiable, systematic, or market, risk

In finance, we call the slope of the line of best fit **beta**. Often we simply use the corresponding Greek letter, β, to refer to this measure of systematic risk. As shown below, a beta of 1 tells us that an asset has just as much systematic risk as the market. A beta higher than or lower than 1 tells us that the asset has more or less systematic risk than the market, respectively. A beta of 0 indicates a risk-free security, such as a U.S. Treasury bill.

A convenient place to find betas for individual companies is MSN Money Central at moneycentral.msn.com/home.asp. Just enter the stock symbol at the top of the page and hit "Enter" on your computer (try CSX, for example). You will get prices, an estimate of the beta, and other financial information.

$\beta = 1$	Same systematic risk as market
$\beta > 1$	More systematic risk than market
$\beta < 1$	Less systematic risk than market
$\beta = 0$	No systematic risk

Now you might ask yourself what happened to the unique risk of GE or Nike stock. This is best illustrated by the GE example, where we have more than two observations. As you can see in Exhibit 7.10, the line of best fit does not go through each data point. That is because some of the change in GE's stock price each month reflected information that did not affect the S&P 500 as a whole. That information is the unsystematic, or unique, component of the risk of GE's stock. The distance between each data point and the line of best fit represents variation in GE's stock return that can be attributed to this unique risk.

The positive slope (β) of the regression line in Exhibit 7.10 tells us that returns for the S&P 500 and for GE stock will tend to move in the same direction. The return on the S&P 500 and the return on GE's stock will not always change in the same direction, however, because the unique risk associated with GE stock can more than offset the effect of the market in any particular period. In the next section, we will discuss the implications of beta for the level (as opposed to the change) in the expected return for a stock such as GE.

Before You Go On

1. Why are returns on the stock market used as a benchmark in measuring systematic risk?
2. How is beta estimated?
3. How would you interpret a beta of 1.5 for an asset? A beta of 0.75?

7.6 Compensation for Bearing Systematic Risk

Now that we have identified the measure of the risk that diversified investors care about—systematic risk—we are in a position to examine how this measure relates to expected returns. Let's begin by thinking about the rate of return that you would require for an investment. First, you would want to make sure that you were compensated for inflation. It would not make sense to invest if you expected the investment to return an amount that did not at least allow you to have the same purchasing power that the money you invested had when you made the investment. Second, you would want some compensation for the fact that you are giving up the use of your money for a period of time. This compensation may be very small if you are forgoing the use of your money for only a short time, such as when you invest in a 30-day Treasury bill, but it might be relatively large if you are investing for several years. Finally, you are also going to require compensation for the systematic risk associated with the investment.

When you invest in a U.S. government security such as a Treasury bill, note, or bond, you are investing in a security that has no risk of default. After all, the U.S. government can always increase taxes or print more money to pay you back. Changes in economic conditions and other factors that affect the returns on other assets do not affect the default risk of U.S. government securities. As a result, these securities do not have systematic risk, and their returns can be viewed as risk free. In other words, returns on government bonds reflect the compensation required by investors to account for the impact of inflation on purchasing power and for their inability to use the money during the life of the investment.

It follows that the difference between required returns on government securities and required returns for risky investments represents the compensation investors require for taking risk. Recognizing this allows us to write the expected return for an asset i as:

$$E(R_i) = R_{rf} + \text{Compensation for taking risk}_i$$

where R_{rf} is the return on a security with a risk-free rate of return, which analysts typically estimate by looking at returns on government securities. The compensation for taking risk, which varies with the risk of the asset, is added to the risk-free rate of return to get an estimate of the expected rate of return for an asset. If we recognize that the compensation for taking risk varies with asset risk and that systematic risk is what matters, we can write the preceding equation as follows:

$$E(R_i) = R_{rf} + (\text{Units of systematic risk}_i \times \text{Compensation per unit of systematic risk})$$

where units of systematic risk_i is the number of units of systematic risk associated with asset i. Finally, if beta, β, is the appropriate measure for the number of units of systematic risk, we can also define compensation for taking risk as follows:

$$\text{Compensation for taking risk}_i = \beta_i \times \text{Compensation per unit of systematic risk}$$

where β_i is the beta for asset i.

Remember that beta is a measure of systematic risk that is directly related to the risk of the market as a whole. If the beta for an asset is 2, that asset has twice as much systematic risk as the market. If the beta for an asset is 0.5, then the asset has half as much systematic risk as the market. Recognizing this natural interpretation of beta suggests that the appropriate "unit of systematic risk" is the level of risk in the market as a whole and that the appropriate "compensation per unit of systematic risk" is the expected return required for the level of systematic risk in the market as a whole. The required rate of return on the market, over and above that of the risk-free return, represents compensation required by investors for bearing a market (systematic) risk. This suggests that:

$$\text{Compensation per unit of systematic risk} = E(R_m) - R_{rf}$$

where $E(R_m)$ is the expected return on the market. The term $E(R_m) - R_{rf}$ is called the *market risk premium.* Consequently, we can now write the equation for expected return as:

$$E(R_i) = R_{rf} + \beta_i[E(R_m) - R_{rf}] \quad (7.9)$$

7.7 The Capital Asset Pricing Model

Capital Asset Pricing Model (CAPM)
a model that describes the relation between risk and expected return

In deriving Equation 7.9, we intuitively arrived at the **Capital Asset Pricing Model (CAPM).** Equation 7.9 is the CAPM, a model that describes the relation between risk and expected return. We will discuss the predictions of the CAPM in more detail shortly, but first let's look more closely at how it works.

Suppose that you want to estimate the expected return for a stock that has a beta of 1.5 and that the expected return on the market and risk-free rate are 10 percent and 4 percent, respectively. We can use Equation 7.9 (the CAPM) to find the expected return for this stock:

$$\begin{aligned} E(R_i) &= R_{rf} + \beta_i[E(R_m) - R_{rf}] \\ &= 0.04 + [1.5 \times (0.10 - 0.04)] = 0.13, \text{ or } 13\% \end{aligned}$$

Note that we must have three pieces of information in order to use Equation 7.9: (1) the risk-free rate, (2) beta, and (3) either the market risk premium or the expected return on the market. Recall that the market risk premium is the difference between the expected return on the market and the risk-free rate $[E(R_m) - R_{rf}]$, which is 6 percent in the above example.

LEARNING BY DOING APPLICATION 7.7

Expected Returns and Systematic Risk

Problem: You are considering buying 100 shares of General Electric stock. Value Line (a financial reporting service) reports that the beta for General Electric is 0.76. The risk-free rate is 4 percent, and the market risk premium is 6 percent. What is the expected rate of return on General Electric stock according to the CAPM?

Approach: Use Equation 7.9 to calculate the expected return on General Electric stock.

Solution: The expected return is

$$\begin{aligned} E(R_{GE}) &= R_{rf} + \beta_{GE}[E(R_m) - R_{rf}] \\ &= 0.04 + (0.76 \times 0.06) = 0.0856, \text{ or } 8.56\% \end{aligned}$$

The Security Market Line

Exhibit 7.11 displays a plot of Equation 7.9 to illustrate how the expected return on an asset varies with systematic risk. This plot shows that the relation between the expected return on an asset and beta is positive and linear. In other words, it is a straight line with a positive slope. The line in Exhibit 7.11 is known as the **Security Market Line (SML)**.

Security Market Line (SML) a plot of the relation between expected return and systematic risk

In Exhibit 7.11 you can see that the expected rate of return equals the risk-free rate when beta equals 0. This makes sense because when investors do not face systematic risk,

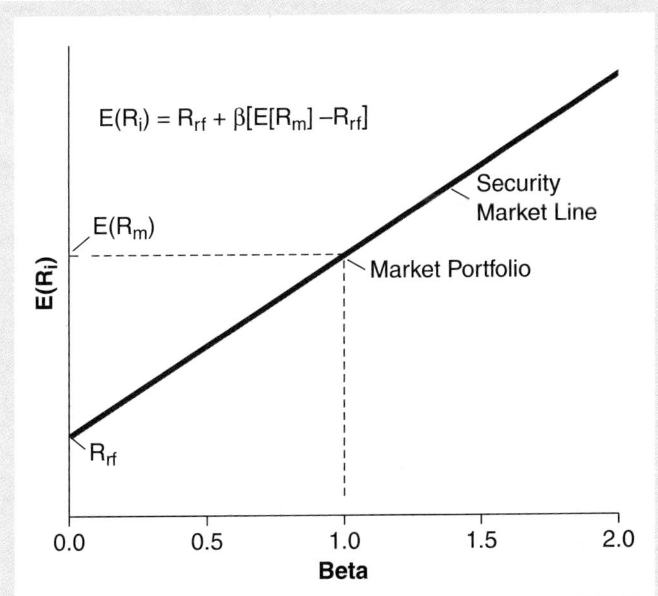

Exhibit 7.11
The Security Market Line
The Security Market Line (SML) is the line that shows the relation between expected returns and systematic risk, as measured by beta. When beta equals zero and there is no systematic risk, the expected return equals the risk free rate. As systematic risk (beta) increases, the expected return increases. This is an illustration of the positive relation between risk and return. The SML shows that it is systematic risk that matters to investors.

they will only require a return that reflects the expected rate of inflation and the fact that they are giving up the use of their money for a period of time. Exhibit 7.11 also shows that the expected return on an asset equals the expected return on the market when beta equals 1. This is not surprising given that both the asset and the market would have the same level of systematic risk if this were the case.

It is important to recognize that the SML illustrates what the CAPM predicts the expected total return should be for various values of beta. The actual expected total return depends on the price of the asset. You can see this from Equation 7.1:

$$R_T = \frac{\Delta P + CF_1}{P_0}$$

where P_0 is the price that the asset is currently selling for. If an asset's price implies that the expected return is greater than that predicted by the CAPM, that asset will plot above the SML in Exhibit 7.11. This means that the asset's price is lower than the CAPM suggests it should be. Conversely, if the expected return on an asset plots below the SML, this implies that the asset's price is higher than the CAPM suggests it should be. The point at which a particular asset plots relative to the SML, then, tells us something about whether the price of that asset might be low or high. Recognizing this fact can be helpful in evaluating the attractiveness of an investment such as the General Electric stock in Learning by Doing Application 7.7.

The Capital Asset Pricing Model and Portfolio Returns

The expected return for a portfolio can also be predicted using the CAPM. The expected return on a portfolio with n assets is calculated using the relation:

$$E(R_{n \text{ Asset portfolio}}) = R_{rf} + \beta_{n \text{ Asset portfolio}}[E(R_m) - R_{rf}]$$

Of course, this should not be surprising since investing in a portfolio is simply an alternative to investing in a single asset.

The fact that the SML is a straight line turns out to be rather convenient if we want to estimate the beta for a portfolio. Recall that the equation for the expected return for a portfolio with n assets was given by Equation 7.5:

$$\begin{aligned} E(R_{\text{Portfolio}}) &= \sum_{i=1}^{n} [x_i \times E(R_i)] \\ &= [x_1 \times E(R_1)] + [x_2 \times E(R_2)] + \cdots + [x_n \times E(R_n)] \end{aligned}$$

If we substitute Equation 7.9 into Equation 7.5 for each of the n assets and rearrange the equation, we find that the beta for a portfolio is simply a weighted average of the betas for the individual assets in the portfolio. In other words:

$$\beta_{n \text{ Asset portfolio}} = \sum_{i=1}^{n} x_i\beta_i = x_1\beta_1 + x_2\beta_2 + x_3\beta_3 + \cdots + x_n\beta_n \tag{7.10}$$

where x_i is the proportion of the portfolio value that is invested in asset i, β_i is the beta of asset i, and n is the number of assets in the portfolio. This formula makes it simple to calculate the beta of any portfolio of assets once you know the betas of the individual assets. As an exercise, you might prove this to yourself by using Equations 7.5 and 7.9 to derive Equation 7.10.

Let's consider an example to see how Equation 7.10 is used. Suppose that you invested 25 percent of your wealth in a fully diversified market fund, 25 percent in risk-free Treasury bills, and 50 percent in a house with twice as much systematic risk as the market. What is the beta of your overall portfolio? What rate of return would you expect to earn from this portfolio if the risk-free rate is 4 percent and the market risk premium is 6 percent?

We know that the beta for the market must equal 1 by definition and that the beta for a risk-free asset equals 0. The beta for your home must be 2 since it has twice the systematic risk of the market. Therefore, the beta of your portfolio is:

$$\begin{aligned}\beta_{\text{Portfolio}} &= x_{\text{Fund}}\beta_{\text{Fund}} + x_{\text{TB}}\beta_{\text{TB}} + x_{\text{House}}\beta_{\text{House}}\\ &= (0.25 \times 1.0) + (0.25 \times 0.0) + (0.50 \times 2.0)\\ &= 1.25\end{aligned}$$

Your portfolio has 1.25 times as much systematic risk as the market. Based on Equation 7.9, you would, therefore, expect to earn a return of 11.5 percent, calculated as follows:

$$\begin{aligned}E(R_{\text{Portfolio}}) &= R_{\text{rf}} + \beta_{\text{Portfolio}}[E(R_{\text{m}}) - R_{\text{rf}}]\\ &= 0.04 + (1.25 \times 0.06) = 0.115, \text{ or } 11.5\%\end{aligned}$$

LEARNING BY DOING APPLICATION 7.8

Portfolio Risk and Expected Return

Problem: You have recently become very interested in real estate. To gain some experience as a real estate investor, you have decided to get together with nine of your friends to buy three small cottages near campus. If you and your friends pool your money, you will have just enough to buy the three properties. Since each investment requires the same amount of money and you will have a 10 percent interest in each, you will effectively have one-third of your portfolio invested in each cottage.

While the cottages cost the same, they are different distances from campus and in different neighborhoods. You believe that this causes them to have different levels of systematic risk, and you estimate that the betas for the individual cottages are 1.2, 1.3, and 1.5. If the risk-free rate is 4 percent and the market risk premium is 6 percent, what will be the expected return on your real estate portfolio after you make all three investments?

Approach: There are two approaches that you can use to solve this problem. First, you can estimate the expected return for each cottage using Equation 7.9 and then calculate the expected return on the portfolio using Equation 7.5. Alternatively, you can calculate the beta for the portfolio using Equation 7.10 and then use Equation 7.9 to calculate the expected return.

Solution: Using the first approach, we find that Equation 7.9 gives us the following expected returns:

$$\begin{aligned}E(R_i) &= R_{\text{rf}} + \beta_i[E(R_{\text{m}}) - R_{\text{rf}}]\\ &= 0.04 + (1.2 \times 0.06) = 0.112, \text{ or } 11.2\%, \text{ for cottage 1}\\ &= 0.04 + (1.3 \times 0.06) = 0.118, \text{ or } 11.8\%, \text{ for cottage 2}\\ &= 0.04 + (1.5 \times 0.06) = 0.130, \text{ or } 13.0\%, \text{ for cottage 3}\end{aligned}$$

Therefore, from Equation 7.5, the expected return on the portfolio is:

$$\begin{aligned}E(R_{\text{Portfolio}}) &= [x_1 \times E(R_1)] + [x_2 \times E(R_2)] + [x_3 \times E(R_3)]\\ &= (1/3 \times 0.112) + (1/3 \times 0.118) + (1/3 \times 0.13) = 0.12, \text{ or } 12.0\%\end{aligned}$$

Using the second approach, from Equation 7.10, the beta of the portfolio is:

$$\beta_{\text{Portfolio}} = x_1\beta_1 + x_2\beta_2 + x_3\beta_3 = (1/3)(1.2) + (1/3)(1.3) + (1/3)(1.5) = 1.33333$$

and from Equation 7.9, the expected return is:

$$\begin{aligned}E(R_{\text{Portfolio}}) &= R_{\text{rf}} + \beta_{\text{Portfolio}}[E(R_{\text{m}}) - R_{\text{rf}}]\\ &= 0.04 + (1.33333 \times 0.06) = 0.120, \text{ or } 12.0\%\end{aligned}$$

DECISION-MAKING EXAMPLE 7.2

Choosing between Two Investments

Situation: You are trying to decide whether to invest in one or both of two different stocks. Stock 1 has a beta of 0.8 and an expected return of 7.0 percent. Stock 2 has a beta of 1.2 and an expected return of 9.5 percent. You remember learning about the CAPM in school and believe that it does a good job of telling you what the appropriate expected return should be for a given level of risk. Since the risk-free rate is 4 percent and the market risk premium is 6 percent, the CAPM tells you that the appropriate expected rate of return for an asset with a beta of 0.8 is 8.8 percent. The corresponding value for an asset with a beta of 1.2 is 11.2 percent. Should you invest in either or both of these stocks?

Decision: You should not invest in either stock. The expected returns for both of them are below the values predicted by the CAPM for investments with the same level of risk. In other words, both would plot below the line in Exhibit 7.11. This implies that they are both overpriced.

Up to this point, we have focused on calculating the expected rate of return for an investment in any asset from the perspective of an investor, such as a stockholder. A natural question that might arise is how these concepts relate to the rate of return that should be used within a firm to evaluate a project. The short answer is that they are the same. The rate of return used to discount the cash flows for a project with a particular level of systematic risk is exactly the same as the rate of return that an investor would expect to receive from an investment in any asset having the same level of systematic risk. In Chapter 13 we will explore the relation between the expected return and the rate used to discount project cash flows in much more detail. By the time we finish that discussion, you will understand thoroughly how businesses determine the rate that they use to discount the cash flows from their investments.

Before You Go On

1. How is the expected return on an asset related to its systematic risk?
2. What name is given to the relation between risk and expected return implied by the CAPM?
3. If an asset's expected return does not plot on the line in question 2 above, what does that imply about its price?

Summary of Learning Objectives

1. **Explain the relation between risk and return.**

   Investors require greater returns for taking greater risk. They prefer the investment with the highest possible return for a given level of risk or the investment with the lowest risk for a given level of return.

2. **Describe the two components of a total holding period return, and calculate this return for an asset.**

   The total holding period return on an investment consists of a capital appreciation component and an income component. This return is calculated using Equation 7.1. It is important to recognize that investors do not care whether they receive a dollar of return through capital appreciation or as a cash dividend. Investors value both sources of return equally.

3. **Explain what an expected return is, and calculate the expected return for an asset.**

   The expected return is a weighted average of the possible returns from an investment, where each of these returns is weighted by the probability that it will occur. It is calculated using Equation 7.2.

4. **Explain what the standard deviation of returns is, explain why it is especially useful in finance, and be able to calculate it.**

   The standard deviation of returns is a measure of the total risk associated with the returns from an asset. It is useful in evaluating returns in finance because the returns on many assets tend to be normally distributed. The standard deviation of returns provides a convenient measure of the dispersion of returns. In other words, it tells us about the probability that a return will fall within a particular distance from the expected value or within a particular range. To calculate the standard deviation, the variance is first calculated using Equation 7.3. The standard deviation of returns is then calculated by taking the square root of the variance.

5. **Explain the concept of diversification.**

Diversification is a strategy of investing in two or more assets whose values do not always move in the same direction at the same time in order to reduce risk. Investing in a portfolio containing assets whose prices do not always move together reduces risk because some of the changes in the prices of individual assets offset each other. This can cause the overall volatility in the value of the portfolio to be lower than if it were invested in a single asset.

6. **Discuss which type of risk matters to investors and why.**

Investors care about only systematic risk. This is because they can eliminate unique risk by holding a diversified portfolio. Diversified investors will bid up prices for assets to the point at which they are just being compensated for the systematic risks they must bear.

7. **Describe what the Capital Asset Pricing Model (CAPM) tells us and how to use it to evaluate whether the expected return of an asset is sufficient to compensate an investor for the risks associated with that asset.**

The CAPM tells us that the relation between systematic risk and return is linear and that the risk-free rate of return is the appropriate return for an asset with no systematic risk. From the CAPM we know what rate of return investors will require for an investment with a particular amount of systematic risk (beta). This means that we can use the expected return predicted by the CAPM as a benchmark for evaluating whether expected returns for individual assets are sufficient. If the expected return for an asset is less than that predicted by the CAPM, then the asset is an unattractive investment because its return is lower than the CAPM indicates it should be. By the same token, if the expected return for an asset is greater than that predicted by the CAPM, then the asset is an attractive investment because its return is higher than it should be.

Summary of Key Equations

Equation	Description	Formula
7.1	Total holding period return	$R_T = R_{CA} + R_I = \frac{P_1 - P_0}{P_0} + \frac{CF_1}{P_0}$
7.2	Expected return on an asset	$E(R_{Asset}) = \sum_{i=1}^{n} (p_i \times R_i)$
7.3	Variance of return on an asset	$Var(R) = \sigma_R^2 = \sum_{i=1}^{n} \{p_i \times [R_i - E(R)]^2\}$
7.4	Coefficient of variation	$CV_i = \frac{\sigma R_i}{E(R_i)}$
7.5	Expected return for a portfolio	$E(R_{Portfolio}) = \sum_{i=1}^{n} [x_i \times E(R_i)]$
7.6	Variance for a two-asset portfolio	$\sigma^2_{R_{2 \text{Asset portfolio}}} = x_1^2\sigma^2_{R_1} + x_2^2\sigma^2_{R_2} + 2x_1x_2\sigma_{R_{1,2}}$
7.7	Covariance between two assets	$\sigma_{R_{1,2}} = \sum_{i=1}^{n} \{p_i \times [R_{1,i} - E(R_1)] \times [R_{2,i} - E(R_2)]\}$
7.8	Correlation between two assets	$\rho = \frac{\sigma_{R_{1,2}}}{\sigma_{R_1}\sigma_{R_2}}$
7.9	Expected return and systematic risk	$E(R_i) = R_{rf} + \beta_i [E(R_m) - R_{rf}]$
7.10	Portfolio beta	$\beta_{n \text{ Asset portfolio}} = \sum_{i=1}^{n} x_i\beta_i$

Self-Study Problems

7.1 Kaaran made a friendly wager with a colleague that involves the result from flipping a coin. If heads comes up, Kaaran must pay her colleague \$15; otherwise, her colleague will pay Kaaran \$15. What is Kaaran's expected cash flow, and what is the variance of that cash flow if the coin has an equal probability of coming up heads or tails? Suppose Kaaran's colleague is willing to handicap the bet by paying her \$20 if the coin toss results in tails. If everything else remains the same, what are Kaaran's expected cash flow and the variance of that cash flow?

7.2 You know that the price of CFI, Inc., stock will be \$12 exactly one year from today. Today the price of the stock is \$11. Describe what must happen to the price of CFI, Inc., today in order for an investor to generate a 20 percent return over the next year. Assume that CFI does not pay dividends.

7.3 Two men are making a bet according to the outcome of a coin toss. You know that the expected outcome of the bet is that one man will lose \$20. Suppose you know that if that same man wins the coin toss, he will receive \$80. How much will he pay out if he loses the coin toss?

7.4 The expected value of a normal distribution of prices for a stock is \$50. If you are 90 percent sure that the price of the stock will be between \$40 and \$60, then what is the variance of the stock price?

7.5 The JCHart Co. common shares have an expected return of 25 percent and a coefficient of variation of 2.0. What is the variance of JCHart Co. common share returns?

Solutions to Self-Study Problems

7.1 Part 1: $\text{E(cash flow)} = (0.5 \times -\$15) + (0.5 \times \$15) = 0$

$$\sigma^2_{\text{Cash flow}} = [0.5 \times (-\$15 - \$0)^2] + [0.5 \times (\$15 - \$0)^2] = \$225$$

Part 2: $\text{E(cash flow)} = (0.5 \times -\$15) + (0.5 \times \$20) = \$2.50$

$$\sigma^2_{\text{Cash flow}} = [0.5 \times (-\$15 - \$2.50)^2] + [0.5 \times (\$20 - \$2.50)^2] = \$306.25$$

7.2 The expected return for CFI based on today's stock price is (\$12 − \$11)/\$11 = 9.09 percent, which is lower than 20 percent. Since the stock price one year from today is fixed, the only way that you will generate a 20 percent return is if the price of the stock drops today. Consequently, the price of the stock today must drop to \$10. It is found by solving the following: $0.2 = (\$12 - x)/x$, or $x = \$10$.

7.3 Since you know that the probability of any coin toss outcome is equal to 0.5, you can solve the problem by setting up the following equation:

$$-\$20 = (0.5 \times \$80) + (0.5 \times x)$$

and solving for x:

$$0.5 \times x = -\$20 - (0.5 \times \$80)$$
$$x = [-\$20 - (0.5 \times \$80)]/0.5 = -\$120$$

which means that he pays \$120 if he loses the bet.

7.4 Since you know that 1.645 standard deviations around the expected return captures 90 percent of the distribution, you can set up either of the following equations:

$$\$40 = \$50 - 1.645\sigma \quad \text{or} \quad \$60 = \$50 + 1.645\sigma$$

and solve for σ. Doing this with either equation yields:

$$\sigma = \$6.079 \text{ and } \sigma^2 = 36.954$$

7.5 Since the coefficient of variation is $CV_i = \dfrac{\sigma_{R_i}}{E(R_i)}$, substituting in the coefficient of variation and $E(R_i)$ allows us to solve for σ^2_{return} as follows:

$$2.0 = \frac{\sigma_{R_i}}{0.25}$$
$$\sigma_{R_i} = 0.5$$
$$\sigma^2_{R_i} = (0.5)^2 = 0.25$$

Critical Thinking Questions

7.1 Given that you know the risk as well as the expected return for two stocks, discuss what process you might utilize to determine which of the two stocks is a better buy. You may assume that the two stocks will be the only assets held in your portfolio.

7.2 What is the difference between the expected rate of return and the required rate of return? What does it mean if they are different for a particular asset at a particular point in time?

7.3 Suppose that the standard deviation of the returns on the shares of stock at two different companies is exactly the same. Does this mean that the required rate of return will be the same for these two stocks? How might the required rate of return on the stock of a third company be greater than the required rates of return on the stocks of the first two companies even if the standard deviation of the returns of the third company's stock is lower?

7.4 The correlation between stocks A and B is 0.50, while the correlation between stocks A and C is −0.5. You already own stock A and are thinking of buying either stock B or stock C. If you want your portfolio to have the lowest possible risk, would you buy stock B or C? Would you expect the stock you choose to affect the return that you earn on your portfolio?

7.5 The idea that we can know the return on a security for each possible outcome is overly simplistic. However, even though we cannot possibly predict all possible outcomes, this fact has little bearing on the risk-free return. Explain why.

7.6 Which investment category has shown the greatest degree of risk in the United States since 1926? Explain why that makes sense in a world where the price of a small stock is likely to be more adversely affected by a particular negative event than the price of a corporate bond. Use the same type of explanation to help explain other investment choices since 1926.

7.7 You are concerned about one of the investments in your fully diversified portfolio. You just have an uneasy feeling about the CFO, Iam Shifty, of that particular firm. You do believe, however, that the firm makes a good product and that it is appropriately priced by the market. Should you be concerned about the effect on your portfolio if Shifty embezzles a portion of the firm's cash?

7.8 The CAPM is used to price the risk in any asset. Our examples have focused on stocks, but we could also price the expected rate of return for bonds. Explain how debt securities are also subject to systematic risk.

7.9 In recent years, investors have correctly agreed that the market portfolio consists of more than just a group of U.S. stocks and bonds. If you are an investor who invests in only U.S. stocks, describe the effects on the risk in your portfolio.

7.10 You may have heard the statement that you should not include your home as an asset in your investment portfolio. Assume that your house will comprise up to 75 percent of your assets in the early part of your investment life. Evaluate the implications of omitting it from your portfolio when calculating the risk of your overall investment portfolio.

Questions and Problems

BASIC

7.1 **Returns:** Describe the difference between a total holding period return and an expected return.

7.2 **Expected returns:** John is watching an old game show rerun on television called *Let's Make a Deal* in which the contestant chooses a prize behind one of two curtains. One of the curtains will yield a gag prize worth \$150, and the other will give a car worth \$7,200. The game show has placed a subliminal message on the curtain containing the gag prize, which makes the probability of choosing the gag prize equal to 75 percent. What is the expected value of the selection, and what is the standard deviation of that selection?

7.3 **Expected returns:** You have chosen biology as your college major because you would like to be a medical doctor. However, you find that the probability of being accepted to medical school is about 10 percent. If you are accepted to medical school, then your starting salary when you graduate will be $300,000 per year. However, if you are not accepted, then you would choose to work in a zoo, where you will earn $40,000 per year. Without considering the additional educational years or the time value of money, what is your expected starting salary as well as the standard deviation of that starting salary?

7.4 **Historical market:** Describe the general relation between risk and return that we observe in the historical bond and stock market data.

7.5 **Single-asset portfolios:** Stocks A, B, and C have expected returns of 15 percent, 15 percent, and 12 percent, respectively, while their standard deviations are 45 percent, 30 percent, and 30 percent, respectively. If you were considering the purchase of each of these stocks as the only holding in your portfolio, which stock should you choose?

7.6 **Diversification:** Describe how investing in more than one asset can reduce risk through diversification.

7.7 **Systematic risk:** Define systematic risk.

7.8 **Measuring systematic risk:** Susan is expecting the returns on the market portfolio to be negative in the near term. Since she is managing a stock mutual fund, she must remain invested in a portfolio of stocks. However, she is allowed to adjust the beta of her portfolio. What kind of beta would you recommend for Susan's portfolio?

7.9 **Measuring systematic risk:** Describe and justify what the value of the beta of a U.S. Treasury bill should be.

7.10 **Measuring systematic risk:** If the expected rate of return for the market is not much greater than the risk-free rate of return, what is the general level of compensation for bearing systematic risk?

7.11 **CAPM:** Describe the Capital Asset Pricing Model (CAPM) and what it tells us.

7.12 **The Security market line:** If the expected return on the market is 10 percent and the risk-free rate is 4 percent, what is the expected return for a stock with a beta equal to 1.5? What is the market risk premium for the set of circumstances described´

INTERMEDIATE

7.13 **Expected returns:** Jose is thinking about purchasing a soft drink machine and placing it in a business office. He knows that there is a 5 percent probability that someone who walks by the machine will make a purchase from the machine, and he knows that the profit on each soft drink sold is $0.10. If Jose expects a thousand people per day to pass by the machine and requires a complete return of his investment in one year, then what is the maximum price that he should be willing to pay for the soft drink machine? Assume 250 working days in a year and ignore taxes and the time value of money.

7.14 **Interpreting the variance and standard deviation:** The distribution of grades in an introductory finance class is normally distributed, with an expected grade of 75. If the standard deviation of grades is 7, in what range would you expect 95 percent of the grades to fall?

7.15 **Calculating the variance and standard deviation:** Kate recently invested in real estate with the intention of selling the property one year from today. She has modeled the returns on that investment based on three economic scenarios. She believes that if the economy stays healthy, then her investment will generate a 30 percent return. However, if the economy softens, as predicted, the return will be 10 percent, while the return will be −25 percent if the economy slips into a recession. If the probabilities of the healthy, soft, and recessionary states are 0.4, 0.5, and 0.1, respectively, then what are the expected return and the standard deviation of the return on Kate's investment?

7.16 **Calculating the variance and standard deviation:** Barbara is considering investing in a stock and is aware that the return on that investment is particularly sensitive to how the economy is performing. Her analysis suggests that four states of the economy can affect the return on the investment. Using the table of returns and probabilities below, find the expected return and the standard deviation of the return on Barbara's investment.

	Probability	Return
Boom	0.1	25.00%
Good	0.4	15.00%
Level	0.3	10.00%
Slump	0.2	−5.00%

7.17 **Calculating the variance and standard deviation:** Ben would like to invest in gold and is aware that the returns on such an investment can be quite volatile. Use the following table of states, probabilities, and returns to determine the expected return and the standard deviation of the return on Ben's gold investment.

	Probability	Return
Boom	0.1	40.00%
Good	0.2	30.00%
OK	0.3	15.00%
Level	0.2	2.00%
Slump	0.2	−12.00%

7.18 **Single-asset portfolios:** Using the information from Problems 7.15, 7.16, and 7.17, calculate each coefficient of variation.

7.19 **Portfolios with more than one asset:** Emmy is analyzing a two-stock portfolio that consists of a Utility stock and a Commodity stock. She knows that the return on the Utility stock has a standard deviation of 40 percent and the return on the Commodity stock has a standard deviation of 30 percent. However, she does not know the exact covariance in the returns of the two stocks. Emmy would like to plot the variance of the portfolio for each of three cases—covariance of 0.12, 0, and −0.12—in order to understand how the variance of such a portfolio would react. Do the calculation for each of the extreme cases (0.12 and −0.12), assuming an equal proportion of each stock in your portfolio.

7.20 **Portfolios with more than one asset:** Given the returns and probabilities for the three possible states listed here, calculate the covariance between the returns of Stock A and Stock B. For convenience, assume that the expected returns of Stock A and Stock B are 11.75 percent and 18 percent, respectively.

	Probability	Return(A)	Return(B)
Good	0.35	0.30	0.50
OK	0.50	0.10	0.10
Poor	0.15	−0.25	−0.30

7.21 **Compensation for bearing systematic risk:** You have constructed a diversified portfolio of stocks such that there is no unsystematic risk. Explain why the expected return of that portfolio should be greater than the expected return of a risk-free security.

7.22 **Compensation for bearing systematic risk:** Write out the equation for the covariance in the returns of two assets, Asset 1 and Asset 2. Using that equation, explain the easiest way for the two asset returns to have a covariance of zero.

7.23 **Compensation for bearing systematic risk:** Evaluate the following statement: By fully diversifying a portfolio, such as by buying every asset in the market, we can completely eliminate all types of risk, thereby creating a synthetic Treasury bill.

7.24 **CAPM:** Damien knows that the beta of his portfolio is equal to 1, but he does not know the risk-free rate of return or the market risk premium. He also knows that the expected return on the market is 8 percent. What is the expected return on Damien's portfolio?

ADVANCED

7.25 David is going to purchase two stocks to form the initial holdings in his portfolio. Iron stock has an expected return of 15 percent, while Copper stock has an expected return of 20 percent. If David plans to invest 30 percent of his funds in Iron and the remainder in Copper, what will be the expected return from his portfolio? What if David invests 70 percent of his funds in Iron stock?

7.26 Sumeet knows that the covariance in the return on two assets is −0.0025. Without knowing the expected return of the two assets, explain what that covariance means.

7.27 In order to fund her retirement, Glenda requires a portfolio with an expected return of 12 percent per year over the next 30 years. She has decided to invest in Stocks 1, 2, and 3, with 25 percent in Stock 1, 50 percent in Stock 2, and 25 percent in Stock 3. If Stocks 1 and 2 have expected returns of 9 percent and 10 percent per year, respectively, then what is the minimum expected annual return for Stock 3 that will enable Glenda to achieve her investment requirement?

7.28 Tonalli is putting together a portfolio of 10 stocks in equal proportions. What is the relative importance of the variance for each stock versus the covariance for the pairs of stocks in her portfolio? For this exercise, ignore the actual values of the variance and covariance terms and explain their importance conceptually.

7.29 Explain why investors who have diversified their portfolios will determine the price and, consequently, the expected return on an asset.

7.30 Brad is about to purchase an additional asset for his well-diversified portfolio. He notices that when he plots the historical returns of the asset against those of the market portfolio, the line of best fit tends to have a large amount of prediction error for each data point (the scatter plot is not very tight around the line of best fit). Do you think that this will have a large or a small impact on the beta of the asset? Explain your opinion.

7.31 The beta of an asset is equal to 0. Discuss what the asset must be.

7.32 The expected return on the market portfolio is 15 percent, and the return on the risk-free security is 5 percent. What is the expected return on a portfolio with a beta equal to 0.5?

7.33 Draw the Security Market Line (SML) for the case where the market risk premium is 5 percent and the risk-free rate is 7 percent. Now suppose an asset has a beta of −1.0 and an expected return of 4 percent. Plot it on your graph. Is the security properly priced? If not, explain what we might expect to happen to the price of this security in the market. Next, suppose another asset has a beta of 3.0 and an expected return of 20 percent. Plot it on the graph. Is this security properly priced? If not, explain what we might expect to happen to the price of this security in the market.

Sample Test Problems

7.1 Friendly Airlines stock is selling at a current price of $37.50 per share. If the stock does not pay a dividend and has a 12 percent expected return, what is the expected price of the stock one year from today?

7.2 Stefan's parents are about to invest their nest egg in a stock that he has estimated to have an expected return of 9 percent over the next year. If the stock is normally distributed with a 3 percent standard deviation, in what range will the stock return fall 95 percent of the time?

7.3 Elaine has narrowed her investment alternatives to two stocks (at this time she is not worried about diversifying): Stock M, which has a 23 percent expected return, and Stock Y, which has an 8 percent expected return. If Elaine requires a 16 percent return on her total investment, then what proportion of her portfolio will she invest in each stock?

7.4 You have just prepared a graph similar to Exhibit 7.9, comparing historical data for Pear Computer Corp. and the general market. When you plot the line of best fit for these data, you find that the slope of that line is 2.5. If you know that the market generated a return of 12 percent and that the risk-free rate is 5 percent, then what would your best estimate be for the return of Pear Computer during that same time period?

7.5 The CAPM predicts that the return of MoonBucks Tea Corp. is 23.6 percent. If the risk-free rate of return is 8 percent and the expected return on the market is 20 percent, then what is MoonBucks's beta?

CHAPTER

10

THE FUNDAMENTALS OF CAPITAL BUDGETING

LEARNING OBJECTIVES

1. Discuss why capital budgeting decisions are the most important investment decisions made by a firm's management.
2. Explain the benefits of using the net present value (NPV) method to analyze capital expenditure decisions, and be able to calculate the NPV for a capital project.
3. Describe the strengths and weaknesses of the payback period as a capital expenditure decision-making tool, and be able to compute the payback period for a capital project.
4. Explain why the accounting rate of return (ARR) is not recommended for use as a capital expenditure decision-making tool.
5. Be able to compute the internal rate of return (IRR) for a capital project, and discuss the conditions under which the IRR technique and the NPV technique produce different results.
6. Explain the benefits of a postaudit review of a capital project.

Getty Images

In March 2007, Intel Corporation announced plans to build a $2.5 billion facility in Dalian, China, to make computer chip wafers. The company expects the plant to be completed in the first half of 2010. The plant will be Intel's largest investment in Asia, and when completed, is expected to employ about five thousand people. To put the $2.5 billion project in perspective, in 2006 Intel's total revenues were $35.4 billion, and its capital expenditures totaled $5.8 billion, or 16.4 percent of sales.

Intel's announcement illustrates not only the large amount of cash involved in a major capital project but also the strategic importance such an investment can have. When he announced the project, Intel's president and CEO, Paul Otellini, pointed out that China was Intel's fastest-growing major market. It was imperative, said Otellini, that Intel invest in markets that will provide for future growth.

The Dalian project involves considerable downside risk for Intel. For example, if the demand for chip wafers proves to be less than expected, the project could be a significant drain on earnings. In addition, international transactions are subject to country risk. If China experiences political or economic instability, the financial consequences for Intel could be severe.

It is clear that investment decisions of this magnitude must be carefully scrutinized, and their costs and benefits carefully weighed. How do firms make capital budgeting decisions that involve billions of dollars? In this chapter, we examine this decision-making process and introduce some of the financial models that aid in the process.

CHAPTER PREVIEW

This chapter is about capital budgeting, a topic we first visited in Chapter 1. Capital budgeting is the process of deciding which capital investments the firm should make.

We begin the chapter with a discussion of the types of capital projects that firms undertake and how the capital budgeting process is managed within the firm. When making capital investment decisions, management's goal is to select projects that will increase the value of the firm.

Next we examine some of the techniques used to evaluate capital budgeting decisions. We first discuss the net present value (NPV) method, which is the capital budgeting approach recommended in this book. The NPV method takes into account the time value of money and provides a direct measure of how much a capital project will increase the value of the firm.

We then examine the payback method and the accounting rate of return. As methods of selecting capital projects, both methods have some serious deficiencies. Finally, we discuss the internal rate of return (IRR), which is the expected rate of return for a capital project. Like the NPV, the IRR involves discounting a project's future cash flows. It is a popular and important alternative to the NPV technique. However, in certain circumstances, the IRR can lead to incorrect decisions. We close by discussing evidence on techniques financial managers actually use when making capital budgeting decisions.

10.1 An Introduction to Capital Budgeting

We begin with an overview of capital budgeting, followed by a discussion of some important concepts you will need to understand in this and later chapters.

LEARNING OBJECTIVE 1

The Importance of Capital Budgeting

Capital budgeting decisions are the most important investment decisions made by management. The objective of these decisions is to select investments in real assets that will increase the value of the firm. These investments *create value* when they are worth more than they cost. Capital investments are important because they can involve substantial cash outlays and, once made, are not easily reversed. They also define what the company is all about—the firm's lines of business and its inherent business risk. For better or worse, capital investments produce most of a typical firm's revenues for years to come.

capital budgeting
the process of choosing the real assets in which the firm will invest

Capital budgeting *techniques* help management systematically analyze potential business opportunities in order to decide which are worth undertaking. As you will see, not all capital budgeting techniques are equal. The best techniques are those that determine the value of a capital project by discounting all of the cash flows generated by the project and thus account for the time value of money. We focus on these techniques in this chapter.

In the final analysis, capital budgeting is really about management's search for the best capital projects—those that add the greatest value to the firm. Over the long term, the most successful firms are those whose managements consistently search for and find capital investment opportunities that increase firm value.

You can read about a real-world example of how capital budgeting techniques are used at www.acq.osd.mil/dpap/contractpricing/vol2chap9.htm.

The Capital Budgeting Process

The capital budgeting process starts with a firm's strategic plan, which spells out its strategy for the next three to five years. Division managers then convert the firm's strategic objectives into business plans. These plans have a one- to two-year time horizon, provide a detailed description of what each division should accomplish during the period covered by the plan, and have quantifiable targets that each division is expected to achieve. Behind each division's business plan is a capital budget that details the resources management believes it needs to get the job done.

The capital budget is generally prepared jointly by the CFO's staff and financial staffs at the divisional and lower levels and reflects, in large part, the activities outlined in the divisional business plans. Many of these proposed expenditures are routine in nature, such as the repair or purchase of new equipment at existing facilities. Less frequently, firms face broader strategic decisions, such as whether to launch a new product, build a new plant, enter a new market, or buy a business. Exhibit 10.1 identifies some reasons that firms initiate capital projects.

Exhibit 10.1 Key Reasons for Making Capital Expenditures

Reason	Description
Renewal:	Over time, equipment must be repaired, overhauled, rebuilt, or retrofitted with new technology to keep the firm's manufacturing or service operations going. For example, a company that has a fleet of delivery trucks may decide to overhaul the trucks and their engines rather than purchase new trucks. Renewal decisions typically do not require an elaborate analysis and are made on a routine basis.
Replacement:	At some point, an asset will have to be replaced rather than repaired or overhauled. This typically happens when the asset is worn out or damaged. The major decision is whether to replace the asset with a similar piece of equipment or purchase equipment that would require a change in the production process. Sometimes, replacement decisions involve equipment that is operating satisfactorily but has become obsolete. The new or retrofitted equipment may provide cost savings with respect to labor or material usage and/or may improve product quality. These decisions typically originate at the plant level.
Expansion:	Strategically, the most important motive for capital expenditures is to expand the level of operating output. One type of expansion decision involves increasing the output of existing products. This may mean new equipment to produce more products or expansion of the firm's distribution system. These types of decisions typically require a more complex analysis than a renewal or replacement decision. Another type of expansion decision involves producing a new product or entering a new market. This type of expansion often involves large dollar amounts and significant business risk and requires the approval of the firm's board of directors.
Regulatory:	Some capital expenditures are required by federal and state regulations. These mandatory expenditures usually involve meeting workplace safety standards and environmental standards.
Other:	This category includes items such as parking facilities, office buildings, and executive aircraft. Many of these capital expenditures are hard to analyze because it is difficult to estimate their cash inflows. Ultimately, the decisions can be more subjective than analytical.

Capital budgeting decisions are the most important investment decisions made by management. Many of these decisions are routine in nature, but from time to time, managers face broader strategic decisions that call for significant capital investments.

Sources of Information

Where does a firm get all of the information it needs to make capital budgeting decisions? Most of the information is generated within the firm, and, for expansion decisions, it often starts with sales representatives and marketing managers who are in the marketplace talking to potential and current customers on a day-to-day basis. For example, a sales manager with a new product idea might present the idea to management and the marketing research group. If the product looks promising, the marketing research group will estimate the size of the market and a market price. If the product requires new technology, the firm's research and development group must decide whether to develop the technology or to buy it. Next, cost accountants and production engineers determine the cost of producing the product and any capital expenditures necessary to manufacture it. Finally, the CFO's staff takes the data and estimates the cost of the project and the cash flows it will generate over time. The project is a viable candidate for the capital budget if the present value of the cash benefits exceeds the project's cost.

Classification of Investment Projects

Potential capital budgeting projects can be classified into three types: (1) **independent projects**, (2) **mutually exclusive projects**, and (3) **contingent projects**.

independent projects
projects whose cash flows are unrelated

mutually exclusive projects
projects for which acceptance of one precludes acceptance of the other

contingent project
a project whose acceptance depends on the acceptance of another project

INDEPENDENT PROJECTS

Projects are independent when their cash flows are unrelated. With independent projects, accepting or rejecting one project does not eliminate the other projects from consideration (assuming the firm has unlimited funds to invest). For example, suppose a firm has unlimited funding and management wants to: (1) build a new parking ramp at its headquarters; (2) acquire a small competitor; and (3) add manufacturing capacity to one of its plants. Since the cash flows for each project are unrelated, accepting or rejecting one of the projects will have no effect on the others.

MUTUALLY EXCLUSIVE PROJECTS

When projects are mutually exclusive, acceptance of one project precludes acceptance of the others. Typically, mutually exclusive projects perform the same function, and thus, only one project needs to be accepted. For example, when BMW decided to manufacture automobiles in the United States, it considered three possible manufacturing sites (or capital projects). Once BMW management had selected the Spartanburg, South Carolina, site, the other two possible locations were out of the running.

CONTINGENT PROJECTS

With contingent projects, the acceptance of one project is contingent on the acceptance of another. There are two types of contingency situations. In the first type of situation, the contingent product is *mandatory*. For example, when a public utility company (such as your local electric company) builds a power plant, it must also invest in suitable pollution control equipment to meet federal environmental standards. The pollution control investment is a mandatory contingent project. When faced with mandatory contingent projects, it is best to treat all of the projects as a single investment for the purpose of evaluation. This provides management with the best measure of the value created by these projects.

In the second type of situation, the contingent project is *optional*. For example, suppose Dell invests in a new computer for the home market. This computer has a feature that allows Dell to bundle a proprietary gaming system. The gaming system is a contingent project but is an optional add-on to the new computer. In these situations, the optional contingent project should be evaluated *independently* and should be accepted or rejected on its own merits.

Basic Capital Budgeting Terms

In this section we briefly introduce two terms that you will need to be familiar with—*cost of capital* and *capital rationing.*

COST OF CAPITAL

cost of capital
the required rate of return for a capital investment

The **cost of capital** is the rate of return that a capital project must earn to be accepted by management. The cost of capital can be thought of as an opportunity cost. Recall from Chapter 8 that an *opportunity cost* is the value of the most valuable alternative given up if a particular investment is made.

Let's consider the opportunity cost concept in the context of capital budgeting decisions. When investors buy shares of stock in a company or loan money to a company, they are giving management money to invest on their behalf. Thus, when a firm's management makes capital investments, they are really investing stockholders' and creditors' money in *real assets*—plant and equipment. Since stockholders and creditors could have invested their money in *financial assets,* the minimum rate of return they are willing to accept on an investment in a real asset is the rate they could have earned investing in financial assets that have similar risk. The rate of return that investors can earn on financial assets with similar risk is an *opportunity cost* because investors lose the opportunity to earn that rate if the money is invested in a real asset instead. It is therefore the rate of return that investors will require for an investment in a capital project. In other words, this rate is the cost of capital. It is also known as the **opportunity cost of capital**. Chapter 13 discusses how we estimate the opportunity cost of capital in practice.

opportunity cost of capital
the return an investor gives up when his or her money is invested in one asset rather than the best alternative asset

BUILDING INTUITION

Investment Decisions Have Opportunity Costs

When any investment is made, the opportunity to earn a return from an alternative investment is lost. The lost return can be viewed as a cost that arises from a lost opportunity. For this reason, it is called an *opportunity cost.* The opportunity cost of capital is the return an investor gives up when his or her money is invested in one asset rather than the best alternative asset. For example, suppose that a firm invests in a piece of equipment rather than returning money to stockholders. If stockholders could have earned an annual return of 12 percent on a stock with cash flows that are as risky as the cash flows the equipment will produce, this is the opportunity cost of capital associated with the investment in the piece of equipment.

CAPITAL RATIONING

When a firm has all the money it needs to invest in all the capital projects that meet its capital selection criteria, the firm is said to be operating without a *funding constraint,* or *resource constraint.* Firms are rarely in this position, especially growth firms. Typically, a firm has a fixed number of dollars available for capital expenditures, and the number of qualified projects that need funding exceeds the funds that are available. Therefore, the firm must allocate its funds to the subset of projects that will provide the largest overall increase in stockholder value. The process of limiting, or rationing, capital expenditures in this way is called **capital rationing**. Capital rationing and its implications for capital budgeting are discussed in Chapter 12.

capital rationing
a situation where a firm does not have enough capital to invest in all attractive projects and must therefore ration capital

Before You Go On

1. Why are capital investments the most important decisions made by a firm's management?
2. What are the differences between capital projects that are independent, mutually exclusive, and contingent?

10.2 Net Present Value

In this section we discuss a capital budgeting method that is consistent with this goal of financial management—to maximize the wealth of the firm's owners. It is called the **net present value (NPV) method**, and it is one of the most basic concepts underlying corporate finance. The NPV method tells us the amount by which the benefits from a capital expenditure exceed its costs. It is the capital budgeting technique recommended in this book.

CCH Business Owner's Toolkit is a valuable Web source for information about running a business, including capital budget analysis. Go to www.toolkit.cch.com/text/p06_6500.asp.

Valuation of Real Assets

LEARNING OBJECTIVE 2

Throughout the book, we have emphasized that the value of any asset is the present value of its future cash flows. In Chapters 8 and 9, we developed valuation models for financial assets, such as bonds, preferred stock, and common stock. We now extend our discussion of valuation models from financial to real assets. The steps used in valuing an asset are the same whether the asset is real or financial:

1. Estimate the future cash flows.
2. Determine the required rate of return, or discount rate, which depends on the riskiness of the future cash flows.
3. Compute the present value of the future cash flows to determine what the asset is worth.

net present value (NPV) method
a method of evaluating a capital investment project which measures the difference between its cost and the present value of its expected cash flows

The valuation of real assets, however, is less straightforward than the valuation of financial assets, for several reasons.

First, in many cases, cash flows for financial assets are well documented in a legal contract. If they are not, we are at least able to make some reasonable assumptions about what they are. For real assets, much less information exists. Specialists within the firm, usually from the finance, marketing, and production groups, often prepare estimates of future cash flows for capital projects with only limited information.

Second, many financial securities are traded in public markets, and these markets are reasonably efficient. Thus, market data on rates of return are accessible. For real assets, no such markets exist. As a result, we must estimate required rates of return on real assets (opportunity costs) from market data on financial assets; this can be difficult to do.

NPV—The Basic Concept

The NPV of a project is the difference between the present value of the project's future cash flows and the present value of its cost. The NPV can be expressed as follows:

$$\text{NPV} = \text{PV (Project's future cash flows)} - \text{PV(Cost of the project)}$$

If a capital project has a positive NPV, the value of the cash flows the project is expected to generate exceeds the project's cost. Thus, a positive NPV project increases the value of the firm and, hence, stockholders' wealth. If a capital project has a negative NPV, the value of the cash flows from the project is less than its cost. If accepted, a negative NPV project will decrease the value of the firm and stockholders' wealth.

To illustrate these important points, consider an example. Suppose a firm is considering building a new marina for pleasure boats. The firm has a genie that can tell the future with perfect certainty. The finance staff estimates that the marina will cost \$3.50 million. The genie volunteers that the market value of the marina is \$4.25 million.

Assuming this information is correct, the NPV for the marina project is a positive \$750,000 (\$4.25 million − \$3.50 million). Management should accept the project because the excess of market value over cost increases the value of the firm by \$750,000. Why is a positive NPV a *direct* measure of how much a capital project will increase the value of the firm? If management wanted to, the firm could sell the marina for \$4.25 million, pay the \$3.50 million in expenses, and deposit \$750,000 in the bank. The value of the firm would increase by the \$750,000 deposited in the bank. In sum, the NPV method tells us which capital projects to select and how much value they add to the firm.

NPV and Value Creation

We have just said that any project with a positive NPV should be accepted because it will increase the value of the firm. Let's take a moment to think about this proposition. What makes a capital asset worth more than it costs? In other words, how does management create value with capital investments?

HOW VALUE IS CREATED

Suppose that when you were in college, you worked part time at a successful pizza parlor near campus. During this time, you learned a lot about the pizza business. After graduation, you purchased a pizza parlor for \$100,000 that was in a good location but had been forced to close because of a lack of profits. The owners had let the restaurant and the quality of the pizzas deteriorate, and the wait staff had been rude, especially to college students. Once you purchased the restaurant, you immediately invested \$40,000 to fix it up: you painted the building, spruced up the interior, replaced some of the dining room furniture, and added an eye-catching, 1950s-style neon sign to attract attention. You also spent \$15,000 for a one-time advertising blitz to quickly build a customer base. More important, you improved the quality of the pizzas you sold, and you built a profitable takeout business. Finally, you hired your wait staff carefully and trained them to be customer friendly.

Almost immediately the restaurant was earning a substantial profit and generating substantial cash flows. The really good news was that several owners of local pizzerias wanted to buy your restaurant. After intense negotiations with several of the potential buyers, you accepted a cash offer of \$475,000 for the business shortly after you purchased it.

What is the NPV for the pizza parlor? For this investment, the NPV is easy to calculate. We do not need to estimate future cash flows and discount them because we already have an estimate of the present value of the cash flows the pizza parlor is expected to produce—\$475,000. Someone is willing to pay you \$475,000 because he or she believes the future cash flows are worth that amount. The cost of your investment includes the purchase price of the restaurant, the cost to fix it up, and the cost of the initial advertising campaign, which totals \$155,000 (\$100,000 + \$40,000 + \$15,000). Thus, the NPV for the pizza parlor is:

$$\begin{aligned} \text{NPV} &= \text{PV (Project's future cash flows)} - \text{PV(Cost of the project)} \\ &= \$475{,}000 - \$155{,}000 \\ &= \$320{,}000 \end{aligned}$$

The \$475,000 price paid for the pizza parlor exceeds the cost (\$155,000) by \$320,000. You have created \$320,000 in value. How did you do this? You did it by improving the food, customer service, and dining ambiance while keeping prices competitive. Your management skills and knowledge of the pizza business resulted in significant growth in the current year's cash flows and the prospect of even larger cash flows in the future.

Where did the \$320,000 in value you created go? The NPV of your investment is the amount that your personal net worth increased because of the investment. For an ongoing business, the result would have been a $320,000 increase in the value of the firm.

How about the original owners? Why would they sell a business worth $475,000 to you for $100,000? The answer is simple; if they could have transformed the business as you did, they would have done so. Instead, when they ran the business, it lost money! They sold it to you because you offered them a price reflecting its value to them.

MARKET DATA VERSUS DISCOUNTED CASH FLOWS

Our pizza parlor example is greatly simplified by the fact that we can observe the price that someone is willing to pay for the asset. In most capital project analyses, we have to estimate the market value of the asset by *forecasting* its future cash flows and discounting them by the cost of capital. The discounted value of a project's future cash flows is an estimate of its value, or the market price for which it can be sold.

Framework for Calculating NPV

We now describe a framework for analyzing capital budgeting decisions using the NPV method. As you will see, the NPV technique uses the discounted cash flow technique developed in Chapters 5 and 6 and applied in Chapters 8 and 9. The good news, then, is that the NPV method requires only the application of what you already know.

The five-step framework discussed in this section and the accompanying cash flow worksheet (Exhibit 10.2) can help you systematically organize a project's cash flow data and compute its NPV. Most mistakes people make when working capital budgeting problems result from problems with cash flows: not identifying a cash flow, getting a cash flow in the wrong time period, or assigning the wrong sign to a cash flow. What can make cash flow analysis difficult in capital budgeting is this: there are often multiple cash flows in a single time period, and some are cash inflows and others are cash outflows.

As always, we recommend that you prepare a time line when doing capital budgeting problems. A sample time line is shown in Exhibit 10.2, along with an identification of the cash flows for each period. Our goal is to compute the net cash flow (NCF) for each time period t, where NCF_t = (Cash inflows − Cash outflows) for the period t. For a capital project, the time periods (t) are usually in years, and t varies from the current

Time line	0	1	2	3	4	5 Year
Cash Flows:						
Initial cost	$-CF_0$					
Inflows (CIF)		CIF_1	CIF_2	CIF_3	CIF_4	CIF_5
Outflows (COF)		$-COF_1$	$-COF_2$	$-COF_3$	$-COF_4$	$-COF_5$
Salvage value						SV
Net cash flow	$-NCF_0$	NCF_1	NCF_2	NCF_3	NCF_4	NCF_5

$$NPV = -NCF_0 + \sum_{t=1}^{5} \frac{NCF_t}{(1+k)^t}$$

Exhibit 10.2
Sample Worksheet for Net Present Value Analysis

In addition to following the five-step framework for solving NPV analysis problems, we recommend that you use a worksheet with a time line like the one shown here to help you determine the proper cash flows for each period.

period ($t = 0$) to some finite time period that is the estimated life of the project ($t = n$). Recall that getting the correct sign on each cash flow is critical to getting the correct answer to a problem. As you have seen in earlier chapters, the convention in finance problem solving is that cash inflows carry a positive sign and cash outflows carry a negative sign. Finally, note that all cash flows in this chapter are on an after-tax basis. We will make adjustments for tax consequences on specific transactions such as the calculation of a project's salvage value.

Our five-step framework for analysis is as follows:

1. **Determine the cost of the project.** We first need to identify and add up all of the expense items related to the cost of the project. In most cases, the cost of a project is incurred during the first year; hence, this cash outflow is already in current dollars. However, some projects have negative cash flows for several years because it takes two or three years to get the projects up and running. If the cash payments for the project extend beyond one year, the dollars paid in the second year and beyond must be discounted for the appropriate time period. Negative cash flows can also occur when a project sustains an operating loss during the start-up years. Turning to Exhibit 10.2, we have incurred a single negative cash flow ($-CF_0$) for the total cost of the project, where $NCF_0 = -CF_0$; thus, NCF_0 has a negative value.

2. **Estimate the project's future cash flows over its expected life.** Capital projects typically generate some cash inflows from revenues (CIF_t) for each period, along with some cash outflows (COF_t) that represent expenses incurred to generate the revenues. In most cases revenues exceed expenses, and thus, NCF_t is positive where $t \geq 1$. However, this may not always be the case. For example, if the project is the purchase of a piece of equipment, it is possible for NCF_3 to have a negative value ($CIF_3 < COF_3$) if the equipment is projected to need a major overhaul or must be replaced during the third year. Finally, you also need to pay attention to a project's final cash flow, which is $t = 5$ in Exhibit 10.2. There may be a salvage value (SV) at the end of the project, which is a cash inflow. In that case $NCF = (CIF_5 - COF_5 + SV)$. The important point is that for each time period, we must identify all the cash flows that take place, assign each cash flow its proper sign, and algebraically add up all the cash flows; the total is the NCF for that time period with the correct sign.

3. **Determine the riskiness of the project and the appropriate cost of capital.** The third step is to identify for each project its risk-adjusted cost of capital, which takes into account the riskiness of the project's cash flows. The riskier the project, the higher its cost of capital. The cost of capital is the discount rate used in determining the present value of the future expected cash flows. In this chapter, the cost of capital and any risk adjustments will be supplied, and no calculations will be required for this step.

4. **Compute the project's NPV.** The NPV, as you know, is the present value of the net cash flows the project is expected to generate minus the cost of the project.

5. **Make a decision.** If the NPV is positive, the project should be accepted because all projects with a positive NPV will increase the value of the firm. If the NPV is negative, the project should be rejected; projects with negative NPVs will decrease the value of the firm.

You might be wondering about how to handle a capital project with an NPV of 0. Technically, management should be indifferent to accepting or rejecting projects such as this because they neither increase nor decrease the value of the firm. At a practical level, projects rarely have an NPV equal to 0, and most firms have more good capital projects (with NPV > 0) than they can fund. Thus, this is not an issue that generates much interest among practitioners.

Net Present Value Techniques

The NPV of a capital project can be stated in equation form as the present value of all net cash flows (inflows − outflows) connected with the project, whether in the current period or in the future. The NPV equation can be written as follows:

$$\begin{aligned} \text{NPV} &= \text{NCF}_0 + \frac{\text{NCF}_1}{1+k} + \frac{\text{NCF}_2}{(1+k)^2} + \cdots + \frac{\text{NCF}_n}{(1+k)^n} \\ &= \sum_{t=0}^{n} \frac{\text{NCF}_t}{(1+k)^t} \end{aligned} \tag{10.1}$$

where:

NCF_t = Net cash flow (cash inflows − cash outflows) in period t, where $t = 1, 2, 3, \ldots, n$
k = The cost of capital
n = The project's estimated life

Next, we will work an example to see how the NPV is calculated for a capital project. Suppose you are the president of a small regional firm located in Chicago that manufactures frozen pizzas, which are sold to grocery stores and to firms in the hospitality and food service industry. Your market research group has developed an idea for a "pocket" pizza that can be used as an entrée with a meal or as an "on the go" snack. The sales manager believes that, with an aggressive advertising campaign, sales of the product will be about $300,000 per year. The cost to modify the existing production line will also be $300,000, according to the plant manager. The marketing and plant managers estimate that the cost to produce the pocket pizzas, to market and advertise them, and to deliver them to customers will be about $220,000 per year. The product's life is estimated to be five years, and the specialized equipment necessary for the project has an estimated salvage value of $30,000. The appropriate cost of capital is 15 percent.

When analyzing capital budgeting problems, we typically have a lot of data to sort through. The worksheet approach introduced earlier is helpful in keeping track of the data in an organized format. Exhibit 10.3 shows the time line and relevant cash flows for the pocket pizza project. The steps in analyzing the project's cash flows and determining its NPV are as follows:

1. *Determine the cost of the capital project.* The cost of the project is the cost to modify the existing production line, which is $300,000. This is a cash outflow (negative sign).

2. *Estimate the capital project's future cash flows over its expected life.* The project's future cash inflows come from sales of the new product. Sales are estimated at $300,000 per year (positive sign). The cash outflows are the costs to manufacture and distribute the new product, which are $220,000 per year (negative sign). The life of the project is five years. The project has a salvage value of $30,000, which is a cash inflow (positive sign). The net cash flow (NCF) per time period is just the sum of the cash inflows and cash outflows for that period. For example, the NCF for period $t = 0$ is −$300,000 the NCF for period $t = 1$ is $80,000, and so on, as you can see in Exhibit 10.3.

3. *Determine the riskiness of the project and appropriate cost of capital.* The discount rate is the cost of capital, which is 15 percent.

4. *Compute the project's NPV.* To compute the project's NPV, we apply Equation 10.1 by plugging in the NCF values for each time period and using the cost of capital, 15 percent, as the discount rate. The equation looks like this (the figures are in thousands of dollars):

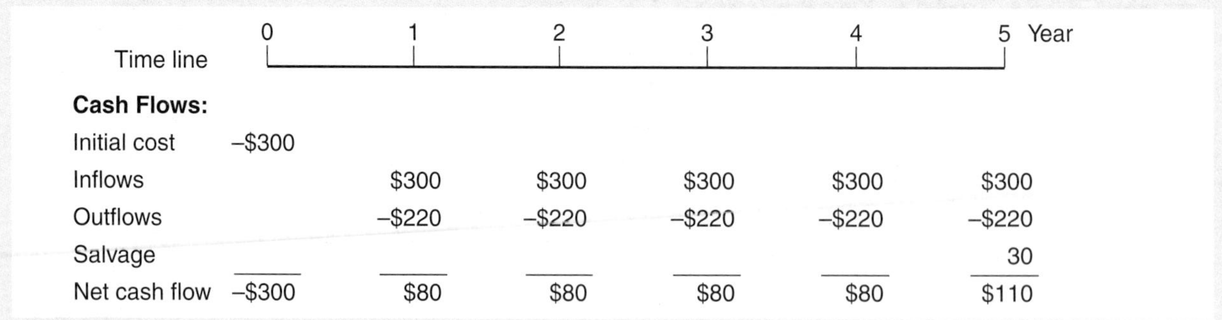

	0	1	2	3	4	5 Year
Time line						
Cash Flows:						
Initial cost	–$300					
Inflows		$300	$300	$300	$300	$300
Outflows		–$220	–$220	–$220	–$220	–$220
Salvage						30
Net cash flow	–$300	$80	$80	$80	$80	$110

Exhibit 10.3
Pocket Pizza Project Time Line and Cash Flows ($ thousands)
The worksheet approach introduced in Exhibit 10.2 is helpful in organizing the data given for the pocket pizza project.

$$
\begin{aligned}
\text{NPV} &= \sum_{t=0}^{n} \frac{\text{NCF}_t}{(1+k)^t} \\
&= -\$300 + \frac{80}{1.15} + \frac{80}{(1.15)^2} + \cdots + \frac{80}{(1.15)^4} + \frac{(80+30)}{(1.15)^5} \\
&= -\$300 + \$69.57 + \$60.49 + \$52.60 + \$45.74 + \$54.69 \\
&= -\$300 + \$283.09 \\
&= -\$16.91
\end{aligned}
$$

The NPV for the pocket pizza project is therefore −\$16,910.

5. *Make a decision.* The pocket pizza project has a negative NPV, which indicates that the project is not a good investment and should be rejected. If management undertook this project, the value of the firm would decrease by \$16,910; and, if the firm had one hundred thousand shares of stock outstanding, we can estimate that the project would decrease the value of each share by about 17 cents (\$16,910/100,000 shares).

CALCULATING NPV WITH A FINANCIAL CALCULATOR

Using a financial calculator is an easier way to calculate the present value of the future cash flows. In this example you should recognize that the cash flow pattern is a five-year ordinary annuity with an additional cash inflow in the fifth year. This is exactly the cash pattern for a bond with annual coupon payments and payment of principal at maturity we saw in Chapter 8. We can find the present value using a financial calculator, with \$80 being the annuity stream for five years and \$30 the salvage value at year 5:

Enter	5	15		80	30
	N	**i**	**PV**	**PMT**	**FV**
Answer			**−283.09**		

The PV of the future cash flows is −\$283.09. With that information, we can compute the NPV using Equation 10.1 as follows:

$$
\begin{aligned}
\text{NPV} &= \sum_{t=1}^{n} \frac{\text{NCF}_t}{(1+k)^t} - \text{NCF}_0 \\
&= \$283.09 - \$300.00 \\
&= -\$16.91
\end{aligned}
$$

LEARNING BY DOING APPLICATION 10.1

The Dough's Up: The Self-Rising Pizza Project

NEED MORE HELP?

Problem: Let's continue our frozen pizza example. Suppose the head of the research and development (R&D) group announces that R&D engineers have developed a breakthrough technology—self-rising frozen pizza dough that, when baked, rises and tastes exactly like fresh-baked dough.

The cost is $300,000 to modify the production line. Sales of the new product are estimated at $200,000 for the first year, $300,000 for the next two years, and $500,000 for the final two years. It is estimated that production, sales, and advertising costs will be $250,000 for the first year and will then decline to a constant $200,000 per year. There is no salvage value at the end of the product's life, and the appropriate cost of capital is 15 percent. Is the project, as proposed, economically viable?

Approach: To solve the problem, work through the steps for NPV analysis given in the text.

Solution: Exhibit 10.4 shows the project's cash flows.

1. The cost to modify the production line is $300,000, which is a cash outflow and the cost of the project.

2. The future cash flows over the expected life of the project are laid out on the time line in Exhibit 10.4. The project's life is five years. The NCFs for the capital project are negative at the beginning of the project and in the first year (−$300,000 and −$50,000) and thereafter are positive.

Time line	0	1	2	3	4	5 Year
Cash Flows:						
Initial cost	–$300					
Inflows		$200	$300	$300	$500	$500
Outflows		–$250	–$200	–$200	–$200	–$200
Salvage						
Net cash flow	–$300	–$50	$100	$100	$300	$300

Exhibit 10.4
Self-Rising Pizza Dough Project Time Line and Cash Flows ($ thousands)
The worksheet shows the time line and cash flows for the self-rising pizza dough project in Learning by Doing Application 10.1. As always, it is important to assign each cash flow to the appropriate year and to give it the proper sign. Once you have computed the net cash flow for each time period, solving for NPV is just a matter of plugging the data into the NPV formula.

(continued)

3. The appropriate cost of capital is 15 percent.

4. The values are substituted into Equation 10.1 to calculate the NPV:

$$\begin{aligned}\text{NPV} &= \text{NCF}_0 + \frac{\text{NCF}_1}{1+k} + \frac{\text{NCF}_2}{(1+k)^2} + \cdots + \frac{\text{NCF}_n}{(1+k)^n}\\ &= -\$300{,}000 - \frac{\$50{,}000}{1.15} + \frac{\$100{,}000}{(1.15)^2} + \frac{\$100{,}000}{(1.15)^3} + \frac{\$300{,}000}{(1.15)^4} + \frac{\$300{,}000}{(1.15)^5}\\ &= -\$300{,}000 - \$43{,}478 + \$75{,}614 + \$65{,}752 + \$171{,}526 + \$149{,}153\\ &= \$118{,}567\end{aligned}$$

5. The decision is based on the NPV. The NPV for the self-rising pizza dough project is $118,567. Because the NPV is positive, management should accept the project. The project is estimated to increase the value of the firm by $118,567.

USING EXCEL

Net Present Value

Net present value problems are most commonly solved using a spreadsheet program. The program's design is good for keeping track of all the cash flows and the periods in which they occur. The following spreadsheet setup for Learning by Doing Application 10.1 shows how to calculate the NPV for the self-rising pizza dough machine:

Notice that the NPV formula does not take into account the cash flow in year zero. Therefore, you only enter into the NPV formula the cash flows in years 1 through 5, along with the discount rate. You then add the cash flow in year zero to the total from the NPV formula calculation to get the NPV for the investment.

◇	A	B	C	D	E
1					
2		Net Present Value Calculations			
3					
4		Year		Cash Flow	
5		0		-$300,000	
6		1		-50,000	
7		2		100,000	
8		3		100,000	
9		4		300,000	
10		5		300,000	
11					
12		Cost of capital		0.15	
13					
14		NPV		$118,567	
15		Formula used		=NPV(D12, D6:D10)+D5	
16					

DECISION-MAKING EXAMPLE 10.1

The IS Department's Capital Projects

Situation: Suppose you are the manager of the information systems (IS) department of the frozen pizza manufacturer we have been discussing. Your department has identified four possible capital projects with the following NPVs: (1) $4,500, (2) $3,000, (3) $0.0, and (4) −$1,000. What should you decide about each project if the projects are independent? What should you decide if the projects are mutually exclusive?

Decision: If the projects are independent, you should accept projects 1 and 2, both of which have a positive NPV, and reject project 4. Project 3, with an NPV of zero, could be either accepted or rejected. If the projects are mutually exclusive and you can accept only one of them, it should be project 1, which has the largest NPV.

Concluding Comments on NPV

Some concluding comments about the NPV method are in order. First, as you may have noticed, the NPV computations are rather mechanical once we have the cash flows and have determined the cost of capital. The real difficulty is estimating or forecasting the future cash flows. Although this may seem to be a daunting task, firms with experience in producing and selling a particular type of product can usually generate fairly accurate estimates of sales volumes, prices, and production costs. However, problems can arise with the cash flow estimates when a project team becomes "enamored" with a project. Wanting a project to succeed, a project team can be too optimistic about the cash flow projections.

Second, we must recognize that the calculated values for NPV are estimates based on management's informed judgment; they are not real market data. Like any estimate, they can be too high or too low. The only way to determine a project's "true" NPV is to put the asset up for sale and see what price market participants are willing to pay for it. An example of this approach was the sale of our pizza parlor; however, situations such as this are the exception, not the rule.

Finally, there is nothing wrong with using estimates to make business decisions as long as they are based on informed judgments and not guesses. Most business managers are routinely required to make decisions that involve expectations about future events. In fact, that is what business is really all about—dealing with uncertainty and making decisions that involve risk.

In conclusion, the NPV approach is the method we recommend for making capital investment decisions. The accompanying table summarizes NPV decision rules and the method's key advantages and disadvantages.

Summary of Net Present Value (NPV) Method

Decision Rule: NPV > 0 ⇨ Accept the project.
NPV < 0 ⇨ Reject the project.

Key Advantages	Key Disadvantages
1. Uses the discounted cash flow valuation technique to adjust for the time value of money.	1. Can be difficult to understand without an accounting and finance background.
2. Provides a direct (dollar) measure of how much a capital project will increase the value of the firm.	
3. Consistent with the goal of maximizing stockholder value.	

Before You Go On

1. What is the NPV of a project?
2. If a firm accepts a project with a $10,000 NPV, what is the effect on the value of the firm?
3. What are the five steps used in NPV analysis?

10.3 The Payback Period

payback period
the length of time required to recover a project's initial cost

The payback period is one of the most widely used tools for evaluating capital projects. The **payback period** is defined as the number of years it takes for the cash flows from a project to recover the project's initial investment. With the payback method for evaluating projects, a project is accepted if its payback period is below some specified threshold. Although it has serious weaknesses, this method does provide some insight into a project's risk; the more quickly you recover the cash, the less risky is the project.

Computing the Payback Period

To compute the payback period, we need to know the project's cost and estimate its future net cash flows. The net cash flows and the project cost are the same values that we used to compute the NPV calculations. The payback (PB) equation can be expressed as follows:

$$\text{PB} = \text{Years before cost recovery} + \frac{\text{Remaining cost to recover}}{\text{Cash flow during the year}} \tag{10.2}$$

Exhibit 10.5 shows the net cash flows (row 1) and cumulative net cash flows (row 2) for a proposed capital project with an initial cost of \$70,000. The payback period calculation for our example is:

$$\begin{aligned}\text{PB} &= \text{Years before cost recovery} + \frac{\text{Remaining cost to recover}}{\text{Cash flow during the year}}\\ &= 2 \text{ years} + \frac{\$70{,}000 - \$60{,}000}{\$20{,}000}\\ &= 2 \text{ years} + \frac{\$10{,}000}{\$20{,}000}\\ &= 2 \text{ years} + 0.5\\ &= 2.5 \text{ years}\end{aligned}$$

Let's look at this calculation in more detail. Note in Exhibit 10.5 that the firm recovers cash flows of \$30,000 in the first year and \$30,000 in the second year, for a total of \$60,000 over the two years. During the third year, the firm needs to recover

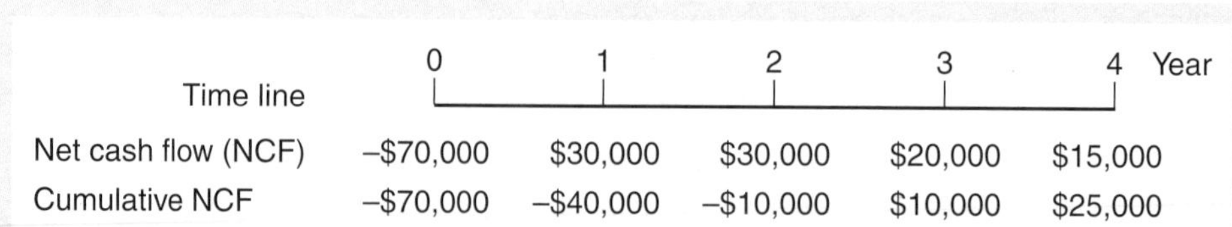

Time line	0	1	2	3	4 Year
Net cash flow (NCF)	–\$70,000	\$30,000	\$30,000	\$20,000	\$15,000
Cumulative NCF	–\$70,000	–\$40,000	–\$10,000	\$10,000	\$25,000

Exhibit 10.5
Payback Period Cash Flows and Calculations
The exhibit shows the net and cumulative net cash flows for a proposed capital project with an initial cost of \$70,000. The cash flow data are used to compute the payback period, which is 2.5 years.

only \$10,000 (\$70,000 − \$60,000) to pay back the full cost of the project. The third-year cash flow is \$20,000, so we will have to wait 0.5 year (\$10,000/\$20,000) to recover the final amount. Thus, the payback period for this project is 2.5 years (2 + 0.5).

The idea behind the payback period method is simple: the shorter the payback period, the faster the firm gets its money back and the more desirable the project. However, there is no economic rationale that links the payback method to stockholder value maximization. Firms that use the payback method accept all projects having a payback period under some threshold and reject those with a payback period over this threshold. If a firm has a number of projects that are mutually exclusive, the projects are selected in order of their payback rank: projects with the shortest payback period are selected first.

A Payback Calculation

LEARNING BY DOING APPLICATION 10.2

NEED MORE HELP?

Problem: A firm has two capital projects, A and B, which are under review for funding. Both projects cost \$500, and the projects have the following cash flows:

Year	Project A	Project B
0	−\$500	−\$500
1	100	400
2	200	300
3	200	200
4	400	100

What is the payback period for each project? If the projects are independent, which project should management select? If the projects are mutually exclusive, which project should management accept? The firm's payback cutoff point is two years.

Approach: Use Equation 10.2 to calculate the number of years it takes for the cash flows from each project to recover the project's initial investment. If the two projects are independent, you should accept the projects that have a payback period that is less than or equal to two years. If the projects are mutually exclusive, you should accept the project with the shortest payback period if that payback period is also less than or equal to two years.

Solution: The payback for project A requires only that we calculate the first term in Equation 10.2—Years before recovery: the first year recovers \$100, the second year \$200, and the third year \$200, for a total of \$500 (\$100 + \$200 + \$200). Thus, in three years, the \$500 investment is fully recovered, so $PB_A = 3.00$.

For project B, the first year recovers \$400 and the second year \$300. Since we need only part of the second-year cash flow to recover the initial cost, we calculate both terms in Equation 10.2 to obtain the payback time.

$$PB = \text{Years before cost recovery} + \frac{\text{Remaining cost to recover}}{\text{Cash flow during the year}}$$

$$PB_A = 3 \text{ years}$$

$$\begin{aligned} PB_B &= 1 \text{ year} + \frac{\$500 - \$400}{\$300} \\ &= 1 \text{ year} + \frac{\$100}{\$300} \\ &= 1.33 \text{ years} \end{aligned}$$

Whether the projects are independent or mutually exclusive, management should accept only project B since project A's payback period exceeds the two-year cutoff point.

Exhibit 10.6 Payback Period with Various Cash Flow Patterns

Year	A	B	C	D	E
0	−$500	−$500	−$500	−$500	−$500
1	200	300	250	500	200
2	300	100	250	0	200
3	400	50	−250	0	200
4	500	0	250	−5,000	5,000
Payback (years)	2.0	∞	2.0/4.0	1.0/∞	2.5
NPV	$450	−$131	−$115	−$2,924	$2,815
Cost of capital = 15%					

Each of the five capital budgeting projects shown in the exhibit calls for an initial investment of $500, but all have different cash flow patterns. The bottom part of the exhibit shows each project's payback period, along with its net present value for comparison.

How the Payback Period Performs

We have worked through some simple examples of how the payback period is computed. Now we will consider several more complex situations to see how well the payback period performs as a capital budgeting criterion. Exhibit 10.6 illustrates five different capital budgeting projects. The projects all have an initial investment of $500, but each one has a different cash flow pattern. The bottom part of the exhibit shows each project's payback period, along with its net present value for comparison. We will assume that management has set a payback period of two years as the cutoff point for an acceptable project.

Project A: The cash flows for project A are $200 in the first year and $300 in the second, for a total of $500; thus, the project's payback period is two years. Under our acceptance criterion, management should accept this project. Project A also has a positive NPV of $450, so the two capital budgeting decision rules agree.

Project B: Project B never generates enough cash flows to pay off the original investment of $500: $300 + $100 + $50 = $450. Thus, the project payback period is infinite. With an infinite payback period, the project should be rejected. Also, as you would expect, Project B's NPV is negative. So far, the payback period and NPV methods have agreed on which projects to accept.

Project C: Project C has a payback period of two years: $250 + $250 = $500. Thus, according to the payback criteria, it should be accepted. However, the project's NPV is a negative $115, which indicates that the project should be rejected. Why the conflict? Look at the cash flows after the payback period of two years. In year 3 the project requires an additional investment of $250 (a cash outflow) and now is in a deficit position; that is, the cash balance is now only $250 ($250 + $250 − $250). Then, in the final year, the project earns an additional $250, recovering the cost of the original investment. The project's payback is really four years. The payback period analysis can lead to erroneous decisions because the rule does not consider cash flows after the payback period.

Projects D and E: Projects D and E dramatically illustrate the problem when a capital budgeting evaluation tool fails to consider cash flows after the payback period. Project D has a payback period of one year, suggesting that it should be accepted, and project E has a payback period of 2.5 years, suggesting that it should be rejected. However, a simple look at the future cash flows suggests otherwise. It is clear that project D, with a negative $5,000 cash flow in year 4, is a disaster and should be rejected, while project E, with a positive $5,000 "windfall" in year 4, should be accepted. Indeed, the NPV analysis confirms these conclusions: project D has a negative NPV of $2,924, and project E has a positive NPV of $2,815. In both instances, the payback rule led to the wrong economic decision. These examples illustrate that a rapid payback does not necessarily mean a good investment.

Discounted Payback Period

One of the weaknesses of the ordinary payback period is that it does not take into account the time value of money. All dollars received before the cutoff period are given equal weight. To address this problem, some financial managers use a variant of the payback period called the **discounted payback period**. This payback calculation is similar to the ordinary payback calculation except that the future cash flows are discounted by the cost of capital.

discounted payback period the length of time required to recover a project's initial cost, accounting for the time value of money

The major advantage of the discounted payback is that it tells management how long it takes a project to reach an NPV of zero. Thus, any capital project that meets a firm's decision rule must also have a positive NPV. This is an improvement over the standard payback calculation, which can accept projects with negative NPVs. Regardless of the improvement, the discounted payback method is not widely used by businesses, and it still ignores all cash flows after the arbitrary cutoff period, which is a major flaw.

To see how the discounted payback period is calculated, turn to Exhibit 10.7. The exhibit shows the net cash flows for a proposed capital project along with both the cumulative and discounted cumulative cash flows; thus, we can compute both the ordinary and the discounted payback periods for the project and then compare them. The cost of capital is 10 percent.

The first two rows show the nondiscounted cash flows, and we can see by inspection that the ordinary payback period is two years. We do not need to make any additional calculations because the cumulative cash flows equal zero at precisely two years. Now let's turn our attention to the lower two rows, which show the project's discounted and cumulative discounted cash flows. Note that the first year's cash flow is $20,000 and its discounted value is $18,182 ($20,000 × 0.9091), and the second year's cash flow is also $20,000 and its discounted value is $16,529 ($20,000 × 0.8264). Now, looking at the cumulative discounted cash flows row, notice that it turns positive between two and three years. This means that the discounted payback period is two years plus some

Time line	0	1	2	3 Year
Net cash flow (NCF)	–$40,000	$20,000	$20,000	$20,000
Cumulative NCF	–$40,000	–$20,000	$0	$20,000
Discounted NCF (at 10%)	–$40,000	$18,182	$16,529	$15,026
Cumulative discounted NCF	–$40,000	–$21,818	–$5,289	$9,737

Payback period = 2 years + $0/$20,000 = 2 years
Discounted payback period = 2 years + $5,289/$15,026 = 2.35 years
NPV = $49,737 –$40,000 = $9,737
Cost of capital = 10%

Exhibit 10.7 Discounted Payback Period Cash Flows and Calculations

The exhibit shows the net and cumulative net cash flows for a proposed capital project with an initial cost of $40,000. The cash flow data are used to compute the discounted payback period for a 10 percent cost of capital, which is 2.35 years.

fraction of the third year's discounted cash flow. The exact discounted payback period computed value is 2 + ($5,289/$15,026) = 2 + 0.35 = 2.35.

As expected, the discounted payback period is longer than the ordinary payback period (2 < 2.35), and in 2.35 years the project will reach a NPV = 0. The project NPV is positive ($9,737); therefore, we should accept the project. But notice that the payback decision criteria are ambiguous. If we use 2.0 years as the payback criterion, we reject the project and if we use 2.5 or 3.0 years as criterion, the project is accepted. The lack of a definitive decision rule remains a major problem with the payback period as a capital budgeting tool.

Evaluating the Payback Rule

In spite of its lack of sophistication, the standard payback period is widely used in business in part because it provides an intuitive and simple measure of a project's liquidity risk. This makes sense because projects that pay for themselves quickly are less risky than projects whose paybacks occur further in the future. There is a strong feeling in business that "getting your money back quickly" is an important standard when making capital investments. Probably the greatest advantage of the payback period is its simplicity; it is easy to calculate and easy to understand, making it especially attractive to business executives with little training in accounting and finance.

When compared with the NPV method, however, the payback method has some serious shortcomings. First, the standard payback method does not use discounting; hence, it ignores the time value of money. Second, it does not adjust or account for differences in the riskiness of projects. Another problem is that there is no economic rationale for establishing cutoff criteria. Who is to say that a particular cutoff, such as two years, is optimal with regard to maximizing stockholder value?

Finally, perhaps the greatest shortcoming of the payback method is its failure to consider cash flows after the payback period, as illustrated by projects D and E in Exhibit 10.6. This is true whether or not the cash flows are discounted. As a result of this feature, the payback method is biased toward shorter-term projects, which tend to free up cash more quickly. Consequently, projects for which cash inflows tend to occur further in the future, such as research and development investments, new product launches, and entry into new lines of business, are at a disadvantage when the payback method is used. The accompanying table summarizes major features of the payback period.

Summary of Payback Method

Decision Rule: Payback period ≤ Payback cutoff point ⇨ Accept the project.
Payback period > Payback cutoff point ⇨ Reject the project.

Key Advantages	Key Disadvantages
1. Easy to calculate and understand for people without a strong finance background.	1. Most common version does not account for time value of money.
2. A simple measure of a project's liquidity.	2. Does not consider cash flows past the payback period.
	3. Bias against long-term projects such as research and development and new product launches.
	4. Arbitrary cutoff point.

Before You Go On

1. What is the payback period?
2. Why does the payback period provide a measure of a project's liquidity risk?
3. What are the main shortcomings of the payback method?

10.4 The Accounting Rate of Return

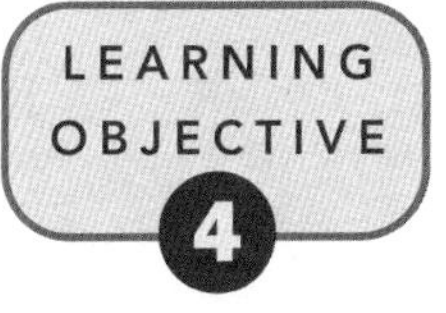

LEARNING OBJECTIVE 4

We turn next to a capital budgeting technique based on the **accounting rate of return (ARR)**, sometimes called the *book value rate of return.* This method computes the return on a capital project using accounting numbers—the project's net income (NI) and book value (BV)—rather than cash flow data. The ARR can be calculated in a number of ways, but the most common definition is:

accounting rate of return (ARR)
a rate of return on a capital project based on average net income divided by average assets over the project's life; also called the *book value rate of return*

$$\text{ARR} = \frac{\text{Average net income}}{\text{Average book value}} \tag{10.3}$$

where:

$$\begin{aligned} \text{Average net income} &= (\text{NI}_1 + \text{NI}_2 + \cdots + \text{NI}_n)/n \\ \text{Average book value} &= (\text{BV}_1 + \text{BV}_2 + \cdots + \text{BV}_n)/n \\ n &= \text{the project's estimated life} \end{aligned}$$

Although ARR is fairly easy to understand and calculate, as you probably guessed, it has a number of major flaws as a tool for evaluating capital expenditure decisions. Besides the fact that AAR is based on accounting numbers rather than cash flows, it is not really even an accounting-based rate of return. Instead of discounting a project's cash flows over time, it simply gives us a number based on average figures from the income statement and balance sheet. Thus, the ARR ignores the time value of money. Also, as with the payback method, there is no economic rationale that links a particular acceptance criterion to the goal of maximizing stockholder value.

Because of these major shortcomings, the ARR technique should not be used to evaluate the viability of capital projects under any circumstances. You may wonder why we even included the ARR technique in the book if it is a poor criterion for evaluating projects. The reason is simply that we want to be sure that if you run across the ARR method at work, you will recognize it and be aware of its shortcomings.

Before You Go On

1. What are the major shortcomings of using the ARR method as a capital budgeting method?

10.5 Internal Rate of Return

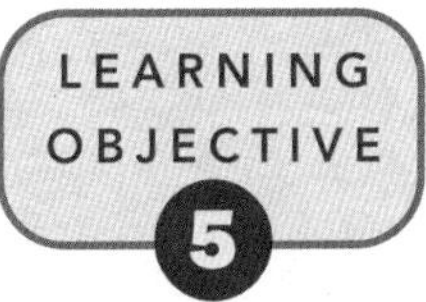

LEARNING OBJECTIVE 5

The **internal rate of return**, known in practice as the **IRR**, is an important and legitimate alternative to the NPV method. The NPV and IRR techniques are closely related in that both involve discounting the cash flows from a project; thus, both account for the time value of money. When we use the NPV method to evaluate a capital project, the discount rate is the rate of return required by investors for investments with similar risk, which is the project's opportunity cost of capital. When we use the IRR, we are looking for the rate of return associated with a project so that we can determine whether this rate is higher or lower than the project's opportunity cost of capital.

internal rate of return (IRR)
the discount rate at which the present value of a project's expected cash inflows equals the present value of the project's outflows

We can define the IRR as the discount rate that equates the present value of a project's expected cash inflows to the present value of the project's outflows:

$$\text{PV(Project's future cash flows)} = \text{PV(Cost of the project)}$$

This means that we can also describe the IRR as the discount rate that causes the NPV to equal zero. This relation can be written in a general form as follows:

$$\text{NPV} = \text{NCF}_0 + \frac{\text{NCF}_1}{1 + \text{IRR}} + \frac{\text{NCF}_2}{(1 + \text{IRR})^2} + \cdots + \frac{\text{NCF}_n}{(1 + \text{IRR})^n} \tag{10.4}$$
$$= \sum_{t=0}^{n} \frac{\text{NCF}_t}{(1 + \text{IRR})^t} = 0$$

Because of their close relation, it may seem that the IRR and the NPV are interchangeable—that is, either should accept or reject the same capital projects. After all, both methods are based on whether the project's return exceeds the cost of capital and, hence, whether the project will add value to the firm. In many circumstances, the IRR and NPV methods do give us the same answer. As you will see later, however, some of the mathematical properties of the IRR equation can lead to incorrect decisions concerning whether to accept or reject a particular capital project.

Calculating the IRR

The IRR is an expected rate of return like the yield to maturity we calculated for bonds in Chapter 8. Thus, in calculating the IRR, we need to apply the same trial-and-error method we used in Chapter 8. We will begin by doing some IRR calculations by trial and error so that you understand the process, and then we will switch to the financial calculator, which provides an answer more quickly and is less prone to mistakes.

TRIAL-AND-ERROR METHOD

Suppose that Ford Motor Company has an investment opportunity with cash flows as shown in Exhibit 10.8 and that the cost of capital is 12 percent. We want to find the IRR for this project. Using Equation 10.4, we will substitute various values for IRR into the equation to compute the project's IRR by trial and error. We continue this process until we find the IRR value that makes Equation 10.4 equal zero.

A good starting point is to use the cost of capital as the discount rate. Note that when we discount the NCFs by the cost of capital, we are calculating the project's NPV:

$$\text{NPV} = \text{NCF}_0 + \frac{\text{NCF}_1}{1 + \text{IRR}} + \frac{\text{NCF}_2}{(1 + \text{IRR})^2} + \cdots + \frac{\text{NCF}_n}{(1 + \text{IRR})^n}$$

$$\text{NPV}_{12\%} = -\$560 + \frac{\$240}{1.12} + \frac{\$240}{(1.12)^2} + \frac{\$240}{(1.12)^3} = \$16.44$$

Exhibit 10.8
Time Line and Expected Net Cash Flows for the Ford Project ($ thousands)
The cash flow data in the exhibit are used to compute the project's IRR, which is 13.7 percent. Since the IRR is higher than Ford's cost of capital, the IRR criterion indicates the project should be accepted. The project's NPV is a positive $16,440, which also indicates that Ford should accept the project. Thus, the IRR and NPV methods have reached the same conclusion.

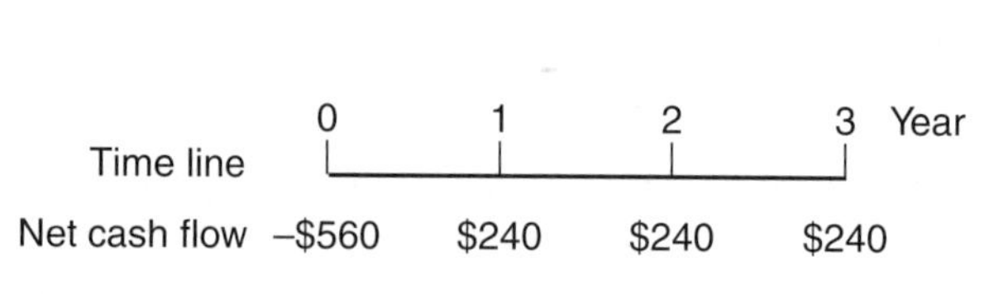

IRR = 13.7%
Cost of capital = 12%
NPV = $576.44 – $560.00 = $16.44

Recall that the result we are looking for is zero. Because our result is \$16.44, the discount rate of 12 percent is too low, and we must try a higher rate. Let's try 13 percent:

$$NPV_{13\%} = -\$560 + \frac{\$240}{1.13} + \frac{\$240}{(1.13)^2} + \frac{\$240}{(1.13)^3} = \$6.68$$

We are very close; let's try 14 percent:

$$NPV_{14\%} = -\$560 + \frac{\$240}{1.14} + \frac{\$240}{(1.14)^2} + \frac{\$240}{(1.14)^3} = -\$2.81$$

Because our result is now a negative number, we know the correct rate is between 13 and 14 percent, and looking at the magnitude of the numbers, we know that the answer is closer to 14 percent. Let's try 13.7 percent.

$$NPV_{13.7\%} = -\$560 + \frac{\$240}{1.137} + \frac{\$240}{(1.137)^2} + \frac{\$240}{(1.137)^3} = 0$$

Good guess! This means that the NPV of Ford's capital project is zero at a discount rate of 13.7 percent. Ford's required rate of return is the cost of capital, which is 12.0 percent. Since the project's IRR of 13.7 percent exceeds Ford's cost of capital, the IRR criterion indicates that the project should be accepted.

The project's NPV is a positive \$16,440, which also indicates that Ford should go ahead with the project. Thus, both the IRR and NPV have reached the same conclusion.

LEARNING BY DOING APPLICATION 10.3

Calculating the IRR at Larry's

Problem: Larry's Ice Cream in the DuPont Circle area of Washington, D.C., is famous for its gourmet ice cream. However, some customers have asked for a health-oriented, low-cal, soft yogurt. The machine that makes this confection is manufactured in Italy and costs \$5,000 plus \$1,750 for installation. Larry estimates that the machine will generate a net cash flow of \$2,000 a year (the shop closes November through March of each year). Larry also estimates the machine's life to be 10 years and that it will have a \$400 salvage value. His cost of capital is 15 percent. Larry thinks the machine is overpriced and it's a bum deal. Is he right?

Approach: The IRR for an investment is the discount rate at which the NPV is zero. Thus, we can use Equation 10.4 to solve for the IRR and then compare this value with Larry's cost of capital. If the IRR is greater than the cost of capital, the project has a positive NPV and should be accepted.

Solution: The total cost of the machine is \$6,750 (\$5,000 + \$1,750), and the final cash flow at year 10 is \$2,400 (\$2,000 + \$400).

Year	0	1	2	3	9	10
15%	−\$6,750	\$2,000	\$2,000	\$2,000	\$2,000	\$2,400

$$NPV = NCF_0 + \frac{NCF_1}{1 + IRR} + \frac{NCF_2}{(1 + IRR)^2} + \cdots + \frac{NCF_n}{(1 + IRR)^n} = 0$$

$$NPV_{15.00\%} = -\$6,750 + \frac{\$2,000}{1.15} + \frac{\$2,000}{(1.15)^2} + \cdots + \frac{\$2,400}{(1.15)^{10}} = \$3,386.41$$

$$NPV_{27.08\%} = -\$6,750 + \frac{\$2,000}{1.2708} + \frac{\$2,000}{(1.2708)^2} + \cdots + \frac{\$2,400}{(1.2708)^{10}} = \$0.00$$

The hand trial-and-error calculations are shown in these equations. The first calculation uses 15 percent, the cost of capital, our recommended starting point, and the answer is \$3,386.41 (which is also the project's NPV). Because the value is a positive number, we need to use a larger discount rate than 15 percent. Our guess is 27.08 percent. At that value, NPV = 0; thus, the IRR for the yogurt machine is 27.08 percent.

(continued)

Because the project's future cash flow pattern resembles that for a bond, we can also solve for the IRR on a financial calculator, just as we would solve for the yield to maturity. Just enter the data directly into the corresponding keys on the calculator and press the interest key and we have our answer—27.08 percent.

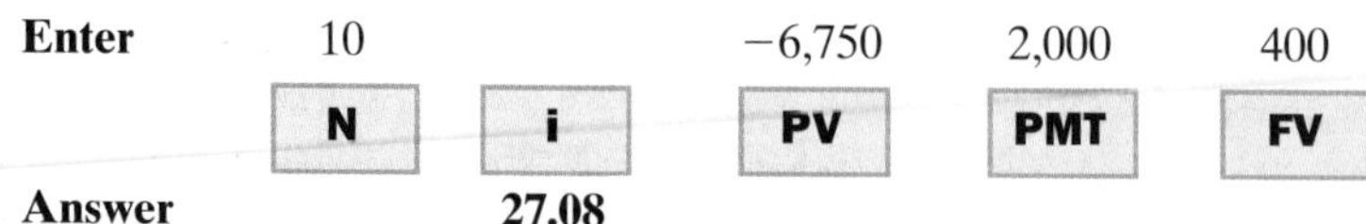

As with present value calculations, for projects with unequal cash flows, you should consult your financial calculator's manual.

Because the project's IRR exceeds Larry's cost of capital of 15 percent, the project should be accepted. Larry is wrong.

USING EXCEL

Internal Rate of Return

You know that calculating IRR by hand can be tedious. The trial-and-error method can take a long time and can be quite frustrating. Knowing all the cash flows and an approximate rate will allow you to use a spreadsheet formula to get an answer instantly.

The accompanying spreadsheet shows the setup for calculating the IRR for the low-cal yogurt machine at Larry's Ice Cream Parlor that is described in Learning by Doing Application 10.3.

Here are a couple of important points to note about IRR calculations using spreadsheet programs:

1. Unlike the NPV formula, the IRR formula accounts for all cash flows, including the initial investment in year 0, so there is no need to add this cash flow later.
2. In order to calculate the IRR, you will need to provide a "guess" value, or a number you estimate is close to the IRR. A good value to start with is the cost of capital. To learn more about why this value is needed, you should go to your spreadsheet's help manual and search for "IRR."

◇	A	B	C	D	E
1					
2		**IRR Calculations**			
3					
4		**Year**		**Cash Flow**	
5		0		-$6,750	
6		1		2,000	
7		2		2,000	
8		3		2,000	
9		4		2,000	
10		5		2,000	
11		6		2,000	
12		7		2,000	
13		8		2,000	
14		9		2,000	
15		10		2,400	
16					
17		Cost of capital		0.15	
18					
19		**IRR**		**27.08%**	
20		Formula used		=IRR(E5:E15, E17)	
21					
22	Remember to keep track of signs - cash outflows are negative and cash inflows are positive.				
23					
24					

When the IRR and NPV Methods Agree

In the Ford example, the IRR and NPV methods agree. The two methods will *always* agree when you are evaluating *independent* projects and the projects' cash flows are *conventional.* As discussed earlier, an independent project is one that can be selected with no effect on any other project, assuming the firm faces no resource constraints. A project with **conventional cash flows** is one with an initial cash outflow followed by one or more future cash inflows. Put another way, after the initial investment is made (cash outflow), all the cash flows in each future year are positive (inflows). For example, the purchase of a bond involves a conventional cash flow. You purchase the bond for a price (cash outflow), and in the future you receive coupon payments and a principal payment at maturity (cash inflows).

conventional cash flow
a cash flow pattern made up of an initial cash outflow that is followed by one or more cash inflows

Let's look more closely at the kinds of situations in which the NPV and the IRR methods agree. A good way to visualize the relation between the IRR and NPV methods is to graph NPV as a function of the discount rate. The graph, called an **NPV profile**, shows the NPV of the project at various costs of capital.

NPV profile
a graph showing NPV as a function of the discount rate

Exhibit 10.9 shows the NPV profile for the Ford project. We have placed the NPVs on the vertical axis, or y-axis, and the discount rates on the horizontal axis, or x-axis. We used the calculations from our earlier example and made some additional NPV calculations at various discount rates, as follows:

Discount Rate	NPV ($ thousands)
0%	$160
5	94
10	37
15	−12
20	−54
25	−92
30	−124

As you can see, a discount rate of 0 percent corresponds with an NPV of $160,000; a discount rate of 5 percent with an NPV of $94,000; and so forth. As the discount rate increases, the NPV curve declines smoothly. Not surprisingly, the curve intersects the x-axis at precisely the point where the NPV is 0 and the IRR is 13.7 percent.

The NPV profile in Exhibit 10.9 illustrates why the NPV and IRR methods lead to identical accept-reject decisions for the Ford project. The IRR of 13.7 percent precisely marks the point at which the NPV changes from a positive to a negative value.

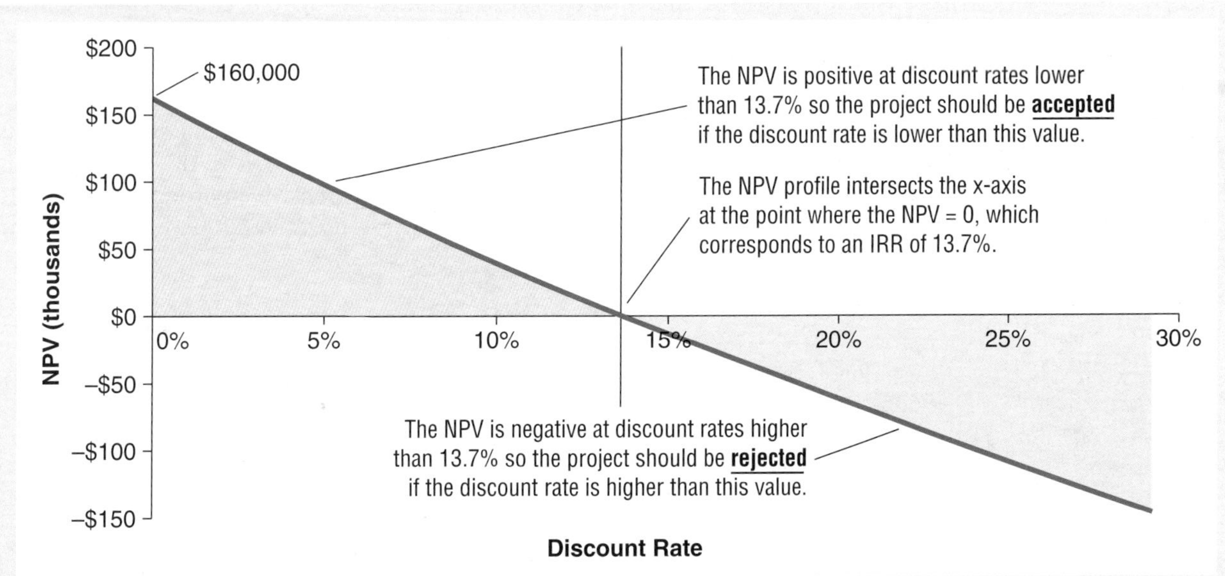

Exhibit 10.9
NPV Profile for the Ford Project
In the NPV profile for the Ford project, the NPV value is on the vertical (y) axis and the discount rate is on the horizontal (x) axis. You can see that as the discount rate increases, the NPV profile curve declines smoothly and intersects the x-axis at precisely the point where the NPV is 0 and the IRR is 13.7 percent—the point at which the NPV changes from a positive to a negative value. Thus, the NPV and IRR methods lead to identical accept-or-reject decisions for the Ford project.

Whenever a project is independent and has conventional cash flows, the result will be as shown in the exhibit. The NPV will decline as the discount rate increases, and the IRR and the NPV methods will result in the same capital expenditure decision.

When the NPV and IRR Methods Disagree

We have seen that the IRR and NPV methods lead to identical investment decisions for capital projects that are independent and that have conventional cash flows. However, if either of these conditions is not met, the IRR and NPV methods can produce different accept-reject decisions.

UNCONVENTIONAL CASH FLOWS

Unconventional cash flows can cause a conflict between the NPV and IRR decision rules. In some instances the cash flows for an unconventional project are just the reverse of those of a conventional project: the initial cash flow is positive, and all subsequent cash flows are negative. For example, consider a life insurance company that sells a lifetime annuity to a retired person. The company receives a single cash payment, which is the price of the annuity (cash inflow), and then makes monthly payments to the retiree for the rest of his or her life (cash outflows). In this case, we need only reverse the IRR decision rule and accept the project if the IRR is *less* than the cost of capital to make the IRR and NPV methods agree. The intuition in this example is that the life insurance company is effectively borrowing money from the retiree and the IRR is a measure of the cost of that money. The cost of capital is the rate at which the life insurance company can borrow elsewhere. An IRR less than the cost of capital means that the lifetime annuity provides the insurance company with money at a lower cost than alternative sources.

When a project's future cash flows include both positive and negative cash flows, the situation is more complicated. An example of such a project is an assembly line that will require one or more major renovations over its lifetime. Another common business situation is a project that has conventional cash flows except for the final cash flow, which is negative. The final cash flow might be negative because extensive environmental cleanup is required at the end of the project, such as the cost for decommissioning a nuclear power plant, or because the equipment originally purchased has little or no salvage value and is expensive to remove.

Consider an example. Suppose a firm invests in a gold-mining operation that costs \$55 million and has an expected life of two years. In the first year, the project generates a cash inflow of \$150 million. In the second year, extensive environmental and site restoration is required, so the expected cash flow is a negative \$100 million. The time line for these cash flows follows.

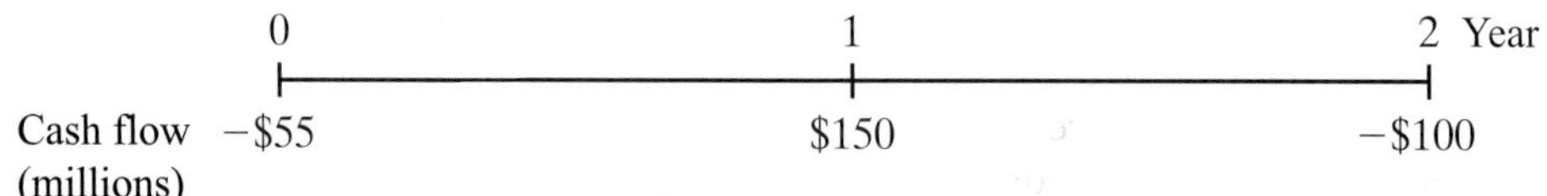

Once again, the best way to understand the effect of these cash flows is to look at an NPV profile. Shown here are NPV calculations we made at various discount rates to generate the data necessary to plot the NPV profile shown in Exhibit 10.10:

Discount Rate	NPV (\$ millions)
0%	−\$5.00
10	−1.28
20	0.56
30	1.21
40	1.12
50	0.56
60	−0.31
70	−1.37

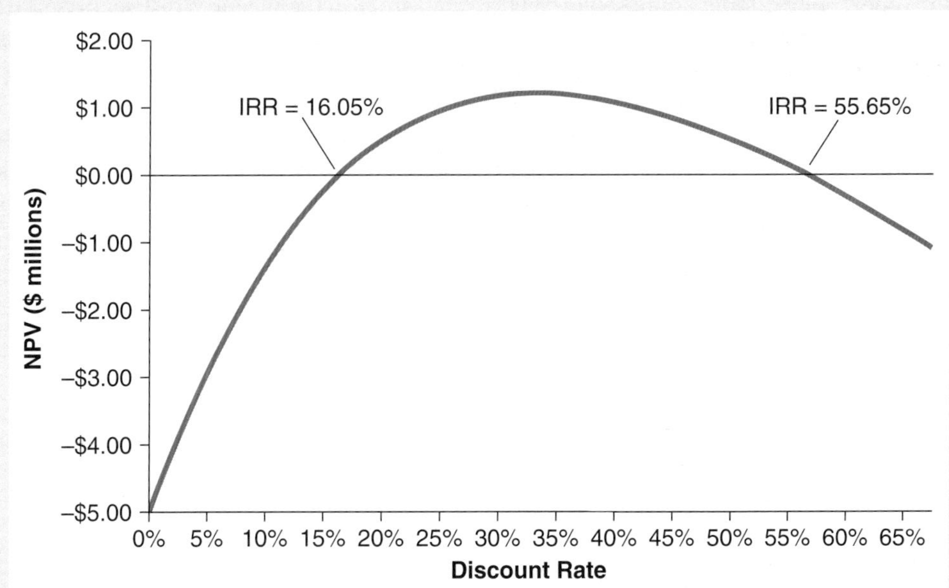

Exhibit 10.10
NPV Profile for Gold-Mining Operation Showing Multiple IRR Solutions
The gold-mining operation has unconventional cash flows. Because there are two cash flow sign reversals, we end up with two IRRs—16.05 percent and 55.65 percent—neither of them correct. In situations like this, the IRR provides a solution that is suspect, and therefore, the results should not be used for capital budgeting decisions.

Looking at the data in the table, you can probably spot a problem. The NPV is initially negative (−$5.00); then, at a discount rate of 20 percent, switches to positive ($0.56); and then, at a discount rate of 60 percent, switches back to negative (−$0.31).

The NPV profile in Exhibit 10.10 shows the results of this pattern: we have two IRRs, one at 16.05 percent and the other at 55.65 percent. Which is the correct IRR, or are both correct? Actually, there is no correct answer; the results are meaningless, and you should not try to interpret them. Thus, in this situation, the IRR technique provides information that is suspect and should not be used for decision making.

How many IRR solutions can there be for a given cash flow? The maximum number of IRR solutions is equal to the number of sign reversals in the cash flow stream. For a project with a conventional cash flow, there is only one cash flow sign reversal; thus, there is only one IRR solution. In our mining example, there are two cash flow sign reversals; thus, there are two IRR solutions.

Finally, for some cash flow patterns, it is impossible to compute an IRR. These situations can occur when the initial cash flow ($t = 0$) is either a cash inflow or outflow and is followed by cash flows with two or more sign reversals. An example of such a cash flow pattern is $NCF_0 = \$15$, $NCF_1 = -\$25$, and $NCF_2 = \$20$. This type of cash flow pattern might occur on a building project where the contractor is given a prepayment, usually the cost of materials and supplies ($15); then does the construction and pays the labor cost (−$25); and finally, upon completion of the work, receives the final payment ($20). Note that when it is not possible to compute an IRR, the project either has a positive NPV or a negative NPV for all possible discount rates. In this example, the NPV is always positive.

MUTUALLY EXCLUSIVE PROJECTS

The other situation in which the IRR can lead to incorrect decisions is when capital projects are mutually exclusive—that is, when accepting one project means rejecting the other. For example, suppose you own a small store in the business district of Seattle that is currently vacant. You are looking at two business opportunities: opening an upscale coffee house or opening a copy center. Clearly, you cannot pursue both projects at the same location; these two projects are mutually exclusive.

When you have mutually exclusive projects, how do you select the best alternative? If you are using the NPV method, the answer is easy. You select the project that has the highest NPV because it will increase the value of the firm by the largest amount. If you are using the IRR method, it would seem logical to select the project with the highest IRR. In this case, though, the logic is wrong! You cannot tell which mutually exclusive project to select just by looking at the projects' IRRs.

Let's consider another example to illustrate the problem. The cash flows for two projects, A and B, are as follows:

Year	Project A	Project B
0	−$100	−$100
1	50	20
2	40	30
3	30	50
4	30	65

The IRR is 20.7 percent for project A and 19.0 percent for project B. Because the two projects are mutually exclusive, only one project can be accepted. If you were following the IRR decision rule, you would accept project A. However, as you will see, it turns out that project B might be the better choice.

The following table shows the NPVs for the two projects at several discount rates:

Discount Rate	NPV of Project A	NPV of Project B
0%	$50.0	$65.0
5%	34.5	42.9
10%	21.5	24.9
13%	14.8	15.7
15%	10.6	10.1
20%	1.3	−2.2
25%	−6.8	−12.6
30%	−13.7	−21.3
IRR	20.7%	19.0%

Notice that the project with the higher NPV depends on what rate of return is used to discount the cash flows. Our example shows a conflict in ranking order between the IRR and NPV methods at discount rates between 0 and 13 percent. In this range, project B has the lower IRR, but it has the higher NPV and should be the project selected. If the discount rate is above 15 percent, however, project A has the higher NPV as well as the higher IRR. In this range there is no conflict between the two evaluation methods.

crossover point
the discount rate at which the NPV profiles of two projects cross and, thus, at which the NPVs of the projects are equal

Now take a look at Exhibit 10.11, which shows the NPV profiles for projects A and B. As you can see, there is a point, called the **crossover point**, at which the NPV profiles for projects A and B intersect. The crossover point here is at a discount rate of 14.3 percent. For any cost of capital above 14.3 percent, the NPV for project A is higher than that for project B; thus, project A should be selected if its NPV is positive. For any cost of capital below the crossover point, project B should be selected.

Another conflict involving mutually exclusive projects concerns comparisons of projects that have significantly different costs. The IRR does not adjust for these differences in size. What the IRR gives us is a rate of return on each dollar invested. In contrast, the NPV method computes the total dollar value created by the project. The difference in results can be significant, as can be seen in Decision-Making Example 10.2.

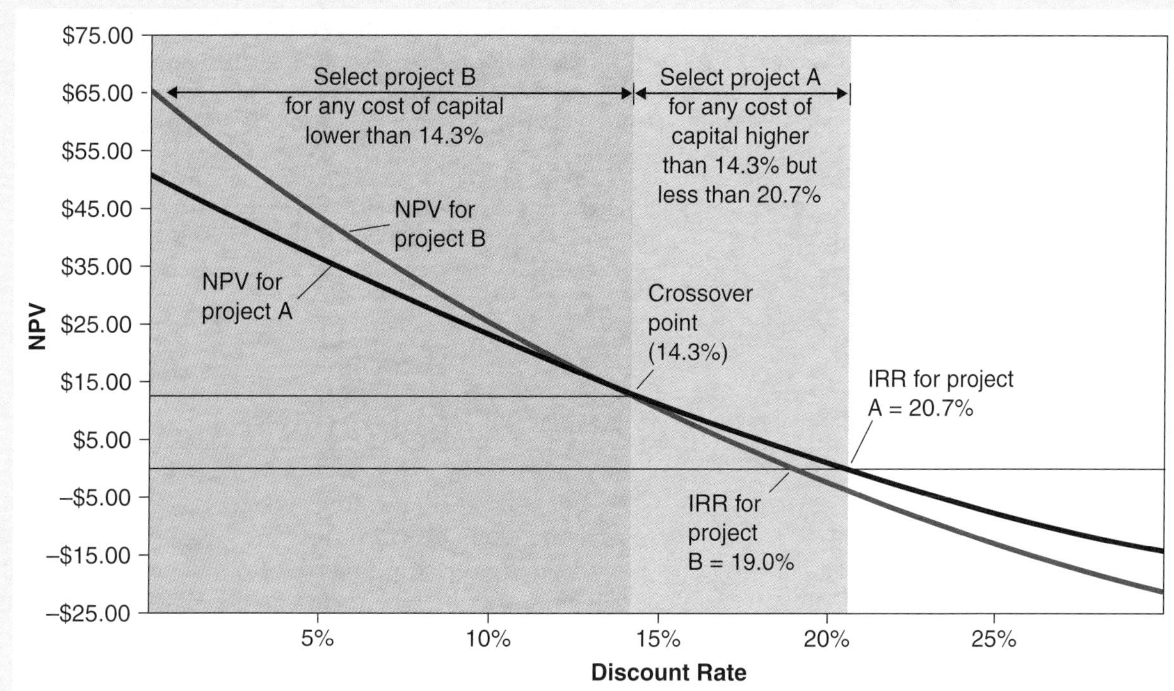

Exhibit 10.11
NPV Profiles for Two Mutually Exclusive Projects
The NPV profiles for two projects often cross over each other. When evaluating mutually exclusive projects, it is helpful to know where this crossover point is. For projects A and B in the exhibit, the crossover point is at 14.3 percent. For any cost of capital above 14.3 percent but below 20.7 percent the NPV for project A is higher than that for project B and is positive; thus, project A should be selected. For any cost of capital below the crossover point, the NPV of project B is higher, and project B should be selected.

DECISION-MAKING EXAMPLE 10.2

The Lemonade Stand versus the Convenience Store

Situation: Suppose you work for an entrepreneur who owns a number of small businesses in Fresno, California, as well as a small piece of property near California State University at Fresno, which he believes would be an ideal site for a student-oriented convenience store. His 12-year-old son, who happens to be in the office after school, says he has a better idea: his father should open a lemonade stand. Your boss tells you to find the NPV and IRR for both projects, assuming a 10 percent discount rate. After collecting data, you present the following analysis:

Year	Lemonade Stand	Convenience Store
0	−$1,000	−$1,000,000
1	850	372,000
2	850	372,000
3	850	372,000
4	850	372,000
IRR	76.2%	18.0%
NPV	$1,694	$179,190

Assuming the projects are mutually exclusive, which should be selected?

(continued)

Decision: Your boss, who favors the IRR method, looks at the analysis and declares his son a genius. The IRR decision rule suggests that the lemonade stand, with its 76.2 percent rate of return, is the project to choose! You point out that the goal of capital budgeting is to select projects or combinations of projects that maximize the value of the firm, his business. The convenience store adds by far the greater value: $179,190 compared with only $1,694 for the lemonade stand. Although the lemonade stand has a high rate of return, its small size precludes it from being competitive against the larger project.[1]

Modified Internal Rate of Return (MIRR)

A major weakness of the IRR method compared with the NPV method concerns the rate at which the cash flows generated by a capital project are reinvested. The NPV method assumes that cash flows from a project are reinvested at the cost of capital, whereas the IRR technique assumes they are reinvested at the IRR. Determining which is the better assumption depends on which rate better represents the rate that firms can actually earn when they reinvest a project's cash flows over time. It is generally believed that the cost of capital, which is often lower than the IRR, better reflects the rate that firms are likely to earn. Using the IRR may thus involve overly optimistic assumptions regarding reinvestment rates.

modified internal rate of return (MIRR)
an internal rate of return (IRR) measure which assumes that cash inflows are reinvested at the opportunity cost of capital until the end of the project

To eliminate the reinvestment rate assumption of the IRR, some practitioners prefer to calculate the **modified internal rate of return (MIRR)**. In this approach, each operating cash flow is converted to a future value at the end of the project's life, compounded at the cost of capital. These values are then summed up to get the project's *terminal value (TV)*. The MIRR is the interest rate that equates the project's cost (PV_{Cost}), or cash outflows, with the future value of the project's cash inflows at the end of the project (PV_{TV}).[2] Because each future value is computed using the cost of capital as the interest rate, the reinvestment rate problem is eliminated.

We can set up the equation for the MIRR in the same way we set up Equation 10.4 for the IRR:

$$\begin{aligned} \text{PV(Cost of the project)} &= \text{PV(Cash inflows)} \qquad (10.5) \\ \text{PV}_{\text{Cost}} &= \text{PV}_{\text{TV}} \\ \text{PV}_{\text{Cost}} &= \frac{\text{TV}}{(1 + \text{MIRR})^n} \end{aligned}$$

To compute the MIRR, we have to make two preliminary calculations. First, we need to calculate the value of PV_{Cost}, which is the present value of the cash outflows that make up the investment cost of the project. Since for most capital projects, the investment cost cash flows are incurred at the beginning of the project, $t = 0$, there is often no need to calculate a present value. If investment costs are incurred over time ($t > 0$), then the cash flows must be discounted at the cost of capital for the appropriate time period.

Second, we need to compute the terminal value (TV). To do this, we find the future value of each operating cash flow at the end of the project's life, compounded at the

[1]The solution ignores the opportunity cost of the land. As we will discuss in Chapter 11, if your boss could sell the land or use it land in some other way that has value, then there is an opportunity cost associated with using it for the convenience store.

[2]As we pointed out in Chapter 5, financial decision-making problems can be solved either by discounting cash flows to the beginning of the project or by using compounding to find the future value of cash flows at the end of a project's life.

cost of capital. We then sum up these future values to get the project's TV. Mathematically, the TV can be expressed as:

$$\begin{aligned} \text{TV} &= \text{CF}_1(1+k)^{n-1} + \text{CF}_2(1+k)^{n-2} + \cdots + \text{CF}_n(1+k)^{n-n} \\ &= \sum_{t=1}^{n} \text{CF}_t(1+k)^{n-t} \end{aligned}$$

where:

TV = the project's terminal value
CF_t = cash flow from operations in period t
k = the cost of capital
n = the project life

Once we have computed the values of PV_{Cost} and TV, we use Equation 10.5 to compute the MIRR.

To illustrate, let's return to the Ford Motor Company example shown in Exhibit 10.8. Recall that the cost of the project is \$560, incurred at $t = 0$, and that the discount rate is 12 percent. To determine the MIRR for the project, we start by calculating the terminal value of the cash flows, as shown on the following time line:

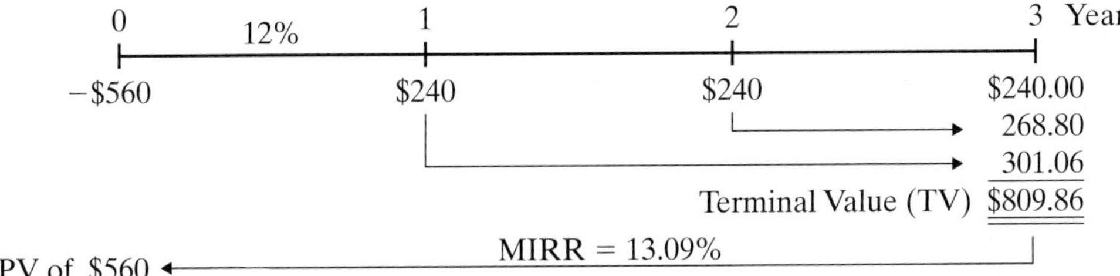

The terminal value of \$809.86 equals the sum of the \$240 in year 1 compounded at 12 percent for two years plus the \$240 in year 2 compounded at 12 percent for 1 year plus the \$240 in year 3. Mathematically, this calculation is:

$$\begin{aligned} \text{TV} &= \text{CF}_1(1+k)^{n-1} + \text{CF}_2(1+k)^{n-2} + \cdots + \text{CF}_n(1+k)^{n-n} \\ &= \$240(1.12)^2 + \$240(1.12) + \$240 = \$809.86 \end{aligned}$$

With the information that the cost of the project is \$560 and the TV is \$809.86, we can calculate the MIRR using Equation 10.5:

$$\begin{aligned} \text{PV}_{\text{Cost}} &= \frac{\text{TV}}{(1+\text{MIRR})^n} \\ \$560 &= \frac{\$809.86}{(1+\text{MIRR})^3} \\ (1+\text{MIRR})^3 &= \frac{\$809.86}{\$560} = 1.4462 \\ (1+\text{MIRR}) &= (1.4462)^{1/3} = 1.1309 \\ \text{MIRR} &= 1.1309 - 1 = 0.1309 \\ &= 13.09\% \end{aligned}$$

At 13.09 percent, the MIRR is higher than Ford's cost of capital of 12 percent, so the project should be accepted.

To read an article that warns finance managers using the IRR about the method's pitfalls, visit www.cfo.com/printable/article.cfm/3304945?f=options.

IRR versus NPV: A Final Comment

The IRR method, as noted, is an important alternative to the NPV method. As we have seen, it accounts for the time value of money, which is not true of methods such as the payback period and accounting rate of return. Furthermore, the IRR technique has great intuitive appeal. Many business practitioners are in the habit of thinking in terms of rates of return, whether the rates relate to their common-stock portfolios or their firms' capital expenditures. To these practitioners, the IRR method just seems to make sense. Indeed, we suspect that the IRR's popularity with business managers results more from its simple intuitive appeal than from its merit.

On the downside, we have seen that the IRR method has several flaws. One of these can be eliminated by using the MIRR. Nevertheless, we believe that the NPV should be the primary method used to make capital budgeting decisions. Decisions made by the NPV method are consistent with the goal of maximizing the value of the firm's stock, and the NPV tells management the dollar amount by which each project is expected to increase the value of the firm.

Review of Internal Rate of Return (IRR)

Decision Rule: IRR > Cost of capital ⇨ Accept the project.
IRR < Cost of capital ⇨ Reject the project.

Key Advantages	Key Disadvantages
1. Intuitively easy to understand.	1. With nonconventional cash flows, IRR approach can yield no usable answer or multiple answers.
2. Based on discounted cash flow technique.	2. A lower IRR can be better if a cash inflow is followed by cash outflows.
	3. With mutually exclusive projects, IRR can lead to incorrect investment decisions.

Before You Go On

1. What is the IRR method?
2. In capital budgeting, what is a conventional cash flow pattern?
3. Why should the NPV method be the primary decision tool used in making capital investment decisions?

10.6 Capital Budgeting in Practice

Capital expenditures are big-ticket items in the U.S. economy. According to the Department of Commerce, U.S. businesses invested $1.15 trillion in capital goods in 2005. The sectors with the largest capital expenditures were manufacturing, $165.2 billion; finance and insurance, $161.6 billion; and real estate and rental and leasing, $103.2 billion. Capital investments also represent large expenditures for individual firms, though the amount spent can vary widely from year to year. For example, over the last several years, Verizon has expanded rapidly to increase its market share in the wireless business. Its capital expenditures, at 20.4 percent of sales, were among the highest for Fortune 1000 firms in 2005. More typical are the capital expenditure figures for Exxon, Cisco, and Kellogg Company, shown in the accompanying table. Given the large dollar amounts and the strategic importance of capital expenditures, it is no surprise that corporate managers spend considerable time and energy analyzing them.

Company	2005 Capital Expenditures ($ billions)	2005 Sales ($ billions)	Capital Expenditures as a Percent of Sales
Verizon	$15.3	$75.1	20.4%
Exxon Mobil	13.8	370.7	3.7
Cisco	0.7	24.8	2.8
Kellogg Co.	0.4	10.2	3.9

Exhibit 10.12 Capital Budgeting Techniques Used by Business Firms

Capital Budgeting Tool	Percent of Surveyed Firms That Use the Technique Frequently	
	1981	1999
Payback period	5.0	56.7
Accounting rate of return (ARR)	10.7	20.3
Internal rate of return (IRR)	65.3	75.7
Net persent value (NPV)	16.5	74.9

Sources: Stanley, Marjorie T. and Stanley B. Block, "A Survey of Multinational Capital Budgeting" *The Financial Review,* March 1984. Graham, John R. and Campbell R. Harvey, "The Theory and Practice of Corporate Finance," *Journal of Financial Economics,* May/June 2001.

The exhibit summarizes evidence from two studies that examined the use of capital budgeting techniques by businesses. As you can see, over time more firms have come to use the NPV and IRR techniques. Surprisingly, though, even in 1999, 20.3 percent still computed the accounting rate of return.

Practitioners' Methods of Choice

Because of the importance of capital budgeting, over the years a number of surveys have asked financial managers what techniques they actually use in making capital investment decisions. Exhibit 10.12, which summarizes the results from two such studies, reveals significant changes over time. As shown, in 1981 only 16.5 percent of the financial managers surveyed frequently used the NPV approach, and the payback period and accounting rate of return approaches were used even less frequently. Most firms, 65.3 percent, used the IRR method. However, practices changed in the 1980s and 1990s. By 1999, 74.9 percent of the firms surveyed were frequently using the NPV technique, 75.7 percent were using the IRR, and 56.7 percent were using the payback period method. As you can see, the most recent findings reflect a much better alignment between practitioners and the academic community. As you can also see, many financial managers use multiple capital budgeting tools.

An article that surveys the use of capital budgeting techniques by the CFOs of Fortune 500 companies can be found at faculty.fuqua.duke.edu/~jgraham/website/SurveyJACF.pdf.

Ongoing and Postaudit Reviews

Management should systematically review the status of all ongoing capital projects and perform postaudit reviews on all completed capital projects. In a **postaudit review**, management compares the actual performance of a project with what was projected in the capital budgeting proposal. For example, suppose a new microchip was expected to earn a 20 percent IRR, but the product's actual IRR turned out to be 9 percent. A postaudit examination would determine why the project failed to achieve its expected financial goals. Project reviews keep all people involved in the capital budgeting process honest because they know that the project and their performance will be reviewed and that they will be held accountable for the results.

postaudit review
an audit to compare actual project results with the results projected in the capital budgeting proposal

Managers should also conduct *ongoing reviews* of capital projects in progress. Such a review should challenge the business plan, including the cash flow projections and the operating cost assumptions. For example, Intel undoubtedly has periodically reviewed the viability of its $2.5 billion computer chip wafer plant in China and made adjustments to reflect changing business conditions. Business plans are management's best estimates of future events at the time they are prepared, but as new information becomes available, the decision to undertake a capital project and the nature of that project must be reassessed.

Management must also evaluate people responsible for implementing a capital project. They should monitor whether the project's revenues and expenses are meeting projections. If the project is not at plan, the difficult task for management is to determine whether the problem is a flawed plan or poor execution by the implementation team. Good plans can fail if they are poorly executed at the operating level.

Before You Go On

1. What shifts have taken place in the capital budgeting techniques used by U.S. companies?

Summary of Learning Objectives

1. **Discuss why capital budgeting decisions are the most important investment decisions made by a firm's management.**

Capital budgeting is the process by which management decides which productive assets the firm should invest in. Because capital expenditures involve large amounts of money, are critical to achieving the firm's strategic plan, define the firm's line of business over the long term, and determine the firm's profitability for years to come, they are considered the most important investment decisions made by management.

2. **Explain the benefits of using the net present value (NPV) method to analyze capital expenditure decisions, and be able to calculate the NPV for a capital project.**

The net present value (NPV) method leads to better investment decisions than other techniques because the NPV method does the following: (1) it uses the discounted cash flow valuation approach, which accounts for the time value of money, and (2) provides a direct measure of how much a capital project is expected to increase the dollar value of the firm. Thus, NPV is consistent with the top management goal of maximizing stockholder value. NPV calculations are described in Section 10.2 and Learning by Doing Application 10.1.

3. **Describe the strengths and weaknesses of the payback period as a capital expenditure decision-making tool, and be able to compute the payback period for a capital project.**

The payback period is the length of time it will take for the cash flows from a project to recover the cost of the project. The payback period is widely used, mainly because it is simple to apply and easy to understand. It also provides a simple measure of liquidity risk because it tells management how quickly the firm will get its money back. The payback period has a number of shortcomings, however. For one thing, the payback period, as most commonly computed, ignores the time value of money. We can overcome this objection by using discounted cash flows to calculate the payback period. Regardless of how the payback period is calculated, however, it fails to take account of cash flows recovered after the payback period. Thus, the payback period is biased in favor of short-lived projects. Also, the hurdle rate used to identify what payback period is acceptable is arbitrarily determined. Payback period calculations are described in Section 10.3 and Learning by Doing Application 10.2.

4. **Explain why the accounting rate of return (ARR) is not recommended as a capital expenditure decision-making tool.**

The ARR is based on accounting numbers, such as book value and net income, rather than cash flow data. As such, it is not a true rate of return. Instead of discounting a project's cash flows over time, it simply gives us a number based on average figures from the income statement and balance sheet. Furthermore, as with the payback method, there is no economic rationale for establishing the hurdle rate. Finally, the ARR does not account for the size of the projects when a choice between two projects of different sizes must be made.

5. **Be able to compute the internal rate of return (IRR) for a capital project, and discuss the conditions under which the IRR technique and the NPV technique produce different results**

The IRR is the expected rate of return for an investment project; it is calculated as the discount rate that equates the present value of a project's expected cash inflows to the present value of the project's outflows—in other words, as the discount rate at which the NPV is equal to zero. Calculations are shown in Section 10.5 and Learning by Doing Application 10.3. If a project's IRR is greater than the required rate of return, the cost of capital, the project is accepted. The IRR rule often gives the same investment decision for a project as the NPV rule. However, the IRR method does have operational pitfalls that can lead to incorrect decisions. Specifically, when a project's cash flows are unconventional, the IRR calculation may yield no solution or more than one IRR. In addition, the IRR technique cannot be used to rank projects that are mutually exclusive because the project with the highest IRR may not be the project that would add the greatest value to the firm if accepted—that is, the project with the highest NPV.

6. **Explain the benefits of a postaudit review of a capital project.**

Postaudit reviews of capital projects allow management to determine whether the project's goals were met and to quantify the benefits or costs of the project. By conducting these reviews, managers can avoid similar mistakes and possibly better recognize opportunities.

Summary of Key Equations

Equation	Description	Formula
10.1	Net present value	$\text{NPV} = \text{NCF}_0 + \frac{\text{NCF}_1}{1+k} + \frac{\text{NCF}_2}{(1+k)^2} + \cdots + \frac{\text{NCF}_n}{(1+k)^n} = \sum_{t=0}^{n} \frac{\text{NCF}_t}{(1+k)^t}$
10.2	Payback period	$\text{PB} = \text{Years before cost recovery} + \frac{\text{Remaining cost to recover}}{\text{Cash flow during the year}}$
10.3	Accounting rate of return	$\text{ARR} = \frac{\text{Average net income}}{\text{Average book value}}$
10.4	Internal rate of return	$\text{NPV} = \sum_{t=0}^{n} \frac{\text{NCF}_t}{(1+\text{IRR})^t} = 0$
10.5	Modified internal rate of return	$\text{PV}_{\text{Cost}} = \frac{\text{TV}}{(1+\text{MIRR})^n}$

Self-Study Problems

10.1 Premium Manufacturing Company is evaluating two forklift systems to use in its plant that produces the towers for a windmill power farm. The costs and the cash flows from these systems are shown here. If the company uses a 12 percent discount rate for all projects, determine which forklift system should be purchased using the net present value (NPV) approach.

	Year 0	Year 1	Year 2	Year 3
Otis Forklifts	−\$3,123,450	\$979,225	\$1,358,886	\$2,111,497
Craigmore Forklifts	−\$4,137,410	\$875,236	\$1,765,225	\$2,865,110

10.2 Rutledge, Inc., has invested \$100,000 in a project that will produce cash flows of \$45,000, \$37,500, and \$42,950 over the next three years. Find the payback period for the project.

10.3 Perryman Crafts Corp. is evaluating two independent capital projects that will each cost the company \$250,000. The two projects will provide the following cash flows:

Year	Project A	Project B
1	\$80,750	\$32,450
2	93,450	76,125
3	40,235	153,250
4	145,655	96,110

Which project will be chosen if the company's payback criterion is three years? What if the company accepts all projects as long as the payback period is less than five years?

10.4 Terrell Corp. is looking into purchasing a machine for its business that will cost \$117,250 and will be depreciated on a straight-line basis over a five-year period. The sales and expenses (excluding depreciation) for the next five years are shown in the following table. The company's tax rate is 34 percent.

	Year 1	Year 2	Year 3	Year 4	Year 5
Sales	\$123,450	\$176,875	\$242,455	\$255,440	\$267,125
Expenses	\$137,410	\$126,488	\$141,289	\$143,112	\$133,556

The company will accept all projects that provide an accounting rate of return (ARR) of at least 45 percent. Should the company accept this project?

10.5 Refer to Problem 10.1. Compute the IRR for each of the two systems. Is the choice different from the one determined by NPV?

Solutions to Self-Study Problems

10.1 NPVs for two forklift systems:
NPV for Otis Forklifts:

$$\begin{aligned} NPV &= \sum_{t=0}^{n} \frac{NCF_t}{(1+k)^t} \\ &= -\$3{,}123{,}450 + \frac{\$979{,}225}{1+0.12} + \frac{\$1{,}358{,}886}{(1.12)^2} + \frac{\$2{,}111{,}497}{(1.12)^3} \\ &= -\$3{,}123{,}450 + \$874{,}308 + \$1{,}083{,}296 + \$1{,}502{,}922 \\ &= \$337{,}076 \end{aligned}$$

NPV for Craigmore Forklifts:

$$\begin{aligned} NPV &= \sum_{t=0}^{n} \frac{NCF_t}{(1+k)^t} \\ &= -\$4{,}137{,}410 + \frac{\$875{,}236}{1+0.12} + \frac{\$1{,}765{,}225}{(1.12)^2} + \frac{\$2{,}865{,}110}{(1.12)^3} \\ &= -\$4{,}137{,}410 + \$781{,}461 + \$1{,}407{,}227 + \$2{,}039{,}329 \\ &= \$90{,}607 \end{aligned}$$

Premium should purchase the Otis forklift since it has a larger NPV.

10.2 Payback period for Rutledge project:

Year	CF	Cumulative Cash Flow
0	(\$100,000)	(\$100,000)
1	45,000	(55,000)
2	37,500	(17,500)
3	42,950	25,450

$$\begin{aligned} \text{Payback period} &= \text{Years before cost recovery} + \frac{\text{Remaining cost to recover}}{\text{Cash flow during the year}} \\ &= 2 + \frac{\$17{,}500}{\$42{,}950} \\ &= 2.41 \text{ years} \end{aligned}$$

10.3 Payback periods for Perryman projects A and B:

Project A

Year	Cash Flow	Cumulative Cash Flows
0	(\$250,000)	(\$250,000)
1	80,750	(169,250)
2	93,450	(75,800)
3	40,235	(35,565)
4	145,655	110,090

Project B

Year	Cash Flow	Cumulative Cash Flows
0	(\$250,000)	(\$250,000)
1	32,450	(217,550)
2	76,125	(141,425)
3	153,250	11,825
4	96,110	107,935

Payback period for project A:

$$\text{Payback period} = \text{Years before cost recovery} + \frac{\text{Remaining cost to recover}}{\text{Cash flow during the year}}$$

$$= 3 + \frac{\$35{,}565}{\$145{,}655}$$

$$= 3.24 \text{ years}$$

Payback period for Project B:

$$\text{Payback period} = \text{Years before cost recovery} + \frac{\text{Remaining cost to recover}}{\text{Cash flow during the year}}$$

$$= 2 + \frac{\$141{,}425}{\$153{,}250}$$

$$= 2.92 \text{ years}$$

If the payback period is three years, project B will be chosen. If the payback criterion is five years, both A and B will be chosen.

10.4 Evaluation of Terrell Corp. project:

	Year 1	Year 2	Year 3	Year 4	Year 5
Sales	$123,450	$176,875	$242,455	$255,440	$267,125
Expenses	137,410	126,488	141,289	143,112	133,556
Depreciation	23,450	23,450	23,450	23,450	23,450
EBIT	($37,410)	$26,937	$77,716	$88,878	$110,119
Taxes (34%)	12,719	9,159	26,423	30,219	37,440
Net Income	($24,691)	$17,778	$51,293	$58,659	$72,679
Beginning Book Value	117,250	93,800	70,350	46,900	23,450
Less: Depreciation	(23,450)	(23,450)	(23,450)	(23,450)	(23,450)
Ending Book Value	$93,800	$70,350	$46,900	$23,450	$0

$$\begin{aligned}
\text{Average net income} &= (-\$24{,}691 + \$17{,}778 + \$51{,}293 + \$58{,}659 + \$72{,}679)/5 \\
&= \$35{,}143.60 \\
\text{Average book value} &= (\$93{,}800 + \$70{,}350 + \$46{,}900 + \$23{,}450 + \$0)/5 \\
&= \$46{,}900.00 \\
\text{Accounting rate of return} &= \$35{,}143.60/\$46{,}900.00 \\
&= 74.93\%
\end{aligned}$$

The company should accept the project.

10.5 IRRs for two forklift systems:

Otis Forklifts:
First compute the IRR by the trial-and-error approach.

NPV (Otis) = $337,075 > 0
Use a higher discount rate to get NPV = 0!
At $k = 15$ percent:

$$\text{NPV} = -\$3{,}123{,}450 + \frac{\$979{,}225}{1 + 0.15} + \frac{\$1{,}358{,}886}{(1.15)^2} + \frac{\$2{,}111{,}497}{(1.15)^3}$$

$$= -\$3{,}123{,}450 + \$851{,}500 + \$1{,}027{,}513 + \$1{,}388{,}344$$

$$= \$143{,}907$$

Try a higher rate. At $k = 17$ percent:

$$\text{NPV} = -\$3{,}123{,}450 + \$836{,}944 + \$992{,}685 + \$1{,}318{,}357$$
$$= \$24{,}536$$

Try a higher rate. At $k = 17.5$ percent:

$$\text{NPV} = -\$3{,}123{,}450 + \$833{,}383 + \$984{,}254 + \$1{,}301{,}598$$
$$= -\$4{,}215$$

Thus, the IRR for Otis is less than 17.5 percent. Using a financial calculator, you can find the exact rate to be 17.43 percent.

Craigmore Forklifts:
First compute the IRR using the trial-and-error approach.

NPV (Craigmore) = \$90,606 > 0

Use a higher discount rate to get NPV = 0!
At k = 15 percent:

$$\begin{aligned} \text{NPV} &= -\$4{,}137{,}410 + \frac{\$875{,}236}{1.15} + \frac{\$1{,}765{,}225}{(1.12)^2} + \frac{\$2{,}865{,}110}{(1.12)^3} \\ &= -\$4{,}137{,}410 + \$761{,}075 + \$1{,}334{,}764 + \$1{,}883{,}856 \\ &= -\$157{,}715 \end{aligned}$$

Try a lower rate. At k = 13 percent:

$$\begin{aligned} \text{NPV} &= -\$4{,}137{,}410 + \$774{,}545 + \$1{,}382{,}430 + \$1{,}985{,}665 \\ &= \$5{,}230 \end{aligned}$$

Try a higher rate. At k = 13.1 percent:

$$\begin{aligned} \text{NPV} &= -\$4{,}137{,}410 + \$773{,}860 + \$1{,}379{,}987 + \$1{,}980{,}403 \\ &= -\$3{,}161 \end{aligned}$$

Thus, the IRR for Craigmore is less than 13.1 percent. The exact rate is 13.06 percent. Based on the IRR, we would still pick Otis over Craigmore forklift systems.

Critical Thinking Questions

10.1 Explain why the cost of capital is referred to as the "hurdle" rate in capital budgeting.

10.2 **a.** A company is building a new plant on the outskirts of Smallesville. The town has offered to donate the land ,and as part of the agreement, the company will have to build an access road from the main highway to the plant. How will the project of building of the road be classified in capital budgeting analysis?

b. Sykes, Inc., is considering two projects: a plant expansion and a new computer system for the firm's production department. Classify each of these projects as independent, mutually exclusive, or contingent projects and explain your reasoning.

c. Your firm is currently considering the upgrading of the operating systems of all the firm's computers. The firm can choose the Linux operating system that a local computer services firm has offered to install and maintain. Microsoft has also put in a bid to install the new Windows Vista operating system for businesses. What type of project is this?

10.3 In the context of capital budgeting, what is "capital rationing"?

10.4 Explain why we use discounted cash flows instead of actual market price data.

10.5 **a.** A firm takes on a project that would earn a return of 12 percent. If the appropriate cost of capital is also 12 percent, did the firm make the right decision? Explain.

b. What is the impact on the firm if it accepts a project with a negative NPV?

10.6 Identify the weaknesses of the payback period method.

10.7 What are the strengths and weaknesses of the accounting rate of return approach?

10.8 Under what circumstances might the IRR and NPV approaches have conflicting results?

10.9 A company estimates that an average-risk project has a cost of capital of 8 percent, a below-average risk project has a cost of capital of 6 percent, and an above-average risk project has a cost of capital of 10 percent. Which of the following independent projects should the company accept? Project A has below-average risk and a return of 6.5 percent. Project B has above-average risk and a return of 9 percent. Project C has average risk and a return of 7 percent.

10.10 Elkridge Construction Company has an overall (composite) cost of capital of 12 percent. This cost of capital reflects the cost of capital for an Elkridge Construction project with average risk. However, the firm takes on projects of various risk levels. The company experience suggests that low-risk projects have a cost of capital of 10 percent and high-risk projects have a cost of capital of 15 percent. Which of the following projects should the company select to maximize shareholder wealth?

Project	Expected Return	Risk
1. Single-family homes	13%	Low
2. Multifamily residential	12	Average
3. Commercial	18	High
4. Single-family homes	9	Low
5. Commercial	13	High

Questions and Problems

BASIC

10.1 Net present value: Riggs Corp. is planning to spend $650,000 on a new marketing campaign. It believes that this action will result in additional cash flows of $325,000 over the next three years. If the discount rate is 17.5 percent, what is the NPV on this project?

10.2 Net present value: Kingston, Inc., is looking to add a new machine at a cost of $4,133,250. The company expects this equipment will lead to cash flows of $814,322, $863,275, $937,250, $1,017,112, $1,212,960, and $1,225,000 over the next six years. If the appropriate discount rate is 15 percent, what is the NPV of this investment?

10.3 Net present value: Crescent Industries is planning to replace some existing machinery in its plant. The cost of the new equipment and the resulting cash flows are shown in the accompanying table. If the firm uses an 18 percent discount rate for projects like this, should the firm go ahead with the project?

Year	Cash Flow
0	−$3,300,000
1	875,123
2	966,222
3	1,145,000
4	1,250,399
5	1,504,445

10.4 Net present value: Franklin Mints, a confectioner, is looking to purchase a new jellybean-making machine at a cost of $312,500. The company projects that the cash flows from this investment will be $121,450 for the next seven years. If the appropriate discount rate is 14 percent, what is the NPV for the project?

10.5 Payback: Quebec, Inc., is purchasing machinery at a cost of $3,768,966. The company expects, as a result, cash flows of $979,225, $1,158,886, and $1,881,497 over the next three years. What is the payback period?

10.6 Payback: Northern Specialties just purchased inventory-management computer software at a cost of $1,645,276. Cost savings from the investment over the next six years will be reflected in the following cash flow stream: $212,455, $292,333, $387,479, $516,345, $645,766, and $618,325. What is the payback period on this investment?

10.7 Payback: Nakamichi Bancorp has made an investment in banking software at a cost of $1,875,000. The institution expects productivity gains and cost savings over the next several years. If the firm is expected to generate cash flows of $586,212, $713,277, $431,199, and $318,697 over the next four years, what is the investment's payback period?

10.8 Average accounting rate of return (ARR): Capitol Corp. is expecting to generate after-tax income of $63,435 over each of the next three years. The average book value of their equipment over that period will be $212,500. If the firm's acceptance decision on any project is based on an ARR of 37.5 percent, should this project be accepted?

10.9 Internal rate of return: Refer to Problem 10.4. What is the IRR that Franklin Mints can expect on this project?

10.10 Internal rate of return: Hathaway, Inc., a resort company, is refurbishing one of its hotels at a cost of $7.8 million. The firm expects that this will lead to additional cash flows of $1.8 million for the next six years. What is the IRR of this project? If the appropriate cost of capital is 12 percent, should it go ahead with this project?

INTERMEDIATE

10.11 Net present value: Champlain Corp. is investigating two computer systems. The Alpha 8300 costs $3,122,300 and will generate annual cost savings of $1,345,500 over the next five years. The Beta 2100 system costs $3,750,000 and will produce cost savings of $1,125,000 in the first three years and then $2 million for the next two years. If the company's discount rate for similar projects is 14 percent, what is the NPV for the two systems? Which one should be chosen based on the NPV?

10.12 Net present value: Briarcrest Condiments is a spice-making firm. Recently, it developed a new process for producing spices. This calls for acquiring machinery that would cost $1,968,450. The machine will have a life of five years and will produce cash flows as shown in the table. What is the NPV if the discount rate is 15.9 percent?

Year	Cash Flow
1	$512,496
2	−242,637
3	814,558
4	887,225
5	712,642

10.13 Net present value: Cranjet Industries is expanding its product line and its production capacity. The costs and expected cash flows of the two independent projects are given in the following table. The firm uses a discount rate of 16.4 percent for such projects.

a. Are these projects independent or mutually exclusive?
b. What are the NPVs of the two projects?
c. Should both projects be accepted? or either? or neither? Explain your reasoning.

Year	Product Line Expansion	Production Capacity Expansion
0	−$2,575,000	−$8,137,250
1	600,000	2,500,000
2	875,000	2,500,000
3	875,000	2,500,000
4	875,000	3,250,000
5	875,000	3,250,000

10.14 Net present value: Emporia Mills is evaluating two heating systems. Costs and projected energy savings are given in the following table. The firm uses 11.5 percent to discount such project cash flows. Which system should be chosen?

Year	System 100	System 200
0	−$1,750,000	−$1,735,000
1	275,223	750,000
2	512,445	612,500
3	648,997	550,112
4	875,000	384,226

10.15 Payback: Creative Solutions, Inc., has invested $4,615,300 on equipment. The firm uses payback period criteria of not accepting any project that takes more than four years to recover costs. The company anticipates cash flows of $644,386, $812,178, $943,279, $1,364,997, $2,616,300, and $2,225,375 over the next six years. Does this investment meet the firm's payback criteria?

10.16 Discounted payback: Timeline Manufacturing Co. is evaluating two projects. The company uses payback criteria of three years or less. Project A has a cost of $912,855, and project B's cost will be $1,175,000. Cash flows from both projects are given in the following table. What are their discounted payback periods, and which will be accepted with a discount rate of 8 percent?

Year	Project A	Project B
1	$86,212	$586,212
2	313,562	413,277
3	427,594	231,199
4	285,552	

10.17 Payback: Regent Corp. is evaluating three competing pieces of equipment. Costs and cash flow projections for all three are given in the following table. Which would be the best choice based on payback period?

Year	Type 1	Type 2	Type 3
0	−$1,311,450	−$1,415,888	−$1,612,856
1	212,566	586,212	786,212
2	269,825	413,277	175,000
3	455,112	331,199	175,000
4	285,552	141,442	175,000
5	121,396		175,000
6			175,000

10.18 Discounted payback: Nugent Communication Corp. is investing $9,365,000 in new technologies. The company expects significant benefits in the first three years after installation (as can be seen by the cash flows), and a constant amount for four more years. What is the discounted payback period for the project assuming a discount rate of 10 percent?

Years	1	2	3	4–7
Cash Flows	$2,265,433	$4,558,721	$3,378,911	$1,250,000

10.19 Modified internal rate of return (MIRR): Morningside Bakeries has recently purchased equipment at a cost of $650,000. The firm expects to generate cash flows of $275,000 in each of the next four years. The cost of capital is 14 percent. What is the MIRR for this project?

10.20 Modified internal rate of return (MIRR): Sycamore Home Furnishings is looking to acquire a new machine that can create customized window treatments. The equipment will cost $263,400 and will generate cash flows of $85,000 over each of the next six years. If the cost of capital is 12 percent, what is the MIRR on this project?

10.21 Internal rate of return: Great Flights, Inc., an aviation firm, is exploring the purchase of three aircrafts at a total cost of $161 million. Cash flows from leasing these aircrafts is expected to build slowly as shown in the following table. What is the IRR on this project? The required rate of return is 15 percent.

Years	Cash Flow
1–4	$23,500,000
5–7	72,000,000
8–10	80,000,000

10.22 Internal rate of return: Compute the IRR on the following cash flow streams:

a. An initial investment of $25,000 followed by a single cash flow of $37,450 in year 6

b. An initial investment of $1 million followed by a single cash flow of $1,650,000 in year 4

c. An initial investment of $2 million followed by cash flows of $1,650,000 and $1,250,000 in years 2 and 4, respectively

10.23 Internal rate of return: Compute the IRR for the following project cash flows.

a. An initial outlay of $3,125,000 followed by annual cash flows of $565,325 for the next eight years

b. An initial investment of $33,750 followed by annual cash flows of $9,430 for the next five years

c. An initial outlay of $10,000 followed by annual cash flows of $2,500 for the next seven years

ADVANCED

10.24 Draconian Measures, Inc., is evaluating two independent projects. The company uses a 13.8 percent discount rate for such projects. Cost and cash flows are shown in the table. What are the NPVs of the two projects?

Year	Project 1	Project 2
0	−$8,425,375	−$11,368,000
1	3,225,997	2,112,589
2	1,775,882	3,787,552
3	1,375,112	3,125,650
4	1,176,558	4,115,899
5	1,212,645	4,556,424
6	1,582,156	
7	1,365,882	

10.25 Refer to Problem 10.24.

a. What are the IRRs for both projects?

b. Does the IRR decision criterion differ from the earlier decisions?

c. Explain how you would expect the management of Draconian Measures to decide.

10.26 Dravid, Inc., is currently evaluating three projects that are independent. The cost of funds can be either 13.6 percent or 14.8 percent depending on their financing plan. All three projects cost the same at $500,000. Expected cash flow streams are shown in the following table. Which projects would be accepted at a discount rate of 14.8 percent? What if the discount rate was 13.6 percent?

Year	Project 1	Project 2	Project 3
1	$ 0	$ 0	$245,125
2	125,000	0	212,336
3	150,000	500,000	112,500
4	375,000	500,000	74,000

10.27 Intrepid, Inc., is looking to invest in two or three independent projects. The costs and the cash flows are given in the following table. The appropriate cost of capital is 14.5 percent. Compute the IRRs and identify the projects that will be accepted.

Year	Project 1	Project 2	Project 3
0	−$275,000	−$312,500	−$500,000
1	63,000	153,250	212,000
2	85,000	167,500	212,000
3	85,000	112,000	212,000
4	100,000		212,000

10.28 Jekyll & Hyde Corp. is evaluating two mutually exclusive projects. Their cost of capital is 15 percent. Costs and cash flows are given in the following table. Which project should be accepted?

Year	Project 1	Project 2
0	−$1,250,000	−$1,250,000
1	250,000	350,000
2	350,000	350,000
3	450,000	350,000
4	500,000	350,000
5	750,000	350,000

10.29 Larsen Automotive, a manufacturer of auto parts, is planning to invest in two projects. The company typically compares project returns to a cost of funds of 17 percent. Compute the IRRs based on the given cash flows, and state which projects will be accepted.

Year	Project 1	Project 2
0	−$475,000	−$500,000
1	300,000	117,500
2	110,000	181,300
3	125,000	244,112
4	140,000	278,955

EXCEL®

10.30 Compute the IRR for each of the following cash flow streams:

Year	Project 1	Project 2	Project 3
0	−$10,000	−$10,000	−$10,000
1	4,750	1,650	800
2	3,300	3,890	1,200
3	3,600	5,100	2,875
4	2,100	2,750	3,400
5		800	6,600

EXCEL®

10.31 Primus Corp. is planning to convert an existing warehouse into a new plant that will increase its production capacity by 45 percent. The cost of this project will be $7,125,000.

It will result in additional cash flows of $1,875,000 for the next eight years. The discount rate is 12 percent.

a. What is the payback period?
b. What is the NPV for this project?
c. What is the IRR?

10.32 Quasar Tech Co. is investing $6 million in new machinery that will produce the next-generation routers. Sales to its customers will amount to $1,750,000 for the next three years and then increase to $2.4 million for three more years. The project is expected to last six years and cost the firm annually $898,620 (excluding depreciation). The machinery will be depreciated to zero by year 6 using the straight-line method. The company's tax rate is 30 percent, and the cost of capital is 16 percent. **EXCEL®**

a. What is the payback period?
b. What is the average accounting return (ARR)?
c. Calculate the project NPV.
d. What is the IRR for the project?

10.33 Skywards, Inc., an airline caterer, is purchasing refrigerated trucks at a total cost of $3.25 million. After-tax net income from this investment is expected to be $750,000 for the next five years. Annual depreciation expense was $650,000. The cost of capital is 17 percent. **EXCEL®**

a. What is the discounted payback period?
b. Compute the ARR.
c. What is the NPV on this investment?
d. Calculate the IRR.

10.34 Trident Corp. is evaluating two independent projects. The costs and expected cash flows are given in the following table. The cost of capital is 10 percent. **EXCEL®**

Year	A	B
0	−$312,500	−$395,000
1	121,450	153,552
2	121,450	158,711
3	121,450	166,220
4	121,450	132,000
5	121,450	122,000

a. Calculate the project's NPV.
b. Calculate the project's IRR.
c. What is the decision based on NPV? What is the decision based on IRR? Is there a conflict?
d. If you are the decision maker for the firm, which project or projects will be accepted? Explain your reasoning.

10.35 Tyler, Inc., is looking to move to a new technology for its production. The cost of equipment will be $4 million. The discount rate is 12 percent. Cash flows that the firm expects to generate are as follows. **EXCEL®**

Years	CF
0	−$4,000,000
1–2	0
3–5	$845,000
6–9	$1,450,000

a. Compute the payback and discounted payback period for the project.
b. What is the NPV for the project? Should the firm go ahead with the project?
c. What is the IRR, and what would be the decision under the IRR?

CFA PROBLEMS

10.36 Given the following cash flows for a capital project, calculate the NPV and IRR. The required rate of return is 8 percent.

Year	0	1	2	3	4	5
Cash Flow	−$50,000	$15,000	$15,000	$20,000	$10,000	$5,000

	NPV	IRR
a.	$1,905	10.9%
b.	$1,905	26.0%
c.	$3,379	10.9%
d.	$3,379	26.0%

10.37 Given the following cash flows for a capital project, calculate its payback period and discounted payback period. The required rate of return is 8 percent.

Year	0	1	2	3	4	5
Cash Flow	−$50,000	$15,000	$15,000	$20,000	$10,000	$5,000

The discounted payback period is
a. 0.16 year longer than the payback period.
b. 0.80 year longer than the payback period.
c. 1.01 years longer than the payback period.
d. 1.85 years longer than the payback period.

10.38 An investment of $100 generates after-tax cash flows of $40 in Year 1, $80 in Year 2, and $120 in Year 3. The required rate of return is 20 percent. The net present value is closest to
a. $42.22
b. $58.33
c. $68.52
d. $98.95

10.39 An investment of $150,000 is expected to generate an after-tax cash flow of $100,000 in one year and another $120,000 in two years. The cost of capital is 10 percent. What is the internal rate of return?
a. 28.19 percent
b. 28.39 percent
c. 28.59 percent
d. 28.79 percent

10.40 An investment has an outlay of 100 and after-tax cash flows of 40 annually for four years. A project enhancement increases the outlay by 15 and the annual after-tax cash flows by 5. As a result, the vertical intercept of the NPV profile of the enhanced project shifts
a. up and the horizontal intercept shifts left.
b. up and the horizontal intercept shifts right.
c. down and the horizontal intercept shifts left.
d. down and the horizontal intercept shifts right.

Sample Test Problems

10.1 Net present value: Techno Corp. is considering developing new computer software. The cost of development will be $675,000, and the company expects the revenue from the sale of the software to be $195,000 for each of the next six years. If the discount rate is 14 percent, what is the net present value of this project?

10.2 Payback method: Parker Office Supplies is looking to replace its outdated inventory-management software. The cost of the new software will be $168,000. Cost savings is expected to be $43,500 for each of the first three years and then to drop off to $36,875 for the next two years. What is the payback period for this project?

10.3 Accounting rate of return: Fresno, Inc., is expecting to generate after-tax income of $156,435 over each of the next three years. The average book value of its equipment over that period will be $322,500. If the firm's acceptance decision on any project is based on an ARR of 40 percent, should this project be accepted?

10.4 Internal rate of return: Refer to Problem 10.1. What is the IRR on this project?

10.5 Net present value: Raycom, Inc., needs a new overhead crane, and two alternatives are available. Crane T costs $1.35 million and will produce cost savings of $765,000 for the next three years. Crane R will cost the firm $1.675 million and will lead to annual cost savings of $815,000 for the next three years. The required rate of return is 15 percent. Which of the two options should Raycom choose based on NPV calculations, and why?

APPENDIX

A

PRESENT VALUE AND FUTURE VALUE TABLES

Table A-1
Future Value Factors for $1 Compounded at *i* Percent for N Periods

Table A-2
Present Value Factors (at *i* Percent) for $1 Received at the End of N Periods

Table A-3
Future Value of Annuity Factors for $1 Compounded at *i* Percent for N Periods

Table A-4
Present Value of Annuity Factors (at *i* Percent Per Period) for $1 Received Per Period for Each of N Periods

Table A-1 **Future Value Factors for $1 Compounded at *i* Percent for N Periods**

					i					
N	1%	2%	3%	4%	5%	6%	7%	8%	9%	10%
1	1.010	1.020	1.030	1.040	1.050	1.060	1.070	1.080	1.090	1.100
2	1.020	1.040	1.061	1.082	1.103	1.124	1.145	1.166	1.188	1.210
3	1.030	1.061	1.093	1.125	1.158	1.191	1.225	1.260	1.295	1.331
4	1.041	1.082	1.126	1.170	1.216	1.262	1.311	1.360	1.412	1.464
5	1.051	1.104	1.159	1.217	1.276	1.338	1.403	1.469	1.539	1.611
6	1.062	1.126	1.194	1.265	1.340	1.419	1.501	1.587	1.677	1.772
7	1.072	1.149	1.230	1.316	1.407	1.504	1.606	1.714	1.828	1.949
8	1.083	1.172	1.267	1.369	1.477	1.594	1.718	1.851	1.993	2.144
9	1.094	1.195	1.305	1.423	1.551	1.689	1.838	1.999	2.172	2.358
10	1.105	1.219	1.344	1.480	1.629	1.791	1.967	2.159	2.367	2.594
11	1.116	1.243	1.384	1.539	1.710	1.898	2.105	2.332	2.580	2.853
12	1.127	1.268	1.426	1.601	1.796	2.012	2.252	2.518	2.813	3.138
13	1.138	1.294	1.469	1.665	1.886	2.133	2.410	2.720	3.066	3.452
14	1.149	1.319	1.513	1.732	1.980	2.261	2.579	2.937	3.342	3.797
15	1.161	1.346	1.558	1.801	2.079	2.397	2.759	3.172	3.642	4.177
16	1.173	1.373	1.605	1.873	2.183	2.540	2.952	3.426	3.970	4.595
17	1.184	1.400	1.653	1.948	2.292	2.693	3.159	3.700	4.328	5.054
18	1.196	1.428	1.702	2.026	2.407	2.854	3.380	3.996	4.717	5.560
19	1.208	1.457	1.754	2.107	2.527	3.026	3.617	4.316	5.142	6.116
20	1.220	1.486	1.806	2.191	2.653	3.207	3.870	4.661	5.604	6.727
21	1.232	1.516	1.860	2.279	2.786	3.400	4.141	5.034	6.109	7.400
22	1.245	1.546	1.916	2.370	2.925	3.604	4.430	5.437	6.659	8.140
23	1.257	1.577	1.974	2.465	3.072	3.820	4.741	5.871	7.258	8.954
24	1.270	1.608	2.033	2.563	3.225	4.049	5.072	6.341	7.911	9.850
25	1.282	1.641	2.094	2.666	3.386	4.292	5.427	6.848	8.623	10.835
30	1.348	1.811	2.427	3.243	4.322	5.743	7.612	10.063	13.268	17.449
35	1.417	2.000	2.814	3.946	5.516	7.686	10.677	14.785	20.414	28.102
40	1.489	2.208	3.262	4.801	7.040	10.286	14.974	21.725	31.409	45.259
45	1.565	2.438	3.782	5.841	8.985	13.765	21.002	31.920	48.327	72.890
50	1.645	2.692	4.384	7.107	11.467	18.420	29.457	46.902	74.358	117.390

				i					
11%	12%	13%	14%	15%	20%	25%	30%	35%	40%
.901	.893	.885	.877	.870	.833	.800	.769	.741	.714
.812	.797	.783	.769	.756	.694	.640	.592	.449	.510
.731	.712	.693	.675	.658	.579	.512	.455	.406	.364
.659	.636	.613	.592	.572	.482	.410	.350	.301	.260
.593	.567	.543	.519	.497	.402	.328	.269	.223	.186
.535	.507	.480	.456	.432	.335	.262	.207	.165	.133
.482	.452	.425	.400	.376	.279	.210	.159	.122	.095
.434	.404	.376	.351	.327	.233	.168	.123	.091	.068
.391	.361	.333	.308	.284	.194	.134	.094	.067	.048
.352	.322	.295	.270	.247	.162	.107	.073	.050	.035
.317	.287	.261	.237	.215	.135	.086	.056	.037	.025
.286	.257	.231	.208	.187	.112	.069	.043	.027	.018
.258	.229	.204	.182	.163	.093	.055	.033	.020	.013
.232	.205	.181	.160	.141	.078	.044	.025	.015	.009
.209	.183	.160	.140	.123	.065	.035	.020	.011	.006
.188	.163	.141	.123	.107	.054	.028	.015	.008	.005
.170	.146	.125	.108	.093	.045	.023	.012	.006	.003
.153	.130	.111	.095	.081	.038	.018	.009	.005	.002
.138	.116	.098	.083	.070	.031	.014	.007	.003	.002
.124	.104	.087	.073	.061	.026	.012	.005	.002	.001
.112	.093	.077	.064	.053	.022	.009	.004	.002	.001
.101	.083	.068	.056	.046	.018	.007	.003	.001	.001
.091	.074	.060	.049	.040	.015	.006	.002	.001	
.082	.066	.053	.043	.035	.013	.005	.002	.001	
.074	.059	.047	.038	.030	.010	.004	.001	.001	
.044	.033	.026	.020	.015	.004	.001			
.026	.019	.014	.010	.008	.002				
.015	.011	.008	.005	.004	.001				
.009	.006	.004	.003	.002					
.005	.003	.002	.001	.001					

Table A-3	Future Value of Annuity Factors for $1 Compounded at *i* Percent for N Periods

					i					
N	1%	2%	3%	4%	5%	6%	7%	8%	9%	10%
1	1.000	1.000	1.000	1.000	1.000	1.000	1.000	1.000	1.000	1.000
2	2.010	2.020	2.030	2.040	2.050	2.060	2.070	2.080	2.090	2.100
3	3.030	3.060	3.091	3.122	3.152	3.184	3.215	3.246	3.278	3.310
4	4.060	4.122	4.184	4.246	4.310	4.375	4.440	4.506	4.573	4.641
5	5.101	5.204	5.309	5.416	5.526	5.637	5.751	5.867	5.985	6.105
6	6.152	6.308	6.468	6.633	6.802	6.975	7.153	7.336	7.523	7.716
7	7.214	7.434	7.662	7.898	8.142	8.394	8.654	8.923	9.200	9.487
8	8.286	8.583	8.892	9.214	9.549	10.897	10.260	10.637	11.028	11.436
9	9.369	9.755	10.159	10.583	11.027	11.491	11.978	12.488	13.021	13.579
10	10.462	10.950	11.464	12.006	12.578	13.181	13.816	14.487	15.193	15.937
11	11.567	12.169	12.808	13.486	14.207	14.972	15.784	16.645	17.560	18.531
12	12.683	13.412	14.192	15.026	15.917	16.870	17.888	18.977	20.141	21.384
13	13.809	14.680	15.618	16.627	17.713	18.882	20.141	21.495	22.953	24.523
14	14.947	15.971	17.086	18.292	19.599	21.015	22.550	24.215	26.019	27.975
15	16.097	17.291	18.599	20.024	21.579	23.276	25.129	27.152	29.361	31.722
16	17.258	18.639	20.157	21.825	23.657	25.673	27.888	30.324	33.003	35.950
17	18.430	20.012	21.762	23.698	25.840	28.213	30.840	33.750	36.974	40.545
18	19.615	21.412	23.414	25.645	28.132	30.906	33.999	37.450	41.301	45.599
19	20.811	22.841	25.117	27.671	30.539	33.760	37.379	41.446	46.018	51.159
20	22.019	24.297	26.870	29.778	33.066	36.786	40.995	45.762	51.160	57.275
21	23.239	25.783	28.676	31.969	35.719	39.993	44.865	50.423	56.765	64.002
22	24.472	27.299	30.537	34.248	38.505	43.392	49.006	55.457	62.873	71.403
23	25.716	28.845	32.453	36.618	41.430	46.996	53.436	60.893	69.532	79.543
24	26.973	30.422	34.426	39.083	44.502	50.816	58.177	66.765	76.790	88.497
25	28.243	32.030	36.459	41.646	47.727	54.865	63.249	73.106	84.701	98.347
30	34.785	40.568	47.575	56.085	66.439	79.058	94.461	113.280	136.300	164.490
35	41.660	49.994	60.462	73.652	90.320	111.430	138.230	172.310	215.710	271.020
40	48.886	60.402	75.401	95.026	120.800	154.760	199.630	259.050	337.880	442.590
45	56.481	71.893	92.720	121.020	159.700	212.740	285.740	386.500	525.850	718.900
50	64.463	84.579	112.790	152.660	209.340	290.330	406.520	573.770	815.080	1163.900

				i					
11%	12%	13%	14%	15%	20%	25%	30%	35%	40%
1.000	1.000	1.000	1.000	1.000	1.000	1.000	1.000	1.000	1.000
2.110	2.120	2.130	2.140	2.150	2.200	2.250	2.300	2.350	2.400
3.342	3.374	3.407	3.440	3.472	3.640	3.813	3.990	4.172	4.360
4.710	4.779	4.850	4.921	4.993	5.368	5.766	6.187	6.633	7.104
6.228	6.353	6.480	6.610	6.742	7.442	8.207	9.043	9.954	10.196
7.913	8.115	8.232	8.536	8.754	9.930	11.259	12.756	14.438	16.324
9.783	10.089	10.405	10.730	11.067	12.916	15.073	17.583	20.492	23.853
11.859	12.300	12.757	13.233	13.727	16.499	19.842	23.858	28.664	34.395
14.164	14.776	15.416	16.085	16.786	20.799	25.802	32.015	39.696	49.153
16.722	17.549	18.420	19.337	20.304	25.959	33.253	42.619	54.590	69.814
19.561	20.655	21.814	23.045	24.349	32.150	42.566	56.405	74.697	98.739
22.713	24.133	25.650	27.271	29.002	39.581	54.208	74.327	101.840	139.230
26.212	28.029	29.985	32.089	34.352	48.497	68.760	97.625	138.480	195.920
30.095	32.393	34.883	37.581	40.505	59.196	86.949	127.910	187.950	275.300
34.405	37.280	40.417	43.842	47.580	72.035	109.680	167.280	254.730	386.420
39.190	42.753	46.672	50.980	55.717	87.442	138.100	218.470	344.890	541.980
44.501	48.884	53.739	59.118	65.075	105.930	173.630	285.010	466.610	759.780
50.396	55.750	61.725	68.394	75.836	128.110	218.040	371.510	630.920	1064.600
56.939	63.440	70.749	78.969	88.212	154.740	273.550	483.970	852.740	1491.500
64.203	72.052	80.947	91.025	102.440	186.680	342.940	630.160	1152.200	2089.200
72.265	81.699	92.470	104.760	118.810	225.020	429.680	820.210	1556.400	2925.800
81.214	92.503	105.491	120.430	137.630	271.030	538.100	1067.200	2102.200	4097.200
91.148	104.600	120.205	138.290	159.270	326.230	673.620	1388.400	2839.000	5737.100
102.170	118.150	136.831	158.650	184.160	392.480	843.030	1806.000	3833.700	8032.900
114.410	133.330	155.620	181.870	212.790	471.980	1054.700	2348.800	5176.500	11247.000
199.020	241.330	293.199	356.780	434.740	1181.800	3227.100	8729.900	23221.000	60501.000
341.590	431.660	546.681	693.570	881.170	2948.300	9856.700	32422.000	104136.000	325400.000
581.820	767.090	1013.704	1342.000	1779.000	7343.800	30088.000	120392.000	466960.000	
986.630	1358.200	1874.165	2490.500	3585.100	18281.000	91831.000	447019.000		
1668.700	2400.000	3459.507	4994.500	7217.700	45497.000	280255.000			

Table A-4 **Present Value of Annuity Factors (at *i* Percent Per Period) for $1 Received Per Period for Each of N Periods**

	i									
N	1%	2%	3%	4%	5%	6%	7%	8%	9%	10%
1	0.990	0.980	0.971	0.962	0.952	0.943	0.935	0.926	0.917	0.909
2	1.970	1.942	1.913	1.886	1.859	1.833	1.808	1.783	1.759	1.736
3	2.941	2.884	2.829	2.775	2.723	2.673	2.624	2.577	2.531	2.487
4	3.902	3.808	3.717	3.630	3.546	3.465	3.387	3.312	3.240	3.170
5	4.853	4.713	4.580	4.452	4.329	4.212	4.100	3.993	3.890	3.791
6	5.795	5.601	5.417	5.242	5.076	4.917	4.767	4.623	4.486	4.355
7	6.728	6.472	6.230	6.002	5.786	5.582	5.389	5.206	5.033	4.868
8	7.652	7.325	7.020	6.733	6.463	6.210	5.971	5.747	5.535	5.335
9	8.566	8.162	7.786	7.435	7.108	6.802	6.515	6.247	5.995	5.759
10	9.471	8.983	8.530	8.111	7.722	7.360	7.024	6.710	6.418	6.145
11	10.368	9.787	9.253	8.760	8.306	7.887	7.499	7.139	6.805	6.495
12	11.255	10.575	9.954	9.385	8.863	8.384	7.943	7.536	7.161	6.814
13	12.134	11.348	10.635	9.986	9.394	8.853	8.358	7.904	7.487	7.103
14	13.004	12.106	11.296	10.563	9.899	9.295	8.745	8.244	7.786	7.367
15	13.865	12.849	11.938	11.118	10.380	9.712	9.108	8.559	8.061	7.606
16	14.718	13.578	12.561	11.652	10.838	10.106	9.447	8.851	8.313	7.824
17	15.562	14.292	13.166	12.166	11.274	10.477	9.763	9.122	8.544	8.022
18	16.398	14.992	13.754	12.659	11.690	10.828	10.059	9.372	8.756	8.201
19	17.226	15.678	14.324	13.134	12.085	11.158	10.336	9.604	8.950	8.365
20	18.046	16.351	14.877	13.590	12.462	11.470	10.594	9.818	9.129	8.514
21	18.857	17.011	15.415	14.029	12.821	11.764	10.836	10.017	9.292	8.649
22	19.660	17.658	15.937	14.451	13.163	12.042	11.061	10.201	9.442	8.772
23	20.456	18.292	16.444	14.857	13.489	12.303	11.272	10.371	9.580	8.883
24	21.243	18.914	16.936	15.247	13.799	12.550	11.469	10.529	9.707	8.985
25	22.023	19.523	17.413	15.622	14.094	12.783	11.654	10.675	9.823	9.077
30	25.808	22.396	19.600	17.292	15.372	13.765	12.409	11.258	10.274	9.427
35	29.409	24.999	21.487	18.665	16.374	14.498	12.948	11.655	10.567	9.644
40	32.835	27.355	23.115	19.793	17.159	15.046	13.332	11.925	10.757	9.779
45	36.095	29.490	24.519	20.720	17.774	15.456	13.606	12.108	10.881	9.863
50	39.196	31.424	25.730	21.482	18.256	15.762	13.801	12.233	10.962	9.915

i									
11%	12%	13%	14%	15%	20%	25%	30%	35%	40%
0.901	0.893	0.885	0.877	0.870	0.833	0.800	0.769	0.741	0.714
1.713	1.690	1.668	1.647	1.626	1.528	1.440	1.361	1.289	1.224
2.444	2.402	2.361	2.322	2.283	2.106	1.952	1.816	1.696	1.589
3.102	3.037	2.974	2.914	2.855	2.589	2.362	2.166	1.997	1.849
3.696	3.605	3.517	3.433	3.352	2.991	2.689	2.436	2.220	2.035
4.231	4.111	3.998	3.889	3.784	3.326	2.951	2.643	2.385	2.168
4.712	4.564	4.423	4.288	4.160	3.605	3.161	2.802	2.508	2.263
5.146	4.968	4.799	4.639	4.487	3.837	3.329	2.925	2.598	2.331
5.537	5.328	5.132	4.946	4.772	4.031	3.463	3.019	2.665	2.379
5.889	5.650	5.426	5.216	5.019	4.192	3.571	3.092	2.715	2.414
6.207	5.938	5.687	5.453	5.234	4.327	3.656	3.147	2.752	2.438
6.492	6.194	5.918	5.660	5.421	4.439	3.725	3.190	2.779	2.456
6.750	6.424	6.122	5.842	5.583	4.533	3.780	3.223	2.799	2.469
6.982	6.628	6.302	6.002	5.724	4.611	3.824	3.249	2.814	2.478
7.191	6.811	6.462	6.142	5.847	4.675	3.859	3.268	2.825	2.484
7.379	6.974	6.604	6.265	5.954	4.730	3.887	3.283	2.834	2.489
7.549	7.120	6.729	6.373	6.047	4.775	3.910	3.295	2.840	2.492
7.702	7.250	6.840	6.467	6.128	4.812	3.928	3.304	2.844	2.494
7.839	7.366	6.938	6.550	6.198	4.843	3.942	3.311	2.848	2.496
7.963	7.469	7.025	6.623	6.259	4.870	3.954	3.316	2.850	2.497
8.075	7.562	7.102	6.687	6.312	4.891	3.963	3.320	2.852	2.498
8.176	7.654	7.170	6.743	6.359	4.909	3.970	3.323	2.853	2.498
8.266	7.718	7.230	6.792	6.399	4.925	3.976	3.325	2.854	2.499
8.348	7.784	7.283	6.835	6.434	4.937	3.981	3.327	2.855	2.499
8.422	7.843	7.330	6.873	6.464	4.948	3.985	3.329	2.856	2.499
8.694	8.055	7.496	7.003	6.566	4.979	3.995	3.332	2.857	2.500
8.855	8.176	7.586	7.070	6.617	4.992	3.998	3.333	2.857	2.500
8.951	8.244	7.634	7.105	6.642	4.997	3.999	3.333	2.857	2.500
9.008	8.283	7.661	7.123	6.654	4.999	4.000	3.333	2.857	2.500
9.042	8.304	7.675	7.133	6.661	4.999	4.000	3.333	2.857	2.500

SOLUTIONS TO SELECTED QUESTIONS AND PROBLEMS

APPENDIX

B

CHAPTER 1

1.1 The two basic sources of funds for all businesses are debt and equity.

1.3 A profitable firm is able to generate enough cash flows from productive assets to cover its operating expenses, taxes, and payments to creditors. Unprofitable firms fail to do this and therefore they may be forced to declare bankruptcy.

1.5 A firm should undertake a capital project only if the value of its future cash flows exceeds the cost of the project.

1.7 Working capital management is the day-to-day management of a firm's current assets and liabilities. The financial manager has to make decisions regarding the level of inventory to hold, the terms of granting credit (account receivables), and the firm's policy on paying accounts payable.

1.9 Advantages: easiest business type to start; least regulated; owners have full control; all income is taxed as personal income. Disadvantages: unlimited liability of proprietor; initial capital limited to proprietor's wealth; difficult to transfer ownership.

1.11 The owners of a corporation are its stockholders and the evidence of their ownership is represented by shares of common stock.

1.13 The owners of a corporation are subject to double taxation—first at the corporate level when the firm's earnings are taxed and then again at a personal level when the dividends they receive are taxed.

1.15 The most important governing body within an organization is the board of directors. Its primary role is to represent the interest of stockholders. The board also hires (and occasionally fires) the CEO, advises him or her on major decisions, and monitors the firm's performance.

1.17 Problems include: difficult to determine what is meant by profits; it does not address the size and timing of cash flows—it does not account for the time value of money; and ignores the uncertainty of risk of cash flows.

1.19 The following factors affect the stock price: the firm, the economy, economic shocks, the business environment, expected cash flows, and current market conditions.

1.21 If a firm's stock price falls sustainably below its maximum potential price, it may attract corporate raiders. These persons look for firms that are fundamentally sound but that are poorly managed, so they can buy the firm, turn it around, and sell it for a handsome profit.

1.23 Business dishonesty and lack of transparency lead to corruption, and that in turn creates inefficiencies in an economy, inhibits growths of capital markets, and slows the rate of economic growth. An example is the Russian economy until it changed its transparency rules in the mid 1990s.

1.25 Insider trading is an example of information asymmetry. The main idea is that investment decisions should be made on an even playing field. Insider trading is considered morally wrong and has been made illegal.

CHAPTER 2

2.1 The role of the financial system is to gather money from businesses and individuals and channel funds to those who need them. The financial system consists of financial markets and financial institutions.

2.3 Saver-lenders are those who have more money than they need right now. The principal saver-lenders in the economy are households. Borrower-spenders are those who need the money saver-lenders are offering. The main borrower-spenders in the economy are businesses and the federal government.

2.5 Your security seems to be marketable, but not liquid. Liquidity implies that when a security is sold, its value will be preserved, marketability does not.

2.7 Trader Inc. is more likely to go public because of its larger size. Though the cost of SEC registration and compliance is very high, larger firms can offset these costs by the lower funding cost in public markets. Smaller companies find the cost prohibitive for the dollar amount of securities they sell.

2.9 **a.** secondary; **b.** secondary; **c.** primary

2.11 **a.** \$300,000; **b.** 3.05%; **c.** \$9,850,000

2.13 Financial intermediaries allow smaller companies to access the financial markets. They do this through converting securities with one set of characteristics into securities with another set of characteristics that meet the needs of smaller companies. By repackaging securities, they are able to meet the needs of different clients.

2.15 Money markets are where short-term debt instruments with maturities of less than one year are bought and sold. Capital markets are where equity securities and debt instruments with maturities of more than one year are sold.

2.17 Dow Jones Industrial Index consists of the 30 largest public companies in the U.S. and it was established to gauge the performance of the U.S. economy, specifically the industrial component of the stock market.

2.19 U.S. treasury bills are short-term debt of the U.S. government. They are the most liquid money market instrument and are considered free of default risk.

2.21 Money markets allow large corporations to adjust their liquidity positions by temporarily investing idle cash in money market instruments and then selling them when cash is needed. In addition, some large firms are able to borrow money by selling commercial paper in the money markets when cash is needed.

2.23 Public markets are wholesale markets for securities open to the public to buy securities. To sell securities publicly, issuers must register their securities with the SEC. Most corporations want access to the public markets because securities can be sold there at the lowest possibly funding cost. Private markets are where securities are sold directly to individual investors. Securities sold privately do not have to be registered with the SEC and, as a result, securities can be brought to market quickly and at very low transactions cost. However, because the securities are not registered, their sale and secondary market activities are severely restricted.

2.25 The real rate of interest measures the return earned on savings and it represents the cost of borrowing to finance capital goods. The real rate of interest is determined by the interaction between firms that invest in capital projects and the rate of return they expect to earn on those investments, and individuals' time preference for consumption. The rate of interest is determined when the desired level of savings equals the desired level of investments in the economy.

2.27 The Fisher effect is the expected annualized change in commodity prices (ΔP_e). The so-called inflation premium is used to protect lenders from losses of purchasing power on their loan contracts due to inflation. It is incorporated into a loan contract by adding it to the real interest rate, as can be seen in Equation 2.2.

2.29 Yes. The CD will be worth $1,067.50 at the end of the year and the price of the trip will be $1,066.

CHAPTER 3

3.1 $97,118

3.3 FIFO makes sense during times of rising prices because it allows the firm to eliminate the lower-priced inventory first resulting in higher profit margin.

3.5 $6,655,610

3.7 $242,401.25

3.9 −$132.085

3.11 Expenses identified on income statement that did not result in cash flows. Depreciation and amortization are examples.

3.13 Marginal tax rates are appropriate because it is the rate at which the next dollar is taxed at.

3.15 $168,022

3.17 $222,764

3.19 $137,263

3.21 $1,804,545.76

3.23 $621,178

3.25 $218,364.32; 34%, 34%.

3.27 $715,719.75

3.29 $198,152

CHAPTER 4

4.1 This measure includes only the most liquid of the current assets and hence gives a better measure of liquidity.

4.3 $1,627,579

4.5 2.87 times; 127.1 days.

4.7 2.65; 0.623; 29.9%.

4.9 Time trend analysis, industry average analysis, and peer group analysis

4.11 $2.55; 21.3 times.

4.13 ($767,243)

4.15 $843,863

4.17 1.27; 2.27.

4.19 51.2%; 19.1%; 12.6%.

4.21 0.41; 36%; 18.32%; 25.92%.

4.23 34.4 times; 22.04 times

4.25 $6,473,600; 5.7%.

4.27 $10,226,559; $88,236,056; 0.82.

4.29 Current ratio = 0.77, quick ratio = 0.57, gross margin = 51.2%, profit margin = 19.1%, debt ratio = 0.70, long-term debt to equity = 0.73, interest coverage = 15.6, ROA = 11.4%, ROE = 37.5%

4.31 Profit margin = 12.61%, total asset turnover = 0.90, equity multiplier = 3.30, return on assets = 11.4%, return on equity = 37.5%

4.33 $292,756.63

4.35 Current ratio = 1.81, quick ratio = 1.19, inventory turnover = 3.50, accounts receivable turnover = 5.16, DSO = 70.76, total asset turnover = 1.23, fixed asset turnover = 7.15, total debt ratio = 1.72, debt to equity ratio = 1.72, equity multiplier = 2.72, times interest earned = 17.56, cash coverage = 37.30, gross profit margin = 0.36, net profit margin = 0.08, ROA = 0.10, ROE = 0.27

CHAPTER 5

5.1 $53,973.12

5.3 $6,712.35

5.5 $3,289.69

5.7 $154,154.24; $154,637.37; $154,874.91; $154,883.03.

5.9 $16,108.92

5.11 $6,507.05

5.13 $734.83

5.15 7.42%

5.17 92,016; 101,218.

5.19 1,045

5.21 10.42%

5.23 11 years

5.25 3.8 years

5.27 **a.** $2,246.57; **b.** $2,073.16; **c.** $2,946.96; **d.** $2,949.88

5.29 13.96%

5.31 Option 1: $26,803.77; Option 2: $23,579.48

5.33 Option C: $ 7,083,096.26

5.35 13.14%

CHAPTER 6

6.1 $74,472.48

6.3 $3,185.40

6.5 $5,747.40

6.7 $5,652.06

6.9 $247,609.95

6.11 $1,361,642.36

6.13 $4,221.07

6.15 **a.** $15,000; **b.** $6,000; **c.** $10,000

6.17 7%

6.19 \$5,391,978

6.21 \$1,496,377.71

6.23 \$1,193,831.54

6.25 \$7,000,000

6.27 **a.** \$17,857.14; **b.** \$114,533.97; **c.** \$4,250.

6.29 **b.** 8.57%

6.31 \$12,847,215.41, \$11,374,540.65, and \$14,519,339.52

6.33 **a.** \$86,124.36; **b.** \$14,156.64; **c.** \$71,967.72; **d.** \$6.627.21.

6.35 \$2,103.89

CHAPTER 7

7.1 Total holding period return represents the percentage return to an investor from holding an asset over a given period of time. The expected return is the probability weighted average of the future performance of an investment under all scenarios.

7.3 \$78,000

7.5 Stock B

7.7 Systematic risk is risk that a security has in common with the market. Because all risky assets in the market have systematic risk, it cannot be eliminated through diversification.

7.9 Since a U.S. Treasury bill has no risk, its beta should equal 0.

7.11 The CAPM describes the relation between systematic risk and the expected return that investors require for bearing that risk.

7.13 \$1,250

7.15 0.145; 0.162.

7.17 0.125; 0.168.

7.19 for $\sigma_{12} = 0.12, 0.1225; \sigma_{12} = -0.12, 0.0025$

7.21 While it has no unsystematic risk, the portfolio still will have an expected return that is higher than that for a risk-free asset if it has systematic risk.

7.23 The statement is false. Even if we could afford such a portfolio and thus completely diversify our portfolio, we would only be eliminating non-systematic risk.

7.25 0.185; 0.165.

7.27 0.19

7.29 Diversified investors are willing to pay the highest prices for assets. They drive prices to the point where investments are expected to yield the returns described by CAPM.

7.31 Risk-free asset

7.33 The first security is underpriced and the second is overpriced.

CHAPTER 8

8.1 \$1,147.20

8.3 \$1,008.15

8.5 \$975.91

8.7 \$359.38

8.9 6.58%; 6.69%.

8.11 9.52%

8.13 \$1,000

8.15 \$912.61

8.17 \$1,079.22

8.19 12.453%

8.21 7.36%

8.23 10.57%

8.25 8.84%

8.27 **a.** \$924.75; **b.** 4.33%.

8.29 **a.** \$904.76; **b.** \$1,086.46, \$832.53; **d.** \$1,063.42, \$866.65.

CHAPTER 9

9.1 \$14.24

9.3 \$27.39

9.5 \$8.50

9.7 \$31.12

9.9 12.15%

9.11 \$56.90

9.13 \$2.46

9.15 \$21.07

9.17 \$23.35

9.19 \$32.34

9.21 \$25.95

9.23 \$2.15

9.25 **a.** \$35.00; **b.** Buy;

9.27 **b.** \$7.87; **c.** \$31.88; **d.** \$24.31; **e.** \$24.32.

9.29 **a.** \$14.09; **b.** \$74.80; **c.** \$51.28.

CHAPTER 10

10.1 \$62,337

10.3 Yes; \$134,986

10.5 2.87 years

10.7 3.45 years

10.9 33.8%

10.11 \$1,496,910; \$1,084,734; Alpha 8300.

10.13 \$27,222; \$732,228; Both.

10.15 No; 4.33 years

10.17 Type 2; 3.6 years

10.19 20.1%

10.21 22.7%

10.23 **a.** 9%; **b.** 12.3%; **c.** 16.3%.

10.25 **a.** 10.7%; 15%; **b.** No to project I, Yes to project II

10.27 7.6%; 19.2%; 25.1%; 2 & 3 Only

10.29 18.8%, 20%; Both

10.31 **a.** 3.8 years; **b.** \$2,189,325; **c.** 20.3%.

10.33 **a.** 3.21years; **b.** 57.7%; **c.** \$1,029,085; **d.** 32.5%.

10.35 **a.** 6 years, 8.8 years; **b.** \$116,980; **c.** 12.5%.

CHAPTER 11

11.1 The main reason is that accounting earnings generally differ from cash flows and cash flows are what stockholders care about.

11.3 Subtract depreciation from EBITDA, multiply by (1− tax rate), and add back depreciation. This enables us to account for the fact that depreciation reduces the taxes that must be paid.

11.5 The average tax rate is the total amount of tax divided by total amount of money earned, while the marginal tax rate is the rate paid on the last dollar earned. Use the marginal tax rate.

11.7 Variable costs are costs that vary directly with the number of units sold. Fixed costs do not vary with the number of units sold.

11.9 \$1,370

11.11 The Equivalent Annual Cost (EAC) is the annual payment from an annuity that has a life equal to that of a project and that has the same NPV as the project.

11.13 \$891.84

11.15 marginal = 35%; average = 34.2%

11.17 \$168,020,000

11.19 $EAC_A = -\$2,866.47$; $EAC_B = -\$2,978.44$; buy Model A

11.21 end of year 3

11.23 end of year 2

11.25 \$4,558.70

11.27 yes; the NPV = \$38,356

11.29 \$532,089.14

11.31 −\$363,805

CHAPTER 12

12.1 Fixed costs are cost which in the short term cannot be changed regardless of how much output the project produces. Variable costs are costs which vary with the number of units of output produced by the project.

12.3 Yes. EBIT is \$375,000 with the new technology and \$250,000 with the old.

12.5 0.392

12.7 To determine how many units are required to make up for the fixed cost we must know the additional positive cash flow or profits from each additional unit sold.

12.9 PI is the ratio of NPV plus initial investment to initial investment. It is useful in ranking projects by the value created per dollar invested.

12.11 Fixed costs could increase by \$230,000 and variable cost per unit could increase by \$15.33.

12.13 15.9%

12.15 340,000 units

12.17 The accounting break-even is higher because the calculation includes depreciation and amortization. This is a non-cash charge that might not accurately reflect an incremental cash flow.

12.19 Since sensitivity analysis assumes independence among variables, this analysis will be most useful when this sort of independence exists.

12.21 Simulation analysis

12.23 Choose projects A, C, and D

12.25 Cash Flow DOL will be less than Accounting DOL

12.27 Changes in revenue and operating leverage

12.29 CO = 300,000 units

CHAPTER 13

13.1 \$98 million

13.3 7.7%

13.5 \$395

13.7 16%

13.9 10%

13.11 15.8%

13.13 9.4%

13.15 The owners of the securities, collectively, own all of the cash flows that the firm generates. The value of these securities must equal the value of these cash flows and, therefore, the value of the firm.

13.17 \$1,000

13.19 decrease

13.21 14%, 12%

13.23 If you can confidently estimate future dividends, and you believe the market is efficient, then one of the methods that rely on dividend projections might be appropriate. If not, the CAPM, which does not require dividend forecasts, would probably be the best.

13.25 9.26%

13.27 Since the firm is financing the project with a different capital mix than it has historically used, then we know the weights and rates for debt, preferred, and common shares in the WACC formula will be different. Therefore, using its historical WACC can cause result in an error in the NPV estimate for the project.

13.29 Use a combination of historical growth information and available information about future growth prospects.

13.31 Under-estimating the dividend growth rate or market inefficiency in the pricing of the stock.

13.33 If the market perceives the risk of the firm to be higher than it actually is due to a lack of information, then the WACC might be too high and the firm might be able to lower it by sharing more information with the market.

CHAPTER 14

14.1 69 days

14.3 −2 days

14.5 73 days

14.7 34.72%

14.9 \$626.91

14.11 11.6%

14.13 75.9 days

14.15 \$1,511,918

14.17 36.5 days

14.19 16 orders

14.21 8.775%

14.23 5.54%

14.25 \$9,324

14.27 28.2 days

14.29 37.1%

14.31 **a.** Increase, Increase; **b.** Increase, Increase; **c.** No change, Decrease; **d.** Increase, Increase; **e.** Increase, Unchanged.

14.33 **a.** 67.9 days; **b.** 80.6 days; **c.** 105.7 days; **d.** 148.5 days; **e.** 42.8 days.

14.35 **a.** \$30,000; **b.** 63.2%; **c.** 85.1%

CHAPTER 15

15.1 A description of the business and industry trends, vision and key strategies for the business, principal products or services and any innovative features or patents, the management team and their experience, market analysis and sales forecast, how the products will be marketed and sold, production costs such as materials and labor, facilities needed and estimated costs, capital required and the use of the proceeds, detailed budget with six years of projected financial statements.

15.3 Sell the business at some period, take it public, or remain a private company.

15.5 Look at comparable companies and see what they are trading for; do a discounted cash flow analysis.

15.7 \$32,465,457

15.9 **a.** false **b.** true **c.** true **d.** false **e.** true

15.11 There are economies of scale in issuing securities, meaning that as the size of the offering increases, the total flotation costs decline.

15.13 Nalco is better off choosing to sell debt in public market, given its size.

15.15 9.43%

15.17 $1,220,000

15.19 $68,700,000

15.21 **a.** $130 million; **b.** $109 million; **c.** $21 million.

15.23 6.52%

CHAPTER 16

16.1 The assumption that there are no information or transaction costs.

16.3 The value of the firm is independent of the proportion of debt and equity utilized by the firm under Modigliani and Miller's Proposition 1.

16.5 20%

16.7 18%

16.9 $150,000,000

16.11 10.5%

16.13 42%

16.15 Information or transaction costs would reduce the total value that is available for the debt holders and the stockholders and, therefore, the value of the firm.

16.17 $530,000,000

16.19 Lower productivity due to lower morale and job hunting and higher recruiting costs are among the costs that the firm will incur.

16.21 Managers expect to lose their jobs in one year whether they take on the project and work hard or not. They have no incentive to take on the project. Declining it makes the shortage to the debt holders, as well as the stockholders, greater than it would be if the firm followed the rule of always accepting positive NPV projects.

16.23 Given the information in the question we would expect that an increase in the marginal tax rate will increase the value of the tax shield and increase the amount of debt in the optimal capital structure.

16.25 That internally generated equity is utilized first as a source of financing does not mean that the internally generated funds are cheaper than debt. Internally generated funds belong to stockholders and are therefore really equity financing, which we know to be more expensive than debt.

16.27 Under these conditions, the value of the firm will increase with the amount of debt financing that is used. The conservative approach will not maximize firm value.

16.29 $810,000,000

16.31 If enough debt is used to finance this firm then the challenges of ensuring that the firm produces enough cash to make interest and principal payments would provide managers of the firm with incentives to work on new positive NPV projects rather than spend their Fridays in Cancun.

CHAPTER 17

17.1 This reduction could indicate that management expects a lower level of profitability in the future (negative signal). It could also indicate that Poseidon requires additional money to invest in positive NPV projects that were not previously available (positive signal).

17.3 (1) Declaration date, (2) Ex-dividend date, (3) Record date, (4) Payment date

17.5 Any cash paid to stockholders through a dividend reduces the value of the assets that are securing the creditors' claims.

17.7 $9.75

17.9 With a stock repurchase, stockholders can decide whether to participate. If they do choose to participate, there are tax advantages for the stockholders, relative to a dividend.

17.11 Relaxing the no transaction cost assumption increases the cost of producing a homemade dividend (the cost of undoing unwanted dividends). This makes a firm's dividend policy a relevant factor when valuing its shares.

17.13 The value of dividend paying stocks should decrease relative to the value of non-dividend-paying stocks.

17.15 Reducing a dividend may indicate that a firm does not have sufficient cash, which would be a negative signal. On the other hand, when a high growth firm increases its dividend, the increase may be interpreted as indicating that the firm's growth rate will decline, which is also a negative signal.

17.17 The announcement of a special dividend is a binding commitment.

17.19 This commits a firm to returning to the capital markets periodically to raise capital, which provides managers with incentives to act in the interest of stockholders.

17.21 A Dutch auction enables a firm to repurchase the number of shares that it wants to repurchase at the lowest possible cost.

17.23 Paying a dividend reduces the value of equity and thereby increases the debt-to-total-capital ratio in a levered firm.

17.25 $15

17.27 $72,500

17.29 $150,000

CHAPTER 18

18.1 The forms of organizations discussed in this chapter include: Sole Proprietorship, Partnership (General Partnership and Limited Partnership), Limited Liability Company (LLC), and Corporation (S-Corporation and C-Corporation).

18.3 With sole proprietors and general partners there is the possibility that personal assets can be taken to satisfy claims on the businesses. In contrast, the liabilities of investors in LLCs and corporations are generally limited to the money that they have invested in the business.

18.5 Equity: friends and family, venture capitalists, or other potential investors that you know. Debt: bank loans, cash advances on credit cards, or loans from other individual investors or other businesses.

18.7 The cost of duplicating the assets of the business in their present form.

18.9 Excess cash is a nonoperating asset because this cash can be distributed to stockholders without affecting the operations of the business and therefore the value of the expected future cash flows. It makes sense to add back the value of excess cash because it represents value over and above that which the business is expected to produce.

18.11 Probably not. The private shares are relatively illiquid and the value would be discounted for this in the market.

18.13 A Limited Liability Company (LLC) is a hybrid of a corporation and a limited partnership. It has limited liability with the tax advantages of a partnership.

18.15 Break-even for TV option = 1,250 units per year. Break-even for flyer option = 150 units per year. Choose the flyer option.

18.17 $1,573.64 million

18.19 The enterprise value/EBITDA multiple is more appropriate since the capital structures of Johnson and Billy's differ considerably.

18.21 $12,675,000

18.23 It is not adequate. $9,400 or additional capital will be required up front. $89,400 is needed to maintain a $5,000 cash balance. The monthly break-even points for the firm are: 4,333.3 bottles in the initial month and 1,833.3 bottles in the following months.

18.25 See outline for a business plan in section 18.2.

18.27 The company has a short history, high investments, no sales, and highly uncertain future cash flows. The cost approach is not valid for such a young biochemical company. It is hard to value the company using multiples because of the lack of sales and negative earnings, and because of lack of comparable public companies. The transaction approach is also likely to be difficult to apply due to the difficulty of finding a comparable transaction.

CHAPTER 19

19.1 It drives all decision making within the firm and covers all areas of a firm's operations.

19.3 Identifies EFN, source of funding, target capital structure, and dividend policy.

19.5 Sales forecasts, pro forma statements, investment decisions, and financing decisions.

19.7 55%

19.9 Measures the amount of assets needed to generate one dollar in sales.

19.11 68%

19.13 6.8%

19.17 Electric utilities industry and the aluminum processing industry.

19.19 8%

19.21 8.2%

19.23 9.9%

19.25 5.2%

19.27 35.9%

19.29 9.6%

19.33 3.37%; 6.26%

19.35 **a.** 4.31%; **b.** 13.9%; **c.** $4,777,333;

CHAPTER 20

20.1 The right to buy or sell an asset at a pre-specified price on or before a pre-specified date.

20.3 $0; $15

20.5 The value of a call option increases as: (1) Current value of the underlying asset increases; (2) Exercise price decreases; (3) Volatility of the value of the underlying asset increases; (4) Time until the expiration of the option increases; or (5) Risk-free rate of interest increases.

20.7 That the value of the underlying asset will remain at or above the exercise price, thereby making it worthless to the owner (buyer).

20.9 No. The losses to the seller of a call option are only limited by the extent to which the value of the underlying asset can increase. There is no other limit.

20.11 Your option is worth very slightly more than zero. There is little chance that the stock price will move above $100 by tomorrow, but the chance is not zero, so the option still has some value.

20.13 The underlying asset of a financial option is financial asset, while the underlying asset of a real option is a non-financial asset, such as a project.

20.15 The payoff functions for lenders and stockholders are like those for different types of options. Agency costs arise because these payoff functions are different.

20.17 The purchaser of a callable bond is simultaneously buying a straight (non-callable) bond and selling the issuer a call option on that bond. The total value of the callable bond would equal the value of the straight bond minus the value of the option. It would be lower than the value for a straight bond.

20.19 Because the buyer pays them. The amount that the seller receives is known as the bond premium.

20.21 $7.01

20.23 $1.18

20.25 A golden parachute can help reduce agency problems by reducing the potential cost to a manager of making decisions that stockholders want, but that could harm the manager. For example, having a golden parachute can provide a manager with stronger incentives to invest in risky projects or approve a merger that could result in the loss of his or her job.

20.27 The payoff of these two portfolios is identical.

20.29 $5 million; $6.5 million; $3.5 million

CHAPTER 21

21.1 $209.30

21.3 **a.** MP 11.8483/$; **b.** 1.6359/£; **c.** C$ 0.0316/Rs

21.5 Same cost in both cities based on the spot rate!

21.7 $9,400

21.9 $2,861,776

21.11 0.069%

21.13 0.45%

21.15 Won 2,120.23/£

21.19 5.4% discount

21.20 3.5% premium

21.21 0.007368/¥

21.23 Rs.43.43/$

21.25 $2,055,201

21.27 $5,286.50

21.29 $7,807.35

21.31 3,685.366 million Won

21.33 2.92%, 2.95% — domestic bond issue

21.35 $62,500; $61,875 — Daiwa's offer

MANAGERIAL ACCOUNTING

Jiambalvo

Third Edition

Volume 2

Selected Chapters

Customized for UMUC • MGMT 640

Financial Decision Making for Managers

CONTENTS

Chapter 1 Managerial Accounting in the Information Age 2

Chapter 4 Cost-Volume-Profit Analysis 125

Chapter 6 Cost Allocation and Activity-Based Costing 209

Chapter 7 The Use of Cost Information in Management Decision Making 261

Chapter 8 Pricing Decisions, Analyzing Customer Profitability, and Activity-Based Pricing 30

Third Edition

JAMES JIAMBALVO
University of Washington

MANAGERIAL ACCOUNTING

John Wiley & Sons, Inc.

To my wife, Cheryl

PUBLISHER Donald Fowley
EXECUTIVE EDITOR Christopher DeJohn
ASSOCIATE EDITOR Brian Kamins
PROJECT EDITOR Ed Brislin
EDITORIAL ASSISTANT Karolina Zarychta
SENIOR PRODUCTION EDITOR Lisa Wojcik
EXECUTIVE MARKETING MANAGER Clay Stone
MARKETING ASSISTANT Tierra Morgan
SENIOR DESIGNER Madelyn Lesure
TEXT DESIGNER Lee Goldstein
COVER PHOTO Reimar Gaertner/Almay Limited
SENIOR ILLUSTRATION EDITOR Anna Melhorn
SENIOR PHOTO EDITOR Elle Wagner
SENIOR MEDIA EDITOR Allison Morris
CHAPTER OPENING ART Michael Jung
ANNIVERSARY LOG DESIGN Richard Pacifico

This book was set in 10/12 New Aster by GGS Book Services and printed and bound by Von Hoffmann Press
This book is printed on acid free paper. ∞

To order books or for customer service please, call 1-800-CALL WILEY (225-5945).
ISBN-13 978-0-470-03815-4
ISBN-10 0-470-03815-2

Printed in the United States of America

10 9 8 7 6 5 4 3 2 1

Surge Performance Beverage Company

CHAPTER 1

LEARNING OBJECTIVES

1. State the primary goal of managerial accounting.
2. Describe how budgets are used in planning.
3. Describe how performance reports are used in the control process.
4. Distinguish between financial and managerial accounting.
5. Define cost terms used in planning, control, and decision making.
6. Explain the two key ideas in managerial accounting.
7. Discuss the impact of information technology on competition, business processes, and the interactions companies have with suppliers and customers.
8. Describe a framework for ethical decision making.
9. Discuss the duties of the controller, the treasurer, the chief information officer (CIO), and the chief financial officer (CFO).

MANAGERIAL ACCOUNTING IN THE INFORMATION AGE

What type of job will you hold in the future? You may be a marketing manager for a consumer electronics firm, you may be the director of human resources for a biotech firm, or you may be the president of your own company. In these and other managerial positions you will have to plan operations, evaluate subordinates, and make a variety of decisions using accounting information. In some cases, you will find information from your firm's balance sheet, income statement, statement of retained earnings, and statement of cash flows to be useful. However, much of the information in these statements is more relevant to *external* users of accounting information, such as stockholders and creditors. In addition, you will need information prepared specifically for firm managers, the *internal* users of accounting information. This type of information is referred to as managerial accounting information.

If you are like most users of this book, you have already studied financial accounting. Financial accounting stresses accounting concepts and procedures that relate to preparing reports for external users of accounting information. In comparison, **managerial accounting** stresses accounting concepts and procedures that are relevant to preparing reports for internal users of accounting information. This book is devoted to the subject of managerial accounting, and this first chapter provides an overview of the role of managerial accounting in planning, control, and decision making. The chapter also defines important cost concepts, and introduces key ideas that will be emphasized throughout the text. The chapter ends with a discussion of the information age and the impact of information technology on business, a framework for ethical decision making, and the role of the controller as the top management accountant. Note that you can enhance and test your knowledge of the chapter using Wiley's online resources and the self-assessment quiz at the end of the chapter.

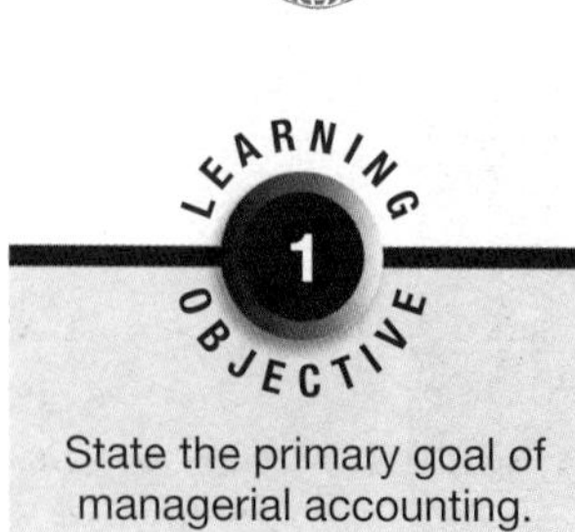

State the primary goal of managerial accounting.

GOAL OF MANAGERIAL ACCOUNTING

Virtually all managers need to plan and control their operations and make a variety of decisions. The goal of managerial accounting is to provide the information they need for *planning, control,* and *decision making*. If *your* goal is to be an effective manager, a thorough understanding of managerial accounting is essential.

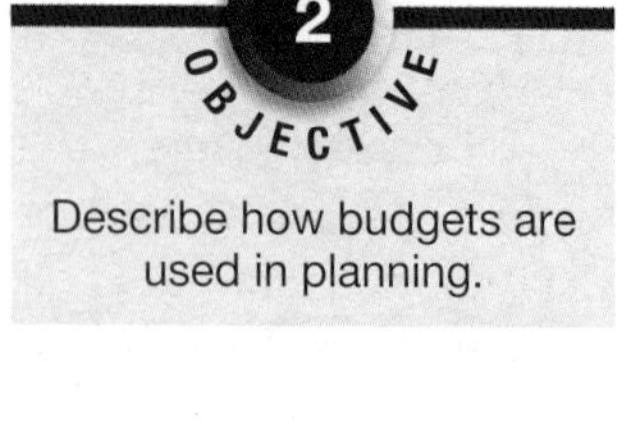

Describe how budgets are used in planning.

PLANNING

Planning is a key activity for all companies. A plan communicates a company's goals to employees aiding coordination of various functions such as sales and production. A plan also specifies the resources needed to achieve company goals.

Budgets for Planning. The financial plans prepared by managerial accountants are referred to as **budgets**. A wide variety of budgets may be prepared. For example, a *profit budget* indicates planned income, a *cash-flow budget* indicates planned cash inflows and outflows, and a *production budget* indicates the planned quantity of production and the expected costs.

Consider the production budget for Surge Performance Beverage Company. In the coming year, the company plans to produce 5,000,000 12-ounce bottles. This amount is based on forecasted sales. To produce this volume, the company estimates it will spend $1,500,000 on bottles, $400,000 on ingredients, $150,000 on water, and pay workers at its bottling plant $300,000. It also expects to pay $60,000 for rent, incur $80,000 of depreciation of equipment, and pay $100,000 for other costs. The production cost budget presented in Illustration 1-1 summarizes this information. This budget informs the managers of Surge about how many bottles the company intends to produce and what the necessary resources will cost.

Describe how performance reports are used in the control process.

CONTROL

Control of organizations is achieved by evaluating the performance of *managers* and the *operations* for which they are responsible. The distinction between evaluating managers and evaluating the operations they control is important. Managers are evaluated to determine how their performance should be rewarded or punished, which in turn motivates them to perform at a high level. Based on an evaluation indicating good performance, a manager might receive a substantial

Illustration 1-1
Production cost budget

SURGE PERFORMANCE BEVERAGE COMPANY

Budgeted Production Costs
For the Year Ended December 31, 2006

Budgeted Production	**5,000,000 Bottles**
Cost of bottles	$1,500,000
Ingredient cost	400,000
Water	150,000
Labor cost	300,000
Rent	60,000
Depreciation	80,000
Other	100,000
Total budgeted production cost	$2,590,000

Managerial accounting information is used to plan and control operations and make decisions at Surge Performance Beverage Company.

bonus. An evaluation indicating a manager performed poorly might lead to the manager being fired. In part because evaluations of managers are typically tied to compensation and promotion opportunities, managers work hard to ensure that they will receive favorable evaluations. (Of course, managers may also work hard because they love their jobs, receive respect from coworkers, or value the sense of accomplishment from a job well done!)

Operations are evaluated to provide information as to whether or not they should be changed (i.e., expanded, contracted, or modified in some way). An evaluation of an operation can be negative even when the evaluation of the manager responsible for the operation is basically positive. For example, the manager of one of the two bottling plants at Surge Performance Beverage Company may do a good job of controlling costs and meeting deadlines given that the plant is old and out of date. Still, senior management may decide to close the plant because, given the outdated equipment in the plant, it is not an efficient operation. In this scenario, the manager receives a positive evaluation whereas the operation receives a negative evaluation.

Company plans often play an important role in the control process. Managers can compare actual results with planned results and decide if corrective action is necessary. If actual results differ from the plan, the plan may not have been followed properly; the plan may have not have been well thought out; or changing circumstances may have made the plan out of date.

Illustration 1-2 presents the major steps in the planning and control process. Once a plan has been made, actions are taken to implement it. These actions lead to results that are compared with the original plan. Based on this evaluation, managers are rewarded (e.g., given substantial bonuses or promoted if performance is judged to be good) or punished (e.g., given only a small bonus, given no bonus, or even fired if performance is judged to be poor). Also, based on the evaluation process, operations may be changed. Changes may consist of expanding (e.g., adding a second shift), contracting (e.g., closing a production plant), or improving operations (e.g., training employees to do a better job answering customer product inquiries). Changes may also consist of revising an unrealistic plan.

Performance Reports for Control. The reports used to evaluate the performance of managers and the operations they control are referred to as **performance reports**. Although there is no generally accepted method of preparing a performance report,

Illustration 1-2
Planning and control process

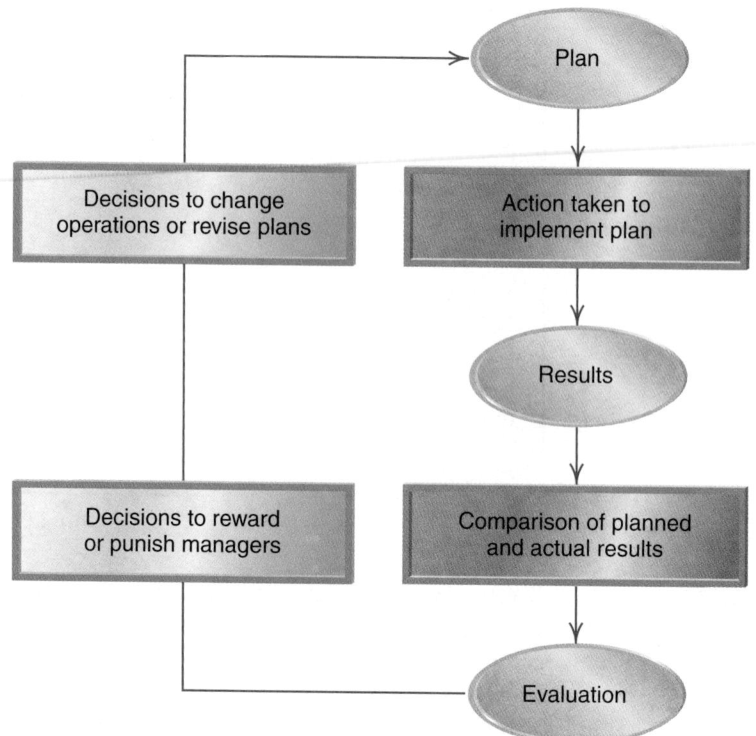

such reports frequently involve a comparison of current period performance with performance in a prior period or with planned (budgeted) performance.

Suppose, for example, that during 2006, Surge Performance Beverage Company actually produced 5,000,000 bottles and incurred the following costs:

Cost of bottles	$1,650,000
Ingredient cost	450,000
Water	152,000
Labor cost	295,000
Rent	60,000
Depreciation	80,000
Other	101,000
Total actual production cost	$2,788,000

A performance report comparing these actual costs to the budgeted costs is presented in Illustration 1-3.

Typically, performance reports only suggest areas that should be investigated; they do not provide definitive information on performance. For example, the performance report presented in Illustration 1-3 indicates that something may be amiss in the control of bottle and ingredient cost. Actual costs are $150,000 more than planned for bottles and $50,000 more than planned for ingredients. There are many possible reasons why these costs are greater than the amounts budgeted. Perhaps the price of bottles or key ingredients increased, or perhaps bottles were damaged in the production process. Management must investigate these possibilities before taking appropriate corrective action.

Although performance reports may not provide definitive answers, they are still extremely useful. Managers can use them to "flag" areas that need closer attention and to avoid areas that are under control. It would not seem necessary, for ex-

Illustration 1-3
Performance report

SURGE PERFORMANCE BEVERAGE COMPANY

Performance Report, Production Costs
For the Year Ended December 31, 2006

	Actual	Budget	Difference (Actual Minus Budget)
Production (number of bottles)	5,000,000	5,000,000	-0-
Cost of bottles	$1,650,000	$1,500,000	$150,000
Ingredient cost	450,000	400,000	50,000
Water	152,000	150,000	2,000
Labor Cost	295,000	300,000	(5,000)
Rent	60,000	60,000	-0-
Depreciation	80,000	80,000	-0-
Other	101,000	100,000	1,000
Total production cost	$2,788,000	$2,590,000	$198,000

ample, to investigate labor, rent, depreciation, or other costs, because these costs are either equal to or relatively close to the planned level of cost. Typically, managers follow the principle of **management by exception** when using performance reports. This means that managers investigate departures from the plan that appear to be exceptional; they do not investigate minor departures from the plan.

DECISION MAKING

As indicated in Illustration 1-2, decision making is an integral part of the planning and control process—decisions are made to reward or punish managers, and decisions are made to change operations or revise plans. Should a firm add a new product? Should it drop an existing product? Should it manufacture a component used in assembling its major product or contract with another company to produce the component? What price should a firm charge for a new product? These questions indicate just a few of the key decisions that confront companies. And how well they make these decisions will determine future profitability and, possibly, the survival of the company. Recognizing the importance of making good decisions, we'll devote all of Chapters 7, 8, and 9 to the topic. And below you'll see that one of the two key ideas of managerial accounting relates to decision making and its focus on so-called incremental analysis. Finally, at the end of each chapter, there is a feature called MAKING BUSINESS DECISIONS. This feature will remind you of how the chapter material is linked to decision making, and it will summarize the knowledge and skills presented in the chapter that will help you make good decisions as a manager.

Distinguish between financial and managerial accounting.

A COMPARISON OF MANAGERIAL AND FINANCIAL ACCOUNTING

As suggested in the opening of this chapter, there are important differences between managerial and financial accounting:

1. Managerial accounting is directed at internal rather than external users of accounting information.
2. Managerial accounting may deviate from generally accepted accounting principles (GAAP).

3. Managerial accounting may present more detailed information.
4. Managerial accounting may present more nonmonetary information.
5. Managerial accounting places more emphasis on the future.

Internal versus External Users. Financial accounting is aimed primarily at external users of accounting information, whereas managerial accounting is aimed primarily at internal users (i.e., company managers). External users include investors, creditors, and government agencies, who need information to make investment, lending, and regulation decisions. Their information needs differ from those of internal users, who need information for planning, control, and decision making.

Need to Use GAAP. Much of financial accounting information is required. The Securities and Exchange Commission (SEC) requires large, publicly traded companies to prepare reports in accordance with generally accepted accounting principles (GAAP). Even companies that are not under the jurisdiction of the SEC prepare financial accounting information in accordance with GAAP to satisfy creditors. Managerial accounting, on the other hand, is completely optional. It stresses information that is *useful* to internal managers for planning, control, and decision making. If a managerial accountant believes that deviating from GAAP will provide more useful information to managers, GAAP need not be followed.

Detail of Information. Financial accounting presents information in a highly summarized form. Net income, for example, is presented for the company as a whole. To run a company, however, managers need more detailed information, for example, information about the cost of operating individual departments versus the cost of operating the company as a whole or sales byproduct versus total company sales.

Emphasis on Nonmonetary Information. Both managerial and financial accounting reports generally contain monetary information (information expressed in dollars such as revenue and expense). But, managerial accounting reports can also contain a substantial amount of nonmonetary information. The quantity of material consumed in production, the number of hours worked by the office staff, and the number of product defects are examples of important nonmonetary data that appear in managerial accounting reports.

Emphasis on the Future. Financial accounting is primarily concerned with presenting the results of past transactions. Managerial accounting, on the other hand, places considerable emphasis on the future. As indicated previously, one of the primary purposes of managerial accounting is planning. Thus, managerial accounting information often involves estimates of the costs and benefits of future transactions.

SIMILARITIES BETWEEN FINANCIAL AND MANAGERIAL ACCOUNTING

We shouldn't overstate the differences between financial accounting and managerial accounting in terms of their respective user groups. Financial accounting reports are aimed *primarily* at external users, and managerial accounting reports are aimed *primarily* at internal users. However, managers also make significant use of financial accounting reports, and external users occasionally request financial information that is generally considered appropriate for internal users. For example, creditors may ask management to provide them with detailed cash-flow projections.

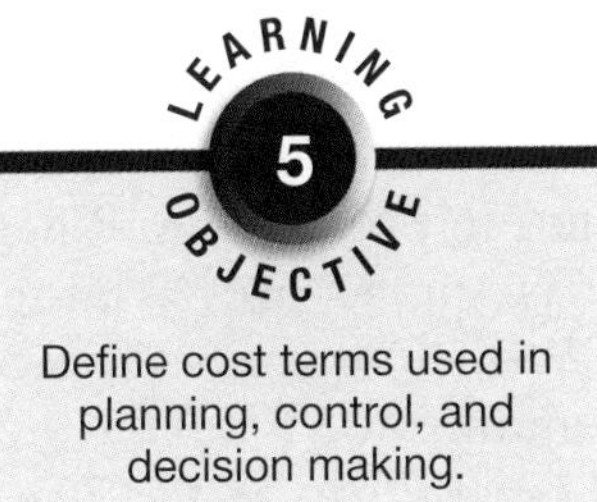

Define cost terms used in planning, control, and decision making.

COST TERMS USED IN DISCUSSING PLANNING, CONTROL, AND DECISION MAKING

When managers discuss planning, control, and decision making, they frequently use the word *cost*. Unfortunately, what they mean by this word is often ambiguous. This section defines key cost terms so that you will have the accounting vocabulary necessary to discuss issues related to planning, control, and decision making. The discussion will be brief because we will return to these cost terms and examine them in detail in later chapters.

VARIABLE AND FIXED COSTS

The classification of a cost as variable or fixed depends on how the cost changes in relation to changes in the level of business activity.

Variable Costs. Costs that increase or decrease in proportion to increases or decreases in the level of business activity are **variable costs**. Material and direct labor are generally considered to be variable costs because in many situations they fluctuate in proportion to changes in production (business activity). Suppose that for Surge Performance Beverage Company the cost of bottles, ingredients, water and labor are variable costs and in the prior month when production was 400,000 bottles, costs were $120,000 for bottles, $32,000 for ingredients, $12,000 for water and $24,000 for labor. How much variable cost should the company plan on for the current month if production is expected to increase by 20 percent to 480,000 bottles? Since the variable costs change in proportion to changes in activity, if production increases by 20 percent, these costs should also increase by 20 percent. Thus, the cost of bottles should increase to $144,000, the cost of ingredients should increase to $38,400, the cost of water to $14,400 and the cost of labor to $28,800.

	Prior Month		Current Month	
Production	400,000 Bottles	Per Unit	480,000 Bottles	Per Unit
Variable costs:				
Cost of bottles	$120,000	$0.30	$144,000	$0.30
Ingredient cost	32,000	0.08	38,400	0.08
Water	12,000	0.03	14,400	0.03
Labor cost	24,000	0.06	28,800	0.06
Total variable cost	$188,000	$0.47	$225,600	$0.47

Note that although the *total variable cost* increases from $188,000 to $225,600 when production changes from 400,000 to 480,000 units, the *variable cost per unit* does not change. It remains $0.47 per bottle. With variable cost of $0.47 per bottle, variable cost increases by $37,600 (i.e., $0.47 × 80,000) when production increases by 80,000 bottles.

Fixed Costs. Costs that remain constant when there are changes in the level of business activity are **fixed costs**. Depreciation and rent are costs that typically do not change with changes in business activity. Suppose that in the prior month, Surge Performance Beverage Company incurred $20,000 of fixed costs including $5,000 of rent, $6,667 of depreciation, and $8,333 of other miscellaneous fixed costs. If the company increases production to 480,000 bottles in the current month, the levels of rent, depreciation, and other fixed costs incurred should remain the same as when production was only 400,000 bottles. However, with fixed costs, the cost per unit does change when there are changes in production. When production increases, the constant amount of fixed cost is spread over a larger number of units. This drives down the fixed cost per unit. With an increase in production from 400,000 to 480,000 units, *total fixed costs* remains at $20,000. Note, however, that *fixed cost per unit* decreases from $0.0500 per unit to $0.0417 per unit.

	Prior Month		Current Month	
Production	400,000 Bottles	Per Unit	480,000 Bottles	Per Unit
Fixed costs:				
Rent	$ 5,000	$0.0125	$ 5,000	$0.0104
Depreciation	6,667	0.0167	6,667	0.0139
Other	8,333	0.0208	8,333	0.0174
Total fixed cost	$20,000	$0.0500	$20,000	$0.0417

SUNK COSTS

Costs incurred in the past are referred to as **sunk costs**. These costs are not relevant to present decisions, because they do not change when these decisions are made. For example, suppose you buy a ticket to a play for $30. Before the play, you run into a friend who invites you to a party. If you go to the party you won't be able to attend the play. The cost of the ticket is irrelevant to the decision as to whether or not you should go to the party. What matters is how much you will enjoy the party versus the play and how much you can *sell* the ticket for (not how much you *paid* for it). Whether you go to the play or go to the party, you are out $30 (the price of the ticket to the play, which is sunk).

OPPORTUNITY COSTS

The values of benefits foregone when one decision alternative is selected over another are **opportunity costs**. For example, suppose Surge Performance Beverage Company refuses an order to produce 50,000 bottles for a grocery chain because taking on the order will require the company to miss delivery deadlines on orders already taken. Suppose the order would have generated $50,000 of additional revenue (the product sells for $1 per bottle) and $23,500 of additional costs. Then the opportunity cost (the net benefit foregone) associated with meeting current delivery deadlines is $26,500 ($50,000 – $23,500).

DIRECT AND INDIRECT COSTS

Costs that are directly traceable to a product, activity, or department are **direct costs**. **Indirect costs** are those that either cannot be directly traced to a product, activity, or department, or are not worth tracing. The distinction between a direct

Illustration 1-4
Insurance as both a direct and indirect cost

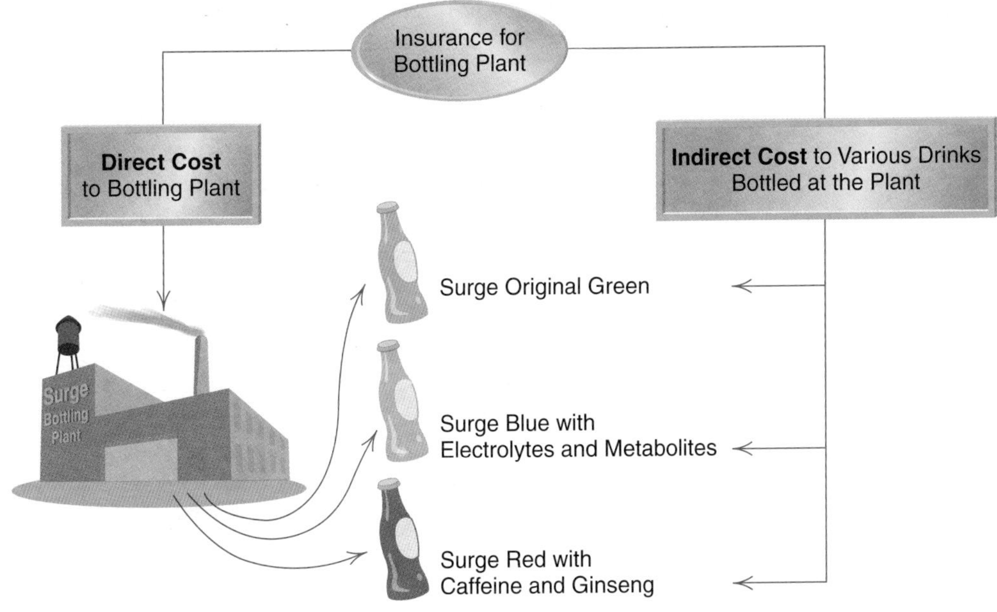

and an indirect cost depends on the object of the cost tracing. For example, Surge Performance Beverage Company has a production facility in Memphis for which it incurs insurance costs. The insurance cost related to the Memphis plant is obviously a direct cost of the Memphis plant. However, the insurance cost is an indirect cost of the individual types of sports drinks produced in the Memphis plant because *direct* tracing of the insurance cost to each type of drink is not possible. This situation is presented in Illustration 1-4.

CONTROLLABLE AND NONCONTROLLABLE COSTS

A manager can influence a **controllable cost** but cannot influence a **noncontrollable cost**. The distinction between controllable and noncontrollable costs is especially important when evaluating manager performance. A manager should not be evaluated unfavorably if a noncontrollable cost sharply increases.

As an example of controllable and noncontrollable costs, consider a plant supervisor. This individual influences labor and material costs by scheduling workers and assuring an efficient production process. Thus, labor and material costs are the supervisor's controllable costs. However, the supervisor cannot determine insurance for a plant. A plant manager or an insurance specialist makes decisions regarding insurance. Therefore, insurance cost is a supervisor's noncontrollable cost but a plant manager's or an insurance specialist's controllable cost.

Explain the two key ideas in managerial accounting.

TWO KEY IDEAS IN MANAGERIAL ACCOUNTING

The subject of managerial accounting has many concepts. However, two ideas are fundamental to understanding the use of managerial accounting information in planning, control, and decision making. Keep these two ideas in mind as you progress through your business career—you'll find them to be invaluable!

Because the ideas are so important, one or both will be emphasized in each chapter of the book and identified with an icon.

1. **Decision making relies on incremental analysis—an analysis of the revenues that increase (decrease) and the costs that increase (decrease) if a decision alternative is selected.**
2. **You get what you measure!**

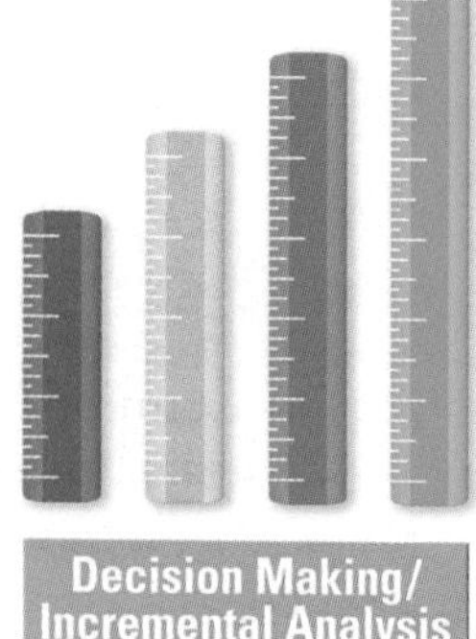

DECISION MAKING RELIES ON INCREMENTAL ANALYSIS

Incremental analysis is the appropriate way to approach the solution to all business problems. Essentially, **incremental analysis** involves the calculation of the difference in revenue and the difference in cost between decision alternatives. The difference in revenue is the **incremental revenue** of one alternative over another, whereas the difference in cost is the **incremental cost** of one alternative over another. If an alternative yields an incremental profit (the difference between incremental revenue and incremental cost), it is the preferred alternative. In the simplified example that follows, decision alternative 1 should be selected because, compared with alternative 2, it yields an incremental profit of $3,000.

Comparison of Decision Alternatives

	Alternative One		Alternative Two			
Revenue	$15,000	–	$10,000	=	$5,000	Incremental Revenue
Cost	8,000	–	6,000	=	2,000	Incremental Cost
Profit	$ 7,000	–	$ 4,000	=	$3,000	Incremental Profit

Although the idea is simple, implementing it in practice can be difficult—that's why we devote all of Chapters 7, 8, and 9 to decision making. For now, let's look at a decision facing Surge Performance Beverage Company to gain a better understanding of incremental analysis.

Recall that at Surge Performance Beverage Company, the budgeted annual production costs for 5,000,000 bottles was $2,590,000 as follows:

Production	5,000,000 bottles
Cost of bottles	$1,500,000
Ingredient cost	400,000
Water	150,000
Labor cost	300,000
Rent	60,000
Depreciation	80,000
Other	100,000
Total production cost	$2,590,000
Cost per unit	$0.518

Currently, Surge sells its product only to grocery and health food stores at $1 per bottle. Now, assume that Surge is approached by a dairy company that offers to buy 200,000 bottles in the coming year for $0.75 per bottle. The dairy plans to use the drink as an ingredient in a new line of frozen yogurt energy bars. In this case there are two decision alternatives: (1) stick with the status quo and decline the offer or (2) accept the offer.

If the offer is accepted, incremental revenue (the increase in revenue due to accepting the offer versus declining the offer) will be $150,000 and incremental cost (the increase in cost due to accepting the offer versus declining the offer) will be $94,000. Thus, the incremental profit of accepting the offer is $56,000. Assuming that the company has the capacity to produce the additional 200,000 bottles and that other orders will not have to be turned down if this large order is accepted (i.e., assuming there are no opportunity costs), Surge Performance Beverage Company should accept this order.

Incremental revenue ($.75 × 200,000 bottles)		$150,000
Less incremental costs:		
Increase in cost of bottles ($.30 × 200,000)	$60,000	
Increase in cost of ingredients ($.08 × 200,000)	16,000	
Increase in cost of water ($.03 × 200,000)	6,000	
Increase in cost of labor ($.06 × 200,000)	12,000	94,000
Incremental profit		$ 56,000

Note that in the analysis, we use only four of the production cost items (cost of bottles, cost of ingredients, cost of water and cost of labor). These are the only costs that increase with the new order, because all other costs (rent, depreciation, and other) are fixed and will not increase with an increase in production. Therefore, they are not incremental costs and are not relevant to the decision at hand. Think about rent expense. If the special order is rejected, rent expense will be $60,000. If the special order is accepted, rent expense will still be $60,000. Since rent expense does not change, it is not incremental, and it is not relevant in analyzing the decision.

YOU GET WHAT YOU MEASURE!

The second key idea in managerial accounting is "You get what you measure!" In other words, performance measures greatly influence the behavior of managers.

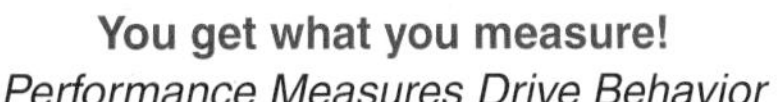

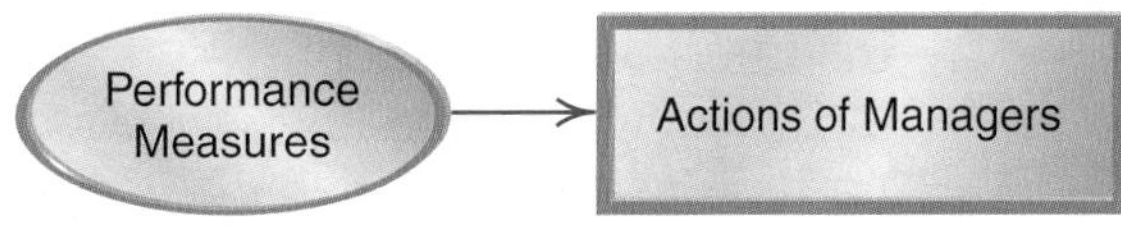

Companies can select from a vast number of performance measures when deciding how they want to assess performance. Profit, market share, sales to new customers, product development time, number of defective units produced, and number of late deliveries are examples of measures in common use. Because rewards often depend on how well an employee performs on a particular measure, employees direct their attention to what is measured and may neglect what isn't measured.

For example, suppose that at Surge Performance Beverage Company, sales to new customers is introduced as a primary measure of the performance of the sales manager. How would this influence the behavior of the sales manager? Most likely, this measure will lead the manager to spend more time developing business with new customers. Although that may be just what senior management wants from the performance measure, it could lead to problems. Suppose a sales manager greatly reduces the time spent attending to the needs of existing customers, and the company loses the business of several key accounts. To avoid this and other unintended consequences, companies need to develop a balanced set of performance measures and avoid placing too much emphasis on any single measure.

Discuss the impact of information technology on competition, business processes, and the interactions companies have with suppliers and customers.

THE INFORMATION AGE AND MANAGERIAL ACCOUNTING

In recent years, advances in information technology have radically changed access to information and, in consequence, the business landscape—so much so, that the current business era is frequently referred to as the *information age*. Since managerial accounting is about *providing information* in order to plan and control operations and to make decisions, part and parcel of an understanding of managerial accounting is an understanding of the impact of information technology on competition, business processes, and the interactions companies have with suppliers and customers. These topics are discussed in this section.

COMPETITION AND INFORMATION TECHNOLOGY

Business competition since the 1970s has been intense. Deregulation of airlines and banking, dropping of trade barriers in response to both the North American Free Trade Agreement (NAFTA), the Central American Free Trade Agreement (CAFTA), and the organization of the European Union, and economic development in Asia have all played a role. Advances in information technology are also redefining the meaning of intense competition. Consider the impact of exchanges: Web sites that are used to conduct auctions. ChemConnect, for example, operates a public on-line marketplace that brings together buyers and sellers of chemicals and plastics. Using their site, a company can place an order for a plastics stabilizer and receive a bid from a U.S. company in minutes, if not seconds. The problem for the potential U.S. supplier, however, is that it will be bidding against other U.S. companies as well as competitors from Asia and Europe whose prices will also be posted almost instantaneously. Local U.S. companies also face stiff competition from online businesses operating in other states. In many cases, consumers will shop their local store to examine merchandise but then make their purchase over the Internet from an out-of-state company with a lower price. But while advances in information technology have increased competition, they have also created opportunities and cost savings for firms that use information for strategic advantage in dealing with customers, suppliers, and improving internal processes.

THE IMPACT OF INFORMATION TECHNOLOGY ON MANAGEMENT OF THE VALUE CHAIN

The **value chain** comprises a company's internal operations and its relationships and interactions with suppliers and customers that are aimed at creating maximum value for the least possible cost. Illustration 1-5 presents a picture of the

Illustration 1-5
The value chain for Milano Clothiers

value chain for Milano Clothiers. Milano has 35 stores throughout the United States and annual sales of over $800 million. For Milano to be successful, its suppliers must provide high quality items, on time, to the right location, at a reasonable price. Also, Milano's own operations must be efficient. It must be able to market effectively and offer products that customers want. How can Milano ensure that this happens? The key is to take advantage of information flows up and down the value chain. This is where advances in information technology are having an impact. Note that in Illustration 1-5 the lines between suppliers and Milano and between customers and Milano are dashed lines. This represents the fact that the organizational boundaries are somewhat permeable because a lot of information is being transmitted both ways. Let's see some examples of how this works.

Information Flows between Milano and Customers. When customers make purchases, a Milano employee scans a bar code attached to the sale item thereby automatically transferring the sale information into a database. This information can be used to update inventory records and ensure the company does not run out of "hot" items. The database also provides information on slow moving merchandise that Milano can sell to a discount department store so that it doesn't take up valuable floor space. Further analysis of the sales data can reveal regional tastes in clothes helping Milano to buy the right styles for stores in different parts of the country. Milano may also track the buying patterns of customers who identify themselves by using Milano's credit card or a special customer discount card. This information can help Milano direct targeted selling messages to different customer types via direct-mail advertising.

Information Flows between Milano and Suppliers. With several key suppliers, Milano has set up processes whereby the suppliers monitor Milano's sales of their merchandise using information from Milano's internal data base. Milano shares this information because the suppliers use it to improve their production scheduling, gain efficiencies, and pass along some of the related cost savings to Milano in the form of lower prices. Milano also tracks the status of its orders using its suppliers' Web sites. Thus, Milano knows the exact time merchandise will be arriving at each of its locations, and this information is available any time of the day. Milano uses this information, in part, to time its advertising campaigns.

Using Information Technology to Gain Internal Efficiencies. Internally, Milano uses information technology to automate purchasing and accounts payable, sales and customer billing, as well as other accounting and finance functions. While in the past the company could not close its books until one month after year end, it can now close in a week. This provides senior managers with timely information on the company's profitability and allows the company to provide timely financial reports to shareholders. The company has over 2,000 employees. Each employee has access to a company human resources (HR) Web site that provides comprehensive information on company policies and allows employees to select from a menu of alternative health and retirement plans. The launch of the Web site has eliminated the need for five full-time HR staff who previously responded to employee questions and processed paperwork.

SOFTWARE SYSTEMS THAT IMPACT VALUE CHAIN MANAGEMENT

Companies use a variety of software systems to process information and improve the operation of the value chain. Here, we'll briefly discuss three systems: Enterprise Resource Planning (ERP) systems, Supply Chain Management (SCM) systems, and Customer Relationship Management systems (CRM).

Enterprise Resource Planning Systems. ERP systems grew out of material requirements planning (MRP) systems that have been used for more than 20 years. MRP systems computerized inventory control and production planning. Key features included an ability to prepare a master production schedule, a bill of materials, and generate purchase orders. ERP systems update MRP systems with better integration, relational databases, and graphical user interfaces. Features now encompass accounting and finance, human resources, and various e-commerce applications including SCM and CRM which are discussed next.

Supply Chain Management Systems. Supply chain management (SCM) is the organization of activities between a company and its suppliers in an effort to provide for the profitable development, production, and delivery of goods to customers. By sharing information, production lead times and inventory holding costs have been reduced, while on-time deliveries to customers have been improved. SCM software systems support the planning of the best way to fill orders and help tracking of products and components among companies in the supply chain. Wal-Mart and Procter & Gamble (P&G) are two companies that have become well known for their cooperation in the use of SCM. When P&G products are scanned at a Wal-Mart store, P&G receives information on the sale via satellite and, thus, knows when to make more product and the specific Wal-Mart stores to which the product should be shipped. Related cost savings are passed on, at least in part, to Wal-Mart customers.

Customer Relationship Management Systems. CRM systems automate customer service and support. They also provide for customer data analysis and support e-commerce storefronts. While CRM is constantly evolving, it has already led to some remarkable changes in the way companies interact with customers. For example, Federal Express allows customers to track their packages on the Web. This service is becoming commonplace, but it didn't exist 10 years ago. Amazon.com uses CRM technology to make suggestions to customers based on their personal purchase histories. The ultimate development of CRM remains to be seen but undoubtedly mobile communication will play a significant role. Many companies are already experimenting with systems to send messages to cell phone users offering them special discounts and buying "opportunities."

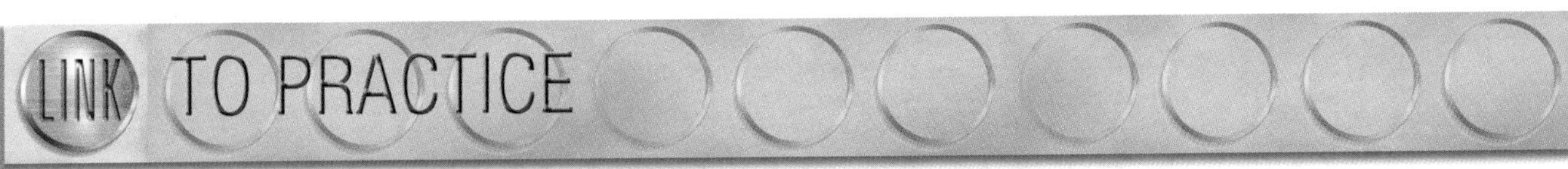

Examples of the Impact of SCM

We noted in the text that supply chain management (SCM) systems utilize improved information flows to reduce costs and improve delivery times. As noted by Mitch Myers, vice president of operations at FW Murphy, an instrument manufacturer in Tulsa, information is replacing crude prediction. "We want to be fast and flexible. We don't want to be dependent on predictions about what's going to happen, like some psychic on a 1-900 number." Here are some additional examples of what's going on with respect to SCM:

1. Dell, long a leader in supply chain management, sends real-time data to suppliers every two hours. Dell is also a leader in rapid inventory turnover.
2. Procter and Gamble is filling retailers' requests for products as diverse as Pringles and Ivory Soap in less than 72 hours.
3. At Russ Berrie & Co., a manufacturer of specialty gift items such as scented candles, managers receive replenishment information weekly from grocery-store operators. Previously, the company admitted that it based production on educated guesses as to what stores needed.
4. At Memphis-based Smith & Nephew Orthopedics, the company has reduced the turnaround time on one set of medical-implant instruments from six months to two days. The company attributes the improvement to better use of technology. One example—product information is scanned into a handheld device as soon as a surgical procedure is completed. The data is then uploaded into Smith & Nephew's purchase-order system.

Source: John Goff, "Start With Demand," *CFO magazine* (January 2005), pp. 53–57.

Describe a framework for ethical decision making.

ETHICAL CONSIDERATIONS IN MANAGERIAL DECISION MAKING

Remember that when we discuss decision making throughout this book, we will focus on incremental analysis as the approach to making good decisions. However, in addition to performing incremental analysis, it is equally important that managers consider the ethical aspects of their decisions. Why focus on ethics? First and foremost, ethical decision making is simply the "right thing to do." But additionally, when managers behave ethically, they gain the confidence of their customers, suppliers, subordinates, and company stockholders and that confidence is likely to translate into gains to the bottom line and the company stock price.

ETHICAL AND UNETHICAL BEHAVIOR

Ethical behavior requires that managers recognize the difference between what's right and what's wrong and then make decisions consistent with what's right. In recent years, we've witnessed a plethora of disclosures, indictments, and convictions, indicating that key managers in major companies either can't tell right from wrong or don't care to make decisions consistent with what's right. Some examples:

> Enron managers mislead investors by hiding debt in so-called special purpose entities. Kenneth Lay, Enron's CEO, touted Enron's stock to employees just weeks before the energy company imploded leaving many with worthless 401(k) retirement accounts.
>
> WorldCom, America's No. 2 long-distance company, disclosed the biggest case of fraudulent accounting in U.S. history with profits overstated by billions. The result—the company declared bankruptcy and began laying off 17,000 employees.
>
> Dennis Kozlowski, who made more than $300 million as head of Tyco, was charged with conspiring with art dealers to avoid sales tax on art he bought for $13.2 million. Tyco's share price took a nosedive following the disclosure.
>
> Sam Waksal, co-founder of ImClone Systems, was charged with insider trading for illegally tipping off family members prior to the public disclosure that the Food and Drug Administration had rejected ImClone's cancer drug.

Sarbanes-Oxley Act. The abuses cited above, along with others, led Congress to enact the Sarbanes-Oxley Act in July of 2002. This law, named after Senator Paul Sarbanes and Representative Michael Oxley, has changed the financial reporting landscape for public companies and their auditors. Some of the act's most important provisions are:

- A requirement that Chief Executive Officers and Chief Financial Officers of a company certify that, based on their knowledge, their financial statements do not contain any untrue statements or omissions of material facts that would make the statements misleading.
- A ban on certain types of work by the company's auditors to ensure their independence. For example, the act bans auditors from performing bookkeeping services and designing or implementing financial information systems for clients.

Andrew Fastow testifies as a witness in the Kenneth Lay trial.

- Longer jail sentences and larger fines for corporate executives who knowingly and willfully misstate financial statements. Fines now run up to $5 million and jail terms up to 20 years.
- A requirement that companies report on the existence and reliability of their internal controls as they relate to financial reports.

The cost of complying with Sarbanes-Oxley has been substantial. According to a survey conducted by Charles River Associates of 90 companies with average annual gross revenue of $8.1 billion, the average cost to comply with the act in the first year was $7.8 million. This amount should be contrasted with the $63 billion lost by shareholders in Enron. Will the net benefits of Sarbanes-Oxley outweigh the costs? Time will tell. There is no doubt, however, that the act has reminded corporate leaders that they have a clear obligation to ensure that financial statements do not mislead investors. And the act has put needed distance between senior managers and auditors of publicly traded companies.

In addition to conspicuous and rather clear-cut examples of unethical behavior, some companies and individuals have been accused of paying unconscionably low wages to workers in Third World countries, using child labor, endangering the environment with toxic chemicals, and bribing officials to promote sales abroad. But are these accusations clearly indicative of ethical lapses? Low wages are better than no wages, and, while child labor is reprehensible, the additional income earned by a child may save a family from starvation. The point is that ethical dilemmas are often complex and the situations managers face are often gray rather than black and white. When this is the case, a framework for ethical decision making may help understanding of "what's right."

A FRAMEWORK FOR ETHICAL DECISION MAKING

The following framework for ethical decision making consists of seven questions.[1] Hopefully, answering these questions will serve as an aid in identifying "what's right." But certainly, answering them doesn't guarantee ethical decision making.

A Seven-Question Framework for Ethical Decision Making

When evaluating a decision, ask:

1. What decision alternatives are available?
2. What individuals or organizations have a stake in the outcome of my decision?
3. Will an individual or an organization be harmed by any of the alternatives?
4. Which alternative will do the most good with the least harm?
5. Would someone I respect find any of the alternatives objectionable?

After deciding on a course of action, but before taking action, ask:

6. At a "gut level," am I comfortable with the decision I am about to make?
7. Will I be comfortable telling my friends and family about this decision?

[1]Developing these questions was aided by three resources located on the Web. The first is *A Guide to Moral Decision Making* by Chris MacDonald in the Department of Bioethics at Dalhousie University (http://www.ethics.ubc.ca/chrismac/publications/guide.html). The second is material developed by the *Center for Applied Ethics* at the University of British Columbia (*http://www.ethics.ubc.ca/resources/business/*), and the third is *Complete Guide to Ethics Management: An Ethics Toolkit for Managers*, by Carter MacNamera (http://www.mapnp.org/library/ethics/ethxgde.htm).

Any Questions?

Q) Why focus on the Seven-Question Framework for ethical decision making? Many, if not most, companies have a written code of ethics, so when managers make decisions, they just need to consult their company's code to determine if their decision stacks up to what's right in their company's environment.

A) Managers should definitely be familiar with their company's code of ethics. However, codes of ethics aren't always a good guide to ethical behavior. Part of the problem is that codes often specify what can't be done rather than what should be done. And some codes focus more on ensuring that decisions are legal rather than right!

A number of exercises, problems, and cases in the end-of-chapter material present ethical dilemmas, and you should refer to this framework when preparing your answers to them. Alternatively, you may wish to consider other ethical perspectives. A large amount of material is available on the Web to help your understanding of ethical decision making.

IMA STATEMENT OF ETHICAL PROFESSIONAL PRACTICE

The Institute of Management Accounting (IMA) is a professional organization that focuses, as its name indicates, on management accounting. One of the contributions of the IMA is the development of a Statement of Ethical Professional Practice which is presented in the Appendix to this chapter. The IMA has also developed an ethics helpline that members can call to discuss ethical dilemmas they face at their companies. Callers are assigned a code number to preserve anonymity and are then referred to a counselor who explains how the dilemma relates to the provisions of the standards of ethical professional practice.

The IMA also publishes *Strategic Finance* and *Management Accounting Quarterly*, and since 1973 it has conducted a comprehensive examination to test what knowledge a management accountant must have in order to be successful in a complex and fast-changing business world. More than 3,000 individuals take the exam each year. Those who pass the exam are issued a Certificate in Management Accounting and are proud to indicate the designation CMA on resumes and business cards. For details on student and professional memberships in the IMA and information on the CMA examination, visit the IMA Web site (www.imanet.org).

Discuss the duties of the controller, the treasurer, the chief information officer (CIO), and the chief financial officer (CFO).

THE CONTROLLER AS THE TOP MANAGEMENT ACCOUNTANT

Who is responsible for preparing the information needed for planning, control, and decision making? In most organizations, the top managerial accounting position is held by the controller. The **controller** prepares reports for planning and evaluating company activities (e.g., budgets and performance reports) and provides the information needed to make management decisions (e.g., decisions related to purchasing office equipment or decisions related to adding or dropping a product). The controller also has responsibility for all financial accounting reports and tax filings with the Internal Revenue Service and other taxing agencies, as well as coordinating the activities of the firm's external auditors.

A simplified example of the organization chart for the controller's office is shown in Illustration 1-6. Note that one of the areas reporting to the controller is cost accounting. Most medium-sized and large manufacturing companies have such a department. Cost accountants estimate costs to facilitate management decisions and develop cost information for purposes of valuing inventory.

Many companies seeking to fill the position of controller send a clear message to applicants; "Bean counters need not apply!" This means that they want a managerial accountant who does more than concentrate on tracking costs ("counting beans"). They want an individual who will be an integral part of the top management team.

It is obvious that if you want a high-level career in managerial accounting you will need strong accounting skills. But this is not enough. To be an important player on the management team, you will need the skills required of all high-level executives: excellent written and oral communication skills, solid interpersonal skills, and a deep knowledge of the industry in which your firm competes.

In addition to the position of controller, many companies have positions called treasurer and chief information officer (CIO). The **treasurer** has custody of cash and funds invested in various marketable securities. In addition to money management duties, the treasurer is generally responsible for maintaining relationships with investors, banks, and other creditors. Thus, the treasurer plays a major role in managing cash and marketable securities, preparing cash forecasts, and obtaining financing from banks and other lenders. The **chief information officer (CIO)** is the person responsible for a company's information technology and computer systems. Both the controller and the treasurer report to the **chief financial officer (CFO)** who is the senior executive responsible for both accounting and financial operations. At some companies, the CIO also reports to the CFO. However, as we saw earlier, information technology is playing a critical role in managing the value chain and, therefore, it's not surprising that the CIO is frequently part of the senior management team reporting directly to the chief executive officer (CEO).

Illustration 1-6
Organization chart for the controller's office

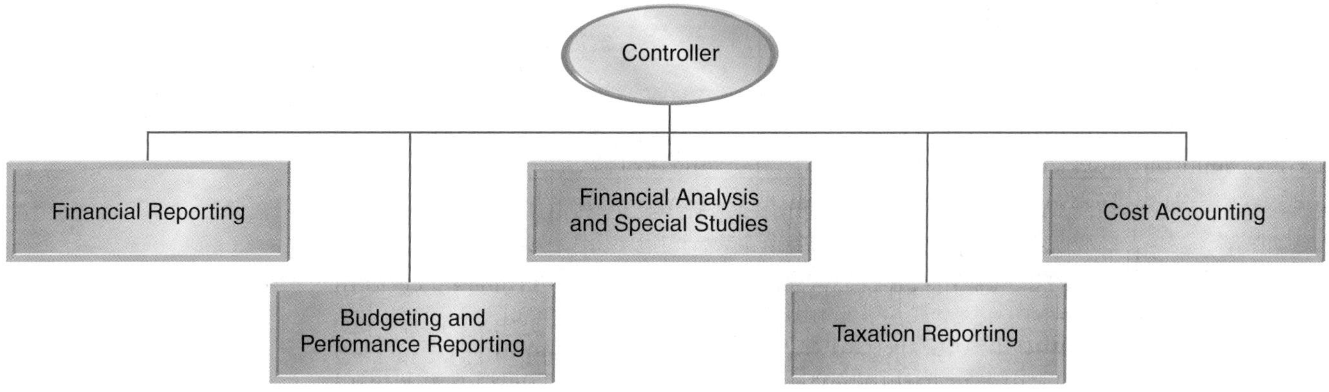

Japanese Companies Creating a New Executive Position—The CFO!

Unlike their U.S. counterparts, most Japanese companies don't have a chief financial officer (CFO), but the situation is changing. In 1999, Sony hired its first CFO and in 2002, Fujitsu, a large chip and computer company, did the same. Why the move to a CFO position? A lot has to do with Japan's economic woes over the last several years. The number of Japanese companies that failed in 2002 is at the third highest level since the 1940s. Also, Japan's banks have their own financial problems, and no longer lend funds to companies just because they are part of the same *keiretsu* (a group of corporations that holds shares in each other's companies and provides mutual support). In this environment, the need for an executive who understands financial markets and who can communicate with investors is crucial, so more and more Japanese companies are hiring their first CFO.

Source: CFO, The Magazine for Senior Financial Executives, Carla Rapoport, July 2002, p. 54–58.

MAKING BUSINESS DECISIONS

As we learned in the chapter, decisions are made to reward or punish managers and to change operations or revise plans. Should a company add a new product? Should it drop an existing product? Should a company outsource a business process or perform it internally? What price should a company charge for a new product? Appropriate answers to these types of questions are critical to firm profitability and much of this book will focus on how to address them. While "gut feel" will always play a role in decision making, so too will careful analysis. And the type of analysis we focus on is called incremental analysis, which is an analysis of the costs and revenues that change when one decision alternative is selected over another.

KNOWLEDGE AND SKILLS (K/S) CHECKLIST

Knowledge and skills are needed to make good business decisions. Check off the knowledge and skills you've acquired from reading this chapter.

- ❒ K/S 1. You have an expanded business vocabulary (see key terms).
- ❒ K/S 2. You understand that incremental analysis is used in decision making.
- ❒ K/S 3. You have a framework for ethical decision making.
- ❒ K/S 4. You know that performance measures impact manager behaviors.
- ❒ K/S 5. You understand that information technology is having a major impact on information flows up and down the value chain.

SUMMARY OF LEARNING OBJECTIVES

1 ***State the primary goal of managerial accounting.*** The primary goal of managerial accounting is to provide information that helps managers plan and control company activities and make business decisions.

2 ***Describe how budgets are used in planning.*** The financial plans prepared by managerial accountants are referred to as budgets. These plans help employees understand company goals and what resources are needed to achieve them.

3 ***Describe how performance reports are used in the control process.*** Control of organizations is achieved by evaluating the performance of managers and the operations for which they are responsible. The reports used to evaluate the performance of managers and the operations they control are referred to as performance reports. Frequently, the reports compare current period performance with performance in a prior period or to planned (budgeted) performance. Since evaluations affect the rewards and punishments managers receive, the evaluation process causes them to work hard to receive good evaluations. Evaluations may also lead to modifications in operations, as needed.

4 ***Distinguish between financial and managerial accounting.*** Managerial accounting differs from financial accounting in many ways. A key difference is that managerial accounting stresses information that is useful to firm managers, whereas financial accounting stresses information that is useful to external parties. In addition, financial accounting information must be prepared in accordance with GAAP, but managerial accounting information need not be.

5 ***Define cost terms used in planning, control, and decision making.*** A number of cost terms are used in discussing planning, control, and decision making. The terms include: *variable cost* (a cost that changes in response to a change in business activity), *fixed cost* (a cost that does not change in response to a change in business activity), *sunk cost* (a cost incurred in the past), *opportunity cost* (a benefit foregone by selecting one decision alternative over another), *direct cost* (a cost that is directly traceable to a product, activity, or department), *indirect cost* (a cost that is not directly traceable to a product, activity, or department or is not worth tracing), *controllable cost* (a cost that a manager can influence), and *noncontrollable cost* (a cost that a manager cannot influence).

6 ***Explain the two key ideas in managerial accounting.*** The first key idea is that "decision making relies on incremental analysis." This means that the solution to business problems involves the calculation of the difference in revenue (incremental revenue) and the difference in costs (incremental costs) between decision alternatives. The second key idea is that "you get what you measure!" In other words, how companies measure performance affects how managers behave. This can create problems if managers spend too much time focused on any single performance measure.

7 ***Discuss the impact of information technology on competition, business processes, and the interactions companies have with suppliers and customers.*** Information technology (IT) allows buyers to reach suppliers with whom, in the past, it would have been too costly to contract. This has had a great impact on competition. Information technology is also having a profound effect on the entire value chain. Companies use IT to coordinate activities with suppliers and to gain information on customers. IT is also being used to improve the internal processes of companies.

8 ***Describe a framework for ethical decision making.*** The framework for ethical decision making consists of seven questions. See page 19.

9 ***Discuss the duties of the controller, the treasurer, the chief information officer, and the chief financial officer.*** The controller is the top management accountant in most organizations. The controller is responsible for preparing reports for planning and evaluating company activities and for preparing information and reports needed to make management decisions. In contrast to the controller, the treasurer is responsible for maintaining relationships with investors, banks, and other creditors. The treasurer also has custody of cash and funds invested in various marketable securities. The chief information officer (CIO) is responsible for information technology. The controller and the treasurer report to the chief financial officer (CFO), who is the senior executive responsible for accounting and financial operations. The chief information officer (CIO) has historically reported to the CFO, but the trend is to have the CIO report to the chief executive officer (CEO).

APPENDIX

IMA STATEMENT OF ETHICAL PROFESSIONAL PRACTICE*

Members of IMA shall behave ethically. A commitment to ethical professional practice includes: overarching principles that express our values, and standards that guide our conduct.

PRINCIPLES

IMA's overarching ethical principles include: Honesty, Fairness, Objectivity, and Responsibility. Members shall act in accordance with these principles and shall encourage others within their organizations to adhere to them.

STANDARDS

A member's failure to comply with the following standards may result in disciplinary action.

I. Competence. Each member has a responsibility to:

1. Maintain an appropriate level of professional expertise by continually developing knowledge and skills.
2. Perform professional duties in accordance with relevant laws, regulations, and technical standards.
3. Provide decision support information and recommendations that are accurate, clear, concise, and timely.
4. Recognize and communicate professional limitations or other constraints that would preclude responsible judgment or successful performance of an activity.

II. Confidentiality. Each member has a responsibility to:

1. Keep information confidential except when disclosure is authorized or legally required.
2. Inform all relevant parties regarding appropriate use of confidential information. Monitor subordinates' activities to ensure compliance.
3. Refrain from using confidential information for unethical or illegal advantage.

III. Integrity. Each member has a responsibility to:

1. Mitigate actual conflicts of interest. Regularly communicate with business associates to avoid apparent conflicts of interest. Advise all parties of any potential conflicts.
2. Refrain from engaging in any conduct that would prejudice carrying out duties ethically.
3. Abstain from engaging in or supporting any activity that might discredit the profession.

---

*Institute of Management Accountants Statement of Ethical Professional Practice, Adapted with permission.

IV. Credibility. Each member has a responsibility to:

1. Communicate information fairly and objectively.
2. Disclose all relevant information that could reasonably be expected to influence an intended user's understanding of the reports, analyses, or recommendations.
3. Disclose delays or deficiencies in information, timeliness, processing, or internal controls in conformance with organization policy and/or applicable law.

RESOLUTION OF ETHICAL CONFLICT

In applying the Standards of Ethical Professional Practice, you may encounter problems identifying unethical behavior or resolving an ethical conflict. When faced with ethical issues, you should follow your organization's established policies on the resolution of such conflict. If these policies do not resolve the ethical conflict, you should consider the following courses of action:

1. Discuss the issue with your immediate supervisor except when it appears that the supervisor is involved. In that case, present the issue to the next level. If you cannot achieve a satisfactory resolution, submit the issue to the next management level. If your immediate superior is the chief executive officer or equivalent, the acceptable reviewing authority may be a group such as the audit committee, executive committee, board of directors, board of trustees, or owners. Contact with levels above the immediate superior should be initiated only with your superior's knowledge, assuming he or she is not involved. Communication of such problems to authorities or individuals not employed or engaged by the organization is not considered appropriate, unless you believe there is a clear violation of the law.
2. Clarify relevant ethical issues by initiating a confidential discussion with an IMA Ethics Counselor or other impartial advisor to obtain a better understanding of possible courses of action.
3. Consult your own attorney as to legal obligations and rights concerning the ethical conflict.

KEY TERMS

Budget (4)
Chief financial officer (CFO) (21)
Chief information officer (CIO) (21)
Controllable cost (11)
Controller (20)
Customer relationship management (CRM) systems (16)
Direct cost (10)
Enterprise resource planning (ERP) systems (16)
Fixed costs (10)
Incremental analysis (12)
Incremental costs (12)
Incremental revenue (12)
Indirect costs (10)
Management by exception (7)
Managerial accounting (4)
Noncontrollable costs (11)
Opportunity costs (10)
Performance report (5)
Supply chain management (SCM) systems (16)
Sunk costs (10)
Treasurer (21)
Value chain (14)
Variable costs (9)

SELF ASSESSMENT *(Answers Below)*

1. The primary goal of managerial accounting is to:

a. Provide information to current and potential investors in the company.
b. Provide information to creditors as well as current and prospective investors.
c. Provide information to creditors, taxing authorities, and current and prospective investors.
d. Provide information for planning, control, and decision making.

2. Match the following terms with the management activities described below:

a. Planning.
b. Control.
c. Decision Making.
(1) This management activity involves changing operations, revising plans, or rewarding/punishing managers.
(2) This management activity compares actual results with planned outcomes as a basis for corrective action.
(3) This management activity formulates goals, communicates them to employees, and specifies the resources needed to achieve them.

3. Which of the following statements about budgets is false?

a. Budgets may be expressed in dollars, quantities, or both.
b. Budgets may reflect projected revenues, projected expenses, projected cash flows, or projected quantities of inputs or outputs.
c. Budgets must be prepared in accordance with GAAP.
d. Budgets are useful both for planning and control.

4. Which of the following statements is false?

a. Managerial accounting statements do not necessarily comply with GAAP.
b. Financial accounting statements normally reflect more detail than would be found in managerial accounting reports.
c. Managerial accounting reports emphasize future activities and future costs.
d. Financial accounting data are directed primarily at external users rather than internal users.

5. Which of the following is most likely to be a variable cost?

a. Depreciation.
b. The cost of material used in production.
c. Rent.
d. Advertising.

6. Which of the following is most likely to be a fixed cost?

a. The cost of material used in production.
b. Rent.
c. Assembly labor cost.
d. Commissions.

7. Costs incurred in the past are:

a. Opportunity costs.
b. Direct costs.
c. Sunk costs.
d. Variable costs.

8. ________________ costs are directly traceable to a product, activity, or department, whereas ________________ costs are not.

9. The salary a student forgoes while in college is an example of:

a. Opportunity cost.
b. Direct cost.
c. Sunk cost.
d. Variable cost.

10. Which of the following is not one of the seven questions in the framework for ethical decision making?

a. Will an individual or an organization be harmed by any of the decision alternatives?
b. Would someone I respect find any of the alternatives objectionable?
c. At a "gut" level, am I comfortable with the decision I am about to make?
d. Are any of the alternatives illegal?

Answers to Self Assessment

1. d; **2.** 1-c, 2-b, 3-a; **3.** c; **4.** b; **5.** b; **6.** b; **7.** c; **8.** Direct, indirect; **9.** a; **10.** d.

INTERACTIVE LEARNING

Enhance and test your knowledge of Chapter 1 using Wiley's online resources.

1. Learning Objectives
2. Multiple Choice
3. Language of Business—Matching of Key Terms
4. Critical Thinking
5. Demonstration—Planning and control process
6. Case—ValuComp Computers; Planning and control process
7. Video—Wizards of the Coast; Use of managerial accounting

Go to our dynamic Web site for more self-assessment, Web links, and additional information.

QUESTIONS

1. What is the goal of managerial accounting?
2. In a performance report, current period performance is compared with some benchmark. What might be a useful benchmark?
3. List three differences between financial and managerial accounting.
4. List three examples of nonmonetary information that might appear in a managerial accounting report.
5. Explain the difference between fixed and variable costs.
6. Consider the manager of the home appliance department at a Sears store. For this manager, list a cost that is controllable and a cost that is non-controllable.
7. What is incremental analysis? How is the concept used in decision making?
8. What is meant by the statement "You get what you measure!"?
9. How have changes in information technology impacted management of the value chain?
10. If an action is legal, is it necessarily ethical? Explain.

EXERCISES

EXERCISE 1-1. Group Assignment A key idea in this book is that *You get what you measure!* Essentially, this means that performance measures have a great influence on the behavior of managers.

Required

Select a company with which you are familiar. Identify three performance measures that the company might use. For each measure, identify a favorable outcome and an unfavorable outcome that might occur because the measure is used to evaluate manager performance.

EXERCISE 1-2. Writing Assignment Rachel Cook owns Campus Copies, a copy business with several high-speed copy machines. One is a color copier that was purchased just last year at a cost of $25,000. Recently a salesperson got Nancy to witness a demo of a new $23,000 color copier that promises higher speed and more accurate color representation. Nancy's interested but she can't get herself to trade in a perfectly good copier for which she paid $25,000 and replace it with one that will only cost $23,000.

Required
Write a paragraph explaining why the cost of the "old" copier is irrelevant to Rachel's decision.

EXERCISE 1-3. Ethics/Internet Assignment Guthrie Wilson is an accountant at Bellwether Systems, a company that sells and installs customer relationship management (CRM) systems. The company sells third-party software at cost plus 20 percent and charges a fee of $200 per hour of installation/integration time spent on each engagement. Recently, Guthrie's boss asked him to charge 60 hours of time to the Bradley account when the time was actually worked servicing the IMG account. The rationale: "Look, IMG is a struggling start-up and they can barely afford our service. We ran over our time estimate due to some unforeseen problems, and they'll balk if we charge them for all of our time. Bradley, on the other hand, is a highly profitable company and we're providing services that are going to make them even more profitable.

They'll have no problem with their bill."

Required
Go to the Web site for the Institute of Management Accounting (http://www.imanet.org). Click on About IMA and go to their Ethics Center. Click on the code of ethics and examine the IMA's ethical standards. What do the standards suggest that Guthrie should do to resolve the issue he's facing?

EXERCISE 1-4. Budgets Megan Kelly is the chief financial officer of a chain of 25 drugstores. Explain how she can use budgets in both planning profit and controlling operations.

EXERCISE 1-5. Performance Reports Which of the following statements related to performance reports is false?

_____ a. Performance reports may provide a comparison of actual performance with planned performance.
_____ b. Performance reports may provide a comparison of actual performance with performance in a prior period.
_____ c. If actual costs exceed planned costs in a performance report, this clearly indicates managerial incompetence.
_____ d. Performance reports are used to evaluate managers and the operations they control.

EXERCISE 1-6. Performance Reports At Designs by Deirdre, the budgeted income statement for December, 2008 indicated sales of $500,000 and cost of sales of $300,000. Actual sales and cost of sales were $600,000 and $325,000, respectively. Should Deirdre Nelson, owner of the company, be concerned that cost of sales is $25,000 greater than planned? Explain the basis for your answer.

EXERCISE 1-7. Financial vs. Managerial Accounting Consider a large manufacturing company like Boeing that rewards its sales force with bonuses based on sales. For this purpose, should the company record sales when orders are placed or, to be consistent with GAAP, wait until orders are delivered?

EXERCISE 1-8. Cost Terms Identify each of the following statements with fixed costs or variable costs.

_____ a. A cost that varies in total with changes in the activity level.
_____ b. A cost that varies on a per-unit basis with changes in the activity level.
_____ c. A cost that remains fixed per unit with changes in the activity level.
_____ d. A cost that remains fixed in total with changes in the activity level.

EXERCISE 1-9. Cost Terms Indicate whether each of the following costs is most likely a fixed cost or a variable cost.

_____ a. Assembly labor.
_____ b. The cost of material used in production.
_____ c. Rent.
_____ d. Depreciation.
_____ e. Fuel cost at an airline.

EXERCISE 1-10. Cost Terms Explain how a cost can be controllable at one administrative level and noncontrollable at another administrative level.

EXERCISE 1-11. Sunk Cost Peter Takesha, the manager of testing services at a medical diagnostics firm, purchased a new lab testing machine last year for $25,000. This year a new machine, which is faster and more reliable than Peter's current model, is available in the market. In deciding whether or not to purchase the new machine, should Peter consider how much he paid for the old machine? Should Peter consider the value of the old machine in the used equipment market?

EXERCISE 1-12. Opportunity Costs Parrish Plumbing provides plumbing services to residential customers from Monday through Friday. Ken Parrish, the owner, believes that it is important for his employees to have Saturday and Sunday off to spend with their families. However, he also recognizes that this policy has implications for profitability, and he is considering staying open on Saturday.

Ken estimates that if his company stays open on Saturday, it can generate $2,000 of daily revenue each day for 52 days per year. The incremental daily costs will be $600 for labor, $400 for parts, $40 for transportation, and $100 for office staff. These costs do not include a share of monthly rent, or a share of depreciation related to office equipment.

Ken is determined not to have employees work on Sunday, but he would like to know the opportunity cost of not working on Saturday. Provide Ken with an estimate of the opportunity cost, and explain why you do not have to consider rent or depreciation of office equipment in your estimate.

EXERCISE 1-13. Opportunity Cost Zachary made plans to visit a friend in New York during the Memorial Day weekend. However, before the trip his employer asked him if he would work overtime for 16 hours at $30 per hour during the weekend. What will be the opportunity cost if Zachary decides to visit his friend in New York?

EXERCISE 1-14. Incremental Analysis Wilmington Chemicals produces a chemical, PX44, which is used to retard fading in exterior house paint. In the past year, the company produced 200,000 gallons at a total cost of $1,000,000 ($5 per gallon). The company is currently considering an order for 10,000 gallons from a paint company in Canada (to date, Wilmington has not sold the product in markets outside the United States). Explain why the incremental cost associated with this order is likely to be less than $50,000.

EXERCISE 1-15. Incremental Analysis In the past year, Williams Mold & Machine had sales of $8,000,000 and total production costs of $6,000,000. In the coming year, the company believes that sales and production can be increased by 30 percent, but this will require adding a second production shift to work from 4:00 P.M. to 1:00 A.M.

Required

a. Indicate three production costs that are likely to increase because of adding a second production shift.

b. What production cost most likely will not increase when the second shift is added?

EXERCISE 1-16. You Get What You Measure! At the start of the current year, Ben Abbot, president of Abbot Products, told his managers that the company was going to begin tracking two new performance measures: customer satisfaction measured via a survey, and percent of orders delivered at the customer request date. Are these new measures likely to affect the behavior of managers? Suggest four possible responses.

EXERCISE 1-17. Information Age In recent years, successful companies have begun to focus on managing cross-company processes with suppliers to reduce costs, increase speed, and improve quality. In its print advertisements, J.D. Edwards, a producer of ERP software systems, notes that companies must "collaborate or die."

Required

Pick a company and discuss how it can collaborate with key suppliers to achieve mutually beneficial outcomes. Your discussion should indicate how information technology can play a role in collaboration.

EXERCISE 1-18. Career Connection Select one or two concepts from this chapter and describe how you might use those concepts in your future career. Briefly describe the career or job you will be performing. Then, specifically describe the type of situation for which the concept could be applied. Also include a discussion of how use of the concept would allow you to make informed decisions or improve your job performance. Envision specific instances where these concepts would be useful to you.

PROBLEMS

PROBLEM 1-1. Budgets in Managerial Accounting Santiago's Salsa is in the process of preparing a production cost budget for May. Actual costs in April were:

Santiago's Salsa
Production Costs
April 2008

Production	20,000 Jars of Salsa
Ingredient cost (variable)	$16,000
Labor cost (variable)	9,000
Rent (fixed)	4,000
Depreciation (fixed)	6,000
Other (fixed)	1,000
Total	$36,000

Required

a. Using this information, prepare a budget for May. Assume that production will increase to 22,000 jars of salsa, reflecting an anticipated sales increase related to a new marketing campaign.

b. Does the budget suggest that additional workers are needed? Suppose the wage rate is $20 per hour. How many additional labor hours are needed in May? What would happen if management did not anticipate the need for additional labor in May?

c. Calculate the actual cost per unit in April and the budgeted cost per unit in May. Explain why the cost per unit is expected to decrease.

PROBLEM 1-2. Incremental Analysis Consider the production cost information for Santiago's Salsa in problem 1. The company is currently producing and selling 250,000 jars of salsa annually. The jars sell for $4.00 each. The company is considering lowering the price to $3.70. Suppose this action will increase sales to 300,000 jars.

Required

a. What is the incremental cost associated with producing an extra 50,000 jars of salsa?

b. What is the incremental revenue associated with the price reduction of $0.30 per jar?

c. Should Santiago's lower the price of its salsa?

PROBLEM 1-3. Budgets in Managerial Accounting Matthew Gabon, the sales manager of Office Furniture Solutions, prepared the following budget for 2008:

Sales Department
Budgeted Costs, 2008
(Assuming Sales of $12,000,000)

Salaries (fixed)	$500,000
Commissions (variable)	180,000
Advertising (fixed)	100,000
Charge for office space (fixed)	2,000
Office supplies & forms (variable)	2,400
Total	$784,400

After he submitted his budget, the president of Office Furniture Solutions reviewed it and recommended that advertising be increased to $120,000. Further, she wanted Matthew to assume a sales level of $13,000,000. This level of sales is to be achieved without adding to the sales force.

Matthew's sales group occupies approximately 250 square feet of office space out of total administrative office space of 20,000 square feet. The $2,000 space charge in Matthew's budget is his share (allocated based on relative square feet) of the company's total cost of rent, utilities, and janitorial costs for the administrative office building.

Required

Prepare a revised budget consistent with the president's recommendation.

PROBLEM 1-4. Performance Reports Below is a performance report that compares budgeted and actual profit in the sporting goods department of Maxwell's Department Store for the month of December.

Maxwell's Department Store
Sporting Goods
Performance Report
December 2008

	Budget	Actual	Difference
Sales	$600,000	$675,000	$75,000
Less:			
Cost of merchandise	300,000	375,000	75,000
Salaries of sales staff	60,000	68,000	8,000
Controllable profit	$240,000	$232,000	($ 8,000)

Required

a. Evaluate the department in terms of its increases in sales and expenses. Do you believe it would be useful to investigate either or both of the increases in expenses?

b. Consider storewide electricity cost. Would this cost be a controllable or a noncontrollable cost for the manager of sporting goods? Would it be useful to include a share of storewide electricity cost on the performance report for sporting goods?

PROBLEM 1-5. Performance Reports At the end of 2008, Cyril Fedako, CFO for Fedako Products, received a report comparing budgeted and actual production costs for the company's plant in Forest Lake, Minnesota:

Manufacturing Costs
Forest Lake Plant
Budget versus Actual 2008

	Budget	Actual	Difference (Actual minus Budget)
Materials	$3,000,000	$3,300,000	$300,000
Direct labor	2,100,000	2,300,000	200,000
Supervisory salaries	375,000	400,000	25,000
Utilities	75,000	85,000	10,000
Machine maintenance	250,000	280,000	30,000
Depreciation of building	50,000	50,000	-0-
Depreciation of equipment	200,000	205,000	5,000
Janitorial	120,000	135,000	15,000
Total	$6,170,000	$6,755,000	$585,000

His first thought was that costs must be out of control since actual costs exceed the budget by $585,000. However, he quickly recalled that the budget was set assuming a production level of 50,000 units. The Forest Lake plant actually produced 55,000 units in 2008.

Required

a. Given that production was greater than planned, should Cyril expect that all actual costs will be greater than budgeted? Which costs would you expect to increase, and which costs would you expect to remain relatively constant?

b. Cyril is extremely busy—the company has six other plants. Therefore, he cannot spend time investigating every departure from the budget. With this in mind, which cost(s) should Cyril concentrate on in his investigation of budget differences?

PROBLEM 1-6. Financial vs. Managerial Accounting SweetTreats.com sells specialty cakes and cookies over the Internet. In its first two years of business the company had relatively high sales but also suffered large losses. The company's income statement for the most recent two years are as follows:

	2008	2007
Sales	$5,860,340	$1,393,500
Cost of sales	4,568,421	1,165,247
Gross profit	1,291,919	228,253
Selling, general and administrative expenses:		
Payroll and payroll taxes	945,672	654,783
Option-based compensation	485,622	125,367
Occupancy & office expenses	523,160	321,456
Contract services and professional fees	704,880	436,050
Internet servicing expenses	201,458	136,598
General and administrative expenses	687,482	359,657
Advertising and promotion	1,257,863	684,571
Depreciation and amortization	19,875	12,458
Total	4,826,012	2,730,940
(Loss) from operations	($3,534,093)	($2,502,687)

Required

a. Assume you are a senior manager for SweetTreats.com. What forward-looking information would you like to see in addition to the income statement?

b. For internal reporting purposes, the company has capitalized certain costs related to employee training and advertising. Management's view is that these costs have increased the value of an important asset—the company's brand name. Would this be allowed for external reporting purposes under GAAP?

c. Is the information in the income statement sufficiently detailed for management's needs? Provide four examples of more detailed information that managers would likely request.

d. Suggest three nonmonetary measures that would be useful to managers of SweetTreats.com but are not included in external financial reports.

e. SweetTreats.com currently reports its income statement on its Web site. Why might management of SweetTreats.com be reluctant to present nonmonetary information along with the income statement on the company's Web site?

PROBLEM 1-7. You get what you measure! Each year, the president of SmartToys selects a single performance measure, and offers significant financial bonuses to all key employees if the company achieves a 10 percent improvement on the measure in comparison to the prior year. She recently expressed the opinion that "this focuses my managers on a single, specific target and gets them all working together to achieve a major objective that will increase shareholder value."

Sarabeth Robbins is a new member of the company's board of directors, and she has begun to question the president's approach to rewarding performance. In particular, she is concerned that placing too much emphasis on a single performance measure may lead managers to take actions that increase performance in terms of the measure but decrease the value of the firm.

Required

a. What negative consequence might occur if the performance measure is *sales to new customers* ÷ *total sales* in the current year versus the prior year? (Note: To receive a bonus, managers would need to increase this ratio compared with the prior year.)

b. What negative consequence might occur if the performance measure is *cost of goods sold* ÷ *sales* in the current year versus the prior year? (Note: To receive a bonus, managers would need to decrease this ratio compared with the prior year.)

c. What negative consequence might occur if the performance measure is *selling and administrative expenses ÷ sales* in the current year versus the prior year? (Note: To receive a bonus, managers would need to decrease this ratio compared with the prior year.)

PROBLEM 1-8. Incremental Analysis The Riverview Hotel is a deluxe four-star establishment. Late on Friday, it had 10 of its 400 rooms available when the desk clerk received a call from the Pines Hotel. The Pines Hotel made a booking error, and did not have room for four guests (each of whom had a "confirmed" room). The Pines wants to send their customers to the Riverview, but pay the rate the guests would have been charged at the Pines ($150 per room) rather than paying the normal rate of $250 per room at the Riverview.

Required

a. If the Riverview accepts the guests, what will be the incremental revenue?

b. Provide examples of incremental costs that the Riverview will incur if it accepts the guests.

c. In your opinion, will the incremental revenue be greater than the incremental cost?

CASES

WILEY PLUS

1-1 LOCAL 635

Local 635 represents kitchen workers at hotels in several Southern cities. Part of their labor agreement states that workers "shall receive one free meal per shift up to a cost of $10, with any cost over $10 being deducted from wages paid to said employee."

A labor dispute arose at the Riverside Hotel shortly after it was opened in June. Kitchen workers who ate dinner on the late shift found that their wages were reduced by $8 for each meal they consumed at the hotel during their dinner break. Josh Parker, a line cook, stated the widely held belief of the workers, "There's no way these dinners cost the Riverside Hotel $10 to make, let alone $18. This is just another case of management trying to rip us off. Take last night. I had the prime rib dinner. The piece of meat cost about $6 and the salad less than $1. That's only $7 in total. Really, there aren't any other costs to speak of. The cook, well he's going to be working in the kitchen and getting paid for eight hours whether he makes my meal or not. This claim that my meal cost $18 is baloney!"

Management of the Riverside Hotel sees the situation differently. Take the case of Josh's dinner. In presenting the hotel's case to a labor arbitration board, Sandy Ross, manager of the hotel, explained, "Look, that dinner goes for $30 on the menu so assigning a cost of $18 represents a very good value to the kitchen workers. The contention that the meal only costs $7 is nonsense. True, the meat costs $6 and the salad ingredients cost $1, but there's also the labor costs related to preparing the meal and numerous overhead costs like the cost of the oven that the prime rib is cooked in. That oven cost more than $18,000. And, there's heat, light, power, etc. Each meal we prepare should be assigned part of these overhead costs. And, don't forget that when the worker finishes his or her meal, someone has to clean up. That costs money too. When you add up all of these items, a prime rib dinner easily adds up to $18!"

Required

a. List examples of costs at the Riverside Hotel that are variable, fixed, and sunk. Provide an example of an opportunity cost.

b. What is the source of conflict between labor and management? What changes would you recommend in the wording of the labor agreement?

1-2 Boswell Plumbing Products

Boswell Plumbing Products produces a variety of valves, connectors, and fixtures used in commercial and residential plumbing applications. Recently, a senior manager walked into the cost accounting department and asked Nick Somner to tell her the cost of the D45 valve. Nick quickly replied, "Why do you want to know?" Noticing that the manager appeared somewhat startled by this statement, he explained, "The cost information you need depends on the decision you're going to make. You might be thinking of increasing a scheduled production run of 3,000 D45s by 100 units, or scheduling an additional production run, or you might even be thinking of dropping the product. For each of these decisions, the 'cost' information that you need is different."

Required

Using the concept of incremental analysis, expand on Nick's response of "Why do you want to know?" What cost information would be relevant to a decision to drop the product that would not be relevant to a decision to increase a production run by 100 units?

CHAPTER 4

LEARNING OBJECTIVES

1. Identify common cost behavior patterns.
2. Estimate the relation between cost and activity using account analysis and the high-low method.
3. Perform cost-volume-profit analysis for single products.
4. Perform cost-volume-profit analysis for multiple products.
5. Discuss the effect of operating leverage.
6. Use the contribution margin per unit of the constraint to analyze situations involving a resource constraint.

COST-VOLUME-PROFIT ANALYSIS

Mary Stuart is the vice president of operations for CodeConnect, a company that manufactures and sells bar code readers. As a senior manager, she must answer a variety of questions dealing with planning, control, and decision making. Consider the following questions that Mary has faced:

Planning: Last year, CodeConnect sold 20,000 bar code readers at $200 per unit. The cost of manufacturing these items was $2,940,000, and selling and administrative costs were $800,000. Total profit was $260,000. In the coming year, the company expects to sell 25,000 units. What level of profit should be in the budget for the coming year?

Control: In April, production costs were $250,000. In May, costs increased to $265,000, but production also increased from 1,750 units in April to 2,000 units in May. Did the manager responsible for production costs do a good job of controlling costs in May?

Decision making: The current price for a bar code reader is $200 per unit. If the price is increased to $225 per unit, sales will drop from 20,000 to 17,000. Should the price be increased?

The answer to each of these questions depends on how costs and, therefore, profit change when volume changes. The analysis of how costs and profit change when volume changes is referred to as **cost-volume-profit (C-V-P) analysis**. In this chapter, we develop the tools to analyze cost-volume-profit relations. These tools will enable you to answer questions like the ones listed above—questions managers face on a daily basis.

Identify common cost behavior patterns.

COMMON COST BEHAVIOR PATTERNS

To perform cost-volume-profit (CVP) analysis, you need to know how costs behave when business activity (e.g., production volume and sales volume) changes. This section describes some common patterns of cost behavior. These patterns may not provide exact descriptions of how costs behave in response to changes in volume or activity, but they are generally reasonable approximations involving variable costs, fixed costs, mixed costs, and step costs.

VARIABLE COSTS

As mentioned in Chapter 1, **variable costs** are costs that change in proportion to changes in volume or activity. Thus, if activity increases by 10 percent, variable costs are assumed to increase by 10 percent. Some common variable costs are direct and indirect materials, direct labor, energy, and sales commissions.

Exactly how activity should be measured in analyzing a variable cost depends on the situation. At McDonald's restaurants, food costs vary with the number of customers served. At United Airlines, fuel costs vary with the number of miles flown. In these situations, number of customers and number of miles are good measures of activity.

Let's consider an example using CodeConnect, the company introduced in the beginning of the chapter. Suppose that CodeConnect has variable production costs equal to $91 per bar code reader. In this case, total variable cost at a production level of 1,000 units (the measure of activity) is equal to $91,000 ($91 × 1,000), while total variable cost at 2,000 units is equal to $182,000 ($91 × 2,000). A graph of the relation between total variable cost and production is provided in Illustration 4-1. The slope of the straight line in the figure measures the change in cost per unit change in activity. Note that while total variable cost increases with production, variable cost per unit remains at $91.

FIXED COSTS

Recall from Chapter 1 that **fixed costs** are costs that do not change in response to changes in activity levels. Some typical fixed costs are depreciation, supervisory salaries, and building maintenance. Suppose that CodeConnect has $94,000 of

Illustration 4-1
Variable cost behavior at CodeConnect

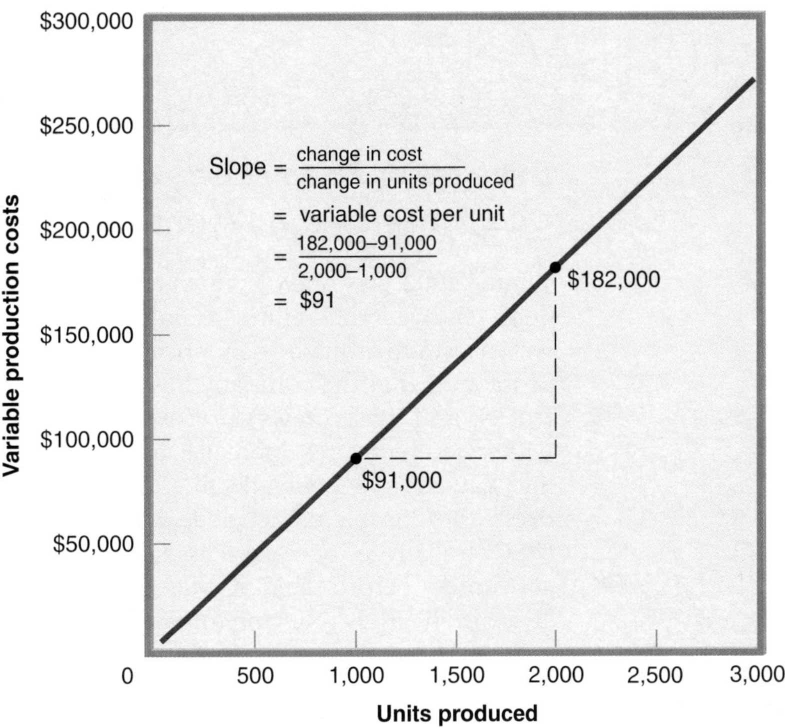

fixed costs per month. A graph of the relation between the company's fixed cost and production is provided in Illustration 4-2. As you can see, whatever the number of units produced, the amount of total fixed cost remains at $94,000. However, the amount of fixed cost per unit does change with changes in the level of activity. When activity increases, the amount of fixed cost per unit decreases because the

Illustration 4-2
Fixed cost behavior at CodeConnect

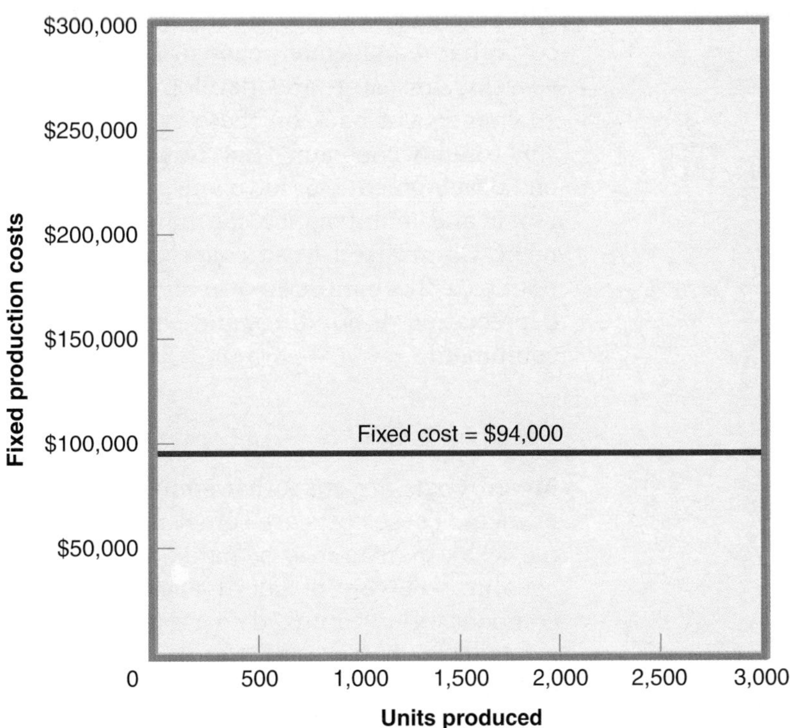

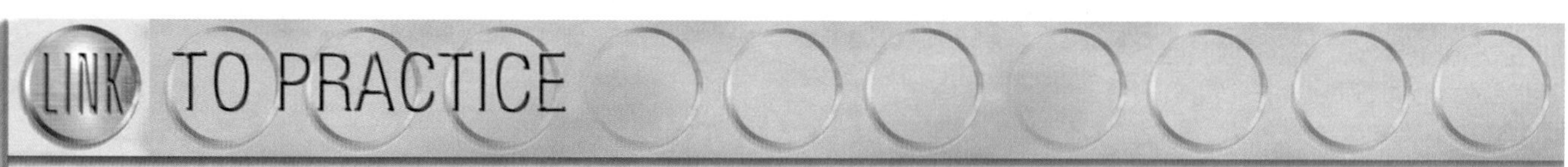

Because of Fixed Costs, Utility Wants Rate Increase to Compensate for a Warmer than Average Winter

Winter 2002 was one of the warmest winters in history for St. Louis. While residents enjoyed the relatively balmy weather, officials at Laclede Gas Company weren't smiling since their profits go down when the temperature goes up. The problem is that the company has the same fixed costs (related to storage capacity, trucks, and work crews) in a warm winter as in a cold winter. However, when winter temperatures increase, consumption of gas for home heating decreases, and Laclede's revenues decline. The result is that profit takes a nosedive. To address the "problem," Laclede asked the Missouri Public Service Commission (PSC) for a rate increase. However, the Missouri Public Counsel who represents consumers before the PSC stated that he would oppose the request, noting that "Essentially, they're trying to pass on costs for gas they didn't sell."

Source: St. Louis Post-Dispatch, March 29, 2002, p. B6. "Laclede Gas Seeks to Recover Distribution Costs While Mitigating Weather on Customer Bills," *Laclede Gas Company*, January 25, 2002. "Laclede Gas Wants Compensation for Warmer Winter," *New Tribune Company*, March 26, 2002.

fixed cost is spread over more units. For example, at 1,000 units, the fixed cost per unit is $94 ($94,000 ÷ 1,000), whereas at 2,000 units, the fixed cost per unit is only $47 ($94,000 ÷ 2,000).

Discretionary versus Committed Fixed Costs. In the short run, some fixed costs can be changed while others cannot. **Discretionary fixed costs** are those fixed costs that management can easily change in the short run. Examples include advertising, research and development, and repair and maintenance costs. Some companies cut back on these expenditures when sales drop so that profit trends stay roughly constant. That, however, may be shortsighted since a cut in research and development can have a negative effect on long-run profitability, and a cut in repair and maintenance can have a negative effect on the life of valuable equipment. **Committed fixed costs**, on the other hand, are those fixed costs that cannot be easily changed in a relatively brief period of time. Such costs include rent, depreciation of buildings and equipment, and insurance related to buildings and equipment.

MIXED COSTS

Mixed costs are costs that contain both a variable cost element and a fixed cost element. These costs are sometimes referred to as **semivariable costs**. For example, a salesperson may be paid $80,000 per year (fixed amount) plus commissions equal to 1 percent of sales (variable amount). In this case, the salesperson's total compensation is a mixed cost. Note especially that **total production cost is also a mixed cost** since it is composed of material, labor, and both fixed and variable overhead cost items.

Illustration 4-3
Mixed cost behavior

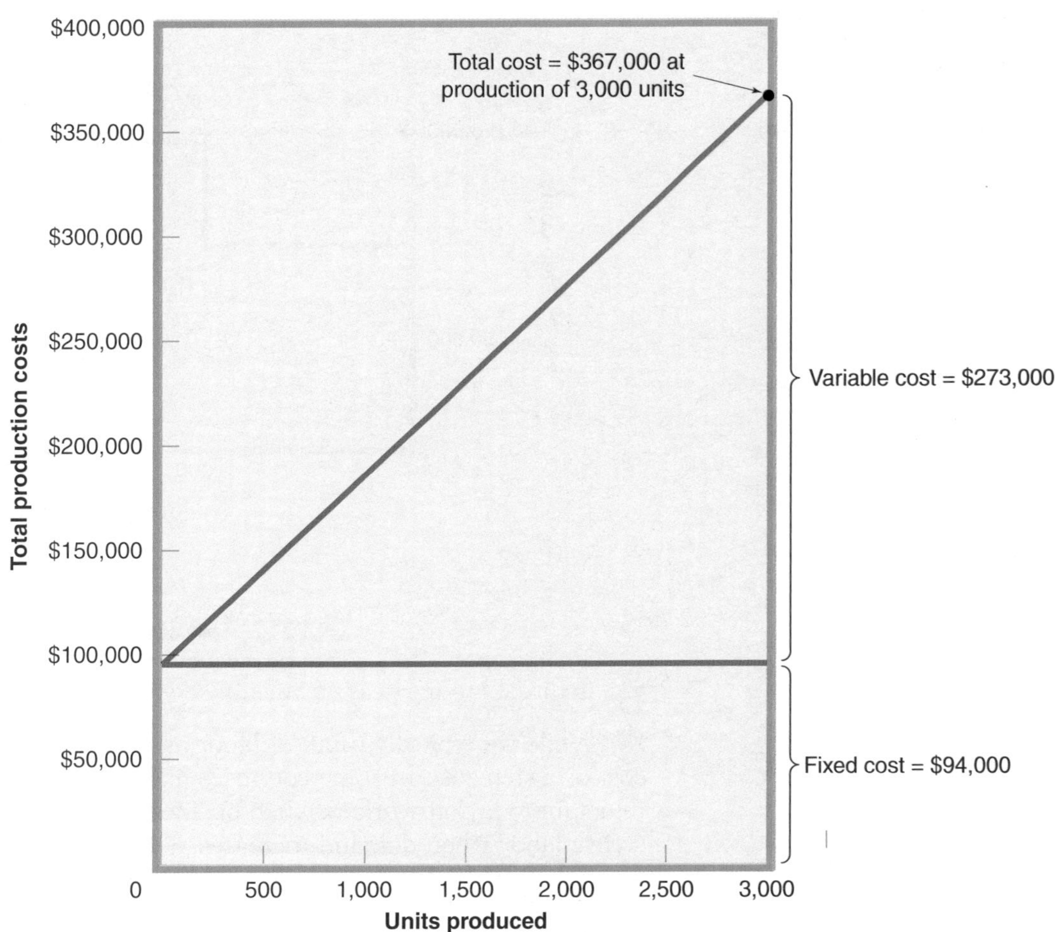

Suppose the total production cost of CodeConnect is composed of $94,000 of fixed cost per month and $91 of variable cost per unit. In this case, total production cost is a mixed cost. A graph of the cost is presented in Illustration 4-3. Note that the total cost line intersects the vertical axis at $94,000 (just below the $100,000 point). This is the amount of fixed cost per month. From this point, total cost increases by $91 for every unit produced. Thus, at 3,000 units, the total cost is $367,000, composed of $94,000 of fixed cost and $273,000 of variable cost ($91 × 3,000).

STEP COSTS

Step costs are those costs that are fixed for a range of volume but increase to a higher level when the upper bound of the range is exceeded. At that point the costs again remain fixed until another upper bound is exceeded. As an example, suppose that CodeConnect can produce up to 3,000 bar code readers with fixed costs of $94,000. However, to produce 3,001 to 6,000 bar code readers the company must add a second shift. Fixed costs related to supervisory salaries, heat, light, and other fixed costs are expected to increase to $144,000. To produce more than 6,000 bar code readers, the company must add a third shift and fixed costs are expected to increase to $194,000. A graph of these step costs is presented in Illustration 4-4.

Illustration 4-4
Step cost behavior

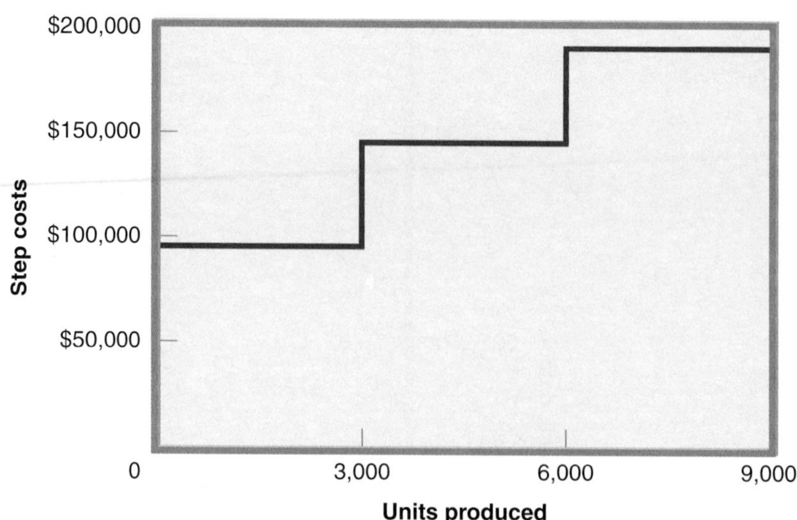

Any Questions?

Q Is direct labor always a variable cost?

A While we typically think of labor as a variable cost, it could also be a fixed cost or a step cost. In some countries like Japan and Korea, companies are very reluctant to lay off workers when business decreases and they are hesitant to increase labor when demand increases. Thus, for many companies in Japan and Korea labor is a fixed cost. In the United States, companies are more willing to hire and fire with fluctuations in demand, making labor more reasonably approximated as a variable cost. But some U.S. companies are so highly automated that they can accommodate wide fluctuations in volume with the same work force, and for them, labor is more reasonably approximated as a fixed cost. To determine whether labor is variable or fixed for a particular company, you must analyze the unique situation facing the company. Also, keep in mind the notion of a relevant range. Within a particular range of activity, labor may be fixed but it may jump to a higher level if the company exceeds the upper limit of the range.

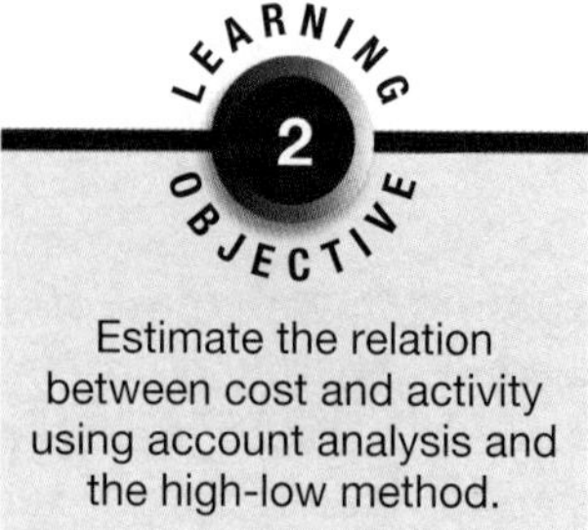

Estimate the relation between cost and activity using account analysis and the high-low method.

COST ESTIMATION METHODS

In order to predict how much cost will be incurred at various activity levels (a critical part of C-V-P analysis), you must know how much of the total cost is fixed and how much is variable. In many cases, cost information is not broken out in terms of fixed and variable cost components; therefore, you must know how to estimate fixed and variable costs from available information. In this section, we cover three techniques for estimating the amount of fixed and variable cost: account analysis, the high-low method, and regression analysis.

ACCOUNT ANALYSIS

Account analysis is the most common approach to estimating fixed and variable costs. This method requires that the manager use professional judgment to classify costs as either fixed or variable. The total of the costs classified as variable can then be divided by a measure of activity to calculate the variable cost per unit of activity. The total of the costs classified as fixed provides the estimate of fixed cost.

To illustrate, let's return to the CodeConnect example. For the month of May, the cost of producing 2,000 units of the DX375 bar code reader was $265,000. Account analysis would require a detailed analysis of the accounts that comprise the $265,000 of production costs. Suppose the costs were as follows:

	May
Production in units	2,000
Production cost	
Component cost	$130,600
Assembly labor	32,400
Utilities	7,100
Rent	22,000
Depreciation of assembly equipment	72,900
Total production cost	$265,000

Using professional judgment, you may decide that component cost and assembly labor are variable costs and all other items are fixed costs. In this case, variable and fixed costs are estimated as in Illustration 4-5. Total production costs would be estimated as $102,000 of fixed cost per month plus $81.50 of variable cost for each unit produced.

Although Illustration 4-5 classifies each individual cost item as either 100 percent fixed or 100 percent variable, the account analysis method does not require that this be so. For example, there may be reason to believe that at least part of utilities is also variable. In this case, the manager can use his or her judgment to refine estimates using account analysis. Suppose the manager believes that approximately 50 percent of utilities are variable. As indicated in Illustration 4-6, the revised estimate of total variable cost would then amount to $166,550, or $83.28 per unit, whereas the revised estimate of fixed costs per month would amount to $98,450.

With these estimates we can project what costs will be at various levels of production. For example, how much cost can CodeConnect expect to incur if

Illustration 4-5
Estimate of variable and fixed costs

CodeConnect

Variable Cost Estimate

Component cost	$130,600	
Assembly labor	32,400	
Total	$163,000	(a)
Production	2,000	(b)
Variable cost per unit	$81.50	(a) ÷ (b)

Fixed Cost Estimate

Utilities	$ 7,100
Rent	22,000
Depreciation	72,900
Total per year	$102,000

Illustration 4-6
Revisited estimate of variable and fixed costs

CodeConnect

Variable Cost Estimate

Component cost	$130,600	
Assembly labor	32,400	
Utilities (50% of $7,100)	3,550	
Total	$166,550	(a)
Production	2,000	(b)
Variable cost per unit	$83.28	(a) ÷ (b)

Fixed Cost Estimate

Utilities (50% of $7,100)	$ 3,550
Rent	22,000
Depreciation	72,900
Total per month	$98,450

2,500 units are produced? With 2,500 units, variable costs are estimated as $208,200 and fixed costs per month are estimated as $98,450. Therefore, total cost of $306,650 would be expected, as shown:

Expected Monthly Cost of 2,500 Units; DX375 Bar Code Reader	
Variable cost (2,500 × $83.28)	$208,200
Fixed cost per month	98,450
Total	$306,650

The account analysis method is subjective in that different managers viewing the same set of facts may reach different conclusions regarding which costs are fixed and which costs are variable. Despite this limitation, most managers consider it an important tool for estimating fixed and variable costs.

SCATTERGRAPHS

In some cases, you may have cost information from several reporting periods available in order to estimate how costs change in response to changes in activity. Weekly, monthly, or quarterly reports are particularly useful sources of cost information. In contrast, annual reports are not as useful because the relation between costs and activity is generally not consistent or stable over several years.

Suppose the monthly production and cost information provided in Illustration 4-7 is available for CodeConnect. We can gain insight into the relation between production cost and activity by plotting these costs and activity levels. The plot of the data is referred to as a **scattergraph**. The scattergraph for the data in Illustration 4-7 is presented in Illustration 4-8.

Typically, as in Illustration 4-8, scattergraphs are prepared with costs measured on the vertical axis and activity level measured on the horizontal axis. Each point on the scattergraph represents one pair of cost and activity values. The graphical features in spreadsheet programs such as Excel® make the preparation of a scattergraph very easy. Essentially, all you need to do is input the data, and then you can rely on the spreadsheet to accurately plot it.

Illustration 4-7
Monthly production cost information

CodeConnect

Month	Production	Cost
January	750	$ 170,000
February	1,000	175,000
March	1,250	205,000
April	1,750	250,000
May	2,000	265,000
June	2,250	275,000
July	3,000	400,000
August	2,750	350,000
September	2,500	300,000
October	1,250	210,000
November	1,000	190,000
December	500	150,000
Total	20,000	$2,940,000

The methods we use to estimate cost behavior assume that costs are linear. In other words, they assume that costs are well represented by straight lines. A scattergraph is useful in assessing whether this assumption is reasonable. The plot in Illustration 4-8 suggests that a linear approximation is quite reasonable since the data points line up in an approximately linear fashion. The scattergraph is also useful in assessing whether there are any outliers. Outliers are data points that are markedly at odds with the trend of other data points. Here, there are no obvious outliers.

Illustration 4-8
Scattergraph of cost and production information

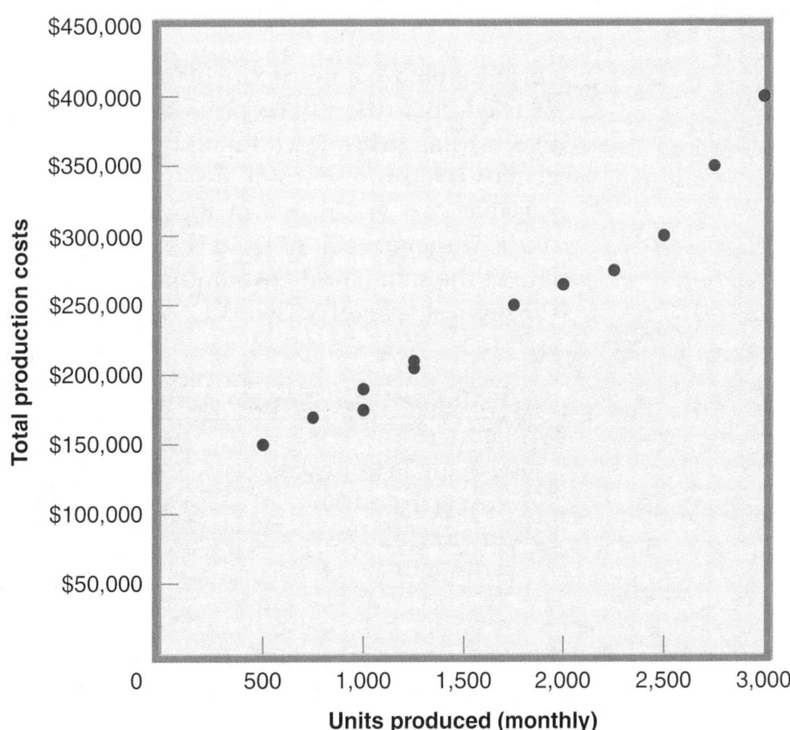

HIGH-LOW METHOD

With the same type of data as that described previously, we can estimate the fixed and variable components of cost at various activity levels using the **high-low method**. This method fits a straight line to the data points representing the highest and lowest levels of activity. The slope of the line is the estimate of variable cost (because the slope measures the change in cost per unit change in activity), and the intercept (where the line meets the cost axis) is the estimate of fixed cost.

We'll use the data in Illustration 4-7 to describe the high-low method. Note in Illustration 4-7 that the highest level of activity is a production level of 3,000 units in July with a corresponding cost of $400,000. The lowest level of activity is a production level of 500 units in December with a corresponding cost of $150,000. Thus, a line connecting these points looks like the one in Illustration 4-9.

We can calculate the slope of the line in Illustration 4-9 fairly easily. The slope is equal to the change in cost divided by the change in activity. In moving from the lowest level of activity to the highest level of activity, the cost changes by $250,000 and activity changes by 2,500 units. Thus, the estimate of variable cost (the slope) is $100 per unit.

$$\text{Estimate of variable cost} = \frac{\text{Change in cost}}{\text{Change in activity}}$$

$$\text{Estimate of variable cost} = \frac{\text{Cost at highest level of activity} - \text{Cost at lowest level of activity}}{\text{Highest level of activity} - \text{Lowest level of activity}}$$

$$\text{Estimate of variable cost} = \frac{\$400{,}000 - \$150{,}000}{3{,}000 - 500}$$

$$\text{Estimate of variable cost} = \frac{\$250{,}000}{2{,}500} = \$100 \text{ per unit}$$

Once we obtain an estimate of variable cost, we can use it to calculate an estimate of fixed cost (the intercept of the line). The fixed cost equals the difference between total cost and estimated variable cost. For example, at the lowest level of activity (500 units), total cost is $150,000. Since variable cost is $100 per unit, variable cost is $50,000 of the total cost. Thus, the remaining cost of $100,000 must be the amount of fixed cost. As indicated in the following calculation, we arrive at the same fixed cost amount ($100,000) whether we work with the lowest or the highest level of activity.

Estimate Using Lowest Activity		Estimate Using Highest Activity	
Total cost	$150,000	Total cost	$400,000
Less: Estimated variable cost (500 × $100)	50,000	Less: Estimated variable cost (3,000 × $100)	300,000
Estimated fixed cost per month	$100,000	Estimated fixed cost per month	$100,000

Be sure to note that because monthly data—the data from Illustration 4-7—are used in this example, the fixed costs calculated are the fixed costs *per month*. If

Illustration 4-9
High-low estimate of production costs

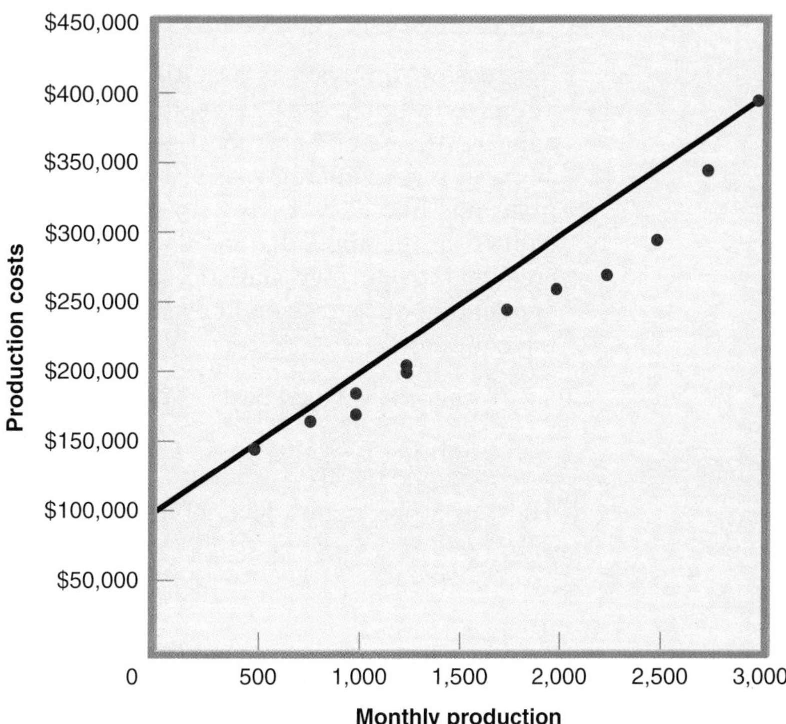

annual data were used, the fixed costs calculated would be the fixed costs *per year*.

Refer back to Illustration 4-9, which shows the high-low line for the cost and activity data from Illustration 4-7. We can describe the total cost at any point along this line by using the following equation:

Total cost = Fixed cost + (Variable cost per unit × Activity level in units)

Thus, we can use the equation to derive an estimate of total cost for a given activity level. For example, at an activity level of 1,500 units, we would estimate that $250,000 of cost would be incurred:

Total cost = $100,000 + ($100 × 1,500)
= $100,000 + $150,000
= $250,000

Looking at Illustration 4-9 should suggest a weakness of the high-low method. Notice that the cost line passes through the high and low data points but the other data points lie below the cost line. In other words, the estimate represented by the line does not adequately fit the available data.

A significant weakness of the high-low method, then, is that it uses only two data points. These two points may not be truly representative of the general relation between cost and activity. The two points may represent unusually high and unusually low levels of activity, and costs at these levels may also be unusual. For example, at the highest level of activity, part-time workers may be used to supplement the normal workforce. They may not work as efficiently as other workers, and costs may be unusually high. Thus, when additional data are available, using more than two data points for estimates is advisable.

REGRESSION ANALYSIS

Regression analysis is a statistical technique that uses all the available data points to estimate the intercept and slope of a cost equation. The line fitted to the data by regression is the best straight-line fit to the data. Software programs to perform regression analysis are widely available and are included in spreadsheet programs like Excel®. How to use Excel® to conduct regression analysis is explained in the appendix to this chapter. The topic of regression analysis is covered in introductory statistics classes. For our purposes, we simply note that application of regression analysis to the data in Illustration 4-7 yields the following equation:

Total cost = Fixed cost + (Variable cost per unit × Activity level in units)

Total cost = \$93,619 + (\$90.83 × Activity level in units)

Thus, at a production level of 1,500 units, the amount of total cost estimated is \$229,864.

Total cost = \$93,619 of fixed cost + (\$90.83 × 1,500)
= \$229,864

This is less than the \$250,000 estimated using the high-low cost equation.

A graph of the regression analysis estimate of cost is presented in Illustration 4-10. Notice that the regression line fits the available data better than the line estimated with the high-low method. Because the regression line is more consistent with the past data of the company, it will probably provide more accurate predictions of future costs.

Illustration 4-10
Regression analysis estimate of production cost

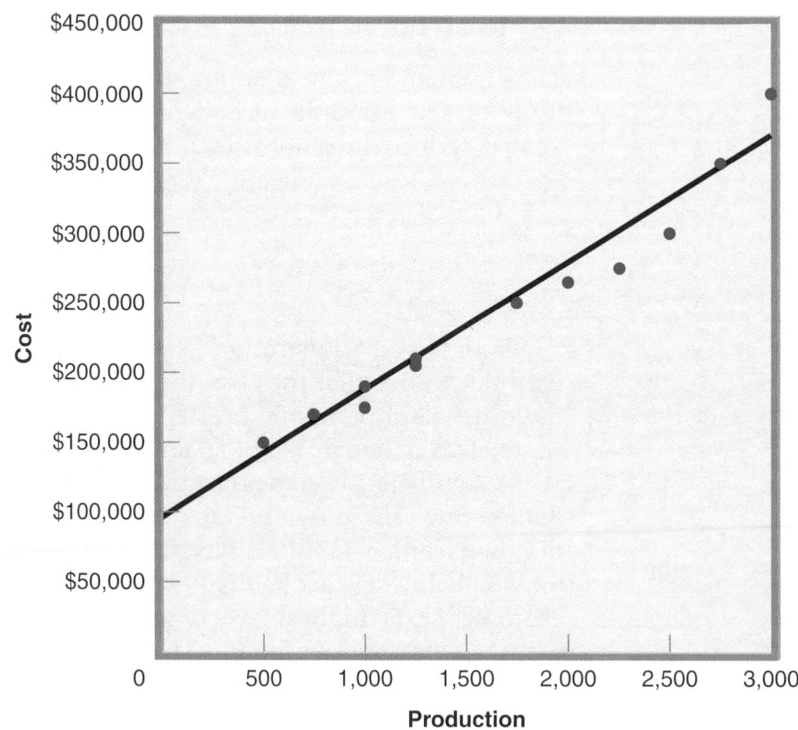

THE RELEVANT RANGE

When working with estimates of fixed and variable costs, remember that they are only valid for a limited range of activity. The **relevant range** is the range of activity for which estimates and predictions are expected to be accurate. Outside the relevant range, the estimates of fixed and variable costs may not be very useful. Often, managers are not confident using estimates of fixed and variable costs when called upon to make predictions for activity levels that have not been encountered in the past. Since the activity levels have not been encountered in the past, past relations between cost and activity may not be a useful basis for estimating costs in this situation. For example, a manager at CodeConnect may not feel confident using the regression estimates of $93,619 fixed cost and $90.83 variable cost per unit to estimate total cost for a production level of 4,000 units. As indicated in Illustration 4-7, the highest prior level of production was 3,000 units and, thus, 4,000 units is outside the relevant range.

In some cases, actual costs behave in a manner that is different from the common cost behavior patterns that we have discussed. All of those patterns imply linear (straight-line) relations between cost and activity. In the real world, some costs are nonlinear. When companies produce unusually large quantities, for example, production may not be efficient, resulting in costs increasing more rapidly than the rate implied by a straight line. This may not be a serious limitation for a straight-line approach as long as the predictions and estimates are restricted to the relevant range. Consider Illustration 4-11. Note that although the relation between cost and activity is nonlinear, within the relevant range a straight line would closely approximate the relation between cost and activity.

Illustration 4-11
Relevant range

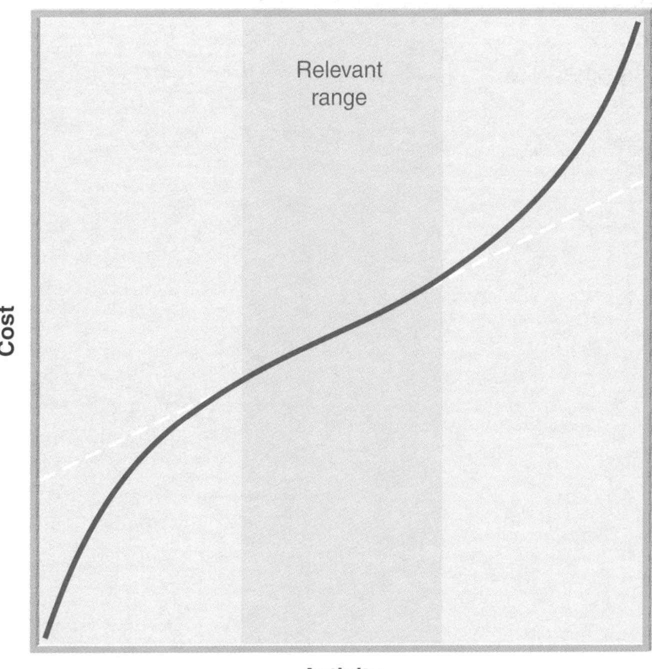

Perform cost-volume-profit analysis for single products.

COST-VOLUME-PROFIT ANALYSIS

Once fixed and variable costs have been estimated, cost-volume-profit analysis (CVP) can be conducted. Basically, CVP analysis is any analysis that explores the relation among costs, volume or activity levels, and profit.

THE PROFIT EQUATION

Fundamental to CVP analysis is the profit equation. The **profit equation** states that profit is equal to revenue (selling price times quantity), minus variable cost (variable cost per unit times quantity), minus total fixed cost.

$$\text{Profit} = \text{SP}(x) - \text{VC}(x) - \text{TFC}$$

where x = Quantity of units produced and sold

SP = Selling price per unit

VC = Variable cost per unit

TFC = Total fixed cost

BREAK-EVEN POINT

One of the primary uses of CVP analysis is to calculate the break-even point. The **break-even point** is the number of units that must be sold for a company to break even—to neither earn a profit nor incur a loss. The break-even point is shown in the profit graph presented in Illustration 4-12. At the point where sales revenue equals total cost (composed of fixed and variable costs), the company breaks even.

To calculate the break-even point, we simply set the profit equation equal to zero, because by definition the break-even point is the point at which profit is

Illustration 4-12
Profit graph and break-even point

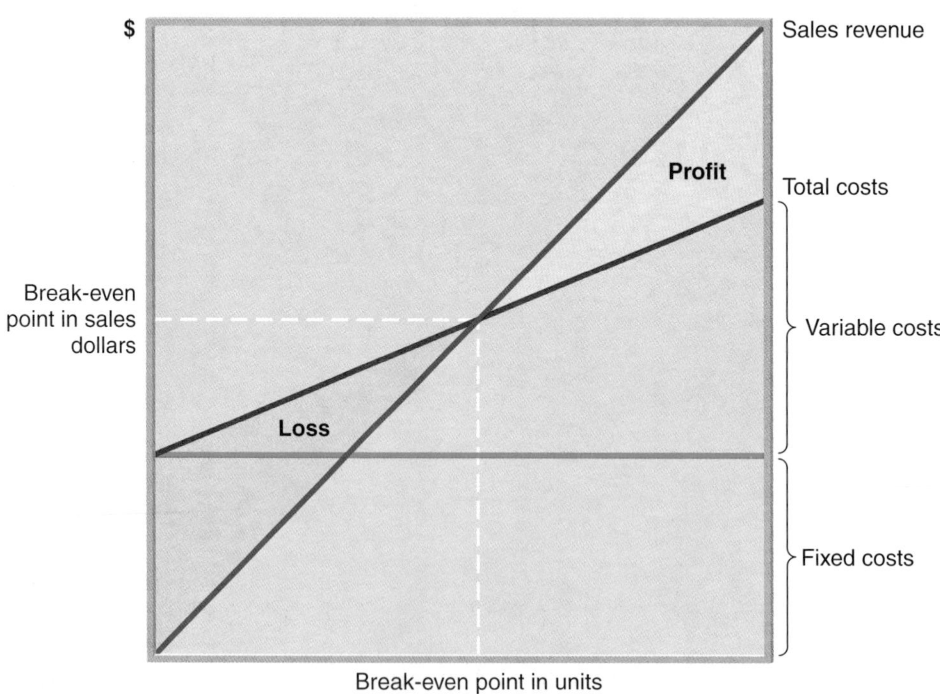

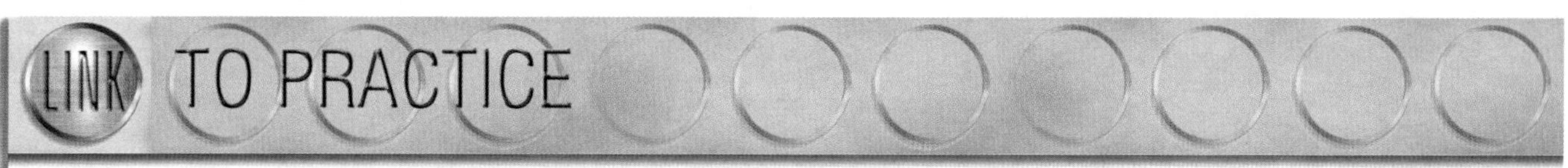

How to Reach Break-Even

In September 2005, Lion Bioscience had a plan to achieve a break-even profit in the fourth quarter of 2005. The plan included reducing its research and development activities to one site and reducing full-time employees from 271 to 190. Other restructuring measures had already reduced expenditures from 40.1 million euros to 20.1 million.

While the plan is to break-even in the fourth quarter, the company still expects a loss of approximately 25 million euros for the fiscal year.

Source: Information on the company Web site (http://www.lionbioscience.com).

zero. Then we insert the appropriate selling price, variable cost, and fixed cost information and solve for the quantity (x).

Let's consider an example. Mary Stuart, the VP of operations at CodeConnect, wants to know the break-even point for the company's model DX375 bar code reader. This will help her assess the possibility of incurring a loss for this product. Suppose CodeConnect sells this model for $200 per unit. Variable costs are estimated to be $90.83 per unit, and total fixed costs are estimated to be $160,285 per month, composed of $93,619 of fixed production costs (estimated above) and $66,666 fixed selling and administrative costs.

Selling price per unit	$200.00
Variable cost per unit	90.83
Fixed production cost per month	$ 93,619
Fixed selling and administrative costs	66,666
Total fixed costs	$160,285

How many units must be sold to break-even in a given month? To answer this question, we solve the profit equation for a particular value of x.

$$0 = \$200(x) - \$90.83(x) - \$160{,}285$$

$$0 = \$109.17(x) - \$160{,}285$$

$$\$109.17(x) = \$160{,}285$$

$$x = 1{,}468 \text{ units}$$

Solving for x yields a break-even quantity of 1,468 units. If management prefers to have the break-even quantity expressed in dollars of sales rather than in units, the quantity is simply multiplied by the selling price of $200 to yield $293,600.

Margin of Safety. Obviously, managers are very concerned that they have a level of sales greater than break-even sales. To express how close they expect to be to the break-even level, managers may calculate the margin of safety. The **margin of safety** is the difference between the expected level of sales and break-even sales. For example, the monthly break-even level of sales for Model DX375 is $293,600.

If management expects to have sales of \$350,000, the margin of safety is \$56,400 (i.e., \$350,000 − \$293,600). Given that the margin of safety is relatively high, Mary Stuart can be reasonably confident that the Model DX375 will break even.

CONTRIBUTION MARGIN

The profit equation can be rewritten by combining the terms containing x in them to yield the **contribution margin** per unit—the difference between the selling price (SP) and variable cost per unit (VC).

$$\text{Profit} = \text{SP}(x) - \text{VC}(x) - \text{TFC}$$

$$\text{Profit} = (\text{SP} - \text{VC})(x) - \text{TFC}$$

$$\text{Profit} = \text{Contribution margin per unit}(x) - \text{TFC}$$

The contribution margin per unit measures the amount each unit sold contributes to covering fixed costs and increasing profit. This may not be obvious at first glance, but consider what happens when sales and production increase by one unit. The firm benefits from revenue equal to the selling price, but it also incurs increased costs equal to the variable cost per unit. Fixed costs are unaffected by changes in volume, so they do not affect the *incremental* profit associated with selling an additional unit. Note that if we multiply the contribution margin per unit by the number of units sold, we obtain the total contribution margin.

If we solve the profit equation for the sales quantity in units (x), we get the following expression:

$$X = \frac{\text{Profit} + \text{TFC}}{\text{SP} - \text{VC}}$$

or

$$X = \frac{\text{Profit} + \text{TFC}}{\text{Contribution margin per unit}}$$

This is a handy formula for calculating the break-even point and solving for the quantity needed to earn various profit levels. For CodeConnect, the amount of fixed cost is \$160,285 per month. With a selling price of \$200 and variable costs of \$90.83, the contribution margin per unit is \$109.17. Using the formula implies that 1,468 units must be sold to break-even each month.

$$1{,}468 = \frac{0 + \$160{,}285}{\$109.17} = \frac{\text{Profit} + \text{TFC}}{\text{Contribution margin per unit}}$$

Now suppose that the management of CodeConnect wants to know how many units must be sold to achieve a profit of \$40,000 in a given month. Using the formula implies that 1,835 units must be sold to achieve a profit of \$40,000.

$$1{,}835 = \frac{\$40{,}000 + \$160{,}285}{\$109.17}$$

CONTRIBUTION MARGIN RATIO

The **contribution margin ratio** provides a measure of the contribution of every sales dollar to covering fixed cost and generating a profit. It is equal to the contribution margin per unit divided by the selling price.

$$\text{Contribution margin ratio} = \frac{\text{SP} - \text{VC}}{\text{SP}}$$

Consider a company whose product has a selling price of $20 and requires variable costs of $15. In this case, the contribution margin ratio is 25 percent. Because the contribution margin per dollar of sales is 25 percent, for every additional dollar of sales, the company will earn $.25.

$$\text{Contribution margin ratio} = \frac{\$20 - \$15}{\$20} = 25\%$$

We can express the profit equation in terms of the contribution margin ratio as:

$$\text{Sales (in dollars)} = \frac{\text{Profit} + \text{TFC}}{\text{Contribution margin ratio}}$$

This formula can be used to calculate the amount of sales dollars needed to earn a profit of $40,000 in a given month for CodeConnect. Its contribution margin ratio is .5459 (contribution margin of $109.17 ÷ selling price of $200). Thus, sales of $366,890 are needed.

$$\$366{,}890 = \frac{\$40{,}000 + \$160{,}285}{.5459}$$

"WHAT IF" ANALYSIS

The profit equation also can show how profit will be affected by various options under consideration by management. Such analysis is sometimes referred to as **"what if" analysis** because it examines *what* will happen *if* a particular action is taken.

Change in Fixed and Variable Costs. Suppose CodeConnect is currently selling 3,000 units per month at a price of $200. Variable costs per unit are $90.83, and total fixed costs are $160,285 per month. Management is considering a change in the production process that will increase fixed costs per month by $50,000 to $210,285, but decrease variable costs to only $80 per unit. How would this change affect monthly profit? Using the profit equation, and assuming that there will be no change in the selling price or the quantity sold, profit under the alternative will be equal to $149,715:

$$\text{Profit} = \$200(3{,}000) - \$80(3{,}000) - \$210{,}285 = \$149{,}715$$

Without the change, profit will equal $167,225:

$$\text{Profit} = \$200(3{,}000) - \$90.83(3{,}000) - \$160{,}285 = \$167{,}225$$

The change in the production process would actually lower profit, so it appears not to be advisable.

Change in Selling Price. Any one of the variables in the profit equation can be considered in light of changes in the other variables. For example, suppose Code-Connect's management wants to know what the selling price would have to be to earn a profit of $200,000 if 3,000 units are sold in a given month. To answer this question, all of the relevant information is organized in terms of the profit equation, and then the equation is solved for the selling price.

$$\$200{,}000 = \text{SP}(3{,}000) - \$90.83(3{,}000) - \$160{,}285$$

$$\text{SP}(3{,}000) = \$632{,}775$$

$$\text{SP} = \$210.93$$

TAXES IN CVP ANALYSIS

So far, our discussion of CVP analysis has ignored taxes on income. Let's see how taxes affect the profit equation. Recall that the profit equation without taxes, otherwise called before-tax profit, is:

$$\begin{aligned} \text{Before tax profit} &= \text{SP}(x) - \text{VC}(x) - \text{TFC} \\ \text{Where } x &= \text{Quantity of units produced and sold} \\ \text{SP} &= \text{Selling price per unit} \\ \text{VC} &= \text{Variable cost per unit} \\ \text{TFC} &= \text{Total fixed cost} \end{aligned}$$

Now, consider a tax rate on income of (t). Then, after-tax profit is:

$$\text{After-tax profit} = [\text{SP}(x) - \text{VC}(x) - \text{TFC}](1\text{-t})$$

Notice that the only difference is that before-tax profit is multiplied by 1 minus the tax rate. Thus, if the tax rate is 40 percent, the after-tax rate of profit is 60 percent.

Suppose CodeConnect sells bar code readers for \$200 per unit, has variable cost per unit of \$90.83, and total fixed costs per month of \$160,285. Further, the company has a tax rate of 40 percent. In this case, how many units must be sold to earn an after-tax profit of \$40,000 per month? Utilizing the after-tax profit equation, we can see that the company must sell approximately 2,079 units.

$$\begin{aligned} \$40{,}000 &= [\$200(x) - \$90.83(x) - \$160{,}285](.6) \\ \$40{,}000 &= [\$109.17(x)].6 - \$96{,}171 \\ \$136{,}171 &= \$65.502(x) \\ x &= 2{,}078.88 \end{aligned}$$

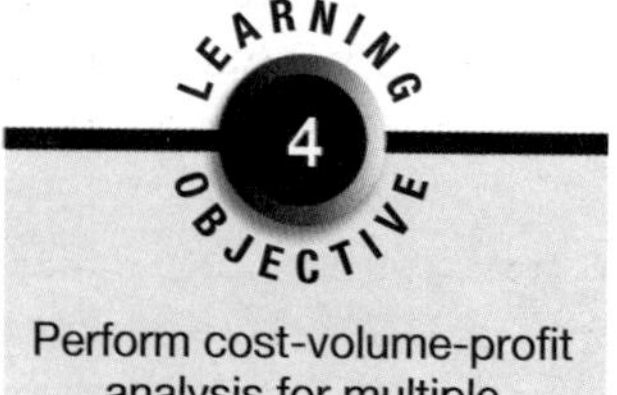

Perform cost-volume-profit analysis for multiple products.

MULTIPRODUCT ANALYSIS

The previous examples illustrated CVP analysis for a single product. But CVP analysis can be extended easily to cover multiple products. In the following sections, we examine the use of the contribution margin and the contribution margin ratio in performing CVP analysis for a company with multiple products.

CONTRIBUTION MARGIN APPROACH

If the products a company sells are similar (e.g., various flavors of ice cream, various types of calculators, various models of similar boats), the weighted average contribution margin per unit can be used in CVP analysis. Let's consider a simple example. Suppose the Master Pen Company produces two types of pens. Model A sells for \$30 and requires \$15 of variable cost per unit. Model B sells for \$50 and requires \$20 of variable cost per unit. Further, Master Pen typically sells two Model A's for one Model B sold. To calculate the weighted average contribution margin per unit, the fact that twice as many A's as B's are sold must be taken into account. Since two Model A's are sold for each Model B, the contribution margin of A is multiplied by 2, and the contribution margin of B is multiplied by 1. The

Illustration 4-13
Calculation of weighted average contribution margin per unit

Master Pen Company

	Contribution Margin Model A	Contribution Margin Model B
Selling Price	$30	$50
Variable cost	15	20
Contribution margin	$15	$30

sum is then divided by 3 units to yield the weighted average contribution margin per unit of $20. (See Illustration 4-13.)

$$\text{Weighted average contribution margin per unit} = \frac{2(\$15) + 1(\$30)}{3} = \$20 \text{ per unit}$$

Now, suppose the Master Pen Company has fixed costs equal to $100,000. How many pens must be sold for the company to break even? Working with the weighted average contribution margin, the break-even point is 5,000 pens.

$$\text{Break-even sales in units} = \frac{\text{Profit} + \text{Total Fixed Costs}}{\text{Weighted average contribution margin per unit}}$$

$$5{,}000 = \frac{0 + \$100{,}000}{\$20}$$

These 5,000 units would be made up of the typical two-to-one mix. Thus, Master Pen must sell 3,333 Model A's (two-thirds of 5,000) and 1,667 Model B's (one-third of 5,000) to break even.

CONTRIBUTION MARGIN RATIO APPROACH

If the products that a company sells are substantially different, CVP analysis should be performed using the contribution margin ratio. Consider a large store like Wal-Mart, which sells literally thousands of different products. In this setting, it does not make sense to ask how many *units* must be sold to break even or how many *units* must be sold to generate a profit of $100,000. Because the costs and selling prices of the various items sold are considerably different, analyzing these types of questions in terms of number of units is not useful. Instead, these questions are addressed in terms of sales dollars. It is perfectly reasonable to ask how much *sales* must be to break even or how much *sales* must be to generate a profit of $100,000. To answer these questions, the contribution margin ratio rather than the contribution margin per unit is used.

Suppose the Packaged Software Products Division of Mayfield Software is interested in using CVP analysis to analyze its product lines. The division has three major product lines—games, learning software, and personal finance software products. All have different costs and selling prices. After performing a detailed study of fixed and variable costs in the prior year, the company prepared the analysis of product-line profitability shown in Illustration 4-14.

Let's review the report. From sales of each product line, the division subtracts variable costs to identify the contribution margin. The contribution margin is then divided by sales to identify the contribution margin ratio. The same procedure can be followed to identify the contribution margin ratio for the entire division. Given

Illustration 4-14
Profitability analysis of product lines

Mayfield Software

Packaged Software Products Division
Profitability Analysis
For the Year Ended December 31, 2006

Packaged Software Products	**Games**	**Learning**	**Personal Finance**	**Total**	
Sales	$20,000,000	$15,000,000	$12,000,000	$47,000,000	(a)
Less variable costs:					
Material/packaging costs	2,000,000	1,200,000	1,440,000	4,640,000	
Order processing labor	1,000,000	900,000	720,000	2,620,000	
Billing labor and materials	800,000	450,000	600,000	1,850,000	
Shipping costs	1,200,000	750,000	720,000	2,670,000	
Sales commissions	400,000	300,000	240,000	940,000	
Total variable costs	5,400,000	3,600,000	3,720,000	12,720,000	
Contribution margin	14,600,000	11,400,000	8,280,000	34,280,000	(b)
Contribution margin ratio	0.73	0.76	0.69	0.73	(a) ÷
Direct fixed costs					
Research and development	2,500,000	1,800,000	1,900,000	6,200,000	
Marketing	6,000,000	4,500,000	3,000,000	13,500,000	
Administrative salaries	1,200,000	900,000	720,000	2,820,000	
Total direct fixed costs	9,700,000	7,200,000	5,620,000	22,520,000	
Product line profit	$ 4,900,000	$ 4,200,000	$ 2,660,000	11,760,000	
Common fixed costs					
Senior management salaries				700,000	
Other common costs				1,500,000	
Total common fixed costs				2,200,000	
Packaged Software Products profit				$ 9,560,000	

the information in the report, what is the break-even level of sales for the Packaged Software Products Division?

To answer this question, the total amount of fixed costs is divided by the contribution margin ratio for the division. Total fixed costs are composed of the direct fixed costs associated with the three product lines plus the common fixed costs. Common fixed costs are related to resources that are shared but not directly identifiable with the product lines. An example is the salary of the division manager. Because the contribution margin ratio for the division is .73 and total fixed costs are $24,720,000 ($22,520,000 direct fixed cost + $2,200,000 common fixed cost), the break-even point is sales of $33,863,014.

$$\text{Break-even point} = \frac{\text{Total fixed costs}}{\text{Contribution margin ratio}}$$

$$\text{Break-even point} = \frac{\$24{,}720{,}000}{.73} = \$33{,}863{,}014$$

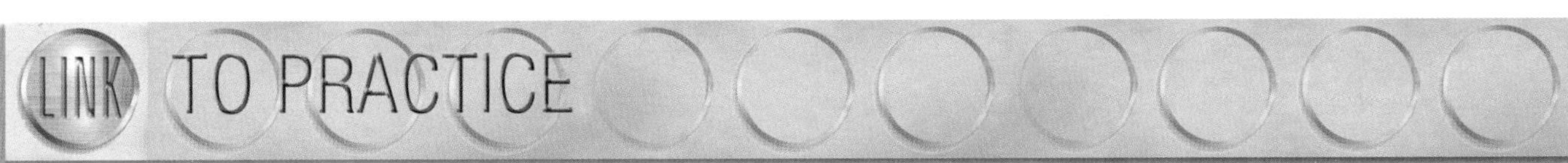

Deciding to Use the Contribution Margin per Unit or the Contribution Margin Ratio

Baskin-Robbins

At an ice cream company like Baskin-Robbins, it is very reasonable for managers to use either the weighted average contribution margin per unit or the weighted average contribution margin ratio in CVP analysis. For example, a manager might want to know the effect on profit of a 1,000,000 gallon increase in sales. Assuming the weighted average contribution margin is \$5 per gallon, profit is expected to increase by \$5,000,000. A manager might also want to know the effect on profit of a \$1,000,000 increase in sales. Assuming a weighted average contribution margin ratio of \$0.30, profit is expected to increase by \$300,000.

Sears

A manager of a Sears store would focus on the weighted average contribution margin ratio, not the weighted average contribution margin per unit. Unlike the units at an ice cream store, the various units at a Sears store are quite different. It doesn't make sense to use a weighted average contribution margin *per unit* when the units are as diverse as refrigerators and shirts. Instead, a manager of a Sears store will focus on the weighted average contribution margin ratio. It would be reasonable for a manager at Sears to ask "What is the weighted average contribution margin ratio for our store?" and use that number to estimate the increase in profit if the store can increase sales by \$20,000,000. Assuming the contribution margin ratio is .20, the expected increase would be \$4,000,000.

The contribution margin ratio can also be used to analyze the effect on net income of a change in total company sales. Suppose in the coming year, management believes that total company sales will increase by 20 percent and is interested in assessing the effect of this increase on overall company profitability. A 20 percent increase in sales is \$9,400,000 (20 percent of \$47,000,000). The weighted average contribution margin ratio of .73 indicates that the company generates \$0.73 of incremental profit on each dollar of sales. Thus, income will increase by $.73 \times \$9,400,000 = \$6,862,000$.

Note that this approach makes one very important assumption: that when overall sales increase, sales of games, learning software, and personal finance software products will increase in the same proportion as current sales. If this assumption is not warranted, then the contribution margin ratios of the three product lines must be weighted by their share of the increase. For example, suppose the company believes sales will increase by \$9,400,000 but expects the increase will be made up of a \$4,000,000 increase in game sales, a \$4,000,000

Which Firm Has the Higher Contribution Margin Ratio?

Listed below are six pairs of firms with different contribution margin ratios (contribution margin per dollar of sales). For each pair, identify the firm with the higher contribution margin ratio. (Answer at bottom.)

Companies

McDonald's versus UAL (United Airlines)

Ford Motor Company versus Kroger (a large grocery chain)

Oracle (a large software company) versus Sears

Nordstrom (a chain of clothing stores) versus E*Trade (an online brokerage firm)

Coca-Cola versus Wal-Mart Stores

Answer United Airlines; Ford Motor Company; Oracle; E*Trade; Coca-Cola.

increase in sales of learning products, and a $1,400,000 increase in sales of personal finance products. To calculate the effect on net income, the contribution margin ratios of the specific departments must be used. The expected increase in profit is $6,926,000.

Department	Increase in Sales	Contribution Margin Ratio	Increase in Profit
Games	$4,000,000	.73	$2,920,000
Learning	4,000,000	.76	3,040,000
Personal Finance	1,400,000	.69	966,000
Total increase in profit			$6,926,000

Why did this analysis yield a larger increase in net income than the preceding analysis? The preceding analysis assumed the increase in sales would be proportionate to the current mix of Games, Learning, and Personal Finance products; the current analysis assumes that of the $9,400,000 increase in sales only $1,400,000 is due to Personal Finance software. Since Personal Finance software is the product line with the lowest contribution margin ratio, profit will be more if proportionately less of this product line is sold.

ASSUMPTIONS IN CVP ANALYSIS

Whenever CVP analysis is performed, a number of assumptions are made that affect the validity of the analysis. Perhaps the primary assumption is that costs can be accurately separated into their fixed and variable components. In some companies, this is a very difficult and costly task. A further assumption is that the fixed costs remain fixed and the variable costs per unit do not change over the activity levels of interest. With large changes in activity, this assumption may not be valid. When performing multiproduct CVP analysis, an important assumption is that the mix remains constant. In spite of these assumptions, most managers find CVP analysis to be a useful tool for exploring various profit targets and for performing "what if" analysis.

CODECONNECT EXAMPLE REVISITED: ANSWERING MARY'S QUESTIONS

Recall that at the beginning of the chapter, Mary Stuart of CodeConnect was faced with several questions related to planning, control, and decision making. Let's go back to these questions and make sure we can answer them.

Planning: Last year, CodeConnect sold 20,000 bar code readers at $200 per unit. The cost of manufacturing these items was $2,940,000, and selling and administrative costs were $800,000. Total profit was $260,000. In the coming year, the company expects to sell 25,000 units. What level of profit should be in the budget for the coming year?

Assume that the $2,940,000 of production costs consist of variable production costs of $90.83 per unit and fixed production costs of $1,123,428 per year. Further, assume that all selling and administrative costs are fixed and equal to $800,000 per year. In this case, expected profit is $805,822.

$$\text{Selling price}(x) - \text{Variable cost}(x) - \text{Fixed costs} = \text{Profit}$$

$$\$200(25{,}000) - \$90.83(25{,}000) - \$1{,}123{,}428 - \$800{,}000 = \$805{,}822$$

Control: In April, production costs were $250,000. In May, costs increased to $265,000, but production also increased from 1,750 units in April to 2,000 units in May. Did the manager responsible for product costs do a good job of controlling costs in May?

Assume that production costs are estimated to be $90.83 per unit of variable cost and $93,619 of fixed costs per month. Then, the expected cost for producing 2,000 bar code readers is $275,279.

$$\text{Variable cost}(x) + \text{Fixed cost} = \text{Total cost}$$

$$\$90.83(2{,}000) + \$93{,}619 = \$275{,}279$$

Because actual costs are somewhat less than expected costs, it appears (based on this limited analysis) that the manager responsible for product costs has done a good job of controlling them.

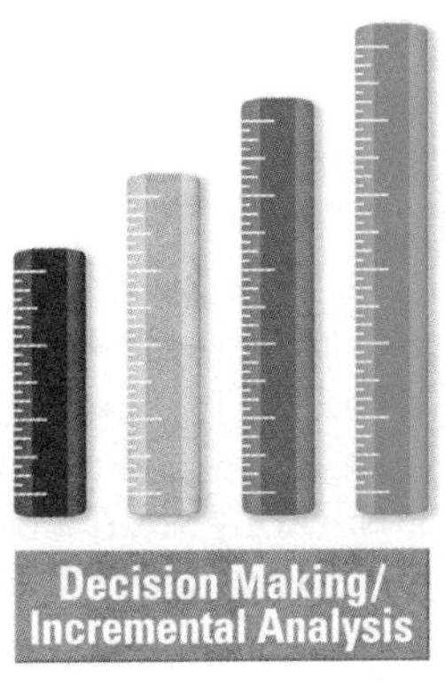

Decision making: The current price for a bar code reader is $200 per unit. If the price is increased to $225 per unit, sales will drop from 20,000 to 17,000. Should the price be increased?

Before answering this question, recall an idea we discussed in Chapter 1: All decisions rely on incremental analysis. For the pricing decision, we can perform an incremental analysis using the contribution margin. Currently, the contribution margin per unit is $109.17 (i.e., $200 − $90.83). Thus, the *total* contribution margin is 20,000 units times $109.17, which equals $2,183,400. If the selling price increases to $225, the contribution margin per unit will increase to $134.17 (i.e., $225 − $90.83). Thus, the *total* contribution margin will increase to $134.17 times 17,000 units, which is $2,280,890. The increase suggests that increasing the selling price is warranted although the effect on profit will be relatively minor. Why aren't fixed costs considered in this analysis? The fixed costs in this decision don't enter into the analysis because they are not incremental costs. Irrespective of the price, the company will have the same level of fixed costs.

Incremental Analysis

Total contribution margin			
	= (Selling price − Variable cost) × Number of units		
$2,183,400	= ($200 − $90.83)	× 20,000	Original price of $200
$2,280,890	= ($225 − $90.83)	× 17,000	New price of $225
$ 97,490	= Incremental profit with new price		

OPERATING LEVERAGE

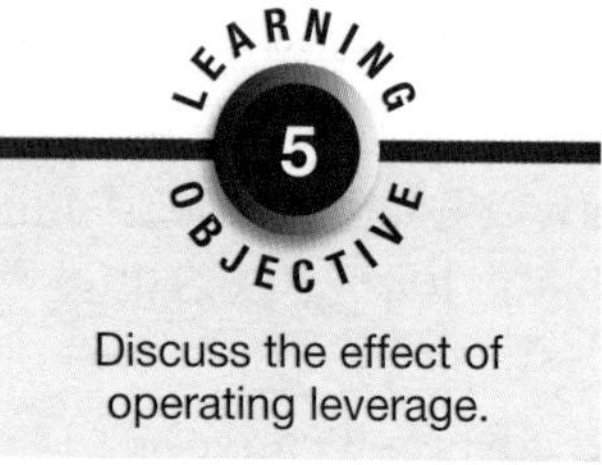

Discuss the effect of operating leverage.

We will cover two additional topics before concluding our discussion of CVP analysis. First, we'll discuss the concept of operating leverage, and then we'll address constraints on output. **Operating leverage** relates to the level of fixed versus variable costs in a firm's cost structure. Firms that have relatively high levels of fixed cost are said to have high operating leverage. To some extent, firms can control their level of operating leverage. For example, a firm can invest in an automated production system using robotics, thus increasing its fixed costs while reducing labor, which is a variable cost. The level of operating leverage is important because it affects the change in profit when sales change. Consider two firms with the same level of profit but different mixes of fixed and variable cost.

	Firm 1	Firm 2
Sales	$10,000,000	$10,000,000
Variable cost	5,000,000	7,000,000
Contribution margin	5,000,000	3,000,000
Fixed costs	3,000,000	1,000,000
Profit	$ 2,000,000	$ 2,000,000

Suppose there is a 20 percent increase in sales. Which firm will have the greatest increase in profit? If Firm 1 has a 20 percent increase in sales, its profit will increase by $1,000,000 (i.e., 20% × the contribution margin) which represents a 50 percent increase in profit. Firm 2, on the other hand will have a profit increase of only $600,000 or 30 percent. Now, suppose there is a 20 percent decrease in sales. Which firm will have the greatest decrease in profit? Again, the answer is Firm 1. This is because it has relatively more fixed costs (higher operating leverage).

Firms that have high operating leverage are generally thought to be more risky because they tend to have large fluctuations in profit when sales fluctuate. However, suppose you are very confident that your firm's sales are going to in-

Governmental Organizations Outsource HR to Turn Fixed Costs into Variable Costs

According to a 2004 report by the Conference Board, federal and state agencies are considering outsourcing their human resource administration functions to private companies. One reason they pursue outsourcing is that it turns fixed costs into variable costs. Consider the State of Florida Department of Management Services. The HR department of this organization must provide services for 189,000 state employees. This entails having a call center to answer questions related to benefits, an automated payroll system and related software and information technology support costs. Many, if not most, of the associated costs are fixed. This can be risky. Suppose the work force shrinks. If costs are primarily fixed, then costs won't decrease. But with outsourcing, the governmental unit pays for services they use. If the unit expands, costs will of course increase. But if the unit contracts, costs will also decline. Since contractions are often associated with fiscal problems, having costs decline can be very important.

Source: The Conference Board, Research Report E-0007-04-RR, *HR Outsourcing in Government Organizations*, 2004.

crease. In that case you would want high operating leverage because the large positive fluctuation in sales will lead to a large positive fluctuation in profit. Unfortunately, many, if not most, managers are not highly confident that their firm's sales will only increase.

A final point on operating leverage: because of fixed costs in the cost structure, when sales increase by 10 percent, profit will increase by more than 10 percent. The only time that you expect profit to increase by the same percent as sales is when all costs are variable. If all costs vary in proportion to sales (i.e., all costs are variable), then profit will vary in proportion to sales.

Use the contribution margin per unit of the constraint to analyze situations involving a resource constraint.

CONSTRAINTS

In many cases (e.g., owing to shortages of space, equipment, or labor) there are constraints on how many items can be produced or how much service can be provided. Under such constraints, the focus shifts from the *contribution margin per unit* to the *contribution margin per unit of the constraint*. For example, suppose a company can produce either Product A or Product B using the same equipment. The contribution margin of A is $200, whereas the contribution margin of B is only $100. However, there are only 1,000 machine hours available, and Product A requires 10 hours of machine time to produce one unit while Product B requires only 2 hours per unit. In this simplified case, the company would only produce Product B. Although its contribution margin is smaller ($100 versus $200), it contributes $50 per machine hour, whereas Product A contributes only $20 per machine hour. In total, with 1,000 available machine hours, Product A can generate

$20,000 of contribution margin while B can generate $50,000 of contribution margin.

	Product A	Product B
Selling price	$500	$300
Variable cost	300	200
Contribution margin	$200	$100
Time to produce 1 unit	10 hours	2 hours
Contribution margin per hour	$20	$50
Contribution margin given 1,000 available hours	$20,000	$50,000

MAKING BUSINESS DECISIONS

In the chapter, we learned how to estimate fixed and variable costs using account analysis, the high-low method, and regression analysis (this latter method is covered in the appendix). All of these methods make the assumption that prior costs are good predictors of future costs. However, decisions that involve significant increases in sales or production may cause prior "fixed" costs to jump to a higher level. This might be due, for example, to the need to hire an additional supervisor.

KNOWLEDGE AND SKILLS CHECKLIST

Knowledge and skills are needed to make good business decisions. Check off the knowledge and skills you've acquired from reading this chapter.

- ❒ K/S 1. You have an expanded business vocabulary (see key terms).
- ❒ K/S 2. You can perform account analysis.
- ❒ K/S 3. You can use the high-low method—and you recognize its limitations.
- ❒ K/S 4. You can use the profit equation to calculate expected profit for various levels of sales.
- ❒ K/S 5. You can perform multiproduct cost-volume-profit analysis.
- ❒ K/S 6. You can use the contribution margin per unit to analyze the effect of selling additional units.
- ❒ K/S 7. You can use the contribution margin ratio to analyze the effect of increasing sales dollars.
- ❒ K/S 8. You know how operating leverage affects the relation between percentage changes in sales and percentage changes in profit.

SUMMARY OF LEARNING OBJECTIVES

1 ***Identify common cost behavior patterns.*** Common cost behavior patterns include those involving variable, fixed, mixed, and step costs. Variable costs are costs that change in proportion to changes in volume or activity. Fixed costs are constant across activity levels. Mixed costs contain both a variable cost component and a fixed cost component. Step costs are fixed for a range of volume but increase to a higher level when the upper bound of the range is exceeded.

2 ***Estimate the relation between cost and activity using account analysis and the high-low method.*** Managers use account analysis, the high-low method, and regression analysis to estimate the relation between cost and activity. Ac-

count analysis requires that the manager use his or her judgment to classify costs as either fixed or variable. The high-low method fits a straight line to the costs at the highest and the lowest activity levels. Regression analysis provides the best straight-line fit to prior cost/activity data.

3 ***Perform cost-volume-profit analysis for single products.*** Once fixed and variable costs have been estimated, cost-volume-profit analysis can be performed. CVP analysis makes use of the profit equation

$$\text{Profit} = \text{SP}(x) - \text{VC}(x) - \text{TFC}$$

to perform "what if" analysis. The effect of changing various components of the equation can be explored by solving the equation for the variable affected by the change. Specific examples include solving for the break-even point or solving the equation to determine the level of volume required to achieve a certain level of profit. The number of units that must be sold or the sales dollars needed to achieve a specified profit level can be determined using the following formulas:

$$\text{Number of units} = \frac{\text{Fixed cost} + \text{Profit}}{\text{Contribution margin}}$$

$$\text{Sales dollars} = \frac{\text{Fixed cost} + \text{Profit}}{\text{Contribution margin ratio}}$$

4 ***Perform cost-volume-profit analysis for multiple products.*** The case of multiple products is easily addressed by using the weighted average contribution margin per unit or the weighted average contribution margin ratio.

5 ***Discuss the effect of operating leverage.*** Operating leverage relates to the level of fixed versus variable costs in a company's cost structure. The higher the level of fixed costs, the greater the operating leverage. Also, the higher the operating leverage, the greater the percentage change in profit for a given percentage change in sales. Firms with high operating leverage are generally considered to be more risky than firms with low operating leverage.

6 ***Use the contribution margin per unit of the constraint to analyze situations involving a resource constraint.*** When there is a constraint, the focus shifts from the contribution margin per unit to the contribution margin per unit of the constraint. The product that has the highest contribution margin per unit of the constraint should be produced because it will generate the greatest contribution to covering fixed costs and generating a profit.

APPENDIX

USING REGRESSION IN EXCEL® TO ESTIMATE FIXED AND VARIABLE COSTS

In this appendix, we will see how to use the Regression function in Excel® to estimate fixed and variable costs using the data for CodeConnect presented in Illustration 4-7. As you will see, the spreadsheet program makes *performing* regression analysis very easy. However, it doesn't make *understanding* regression analysis easy! While we will discuss the interpretation of the output of the regression program, it would be wise to consult the treatment of regression analysis in an introductory statistics book before doing any real-world analysis.

SETTING UP THE SPREADSHEET

In a normal installation of Excel®, data analysis programs such as Regression are not installed. So, before trying to perform regression, make sure you have installed the data analysis programs.

Once you have installed the data analysis programs, open a spreadsheet and enter the cost and production data from Illustration 4-7 in columns A and B. Now go under *Tools* and scroll down to *Data Analysis* (see Illustration A4-1). When the

Illustration A4-1
Under *Tools*, select *Data Analysis*

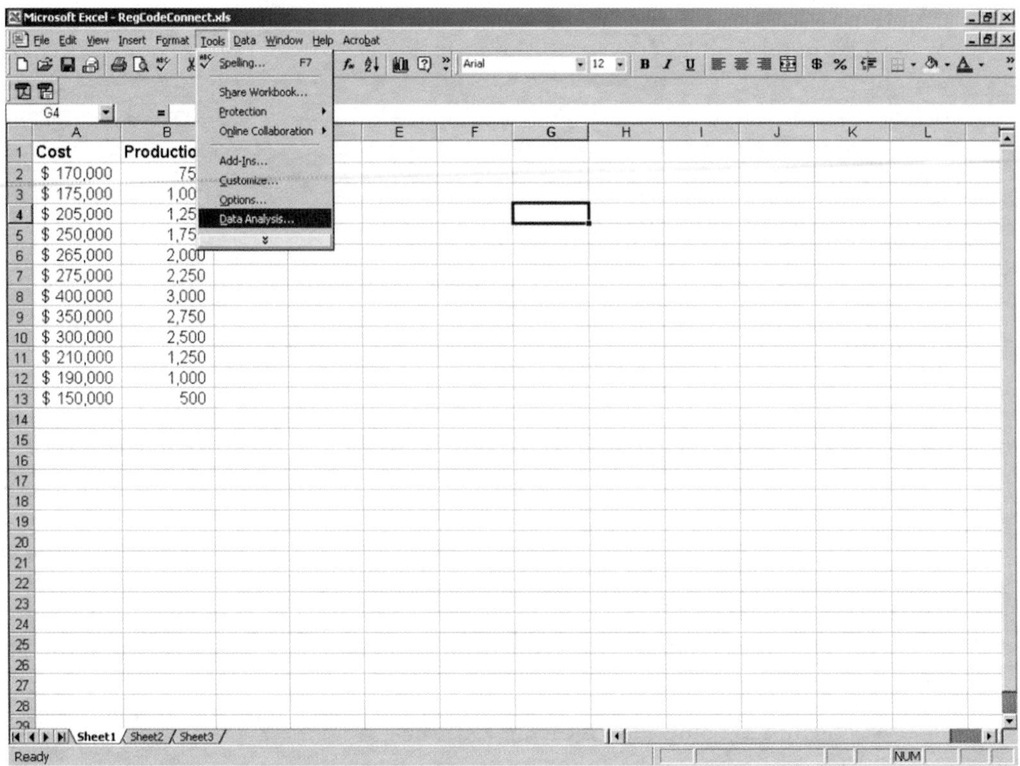

Data Analysis box opens up, scroll down to *Regression* and click *OK* (see Illustration A4-2).

Once the Regression program opens, under *Input Y*, scroll down from A1 to A13. Note that this includes the heading "Cost." Under *Input X*, scroll down from B1 to B13. Note that this includes the heading "Production." Click on Labels, which indicates that you have labels for Production and Cost data columns.

Under *Output options*, click on *New workbook*. Under *residuals*, click on *Line fit plot*. This indicates that you want a plot of the data and the regression line. At this point, your spreadsheet should look like the one in Illustration A4-3. Now click on *OK* and the Regression program will yield the output presented in Illustration A4-4.

INTERPRETING THE OUTPUT OF THE *REGRESSION* PROGRAM

Let's interpret the most critical elements of the regression output.

The Plot. The plot of the data and the plot of the regression line indicate that the data line up quite close to the regression line. This suggests that a straight-line fit to the data will be quite successful.

R Square. R Square is a statistical measure of how well the regression line fits the data. Specifically, it measures the percent of variance in the dependent variable (cost in the current case) explained by the independent variable (production). R Square ranges from a low of 0, indicating that there is no linear

Illustration A4-2
Under *Data Analysis*, select *Regression*

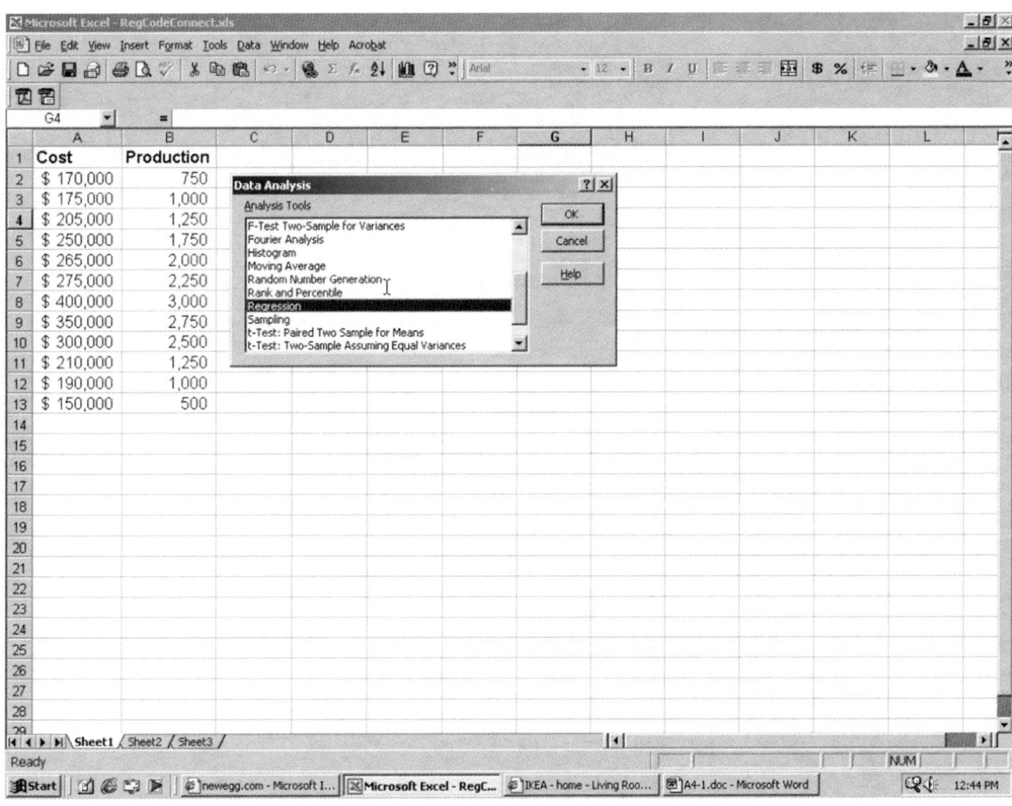

Illustration A4-3
Regression Program

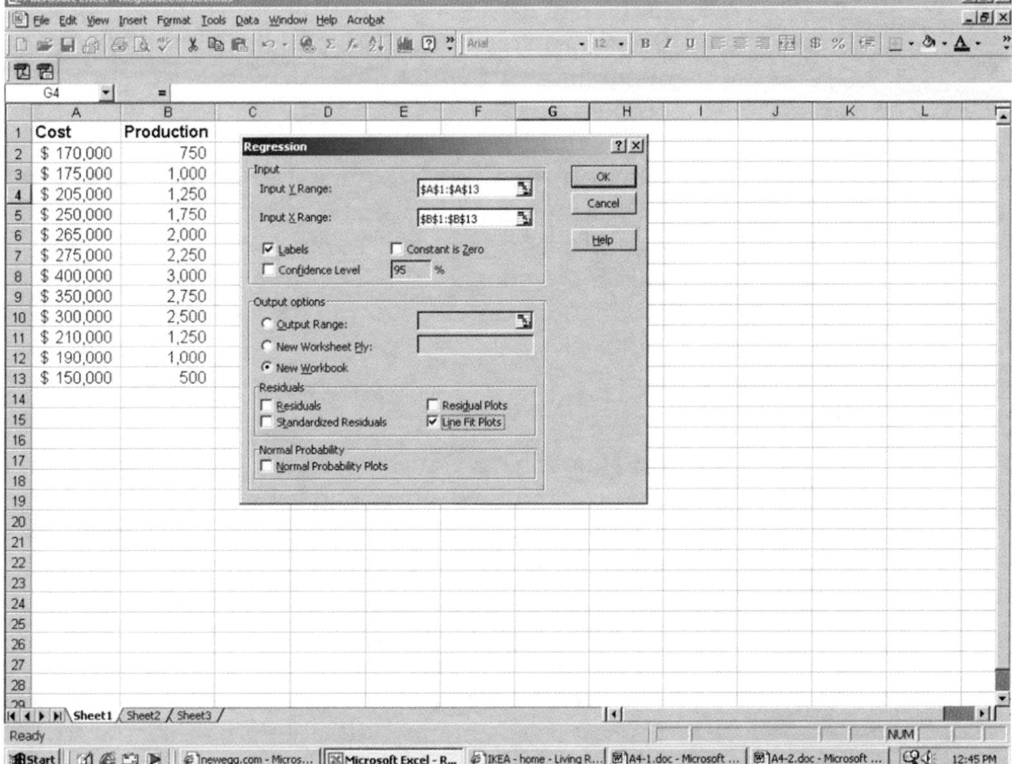

Illustration A4-4
Regression Output

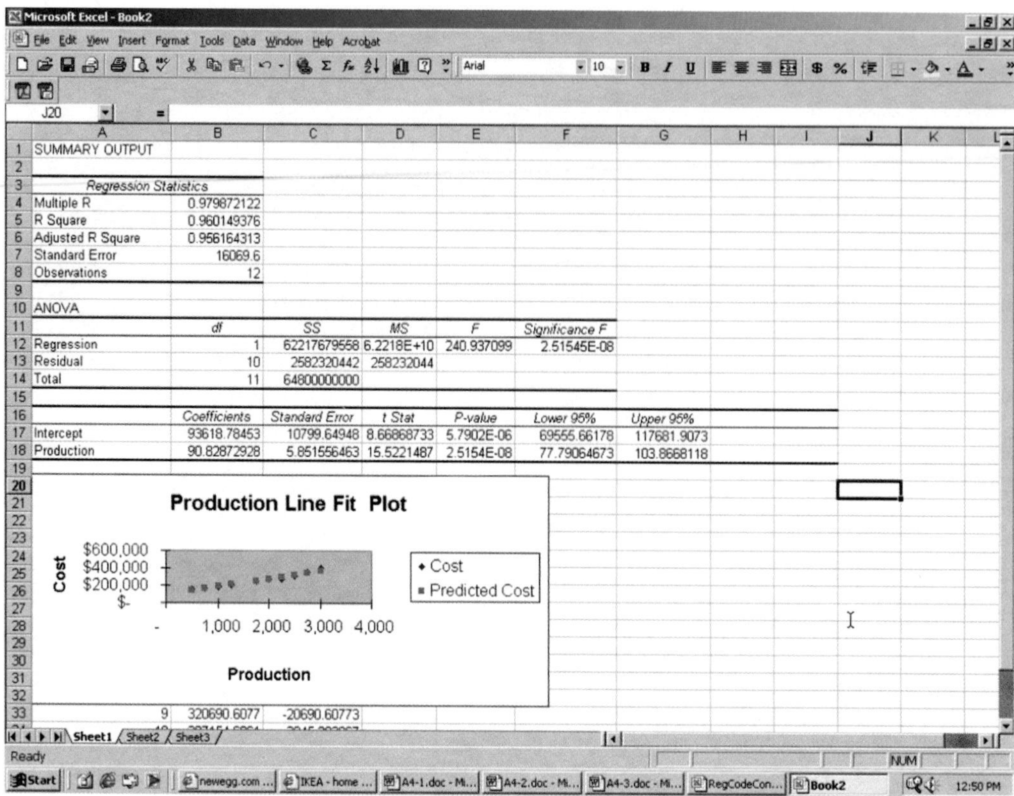

SUMMARY OUTPUT

Regression Statistics	
Multiple R	0.979872122
R Square	0.960149376
Adjusted R Square	0.956164313
Standard Error	16069.6
Observations	12

ANOVA

	df	*SS*	*MS*	*F*	*Significance F*
Regression	1	62217679558	6.2218E+10	240.937099	2.51545E-08
Residual	10	2582320442	258232044		
Total	11	64800000000			

	Coefficients	*Standard Error*	*t Stat*	*P-value*	*Lower 95%*	*Upper 95%*
Intercept	93618.78453	10799.64948	8.66868733	5.7902E-06	69555.66178	117681.9073
Production	90.82872928	5.851556463	15.5221487	2.5154E-08	77.79064673	103.8668118

relation between cost and production, to a high of 1, indicating that there is a perfect linear relation between cost and production. In the current case, R Square is .96 which is quite high. This reinforces our conclusion from looking at the plot of the data that there is a strong linear relation between cost and production.

Intercept and Slope of the Regression Line. The intercept of the regression line is interpreted as the estimate of fixed cost while the slope of the regression line is interpreted as the variable cost per unit. The output from the regression indicates that the intercept is $93,618.78 while the coefficient on production (the slope of the regression line) is $90.83. Thus, the regression line indicates that:

$$\text{Cost} = \$93{,}618.78 + \$90.83\ (\text{Production})$$

P-Value. The p-values corresponding to the intercept and the slope measure the probability of observing values as large as the estimated coefficients when the true values are zero. In other words, there is some probability that even when the true fixed cost is zero we will observe an estimate as large as $93,618.78. We would, of course, like this probability to be quite low (at least less than .05). In the current case the probability is very low (.00000579022). Likewise, the probability that we will observe an estimate as large as $90.83 when the true variable cost per unit is zero is also very low (.0000000251545). Thus, it seems highly unlikely that either the true fixed cost is zero or that the true variable cost per unit is zero.

REVIEW PROBLEM 1

Potter Janitorial Services provides cleaning services to both homes and offices. In the past year, income before taxes was $4,250 as follows:

	Home	Office	Total
Revenue	$250,000	$425,000	$675,000
Less variable costs:			
Cleaning staff salaries	175,000	276,250	451,250
Supplies	30,000	42,500	72,500
Contribution margin	$ 45,000	$106,250	151,250
Less common fixed costs:			
Billing and accounting			25,000
Owner salary			90,000
Other miscellaneous common fixed costs			32,000
Income before taxes			$ 4,250

For the coming year, Janice Potter, the company owner, would like to perform CVP analysis and she has asked you to help her address the following independent questions.

Required

a. What are the contribution margin ratios of the Home and Office segments and what is the overall contribution margin ratio?
b. Assuming the mix of home and office services does not change, what amount of revenue will be needed for Janice to earn a salary of $125,000 and have income before taxes of $4,000?
c. Suppose staff salaries increase by 20 percent. In this case, how will break-even sales compare in the coming year to the prior year?

Answer

a. Contribution margin ratio for Home = $45,000 ÷ $250,000 = .18
   Contribution margin ratio for Office = $106,250 ÷ $425,000 = .25
   Overall contribution margin ratio = $151,250 ÷ $675,000 = .22407
b. ($25,000 + $125,000 + $32,000 + $4,000) ÷ .22407 = $830,097.34
c. Break-even in the prior year = ($25,000 + $90,000 + $32,000) ÷ .22407 = $656,044.99.

   If staff salaries increase by 20 percent, then the contribution margin ratios will be as follows:

Revenue	$250,000	$425,000	$675,000
Less variable costs:			
Cleaning staff salaries	210,000	331,500	541,500
Supplies	30,000	42,500	72,500
Contribution margin	10,000	51,000	61,000
Contribution margin ratios	0.0400	0.1200	0.09037

   In this case, the break-even level of sales will be = ($25,000 + $90,000 + $32,000) ÷ .09037 = $1,626,646.01. Obviously, a 20% increase in staff salaries will have a very significant impact on the break-even level of sales.

REVIEW PROBLEM 2

The Antibody Research Institute (ARI) is a biotechnology company that develops humanized antibodies to treat various diseases. Antibodies are proteins that bind with a foreign substance such as a virus and render it inactive. The company operates a research lab in Boston and currently employs 23 scientists. Most of the company's work involves development of humanized antibodies for specific pharmaceutical companies. Revenue comes from this contract work and from royalties on products that ultimately make use of ARI developed antibodies.

In the coming year, the company expects to incur the following costs:

Expense Summary

Salaries of 23 research scientists	$2,760,000
Administrative salaries	785,000
Depreciation of building and equipment	3,200,000
Laboratory supplies	765,000
Utilities and other miscellaneous (fixed) expenses	285,000
Total	$7,795,000

Annual contract revenue is projected to be $4,000,000. The company also anticipates royalties related to the sale of Oxacine, which is a product that will come to market next year. Oxacine is marketed by Reach Pharmaceuticals and makes use of an antibody developed under contract with ARI. The product is scheduled to sell for $120 per unit and ARI will receive a royalty of 20 percent of sales. ARI, in turn, has a contractual commitment to pay 10 percent of royalties it receives (i.e., 10% of the 20%) to the scientists who were on the team that developed the antibody.

Required

a. How many units of Oxacine must be sold for ARI to achieve its break-even point?
b. Reach Pharmaceuticals has projected annual sales of 180,000 units of Oxacine. Assuming this level of sales, what will be the before-tax profit of ARI?
c. What if Reach Pharmaceuticals sells only 160,000 units of Oxacine? Assuming that the average salary of scientists is $120,000, how many scientists must be "downsized" to achieve the break-even point?
d. Do you consider ARI to be high or low with respect to operating leverage? Explain.

Answer

a. $4,000,000 + .20($120)(Q) − .10(.20)($120)(Q) − $7,795,000 = $–0–
 $21.6(Q) = $3,795,000
 Q = 175,694.44
b. $4,000,000 + .20($120)(180,000) − .10(.20)($120)(180,000) − $7,795,000 = $93,000
c. $4,000,000 + .20($120)(160,000) − .10(.20)($120)(160,000) − $7,795,000 = ($339,000)
 Average salary = $2,760,000 ÷ 23 = $120,000
 ($339,000) ÷ $120,000 = (2.825)
 This implies that approximately 3 scientists must be "downsized."
d. ARI is extremely high with respect to operating leverage since costs other than royalty payments to scientists are generally fixed. The fact that the costs are fixed does not mean, however, that they cannot be cut. Some costs such as the salaries of the scientists are discretionary fixed costs. Other costs such as depreciation are committed fixed costs.

KEY TERMS

Account analysis (130)
Break-even point (138)
Committed fixed costs (128)
Contribution margin (140)
Contribution margin ratio (140)
Cost-volume-profit (CVP) analysis (126)
Discretionary fixed costs (128)
Fixed costs (126)
High-low method (134)
Margin of safety (139)
Mixed costs (128)
Operating leverage (148)
Profit equation (138)
Regression analysis (136)
Relevant range (137)
Scattergraph (132)
Semivariable costs (128)
Step costs (129)
Variable costs (126)
"What-if" analysis (141)

SELF ASSESSMENT *(Answers Below)*

1. At Branson Corporation, the selling price per unit is $800 and variable cost per unit is $500. Fixed costs are $1,000,000 per year. In this case, the contribution margin per unit is:

a. $300
b. $0.375
c. 2,500 units.
d. None of the above.

2. At Branson Corporation, the selling price per unit is $800 and variable cost per unit is $500. Fixed costs are $1,000,000 per year. Assuming sales of $3,000,000, profit will be:

a. $125,000
b. $680,000
c. $750,000
d. None of the above.

3. The contribution margin ratio measures:

a. Profit per unit.
b. Contribution margin per dollar of sales.
c. Profit per dollar of sales.
d. The ratio of variable to fixed costs.

4. In March, Octavius Company had the following costs related to producing 5,000 units:

Direct materials	$60,000
Direct labor	20,000
Rent	5,000
Depreciation	4,000

Estimate variable cost per unit using account analysis.

a. $17.80
b. $4.00
c. $5.80
d. $16.00

5. Using the following production/cost data, estimate variable cost per unit using the high-low method:

Month	Production	Cost
January	2,000	$20,000
February	2,500	$21,000
March	3,000	$23,000
April	1,900	$18,500

a. $4.00
b. $3.70
c. $4.20
d. $4.09

6. At Branson Corporation, the selling price per unit is $800 and variable cost per unit is $500. Fixed costs are $1,000,000 per year. In this case, the break-even point is approximately:

a. 3,333 units.
b. 6,667 units.
c. 5,500 units.
d. None of the above.

7. Consider the sales and variable cost information for the three departments at Fortesque Drug in May:

	Drugs	Cosmetics	Housewares
Sales	$80,000	$40,000	$30,000
Variable cost	40,000	15,000	25,000
Contribution margin	$40,000	$25,000	$ 5,000

Based on this information, estimate the increase in profit for a $10,000 increase in sales (assuming the sales mix stays the same).

a. $4,667
b. $5,667
c. $3,334
d. None of the above.

8. Consider the sales and variable cost information in Question 7. Assuming that total fixed costs at Fortesque Drug are $30,000 per month, what is the break-even level of sales in dollars?

a. $86,326
b. $45,876
c. $72,284
d. $64,286.

9. If a firm has relatively high operating leverage, it has:

a. Relatively high variable costs.
b. Relatively high fixed costs.
c. Relatively low operating expenses.
d. Relatively high operating expenses.

10. Product A has a contribution margin per unit of $500 and requires 2 hours of machine time. Product B has a contribution margin per unit of $1,000 and requires 5 hours of machine time. How much of each product should be produced given there are 100 hours of available machine time?

a. 50 units of A.
b. 25 units of B.
c. 50 units of A and 25 units of B.
d. None of the above.

Answers to Self Assessment

1. a; **2.** a; **3.** b; **4.** d; **5.** d; **6.** a;
7. a; **8.** d; **9.** b; **10.** a.

INTERACTIVE LEARNING

Enhance and test your knowledge of Chapter 4 using Wiley's online resources.

1. Learning Objectives
2. Multiple Choice
3. Language of Business—Matching of Key Terms
4. Critical Thinking
5. Demonstration—How variable costs, fixed costs, and the selling price affect the break-even point
6. Case—The Games Division of Mayfield Software; Calculating the break-even point
7. Video—Holland America West Tours; Fixed and variable costs of a cruise.

Go to our dynamic Web site for more self-assessment, Web links, and additional information.

QUESTIONS

1. Define the term "mixed cost" and provide an example of such a cost.
2. Distinguish between discretionary and committed fixed costs.
3. Provide two examples of costs that are likely to be variable costs.
4. Provide two examples of costs that are likely to be fixed costs.
5. Explain why total compensation paid to the sales force is likely to be a mixed cost.
6. Explain how one uses account analysis to estimate fixed and variable costs.
7. Explain the concept of a relevant range.
8. What is the difference between the contribution margin and the contribution margin ratio?
9. In a multiproduct setting, when would it not be appropriate to focus on a weighted average contribution margin per unit?
10. Which company would have higher operating leverage: a software company that makes large investments in research and development, or a manufacturing company that uses expensive materials and relies on highly skilled manual labor rather than automation? Why?

EXERCISES

EXERCISE 4-1. Group Assignment Audrey Bard is planning on opening a 3,000-square-foot restaurant in Columbus, Ohio. As a small business owner, Audrey is concerned about controlling her mix of fixed and variable costs. As Audrey noted, "If I have too much fixed cost and sales don't take off right away, I'll have tremendous losses and may even go bust."

Required

Expand on Audrey's comment. Why is it crucial that small businesses limit their exposure to fixed costs? Identify a way that Audrey can turn potential fixed costs into variable costs.

EXERCISE 4-2. Writing Assignment During the 1990s, profits at Microsoft grew by an average of 47.5 percent per year, far faster than the 38.1 percent average annual growth in sales. Since profit growth drives stock prices, it is not surprising that the huge increases in the bottom line translated into huge increases in Microsoft's stock price.

Required
Write a paragraph explaining how Microsoft managed to grow profits at a rate substantially higher than its rate of growth for sales. Be sure to comment on the cost structure at Microsoft.

EXERCISE 4-3. Internet Assignment Go to the Web site for Men's Wearhouse (http://www.menswearhouse.com). From there, go to Investor Relations and locate the company's annual report. Examine the line item "Gross Margin" on the company income statement. Explain why the gross margin divided by net sales is likely to underestimate the company's weighted average contribution margin ratio.

Now go to the Web site for Best Buy (http://www.bestbuy.com/) and locate their annual report. Consider their gross profit, which is equivalent to a gross margin. Explain why dividing their gross profit by revenues may provide a reasonable estimate of the firm's weighted average contribution margin ratio.

EXERCISE 4-4. Cost Behavior Information for three costs incurred at Boole Manufacturing in the first quarter follows:

	Month	Cost	Units Produced
Depreciation	January	$550,000	6,000
	February	$550,000	9,000
	March	$550,000	12,000
Direct labor	January	$210,000	6,000
	February	$315,000	9,000
	March	$420,000	12,000
Telecommunications	January	$225,000	6,000
	February	$300,000	9,000
	March	$375,000	12,000

Required
Plot each cost, making the vertical axis cost and the horizontal axis units produced. Classify each cost (depreciation, direct labor, and telecommunications) as either fixed, variable, or mixed.

EXERCISE 4-5. High-Low Method Campus Copy & Printing wants to predict copy machine repair expense at different levels of copying activity (number of copies made). The following data have been gathered:

	Copy Machine	
Month	**Repair Expense**	**Copies Made**
May	$ 4,000	200,000
June	6,000	400,000
July	10,000	800,000
August	8,000	600,000
September	5,000	300,000

Required
Determine the fixed and variable components of repair expense using the high-low method. Use copies made as the measure of activity.

EXERCISE 4-6. High-Low Method Madrigal Theater Company is interested in estimating fixed and variable costs. The following data are available:

	Cost	No. of Tickets Sold
January	$180,000	18,000
February	212,000	21,000
March	232,000	25,000
April	239,000	27,000
May	231,000	27,500
June	208,000	21,500
July	199,000	20,000
August	165,000	15,000
September	212,000	22,500
October	217,000	24,000
November	230,000	28,000
December	255,000	30,000

Required

a. Use the high-low method to estimate fixed cost per month and variable costs per ticket sold [i.e., estimate a and b in the equation Cost = a + (b × # of tickets) using the high-low method].

b. Madrigal Theater Company is considering an advertising campaign that is expected to increase annual sales by 12,000 tickets. Assume that the ticket selling price is $30. Ignoring the cost of the advertising campaign, what is the expected increase in profit associated with the advertising campaign?

c. (optional) Repeat part a using regression analysis. In light of the result, how would you answer Part b?

EXERCISE 4-7. Scattergraph Reef Office Supplies is interested in estimating the relationship between customer service costs and sales. The following data are available:

Month	Customer Service Cost	Sales
May	$6,000	$100,000
June	$6,500	$140,000
July	$7,300	$170,000
August	$10,200	$200,000
September	$10,800	$225,000

Required

a. Prepare a scattergraph of customer service cost (vertical axis) and sales (horizontal axis).

b. Comment on whether there appears to be a linear relation between cost and sales and whether any of the observations appear to be outliers.

EXERCISE 4-8. Account Analysis Reef Office Supplies is interested in estimating the cost involved in hiring new employees. The following information is available regarding the costs of operating the Human Resource department at Reef Office Supplies in May when there were 50 new hires.

Human Resource Department
May

Staff salaries	$25,000
Manager salary	7,000
Office supplies	200
Depreciation of office equipment	300
Share of building cost (based on square feet occupied by Human Resources)	1,500
Total	$34,000

Required

a. Use account analysis to determine fixed cost per month and variable cost per new hire.

b. The company is planning to hire 60 employees in June. Estimate the total cost of Human Resources for June.

c. What is the expected incremental cost associated with hiring 10 more employees than were hired in May?

EXERCISE 4-9. Account analysis Madrigal Theater Company is interested in estimating fixed and variable costs. The following data are available for the month of December.

	No. of Tickets Sold	Cost
December	30,000	$255,000
Detail of Cost:		
Author royalties/fees*	$ 75,000	
Wages (ticket office, ushers, etc.)	103,000	
Rent	50,000	
Utilities	6,000	
Depreciation—theater equipment	12,000	
Owner's salary	9,000	
Total	$255,000	

Author royalties/fees are fixed because the theater pays for the right to put on the play; royalties and fees are not paid based on the number of tickets sold.

Required

a. Use account analysis to estimate fixed cost per month and variable costs per dollar of sales [i.e., estimate a and b in the equation Cost = a + (b × Sales)].

b. Assume that the selling price per ticket is $30. Based on your answer to part a, what is your estimate of the contribution margin ratio at Madrigal Theater?

EXERCISE 4-10. Account analysis Scherzo Industrial is interested in estimating fixed and variable manufacturing costs using data from October. Based on judgment, the plant manager classified each manufacturing cost as fixed, variable, or part fixed and part variable.

	Units Produced	Cost	
October	1,000	$101,600	
Detail of Cost			**Cost Behavior**
Material		$ 42,000	*Variable*
Direct labor		15,000	*Variable*
Depreciation		8,000	*Fixed*
Phone		200	*Fixed*
Other utilities		4,000	*20% Fixed*
Supervisory salaries		20,000	*80% Fixed*
Equipment repair		6,000	*10% Fixed*
Indirect materials		400	*Variable*
Factory maintenance		6,000	*90% Fixed*
Total		$101,600	

Required

a. Use account analysis to estimate fixed cost per month and variable costs per unit produced.

b. Based on your answer to Part a, what is your estimate of the incremental cost of producing 200 units?

EXERCISE 4-11. CVP Analysis Gabby's Wedding Cakes creates elaborate wedding cakes. Each cake sells for $500. The variable cost of making the cakes is $200 and the fixed cost per month is $6,000.

Required

a. Calculate the break-even point for a month in units.

b. How many cakes must be sold to earn a monthly profit of $9,000?

EXERCISE 4-12. CVP Analysis, Profit Equation Clyde's Marina has estimated that fixed costs per month are $240,000 and variable cost per dollar of sales is $0.60.

Required

a. What is the break-even point per month in sales?

b. What level of sales is needed for a monthly profit of $60,000?

c. For the month of July, the marina anticipates sales of $1,200,000. What is the expected level of profit?

EXERCISE 4-13. Contribution Margin Rhetorix, Inc. produces stereo speakers. The selling price per pair of speakers is $800. The variable cost of production is $300 and the fixed cost per month is $50,000.

Required

a. Calculate the contribution margin associated with a pair of speakers.

b. In August, the company sold five more pairs of speakers than planned. What is the expected effect on profit of selling the additional speakers?

c. Calculate the contribution margin ratio for Rhetorix associated with a pair of speakers.

d. In October, the company had sales that were $5,000 higher than planned. What is the expected effect on profit related to the additional sales?

EXERCISE 4-14. Margin of Safety Rhetorix, Inc. produces stereo speakers. The selling price per pair of speakers is $800. The variable cost of production is $300 and the fixed cost per month is $50,000. For November, the company expects to sell 120 pairs of speakers.

Required

a. Calculate expected profit.

b. Calculate the margin of safety in dollars.

EXERCISE 4-15. "What If" Analysis Rhetorix, Inc. produces stereo speakers. The selling price per pair of speakers is $800. The variable cost of production is $300 and the fixed cost per month is $50,000.

Required
Calculate the expected profit for November assuming the company sells 120 pairs of speakers as planned (see Exercise 14), but the selling price changes to $1,000.

EXERCISE 4-16. Multiproduct, Contribution Margin Ratio Wilde Home & Garden is organized into three departments. The following sales and cost data are available for the prior year:

	Dept A	Dept B	Dept C	Total
Sales	$265,000	$850,000	$900,000	$2,015,000
Less variable costs	106,000	510,000	720,000	1,336,000
Contribution margin	159,000	340,000	180,000	679,000
Less fixed costs	60,000	85,000	92,000	237,000
Profit	$ 99,000	$255,000	$ 88,000	$ 442,000

Required

a. What is the weighted average contribution margin ratio?

b. What level of sales is needed to earn a profit of $500,000 assuming the current mix?

c. Wilde Home & Garden places an advertisement in the local paper each week. All else equal, which department would you emphasize in the advertisement?

EXERCISE 4-17. Operating Leverage Refer to the data in Exercise 16.

Required

a. Calculate profit as a percent of sales in the prior year.

b. Suppose sales in the current year increase by 20 percent. Calculate profit as a percent of sales for the new level of sales and explain why the percent is greater than the one calculated in Part a.

EXERCISE 4-18. Constraints Dvorak Music produces two durable music stands:

	Stand A	Stand B
Selling price	$80	$70
Less variable costs	20	40
Contribution margin	$60	$30

Stand A requires 5 labor hours and stand B requires 2 labor hours. The company has only 320 available labor hours per week. Further, the company can sell all it can produce of either product.

Required

a. Which stand(s) should the company produce?

b. What would be the incremental benefit of obtaining 10 additional labor hours?

PROBLEMS

PROBLEM 4-1. Cost Behavior Hotel Majestic is interested in estimating fixed and variable costs so that the company can make more accurate projections of costs and profit. The hotel is in a resort area that is particularly busy from November through February. In July and August, however, the hotel has only a 50 percent occupancy rate.

Required

Classify each of the following costs as fixed (F), variable (V), or mixed (M) with respect to the number of hotel guests per month:

_____ a. Depreciation of the building
_____ b. Salaries of restaurant staff
_____ c. Salaries of administrative staff (hotel manager, desk clerks, accountants, etc.)
_____ d. Soap, shampoo, and other toiletries in rooms
_____ e. Laundry costs (cost of linens, cleaning products, depreciation of laundry equipment, etc.)
_____ f. Food and beverage costs
_____ g. Grounds maintenance

PROBLEM 4-2. Account Analysis Lancer Audio produces a high-end DVD player that sells for $1,250. Total operating expenses for July were as follows:

Units produced and sold	**140**
Component cost	$ 67,000
Supplies	1,680
Assembly labor	23,500
Rent	2,200
Supervisor salary	5,500
Electricity	250
Telephone	180
Gas	200
Shipping	1,540
Advertising	2,500
Administrative costs	14,500
Total	$119,050

Required

a. Use account analysis to determine fixed cost per month and variable cost per DVD player.

b. Project total cost for August assuming production and sales of 160 units.

c. What is the contribution margin per DVD player?

d. Estimate total profit assuming production and sales of 160 units.

e. Lancer Audio is considering an order for 100 DVD players, to be produced in the next 10 months, from a customer in Canada. The selling price will be $900 per unit (well under the normal selling price). However, the Lancer Audio brand name will not be attached to the product. What will be the impact on company profit associated with this order?

PROBLEM 4-3. High-Low, Break-Even Lancer Audio produces a high-end DVD player that sells for $1,250. Total operating expenses for the past 12 months are as follows:

	Units Produced and Sold	Cost
August	125	$112,670
September	145	121,990
October	150	129,500
November	160	131,500
December	165	139,700
January	140	117,400
February	145	125,600
March	135	115,400
April	130	116,140
May	135	119,220
June	145	121,700
July	140	119,050

Required

a. Use the high-low method to estimate fixed and variable costs.

b. Based on these estimates, calculate the break-even level of sales in units.

c. Calculate the margin of safety for the coming August assuming estimated sales of 160 units.

d. Estimate total profit assuming production and sales of 160 units.

e. Comment on the limitations of the high-low method in estimating costs for Lancer Audio.

PROBLEM 4-4. Regression Analysis (see Appendix) Lancer Audio produces a high-end DVD player that sells for $1,250. Total operating expenses for the past 12 months are as follows:

	Units Produced and Sold	Cost
August	125	$112,670
September	145	121,990
October	150	129,500
November	160	131,500
December	165	139,700
January	140	117,400
February	145	125,600
March	135	115,400
April	130	116,140
May	135	119,220
June	145	121,700
July	140	119,050

Required

a. Use regression analysis to estimate fixed and variable costs.

b. Compare your estimates to those obtained using account analysis (Problem 2) or the high-low method (Problem 3). Which method provides the best estimates of fixed and variable costs?

PROBLEM 4-5. Break-Even, "What If" Michael Bordellet is the owner/pilot of Bordellet Air Service. The company flies a daily round trip from Seattle's Lake Union to a resort in Canada. In 2007, the company reported an annual income before taxes of $4,100 although that included a deduction of $60,000 reflecting Michael's "salary."

Revenue		$436,800
($350 × 1,248 passengers)		
Less costs:		
Pilot (owner's salary)	$ 60,000	
Fuel (35,657 gallons × $4)	142,628	
Maintenance (variable)	124,800	
Depreciation of plane	20,000	
Depreciation of office equipment	1,500	
Rent expense	36,000	
Insurance	18,000	
Miscellaneous (fixed)	6,000	432,700
Income before taxes		$ 4,100

Revenue of $436,800 reflects six round trips per week for 52 weeks with an average of four passengers paying $350 each per round trip (6 × 52 × 4 × $350 = $436,800). The flight to the resort is 400 miles one way. With 312 round trips (6 per week × 52 weeks), that amounts to 249,600 miles. The plane averages 7 miles per gallon.

Required

a. How many round trips is Michael currently flying, and how many round trips are needed in total to break even?

b. How many round trips are needed so that Michael can draw a salary of $100,000 and still not show a loss?

c. What is the average before-tax profit of a round trip flight in 2007?

d. What is the incremental profit associated with adding a round trip flight?

PROBLEM 4-6. Account Analysis, High-Low, Contribution Margin Information on occupancy and costs at the New Light Hotel for April, May, and June are indicated below:

	April	**May**	**June**
Occupancy	1,500	1,650	1,800
Day manager salary	$ 4,200	$ 4,200	$ 4,200
Night manager salary	3,700	3,700	3,700
Cleaning staff	15,300	15,600	15,900
Depreciation	12,000	12,000	12,000
Complimentary continental breakfast:			
food and beverages	4,600	5,300	5,800
Total	$39,800	$40,800	$41,600

Required

a. Calculate the fixed costs per month and the variable cost per occupied room using account analysis for April.

b. Calculate the fixed costs per month and the variable cost per occupied room using the high-low method.

c. Average room rates are $110 per night. What is the contribution margin per occupied room? In answering this question, use your variable cost estimate from Part b.

PROBLEM 4-7. Fixed and Variable Costs, The Profit Equation Last year, Emily Sanford had a booth at the three-day Indianapolis Craft Expo where she sold a variety of silver jewelry handcrafted in India. Her before-tax profit was as follows:

Sales	$17,800
Cost of jewelry sold	10,680
Gross margin	7,120
Registration fee	1,500
Booth rental (5% sales)	890
Salary of Mindy Orwell	425
Before tax profit	$ 4,305

Mindy Orwell is a friend who takes care of the booth for approximately 5 hours from 9 A.M. until 2 P.M. Emily takes over from 2 P.M. until closing at 9 P.M. Emily has added several new designs to her collection and anticipates that in the coming year, her sales will increase by 25 percent to $22,250. In light of this, she has forecasted before-tax profit as follows:

Before-tax profit in prior year	$ 4,305	a
Sales in prior year	17,800	b
Before-tax profit per dollar of sales	0.24185	a ÷ b
Forecasted sales	$22,250	
Profit per dollar of sales	0.24185	
Forecasted before-tax profit	$ 5,381	

Required

a. What is the fundamental assumption that Emily is making and why is it obviously wrong?

b. Prepare a more appropriate forecast of before-tax profit related to the Indianapolis Craft Expo.

PROBLEM 4-8. The Profit Equation Gaming Solutions is a small company that assembles PCs to gamer customer specifications. The company buys all of its component parts from Northern Oregon Computer Warehouse. In the past year, the company had the following before tax profit:

Sales		$1,550,000
Less:		
Cost of components	$1,085,000	
Staff salaries	225,000	
Rent	36,000	
Utilities	7,500	
Advertising	6,000	1,359,500
Operating profit before bonuses		$ 190,500
Staff bonuses		76,200
Profit before taxes and owner "draw"		$ 114,300

The company, owned by Steven Rich, has six full-time employees. These employees are each paid a base salary of $37,500 per year. In addition, they receive a bonus equal to 40 percent of operating profits before bonuses. Owner "draw" is the amount Steven pays himself out of company profits.

The company is in the process of planning profit for the coming year. Northern Oregon Computer Warehouse has agreed that their prices to Gaming Solutions will be reduced by 20 percent on all purchases over $900,000.

Required

Estimate profit before taxes and owner "draw" for five levels of sales: $1,300,000; $1,400,000; $1,500,000; $1,600,000; $1,700,000.

PROBLEM 4-9. High-Low, Profit Equation Rhetorix, Inc. produces stereo speakers. Each unit (a pair of speakers) sells for $800. Below is information on production/sales and costs for 2007.

	Production and Sales in Units	Production Costs	Selling and Admin. Costs
January	100	$ 83,400	$ 22,700
February	112	92,300	24,500
March	92	79,000	21,700
April	101	82,900	23,300
May	110	89,800	24,200
June	120	96,500	25,300
July	123	98,900	26,000
August	127	102,300	26,200
September	133	108,900	27,200
October	121	98,000	25,600
November	119	96,000	26,100
December	103	89,500	24,100
Total	1,361	$1,117,500	$296,900
Average cost per unit		$821.08744	$218.14842

Required

a. Use the high-low method to identify the fixed and variable cost components for both production costs and selling and administrative costs.

b. The company estimates that production and sales in 2008 will be 1,500 units.

Based on this estimate, forecast income before taxes for 2008.

PROBLEM 4-10. High-Low Method; Scattergraph; Break-Even Analysis FirstTown Mortgage specializes in providing mortgage refinance loans. Each loan customer is charged a $400 loan processing fee by FirstTown when the loan is processed. Their costs over the past year associated with processing the loans follow.

	Loans Processed	Cost
January	160	$47,000
February	180	47,900
March	190	48,500
April	201	48,600
May	225	49,900
June	300	54,100
July	275	51,300
August	230	50,450
September	209	49,400
October	175	47,500
November	165	47,200
December	150	47,100

Required:

a. Use the high-low method to estimate fixed and variable costs.

b. Based on these estimates, calculate the number of loans that must be made to break even.

c. Estimate total profit in a month when 250 loans are processed.

d. Prepare a scattergraph of loan processing cost (vertical axis) and number of loans processed (horizontal axis).

5. Comment on whether the high-low method produces a reasonable estimate of costs. Look at whether the relationship between the number of loans processed and the cost is linear. Are there any outliers? Does an outlier affect the high-low estimate?

PROBLEM 4-11. Break-Even Analysis, Margin of Safety, Increase In Profit Edison Entrepreneur Services, Inc., is a legal services firm that files the paperwork to incorporate a business. Edison charges $1,000 for the incorporation application package and plans to file 1,600 applications next year. The company's projected income statement for the coming year is:

Sales	$1,440,000
Less variable expenses	1,008,000
Contribution margin	432,000
Less fixed expenses	250,000
Operating income	$ 182,000

Required:

1. Compute the contribution margin per application and calculate the break-even point in number of applications (round to the nearest whole unit, since it is not possible to file a partial application). Calculate the contribution margin ratio and the break-even sales revenue.
2. What is the current margin of safety in terms of the number of units? What is the current margin of safety in terms of the sales dollars?
3. If Edison wants to have operating income of $350,000 next year, how many applications must they process (round to the nearest whole unit)? What dollar level of sales is required to achieve operating income of $350,000?
4. The office manager for Edison has proposed that Edison increase advertising (a fixed cost) for the upcoming year by $75,000; she feels that this increase in advertising will lead to an increase in sales of $300,000. Prepare a new projected income statement for this projection. Should Edison increase its advertising to this new level?

PROBLEM 4-12. Multiproduct CVP Fidelity Multimedia sells audio and video equipment and car stereo products. After performing a study of fixed and variable costs in the prior year, the company prepared a product-line profit statement as follows:

Fidelity Multimedia
Profitability Analysis
For the Year Ended December 31, 2007

	Audio	**Video**	**Car**	**Total**
Sales	$3,000,000	$1,800,000	$1,200,000	$6,000,000
Less variable costs:				
Cost of merchandise	1,800,000	1,260,000	600,000	3,660,000
Salary part-time staff	120,000	80,000	30,000	230,000
Total variable costs	1,920,000	1,340,000	630,000	3,890,000
Contribution margin	1,080,000	460,000	570,000	2,110,000
Less direct fixed costs:				
Salary, full-time staff	300,000	250,000	210,000	760,000
Less common fixed costs:				
Advertising				110,000
Utilities				20,000
Other administrative costs				560,000
Total common fixed costs				690,000
Profit				$ 660,000

Required

a. Calculate the contribution margin ratios for the audio, video, and car product lines.

b. What would be the effect on profit of a $100,000 increase in sales of audio equipment compared with a $100,000 increase in sales of video equipment, or a $100,000 increase in sales of car equipment? Based on this limited information, which product line would you recommend expanding?

c. Calculate the break-even level of sales for the company as a whole.

d. Calculate sales needed to achieve a profit of $1,500,000 assuming the current mix.

e. Determine the sales of audio, video, and car products in the total sales amount calculated for Part d.

PROBLEM 4-13. Multiproduct, Contribution Margin Ratio ComputerGuard offers computer consulting, training, and repair services. For the most recent fiscal year, profit was $230,000 as follows:

	Consulting	Training	Repair	Total
Sales	$500,000	$400,000	$300,000	$1,200,000
Less variable costs:				
Salaries	250,000	160,000	180,000	590,000
Supplies/parts	20,000	30,000	60,000	110,000
Other	1,000	2,000	4,000	7,000
Contribution margin	229,000	208,000	56,000	493,000
Less common fixed costs:				
Rent				40,000
Owner's salary				200,000
Utilities				15,000
Other				8,000
Profit				$ 230,000

Required

a. Linda O'Flaherty, the owner of ComputerGuard, believes that in the coming year she can increase sales by 20 percent. Assuming the current mix of services, what will be the percentage increase in profit associated with a 20 percent increase in sales? Why will profit increase at a greater percent than sales?

b. If Linda were to focus on the contribution margin per unit (rather than the contribution margin ratio), what would be a likely unit of service?

PROBLEM 4-14. Multiproduct, Contribution Margin National Tennis Racquet Co. produces and sells three models:

	Smasher	Basher	Dinker	Total
Units sold	1,000	2,000	2,000	5,000
Sales	$100,000	$120,000	$80,000	$300,000
Less variable costs	50,000	48,000	24,000	122,000
Contribution margin	$ 50,000	$ 72,000	$56,000	178,000
Less common fixed costs				103,000
Profit				$ 75,000

Required

a. What is the weighted average contribution margin per unit?

b. Calculate the break-even point in units assuming the current mix.

c. What would be the number of Smashers, Bashers, and Dinkers in the break-even level of sales?

d. What is the weighted average contribution margin ratio?

e. What level of sales (in dollars) would be needed to earn a profit of $100,000 assuming the current mix?

f. What would be the sales (in dollars) of Smashers, Bashers, and Dinkers for total sales calculated in Part e?

PROBLEM 4-15. Operating Leverage Equillion, Inc. and Stoichran, Inc. are two companies in the pharmaceutical industry. Equillion has relatively high fixed costs related to research and development. Stoichran, on the other hand, does little research and development. Instead, the company pays for the right to produce and market drugs that have been developed by other companies. The amount paid is a percent of sales. Thus, Stoichran has relatively high variable costs and relatively low fixed costs.

	Equillion, Inc.	Stoichran, Inc.
Sales	$80,000,000	$80,000,000
Less variable costs	20,000,000	50,000,000
Less fixed costs	50,000,000	20,000,000
Profit	$10,000,000	$10,000,000

Required

a. Which company has the higher operating leverage?

b. Calculate the expected percentage change in profit for a 10 percent increase (and for a 10 percent decrease) in sales for each company.

c. Which company is more risky?

PROBLEM 4-16. Value of Loosening a Constraint For the past three years, Rhetorix, Inc. has produced the model X100 stereo speaker. The model is in high demand, and the company can sell as many pairs as it can produce. The selling price per pair is $800. Variable costs of production are $300, and fixed costs per year are $600,000. Each pair of speakers requires four hours of assembly time. Currently, the company has four assembly workers who are highly skilled and can work a total of 8,000 hours per year. With a tight labor market, the company finds it difficult to hire additional assembly workers with the skill needed to assemble the X100. Jurgis Rand, the owner of Rhetorix, is considering offering assembly workers an overtime premium (wages in excess of regular hourly wages) to get them to work more than 8,000 hours per year. In thinking about how much to offer, Jurgis performed the following calculation:

Sales (2,000 units × $800)	$1,600,000
Less variable costs (2,000 × $300)	600,000
Less fixed costs	600,000
Profit	$ 400,000
Profit/assembly hours ($400,000/8,000)	$50 per assembly hour

After seeing this calculation, Jurgis decided to offer an overtime premium of $25 per hour to his assembly workers. Jurgis reasoned that "This is a great deal. Both the workers and I make an extra $25 when they work an hour of overtime!"

Required

a. How much would profit increase if four more assembly hours were available at the regular hourly wage for assembly workers?

b. Compare your answer in Part a to the answer that Jurgis would provide to the question in Part a (i.e., $50 × 4 = $200). What is the flaw in Jurgis's calculation of the value of additional assembly time?

c. Suppose Jurgis pays assembly workers $25 per hour of overtime premium. On average, what will be the incremental benefit to Jurgis of an hour of extra assembly time?

PROBLEM 4-17. Constraints Fleet Valley Shoes produces two models: the Nx100 (a shoe aimed at competitive runners) and the Mx100 (a shoe aimed at fitness buffs). Sales and costs for the most recent year are indicated:

	Nx100	**Mx100**
Sales (pairs)	15,000	75,000
Sales	$2,250,000	$8,250,000
Variable costs	525,000	1,125,000
Contribution margin	1,725,000	7,125,000
Fixed costs	100,000	1,400,000
Profit	$1,625,000	$5,725,000
Assembly time per pair	2 hours	1.5 hours
Profit per assembly hour	$54.17	$50.89
CM per assembly hour	$57.50	$63.33

Required

a. Suppose the company has 138,000 assembly hours available. Further, management believes that at least 2,000 pairs of each model must be produced so that the company has a presence in both market segments. How many pairs of each model should be produced in the coming year?

b. Suppose management decides that at least 4,000 pairs of each model must be produced. What is the opportunity cost of this decision versus requiring only 2,000 pairs?

PROBLEM 4-18. Regression Analysis (see Appendix), Profit Equation Cindy Havana is a vice president of finance for Captain Wesley's Restaurant, a chain of 12 restaurants on the East Coast, including five restaurants in Florida. The company is considering a plan whereby customers will be mailed coupons, in the month of their birthday, entitling them to 20 percent off their total bill. The cost of the mailing (printing, paper, postage, etc.) is estimated to be $400,000. Cindy estimates that the campaign will result in an annual increase in sales of $2,500,000 at normal prices ($2,000,000 after the 20 percent discount).

As part of her analysis of the financial impact of the plan, Cindy ran a regression of total monthly operating costs on sales using data from the past year. The results of this analysis are indicated in the Summary Output table:

	Operating Costs	**Sales**
January	$3,366,650	$3,641,000
February	3,352,250	3,565,000
March	3,541,500	3,910,000
April	3,566,625	4,002,500
May	3,502,500	4,250,000
June	3,793,800	4,352,000
July	3,912,000	4,380,000
August	3,760,550	4,247,000
September	3,633,250	4,125,000
October	3,589,600	3,984,000
November	3,375,250	3,765,000
December	3,682,250	4,165,000
	$43,076,225	$48,386,500

Summary Output

Regression Statistics				
Multiple R	0.89547667			
R Square	0.80187846			
Adjusted R Squ	0.78206631			
Standard Error	83006.2325			
Observations	12			
ANOVA				
	df	*SS*	*MS*	*F*
Regression	1	2.78868E+11	2.7887E+11	40.4740682
Residual	10	68900346361	6890034636	
Total	11	3.47768E+11		
	Coefficients	*Standard Error*	*t Stat*	*P-value*
Intercept	1214820.06	374061.8848	3.24764459	0.00875534
Sales	0.58897387	0.092577959	6.36192331	8.2247E-05

Required

Based on the limited information provided, give Cindy an estimate of the net effect of the coupon campaign on annual profit (ignore taxes).

CASES

4-1 ROTHMUELLER MUSEUM

In 1928, Francis P. Rothmueller, a Northwest railroad magnate, established an endowment to fund the Rothmueller Museum in Minneapolis. Whereas the museum currently has a 30 million dollar endowment, it also has substantial operating costs and continues to add to its eclectic collection that encompasses paintings, photographs, drawings, and design objects post-1900. Annual earnings from the endowment (approximately $2,100,000 in 2007) are not sufficient to cover operations and acquisitions, and the museum's trustees and president are conscious of the need to generate income from admissions, special exhibits, and museum store sales.

Alice Morgan, photographic curator, is in the process of planning an exhibition of Ansel Adams photographs, that will run from September through November of 2008. Below is a preliminary budget, prepared by Alice, of revenue and costs associated with the exhibition:

Revenue (9,000 × $12)		$108,000	1
Less:			
Lease of photographs from other museums and collectors	$80,000		2
Packing and transportation of photographs from other museums and collectors	4,000		3
Event insurance	2,000		4
Alice Morgan salary (25%)	12,000		5
William Jacob salary (25%)	8,000		6
Guard service	9,000		7
Installation costs	1,000		8
Advertising	5,000		9
Exhibition printed programs	2,000	123,000	10
Profit (loss)		$(15,000)	

1. Estimated attendance is 9,000 and admission to the exhibit is $12.
2. Some photographs will come from the Rothmueller collection while others will be leased from other museums and collectors.
3. Cost of packing and transportation to and from Rothmueller.
4. Insurance to cover photographs during the run of the exhibition.
5. Twenty-five percent of annual salary for Alice Morgan, head photography curator.
6. Twenty-five percent of annual salary for William Jacob, assistant photography curator.
7. Cost of guard service for exhibition.
8. Painting of exhibition room to off-white background.
9. Advertising in newspapers and public radio.
10. Cost of programs describing the work of Ansel Adams and pictures at exhibition.

Additional Information

In preparing the budget, Alice assigned 25 percent of her and her assistant's annual salaries to the exhibition since they will each spend approximately three months on the project. An admission fee of $5 is charged to enter the museum, and attendance at the exhibition is an additional $12 per person. Approximately one-fifth of the individuals who are estimated to attend the exhibition would have come to the museum whether or not the exhibition was being held. (Alternatively, four-fifths of the individuals are coming specifically to attend the exhibition.)

Analysis of prior data indicates that 20 percent of individuals make a purchase at the museum store, and the average purchase price is $7. The store has a 30 percent gross margin (sales minus cost of sales) and profit (sales minus cost of sales minus staff salaries and other operating costs) per dollar of sales of 5 percent.

Required

a. Prepare an analysis of the financial impact of the exhibition on the Rothmueller Museum assuming attendance is 9,000. Does offering the exhibition appear to be a good decision from a financial standpoint?

b. How many people must attend the exhibition for its financial impact to be profit neutral (i.e., the museum will not be better or worse off financially)?

4-2 MAYFIELD SOFTWARE, CUSTOMER TRAINING

Marie Stefano is the group director of customer training for Mayfield Software. In this capacity, she runs a center in Kirkland, Washington that provides training to employees of companies that use Mayfield's inventory control, customer management, and accounting software products. Her group employs a receptionist and an office manager/bookkeeper, and she has arrangements with several part-time trainers who are hired on an as-needed basis (they are all retired employees of Mayfield Software). Trainers are paid

$3,750 per daylong class. Mayfield is a decentralized company and Marie is given considerable authority to advertise and conduct classes as she sees fit.

During 2007, the group conducted 810 day-long classes with an average enrollment of 18 students paying $350. The group's Report of Operating Results for 2007 is detailed next.

Report of Operating Results, 2007

Revenue	$5,103,000
Less operating costs:	
Trainer costs	3,037,500
Director salary	165,000
Receptionist	51,000
Office manager	75,000
Utilities, phone, etc.	32,000
Lease expense related to computers, servers, etc.	360,000
Rent	96,000
Operating manuals for participants	437,400
Postage, envelopes, paper, etc.	10,935
Advertising	157,000
Total operating costs	4,421,835
Profit before central charges	681,165
Central charges	765,450
Group profit	($ 84,285)

Additional facts

1. All equipment is leased on a yearly basis. Costs include 80 workstations for students (one workstation for every seat in each of the four 20-student classrooms), plus servers and other miscellaneous equipment. While average class enrollment is 18 students, some classes are full (20 students) and classes are cancelled if enrollment is less than 12 students. Classes are typically held Monday through Friday, although some classes are held on Saturdays and Sundays.
2. Rent relates to the training center in Kirkland, which is not part of Mayfield's main campus located in Bellevue, Washington.
3. Advertising costs relate to the cost of monthly advertisements in trade journals such as *TechWorker* and *Inventory Management*. These ads provide information on upcoming training sessions.
4. Operating manuals are provided to each participant.
5. Postage, envelopes, and paper costs relate primarily to billing companies for employees who participate in classes. This cost varies with the number of participants.
6. Central charges are assigned to each group at Mayfield Software based on actual sales. The allocation relates to costs incurred for the benefit of the company as a whole including salaries of the CEO and company president, legal costs, cost related to the company's central office building, brand advertising, etc. The charge is 15 percent of revenue.

Required

a. As indicated, the training group suffered a loss in 2007. Thus, unbeknownst to Marie, management of Mayfield is considering shutting down the training center. Given the results of 2007, what would be the effect on Mayfield Software's total company profit in 2008 if the training center is closed at the start of the year?

b. Given the current room configuration and approach to allocation of central charges (15 percent of revenue), calculate the number of classes that must be offered (with an average enrollment of 18 students) for Marie's group to break-even on the Report of Operating Results.

c. Recalculate your answer to part b assuming Marie can lower the amount paid to instructors to $3,000 per class. Should Marie seriously pursue this option?

d. Mayfield Software is releasing version 4.0 of "CustomerTrack" in 2008. Marie believes that this will create a demand for 30 additional day-long classes with an average enrollment of 18 students per class. What effect will this have on "group profit" on Marie's Report of Operating Results? Assume instructors will be paid $3,750 per class.

4-3 KROG'S METALFAB, INC.

John Krog is President, Chairman of the Board, Production Supervisor, and majority shareholder of Krog's Metalfab, Inc. He formed the company in 1991 to manufacture custom-built aluminum storm windows for sale to contractors in the greater Chicago area. Since that time the company has experienced tremendous growth and currently operates two plants: one in Chicago, the main production facility, and a smaller plant in Moline, Illinois. The company now produces a wide variety of metal windows, framing materials, ladders, and other products related to the construction industry. Recently, the company developed a new line of bronze-finished storm windows and initial buyer reaction has been quite favorable. The company's future seemed bright but on January 3, 2005, a light fixture overheated causing a fire that virtually destroyed the entire Chicago plant. Three days later, Krog had moved 50 percent of his Chicago workforce to the Moline plant. Workers were housed in hotels, paid overtime wages, and provided with bus transportation home on weekends. Still, the company could not meet delivery schedules because of reduced operating capacity, and total business began to decline. At the end of 2005, Krog felt that the worst was

Krog's Metalfab
Income from Operations, 2004 and 2005

2004	**January**	**February**	**March**	**April**	**May**	**June**
Sales	$500,260	$348,260	$360,250	$302,685	$434,650	$510,650
Less:						
Cost of goods sold	391,254	440,304	333,107	320,074	370,285	405,271
Selling expense	21,200	15,670	15,500	13,260	18,386	21,430
Administrative expense	20,250	20,250	20,250	20,250	20,250	20,250
Total expense	432,704	476,224	368,857	353,584	408,921	446,951
Income from operations	$ 67,556	($127,964)	($ 8,607)	($ 50,899)	$ 25,729	$ 63,699
2005	**January**	**February**	**March**	**April**	**May**	**June**
Sales	$446,252	$235,362	$290,370	$215,265	$277,165	$315,441
Less:						
Cost of goods sold	394,560	310,478	329,585	299,840	326,598	342,512
Selling expense	19,300	10,864	13,065	10,061	12,537	14,068
Administrative expense	22,250	23,465	23,860	24,600	23,695	24,740
Total expense	436,110	$344,807	$366,510	$334,501	$362,830	$381,320
Income from operations	$ 10,142	($109,445)	($ 76,140)	($119,236)	($ 85,665)	($ 65,879)

over. A new plant had been leased in Chicago, and the company was almost back to normal.

Finally, Krog could turn his attention to a matter of considerable importance: settlement with the insurance company. The company's policy stipulated that the building and equipment loss be calculated at replacement cost. This settlement had been fairly straightforward and the proceeds had aided the rapid rebuilding of the company. A valued feature of the insurance policy was "lost profit" coverage. This coverage was to "compensate the company for profits lost due to reduced operating capacity related to fire or flood damage." The period of "lost profit" was limited to 12 months. Interpreting the exact nature of this coverage proved to be difficult. The insurance company agreed to reimburse Krog for the overtime premium, transportation, and housing costs related to operating out of the Moline plant. These expenses obviously minimized the damages related to the 12 months of lost or reduced profits. But was the company entitled to any additional compensation?

Krog got out the latest edition of *Construction Today*. According to this respected trade journal, sales of products similar to products produced by Krog's Metalfab had increased by 7 percent during 2005. Krog felt that were it not for the fire, his company could also have increased sales by this percentage.

Income statement information is available for 2004 (the year prior to the fire) and 2005 (the year during which the company sustained "lost profit"). The expenses in 2005 include excess operating costs of $240,000. Krog has documentation supporting these items, which include overtime costs, hotel costs, meals, and such related to operating out of Moline. The insurance company is quite willing to pay for these costs since they reduced potential lost profit.

The chief accountant at Krog, Peter Newell, has estimated lost profit to be only $34,961. Thus, he does not feel that it's worthwhile spending a lot of company resources trying to collect more than the $240,000. Peter arrived at his calculation as follows.

Sales in 2004	$5,079,094
Predicted sales in 2005 assuming a 7% increase	$5,434,630
Actual sales in 2005	3,845,499
(A) Lost sales	1,589,131
(B) Profit in 2004 as a percent of 2004 sales ($111,928 ÷ 5,079,094)	.0220
Lost profit (A × B)	$ 34,961

Required

a. Mr. Krog is not convinced by Peter's analysis and has turned to you, an outside consultant, to provide a preliminary estimate of lost profit. Using the limited

July	August	September	October	November	December	Total
$560,625	$602,210	$420,210	$330,025	$329,009	$380,260	$5,079,094
421,256	439,890	369,555	331,252	332,125	353,125	4,507,498
23,550	24,980	17,753	14,340	14,258	16,341	216,668
20,250	20,250	20,250	20,250	20,250	20,250	243,000
465,056	485,120	407,558	365,842	366,633	389,716	4,967,166
$ 95,569	$117,090	$ 12,652	($ 35,817)	($ 37,624)	($ 9,456)	$ 111,928

July	August	September	October	November	December	Total
$356,662	$452,245	$362,772	$314,427	$263,273	$316,265	$3,845,499
356,880	394,570	361,258	339,652	319,586	342,500	4,118,019
15,716	19,540	15,961	14,027	11,981	14,101	171,221
23,695	23,472	23,620	22,741	22,659	22,940	281,737
396,291	437,582	400,839	376,420	354,226	379,541	4,570,977
($ 39,629)	$ 14,663	($ 38,067)	($ 61,993)	($ 90,953)	($ 63,276)	($ 725,478)

information contained in the financial statements for 2004 and 2005, estimate lost profit. (Hint: You can proceed as follows.)

Step 1. Determine the level of fixed and variable costs in 2004 as a function of sales. You can use account analysis, the high-low method, or regression if you are familiar with that technique.

Step 2. Predict what sales would have been in 2005 if there was no fire. Using this level of sales and the fixed and variable cost information from step 1, estimate what profit would have been in 2005.

Step 3. The difference between actual profit in 2005 and the amount estimated in step 2 is lost profit.

b. Based on your preliminary analysis, do you recommend that Mr. Krog aggressively pursue a substantial claim for lost profit?

c. What is the fundamental flaw in Peter Newell's analysis?

Gardenrite

CHAPTER 6

LEARNING OBJECTIVES

1. Explain why indirect costs are allocated.
2. Describe the cost allocation process.
3. Discuss allocation of service department costs.
4. Identify potential problems with cost allocation.
5. Discuss activity-based costing (ABC) and cost drivers.
6. Distinguish activity-based costing (ABC) from activity-based management (ABM).

COST ALLOCATION AND ACTIVITY-BASED COSTING

Gardenrite Manufacturing Company produces garden tools and lawn maintenance products that are sold through a national chain of hardware stores. The company manufactures more than 60 products. Approximately 80 percent of its revenue comes from selling small home garden tools such as rakes, pruners, and spades. The company also manufactures high-quality lawn mowers, edgers, and blowers that are popular with professional lawn service companies, but sales of these products have not been a major source of revenue.

In recent months, Ben Jakes, the CFO at Gardenrite, has become concerned about the apparent profitability of several products. In particular, some high-volume products like the Model 250 spade are barely breaking even, whereas some low-volume products like the new Model 900 mower are selling for much more than the cost of production. The high profit earned by the Model 900 mower is particularly surprising. The company only recently began manufacturing mowers, and Ben expected production inefficiencies, associated with the new product, to keep profit margins low. Ben knows that manufacturing overhead is allocated to products based on labor cost. The approach is simple, but he suspects it may be causing allocations of cost that are too high for spades and too low for mowers.

Firms that produce more than one product or provide more than one type of service invariably have indirect costs because resources are shared by the products or services (e.g., two different products may be manufactured using the same piece of equipment). Various departments may also have common or shared resources (e.g., the marketing and human resources departments may share a high-speed copy machine). Because indirect costs associated with shared resources cannot be directly traced to products or services, some means of assigning them must be developed. The process of assigning indirect costs is referred to as **cost allocation**, which we first discussed in Chapter 2. Unfortunately, cost allocation frequently results in problems like the one faced by Ben Jakes. To prepare yourself to deal with them, you need a good understanding of why and how costs are allocated. Providing you with that understanding is the purpose of this chapter. One of the key points of the chapter is that costs are allocated for a variety of purposes; allocations that are adequate for one purpose may not be adequate for another purpose.

Many managers have expressed concern that the way overhead is typically allocated may seriously distort product cost for manufacturing firms. The problem arises because most product costing systems allocate overhead using measures related to production volume. This is the case at Gardenrite, where manufacturing overhead is allocated based on labor cost. However, many overhead costs are not proportional to volume. Activity-based costing (ABC) is an approach to allocating overhead costs that addresses this problem. We briefly discussed ABC in Chapter 2. Here you will gain a better understanding of the general process of cost allocation, which allows for a more detailed treatment of ABC.

In our discussion of ABC, we will build on the Gardenrite Manufacturing Company example. However, it is important to note that ABC is not restricted to manufacturing firms. Banks, hospitals, insurance companies, and other service firms find that ABC provides insight into the costs of providing services to customers. Several of the problems and cases at the end of this chapter are in a service firm context and will provide you with an opportunity to generalize the ideas of ABC to this important business setting.

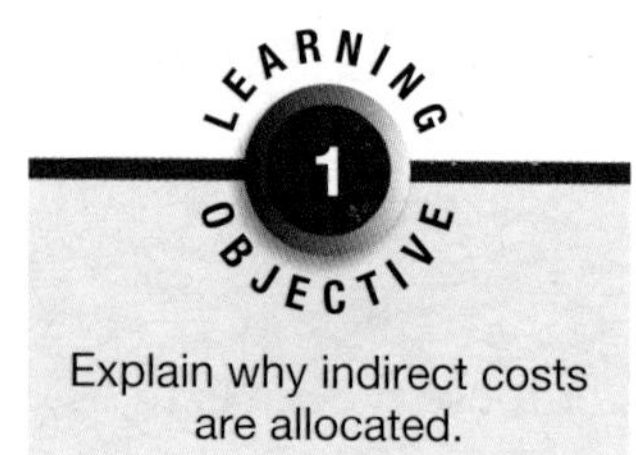

Explain why indirect costs are allocated.

PURPOSES OF COST ALLOCATION

Companies allocate costs to products, services, and departments for four major reasons: (1) to provide information needed to make appropriate decisions, (2) to reduce the frivolous use of common resources, (3) to encourage managers to evaluate the efficiency of internally provided services, and (4) to calculate the "full cost" of products for financial reporting purposes and for determining cost-based prices (see Illustration 6-1). We will now discuss each of these purposes.

TO PROVIDE INFORMATION FOR DECISION MAKING

When managers use a company resource and receive an allocation of its cost, they are, in essence, receiving a charge for use. For example, when Malinda Smith, a product manager at Mayfield Software, asks the art department to de-

Illustration 6-1
Reasons why firms allocate costs

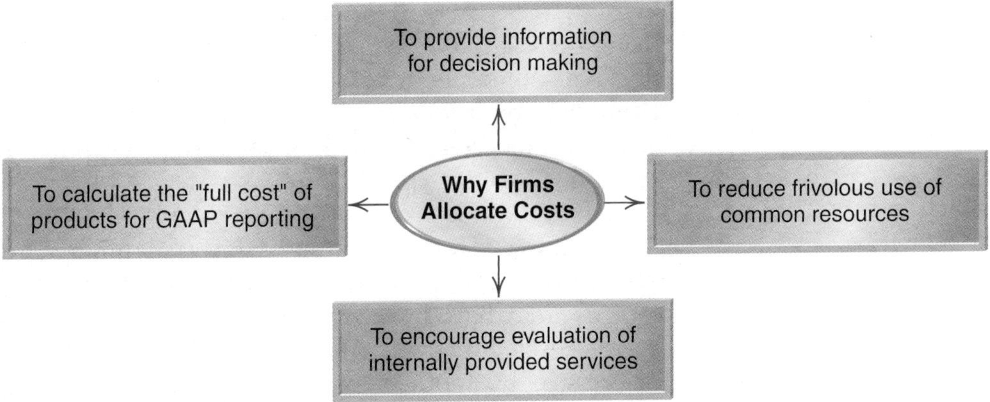

sign a prototype box for a product under development, she will likely receive an allocation, on her product-line profit and loss statement, of costs incurred in the art department. The more art work she orders, the more cost she will receive, reducing the profit for which she is responsible. But what is the appropriate allocation?

From a decision making standpoint, the allocated cost should measure the opportunity cost of using a company resource. Let's see why this is the case. Suppose the art department has excess capacity and the design work does not create additional costs other than very minor material cost. In this case, the opportunity cost is approximately zero, and the appropriate allocation is also zero. Malinda's company, after all, does not want to discourage her from using the art department's services since this use does not lead to additional costs.

Suppose, however, the art department is extremely busy. If it takes on Malinda's job, other work will be delayed. In fact, a different product-line manager will be forced to go outside the company to get art work done on time, incurring a cost of $5,000. In this case, Malinda's use of a company resource has led to a $5,000 opportunity cost. Thus, $5,000 would be an appropriate allocation, or charge, to Malinda's operation. If she does not believe that the art department's services represent a $5,000 benefit to her operation, then she will not demand these services, and the other product manager can make use of them and avoid incurring $5,000 of costs outside the company.

Although allocated costs should measure the opportunity cost of using a company resource, in practice this is difficult to operationalize. One reason is that the opportunity cost may quickly change. For example, on Wednesday, the art department may be dealing with a rush job and working overtime. But by Friday, the rush job may be completed, and there may be excess capacity. Thus, the opportunity cost would be much higher on Wednesday than on Friday.

Still, the opportunity cost idea is a useful benchmark. Whenever you are discussing allocations of cost, you should ask yourself, "How close is this allocation to the opportunity cost of use?" The closer it is, the better the allocation.

TO REDUCE FRIVOLOUS USE OF COMMON RESOURCES

As already noted, allocated costs serve as charges, or fees, for use of internal resources or services. Consider a company that purchases a computer to be used by all three of its divisions. Almost all of the costs associated with running the computer are fixed, and they amount to $100,000 per year. Some accountants would argue that because these costs are fixed, the divisions should not be charged for using the computer, since use creates no incremental cost. However, if the three divisions do not incur any charge for using the computer, they may tend to use the computer for frivolous or nonessential purposes (e.g., playing computer games, sending unnecessary e-mail, or preparing computer-generated reports that are not really needed).

This situation may not seem to be that detrimental to the company's welfare. After all, the costs associated with the computer are primarily fixed. If frivolous use does not create additional costs, why discourage it? The reason is that frivolous use may have hidden costs. The primary hidden cost in the example is slower service to departments that need to use the computer when it is being used unnecessarily by another department. In other words, an opportunity cost is associated with the use of the computer. Reports that take minutes to prepare when the computer is being used efficiently may take hours to produce when the computer is being used to prepare reports that are not important.

One way to eliminate frivolous use is to charge for the use of centrally provided services. And one of the most common ways to charge for use is to allocate the cost of the service. For example, suppose Division 1 plans to use the computer for 1,000 hours per year, Division 2 plans to use it for 1,000 hours, and Division 3 for 2,000 hours. A charge of $25 per hour ($100,000 ÷ 4,000 hours) could be assessed. Note that this rate would allocate the entire cost of the computer ($100,000) among the three users, assuming that their plans worked out as expected. Divisions 1 and 2 would each be charged $25,000, and Division 3 would be charged $50,000. If division managers knew that this method of cost allocation would be used, they would have an incentive to reduce their division's frivolous use of the computer, because use of the computer reduces the reported profit of their division.

TO ENCOURAGE EVALUATION OF SERVICES

Cost allocation is also useful because it encourages managers to evaluate the services for which they are being charged. If no costs are allocated to users of centrally administered services, such as computer services or janitorial services, then the users of the services do not have an incentive to evaluate these services carefully. After all, the services are free. However, if the users are charged for the services (i.e., if they receive an allocation of the cost of the services), then the users have a strong incentive to look critically at the services and consider the possibility of lower-cost alternatives. If lower-cost alternatives exist, the users will certainly bring them to the company's attention. The company can then evaluate whether the services are being provided in an efficient manner.

Consider the example of the three divisions using a central computer system. Because the three divisions are being charged for using the system (through an allocation of its costs), the managers of the divisions have an incentive to evaluate the cost and quality of the service being provided. Suppose the manager of Division 3 determines that similar computing services can be purchased outside the company for less than the $50,000 currently being allocated to Division 3 for its use of the central computer system. The manager of Division 3 will bring this matter to high-level company officials, who will encourage the manager of the computer system to lower that operation's costs, perhaps by reducing staffing. If the costs of the computer system cannot be lowered, the company may consider replacing the computer system with separate computers for the divisions or buying computer services outside the company.

TO PROVIDE "FULL COST" INFORMATION

As we have mentioned, GAAP requires full costing for external reporting purposes. Indirect production costs must be allocated to goods produced to meet this requirement. In addition, full cost information is required when a company has an agreement whereby the amount of revenue received depends on the amount of cost incurred. For example, defense contractors with the federal government often have contracts that specify they will be paid the cost of production as well as some fixed amount or percentage of cost. Such contracts are commonly called "cost-plus" contracts. An interesting feature of these contracts is that the cost of production specified often includes not only manufacturing costs but also a share of general and administrative costs. Thus, a substantial amount of cost allocation is required to assign indirect manufacturing costs and indirect general and administrative costs to the contract work.

A major problem with cost-plus contracts is that they create an incentive to allocate as much cost as possible to the goods produced on a cost-plus basis and little cost to goods that are not produced on a cost-plus basis. The more cost allocated to cost-plus contracts, the higher the amount paid to the company.

In spite of this limitation, cost-plus contracts serve a useful purpose. Without the assurance that they will be reimbursed for their costs and that they will earn some profit, many manufacturers would not be willing to bear the financial risks associated with producing state-of-the-art products for the government, using untried technologies. For example, not many companies would be willing to develop a new fighter aircraft without assurance that they would be reimbursed for all costs incurred in its development.

Lack of Oversight for Cost-Plus Contracts

Halliburton is a Houston-based oilfield services company that has received U.S. government contracts to help with the rebuilding of Iraq. Frequently, its contracts are on a cost-plus basis. Advocates of this type of contract say that companies would not be willing to work in a war zone if they were not sure they would earn a profit. However, such contracts do not create an incentive to control costs. The problem might not be severe if there was high-quality oversight of the contracts by the federal government. But from 1990 to 1999 the Defense Department's accounting and budget staff dropped from 17,504 to 6,432. A Pentagon inspector general report indicated that there was little or no government oversight on 13 of 14 rebuilding contracts. In fact, a single Halliburton contract extension that was worth over $500 million was renewed in just 10 minutes with only six pages of documentation.

Source: Joshua Chaffin, "Focus on Halliburton Masks Deeper Problems With Iraq Contracts," by Joshua Chaffin from *Financial Times*, March 30, 2004. Copyright © 2004. Reprinted by permission of *Financial Times*.

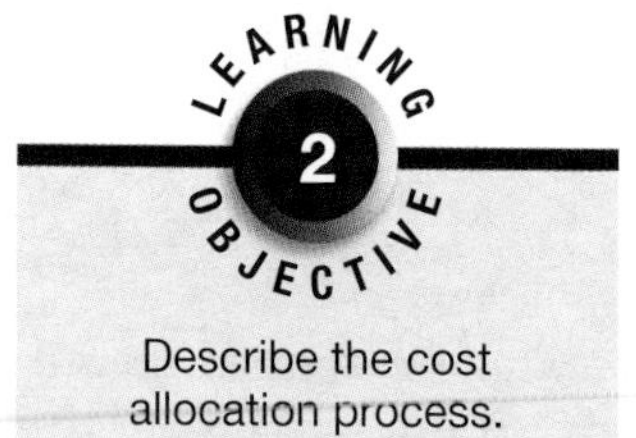

Describe the cost allocation process.

PROCESS OF COST ALLOCATION

We have seen that cost allocation is often necessary. But how is it achieved? The cost allocation process has three steps: (1) identify the cost objectives, (2) form cost pools, and (3) select an allocation base to relate the cost pools to the cost objectives. The three steps are shown in Illustration 6-2.

Illustration 6-2
The cost allocation process

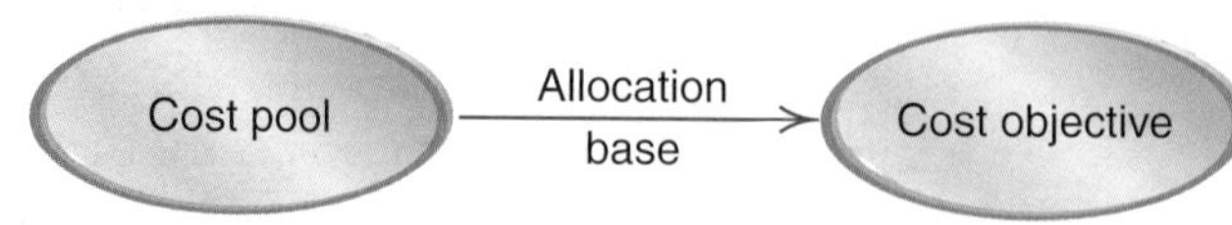

DETERMINING THE COST OBJECTIVE

The first step in the cost allocation process is to determine the product, service, or department that is to receive the allocation. The object of the allocation is referred to as the **cost objective**. For example, if a company allocates depreciation of a drilling press to products such as flanges and brackets, the products are the cost objectives. If computer-processing costs are allocated to the contracts worked on by a computer-aided design group, the contracts are the cost objectives. If a bank allocates general and administrative costs to product lines (e.g., loan services and estate-planning services), the product lines are the cost objectives (see Illustration 6-3).

FORMING COST POOLS

The second step in the cost allocation process is to form **cost pools**. A cost pool is a grouping of individual costs whose total is allocated using one allocation base. For example, all of the costs in the maintenance department could be treated as a

Illustration 6-3
Cost objectives

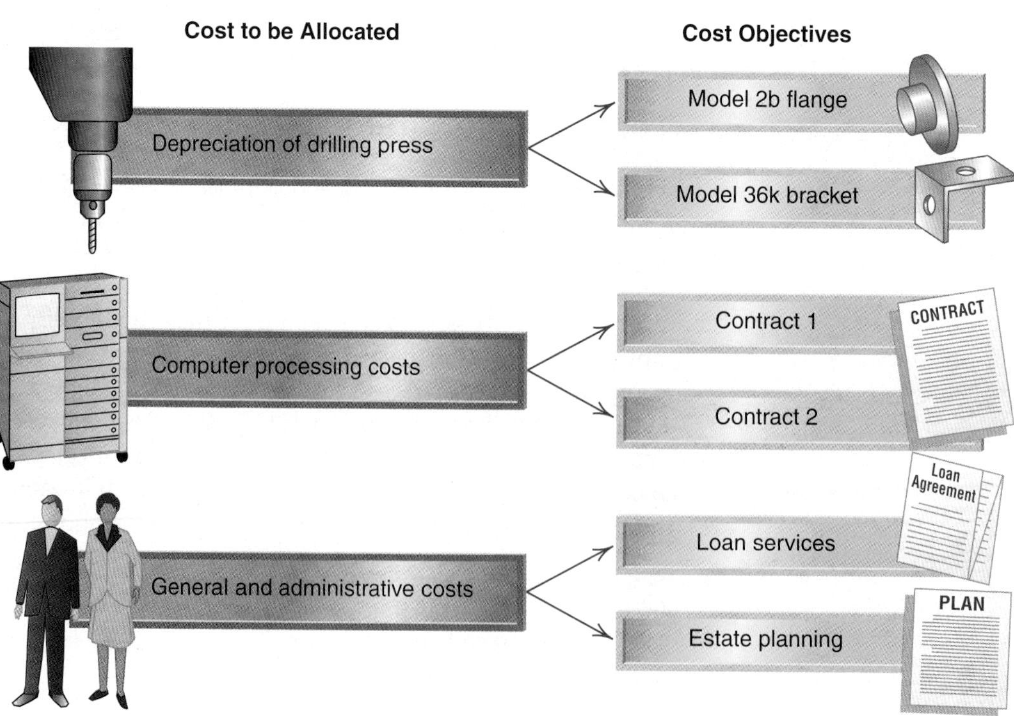

cost pool. In this case, the cost pool would include the wages of workers in the maintenance department, supplies, small tools, and a variety of additional cost items. Cost pools are often formed along departmental lines (for example, maintenance department costs in one cost pool and personnel department costs in another cost pool). They may also be formed according to major activities. For example, costs related to equipment setups, a major activity in most manufacturing firms, are in one cost pool, and costs related to inspecting products for defects, another major activity, are in another cost pool.

The overriding concern in forming a cost pool is to ensure that the costs in the pool are homogeneous, or similar. One way to determine whether these costs are homogeneous is to compare the allocations with the allocations that result from breaking the pool up into smaller pools and using a variety of allocation bases. If there is not a substantial difference in the allocations, then, for practical purposes, the costs in the pool are considered to be homogeneous.

Some manufacturing companies include all manufacturing overhead (power costs, computing costs, material handling costs, etc.) in a single cost pool. However, allocations from a large pool containing costs related to very different activities are not likely to provide useful information. (We discuss this problem later in the chapter.) Although use of a single cost pool for overhead seems too broad, exactly how many cost pools are appropriate is not clear. Managers must make a cost-benefit decision. More pools involve more analysis and recordkeeping, which is costly. However, more pools also result in the benefit of more accurate information.

SELECTING AN ALLOCATION BASE

The third step in the allocation process is to select an allocation base that relates the cost pool to the cost objectives. The allocation base must be some characteristic that is common to all of the cost objectives. If the cost objectives are manufactured products, then direct labor hours, direct labor cost, and machine hours are examples of characteristics that could be used as allocation bases. If the cost objectives are the divisions of a multidivisional firm, then sales dollars, total assets, and divisional profit are examples of characteristics that could be used as allocation bases.

Deciding which of the possible allocation bases to use is not an easy matter. Ideally, the allocation base selected should relate costs to cost objectives that *caused* the costs to be incurred. In this case, the allocation is based on a **cause-and-effect relationship**. For example, if additional activity in a production department causes an increase in the costs incurred by the maintenance department, then the allocation base selected should result in the additional costs being allocated to the production department when there is additional activity. Direct labor hours, direct labor cost, or machine hours in the production department would be likely choices for the allocation base because they represent the increase in activity that leads to the increase in cost in the Maintenance Department. However, it would be difficult to argue that one of these allocation bases is better than another on cause-and-effect grounds. As we will see next, this is one of the problems of cost allocation. A number of allocation bases may appear to be equally valid, but they may result in substantially different costs being assigned to the cost objectives.

Let's consider an example. Watts Equipment Company has two producing departments, Assembly and Finishing, that receive allocations of indirect costs from the Maintenance department. In the coming year, the Maintenance Department expects to incur variable costs of $200,000. These costs are related to both the labor hours and the machine hours incurred in the producing departments. The quantities of labor and machine hours are indicated here. With labor hours as the allocation base, the allocation rate is $4 per labor hour, and the Assembly Department receives an $80,000 allocation of cost from the Maintenance Department. However, with machine hours as the allocation base, the allocation rate is $10 per machine hour, and the Assembly Department receives a $110,000 allocation of cost from the Maintenance Department. The $30,000 difference in the allocations occurs even though both labor hours and machine hours are reasonable allocation bases to use.

	Labor Hours	Allocations	Machine Hours	Allocations
Assembly	20,000	$ 80,000	11,000	$110,000
Finishing	30,000	120,000	9,000	90,000
Total	50,000	$200,000	20,000	$200,000
Allocation Rate	$4 per labor hour		$10 per machine hour	

When indirect costs are fixed, establishing cause-and-effect relationships between costs and cost objectives is not feasible. In these cases, accountants turn to other criteria, such as relative benefits, ability to bear costs, and equity. Unfortunately, these terms are rather vague and difficult to implement in an unambiguous manner.

The **relative benefits approach to allocation** suggests that the base should result in more costs being allocated to the cost objectives that benefit most from incurring the cost. This might suggest, for example, that computer costs should be allocated to departments based on time spent using the computer, since greater use implies greater benefit. However, this could result in fixed computer cost being allocated to departments that did not exist when the computer was acquired (and so could not have caused the cost of the computer to be incurred).

The **ability to bear costs** notion suggests that the allocation base should result in more costs being allocated to products, services, or departments that are more profitable. Because they are more profitable, they can *bear* the increased costs from the higher allocations.

The **equity approach to allocation** suggests that the base should result in allocations that are perceived to be fair or equitable. Obviously, this is a difficult criterion to apply, because different individuals have different perceptions of what is equitable.

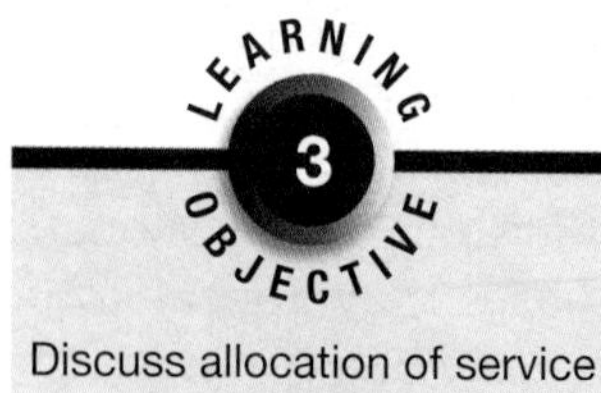

Discuss allocation of service department costs.

ALLOCATING SERVICE DEPARTMENT COSTS

The organizational units in most manufacturing firms can be classified as either production departments or service departments. Production departments engage in direct manufacturing activity, whereas service departments provide indirect support. For example, in a furniture manufacturing company, the assembly and finishing departments are production departments, whereas maintenance, janitorial, personnel, cafeteria, cost accounting, and power are service departments.

Cost pools are often formed by service departments, and these costs are allocated to production departments—the cost objectives. Ultimately, production departments allocate their costs to specific products.

DIRECT METHOD OF ALLOCATING SERVICE DEPARTMENT COSTS

The method of allocating service department costs that we cover is called the direct method. In the **direct method of allocating cost**, service department costs are allocated to production departments but not to other service departments.[1] Thus, even though the Janitorial Department provides a service to the Personnel Department, under the direct method no janitorial costs are allocated to the Personnel Department. The process is diagrammed in Illustration 6-4. The illustration includes no arrow between janitorial costs and personnel costs because there is no allocation of costs between the Janitorial Service Department and the Personnel Department.

We'll consider an example involving the Mason Furniture Company. Suppose the company's janitorial costs are $100,000. The company decides to allocate these costs to Assembly and Finishing based on the number of square feet in each production department. Since Assembly has 20,000 square feet and Finishing has 30,000 square feet, the allocation rate is $2 per square foot ($100,000 ÷ 50,000 square feet). Assembly receives an allocation of $40,000 (20,000 square feet × $2), and Finishing receives an allocation of $60,000 (30,000 square feet × $2).

Now suppose the personnel costs at Mason are $200,000. These costs are allocated based on the number of employees in each production department. The Assembly Department has 60 employees, and the Finishing Department has 40 employees. Thus, the allocation rate for personnel costs is $2,000 per employee ($200,000 ÷ 100 employees). The Assembly Department receives an allocation of

Illustration 6-4
Allocating service department costs with the direct method

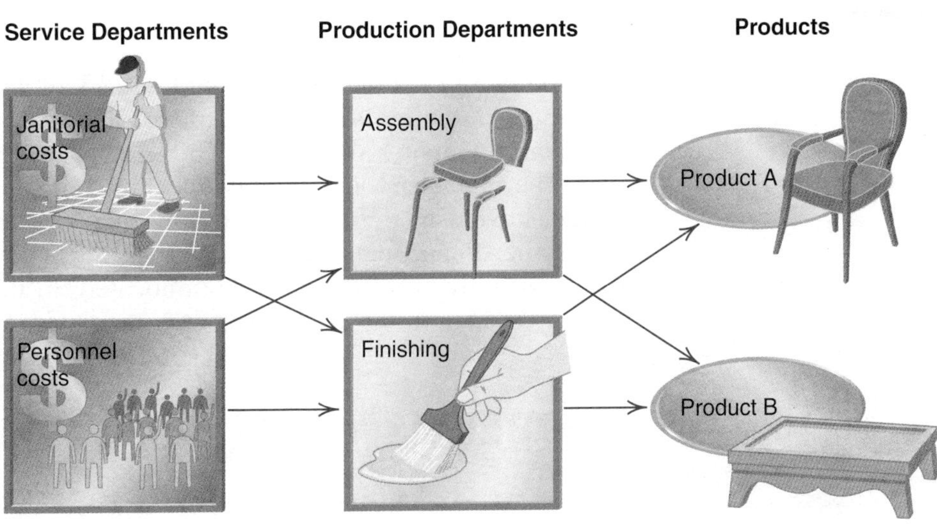

[1]Alternatives to the direct method that recognize that service departments make use of each other's resources (including the sequential and the reciprocal methods) are covered in cost accounting texts.

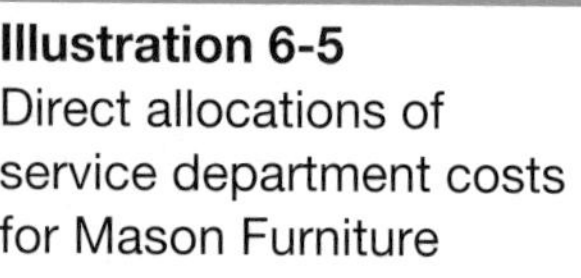

Illustration 6-5
Direct allocations of service department costs for Mason Furniture

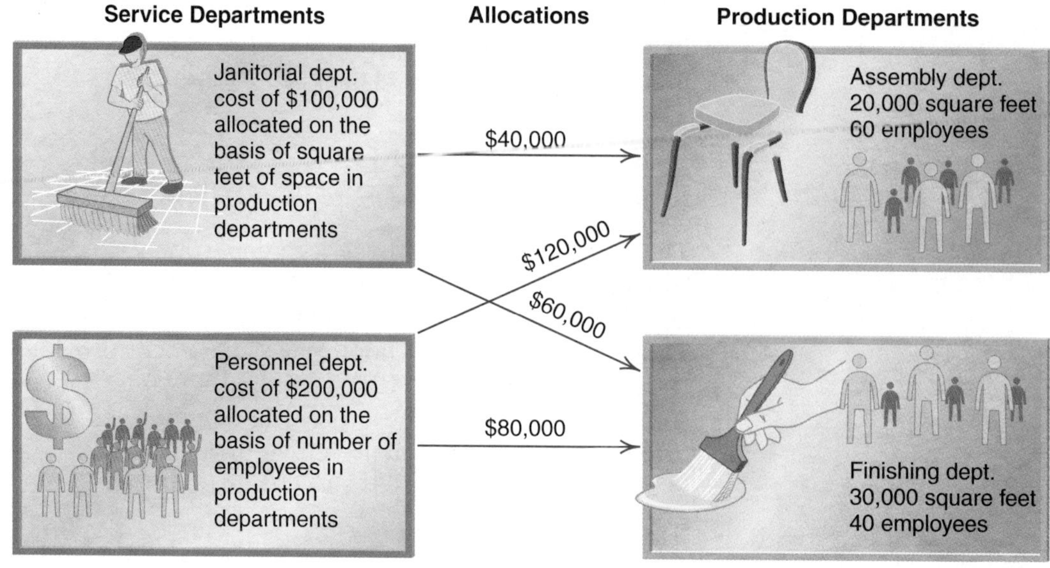

$120,000 (60 × $2,000), and the Finishing Department receives an allocation of $80,000 (40 × $2,000). The allocations are presented in Illustration 6-5.

ALLOCATING BUDGETED AND ACTUAL SERVICE DEPARTMENT COSTS

It is generally a good idea to allocate budgeted rather than actual service department costs. If budgeted costs are allocated, service departments cannot pass on the cost of inefficiencies and waste. For example, suppose at the start of the year, budgeted costs in the Janitorial Department are $100,000, and the accounting department informs Assembly and Finishing that they will receive allocations of $2 per square foot ($100,000 ÷ 50,000 square feet).

But suppose that the Janitorial Department actually incurs $130,000 of cost ($30,000 more than planned) owing to a lack of good cost control. If actual costs are allocated, the Janitorial Department can pass the extra costs on to the production departments by allocating $2.60 per square foot ($130,000 ÷ 50,000 square feet). The managers of Assembly and Finishing would strongly resist the higher charge. Obviously, they would not want their costs to be increased simply because some other department was not performing its job efficiently. This problem is avoided if only budgeted costs are allocated; in that case, the Janitorial Department must stick to the allocation of $2 per square foot.

PROBLEMS WITH COST ALLOCATION

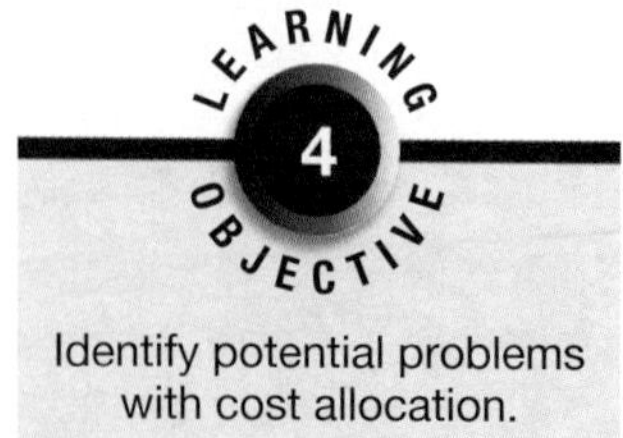

Identify potential problems with cost allocation.

Our discussion so far has focused on ideas about how costs should be allocated. In practice, when costs are allocated, a number of problems may arise. Here we discuss problems brought about by (1) allocations of costs that are not controllable, (2) arbitrary allocations, (3) allocations of fixed costs that make the fixed costs appear to be variable costs, (4) allocations of manufacturing overhead to products using too few overhead cost pools, and (5) use of only volume-related allocation bases.

RESPONSIBILITY ACCOUNTING AND CONTROLLABLE COSTS

In Chapter 1 we learned that one of the primary uses of managerial accounting is to evaluate the performance of managers and the operations under their control. Performance evaluation is facilitated by a system of accounting that traces revenues and costs to organizational units (e.g., departments and divisions) and individuals (e.g., plant manager, supervisor of assembly workers, vice president of operation), with related responsibility for generating revenue and controlling costs. Such a system is referred to as a **responsibility accounting system**.

Consider a company that produces tennis rackets and tennis clothes in two separate plants. The company could prepare monthly production cost reports that list the total amount of material, labor, and overhead cost for the two plants combined. However, this would *not* be consistent with responsibility accounting because the reports would not trace the production costs to the plants responsible for controlling them. A responsibility accounting system would require not only that the costs of producing the tennis rackets and tennis clothes be traced to their respective plants but also that the costs in each plant be traced to the departments or other units responsible for those costs. For example, within the plant producing the tennis rackets, labor costs should be traced to each foreman responsible for an identifiable group or team of workers (e.g., assembly workers and finishing workers).

Cost allocation is generally required in a responsibility accounting system because one organizational unit is often responsible for the costs incurred by another organizational unit. For example, activity in a Production Department increases the costs incurred in the Machine Repair Department. Because the Production Department is responsible for the incurrence of costs in the Machine Repair Department, the Production Department's performance reports should reflect some share of the Machine Repair Department cost. This can be achieved by allocating Machine Repair Department costs to the Production Department.

Some allocations of costs, however, are not consistent with a responsibility accounting system. Most accountants believe that managers should be held responsible only for costs they can control. These costs, called **controllable costs**, are affected by the manager's decisions. Allocating the cost of a building to the performance report of a supervisor responsible for controlling labor costs is not appropriate because the supervisor cannot control building costs.

If allocated costs beyond the manager's control appear on the manager's performance reports, they may cause considerable frustration. Managers want their performance evaluations to reflect their own strengths and weaknesses. In some cases, managers are allocated costs beyond their control simply to make them aware that the costs exist and must be covered by the firm's revenue. In such situations, the costs should be clearly labeled noncontrollable, indicating to the manager that company officials are aware that the items are not affected by his or her decisions. This should minimize possible resentment.

ARBITRARY ALLOCATIONS

In practice, cost allocations are the topic of numerous and often heated discussions. Managers may feel that their departments receive unnecessarily large allocations of indirect costs, causing the departments to appear less profitable. Governmental agencies that have cost-plus contracts may feel that products produced by contractors on a cost-plus basis receive allocations of indirect costs that are unfairly high. Unfortunately, such discussions are likely to continue in the future. The reason is that allocations of costs are to a great extent inherently arbitrary.

In almost all cost allocation situations, determining the one "true," "correct," or "valid" allocation is not possible. As noted earlier in the chapter, various allocation bases (e.g., labor hours, labor cost, and machine hours) may be equally justifiable but may result in substantially different allocations. These situations naturally lead managers to support the allocation that makes their performance look best and reject allocations that cast an unfavorable light on their performance.

UNITIZED FIXED COSTS AND LUMP-SUM ALLOCATIONS

One of the most significant problems associated with cost allocation is due to the fact that the allocation process may make fixed costs appear to be variable costs. This happens when fixed costs are **unitized**—that is, stated on a per unit basis. To illustrate the problem, consider the Smith Tool Company, which has two divisions. At the start of each year, the company estimates the amount of general and administrative costs that are incurred centrally on behalf of the operations of both divisions. Such costs include administrative salaries, clerical costs, central accounting costs, and a variety of others, all of which are essentially fixed in the short run. In the current year, these costs are expected to amount to \$2,000,000. Smith has decided that it would be useful for the divisions to know that these costs are being incurred on their behalf. Therefore, it allocates the costs among the divisions based on their relative sales. In the current year, divisional sales are expected to be \$50,000,000. Thus, Smith has decided to allocate general and administrative costs to the divisions at a rate of \$0.04 per dollar of sales (i.e., \$2,000,000 ÷ \$50,000,000).

We have said that the general and administrative costs are essentially fixed, but how will they appear to the division managers? Let's look, for instance, at Bob Gallegos, the manager of the Carpenter Division, which produces a variety of carpenter tools (e.g., hammers, saws, and drills). Bob observes that as divisional revenue increases, the allocated costs increase. Thus, to him, the costs appear to be variable. This may lead Bob to make decisions that are not in the best interest of the company as a whole but that appear to maximize divisional profitability. For example, suppose the Carpenter Division is considering producing a new hammer that will sell for \$20. At this price, the division expects to sell 100,000 units. Production of the hammer will require \$12 of direct material cost, \$6 of direct labor cost, and an increase in manufacturing overhead costs of \$130,000. An analysis of the effect on the profit of the Carpenter Division is presented in Illustration 6-6.

As indicated in the illustration, sale of the hammer is expected to result in an increase of \$2,000,000 in sales. There will also be a \$1,800,000 increase in variable costs (direct material and direct labor) and a \$130,000 increase in manufac-

Illustration 6-6
Problem of unitized fixed costs

Sales of hammers		
(100,000 × \$20)		\$2,000,000
Less: additional costs		
Direct material (100,000 × \$12)	\$1,200,000	
Direct labor (100,000 × \$6)	600,000	
Additional manufacturing overhead cost	130,000	1,930,000
Real increase in profit		\$70,000
Less: allocated fixed costs		
(\$2,000,000 increase in sales × \$.04)		80,000
Perceived loss on sale of hammers		(\$10,000)

turing overhead cost. Thus, production and sale of the hammer will result in a $70,000 increase in profit. From this information, the hammer appears to be a profitable addition to the product line of the division. However, will the manager of the division be motivated to produce the hammer? Probably not.

The reason is that, with the increase in sales, the division will receive a larger allocation of central general and administrative costs. With an allocation rate of $.04 per dollar of sales and an expected increase in sales of $2,000,000, the division would expect its allocated costs to increase by $80,000. To the manager of the division, the additional allocated costs appear to be variable even though, in fact, they are fixed (that is, central administration salaries, clerical costs, and accounting costs will not increase if the hammer is produced). The result is that the manager of the division would expect production of the hammer to result in a loss of $10,000 ($70,000 − $80,000) for the division.

To remedy this problem, allocations of *fixed costs* must be made in such a way that they *appear fixed* to the managers whose departments receive the allocations. This is achieved by **lump-sum allocations** of fixed costs. A lump-sum allocation is an allocation of a predetermined amount that is not affected by changes in the activity level of the organizational unit receiving the allocation. Resources are acquired taking into account the long-run needs of users. Thus, allocations of fixed costs should be based on the projected long-run needs that lead managers to incur the costs. For example, suppose Smith Tool Company purchases a computer to serve each of its two divisions. Purchase of the computer results in annual fixed costs of $40,000. In deciding what type of computer to purchase, management estimated that the Carpenter Division would use the computer for 2,000 hours per year and the Specialty Tools Division would use the computer for 3,000 hours per year. Thus, allocating $16,000 to the Carpenter Division ($40,000 × 2/5) and $24,000 to the Specialty Tools Division ($40,000 × 3/5) is appropriate.

Lump-sum allocations should generally remain the same year after year, even though, over time, the activity of the organizational units involved may deviate from expectations. Suppose, for example, that the Carpenter Division expanded and required 3,000 hours of computer time per year, whereas the Specialty Tools Division lost business and required only 2,000 hours. Should the lump-sum allocations of the two divisions be reversed? Probably not. Reversing the allocations would make it appear to the managers of the two divisions that their allocations do indeed depend on their activity levels. In other words, the fixed costs would again appear to be variable. If lump-sum allocations of *fixed* costs are to *appear fixed*, the amount of the allocation must not depend on changes in activity.

It follows that, with lump-sum allocations, the allocations of a division do not depend on the activity level of other divisions. Suppose the activity of the Carpenter Division stayed at 2,000 hours, but the activity level of the Specialty Tools Division decreased from 3,000 hours to 2,000 hours. If the cost of the computer were allocated based on current activity levels, the amount allocated to the Carpenter Division would increase from $16,000 to $20,000, in spite of the fact that its use of the computer had not changed. Obviously, this could cause considerable dissatisfaction on the part of the manager of the Carpenter Division. It could also make planning more difficult, because the costs of the division would depend on the activity of other divisions. This is not the case with a lump-sum allocation. Once the amount of the lump-sum is determined, it does not vary in response to changes in activity.

How can lump-sum allocations improve a manager's decisions? Refer back to the decision Bob Gallegos at the Carpenter Division of Smith Tool Company faced regarding sale of a new hammer. If the general and administrative costs at

Smith Tool Company are allocated on a lump-sum basis and the amount allocated to the Carpenter Division is $700,000 regardless of its activity, then Bob will perceive that general and administrative costs are indeed fixed. Thus, he will correctly determine that, in the interest of maximizing divisional profit, the hammer should be produced because it contributes $70,000 toward covering the allocated costs that will be incurred whether or not the hammer is produced.

THE PROBLEM OF TOO FEW COST POOLS

Some companies assign overhead to products using only one or two overhead cost pools. Although the approach has the benefit of being simple and easy to use, product costs may be seriously distorted when only a small number of cost pools are used.

Consider the problem in the context of the Reed Manufacturing Company, which manufactures products in two departments: Assembly and Finishing. Electra has total manufacturing overhead of $1,000,000, and each year the company incurs 50,000 labor hours. If the company includes all overhead in one cost pool and allocates overhead using labor hours, the overhead rate will be $20 per labor hour ($1,000,000 ÷ 50,000 labor hours). But suppose that of the $1,000,000 of overhead, $600,000 is incurred in Assembly and $400,000 is incurred in Finishing. Furthermore, Assembly requires 40,000 labor hours, and Finishing requires only 10,000 labor hours. You can see that overhead per labor hour is much more expensive in the Finishing Department: $15 per labor hour in Assembly and $40 per labor hour in Finishing. (See Illustration 6-7.)

Now, assume that Reed has two products (A and B) that require 10 labor hours each. Product A requires two hours of assembly time and eight hours of finishing, whereas Product B requires eight hours of assembly time and two hours of finishing. How much overhead will be allocated to each product if all overhead is included in a single cost pool and allocated on the basis of labor hours? The answer is that both products will receive the same allocation. They both require 10 hours of total labor, and use of a single cost pool allocates the average cost per labor hour. Both will be allocated $200 of overhead ($20 × 10 labor hours).

Which product is being undercosted and which product is being overcosted? Product A is undercosted because it requires relatively more production time in finishing, which is a high-cost department in terms of overhead cost. Product B is overcosted because it requires relatively more production time in assembly, which is a cheap department in terms of overhead. Still, Product B receives the same charge per labor hour as Product A when only a single cost pool is used. Reed's problem is easily solved by setting up separate cost pools for overhead in each department.

Illustration 6-7
Overhead rates using one versus two cost pools

One cost pool

$$\frac{\text{Total overhead}}{\text{Total labor hours}} = \frac{\$1{,}000{,}000}{50{,}000} = \$20 \text{ per labor hour}$$

Two cost pools (one for Assembly and one for Finishing)

$$\frac{\text{Assembly overhead}}{\text{Assembly labor hours}} = \frac{\$600{,}000}{40{,}000} = \$15 \text{ per assembly labor hour}$$

$$\frac{\text{Finishing overhead}}{\text{Finishing labor hours}} = \frac{\$400{,}000}{10{,}000} = \$40 \text{ per finishing labor hour}$$

In general, product costs will be more accurate when more overhead cost pools are used. And decisions that rely on product cost information, such as product pricing decisions, will be improved. However, the more pools that are formed, the more costly will be the cost of record keeping. Companies must make a cost-benefit tradeoff. Is the cost of forming more cost pools worth the benefit of improved information? Similar questions must always be addressed when considering improvements in accounting information.

USING ONLY VOLUME-RELATED ALLOCATION BASES

We now turn to a final problem involved in cost allocations. Some manufacturing companies allocate manufacturing overhead to products using only measures of production volume (e.g., direct labor or machine hours) as allocation bases. However, not all overhead costs vary with volume. We discuss this issue in the next section along with activity-based costing (ABC), because ABC solves the problem.

Discuss activity-based costing (ABC) and cost drivers.

ACTIVITY-BASED COSTING

Activity-based costing (ABC) is a relatively recent development in managerial accounting, and it has received a tremendous amount of attention from both academics and practitioners interested in improving managerial accounting information.[2] We introduced ABC in Chapter 2, dealing with job-order costing. Now we discuss it in more detail.

THE PROBLEM OF USING ONLY MEASURES OF PRODUCTION VOLUME TO ALLOCATE OVERHEAD

Manufacturing companies commonly use direct labor hours, direct labor cost, and machine hours as allocation bases when assigning overhead to products. Each of these items is a measure of production volume. Because most companies continue to allocate overhead using only measures of production volume as allocation bases, we refer to this approach as the "traditional approach." The problem with the traditional approach is that it assumes that all overhead costs are proportional to production volume. By "proportional," we mean that, for example, when volume increases by 20 percent, overhead increases by 20 percent; when volume increases by 50 percent, overhead increases by 50 percent, and so forth. However, many overhead costs (such as the cost of setting up equipment for a production run, the cost of inspecting raw materials, and the cost of handling materials) are not proportional to volume. In fact, many overhead costs are affected by product complexity rather than volume. The result is that simple high-volume products are often overcosted, whereas complex low-volume products are undercosted.

Consider the overhead costs created by starting up a production line. Both a high-volume product (which is associated with a large amount of labor and machine time) and a low-volume product (which is associated with a small amount of labor and machine time) may require the same amount of setup time and setup cost. However, since setup costs (along with all other overhead) are allocated only

---

[2]Credit for developing activity-based costing is usually given to Robin Cooper and Robert Kaplan. See R. Cooper, "The Rise of Activity-Based Costing—Part One: What Is an Activity-Based Cost System?" *Journal of Cost Management*, Summer 1988, pp. 45–54, and R. Cooper and R. Kaplan, "How Cost Accounting Distorts Product Costs," *Management Accounting*, April 1988, pp. 20–27.

The Activity-Based Costing Portal

http://www.offtech.com.au/abc/Home.asp

This site offers a free ABC magazine, links to articles, and a forum for discussion of ABC related topics. A special feature allows students to submit questions on ABC.

Articles recently featured on the site in May, 2006 include:

- *A Procedure for Smooth Implementation of Activity-Based Costing in Small Companies*
- *The Association Between Activity-Based Costing and Improvement in Financial Performance*
- *Using Activity-Based Costing to Manage More Effectively*
- *Activity-Based Costing Approach to Equipment Selection Problem for Flexible Manufacturing Systems*
- *Quality, Cost, and Value-Added in Comprehensive Institutions of Higher Education*

on the basis of production volume, the high-volume product will receive a larger *allocation* of setup cost. Thus, the high-volume product is overcosted. Let's see how the ABC approach avoids this problem.

THE ABC APPROACH

In the ABC approach, companies identify the major activities that cause overhead costs to be incurred. Some of these activities are related to production volume, but others are not. The costs of the resources consumed performing these activities are grouped into cost pools. Finally, the costs are assigned to products using a measure of activity referred to as a **cost driver** (an allocation base in an ABC system). The steps involved in the ABC approach, then, are:

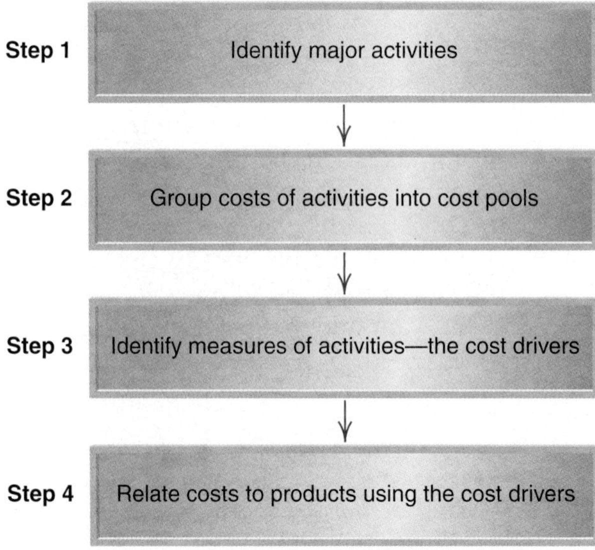

Illustration 6-8
Common activities and associated cost drivers

Major Activities	Associated Costs	Cost Driver
Processing purchase orders for materials and parts	Labor cost for workers determining order quantities, contracting vendors, and preparing purchase orders	Number of purchase orders processed
Handling material and parts	Labor cost for workers handling material and parts, depreciation of equipment used to move material and parts (e.g., depreciation of fork lift trucks), etc.	Number of material requisitions
Inspecting incoming material and parts	Labor cost for workers performing inspections, depreciation of equipment used to test strength of materials, tolerances, etc.	Number of receipts
Setting up equipment	Labor cost for workers involved in setups, depreciation of equipment used to adjust equipment	Number of setups
Producing goods using manufacturing equipment	Depreciation on manufacturing equipment	Number of machine hours
Supervising assembly workers	Salary of assembly supervisors	Number of assembly labor hours
Inspecting finished goods	Labor cost for finished goods inspectors, depreciation of equipment used to test whether finished goods meet customer specifications, etc.	Number of inspections
Packing customer orders	Labor cost for packing workers, cost of packing materials, etc.	Number of boxes shipped

Some common activities and associated cost drivers are listed in Illustration 6-8. Note that some of the cost drivers are volume related; machine hours and assembly labor hours are examples. Other cost drivers are not related to production volume; one example is the number of inspections. Some low-volume products that involve complex or fragile parts may need a large number of inspections, whereas some high-volume products that involve simple or rugged parts may need relatively few inspections. Number of setups, as suggested earlier, is another cost driver that may not be related to volume. Both low-volume and high-volume products may require the same number of setups.

Each firm must decide how many separate activities (and related cost pools and cost drivers) to identify. If too many activities are identified, the system will be unnecessarily costly and confusing. For example, consider a company that produces 200 products and identifies 100 key activities. This company must account for 20,000 (200 × 3 × 100) product-activity relations. On the other hand, if too few activities are used, the ABC system is not likely to produce accurate data. Most companies that design ABC systems use 25 to 100 distinct activities.[3]

[3]See R. Cooper, R. Kaplan, L. Maisel, E. Morrissey, and R. Oehm, "Implementing Activity-Based Cost Management: Moving from Analysis to Action," *Institute of Management Accountants*, 1992, p. 13.

RELATING COST POOLS TO PRODUCTS USING COST DRIVERS

Let's take a moment to look at the last step in the ABC approach: relating cost pools to products using cost drivers as the allocation bases. Understanding how this step is accomplished will allow us to move on to a comprehensive example.

Kim Electronics produces a variety of electronic products ranging from simple hand-held calculators to hard disk drives. Inspection to ensure that products are of high quality is a major activity at Kim. In the coming year, the company expects to incur inspection costs of $2,500,000. Forty workers are employed in the inspection process, and they are expected to perform 1,000,000 product inspections in the coming year. Using inspection cost as a cost pool and the number of inspections as a cost driver, the company arrives at a rate of $2.50 per inspection for purposes of allocating inspection costs to products.

Kim produces 20,000 Model ZX disk drives. Each drive is inspected three times during the production process, and various functions are tested for conformance with rigorous standards set by the company. How much of the total $2,500,000 inspection cost will be allocated to the Model ZX? With 20,000 disk drives and three inspections per drive, a total of 60,000 inspections will be performed. A rate of $2.50 per inspection implies that $7.50 of inspection cost will be allocated to each disk drive ($2.50 rate × 3 inspections) for a total of $150,000 ($7.50 × 20,000). A similar approach will be taken to determine the amount of inspection cost to be allocated to the other products produced by Kim.

Budgeted inspection cost	$2,500,000
Divided by budgeted number of inspections	1,000,000
Cost per inspection	$2.50
Times number of inspections per unit for the Model ZX disk drive	3
Inspection cost per unit for Model ZX	$7.50

THE ABC APPROACH AT GARDENRITE MANUFACTURING: A COMPREHENSIVE EXAMPLE

Our comprehensive example of the ABC approach uses the situation faced by the Gardenrite Manufacturing Company presented at the start of the chapter. As you read through the example, make sure you can explain why using the ABC approach reduces the cost of the high-volume product (the Model 250 spade) and increases the cost of the low-volume product (the Model 900 mower).

Gardenrite's Costs Under the Traditional Approach. For product costing purposes, Gardenrite traces labor and material costs directly to products produced. Manufacturing overhead is allocated to products based on labor cost. At the start of 2008, estimated manufacturing overhead was $40,000,000, and estimated labor cost was $8,000,000. Thus, the overhead allocation rate was $5 per dollar of labor.

For 2008, the following costs and revenues are expected from sale of the Model 250 spade and the Model 900 mower.

	Model 250 Spade	Model 900 Mower
Number of units	85,000	800
Sales revenue	$765,000	$240,000
Direct labor	91,800	12,000
Direct material	153,000	48,000
Overhead	459,000	60,000
Total cost	703,800	120,000
Gross profit	$ 61,200	$120,000
Cost per unit	$8.28	$150.00
Gross profit per unit	$.72	$150.00
Gross profit as a % of sales	8.00%	50.00%

Note that the overhead allocated to the Model 250 spade, $459,000, is equal to the overhead rate of $5 per dollar of labor times the $91,800 of direct labor incurred in production of the spade.

The production process for spades is fairly simple. The company uses one supplier for the metal handle and blade. The company produces shafts on an automatic lathe, and the handles, blades, and shafts are assembled by hand at a single workstation.

Two years ago, the company began manufacturing lawn mowers. The production process for lawn mowers is much more complicated than that used for spades. Twenty suppliers are used to provide the 50 components involved in producing the Model 900 mower. Furthermore, assembly of mowers makes use of 15 separate assembly workstations.

Recall that Ben Jakes, the CFO at Gardenrite, suspects that the low gross profit (less than 10 percent of sales) for spades may be due to problems with the costing system in use. Furthermore, he is somewhat surprised that the company is able to earn such a high gross profit on mowers (50 percent of sales). Since the company only recently began manufacturing mowers, he expected production inefficiencies to keep gross profit low for at least three years.

Gardenrite's Costs under the ABC Approach. The CFO is right to be concerned about the product costing system at Gardenrite. The company's approach to allocating overhead assumes that all overhead is proportional to a single measure of production volume—labor cost. However, overhead is likely caused by several key activities.

Suppose the CFO authorizes a study of how the costs of the Model 250 spade and the Model 900 mower will change if an ABC approach is taken. The study determines that the $40,000,000 of overhead cost is related to the four cost drivers identified in Illustration 6-9. As indicated in the illustration, setup costs are related to the number of setups, material handling costs are related to the number of material requisitions, and depreciation of equipment is related to the number of machine hours required to produce products. All other overhead is categorized in a cost pool simply referred to as "Other." Gardenrite has decided that "manufacturing complexity" is a major factor contributing to the incurrence of other overhead costs. The cost driver for complexity is the number of workstations required to produce a product. Products that require many workstations to produce are more complex and cause more overhead.

Illustration 6-9
Overhead cost items and cost drivers

Overhead Cost Items	Annual Cost	Cost Driver	Estimated Annual Value	Cost per Driver Unit
Setup costs	$4,000,000	Number of setups	1,000	$4,000 per setup
Material handling costs	$2,000,000	Number of material requisitions	2,000	$1,000 per requisition
Depreciation of equipment	$10,000,000	Number of machine hours	20,000	$500 per machine hour
Other	$24,000,000	Number of workstations used in production of a product	3,000 workstations used across all products	$8,000 per workstation

Manufacturing spades requires two setups and three material requisitions. Forty machine hours are used to produce the 85,000 Model 250 spades. Assembly of spades requires one workstation. Production of the 800 Model 900 mowers requires five setups and 50 material requisitions. One hundred machine hours are used to produce the 800 mowers. Assembly of mowers requires 15 workstations. This information is summarized in Illustration 6-10.

Using this information, we can calculate the cost per unit of Model 250 spades and the cost per unit of Model 900 mowers assuming the company changes to an ABC system. The calculations are presented in Illustration 6-11. With the ABC approach, the cost of the Model 250 spade drops from $8.28 to $3.34 per unit, whereas the cost of the Model 900 mower increases from $150 to $375 per unit.

	Model 250 Spade	Model 900 Mower
Cost per unit using traditional approach to allocating overhead	$8.28	$150.00
Cost per unit using ABC approach to allocating overhead	$3.34	$375.00

Recall that the Model 250 spades sell for $9 per unit. Thus, the ABC approach reveals that this high-volume product is very profitable. However, the Model 900 mower sells for only $300 per unit. The ABC approach reveals that the selling

Illustration 6-10
Production information for 85,000 spades and 800 mowers

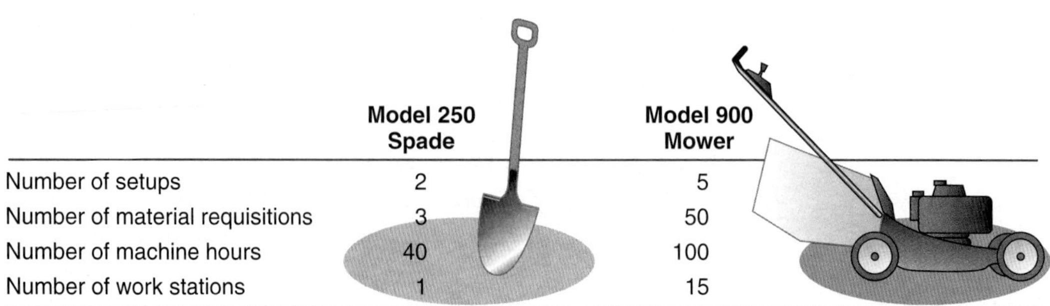

	Model 250 Spade	Model 900 Mower
Number of setups	2	5
Number of material requisitions	3	50
Number of machine hours	40	100
Number of work stations	1	15

Illustration 6-11
Costs of Model 250 spade and Model 900 mower using an ABC approach

	Model 250 Spade		Model 900 Mower
Number of units	85,000	Number of units	800
Direct labor	$ 91,800	Direct labor	$ 12,000
Direct material	153,000	Direct material	48,000
Overhead:		Overhead:	
Setup cost ($4,000 × 2)	8,000	Setup cost ($4,000 × 5)	20,000
Material handling cost ($1,000 × 3)	3,000	Material handling cost ($1,000 × 50)	50,000
Depreciation of equipment ($500 × 40)	20,000	Depreciation of equipment ($500 × 100)	50,000
Other ($8,000 × 1)	8,000	Other ($8,000 × 15)	120,000
Total overhead	39,000	Total overhead	240,000
Total cost	$283,800	Total cost	$300,000
Cost per unit	$3.34	Cost per unit	$375.00
Selling price per unit	$9.00	Selling price per unit	$300.00
Gross profit per unit	$5.66	Gross profit (loss) per unit	($75.00)
Gross profit as a % of sales	63%	Gross profit (loss) as a % of sales	(25%)

price does not even cover the full cost of this low-volume product.[4] The CFO's intuition that the traditional product costing system at Gardenrite might be providing misleading information was correct. Because the traditional system only allocated costs using a volume-related allocation base, the high-volume product (spades) was overcosted and did not appear to be particularly profitable. The low-volume product (mowers) was undercosted and appeared to be highly profitable, when in fact it was not covering its full costs.

PROS AND CONS OF ABC

Although, as you can see, ABC offers some real advantages, it is not without problems. This section describes two major benefits of ABC and two major limitations.

Benefits. ABC is less likely than traditional costing systems to undercost complex, low-volume products and overcost simple, high-volume products. This follows because ABC uses more cost drivers to assign costs and the drivers are not necessarily volume related.

A second benefit is that ABC may lead to improvements in cost control. With ABC, managers see costs broken out by a number of activities rather than buried in one or two overhead cost pools. Unless managers know the costs of

[4]The fact that costs exceed revenue for the Model 900 mower does not *necessarily* imply that the product should be immediately dropped. Some of the costs included in the cost of the mower (like depreciation) will exist whether or not the mower is produced. See the discussion in Chapter 7 dealing with cost information and management decisions.

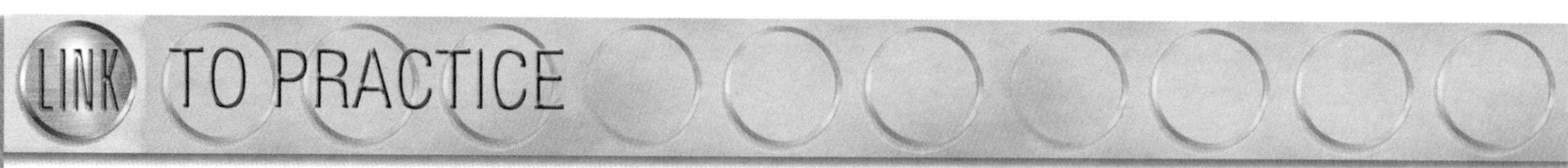

Avoiding a Disastrous Decision by Using ABC

Mike Paris is a principal at Paris Consultants, Inc., a Hinsdale, Illinois firm that performs ABC consulting. Here's one of his "war stories" on how ABC saved a client from a potentially disastrous decision.

> "A gear maker produces standard industrial gearboxes and very large specially engineered ring gears for ships and mining machinery. The special-gear business employed 86 engineers and a technically trained sales force, which ran up lots of sales-related travel costs. The standard gearboxes, however, required just four engineers, and sales expenses were minimal since most sales were to distributors and by catalog.
>
> The indirect costs averaged a worrisome 40% and were badly skewed. Burden rates were allocated on the basis of direct labor hours worked. Despite the 86:4 engineering ratio, the big special gears required less labor than the standard gearboxes. The accounting system shifted a large chunk of the big special gears' overhead costs for engineering, sales, and tooling onto the standard products because they used more total direct labor.
>
> This led management to believe the standard gears lost money when the truth was they were very profitable. The big gears lost money. The company almost sold the profitable part of its business to focus on specials that were killing them. Until we pointed out the unintended cross-subsidy, no one perceived the competitive advantages and disadvantages."

Source: Michael Paris and Dan Brassard, "Reading Between the Numbers," *Strategic Finance*, (December 2004), pp. 41–45.

setups, inspections, order taking, stocking, moving inventory, and other key activities, they are not likely to see a need to improve efficiency and reduce these costs.

Recall that under its traditional overhead allocation system, managers at Gardenrite knew that overhead was $5 per labor dollar. What they didn't know was the cost of the key activities that determine total overhead. With the ABC system, however, they now know that (1) setup costs are $4,000,000 in total or $4,000 per setup; (2) material handling costs are $2,000,000 in total or $1,000 per requisition; (3) depreciation of equipment is $10,000,000 in total or $500 per machine hour and (4) other overhead costs are $24,000,000. With this information, managers are likely to be spurred to action leading to process improvements and increased efficiency. One can easily imagine a manager saying "Wow, I had no idea we were spending $2 million on material handling. We've got to be able to get this cost down below $1,000 per requisition. Let's take a look at the steps involved in material handling and cost them out. Now that I think of it, we have 15 people working the receiving dock and they don't seem that busy. Maybe that's a place to start."

Limitations. A major disadvantage of ABC is its expense; an ABC system is more costly to develop and maintain than a traditional costing system. Consider an ABC system with 20 cost pools applied to 100 different products. Assigning costs to each of the 20 pools will be costly, and then 2,000 allocations will have to be made (20 pools × 100 products) to assign costs to products.

Decision Making/ Incremental Analysis

Perhaps the major limitation of ABC is that, in practice, it is used to develop the *full cost* of products. Because full costs include allocations of costs that are fixed (e.g., depreciation of plant and equipment and supervisory salaries), the cost per unit generated by the ABC system does not measure the incremental costs needed to produce an item. And incremental information is what is needed to make decisions. (Remember that Chapter 1 made this point: Decision making relies on incremental analysis.)

Consider the example of the mower produced by Gardenrite analyzed in the previous section. The ABC system indicated that the cost per unit was $375 and that the selling price was only $300. However, will Gardenrite's costs really increase by $375 if another mower is produced? The answer is no. Much of the cost of producing the mower relates to depreciation on equipment that has already been incurred. This cost is not just fixed, it's also sunk, and sunk costs are not relevant for decisions since they're not incremental. Thus, in many cases, ABC does not provide clear-cut information applicable to decision making. Do the disadvantages of ABC outweigh the advantages? After assessing the pros and cons, we can reasonably conclude that, for companies that don't use the information in an overly simplistic way (i.e., treat the full cost information as if it were incremental cost information), an ABC system is likely to be quite beneficial.

Any Questions?

Q According to the book, a major limitation of ABC is that it doesn't distinguish between fixed and variable costs. Isn't there a simple fix to this problem? Just separate fixed costs and variable costs in each cost pool and allocate the variable costs per unit of each cost driver to products, but don't allocate the fixed costs on a per unit basis.

A Your idea is a good one. Most likely, managers would find the variable cost per setup, the variable cost per material requisition, the variable cost per inspection, etc. to be very useful information. Unfortunately, the "simple fix" you suggest isn't common in practice. Perhaps this is due to the fact that, in practice, the fix isn't all that simple—a great deal of analysis would be needed to separate fixed and variable costs in each overhead cost pool.

ACTIVITY-BASED MANAGEMENT (ABM)

Distinguish activity-based costing (ABC) from activity-based management (ABM).

Activity-based management (ABM) is a management tool that involves analyzing and costing activities with the goal of improving efficiency and effectiveness. As you would expect, ABM is closely related to ABC, but the two schemes differ in their primary goals. Whereas ABC focuses on activities with the goal of measuring the costs of products and services produced by them, ABM focuses on activities with the goal of managing the activities themselves. This difference is shown graphically in Illustration 6-12.

Illustration 6-12
Comparison of ABC and ABM

ABC focus is better costing of products and services.
Resources are traced to activities to facilitate costing of products and services.

ABM focus is improvement of efficiency and effectiveness of activities.
Resources are traced to activities to facilitate evaluation of activities.

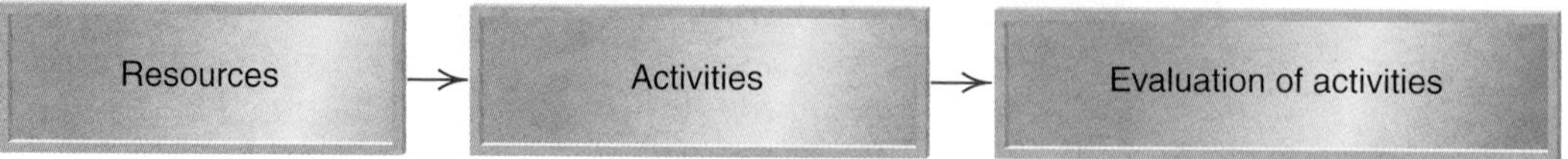

To clarify the difference, consider activities involved in setting up equipment for a production run. ABC seeks to measure the cost of setups and then assign a cost to products based on how many setups each product requires. The goal of ABM, however, is to improve the efficiency and effectiveness of the activities. Thus, for example, ABM would focus on ways to improve the setup process and ways to eliminate the demand for setup activity (thus reducing setup cost).

Managers using ABM want to know the costs of activities because this information may provide insight into how well the activities are being performed. For example, by knowing the cost of setups, managers can benchmark performance by comparing setup costs at one plant to setup costs at another plant. If the costs per setup are much higher at Plant A than at Plant B (and the plants are producing similar items), there is a good chance that costs are out of control in Plant A. In essence, ABM supports the management dictum, "You can't manage what you can't measure." In other words, you need to know the costs of activities before you can do a good job managing them. ABM is discussed in more detail in the appendix to this chapter.

REMEMBER—YOU GET WHAT YOU MEASURE!

Before concluding our discussion of cost allocation, let's return to one of the key points raised in Chapter 1: You get what you measure! How does this point relate to cost allocation? Allocations affect the profit that managers have reported on their performance reports. Thus, managers pay attention to controlling the allocation base, since more use of the allocation base results in higher costs and lower profit.

Consider two companies that are initially identical. Company A allocates production overhead based on labor hours, whereas Company B allocates production overhead based on machine hours. Managers at both companies must make decisions about how much labor and equipment to use in their production processes. All else being equal, the managers at Company A will view labor as more expensive, because when they use more labor to make products, the products receive higher allocations of overhead. Managers at Company B will view equipment as more expensive because when they use more machine time to produce products, the products receive higher allocations of overhead. Thus, over time, we might expect the managers of Company A to increase use of equipment and the managers of Company B to increase use of labor to produce their products.

Similarly, if you calculate overhead using the number of setups as the allocation base, managers are likely to want to reduce the number of setups. If you calculate overhead using the number of inspections as the allocation base, managers are likely to want to reduce the number of inspections. And if you calculate overhead using labor costs as the allocation base, managers are likely to want to reduce labor costs. These actions, which are driven by the way companies measure profit, are not necessarily good or bad. For example, it may be useful to *reduce* the number of inspections in order to reduce cost, but it might also be useful to *increase* the number of inspections in order to increase product quality. The point is not that the number of setups, the number of inspections, or labor costs are or are not good allocation bases. The point is that the choice of an allocation base affects other management decisions in ways that may not be obvious.

MAKING BUSINESS DECISIONS

Decision making relies on incremental analysis. A potential problem with cost allocation is that it may make a fixed cost appear to be a variable cost and, therefore, incremental. Suppose, for example, that fixed costs are allocated based on sales dollars. This makes it appear that if sales increase, the costs will increase. When making decisions using cost information that involves allocation—beware!

KNOWLEDGE AND SKILLS (K/S) CHECKLIST

Knowledge and skills are needed to make good business decisions. Check off the knowledge and skills you've acquired from reading this chapter.

❐ K/S 1. You have an expanded business vocabulary (see key terms).

❐ K/S 2. You can explain why costs are allocated.

❐ K/S 3. You can allocate service department costs to production departments.

❐ K/S 4. You recognize that cost allocation can lead to a number of significant problems.

❐ K/S 5. You understand activity-based costing (ABC) and can explain why it results in a cost that is different from that obtained using a traditional product costing approach.

❐ K/S 6. You can explain the difference between activity-based costing (ABC) and activity-based management (ABM).

SUMMARY OF LEARNING OBJECTIVES

1 ***Explain why indirect costs are allocated.*** Indirect costs are allocated to provide information for decision making, to calculate the full cost of products, to reduce the frivolous use of common resources, and to encourage managers to evaluate the efficiency of internally provided services. From a decision making standpoint, the allocation should measure the opportunity cost of using a company resource. However, this is difficult to operationalize in practice, since opportunity costs often change quickly.

2 ***Describe the cost allocation process.*** The cost allocation process has three steps: (1) identify the cost objectives, (2) form cost pools, and (3) select an allocation base to relate the costs to the cost objectives.

3 ***Discuss allocation of service department costs.*** Service department costs are allocated to production departments, which in turn allocate these costs to products. The direct method allocates service department costs to production departments but not to other service departments.

4 ***Identify potential problems with cost allocation.*** A number of problems are associated with cost allocation in practice: (1) the allocated costs

may not be controllable by the manager receiving the allocation; (2) allocations may be arbitrary; (3) allocations may make fixed costs appear to be variable; (4) allocations may be made using too few cost pools; and (5) allocation may be made using only volume-related allocation bases.

5 ***Discuss activity-based costing (ABC) and cost drivers.*** Activity-based costing (ABC) is a costing method that recognizes that costs are caused by activities. Measures of the key activities that cause costs to be incurred are referred to as cost drivers. The cost drivers are used as the allocation bases to relate indirect costs to products. Unlike traditional systems, ABC does not focus solely on volume-related cost drivers.

6 ***Distinguish activity-based costing (ABC) from activity-based management (ABM).*** Whereas ABC focuses on the costs of activities in order to develop the cost of goods and services produced by the activities, ABM focuses on the costs of activities in order to help manage the activities themselves (you can't manage what you can't measure).

APPENDIX

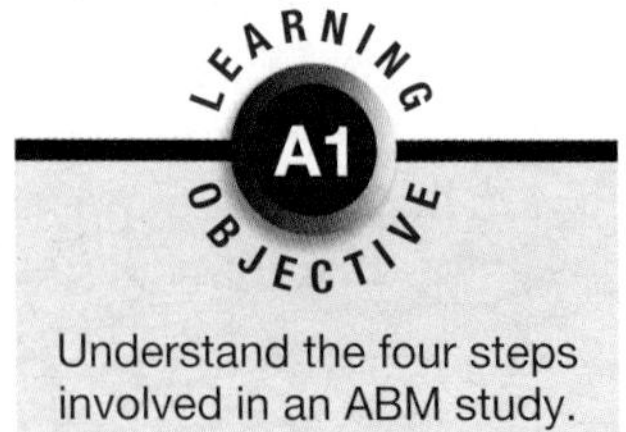

Understand the four steps involved in an ABM study.

ACTIVITY-BASED MANAGEMENT

Activity-based management is a method of activity analysis aimed at improving the efficiency and effectiveness of business processes. Let's look at two process improvement examples that will help make the goal of ABM more concrete. Then we'll discuss a four-step approach to conducting an ABM study.

Consider the activity *shipping goods to stores* conducted by a large retailer with multiple stores. This activity involves having suppliers unload deliveries at the company's warehouse. Subsequently, goods are moved from the warehouse to the company's trucks and sent to stores. How could this process be improved? Wal-Mart uses *cross-docking* whereby deliveries from suppliers are loaded directly from suppliers' trucks onto Wal-Mart trucks and then sent to stores. With this approach, there is no need to move products into and around a warehouse.

As another example, consider the activity *checking into a hotel*. A number of hotels have improved this process using computer technology. Based on information obtained from initial visits, a computerized database knows customer preferences for room location and for a smoking versus nonsmoking room. Credit card information, addresses, and phone numbers are also in the database. With this information readily available, hotel workers at the registration desk can check customers in more rapidly and in a way that recognizes their individual preferences, leading to gains in customer loyalty.

Hopefully, these two examples have provided some insight into the goal of an ABM study—process improvement. Now, let's discuss a four step process for conducting one. In our discussion, we'll consider the case of Mattress Warehouse, a discount store that sells beds and mattresses. The company has a single warehouse and 15 stores in the Dallas/Fort Worth area. Stores do not hold inventory except for display. Thus, all shipments originate from the warehouse. The company offers free delivery within 100 miles of any store and for the first time in its 25-year history has decided to study the delivery process to determine its cost and identify potential improvements. Solutions Analysis, a consulting firm, has been hired to undertake the study.

STEP 1: DETERMINE MAJOR ACTIVITIES

The first step in the ABM study is to determine major activities. This is usually accomplished through interviews and observation. Solutions Analysis has determined that the key activities are:

a. Determine customer locations, determine availability of stock, and prepare delivery schedules.

b. Pick orders from warehouse.

c. Load trucks.

d. Deliver merchandise.

e. Return merchandise to stock if not acceptable to customer or customer not home to receive delivery.

f. Wash delivery trucks (performed each night).

g. Schedule trucks for routine service (e.g., oil change) and nonroutine repairs.

STEP 2: IDENTIFY RESOURCES USED BY EACH ACTIVITY

The second step is to identify the resources used by each activity. Let's consider the resources used by activities (e) and (f).

Return Merchandise to Stock If Not Acceptable to Customer or Customer Not Home to Receive Delivery. Solutions Analysis has determined that in a typical month, 25 orders are returned because customers receive a slightly different mattress or box spring than expected. For example, a customer may have picked out a mattress in the store with blue stitching but the one delivered has red stitching. Or, the model name on the mattress delivered is different (due to a change by the manufacturer) from the model name on the mattress in the store although items are identical in all other respects. Additionally, 40 orders are returned each month due to customers not being home to receive delivery. The monthly cost of this activity is $2,050.

Wash Delivery Trucks. Solutions Analysis has determined that each of the 15 delivery trucks is washed each night. Costs include the salaries of three employees, supplies, depreciation, water and other miscellaneous costs. The total cost is $8,450 each month.

Monthly Cost of Returning Merchandise to Stock when Not Acceptable to the Customer or the Customer Is Not Home to Receive Delivery.	
Salaries related to returning merchandise to stock (15 hours × $20)	$ 300
Costs to process paperwork for corrected shipment	250
Salaries to re-pick shipment (10 hours × $20)	200
Transportation cost to re-ship order (includes fuel, repair cost, and driver salary)	1,300
Total	$2,050
Monthly Cost to Wash 15 Delivery Trucks.	
Monthly salaries (three full-time employees)	$7,500
Supplies	450
Depreciation of equipment	300
Water and other miscellaneous costs	200
Total	$8,450

STEP 3: EVALUATE THE PERFORMANCE OF THE ACTIVITIES

Once Solutions Analysis has determined the cost of key activities, they can turn their attention to an evaluation of them. This is the third step in an ABM study. One way they can do this is by benchmarking the activities against similar activities performed by other clients they have dealt with. For example, Solutions Analysis now knows that it costs the company $101,400 a year ($8,450 × 12 months) to wash its 15 trucks. That's $6,760 per truck. From their work with other retail companies that perform delivery services, they have calculated an average cost of under $3,000 per truck. Thus, the cost of this activity to Mattress Warehouse appears to be too high.

STEP 4: IDENTIFY WAYS TO IMPROVE THE EFFICIENCY AND/OR EFFECTIVENESS OF THE ACTIVITIES

The most satisfying part of the ABM process is identifying ways to improve the efficiency and/or effectiveness of activities, the fourth and last step of the ABM process. Pause for a minute and consider the two activities analyzed. Can you suggest any process improvements?

To identify process improvements, the consultants at Solutions Analysis would think about best practices they've identified at other clients, they would brainstorm with each other, and they would solicit input from managers at Mattress Warehouse. Possible improvements are listed in Illustration A6-1.

Illustration A6-1
Possible process improvements for mattress warehouse

- Ask the sales force to discuss the possibility of minor variations in stitching color with customers. If customers have a strong preference, confirm current colors with the warehouse before shipping. This should reduce returns.
- Have a clerk call customers the day before a delivery to confirm that the customers will be home. This should reduce the problem of customers not being home to accept deliveries.
- Reduce staffing in the wash operation from three full-time employees to two full-time employees. This will save approximately $2,500 per month. Alternatively, consider outsourcing the wash operation.

CONCLUSION

Hopefully, this brief treatment of ABM has provided you with insight into the nature of an ABM study.[1] Unlike ABC, which is focused on better costing of goods and services, ABM is focused on process improvements. Still, ABM like ABC re-

[1]The following books will provide you with additional information on activity-based management: Judith J. Baker, *Activity-Based Costing and Activity-Based Management for Health Care*, Aspen Publishers, (1998); James A. Brimson and John Antos, *Activity-Based Management*, John Wiley and Sons, (1994); and Robin Cooper, Robert Kaplan, Lawrence Maisel, Eileen Morrissey, and Ronald Oehm, *Implementing Activity-Based Cost Management: Moving From Analysis to Action*, Institute of Management Accountants, (1992).

quires costing activities. Once activities are costed, a manager conducting an ABM study can identify the so-called "low hanging fruit." That is, the manager can identify activities whose costs are large and apparently out of line. These are the activities that deserve immediate management attention.

One reason ABM studies have become so popular is that they often generate very substantial financial returns. Consider the case of Mattress Warehouse. If it turns out that eliminating one employee from the wash operation is appropriate, the company will save $2,500 per month or $30,000 per year. Over five years, that's $150,000. To analyze the wash operation, a consultant from Solutions Analysis likely spent less than 8 hours and billed Mattress Warehouse less than $4,000.

REVIEW PROBLEM

Bender Electric Motors produces electric motors used by home appliance and other manufacturing companies. Each motor is built to customer specifications although the number of units requested may vary from 1 to as many as 2,000.

Bender has recently adopted an activity-based costing system with the following overhead costs and drivers.

Cost Pool	Annual Amount		Annual Driver
Direct labor related	$ 400,000	$1,000,000	direct labor cost
Material ordering	100,000	5,000	purchase orders
Material inspection	600,000	4,000	receiving reports
Equipment setup	200,000	1,000	setups
Quality control	400,000	2,000	inspections of motors
Machine related	800,000	40,000	machine hours
Miscellaneous	400,000	$4,000,000	of product costs other than miscellaneous overhead
Total overhead	$2,900,000		

Recently, the company received an order from Kromer's Department Stores for 10 identical motors for use in a holiday display. Bender estimates the following costs and activities related to the order:

Material cost	$500
Labor cost	$200
Purchase orders	2
Receiving reports	2
Setups	1
Inspections	1
Machine hours	10

Note that the costs indicated are *for all 10 motors*—they are *not* per motor.

Required

a. Calculate the cost of the Kromer job using the new ABC system.
b. Calculate the cost of the Kromer job assuming the company used a traditional costing system with labor cost as the only allocation base.
c. Briefly explain why costs are higher or lower using the ABC system in part a compared to the traditional system in part b.

Answer

a.

Cost Pool	Overhead Rate
Direct labor related	$ 0.40 per direct labor dollar
Material ordering	$ 20.00 per purchase order
Material inspection	$150.00 per receiving report
Equipment setup	$200.00 per setup
Quality control	$200.00 per inspection
Machine related	$ 20.00 per machine hour
Miscellaneous	$ 0.10 per dollar of product costs other than misc.

ABC Cost of Kromer Job

Material	$ 500
Labor	200
Overhead:	
Labor related ($0.40 × $200)	80
Material ordering ($20 × 2)	40
Material inspection ($150 × 2)	300
Setup ($200 × 1)	200
Quality control ($200 × 1)	200
Machine related ($20 × 10)	200
Miscellaneous (= .10 × cost other than misc.)	172
Total overhead	1,192
Total cost	$1,892

Cost other than misc. = $1,720

b.

Traditional Overhead Rate

Total overhead	$2,900,000
Total labor cost	$1,000,000
Rate	$2.90 per labor dollar

Traditional Cost of Kromer Job

Material	$ 500
Labor	200
Overhead ($2.90 × $200)	580
Total cost	$1,280

c. Costs are higher with ABC because the Kromer job is relatively small and makes use of a number of activities whose costs are not proportionate to volume.

KEY TERMS

Ability to bear costs (216)
Activity-based costing (ABC) (223)
Activity-based management (ABM) (231)
Cause-and-effect relationship (215)
Controllable cost (219)
Cost allocation (210)
Cost driver (224)
Cost objective (214)
Cost pools (214)
Direct method of allocating cost (217)
Equity approach to allocation (216)
Lump-sum allocations (221)
Relative benefits approach to allocation (216)
Responsibility accounting system (219)
Unitized (220)

SELF ASSESSMENT *(Answers Below)*

1. Costs are allocated:

a. To provide information useful for decision making.
b. To reduce frivolous use of resources.
c. To encourage evaluation of internally provided services.
d. To calculate the "full cost" of products/services for GAAP reporting.
e. All of the above are reasons to allocate costs.

2. An important concern in forming a cost pool is to:

a. Avoid placing similar costs in the same pool.
b. Limit the number of costs that make up the pool.
c. Ensure that the costs in the pool are homogeneous, or similar.
d. None of the above.

3. In the cost allocation process, an allocation base:

a. Must be some characteristic that is common to all of the cost objectives.
b. Ideally should result in cost being allocated based on a cause-and-effect relationship.
c. Both a and b.
d. None of the above.

4. The direct method of allocating costs:

a. Allocates service department costs to other service departments.
b. Allocates only direct costs.
c. Allocates service department costs to producing departments only.
d. Both b and c.

5. When fixed costs are stated on a per unit basis:

a. Fixed costs are said to be "unitized."
b. Fixed costs may appear to be variable to managers receiving allocations.
c. Decision making is greatly improved.
d. Both a and b.

6. One way to avoid the problems associated with unitized fixed costs is to:

a. Not allocate fixed costs.
b. Use a lump-sum method of allocating fixed costs.
c. Combine fixed and variable costs in a single cost pool.
d. None of the above.

7. Controllable costs for the manager of Production Department A include:

a. Costs of the finance department
b. Costs of material and labor used in Department A.
c. All costs related to Department A's final product.
d. All the above.

8. In allocating costs to products, more accurate costing is generally obtained by:

a. Allocating costs using labor hours as the allocation base.
b. Having more than one cost pool.
c. Always using allocation bases that are based on production volume.
d. None of the above.

9. Cost drivers in activity-based costing:

a. Are always related to production volume.
b. Are workers who influence cost control.
c. Often assign more costs to low-volume products than traditional allocation methods.
d. None of the above.

10. Most companies that use an activity-based costing system use:

a. No cost pools.
b. One or two cost pools.
c. Two to five cost pools.
d. More than five cost pools.

Answers to Self Assessment

1. e; **2.** c; **3.** c; **4.** c; **5.** d; **6.** b;
7. b; **8.** b; **9.** c; **10.** d.

INTERACTIVE LEARNING

Enhance and test your knowledge of Chapter 6 using Wiley's online resources.

1. Learning Objectives
2. Multiple Choice
3. Language of Business—Matching of Key Terms
4. Critical Thinking
5. Demonstration—How allocation using a single overhead rate can distort the apparent profitability of products
6. Case—Andrews Consulting; Use ABM to analyze the process of acquiring technology at a consulting firm
7. Video—Activity-based management (ABM) at Microsoft

Go to our dynamic Web site for more self-assessment, Web links, and additional information.

QUESTIONS

1. Is the following statement true? "Cost allocation refers to the process of assigning direct costs." Discuss.
2. Explain what a cost objective is and give two examples.
3. Explain one possible advantage to having two cost pools for each service department; one for variable costs and one for fixed costs.
4. If a company is allocating cafeteria costs to all departments within the company, what allocation base might result in a cause-and-effect relationship?
5. Why is it generally a good idea to allocate budgeted, rather than actual, service department costs?
6. What is a responsibility accounting system?
7. Why might noncontrollable costs be allocated to a department?
8. Briefly explain how traditional methods of allocating overhead to products might underallocate costs to low production-volume products.
9. How does activity-based costing differ from the traditional costing approach?
10. When would activity-based costing give more accurate costs than traditional costing systems?

EXERCISES

EXERCISE 6-1. Group Assignment Explain how the allocation process can make a fixed cost appear variable, leading to a poor decision.

EXERCISE 6-2. Writing Assignment Mansard Hotels has five luxury hotels located in Boston, New York, Chicago, San Francisco, and Los Angeles. For internal reporting purposes, each hotel has an income statement showing its revenue and direct expenses. Additionally, the company allocates to each hotel a share of general administrative and advertising costs (e.g., salary of the company president, salary of the company CFO, hotel chain advertising, etc.) based on relative revenue.

Required
Write a paragraph explaining why the allocation of general administrative and advertising costs to the specific hotels is potentially useful or potentially harmful.

EXERCISE 6-3. Internet Assignment Many organizations have issued guidelines for indirect cost allocations. Using an Internet search engine such as Google.com, search for the term "indirect cost allocation guidelines" and select one site from those

returned by the search. Answer the following questions from the information you find on this site:

1. What is the organization that is issuing the guidelines? What audience are the guidelines created for?
2. What costs are considered to be "indirect" within this industry?
3. How should the targeted organizations allocate their indirect costs? What allocation base or bases should they use to allocate their indirect costs?
4. Are these allocations consistent with "cause and effect" or "relative benefits"?

EXERCISE 6-4. Reasons for Allocating Indirect Costs Warner Development Company has a security department that provides security services to other departments within the company. Department managers are responsible for working with the head of security to ensure that their departments are protected. Explain why Warner might want to allocate security department costs to other departments.

EXERCISE 6-5. Choice of Allocation Base (Cost Driver) For Service Departments Auburn Banking and Loans Company has six service departments:

Human Resources (hires employees and manages benefits)
Duplicating (performs copy services)
Janitorial (provides routine cleaning services)
Accounting (provides accounting services)
Graphic Design (designs forms)
Food Services (provides free breakfast and lunch to employees)

The services are used by the company's two subsidiaries (Auburn Personal Banking and Auburn Business Banking).

Required

a. Suggest allocation bases to be used in allocating the service department costs to the two subsidiaries.

b. Food Services are used by employees in the Human Resources Department. Would a share of Food Service costs be allocated to Human Resources under the direct method of allocation?

EXERCISE 6-6. Cost Allocation Process Apex Company's Copy Department, which does almost all of the photocopying for the Sales Department and the Administrative Department, budgets the following costs for the year, based on the expected activity of 6,000,000 copies:

Salaries (fixed)	$90,000
Employee benefits (fixed)	15,000
Depreciation of copy machines (fixed)	15,000
Utilities (fixed)	6,000
Paper (variable, 1 cent per copy)	60,000
Toner (variable, 1 cent per copy)	60,000

The costs are assigned to two cost pools, one for fixed and one for variable costs. The costs are then assigned to the Sales Department and the Administrative Department. Fixed costs are assigned on a lump-sum basis, 60 percent to sales and 40 percent to administration. The variable costs are assigned at a rate of 2 cents per copy.

Required

Assuming 5,800,000 copies were made during the year, 3,000,000 for Sales and 2,800,000 for Administration, calculate the Copy Department costs allocated to Sales and Administration.

EXERCISE 6-7. Allocation of Service Department Costs The building maintenance department for Taylor Bath Manufacturing Company budgets annual costs of $3,000,000 based on the expected operating level for the coming year. The costs are allocated to two production departments. Taylor Bath is considering two allocation bases for assignment of costs to departments: (1) square footage and (2) direct labor hours. The following data relate to the potential allocation bases:

	Production Dept. 1	Production Dept. 2
Square footage	20,000	30,000
Direct labor hours	30,000	20,000

Required

Calculate the costs allocated to the production departments using each allocation base. Comment on which allocation base is preferable.

EXERCISE 6-8. Allocation of Service Department Costs Marvin Company has three service departments (S1, S2, S3) and two production departments (P1, P2). The following data relate to Marvin's allocation of service department costs:

	Budgeted Costs	Number of Employees
S1	$3,000,000	75
S2	2,000,000	50
S3	1,000,000	25
P1		150
P2		225

Service department costs are allocated by the direct method. The number of employees is used as the allocation base for all service department costs.

Required

a. Allocate service department costs to production departments.

b. Calculate the total service department cost allocated to each production department.

EXERCISE 6-9. Problems Associated with Cost Allocation Custom Metal Works received an offer from a "big box" retail company to purchase 2,000 metal outdoor tables for $195 each. Custom Metal Works accountants determine that the following costs apply to the tables:

Direct material	$ 90
Direct labor	42
Manufacturing overhead	65
Total	$197

Of the $65 of overhead, $10 is variable and $55 relates to fixed costs. The $55 of fixed overhead is allocated as $1.50 per direct labor dollar.

Required

a. What will be the real effect on profit if the order is accepted?

b. Explain why managers who focus on reported cost per unit may be inclined to turn down the order.

EXERCISE 6-10. Responsibility Accounting, Controllable Costs Chance Morton, the manager of the service department at the Proton Electronics Company, is evaluated based on the profit performance of his department. The profit of the department is down this year because the service department's share of allocated general and administrative costs (allocated based on relative sales dollars) is much higher than last year. In the current year, service revenue has increased slightly while sales of handheld electronic game devices, the company's major product, have decreased substantially.

Required

a. Explain why the allocation of general and administrative costs to the service department is higher in the current year.

b. Discuss how this situation relates to a responsibility accounting system and controllable costs.

EXERCISE 6-11. Problems with Cost Allocation Auburn Banking and Loan Company has six service departments (Human Resources, Duplicating, Janitorial, Accounting, Graphic Design and Food Services) whose costs are allocated to the company's two subsidiaries (Auburn Personal Banking and Auburn Business Banking) on the basis of their relative sales.

Required

a. Suppose you are the president of Auburn Business Banking. Will you perceive the allocated service department costs to be fixed costs, variable costs, or mixed costs?

b. In performing incremental analysis, related to expanding or contracting her business, will the president of Auburn Business Banking tend to overestimate or underestimate incremental costs? Explain.

EXERCISE 6-12. Problems Associated with Too Few Cost Pools Mott Manufacturing allocates factory overhead using one cost pool with direct labor hours as the allocation base. Mott has two production departments (P1 and P2). The new accountant at Mott estimates that next year the total factory overhead costs will be $3,000,000 and approximately 400,000 direct labor hours will be worked. The accountant also estimates that P1 will use 100,000 direct labor hours and there will be about $2,000,000 in overhead costs in P1. P2 will use 300,000 direct labor hours and there will be $1,000,000 in overhead costs in P2. Mott has two products: A1 and B1. It takes two direct labor hours in P1 and three direct labor hours in P2 to complete one unit of A1. It takes one direct labor hour in P1 and four direct labor hours in P2 to complete one unit of B1.

Required

Which product will be undercosted and which will be overcosted with the one cost pool system? Support your answer with appropriate calculations.

EXERCISE 6-13. Cost Allocation and Opportunity Cost Auburn Banking and Loan Company has a graphic design department that designs loan forms and other documents used by the company's two subsidiaries (Auburn Personal Banking and Auburn Business Banking). For practical purposes, the costs of the graphic design department are primarily fixed and relate to the salaries of the department's two employees.

Required

Analyze the following four independent cases:

a. Assume there is no allocation of graphic design costs to the subsidiaries. Jobs requested by the subsidiaries are completed promptly (generally by the next business day). How does the allocation (which is zero) compare to the opportunity cost of using design services?

b. Assume there is no allocation of graphic design costs to the subsidiaries. Jobs requested by the subsidiaries generally take weeks to complete; the subsidiaries often go outside the company for design services. How does the allocation (which is zero) compare to the opportunity cost of using design services?

c. Assume subsidiaries receive an allocation of $50 per design hour. Jobs requested by the subsidiaries generally take weeks to complete; the subsidiaries often go outside the company for design services rather than wait for jobs to be completed. They generally pay $70 per hour outside the company. How does the allocation ($50 per design hour) compare to the opportunity cost of using design services?

d. Assume subsidiaries receive an allocation of $50 per design hour. Although the graphic design department is busy, jobs requested by the subsidiaries are completed promptly (generally by the next business day). How does the allocation ($50 per design hour) compare to the opportunity cost of using design services?

EXERCISE 6-14. Activity-Based Costing The following are six cost pools established for a company using activity-based costing. The pools are related to the company's products using cost drivers.

Cost Pools:

(1) Inspection of raw materials

(2) Production equipment repairs and maintenance

(3) Raw materials storage

(4) Plant heat, light, water, and power

(5) Finished product quality control

(6) Production line setups

Required

For each of the preceding cost pools, identify a possible cost driver.

EXERCISE 6-15. Relating Cost Pools to Products Using Cost Drivers Power Electronics manufactures portable power supply units. Power has recently decided to use an activity-based approach to cost its products. Production line setups is a major activity at Power. Next year Power expects to perform 1,000 setups at a total cost of $1,500,000. Power plans to produce 750 units of product EP150, which will require two setups. How much setup cost will be allocated to each unit of EP150 produced?

EXERCISE 6-16. Relating Cost Pools to Products Using Cost Drivers Classy Attire is the designer and maker of elaborate prom dresses. The president of Classy wants to switch to an activity-based approach in the upcoming year to assign prices to the gowns. Production line setups are a major activity at Classy. Next year Classy expects to perform 1,200 setups at a total cost of $90,000. Classy plans to produce 300 dresses of the A128 design, which will require three setups. How much setup cost will be allocated to each dress of the A128 design that is produced?

EXERCISE 6-17. Activity-Based Management Eldon Company has two production plants. Recently, the company conducted an ABM study to determine the cost of activities involved in processing orders for parts at each of the plants. How might an operations manager use this information to manage the cost of processing orders?

EXERCISE 6-18. Activity-Based Management Hearthstone Appliances supplies parts for laundry and kitchen appliances. Customer orders are placed over the Internet and are generally filled in one or two days using express mail services.

Angela Farnsworth, a consultant with ABM Services, has been asked to conduct an ABM study of inventory management at Hearthstone Appliances. In this regard she has determined that the cost of filling customer orders in the past year consisted primarily of $250,000 of salary expense related to five workers who "pick" parts from the warehouse and $300,000 of salary expense related to six workers who pack the orders for shipment. In the past year, the company filled 100,000 orders. Based on work performed for a chain of auto supply stores, Angela has determined a benchmark cost of $4 per order.

Required

a. Comment on the advisability of comparing the costs at Hearthstone Appliances to those at an auto supply chain store.

b. Angela has observed the following: Workers go to a box that contains individual customer order sheets. They take the bottom order (the "oldest") and go into the warehouse with a handcart and a box. They then fill the order and carry the parts to a packing station. Can you suggest ways of improving this process?

PROBLEMS

PROBLEM 6-1. Number of Cost Pools Icon.com sells software and provides consulting services to companies that conduct business over the Internet. The company is organized into two lines of business (software and consulting), and profit statements are prepared as follows:

	Software	**Consulting**
Sales	$10,000,000	$5,000,000
Less direct costs	5,000,000	3,000,000
Less allocated costs	3,000,000	1,000,000
Income before taxes	$ 2,000,000	$1,000,000

Direct costs include costs that are easily associated with each line of business. For software, this includes the salary of programmers, the cost of computers used by programmers, and the cost of CDs sold to customers. For consulting, direct costs include consultant salaries, computer costs, and travel costs. Allocated costs include costs that are not directly traced to the business units. These costs include employee benefits, rent, telecommunications costs, and general and administrative costs such as the salary of the CEO of Icon.com.

At the start of 2008, allocated costs were estimated as follows:

Employee benefits	$1,000,000
Rent	600,000
Telecommunications	400,000
General and administrative costs	2,000,000
Total	$4,000,000

In the past, allocations have been based on headcount (the number of employees in each business unit). Software had 300 employees and consulting had 100 employees. The new controller of Icon.com believes that the key driver of employee benefits and telecommunications costs is headcount. However, rent is driven by space occupied, and general and administrative costs are driven by relative sales. Icon.com rents 30,000 square feet; approximately 15,000 is occupied by software employees and 15,000 by consulting personnel.

Required

a. Prepare profit reports for software and consulting assuming the company allocates costs using headcount, space occupied, and sales as allocation bases. Compare the new levels of profit to the levels that result using a single allocation base (headcount).

b. Which provides the best information on profitability—a single overhead cost pool with headcount as the allocation base, or multiple cost pools using headcount, sales, and space occupied?

PROBLEM 6-2. Number of Cost Pools Ball O' Fluff Company manufactures and ships children's stuffed animals across the nation. The following are profit statements for the company's two lines of business:

	Stock Stuffed Animals ("Stock")	Custom Stuffed Animals ("Custom")
Sales	$4,000,000	$3,000,000
Less direct costs	1,500,000	2,100,000
Less allocated costs	1,000,000	1,000,000
Income (loss) before taxes	$1,500,000	($100,000)

Costs that are easily associated with each line of business are included in the direct costs. Allocated costs include costs that are not directly traced to the business units. These costs include employee benefits, rent, telecommunications costs, and general and administrative costs such as the salary of the CEO of Ball O' Fluff.

At the start of 2008, allocated costs were estimated as follows:

Employee benefits	$ 500,000
Rent	750,000
Telecommunications	250,000
General and administrative costs	500,000
Total	$2,000,000

In the past, allocations have been based on headcount (the number of employees in each business unit). There were 100 employees in "Stock" and 50 employees in "Custom." The new controller of Ball O' Fluff believes that the key driver of employee benefits and telecommunications costs is headcount. However, rent is driven by space occupied, and general and administrative costs are driven by relative sales. Ball O' Fluff rents 10,000 square feet; approximately 5,000 is occupied by "Stock" employees, and 5,000 by "Custom" personnel.

Required

a. Prepare profit reports for Stock and Custom, assuming the company allocates costs using headcount, space occupied, and sales as allocation bases. Compare the new levels of profit to the levels that result using a single allocation base (headcount).

b. Which provides the best information on profitability—a single overhead cost pool with headcount as the allocation base, or multiple cost pools using headcount, sales, and space occupied?

PROBLEM 6-3. Allocated Cost and Opportunity Cost Binder Manufacturing produces small electric motors used by appliance manufacturers. In the past year, the company has experienced severe excess capacity due to competition from a foreign company that has entered Binder's market. The company is currently bidding on a potential order from Dacon Appliances for 7,000 Model 350 motors. The estimated cost of each motor is $55, as follows:

Direct material	$25
Direct labor	10
Overhead	20
Total	$55

The predetermined overhead rate is $2 per direct labor dollar. This was estimated by dividing estimated annual overhead ($10,000,000) by estimated annual direct labor ($5,000,000). The $10,000,000 of overhead is composed of $4,000,000 of variable costs and $6,000,000 of fixed costs. The largest fixed cost relates to depreciation of plant and equipment.

Required

a. With respect to overhead, what is the opportunity cost of producing a Model 350 motor?

b. Suppose Binder can win the Dacon business by bidding a price of $53 per motor (but no higher price will result in a winning bid). Should Binder bid $53?

c. Discuss how an allocation of overhead based on opportunity cost would facilitate an appropriate bidding decision.

PROBLEM 6-4. Allocated Cost and Opportunity Cost Mighty Mint Co. produces a mint syrup used by gum and candy companies. Recently, the company has had excess capacity due to a foreign supplier entering its market. Mighty Mint is currently bidding on a potential order from Quality Candy for 5,000 cases of syrup. The estimated cost of each case is $18, as follows:

Direct material	$ 6
Direct labor	4
Overhead	8
Total	$18

The predetermined overhead rate is $2 per direct labor dollar. This was estimated by dividing estimated annual overhead ($1,000,000) by estimated annual direct labor ($500,000). The $1,000,000 of overhead is composed of $250,000 of variable costs and $750,000 of fixed costs. The largest fixed cost relates to depreciation of plant and equipment.

Required

a. With respect to overhead, what is the opportunity cost of producing a case of syrup?

b. Suppose Mighty Mint can win the Quality Candy business by bidding a price of $16 per case (but no higher price will result in a winning bid). Should Mighty Mint bid $16?

c. Discuss how an allocation of overhead based on opportunity cost would facilitate an appropriate bidding decision.

PROBLEM 6-5. Cost-Plus Contracts, Allocations and Ethics Pelton Instrumentation manufactures a variety of electronic instruments that are used in military and civilian applications. Sales to the military are generally on a cost-plus profit basis with profit equal to 10 percent of cost. Instruments used in military applications require more direct labor time because "fail-safe" devices must be installed. (These devices are generally omitted in civilian applications.)

At the start of the year, Pelton estimates that the company will incur $50,000,000 of overhead, $5,000,000 of direct labor, and 500,000 machine hours. Consider the Model KV10 gauge that is produced for both civilian and military uses:

	Civilian	**Military**
Direct material	$2,000	$2,500
Direct labor	$ 600	$ 900
Machine hours	80	80

Required

a. Calculate the cost of civilian and military versions of Model KV10 using both direct labor dollars and machine hours as alternative allocation bases.

b. Explain why Pelton Instruments may decide to use direct labor as an overhead allocation base.

c. Is it ethical for Pelton to select an allocation base that tends to allocate more of overhead costs to government contracts? Explain.

PROBLEM 6-6. Allocating Service Department Costs World Airlines has three service departments: (1) ticketing, (2) baggage handling, and (3) engine maintenance. The service department costs are estimated for separate cost pools formed by department and are allocated to two revenue-producing departments: (1) domestic flights and (2) international flights. World does not differentiate between fixed and variable costs in making allocations. The following data relate to the allocations:

	Budgeted Data	
	Costs	**Air Miles**
Ticketing	$4,000,000	
Baggage handling	$2,000,000	
Engine maintenance	$6,000,000	
Domestic flights		5,000,000
International flights		20,000,000

Required

a. Allocate the service department costs to the revenue-producing departments using air miles as the allocation base.

b. Evaluate the cause-and-effect relationship resulting from the use of air miles as the allocation base. In which of the cost pools do you think the cause-and-effect relationship is the strongest? Suggest alternative allocation bases for the two remaining cost pools with the weakest cause-and-effect relationship.

PROBLEM 6-7. Allocating Service Department Costs Armstrong Industries produces electronic equipment for the marine industry. Armstrong has two service departments (maintenance and computing) and two production departments (assembly and testing). Maintenance costs are allocated on the basis of square footage occupied, and computing costs are allocated on the basis of the number of computer terminals. The following data relate to allocations of service department costs:

	Maintenance	Computing	Assembly	Testing
Service department costs	$400,000	$600,000		
Square footage			70,000	30,000
Terminals			5	10

Required

Allocate the service department costs to production departments using the direct method.

PROBLEM 6-8. Allocating Service Department Costs Snowcap Electronics is a manufacturer of data storage devices. Snowcap consists of two service departments, maintenance and computing, and two production departments, assembly and testing. Maintenance costs are allocated on the basis of square footage occupied, and computing costs are allocated on the basis of the number of computer terminals. The following data relate to allocations of service department costs:

	Maintenance	Computing	Assembly	Testing
Service department costs	$600,000	$800,000		
Square footage			90,000	45,000
Terminals			15	30

Required

Allocate the service department costs to production departments using the direct method.

PROBLEM 6-9. Choice of Allocation Base, Problems with Cost Allocation Tilden Financial Services has two divisions: Financial Planning and Business Consulting. The firm's accountants are in the process of selecting an allocation base to allocate centrally provided personnel costs to the divisions. Two allocation bases have been proposed—salary and headcount (number of employees). Personnel costs are expected to be $1,000,000. The following data relate to the allocation:

	Financial Planning	Business Consulting
Salaries	$10,000,000	$5,000,000
Headcount	150	50

Required

a. Prepare a schedule showing the allocations to the two divisions using each allocation base.

b. Referring to your answer to part a, explain why allocations are sometimes considered arbitrary.

PROBLEM 6-10. Cost Allocation and Apparent Profitability Diamonds, Etc. manufactures jewelry settings and sells them to retail stores. In the past, most settings were made by hand, and the overhead allocation rate in the prior year was $10 per labor hour ($2,000,000 overhead ÷ 200,000 labor hours). In the current year, overhead increased by $400,000 due to acquisition of equipment. Labor, however, decreased by 50,000 hours because the equipment allows rapid creation of the settings. One of the company's many customers is a local jewelry store, Jasmine's Fine Jewelry. This store is relatively small and the time to make an order of jewelry pieces is typically less than 8 labor hours. On such jobs (less than 8 labor hours), the new equipment is not used, and thus the jobs are relatively labor intensive.

Required

a. Assume that in the current year, the company continues to allocate overhead based on labor hours. What would be the overhead cost of an 8-labor-hour job requested by Jasmine's Fine Jewelry? How does this compare to the overhead cost charged to such a job in the prior year?

b. Assume that the price charged for small jobs does not change in the current year. Are small jobs less profitable than they were in the past?

PROBLEM 6-11. Activity-Based Costing The Summit Manufacturing Company produces two products. One is a recreational whitewater kayak molded from plastic and designed to perform as a durable whitewater play boat. The other product is a high-performance competition kayak molded with high-tech fiberglass materials that are very light. The recreation boat is uniform in its dimensions and style. However, the competition boat is custom designed to fit the individual (e.g., rocker and cockpit size are adjusted).

Most of the sales come from the recreation boat, but recently sales of the competition boat have been increasing. The following information is related to the products for the most recent year.

	Recreation Kayak	Competition Kayak
Sales and production (number of boats)	900	100
Sales price per boat	$600	$660
Unit costs:		
Direct materials	150	200
Direct labor	100	100
Overhead*	135	135
Total unit cost	385	435
Gross profit	$215	$225

*Overhead costs:

Building depreciation	$ 25,000
Equipment depreciation	25,000
Materials ordering	15,000
Quality control	10,000
Maintenance and security	10,000
Setup and drafting	20,000
Supervision	30,000
Total	$135,000

Overhead rate based on direct labor dollars:

Total overhead	$135,000
Total labor ($100 × 900) + ($100 × 100)	$100,000
Overhead rate = $1.35 per direct labor dollar	

Victoria Mason, the president of Summit Manufacturing, is concerned that the traditional cost system used by Summit may not be providing accurate cost information and that the sales price of the competition boat might not be enough to cover its true cost.

Required

a. The traditional system that Summit is using assigns 90 percent of the $135,000 total overhead to the recreational boats because 90 percent of the direct labor dollars are spent on the recreational boats. Discuss why this might not be an accurate way to assign overhead to boats.

b. Discuss how Summit might be able to improve cost allocation by using an ABC system.

c. Assume that Summit retains a consultant to create an activity-based costing system, and the consultant develops the following data:

			Driver Activity	
Cost Pool	**Amount**	**Driver**	**Rec. Boats**	**Comp. Boats**
Building	$ 25,000	Square footage	6,000	1,000
Equipment	25,000	Machine hours	3,400	600
Materials ordering	15,000	Number of orders	200	100
Quality control	10,000	Number of inspections	300	150
Maint. & security	10,000	Square footage	6,000	1,000
Setup and drafting	20,000	Number of setups	20	40
Supervision	30,000	Direct labor cost	$90,000	$10,000
	$135,000			

Determine the overhead allocation to each line of boats using an activity-based costing approach and compute the total unit costs for each model boat.

d. Discuss why activity-based allocations are different from those generated by the traditional allocation method used by Summit.

PROBLEM 6-12. Activity-Based Costing The Divine Cheesecake Shoppe is a national bakery that is known for its strawberry cheesecake. They also make 12 different kinds of cheesecake as well as several other types of bakery items. They have recently adopted an activity-based costing system to assign manufacturing overhead to products. The following data relate to their strawberry cheesecake and the ABC cost pools:

Strawberry Cheesecake:	
Annual production	40,000 units
Direct materials per unit	$5
Direct labor per unit	$1

Cost Pool	Cost	Cost Driver
Materials ordering	$60,000	Number of purchase orders
Materials inspection	80,000	Number of receiving reports
Equipment setup	75,000	Number of setups
Quality control	45,000	Number of inspections
Other	75,000	Direct labor cost
Total mfg. overhead	$335,000	

Annual activity information related to cost drivers:

Cost Pool	All Products	Strawberry Cheesecake
Materials ordering	7,500 orders	2,000
Materials inspection	400 receiving reports	50
Equipment setup	2,000 setups	20
Quality control	2,000 inspections	100
Other	$1,500,000 direct labor	$25,000

Required

a. Calculate the overhead rate per unit of activity for each of the five cost pools.

b. Calculate the total overhead assigned to the production of the Strawberry Cheesecake.

c. Calculate the overhead cost per unit for the Strawberry Cheesecake.

d. Calculate the total unit cost for the Strawberry Cheesecake.

e. Suppose that The Divine Cheesecake Shoppe allocates overhead by a traditional production volume-based method using direct labor dollars as the allocation base and one cost pool. Determine the overhead rate per direct labor dollar and the per unit overhead assigned to the Strawberry Cheesecake. Discuss the difference in cost allocations between the traditional method and the activity-based costing approach.

PROBLEM 6-13. Activity-Based Costing at a Service Company Tannhauser Financial is a banking services company that offers many different types of checking accounts. They have recently adopted an activity-based costing system to assign costs to their various types of checking accounts. The following data relate to one of their checking accounts, the money market checking account, and the ABC cost pools:

Money Market Checking Account:

Annual number of accounts 50,000 accounts

Checking account cost pools:

Cost Pool	Cost	Cost Driver
Returned check costs	$2,250,000	Number of returned checks
Checking account reconciliation costs	50,000	Number of account reconciliation requests
New account setup	600,000	Number of new accounts
Copies of cancelled checks	360,000	Number of cancelled check copy requests
Web site maintenance (for online banking)	185,000	Per product group (type of checking account)
Total checking account costs	$3,445,000	

Annual activity information related to cost drivers:

Cost Pool	All Products	Money Market Checking
Returned checks	150,000 returned checks	12,000
Check reconciliation costs	2,500 checking account reconciliations	350
New accounts	50,000 new accounts	12,000
Cancelled check copy requests	90,000 cancelled check copy requests	55,000
Web site costs	10 types of checking accounts	1

Required

a. Calculate the cost rate per cost driver activity for each of the five cost pools.

b. Calculate the total cost assigned to the money market checking account.

c. Suppose that Tannhauser Financial allocates overhead using the number of checking accounts as the allocation base and one cost pool. Determine the cost rate per checking account and the per-account cost assigned to the money market checking account. Discuss the difference in cost allocations between this method and the activity-based costing approach.

PROBLEM 6-14. Traditional Allocation vs. ABC Allocation of Manufacturing Overhead Costs TriTech Company has been allocating overhead to individual product lines based on each line's relative shares of direct labor hours. For the upcoming year, the company estimated that manufacturing overhead will be $1,400,000 and estimated direct labor hours will be 100,000. The company has the following cost information:

Cost Pool	Cost Driver	Total Amount	Total Amount of Activity
Maintenance costs	Direct labor hours	$600,000	100,000
Setup costs	Number of setups	$450,000	225
Professional services costs	Number of design changes	$300,000	250

TriTech has two products, Standard and Elite switches. Standard switches is a high-volume product that the company makes in large batches, while Elite switches are a specialty product that is fairly low in sales volume.

Information about Standard and Elite usage of the different activities follows:

	Standard	Elite
Direct labor hours	1,500	120
Number of setups	7	13
Number of design changes	5	20

Required:

a. Calculate the predetermined overhead rate based on direct labor hours (traditional allocation). Use this predetermined overhead rate to calculate the amount of overhead to apply to Standard and Elite Switches, based on their usage of direct labor hours.

b. Calculate the individual ABC pool rates by taking the total amount of overhead for each cost pool and dividing that total by the total amount of activity for that pool. Allocate overhead to each of the two products using these three activity rates.

c. Compare the overhead calculated in part a to that calculated in part b. Why are they different? Which allocation method (traditional or ABC) most likely results in a better estimate of product cost?

PROBLEM 6-15. Activity-Based Costing—Comprehensive Problem Riverdale Printing Company is the publisher for many of the local newspapers and magazines. They publish nine periodicals and several other types of literature, including handouts and pamphlets. They have recently adopted an activity-based costing system to assign manufacturing overhead to products. The following data relate to one of their products, *The Riverdale Weekly*, and the ABC cost pools:

The Riverdale Weekly:	
Annual production	20,000 units
Direct material per unit	$31
Direct labor per unit	$6

Manufacturing overhead cost pools:

Cost Pool	Cost	Cost Driver
Materials ordering	$800,000	Number of purchase orders
Materials inspection	400,000	Number of receiving reports
Equipment setup	2,000,000	Number of setups
Quality control	900,000	Number of inspections
Other	15,000,000	Direct labor cost
Total mfg. overhead	$19,100,000	

Annual activity information related to cost drivers:

Cost Pool	All Products	The Riverdale Weekly
Materials ordering	100,000 orders	1,000
Materials inspection	2,000 receiving reports	300
Equipment setup	100 setups	1
Quality control	4,000 inspections	400
Other	$10,000,000 direct labor	$120,000

Required

a. Calculate the overhead rate per unit of activity for each of the five cost pools.

b. Calculate the total overhead assigned to the production of *The Riverdale Weekly*.

c. Calculate the overhead cost per unit for *The Riverdale Weekly*.

d. Calculate the total unit cost for *The Riverdale Weekly*.

e. Suppose that Riverdale Printing allocates overhead by a traditional production volume-based method using direct labor dollars as the allocation base and one cost pool. Determine the overhead rate per direct labor dollar and the per unit overhead assigned to *The Riverdale Weekly*. Discuss the difference in cost allocations between the traditional method and the activity-based costing approach.

PROBLEM 6-16. (Appendix) Activity-Based Management Talbot Partners is a consulting firm with clients across the nation. Within the company is a travel group that arranges flights and hotel accommodations for its over 1,000 consultants. The cost of operating the travel group (excluding the costs associated with actual travel such as hotel cost and air fare) amounts to approximately $800,000.

Recently, Talbot Partners has conducted an ABM study that has determined the following:

a. Each consultant takes approximately 20 business trips per year.

b. On average, 30 percent of trips are rescheduled due to conflicts and poor planning.

c. The travel group employs 14 individuals at $45,000 each to book travel. In addition, there is a travel manager and an assistant travel manager.

d. Benchmarking with a Talbot Partners' client indicates that the client incurs $30 cost per completed trip to book travel.

Required

a. Evaluate the cost incurred by Talbot Partners compared to the benchmark cost.

b. Talbot Partners is planning a process improvement initiative aimed at reducing scheduling conflicts. What would be the savings if rescheduling could be reduced by 50 percent? Assume that the only variable cost in travel services is the wages paid to employees who book travel.

PROBLEM 6-17. (Appendix) Activity-Based Management Primary Savings and Loan of Denver is conducting an ABM study of its teller operations. In this regard, the company has identified the following major activities performed by bank tellers:

a. Process deposits

b. Process withdrawals

c. Process requests for certificates of deposits

d. Answer customer questions related to balances, overdrafts, interest rates, etc.

e. Print out customer activity statements

f. Provide access to safe deposit boxes

g. Reconcile cash drawer

The company benchmarked its operations against banks in other cities and has found that it has many more tellers in comparison to banks of similar size. Further, the company has a relatively unsophisticated Web site and call center.

Required

a. How do the company's Web site and call center affect the demand for teller activities and the cost of teller services?

b. Identify two or three ways that technology can be used to reduce the cost of teller services.

PROBLEM 6-18. (Appendix) Activity-Based Management Each month, senior managers at Vermont Wireless Technologies review cost reports for the company's various departments. The report for the human resource (HR) group for April is as follows:

Human Resources
April, 2006

Salaries and benefits	$63,500
Supplies	1,900
Depreciation of office equipment	1,300
Total	$66,700

Jason Fox, the new vice president of operations, expressed his dissatisfaction with the report at a meeting with the company president, CFO, and controller. "This report is garbage," he began. "It shows that $63,500 is being spent on salaries in HR but it doesn't provide any information on what we're paying for. We need to know the activities of HR and what they cost. How are we supposed to manage the activities without that information? At my previous company, we routinely did activity-based management studies and they really helped us get a handle on operations and our costs."

Maxwell Davies, the controller responded that he'd get to work on ABM studies right away. Two weeks later, his staff had developed the following information for the HR operation:

Activities in HR	**Monthly Cost**
General administration of department	
Salary of HR head	$ 8,500
Salary of assistant to HR head	4,000
Depreciation of equipment	200
Supplies	150
	12,850
Benefits administration	
Salary of administrator	6,500
Depreciation of equipment	150
Supplies	300
	6,950
HR Web site development/maintenance	
One half-time staff person	2,000
Depreciation of equipment	400
Supplies	150
	2,550
Operations	
Salary of five clerks who process paperwork related to hiring, retirements, terminations	12,500
Depreciation of equipment	600
Supplies	450
	13,550
Training	
Salary of six staff members who train new employees on company policies	30,000
Depreciation of equipment	550
Supplies	250
	30,800
Total	$66,700

Additional Information: The company has approximately 6,000 employees and annual employee turnover of approximately 15 percent.

Required

Comment on the insights provided by the ABM study to date. Where's the "low hanging fruit?" In other words, what activities appear to be good candidates for further study and significant cost savings?

CASES

6-1 EASTSIDE MEDICAL TESTING

Eastside Medical Testing performs five different tests (T1–T5) to detect drug use. Most clients are referred to the company by potential employers who pay for the tests. Revenue and costs related to the tests, for the most recent fiscal year, are detailed in Table 1.

Setting up equipment to conduct a test is the responsibility of three highly skilled technicians, one of whom is Emmet Wilson, founder and owner of the company. Tests T2–T5 are high-volume tests that are conducted in batches of 100 tests per batch. Thus, for example, T5 is run approximately twice a day to annually process 70,000 tests in 700 batches. On the other hand, T1 is a test with relatively low demand. However, it is run almost every day (300 runs per year), so that results can be quickly communicated to employers. This fast turnaround represents a significant competitive advantage for the company.

Nuclear Systems, Inc., is one of the few companies that requires T1. Indeed, it accounted for almost half of the 3,000 T1 tests conducted in the past year. Recently, Ron Worth, vice president of operations at Nuclear Systems, questioned the relatively high price being charged for T1. In a letter to Emmet Wilson he noted that

> We pay $31 for each T1 test, which is about 50% higher than your next most expensive test. Is this charge warranted? Frankly, this isn't just a matter of dollars and cents. We believe that we are being taken advantage of because we are one of the few companies that requires the test, and you are one of the few companies that provide it. If we believed that the high price was justified in terms of significantly higher costs, we would not be writing this letter.

Before responding to Worth's letter, Emmet reviewed the revenue and cost data presented in Table 1. As indicated, T1 produced a profit of $6.80 per test which was much higher than the profit per test of any of the other procedures. However, since taking a day-long continuing education course at City College (entitled "ABC and Managing by the Right Numbers!"), Emmet has wondered whether the profitability of tests is being distorted by the company's simple approach to allocating overhead—overhead allocation is based on direct labor cost. Direct labor consists of wages and benefits paid to relatively unskilled technicians who

Table 1 Profitability of Tests for the Fiscal Year Ending December 31, 2008

	T1	T2	T3	T4	T5	Total
Number of tests per year	3,000	40,000	55,000	60,000	70,000	228,000
Number of runs	300	400	550	600	700	2,550
Price per test	$ 31.00	$ 22.00	$ 20.00	$ 18.00	$ 17.00	
Less:						
Material cost	11.00	9.00	7.00	6.85	5.35	
Direct labor at $18 per hour	1.20	0.85	0.85	0.85	0.85	
Overhead at $10 per labor dollar	12.00	8.50	8.50	8.50	8.50	
Total cost	24.20	18.35	16.35	16.20	14.70	
Profit per test	$ 6.80	$ 3.65	$ 3.65	$ 1.80	$ 2.30	
Total profit	$20,400	$146,000	$200,750	$108,000	$161,000	$ 636,150
Total overhead	$36,000	$340,000	$467,500	$510,000	$595,000	$1,948,500
Total labor	$ 3,600	$ 34,000	$ 46,750	$ 51,000	$ 59,500	$ 194,850

prepare samples for testing. This cost, $194,850, is only 10 percent of total overhead.

With help from his bookkeeper, Emmet began to analyze overhead costs in an attempt to calculate the ABC cost of the five tests. In the past year, overhead amounted to $1,948,500 as follows.

Overhead	Costs
Setup labor	$ 525,000
Equipment	1,050,000
Rent	140,000
Billing	84,000
Clerical	68,000
Other	81,500
Total	$1,948,500

Emmet's analysis of these six overhead cost categories was as follows.

Setup labor ($525,000). This amount is essentially the salary and benefits paid to Emmet and the two other skilled technicians who set up equipment for testing batches of T1–T5. Emmet believes that the number of runs (batches of tests) is a valid driver for this cost pool. In the past year, there were 2,550 runs.

Equipment ($1,050,000). This amount is depreciation on equipment used to process the tests. All of the major pieces of equipment are used in each test. (In other words, no major piece of equipment is used exclusively for any individual test.) Emmet believes that the amount of direct labor cost is a valid driver for this cost pool. This follows because equipment hours vary with direct labor hours and direct labor cost. In the past year, total direct labor was $194,850.

Rent ($140,000). This amount is the annual rent on the facility occupied by Eastside Medical Testing. Emmet believes that the number of tests (228,000 in the prior year) is a valid driver for this cost pool since each test benefits equally from the incurrence of rent expense.

Billing ($84,000). This amount is the annual salary and benefits of two billing clerks as well as a variety of other charges (e.g., billing software costs). Emmet believes that the number of tests (228,000 in the prior year) is a valid driver for this cost pool since each test requires a separate billing charge.

Clerical ($68,000). This amount is the annual salary and benefits of two general clerical employees who process orders for supplies, file records, and so on. Emmet believes that the number of tests (228,000 in the prior year) is a valid driver for this cost pool since each test benefits equally from the incurrence of clerical expense.

Other ($81,500). This amount includes the salary and benefits of the bookkeeper, depreciation on office equipment, utilities, and so on. Emmet believes that the number of tests (228,000 in the prior year) is a valid driver for this cost pool since each test benefits equally from the incurrence of these expenses.

Required

a. Based on Emmet's assumptions, calculate the ABC cost per unit and profit per unit of each test.

b. Should Emmet lower the price of the T1 test, or keep the current price and risk losing the business of Nuclear Systems?

c. Assume that Emmet, based on his ABC analysis, decides not to lower the price of the T1 test. What will be the effect on annual company profit if the company loses the business of Nuclear Systems (i.e., T1 tests decrease by 1,500)?

6-2 QuantumTM

QuantumTM manufactures electronic testing and measurement instruments. Many products are custom-designed with recent orders for function generators, harmonic analyzers, logic analyzers, temperature measurement instruments, and data logging instruments. The company prices its instruments at 35 percent over estimated cost (excluding administrative and selling costs).

Recently, senior management has noted that its product mix has changed. Specifically, the company is receiving fewer large orders for instruments that are relatively simple to produce and customers are saying that the company is not price competitive. On the other hand, the company is receiving more small orders for complex instruments and customers appear quite happy to pay QuantumTM's price. This situation was discussed at a weekly management meeting and Jason Norton, VP operations, blamed the company's antiquated cost-accounting system. "Look," he said. "If you have bad cost information, you're going to have bad prices, and we're still doing product costing the way companies did it in the 1930s. I've been reading articles about activity-based costing and they indicate that out-of-date costing systems make simple products look too costly and complex products too cheap. If that's true, it would explain why we're not price competitive for simple products."

The meeting ended with a decision to hire a consultant to conduct a preliminary ABC study to determine how a switch to ABC would affect product cost. The consulting firm selected two recent orders for study: an 800 unit order for a temperature monitoring

Exhibit 1 Cost Pools and Drivers

Cost Pools	Annual Cost	Annual Driver Value	
Cost Pools	$ 6,000,000	120,000	design hours
Product design	8,000,000	100,000	unique part #s
Material ordering and handling	2,500,000	400,000	inspections
Inspection	1,500,000	50,000	set-ups
Set-up	6,000,000	$8,000,000	direct labor
Labor related overhead	16,000,000	200,000	machine hours
Depreciation of plant and equipment	$40,000,000		

device and an order for one harmonic analyzer. The costs and prices charged were as follows:

	Temperature Monitor	Harmonic Analyzer
Component cost per unit	$200	$2,000
Direct labor per unit	20	400
Overhead per unit	100	2,000
Cost per unit	320	4,400
Mark-up at 30%	96	1,320
Price per unit	$416	$5,720
Number of units	800	1
Value of order	$332,800	$5,720

In the current system, overhead is applied based on an estimate of $40,000,000 of annual overhead and $8,000,000 of direct labor cost. The consultants have broken the $40,000,000 of annual overhead down into six cost pools and identified related cost drivers as indicated in Exhibit 1. The consultants have also found that the monitor and analyzer make use of the cost drivers as indicated in Exhibit 2.

Required

a. Based on the consultants work to date, calculate the ABC cost per unit of each product.

b. The consultants have completed their job and QuantumTM has adopted an ABC system as indicated in Exhibit 1. Recently, the company received an order for a unique data-logging device. The device will re-

Exhibit 2 Use of Cost Driver

The following values relate to the entire order of 800 Monitors (this is not per monitor):	
Number of design hours	42
Number of unique parts	15
Number of inspections	200
Number of setups	1
Machine hours	100

The following values relate to the order for one Analyzer:	
Number of design hours	100
Number of unique parts	20
Number of inspections	15
Number of setups	1
Machine hours	5

quire $8,000 of components and $2,000 of direct labor along with the following requirements:

Use related to a data logging device:	
Number of design hours	25
Number of unique parts	15
Number of inspections	10
Number of setups	1
Machine hours	8

The customer has indicated that they currently have a low bid from another company of $19,000. Calculate the ABC cost of the data logging device.

c. Suppose QuantumTM meets their competitor's price and gets the job. What will be the impact on company profit? In answering this question, make the following assumptions:

a. 40 percent of design costs are fixed and 60 percent vary with design hours.
b. 30 percent of material ordering and handling costs are fixed and 70 percent vary with the number of unique parts.
c. 50 percent of inspection costs are fixed and 50 percent are variable.
d. 80 percent of setup costs are fixed and 20 percent are variable.
e. 20 percent of labor-related costs are fixed and 80 percent are variable.
f. Prices charged to this customer or other customers in the future will not be impacted by the current deal. This follows because each order is somewhat unique.

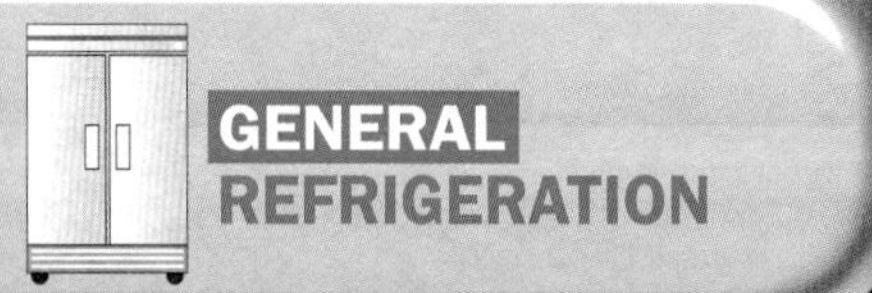

CHAPTER 7

LEARNING OBJECTIVES

1. Explain the role of incremental analysis (analysis of incremental costs and revenues) in management decisions.
2. Define sunk cost, avoidable cost, and opportunity cost and understand how to use these concepts in analyzing decisions.
3. Analyze decisions involving joint costs.
4. Discuss the importance of qualitative considerations in management decisions.

THE USE OF COST INFORMATION IN MANAGEMENT DECISION MAKING

At the start of the year, the president of General Refrigeration Company asked his three plant managers to examine their operations and search for ways to cut costs and improve profitability. Substantial bonuses were promised to managers who achieved cost savings in excess of $1,000,000.

Wendy Grant, manager of the Tennessee plant, thought she had a surefire way to save money. Her plant manufactures refrigeration units used by food processors and retail food stores. One of the main components of the refrigeration units is a compressor. Wendy anticipates producing 50,000 compressors in the coming year at a cost per unit of $345. Because she is concerned that production of compressors is not efficient, Wendy asked Dillard Compressor Corporation to bid on supplying the 50,000 units. After studying the specifications of the compressor, Dillard has indicated that it is willing to supply the compressors at $310 per unit.

"Look," Wendy explained to Ed Anderson, the plant accountant, "if we close the compressor operation and buy compressors from Dillard, we'll save about $1,750,000 a year! That kind of cost saving ought to really grab the president's attention." Ed seemed skeptical. "Wendy, let's look at the costs of producing the compressors. More than $1,000,000 of the cost is depreciation on plant and equipment purchased years ago. Another $500,000 represents the salaries of production supervisors. I don't think all of those costs will go away just because we shut down the compressor operation and turn to an outside supplier. Perhaps you'd better let me analyze the cost information in some detail before you make a recommendation."

Ed's point is well taken. Before making a decision, managers must gain a thorough understanding of the cost information that is relevant. In previous chapters, we have examined various issues involving costs: determining the costs of products and services using job-order and process costing systems (Chapters 2 and 3), examining cost-volume-profit relations (Chapter 4), and discussing the allocation of costs (Chapter 6). In the course of those discussions, we considered several examples of how cost information is used in decision making. Now, we discuss the topic in more detail.

INCREMENTAL ANALYSIS

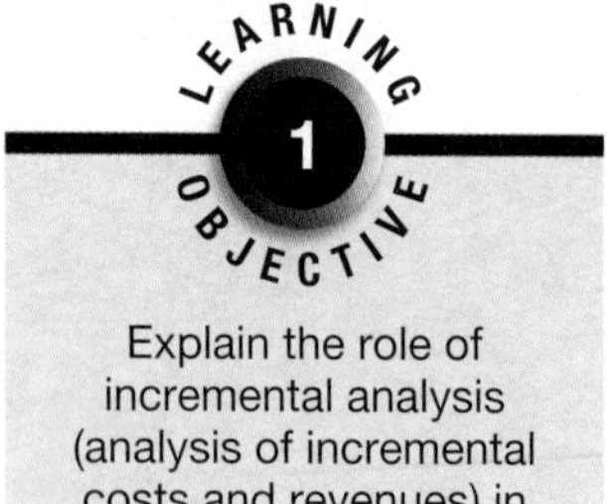

Explain the role of incremental analysis (analysis of incremental costs and revenues) in management decisions.

All decisions involve a choice among alternative courses of action. In Chapter 1, we learned that the solution to all business problems involves **incremental analysis**—the analysis of the *incremental* revenue and the *incremental* costs incurred when one decision alternative is chosen over another. **Incremental revenue** is the additional revenue received as a result of selecting one decision alternative over another. **Incremental cost** is the additional cost incurred as a result of selecting one decision alternative over another. If an alternative yields an incremental profit (the difference between incremental revenue and incremental cost), then it should be selected. Incremental costs are sometimes referred to as **relevant costs**, because they are the only costs that are *relevant* to consider when analyzing decision alternatives. They are also referred to as **differential costs**, because they are the costs that differ between decision alternatives.

Let's go over a simple example of incremental analysis to ensure that the approach is understood. The example we'll consider is a decision faced by Jensen Rapid Copy Center. Later, we'll apply incremental analysis to somewhat more complicated decisions including the decision faced by Wendy Grant of General Refrigeration, which was presented at the start of the chapter .

Currently, Jensen Rapid Copy Center is open from 6 A.M. until 8 P.M. The owner of the company, Jon Jensen, is trying to decide whether or not hours should be extended until midnight. In this case, Jensen is facing a choice between two alternatives: closing at 8 P.M., which is the status quo, or closing at midnight. Incremental analysis of this decision is presented in Illustration 7-1. Note that there are three columns. In the first column, we show the revenue and costs asso-

ciated with the status quo (decision alternative 1) for a one-year time horizon. In the second column, we show the revenue and costs associated with the decision to stay open until midnight (decision alternative 2). In the third column, we show the difference in the revenue and costs between the two decision alternatives. This is the incremental revenue and incremental costs associated with the decision to stay open later. Since we are using a one year time horizon, this is obviously the incremental revenue and costs associated with that time period. We could also perform the analysis for multiple years. However, when multiple years are considered, it is generally important to consider the time value of money. That is, we need to take into account the fact that a dollar today is worth more than a dollar in the future. We'll go into that topic in Chapter 9.

As indicated in Illustration 7-1, if hours are extended, revenue will increase by $288,000. This is the incremental revenue. However, labor, paper, toner and other supplies, utilities, and insurance will increase. The total increase in expense is $232,981. This is the incremental cost of extending hours. Incremental profit, the difference between incremental revenue and incremental cost, is $55,019. Since incremental profit is positive, the second alternative (extending hours) should be selected.

Illustration 7-1
Incremental analysis of decision to extend hours of operation until midnight

	Alternative 1 Current Hours	**Alternative 2 Extend Hours to Midnight**	**Incremental Revenue and Costs (Alternative 2 minus Alternative 1)**
Revenue	$3,600,000	$3,888,000	$288,000
Less:			
Labor	576,000	604,800	28,800
Paper, toner and other supplies	2,520,000	2,721,600	201,600
Utilities	26,640	28,771	2,131
Insurance	7,800	8,250	450
Depreciation	60,000	60,000	-0-
Rent	55,000	55,000	-0-
Other fixed costs	3,000	3,000	
Total expense	3,248,440	3,481,421	232,981
Profit	$ 351,560	$ 406,579	$ 55,019

Note that depreciation, rent and other fixed costs are not incremental in this decision, since none of these costs changed. Thus, they are not relevant to decision at hand. This is not to say that a fixed cost is never incremental. As we will see in later examples, sometimes decisions have a major impact on operations and cause costs that are normally considered to be fixed to change. For example, suppose expanded operations required Jon Jensen to rent additional space to store supplies. In this case, rent (which is normally considered to be a fixed cost) would, in fact, be an incremental cost.

Incremental analysis can be easily extended beyond two decision alternatives. Suppose Jensen is also considering the option of keeping the copy center open 24 hours per day. Now there are three choices: close at 8 P.M., close at midnight or stay open twenty four hours. There are two ways we can deal with the third choice. We can compare it to the status quo and see if it yields an incremental profit greater than the incremental profit associated with staying open until midnight, which is $55,019—if so, it is preferred to the midnight alternative. Or, we can compare the all-day alternative directly to the midnight option, which, as we know, dominates the status quo. Let's do the latter. The analysis is presented in Illustration 7-2. As indicated, the incremental revenue associated with staying open 24 hours is $36,000. However, the incremental cost is $68,917. Thus, if Jensen were to stay open 24 hours, he would lose $32,917 compared to staying open until midnight. Jensen's best decision of the three alternatives, therefore, is to stay open until midnight.

WHEN YOUR BOSS ASKS "WHAT DOES THIS PRODUCT (SERVICE) COST?" YOU SHOULD SAY "WHY DO YOU WANT TO KNOW?"

If you're ever in a situation where your boss asks you how much a product or service costs, you should reply "Why do you want to know?" While that reply may seem a bit rude, it makes an important point about incremental analysis. There is

Illustration 7-2
Incremental analysis of the decision to stay open 24 hours versus staying open until midnight

	Alternative 2 Stay Open Until Midnight	Alternative 3 Stay Open 24 Hours	Incremental Revenue and Costs (Alternative 3 minus Alternative 2)
Revenue	$3,888,000	$3,924,000	$ 36,000
Less:			
Labor	604,800	648,000	43,200
Paper, toner and other supplies	2,721,600	2,746,800	25,200
Utilities	28,771	29,038	267
Insurance	8,250	8,500	250
Depreciation	60,000	60,000	–0–
Rent	55,000	55,000	–0–
Other fixed costs	3,000	3,000	–0–
Total expense	3,841,421	3,550,338	68,917
Profit	$ 406,579	$ 373,662	$(32,917)

no single cost number that is relevant for all decisions. Thus, you need to know what decision your boss is planning to make so you can identify the incremental cost information that is applicable to the decision. Suppose your boss is trying to decide whether to accept a special order for a particular product. In this case, your boss wants to know whether the incremental cost of producing the order will exceed the incremental revenue from accepting it. Some costs such as the salary of a production supervisor will not change as a result of accepting the order and should not be considered as an incremental cost.

On the other hand, your boss may be considering dropping the product. If the product is dropped, the supervisor may be laid off and the cost savings related to the supervisor's salary is incremental. Thus, whether supervisory salary is an incremental cost and relevant to a decision depends on the decision being made. So, whenever, you're asked what a product or service costs, you want to respond "Why do you want to know?"

ANALYSIS OF DECISIONS FACED BY MANAGERS

Now let's turn our attention to the use of incremental analysis for three decisions that managers frequently face:

1. The decision to engage in additional processing of a product.
2. The decision to make or buy a product.
3. The decision to drop a product line.

ADDITIONAL PROCESSING DECISION

Occasionally, manufacturers must decide whether to sell a product in a partially completed stage or incur the additional processing costs required to complete the product. As an example, consider Bridge Computer, a manufacturer of personal computers. Bridge Computer has already decided to discontinue its Model 250 computer. Currently, it has 5,000 partially completed units on hand. To date, the company has spent $800 per unit, or $4,000,000, to bring these computers to their current stage of completion. The company estimates that costs of $400 per unit must be incurred to complete the computers. The costs are summarized below:

Bridge Computer

Costs of Model 250 Computer

	Costs per Unit Incurred to Date	Costs per Unit to Complete
Material	$300	$200
Labor	200	100
Variable overhead	100	100
Fixed overhead	200	
	$800	$400

Because the company has announced that the Model 250 is going to be discontinued, the price of the computer has fallen. If the units are completed, they can only be sold for $1,000 per unit. That is less than the total cost of producing the computers—$1,200 per unit ($800 cost to date plus $400 of additional cost). An alternative to finishing the units is to sell them as they are. A small computer assembly company in another state is willing to buy the units in their current partial state of completion for $500 per unit.

Which action should be taken? Should the computers be sold in their current state of completion, or should the additional processing costs be incurred? Without a thorough understanding of accounting information and incremental analysis, a manager at Bridge Computer might conclude that further processing is not appropriate. After all, with further processing, total costs will amount to $1,200 per unit, which is more than the selling price of $1,000 per unit.

The error of this conclusion is revealed by incremental analysis. The facts for our analysis are presented in Illustration 7-3. Note that the illustration contains three columns. The first column lists the revenue and costs related to selling the computers in their current state of completion (Alternative 1). The second column lists the revenue and costs related to selling completed computers (Alternative 2). The third column lists the incremental revenue and costs that will be incurred by completing the computers.

We'll begin by examining incremental revenue. Recall that incremental revenue is simply the difference in revenue between two alternatives. Bridge Computer can sell completed units for $1,000 each, whereas it can sell the units in

Illustration 7-3
Incremental analysis of additional processing decision

Bridge Computer

Incremental Analysis of Additional Processing

	Sell in Current State of Completion (Alternative 1)	Complete Processing (Alternative 2)	Incremental Revenue and Costs (Alternative 2 minus Alternative 1)	
Revenue	$500	$1,000	$500	← Incremental revenue associated with Alternative 2
Less:				
Prior production costs				
Material	300	300	0	
Labor	200	200	0	
Variable overhead	100	100	0	
Fixed overhead	200	200	0	
	800	800	0	
Additional processing costs				
Material	0	200	200	
Labor	0	100	100	
Variable overhead	0	100	100	
	0	400	400	← Incremental cost associated with Alternative 2
Gain (loss) per unit	($300)	($200)	$100	← Incremental profit associated with Alternative 2

their current state of completion for $500 each. Thus, incremental revenue of $500 per unit is associated with choosing Alternative 2 and completing processing.

Now let's turn to incremental cost. Before going any further, we need to recall another cost term from Chapter 1—*sunk costs*, or costs incurred in the past. Sunk costs are not incremental costs. Since they've already been incurred, they won't increase or decrease with the choice of one alternative over another. In the case of Bridge Computer, the prior production costs are sunk costs, not incremental costs. Thus, they do not enter our analysis.

What, then, are the incremental costs for Bridge Computer? An incremental cost, remember, is the difference in cost between two alternatives. The $400 cost of completing the units ($200 material, $100 labor, and $100 variable overhead) will be incurred if the units are completed and, thus, $400 is the incremental cost associated with completing processing.

You can see that by choosing Alternative 2 the company will be better off by $100 per unit ($500 incremental revenue − $400 incremental cost). In other words, choosing this alternative produces an incremental profit. As we noted earlier, if an alternative yields an incremental profit, it should be selected.

MAKE-OR-BUY DECISIONS: THE GENERAL REFRIGERATION EXAMPLE

Most manufactured goods are made up of numerous components. In some cases, a company may purchase one or more of the components from another company. This may lead to considerable savings if the outside supplier is particularly efficient at manufacturing the component and can offer it at a reasonable price. Two decision alternatives arise in this situation: make or buy the component. No incremental revenues are involved. Therefore, the analysis of this decision concentrates solely on incremental costs.

Recall that Wendy Grant, manager of the Tennessee plant of General Refrigeration Company, is considering an offer by Dillard Compressor Corporation to supply 50,000 compressors at $310 per unit. Last year, when her plant produced 50,000 compressors, the following costs were incurred.

GENERAL REFRIGERATION

Cost of Manufacturing 50,000 Compressors

Variable costs:	
Direct material ($100 per unit)	$ 5,000,000
Direct labor ($120 per unit)	6,000,000
Variable overhead ($80 per unit)	4,000,000
Total variable cost	15,000,000
Fixed costs:	
Depreciation of building	600,000
Depreciation of equipment	800,000
Supervisory salaries	500,000
Other	350,000
Total fixed cost	2,250,000
Total cost	$17,250,000
Cost per unit	$345

Additional analysis reveals the following: (1) The market value of the machinery used to produce the compressors is approximately zero. (2) Five of the six production supervisors will be fired if production of compressors is discontinued. However, one of the supervisors, who has more than 10 years of service, is protected by a clause in a labor contract, and will be reassigned to other duties, although his services are not really needed. His salary is $110,000.

At first, you might assume that General should buy the compressors rather than manufacture the units internally since the company can buy the units for $310 each, whereas the cost of manufacturing them is $345 each ($17,250,000 ÷ 50,000 units). However, careful consideration of the incremental costs reveals that it is cheaper to manufacture the compressors internally.

To demonstrate, we'll work through an incremental analysis, which is presented in Illustration 7-4. Like previous examples, Illustration 7-4 uses a three-column format. The first two columns present the costs of the two alternatives, while the third column presents the incremental costs. Another option is to use a single-column format that concentrates only on the incremental costs and benefits. A single-column analysis of the make or buy decision faced by the General Refrigeration Company is presented in Illustration 7-5.

A key issue in our analysis involves determining which of the costs listed earlier are, in fact, incremental costs. Clearly, none of the $15,000,000 of variable manufacturing costs will be incurred if the compressors are purchased outside the company. Thus, this is an incremental cost *savings* between the two alternatives.

What about the fixed costs? Let's consider them item by item. The fixed costs associated with depreciation on the building and equipment do not represent a cost savings. The costs of purchasing the building and equipment were incurred in prior periods. Remember that the approach to analyzing decisions requires consideration of only the incremental revenues and costs of decision alternatives. The sunk costs related to purchasing the building and the pieces of equipment are not incremental costs because they have already been incurred and will not change no matter which decision alternative is selected.

Illustration 7-4
Incremental analysis of make-or-buy decision

GENERAL REFRIGERATION

Incremental Cost Analysis

	Cost of Manufacturing 50,000 Compressors	Cost of Buying 50,000 Compressors	Incremental Cost (Savings)
Variable costs:			
Direct material	$ 5,000,000	–0–	($5,000,000)
Direct labor	6,000,000	–0–	(6,000,000)
Variable overhead	4,000,000	–0–	(4,000,000)
Total variable cost	15,000,000	–0–	(15,000,000)
Fixed costs:			
Depreciation of building	600,000	600,000	–0–
Depreciation of equipment	800,000	800,000	–0–
Supervisory salaries	500,000	110,000	(390,000)
Other	350,000	350,000	–0–
Total fixed costs	2,250,000	1,860,000	(390,000)
Cost of buying compressors	-0-	15,500,000	15,500,000
Total	$17,250,000	$17,360,000	$ 110,000

Illustration 7-5
Single-column format for incremental analysis

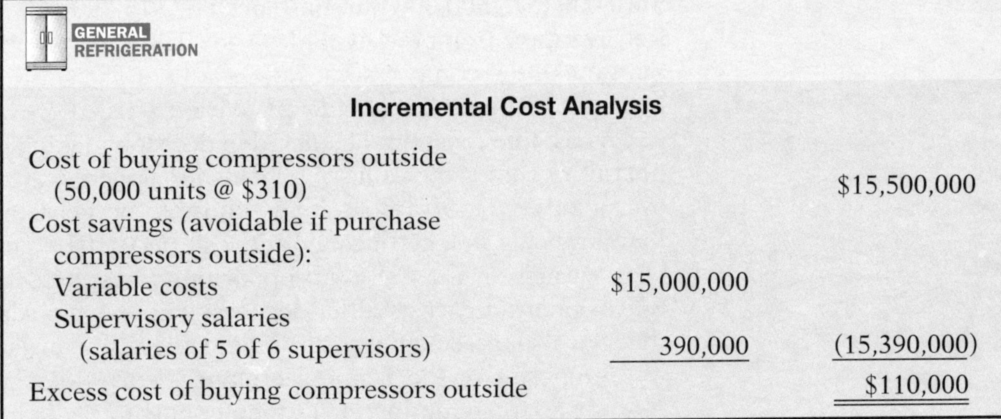

GENERAL REFRIGERATION

Incremental Cost Analysis

Cost of buying compressors outside (50,000 units @ $310)		$15,500,000
Cost savings (avoidable if purchase compressors outside):		
Variable costs	$15,000,000	
Supervisory salaries (salaries of 5 of 6 supervisors)	390,000	(15,390,000)
Excess cost of buying compressors outside		$110,000

The example assumes that fixed costs classified as "other" are also irrelevant sunk costs. But note that not all fixed costs are irrelevant sunk costs. Some fixed costs are **avoidable costs**—costs that can be avoided if a particular action is undertaken. In our example, if compressors are purchased outside the company, the salaries of five production supervisors will be saved. The saving totals $390,000 (total supervisory salaries of $500,000 less the $110,000 that must still be paid to the supervisor who will be retained). In other words, supervisory salaries of $390,000 represent an avoidable cost and thus an incremental cost.

We can see, then, that $15,000,000 of variable costs and $390,000 of fixed costs can be eliminated if the compressors are purchased from Dillard Compressor Corporation, for a total cost savings of $15,390,000. But the cost of purchasing the compressors from Dillard is $15,500,000 (50,000 units × $310). The difference is

Alaska Airlines Outsources Baggage Handling

The make-or-buy decision that we just analyzed for General Refrigeration is much like the outsourcing decisions faced by many companies. Consider Alaska Airlines. In 2005, the company outsourced the handling of baggage to Menzies Aviation, which also performs this service for Continental, United, Northwest and Delta Air Lines. Alaska estimates that it will save $13 million a year. The downside, however, is that 472 of the company's baggage handlers lost their jobs.

The former baggage handlers at Alaska are members of the International Association of Machinists and Aerospace Workers union. The airline made the decision to outsource a week after the union workers rejected a new contract that would have cut pay and benefits.

Source: "Alaska Airlines Outsources Baggage Handling" by Melissa Allison, Seattle Times business reporter from *The Seattle Times*, May 16, 2005. Preprinted by permission.

\$110,000 (\$15,500,000 purchase price − \$15,390,000 cost saving), and the General Refrigeration Company would be \$110,000 worse off if it decided to buy rather than make the compressors. Before a final decision is reached, however, qualitative factors should be considered. We'll discuss these factors later in the chapter.

A cost that must be considered in decision making is an opportunity cost. An **opportunity cost** is the value of benefits foregone by selecting one decision alternative over another. For example, if you chose to purchase a \$1,000 stereo system rather than investing in a certificate of deposit (CD), the potential interest that could have been earned on the CD is an opportunity cost associated with buying the stereo. Since opportunity costs differ depending upon which decision alternative is selected, they are also incremental costs and are relevant in evaluating decision alternatives.

Suppose that the Tennessee plant is currently spending \$500,000 per year to rent space for manufacturing metal shelving, which is used in the refrigeration units. If production of compressors is discontinued, the company will move the shelving operation to space currently occupied by the compressor operation. Thus, in continuing to produce the compressors the company gives up rent savings of \$500,000. The foregone rent savings represents an opportunity cost. An analysis that includes this opportunity cost is presented in Illustration 7-6. According to this analysis, purchasing the compressors outside is the best alternative because it results in a net annual cost saving of \$390,000.

DROPPING A PRODUCT LINE

Dropping a product line is a very significant decision and one that receives a great deal of attention. The proper approach to analyzing the problem is to calculate the change in income that will result from dropping the product line. If income will increase, the product line should be dropped. If income will decrease, the product line should be kept. This amounts to comparing the incremental revenues and costs that result from dropping the product line.

Let's consider an example involving a retailer. Mercer Hardware sells three product lines: tools, hardware supplies, and garden supplies. Illustration 7-7 presents a product line income statement for the prior year. To arrive at net income for each product line, both direct fixed costs and allocated fixed costs are deducted from each product line's contribution margin.

Illustration 7-6
Make-or-buy analysis with opportunity costs considered

GENERAL REFRIGERATION

Incremental Cost Analysis

Cost of buying compressors outside (50,000 units @ \$310)		\$15,500,000
Cost savings (avoidable if purchase compressors outside)		
Variable costs	\$15,000,000	
Supervisory salaries (salaries of 5 or 6 supervisors)	390,000	
Opportunity cost of using the plant to produce compressors (foregone rent savings)	**500,000**	(15,890,000)
Net savings resulting from buying the compressors outside		(\$390,000)

Illustration 7-7
Product line income statement for Mercer Hardware

Mercer Hardware

Product Line Income Statement
For the Year Ended December 31, 2006

	Tools	Hardware Supplies	Garden Supplies	Total
Sales	$120,000	$200,000	$80,000	$400,000
Cost of goods sold	81,000	90,000	60,000	231,000
Gross margin	39,000	110,000	20,000	169,000
Other variable costs	2,000	4,000	1,000	7,000
Contribution margin	37,000	106,000	19,000	162,000
Direct fixed costs	8,000	5,000	3,500	16,500
Allocated fixed costs	24,000	40,000	16,000	80,000
Total fixed costs	32,000	45,000	19,500	96,500
Net income (loss)	$ 5,000	61,000	$ (500)	$ 65,500

Direct fixed costs are fixed costs that are directly traceable to a product line. For example, the salary of a worker who spends 100 percent of his or her time working in the tool section of the hardware store is a direct fixed cost to the tool product line.

Allocated fixed costs are those fixed costs that are not directly traceable to an individual product line. These costs are also referred to as **common costs**, because they are incurred for the common benefit of all product lines. An example of an allocated fixed cost is the salary of the owner/manager of the hardware store. Mercer Hardware allocates common fixed costs to product lines based on their relative sales revenues. For example, sales of tools are 30 percent of sales ($120,000 tool sales ÷ $400,000 total sales). Thus, of the $80,000 of common costs, $24,000 (30% of $80,000) is allocated to tools.

In examining the product line income statement, the owner of Mercer Hardware observes that the garden supplies line is currently showing a loss of $500. Would dropping this product line increase the profitability of the hardware store? To answer this question, we turn again to incremental analysis. As indicated in Illustration 7-8, sales revenue will decline by $80,000 if garden supplies are dropped. However, some costs will decrease or be eliminated altogether. Cost of goods sold will decrease by $60,000, and other variable costs will decrease by

Illustration 7-8
Effect of dropping garden supplies at Mercer Hardware

	Income With Garden Supplies				Income Without Garden Supplies			Difference
	Tools	Hardware Supplies	Garden Supplies	Total	Tools	Hardware Supplies	Total	
Sales	$120,000	$200,000	$80,000	$400,000	$120,000	$200,000	$320,000	$(80,000)
Cost of goods sold	81,000	90,000	60,000	231,000	81,000	90,000	171,000	(60,000)
Gross margin	39,000	110,000	20,000	169,000	39,000	110,000	149,000	(20,000)
Other variable costs	2,000	4,000	1,000	7,000	2,000	4,000	6,000	(1,000)
Contribution margin	37,000	106,000	19,000	162,000	37,000	106,000	143,000	(19,000)
Direct fixed costs	8,000	5,000	3,500	16,500	8,000	5,000	13,000	(3,500)
Allocated fixed costs	24,000	40,000	16,000	80,000	30,000	50,000	80,000	–
Total fixed costs	32,000	45,000	19,500	96,500	38,000	55,000	93,000	(3,500)
Net income	$ 5,000	$ 61,000	$ (500)	$ 65,500	$ (1,000)	$ 51,000	$ 50,000	$(15,500)

$1,000. Whether or not the direct fixed costs will decrease depends on the nature of these costs. For purposes of this example, assume that the direct fixed cost of $3,500 for garden supplies represents the wages paid to a part-time employee. If the garden supplies product line is dropped, this employee will not be retained by the store. In this case, the direct fixed cost of $3,500 is avoidable and represents a cost savings achieved by dropping garden supplies.

Allocated common fixed costs are generally not avoidable. Thus, no cost savings will be achieved with respect to the $16,000 of fixed costs allocated to garden supplies. For example, one component of the allocated fixed cost is rent of the hardware store. The rent will not decrease simply because one of the product lines is eliminated. Another allocated fixed cost is the cost of electricity. This cost is also unlikely to decrease if garden supplies are eliminated, because the store will still need approximately the same amount of heat and light. If garden supplies are eliminated, the share of fixed costs allocated to tools and hardware supplies will simply increase.

To summarize, the analysis of incremental costs and revenues indicates that income of $15,500 will be lost if garden supplies are dropped.

Incremental Analysis
Dropping Garden Supplies

Lost sales	($80,000)
Cost savings:	
Cost of goods sold	60,000
Other variable costs	1,000
Direct fixed costs	3,500
Total cost savings	64,500
Net loss from dropping	($15,500)

BEWARE OF THE COST ALLOCATION DEATH SPIRAL!

Whenever you analyze a decision involving dropping a product or service, remember that common fixed costs are not incremental. This will allow you to avoid what is sometimes referred to as the *cost allocation death spiral*! In many cases, products or services may not appear to be profitable because they receive allocations of common fixed costs. But what will happen to the common costs if the product or service is dropped? They'll be allocated over the remaining products and services. That may result in another product or service appearing to be unprofitable.

Consider Mercer Hardware as an example. If the company had decided to drop garden supplies, the $80,000 of common fixed costs would have been allocated over tools and hardware supplies. The new allocation would be $6,000 higher for tools, and it no longer would appear profitable—it would show a $1,000 loss. But what will happen to the common costs if it's dropped? That's right, they'll be allocated to hardware supplies. Before long, the store (which is reasonably profitable) would be out of business!

Define sunk cost, avoidable cost, and opportunity cost and understand how to use these concepts in analyzing decisions.

SUMMARY OF INCREMENTAL, AVOIDABLE, SUNK, AND OPPORTUNITY COSTS

A number of costs terms have been used earlier, and in this section we briefly review them. Recall that the basic approach to decision making is to compare decision alternatives in terms of costs and revenues that are incremental. Costs that

Illustration 7-9
Fixed costs and decision relevance

Fixed costs	Classification
Depreciation on equipment already purchased	Sunk and irrelevant (not incremental)
President's salary which will not change for both action A and action B	Not sunk but still irrelevant (not incremental)
Salary of supervisor who will be retained if action A is taken and fired if action B is taken	Not sunk and relevant (incremental)

can be *avoided* by taking a particular course of action are always incremental costs and, therefore, relevant to the analysis of a decision. Costs that are *sunk* (i.e., already incurred and not reversible) are never incremental costs because they do not differ among the decision alternatives. Therefore, they are not relevant in making a decision.

Students of managerial accounting often assume that fixed costs are equivalent to sunk costs and are thus irrelevant (i.e., are not incremental costs), but this is not always the case. Fixed costs may be sunk and, therefore, irrelevant. Fixed costs may not be sunk but still irrelevant. Finally, fixed costs may not be sunk and may be relevant. Examples of these three possibilities are presented in Illustration 7-9.

Finally, *opportunity costs* represent the benefit foregone by selecting a particular decision alternative over another. By their nature, they are always incremental costs, and they must be considered when making a decision. To illustrate opportunity costs, consider the Mercer Hardware example presented earlier. In this example, the company is considering dropping the garden supplies product line. Suppose that if garden supplies are dropped, more space can be devoted to selling tools, sales of tools will increase and the contribution margin associated with tools will increase by $20,000. In this case, there is a $20,000 opportunity cost associated with the decision to keep the garden supplies product line. This opportunity cost would make dropping the product line desirable rather than undesirable. Recall that our previous analysis indicated a $15,500 decrease in income from dropping the product line. However, considering the $20,000 opportunity cost due to foregone sales of tools, it appears that the store will be better off by $4,500 (i.e., $20,000 − $15,500) if garden supplies are dropped.

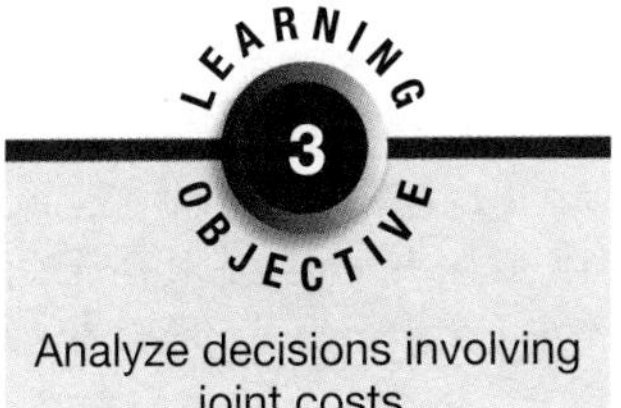

Analyze decisions involving joint costs.

DECISIONS INVOLVING JOINT COSTS

When two or more products *always* result from common inputs, they are known as **joint products**. The costs of the common inputs are referred to as **joint costs**. Joint costs are common in the food processing, extractive, and chemical industries. For example, in the dairy processing business, the common input of raw milk is converted into cream, skim milk, and whole milk. For lumber companies, the common input of a log is converted into various grades of lumber. For fuel companies, the common input of crude oil is converted into a variety of fuels and lubricants.

A graphical treatment of a joint products and joint costs problem is presented in Illustration 7-10. In the illustration, joint costs are incurred, leading to two

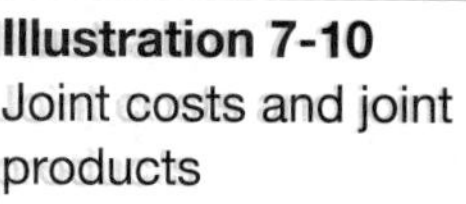

Illustration 7-10
Joint costs and joint products

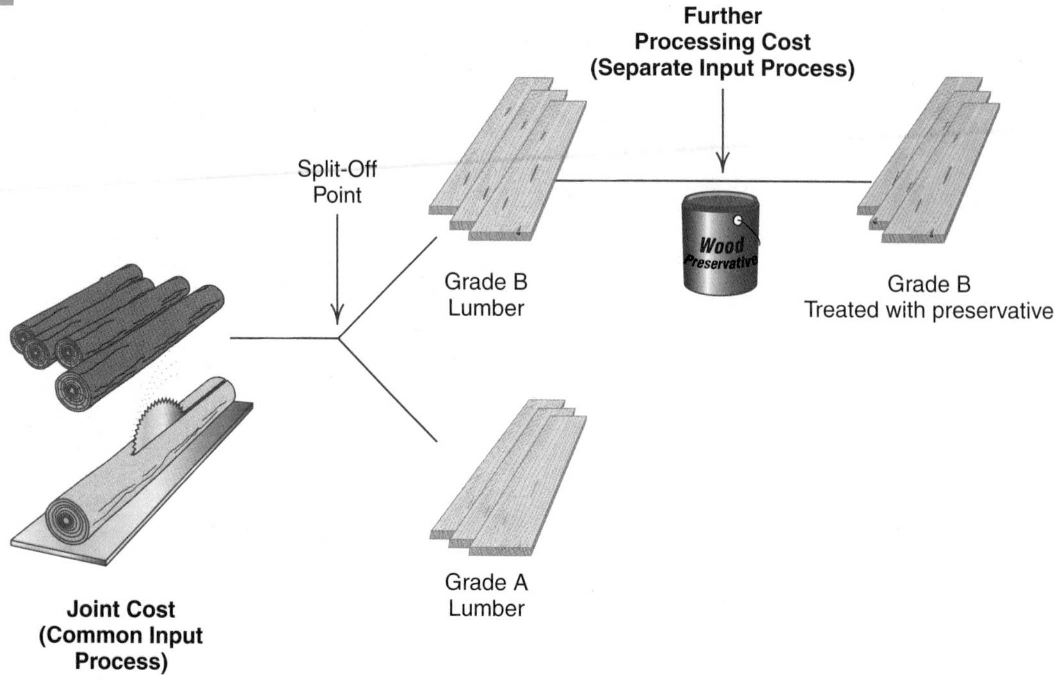

joint products. The stage of production at which individual products are identified is referred to as the **split-off point**. Beyond this point each product may undergo further separate processing and may incur additional costs.

ALLOCATION OF JOINT COSTS

For financial reporting purposes, the cost of the common inputs must be allocated to the joint products. However, care must be taken to ensure that the resulting information does not mislead managers about the profitability of the joint products. For example, suppose a lumber company spends $600 for an oak log and $20 to saw the log into two grades of lumber. The process results in 500 board feet of grade A lumber that sells for $1 per board foot and 500 board feet of grade B lumber that sells for $0.50 per board foot. How should the $620 joint cost be allocated to the joint products? One approach might be to allocate the cost based on the physical quantity of output. Since the production process results in equal quantities of physical output, it might seem reasonable to allocate an equal share of the joint cost to each of the grades of lumber. In this case both the grade A lumber and the grade B lumber would show a cost of $310. This allocation could lead managers to think that grade B lumber is not profitable and should be scrapped—after all, its cost is $310, while revenue from its sale is only $250. But this logic is faulty. If the grade B lumber were scrapped, the company would lose $250 that helped cover the joint cost of $620.

It is important to realize that the total joint cost will be incurred no matter what the company does with the joint products beyond the split-off point. Because the joint cost is not incremental to production of an individual joint product, it is irrelevant to any decision regarding an individual joint product. However, the joint cost is relevant to decisions involving the joint products as a group. If the total revenue from the sale of the joint products is less than the joint cost, production of all of the joint products should cease.

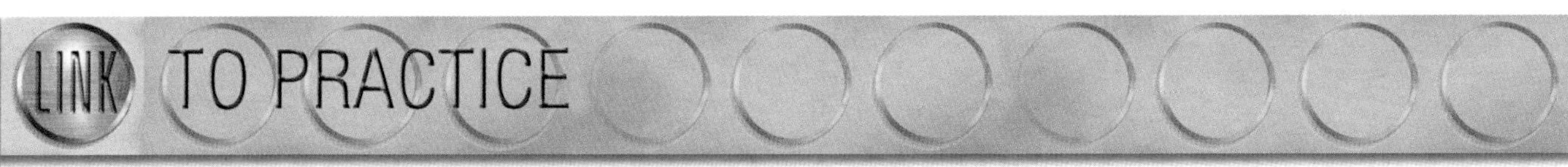

The Sunk Cost Effect

When managers make decisions, they need to be careful that they are not influenced by sunk costs. That's difficult because, psychologically, people are pre-disposed to take sunk costs into account. Psychologists refer to this "irrational" economic behavior as the sunk cost effect. Consider an immensely expensive waterway project that was scheduled for Congressional review. Proponents of the project suggested that its elimination would be inappropriate because so much money had already been spent on its completion. That is, proponents rationalized continuation of the project in terms of sunk costs!

Two psychologists, Hal Arkes and Catherine Blumer, have investigated the sunk cost effect. In a research study, they presented 61 college students in Ohio and Oregon with the following question.

> Assume that you have spent $100 on a ticket for a weekend ski trip to Michigan. Several weeks later you buy a $50 ticket for a weekend ski trip to Wisconsin. You think you will enjoy the Wisconsin ski trip more than the Michigan ski trip. As you are putting your just-purchased Wisconsin ski trip ticket in your wallet, you notice that the Michigan ski trip and the Wisconsin ski trip are for the same weekend! It's too late to sell either ticket, and you cannot return either one. You must use one ticket and not the other. Which trip will you go on?

More than half of the respondents chose the Michigan trip, even though the Wisconsin trip was identified as more enjoyable. Based on this result and other experiments, Arkes and Blumer suggest that the psychological justification for the irrational behavior is a desire not to appear wasteful.

Arkes and Blumer also presented the question above to a group of students enrolled in an economics course where they had studied the concept of sunk cost. Even in this group, about a third favored the Michigan trip. Apparently, training in economics does not greatly lessen the sunk cost effect. On the other hand, I gave the question to a group of students who had studied sunk cost in their managerial accounting course. Almost none of the students selected the Michigan trip. Maybe accounting instructors are more effective in getting across the message—Beware of sunk costs when making decisions!

Source: "The Psychology of Sunk Cost," by Arkes, H. R. and C. Blumer, from *Organizational Behavior and Human Decision Processes,* 35 (1985) pp. 124–140. Reprinted by permission of Elsevier.

A better way of allocating the joint cost is to use the **relative sales value method**. With this method, the amount of joint cost allocated to products depends on the relative sales values of the products at the split-off point.

$$\text{Joint cost allocated to product A} = \frac{\text{Sales value of A}}{\text{Sales value of A} + \text{Sales value of B}} \times \text{Joint Cost}$$

$$\text{Joint cost allocated to product B} = \frac{\text{Sales value of B}}{\text{Sales value of A} + \text{Sales value of B}} \times \text{Joint Cost}$$

In the previous example, the grade A lumber would receive an allocation of \$413.33 [i.e., \$620 × (\$500 ÷ \$750)]. The grade B lumber would receive an allocation of \$206.67 [i.e., \$620 × (\$250 ÷ \$750)]. A good feature of this method is that the amount of joint cost allocated to a product cannot exceed its sales value at the split-off point. Thus, products that make a positive contribution to covering joint cost will not look unprofitable.

The costs allocated to the two grades of lumber using the physical quantity and the relative sales value approaches are compared in Illustration 7-11. In particular, note that for grade B lumber, the physical quantity approach yields a negative gross margin of \$60, whereas the relative sales value approach yields a positive gross margin of \$43.33.

ADDITIONAL PROCESSING DECISIONS AND JOINT COSTS

Suppose the manager of a lumber company is considering whether or not to pressure-treat grade B lumber so that it will be resistant to rot. The additional processing costs per board foot will be \$0.20. The pressure-treated lumber can be sold for \$0.75 per board foot, compared with \$0.50 for nontreated lumber. Should the additional processing be undertaken? Ask yourself, "What will be the incremental revenue and the incremental costs?" The incremental revenue will be \$0.25 per board foot (i.e., \$0.75 − \$0.50). The incremental cost will be \$0.20. Therefore, the incremental profit will be \$0.05, indicating the further processing is warranted.

Illustration 7-11
Comparison of physical quantity and relative sales value approaches to allocation of joint costs

Joint cost:	
Cost of log	\$600.00
Cost of sawing	20.00
Total	\$620.00

Joint process yields:

500 board feet of grade A lumber selling for \$1.00 per board foot

500 board feet of grade B lumber selling for \$.50 per board foot

Results using physical quantities to allocate joint costs

	Grade A	**Grade B**
Sales revenue		
500 b.f. × \$1.00	\$500.00	
500 b.f. × \$.50		\$250.00
Cost		
\$620 × (500 b.f. ÷ 1,000 b.f.)	310.00	
\$620 × (500 b.f. ÷ 1,000 b.f.)		310.00
Gross margin	\$190.00	(\$60.00)

Results using relative sales values to allocate joint costs

	Grade A	**Grade B**
Sales revenue		
500 b.f. × \$1.00	\$500.00	
500 b.f. × \$.50		\$250.00
Cost		
\$620 × (\$500 ÷ \$750)	413.33	
\$620 × (\$250 ÷ \$750)		206.67
Gross margin	\$ 86.67	\$ 43.33

Where do the joint costs enter into this decision? They don't, because they are not incremental! Whether or not further processing will take place, the company must obtain a log and cut it into grade A and grade B lumber (unless the company wants to get out of the business of producing both grade A and grade B lumber).

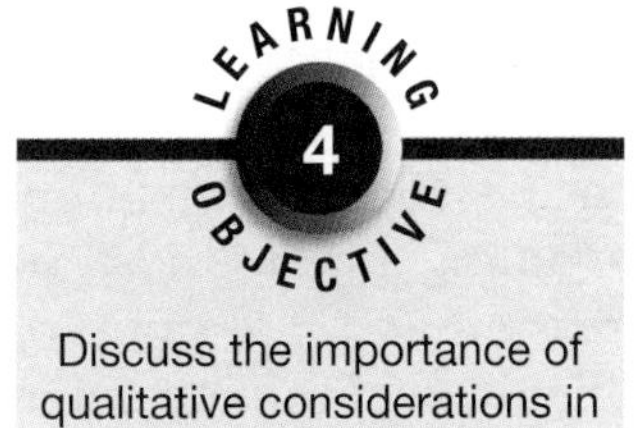

Discuss the importance of qualitative considerations in management decisions.

QUALITATIVE CONSIDERATIONS IN DECISION ANALYSIS

The solutions to the problems presented above have focused on the *quantitative* features of the decision situations. In particular, we have concentrated on quantitative differences in costs and revenues among decision alternatives. However, most important problems have one or more features that are very difficult, if not impossible, to quantify. These *qualitative* aspects of the problem must receive the same careful attention as the quantitative components.

The importance of qualitative considerations can be illustrated in the context of the make-or-buy decision discussed earlier. Recall that the Tennessee plant of the General Refrigeration Company was considering whether to continue producing

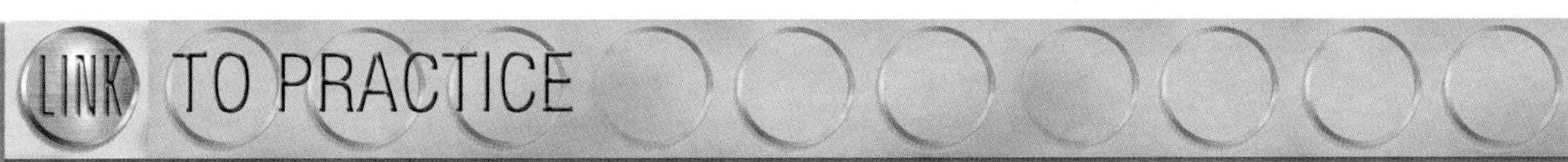

Qualitative Considerations in Outsourcing to China

Labor rates in China are about 10 percent of those in the U.S. and raw material costs may also be much lower. Therefore, it's not surprising that many U.S. companies have outsourced manufacturing to China even though transportation costs back to the U.S. may be significant.

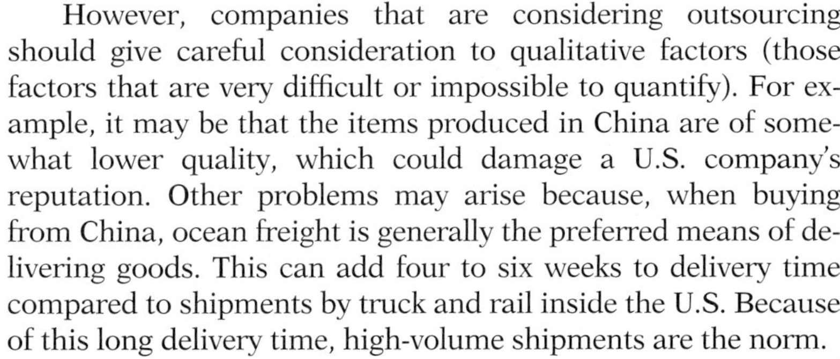

However, companies that are considering outsourcing should give careful consideration to qualitative factors (those factors that are very difficult or impossible to quantify). For example, it may be that the items produced in China are of somewhat lower quality, which could damage a U.S. company's reputation. Other problems may arise because, when buying from China, ocean freight is generally the preferred means of delivering goods. This can add four to six weeks to delivery time compared to shipments by truck and rail inside the U.S. Because of this long delivery time, high-volume shipments are the norm.

This, however, leads to higher inventory holding costs. And the U.S. buyer faces a risk that inventory may become obsolete before all of it is sold. Also, consider the risk of a manufacturing defect in the shipment. That's obviously a much greater problem when the volume is 20,000 units as opposed to 500.

Source: Excerpt from "The China Syndrome: A Five–Dimension Analytical Model for Deciding When (and When Not) to Purchase from the East" by Mitchell Quint and Dermot Shorten in *Strategy & Business*, Issue 38, Spring 2005, pp. 20–24. Adapted and reprinted with permission from *Strategy & Business*, the award-winning management quarterly published by Booz Allen Hamilton, www.strategy-business.com.

compressors or purchase them from another firm. The goal of our analysis was to determine whether it would cost General more to produce the compressors or to buy them from an outside supplier. However, our analysis only considered the easily quantifiable differences in costs between the two decision alternatives. In addition, there are qualitative benefits and costs associated with using an outside supplier.

Perhaps the primary benefit of using an outside supplier is that the adverse effect of a downturn in business is less severe. Suppose there is a temporary downturn in the demand for refrigeration units. In this case, General can simply order fewer compressors from its outside supplier, thus avoiding a major cost. In contrast, if General continues to manufacture the compressors and a temporary downturn in business is experienced, it is much more difficult to eliminate some of the fixed costs associated with manufacturing the compressors. For example, the company probably cannot eliminate the fixed costs of supervisors if the downturn is thought to be only temporary. Experienced supervisors are difficult to find, and they cannot be hired and fired based on temporary fluctuations in business.

A disadvantage of using an outside supplier is the associated loss of control over the production process. Purchased items may not be of sufficiently high quality and delivery schedules may not be honored. Furthermore, knowing that it would be costly for the company to restart internal production, the outside supplier may believe that it has the company "over a barrel" and that it can raise prices significantly in the future. Also, employee morale may suffer when a company decides to purchase a component outside and employees are fired or transferred as a result. The cost to the firm of reduced morale is difficult to quantify, but it may have a significant effect on the quantity and quality of the products produced by remaining employees.

MAKING BUSINESS DECISIONS

Throughout the book, and in particular in this chapter, we've stressed the idea that decision making relies on incremental analysis. A problem with implementing this approach, however, is that some incremental costs and incremental benefits are very difficult to quantify. What if a decision has a negative impact on employee morale? How will we quantify this as an incremental cost? Or what if a decision has a positive impact on customer satisfaction? How do we go from knowledge of this qualitative benefit to an estimate of incremental revenue? Whenever you make a decision, carefully think about items that are difficult to quantify. These so-called qualitative factors may be the most important aspect of the decision.

KNOWLEDGE AND SKILLS (K/S) CHECKLIST

Knowledge and skills are needed to make good business decisions. Check off the knowledge and skills you've acquired from reading this chapter.

❐ K/S 1. You have an expanded business vocabulary (see key terms).

❐ K/S 2. You have an enhanced ability to analyze decision alternatives using incremental analysis. In particular, you can appropriately deal with avoidable, sunk, and opportunity costs in decision making.

❐ K/S 3. You can appropriately analyze additional processing decisions involving joint costs.

❐ K/S 4. You understand the importance of qualitative considerations in decision making.

SUMMARY OF LEARNING OBJECTIVES

1 ***Explain the role of incremental analysis (analysis of incremental costs and revenues) in management decisions.*** Decisions involve a choice between two or more alternatives. The best decision can be determined by comparing alternatives in terms of the costs and revenue items that differ between them. These costs and revenues are referred to as incremental costs and revenues.

2 ***Define sunk cost, avoidable cost, and opportunity cost and understand how to use these concepts in analyzing decisions.*** Sunk costs are costs that have been incurred in the past and are irrelevant to present and future decisions. Avoidable costs are costs that can be avoided by taking a particular action. The term *opportunity cost* refers to the benefit foregone by selecting a particular decision alternative over another. Avoidable costs and opportunity costs are always incremental and relevant in decision analysis.

3 ***Analyze decisions involving joint costs.*** Joint costs are the costs of common inputs that result in two or more joint products. Joint costs are not relevant to analyzing decisions that involve only one of the joint products, because they are only incremental to producing all of the joint products. In analyzing decisions related to further processing beyond the split-off point, consider only the incremental revenue (the extra revenue related to further processing) and incremental costs (the costs incurred beyond the split-off point).

4 ***Discuss the importance of qualitative considerations in management decisions.*** A variety of qualitative factors (e.g., quality of goods, employee morale, and customer service) need to be considered in making a decision. Qualitative factors are often even more important than costs and benefits that are easy to quantify.

APPENDIX

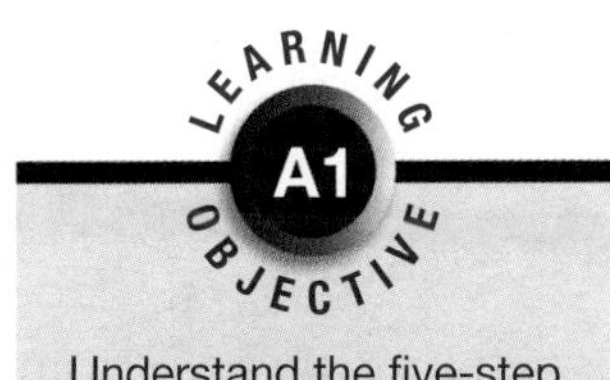

Understand the five-step approach to the Theory of Constraints (TOC).

THE THEORY OF CONSTRAINTS (TOC)

In this chapter, we focused on the general approach to decision making—incremental analysis. Here we discuss decisions related to constraints and show how large increases in profit can be achieved by elimination of bottlenecks in production processes. Specifically, we will focus on the Theory of Constraints (TOC), which is an approach to production and constraint management, developed by Eli Goldratt.[1]

To facilitate our discussion, let's consider the production process of Dwyer Electronics, a producer of electronic measurement instruments. Production takes place in 4 departments as indicated in Illustration A7-1. Subassemblies are produced in Departments 1 and 2. The subassemblies are transferred to Department 3, which makes and tests connections and installs the subassemblies in housing units. Units are then transferred to Department 4, which completes final testing and packages units for shipping.

THE FIVE-STEP PROCESS OF TOC

Goldratt specifies a five-step process for dealing with constraints. In this section, we discuss each step.

[1]For additional information on TOC, see E. Goldratt and J. Cox, *The Goal*, North River Press (1984). Also see D. Smith, *The Measurement Nightmare, How the Theory of Constraints Can Resolve Conflicting Strategies, Policies, and Measures*, The St. Lucie Press/APICS Series on Constraints Management (2000).

Illustration A7-1
Production flow at Dwyer Electronics

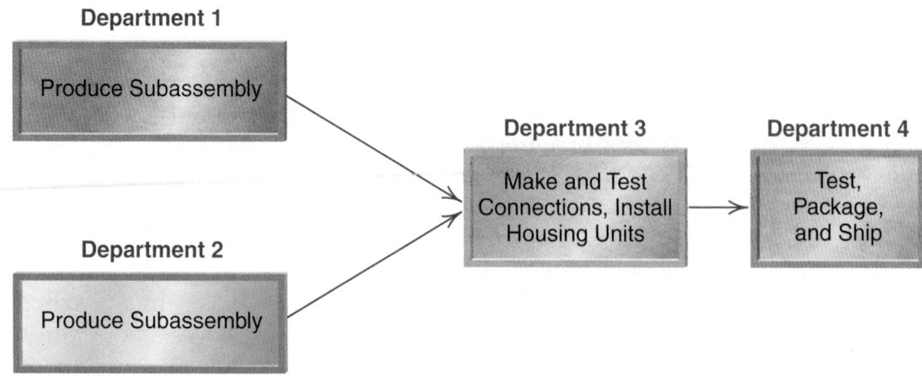

STEP 1. IDENTIFY THE BINDING CONSTRAINT

The first step in the TOC process is to identify the bottleneck or binding constraint. This is the process that limits throughput (throughput is the amount of inventory produced in a period). Every manufacturing company has a binding constraint unless capacity in all departments exceeds demand for the company's product. And in this case, demand is the binding constraint. For Dwyer Electronics, lets assume that Department 3 is the bottleneck. Management has identified this department as the bottleneck since production from Departments 1 and 2 is stacking up in front of the Department 3 work area.

In the TOC, the department that is the bottleneck is equated to a drum since it "beats a rhythm" that coordinates the production in other departments. At Dwyer Electronics, the production in Departments 1 and 2 should be tied to the needs of Department 3. Even though they can produce more than Department 3, there is no need for them to do so. Production beyond the needs of Department 3 just ties up company funds in excess work in process inventory.

STEP 2. OPTIMIZE USE OF THE CONSTRAINT

The second step is to optimize use of the constraint. This requires that the company use the constraint to produce products with the *highest contribution margin per unit of the constraint*.[2] Consider the following two testing instruments produced by Dwyer:

	Model A70	Model B90
Selling price per unit	$1,000	$2,000
Variable costs per unit:		
Direct materials	400	900
Direct labor	200	300
Contribution margin per unit	**400**	**800**
Fixed costs per unit	100	300
Profit per unit	$ 300	$ 500
Time to complete 1 unit in Department 3	.1 hour	.3 hour
Contribution margin per hour in Dept. 3	$4,000	$2,667

[2]Goldratt takes the somewhat extreme position that the only variable cost is material. While this is undoubtedly true in some situations, it is also undoubtedly true that in other situations additional cost elements are variable. For example, in the production of aluminum, which requires a great deal of electricity, power is clearly a variable cost.

Which product optimizes use of the constraint—the Model A70 or the Model B90? The answer is the Model A70. Note that its contribution margin is $400 per unit but it only takes .1 hour to produce a unit in Department 3, which is the constrained department. Thus, each hour this product generates $4,000 of incremental profit. So if managers of Dwyer face a choice between using scarce time in Department 3 to produce the Model A70 or the Model B90, they should definitely choose the Model A70.

STEP 3. SUBORDINATE EVERYTHING ELSE TO THE CONSTRAINT

The third step is to subordinate everything else to the constraint. This means that managers of Dwyer should focus their attention on trying to loosen the constraint and not concentrate on process improvements in other departments. Why, for example, should managers work to improve processes 1, 2, or 4 if they are not limiting production? Only the binding constraint limits production and attention should be focused completely on this department.

There are a number of things that managers can do to loosen the constraint in Department 3. For example, suppose the workers in Department 3 all take their breaks at the same time. Capacity could be gained by staggering breaks. And note that this would generate substantial sums of money. Product Model A70 generates $4,000 per hour. If breaks are staggered and the company gains an hour a day of additional capacity in Department 3, then it is generating an additional $20,000 of profit per week (5 hours × $4,000 per hour).

STEP 4. BREAK THE CONSTRAINT

The fourth step in the TOC process is to break the constraint. This can be accomplished in many ways. Here are some examples:

- Cross-train workers in Departments 1 and 2 so they can help out in Department 3.
- Outsource some of Department 3's work.
- Purchase additional equipment for Department 3.
- Hire additional workers for Department 3.
- Train workers in Department 3 so that they can perform their jobs more efficiently.

STEP 5. IDENTIFY A NEW BINDING CONSTRAINT

The final step is to identify a new binding constraint. Once, the constraint is broken in Department 3, either Department 1, 2, or 4 will become the bottleneck. Or, if the company has excess capacity in all departments, it should focus its attention on building demand.

IMPLICATIONS OF TOC FOR INSPECTIONS, BATCH SIZES, AND ACROSS THE BOARD CUTS

TOC has implications for a number of decisions faced by managers. Here, we'll discuss three: implications for inspections, batch sizes, and across the board cuts.

Inspections. Time in a constrained department should never be wasted. Thus, whenever possible, inspections should take place *before* work is transferred to a constrained department. That way, the valuable time of the constrained department will not be wasted working on defective items.

Batch Sizes. In recent years, many companies have gone to small batch sizes to gain flexibility in responding to new orders and to avoid producing large quantities of defective items if a process goes out of control. However, when a production process is a binding constraint, it may be better to have large batch sizes. The reason is that then the valuable time of the constrained department is not wasted setting up equipment for numerous small batches of production.

Across the Board Cuts. The decision to have across the board cuts is completely at odds with TOC. Cuts in nonbottleneck departments may make sense, but across the board cuts, even to the department that is the binding constraint, can have a severe, negative impact on profit. Recall that at Dwyer Electronics, each hour gained in Department 3 results in $4,000 of incremental profit if the time is spent producing Model A70. Likewise, each hour lost reduces profit by $4,000. If an across the board cut reduced capacity by the equivalent of just an hour a day, more than a $1 million of profit would be lost in a year (1 hour × 5 days per week × 52 weeks × $4,000 per hour = $1,040,000).

YOU GET WHAT YOU MEASURE AND TOC

As you know, a major theme of this book is "You get what you measure!" In other words, performance measures drive the behavior of managers. TOC points out that performance measures related to production volume (e.g., units produced per hour) can have a negative impact on shareholder value *when they are applied to nonbottleneck departments*. Suppose at Dwyer Electronics, the company measures and rewards Departments 1 and 2 for units produced per hour. In this case, the departments have an incentive to produce more items than Department 3 can deal with since it is a bottleneck. The result will be large levels of work in process inventory accumulating in front of Department 3. That excess inventory is an investment of shareholder funds, but shareholders will not receive a reasonable return on the investment since it serves no useful purpose. Remember—be careful of performance measures that encourage overproduction in nonbottleneck departments!

REVIEW PROBLEM

Mayfield Software has a 2,000 square foot cafeteria located on the lower level of Building No. 3, the company's largest building. The vice president of operations for Mayfield insists that meal prices be reasonable so workers will stay on campus and avoid "wasting time" driving to restaurants with slow service. Employees at Mayfield are generally happy with the quality of food and the level of service in the cafeteria. Still, Mayfield is considering outsourcing to Regal Food Service. Mayfield is expanding and realizes that the future success of the company will require increased focus on its core competencies (and food service is not a core competency!).

A cafeteria profit report for 2008 follows. In the report, the cafeteria is charged $20 per year per square foot for space and three percent of sales for general overhead (to cover the centrally administered costs of Mayfield Software such as legal, brand advertising, salary of the CFO, etc.). All business units receive the same three percent charge.

Cafeteria Profit Report for 2008

Sales		$1,095,000
Less expenses:		
Cost of food and supplies	$657,000	
Salaries	342,000	
Space charge	40,000	
Depreciation of equipment	6,000	
General overhead charge	32,850	1,077,850
Cafeteria profit		$ 17,150

The terms of the agreement with Regal (which has not yet been signed) call for Regal to provide similar quality meals and service at the same prices that were charged in 2008. Regal will use the current cafeteria space and existing equipment without cost to them. Regal will keep 96 percent of sales revenue and remit four percent of sales revenue back to Mayfield. Regal will pay for all food and supplies and hire and pay the salaries of all staff including the cafeteria manager, cooks and servers.

Required

Evaluate the annual financial impact of the outsourcing decision assuming sales in the coming year, under Regal, will be the same as in 2008.

Answer

Incremental Revenue and Costs

Lost sales	($1,095,000)
4% payment from Regal	43,800
Food savings	657,000
Salary savings	342,000
Net effect	($52,200)

Food services should not be outsourced since the effect is to reduce profit by $52,200. Note that the general overhead charge is not included in the analysis because these costs will not actually change due to the outsourcing decision. Thus, they are not incremental costs.

KEY TERMS

Avoidable costs (269)
Common costs (271)
Differential costs (262)
Incremental analysis (262)
Incremental cost (262)
Incremental revenue (262)
Joint costs (273)
Joint products (273)
Opportunity cost (270)
Relative sales value method (275)
Relevant costs (262)
Split-off point (274)

SELF ASSESSMENT *(Answers Below)*

1. Differential costs are sometimes referred to as ______________ costs.

2. Which of the following costs should **not** be taken into consideration when making a decision?

a. Opportunity costs.
b. Sunk costs.
c. Relevant costs.
d. Differential costs.

3. Which of the following is often **not** a differential cost?
   a. Material.
   b. Labor.
   c. Variable overhead.
   d. Fixed overhead.

4. True or false? Fixed costs are never incremental costs.

5. Which of the following is **not** relevant when considering whether or not to drop a product?
   a. The contribution margin.
   b. Qualitative factors.
   c. The potential impact on demand for other products.
   d. Allocated common costs.

6. Opportunity costs are:
   a. Never incremental costs.
   b. Always incremental costs.
   c. Sometimes sunk costs.
   d. None of the above.

7. The joint costs incurred in a joint product situation:
   a. Are incurred before the split-off point.
   b. Are incurred after the split-off point.
   c. Should only be allocated based on physical attributes.
   d. None of the above.

8. A joint product's cost is $18, which includes $6 of allocated joint cost. Its sales price is $16. In this case:
   a. Profit will improve if the company discontinues production of the product.
   b. The company should sell as few of the items as possible to minimize the loss on sales.
   c. The data are misleading because the $6 allocated joint cost will be incurred even if the product is discontinued.
   d. Both a and b are correct.

9. (Appendix) According to the Theory of Constraints, optimizing use of a constraint requires:
   a. Production of the product with the highest profit per unit.
   b. Production of the product with the shortest production time.
   c. Production of the product with the highest contribution margin.
   d. Production of the product with the highest contribution margin per unit of the constrained resource.

10. (Appendix) True or false? Generally, parts should be inspected prior to being sent to a department that is a bottleneck.

Answers to Self Assessment

1. relevant; **2.** b; **3.** d; **4.** False; **5.** d; **6.** b; **7.** a; **8.** c; **9.** d; **10.** True.

INTERACTIVE LEARNING

Enhance and test your knowledge of Chapter 7 using Wiley's online resources.

1. Learning Objectives
2. Multiple Choice
3. Language of Business—Matching of Key Terms
4. Critical Thinking
5. Demonstration—The cost allocation death spiral!
6. Case—West Coast Grocery Supply; Incremental analysis

Go to our dynamic Web site for more self-assessment, Web links, and additional information.

QUESTIONS

1. What are differential costs and revenues?
2. Why are sunk costs irrelevant in decision making?
3. What are avoidable costs?
4. Why are opportunity costs relevant when making decisions?
5. What is the proper approach to analyzing whether or not a product line should be dropped?
6. Give an example of a fixed cost that is not sunk but is still irrelevant.
7. What is a qualitative advantage of making rather than buying a component?
8. Why is the relative sales value a more logical basis for allocating joint costs than physical quantity?
9. (Appendix) Why are batch sizes generally larger in bottleneck departments?
10. (Appendix) Why is the bottleneck department referred to as a "drum" in the Theory of Constraints?

EXERCISES

EXERCISE 7-1. Group Assignment Describe a decision and provide an example of a fixed cost that is incremental in the context of the decision. Then, provide an example of a fixed cost that is not incremental in the context of the decision.

EXERCISE 7-2. Writing Assignment Jordan Walken owns and operates an electronics store in Seattle, Washington. His accountant has prepared a product line income statement that is reproduced below (Jordan's two lines are MP3 players and accessories). In preparing the income statement, the accountant allocated all common costs including rent, Jordan's salary, and the salary of his two assistants, utilities, and other common costs based on relative sales. His reason was that "Each product line needs to cover its share of common costs."

In light of this report, Jordan is considering eliminating accessories and concentrating solely on the sale of MP3 players (although he does not expect an increase in MP3 player sales).

	MP3 players	Accessories	Total
Sales	$850,000	$125,000	$975,000
Cost of merchandise	595,000	93,750	688,750
Gross margin	255,000	31,250	286,250
Rent	41,760	6,240	48,000
Salaries	191,400	28,600	220,000
Utilities	5,220	780	6,000
Other	4,350	650	5,000
Total	242,730	36,270	279,000
Income before taxes	$ 12,270	$ (5,020)	$ 7,250

Required
Analyze the effect on profit of dropping accessories. Then, write a paragraph explaining the role of common costs in your analysis and how allocation of common costs can lead to the cost allocation death spiral!

EXERCISE 7-3. Internet Assignment Go to the financial glossary Investorwords.com at http://www.investorwords.com/ and look up the words "sunk cost" and "opportunity cost." Why is it that sunk costs are never relevant to a decision whereas opportunity costs are always relevant?

EXERCISE 7-4. Incremental Analysis Rustic Interiors, an interior design company, has experienced a drop in business due to an increase in interest rates and a corresponding slowdown in remodeling projects. To stimulate business, the company is considering exhibiting at the Middleton Home and Garden Expo. The exhibit will cost the company $12,000 for space. At the show, Rustic Interiors will present a slide show on a PC, pass out brochures that were printed previously (the company printed more than needed), and show its portfolio of previous jobs.

The company estimates that revenue will increase by $36,000 over the next year as a result of the exhibit. For the previous year, profit was as follows:

Revenue		$201,000
Less:		
Design supplies	$15,000	
Salary of Samantha Spade (owner)	80,000	
Salary of Kim Bridesdale (full time employee)	55,000	
Rent	18,000	
Utilities	6,000	
Depreciation of office equipment	3,600	
Printing of advertising materials	700	
Advertising in Middleton Journal	2,500	
Travel expenses other than depreciation of autos	2,000	
Depreciation of company cars	9,000	191,800
Net income		$ 9,200

Required

Calculate the impact of the exhibit on company profit. Should the company exhibit at the home show?

EXERCISE 7-5. Incremental Analysis Each year, Knight Motors surveys 7,500 former and prospective customers regarding satisfaction and brand awareness. For the current year, the company is considering outsourcing the survey to RBG Associates, who have offered to conduct the survey and summarize results for $30,000. Craig Knight, the president of Knight Motors, believes that RBG will do a higher-quality job than his company has been doing, but is unwilling to spend more than $10,000 above current costs. The head of bookkeeping for Knight has prepared the following summary of costs related to the survey in the prior year.

Mailing	$16,000
Printing (done by Lester Print Shop)	4,500
Salary of Pat Fisher, part-time employee who stuffed envelopes and summarized data when surveys were returned (100 hours × $15)	1,500
Share of depreciation of computer and software used to track survey responses and summarize results	1,100
Share of electricity/phone/etc. based on square feet of space occupied by Pat Fisher vs. entire company	500
Total	$23,600

Required

What is the incremental cost of going outside versus conducting the survey as in the past? Will Craig Knight accept the RBG offer?

EXERCISE 7-6. Incremental Analysis and Opportunity Costs Finn's Seafood Restaurant has been approached by New England Investments, which wants to hold an employee recognition dinner next month. Lillian Sumner, a manager of the restaurant, agreed to a charge of $65 per person, for food, wine, and dessert, for 150 people. She estimates that the cost of unprepared food will be $30 per person and beverages will be $12 per person.

To be able to accommodate the group, Lillian will have to close the restaurant for dinner that night. Typically, she would have served 160 people with an average bill of $50 per person. On a typical night, the cost of unprepared food is $18 per person and beverages are $13 per person. No additional staff will need to be hired to accommodate the group from New England Investments.

Required

a. Calculate the incremental profit or loss associated with accepting the New England Investments group.

b. What was the opportunity cost of accepting the New England Investments group?

c. Should Lillian have considered any qualitative factors in her decision? Explain.

EXERCISE 7-7. Make or Buy Decision: Relevant Costs The Tufanzi Furniture Company manufactures leather furniture. The manufacturing process uses a variety of metal pieces such as brackets, braces, and casters. Carla Reid, the resource officer of Tufanzi, has been asked to determine if it is advisable to purchase these pieces rather than make them internally (the current practice). Identify which of the following items are relevant to her decision.

a. The original cost of equipment currently used to make metal pieces.

b. The market value of equipment currently used to make metal pieces.

c. The cost of buying metal pieces from suppliers.

d. The space freed up if metal pieces are not made internally.

e. The salary of the president of Tufanzi Furniture.

f. The quality of the metal pieces made internally.

g. The quality of the metal pieces purchased from suppliers.

h. Depreciation on equipment used to make metal pieces (ignore taxes).

i. The labor contract with production workers.

j. The selling prices of furniture pieces.

EXERCISE 7-8. Make-or-Buy Decision Howell Corporation produces an executive jet for which it currently manufactures a fuel valve; the cost of the valve is indicated below:

	Cost per Unit
Variable costs	
Direct material	$ 800
Direct labor	500
Variable overhead	200
Total variable costs	1,500
Fixed costs	
Depreciation of equipment	400
Depreciation of building	100
Supervisory salaries	200
Total fixed costs	700
Total cost	$2,200

The company has an offer from Duvall Valves to produce the part for $1,800 per unit and supply 1,000 valves (the number needed in the coming year). If the company accepts this offer and shuts down production of valves, production workers and supervisors will be reassigned to other areas needing their services. The equipment cannot be used elsewhere in the company, and it has no market value. However, the space occupied by the production of the valve can be used by another production group that is currently leasing space for $50,000 per year.

Required
Should the company make or buy the valve?

EXERCISE 7-9. Sunk, Avoidable, and Opportunity Costs Consider the information in Exercise 7-8 and identify the following statements as true or false.

a. Supervisory salary is an avoidable cost if the company decides to buy the valves.

b. Depreciation of building is an avoidable cost if the company decides to buy the valves.

c. The $50,000 cost of leasing space is an opportunity cost associated with continuing production of the valve.

d. The depreciation of equipment is an opportunity cost associated with continuing production of the valve.

e. Depreciation of building is a sunk cost even if the company continues with production of the valve.

f. Supervisory salary is a sunk cost even if the company continues with production of the valve.

EXERCISE 7-10. Dropping a Product: Relevant Costs E-Teller Inc. manufactures ATM machines. Recently, the company has begun manufacturing and marketing a machine that can recognize customer fingerprints. Demand for this machine is very strong and the chief executive officer (CEO) of E-Teller is considering dropping production of the company's original model that relies on bankcards and passwords. This will give the company increased capacity to devote to the new model. Which of the following items are relevant to the CEO's decision to drop the old model machine?

a. The original cost of equipment used to manufacture the old model.

b. Depreciation of the equipment used to manufacture the old model (ignore taxes).

c. The CEO's salary.

d. The time it takes to manufacture each model.

e. The production manager's salary.

f. The selling price of the new model.

g. The variable cost of producing the new model.

h. The cost of retraining personnel to make the newer model.

i. Depreciation of the factory building allocated to the old model.

EXERCISE 7-11. Additional Processing Decision DataPoint Inc. has decided to discontinue manufacturing its Quantum model personal organizer. Currently, the company has a number of partially completed personal organizers on hand. The company has spent $105 per unit to manufacture these organizers. To complete each unit, costs of $12 for material and $13 for direct labor will be incurred. In addition, $10 of variable overhead and $30 of allocated fixed overhead (relating primarily to depreciation of plant and equipment) will be added per unit.

If DataPoint Inc. completes the organizers, they can sell them for $125 per unit. On the other hand, another manufacturer is interested in purchasing the partially completed organizers for $100 per unit and converting them into inventory tracking devices.

Determine if DataPoint Inc. should complete the personal organizers or sell them in their current state.

EXERCISE 7-12. Make or Buy Decision Imperial Corp. produces whirlpool tubs. Currently, the company uses internally manufactured pumps to power water jets. Imperial Corp. has found that 40 percent of the pumps have failed within their 12-month warranty period, causing huge warranty costs. Because of the company's inability to manufacture high-quality pumps, management is considering buying pumps from a reputable manufacturer who will also bear any related warranty costs. Imperial's unit cost of manufacturing pumps is $72.85 per unit, which includes $16.75 of allocated fixed overhead (primarily depreciation of plant and equipment). Also, the company has spent an average of $19.75 (labor and parts) repairing each pump returned. Imperial Corp. can purchase pumps for $85.25 per pump.

Required
During 2008, Imperial Corp. plans to sell 14,200 whirlpools (requiring 14,200 pumps). Determine whether the company should make or buy the pumps and the amount of cost savings related to the best alternative. What qualitative factors should be considered in the outsourcing decision?

EXERCISE 7-13. Dropping a Product Line Computer Village sells computer equipment and home office furniture. Currently, the furniture product line takes up approximately 50 percent of the company's retail floor space. The president of Computer Village is trying to decide whether the company should continue offering furniture or just concentrate on computer equipment. Below is a product line income statement for the company. If furniture is dropped, salaries and other direct fixed costs can be avoided. In addition, sales of computer equipment can increase by 20 percent without affecting direct fixed costs. Allocated fixed costs are assigned based on relative sales.

	Computer Equipment	Home Office Furniture	Total
Sales	$1,000,000	$700,000	$1,700,000
Less cost of goods sold	600,000	420,000	1,020,000
Contribution margin	400,000	280,000	680,000
Less direct fixed costs:			
Salaries	150,000	150,000	300,000
Other	50,000	50,000	100,000
Less allocated fixed costs:			
Rent	11,765	8,235	20,000
Insurance	2,941	2,059	5,000
Cleaning	3,529	2,471	6,000
President's salary	70,588	49,412	120,000
Other	5,882	4,118	10,000
Net income	$ 105,295	$ 13,705	$ 119,000

Required
Determine whether Computer Village should discontinue the furniture line and the financial benefit (cost) of dropping it.

EXERCISE 7-14. Qualitative Factors in Decision Making For each of the following situations, indicate a qualitative factor that should be considered prior to making a decision:

a. A company that produces and sells bottled water is considering outsourcing its bottling operation. The company will still source the water and deliver it to bottling companies.

b. A wine producer is considering dropping its premium brand wine and concentrating exclusively on less costly wines.

c. A software company currently has a large facility for producing videos used in games and advertisements. The company is considering shutting down the facility and using resources provided by other companies.

EXERCISE 7-15. Joint Cost Allocation with Physical Quantity of Output Bailey Products produces two joint products (A and B). Prior to the split-off point, the company incurs costs of $5,000. Product A weighs 25 pounds and product B weighs 100 pounds. Product A sells for $90 per pound and product B sells for $30 per pound.

Required

a. Based on a physical measure of output, allocate joint costs to products A and B.

b. Compare the costs to the selling prices. Should the company sell products whose selling price is less than the allocated joint cost?

EXERCISE 7-16. Joint Cost Allocation with Relative Sales Values Bailey Products produces two joint products (A and B). Prior to the split-off point, the company incurs costs of $5,000. Product A weighs 25 pounds and product B weighs 100 pounds. Product A sells for $90 per pound and product B sells for $30 per pound.

Required

a. Based on relative sales values at the split-off point, allocate joint costs to products A and B.

b. Under what condition would the cost allocated using relative sales values be greater than the selling price of a joint product?

EXERCISE 7-17. Allocating Joint Costs The American Produce Company purchased a truckload of cantaloupes (weighing 5,000 pounds) for $1,000. American Produce separated the cantaloupes into two grades: superior and economy. The superior grade cantaloupes had a total weight of 4,000 pounds and the economy grade cantaloupes totaled 1,000 pounds. Fresh Produce sells the superior grade at $0.30 per pound and the economy grade at $0.10 per pound.

Required
Allocate the $1,000 cost of the truckload to the superior grade and economy grade cantaloupes using the physical quantity method and the relative sales value method.

EXERCISE 7-18. (Appendix) Calculating the Value of Loosening a Constraint At RM Sharpton Corporation, the engraving department is a bottleneck, and the company is considering hiring an extra worker, whose salary will be $40,000 per year, to mitigate the problem.

With the extra worker, the company will be able to produce and sell 8,000 more units per year. The selling price per unit is $15. Cost per unit currently is $8 as follows:

Direct material	$3.00
Direct labor	1.00
Variable overhead	.25
Fixed overhead (primarily depreciation of equipment)	3.75
Total	$8.00

Required
Calculate the annual financial impact of hiring the extra worker.

PROBLEMS

PROBLEM 7-1. Decision Making and Ethics Joan Paxton, VP of marketing for Supertone Recording Equipment, has developed a marketing plan for presentation to the company's president. The plan calls for television ads, something the company has never used. As part of her presentation, she will indicate the impact of the TV ads on company profit as follows:

Incremental sales from increased exposure		$8,000,000
Less:		
Incremental cost of goods sold	$3,500,000	
Cost of TV ads	2,250,000	5,750,000
Incremental profit		$2,250,000

While Joan is quite confident in the cost of the ads and the incremental cost of goods sold if sales are $8,000,000, she is quite uncertain about the sales increase. In fact, she believes that her estimate is on the "high side." However, she also believes that if she puts in a more conservative estimate such as $6,000,000, the president will not go along with the TV ads even though they will still generate substantial profits at $6,000,000 of incremental sales.

Required

Is it unethical of Joan to bias her estimate of incremental sales on the "high side" given she believes the ultimate outcome is in the best interest of the company?

PROBLEM 7-2. Incremental Analysis of Outsourcing Decision Oakland College is considering outsourcing their grounds maintenance. In this regard, Oakland has received a bid from Highline Grounds Maintenance for $275,000 per year. Highline states that their bid will cover all services and planting materials required to "keep Oakland's grounds in a condition comparable to prior years." Oakland's cost for grounds maintenance in the preceding year were $280,500 as follows:

Salary of three full-time gardeners	$182,000
Plant materials	75,000
Fertilizer	6,000
Fuel	7,500
Depreciation of tractor, mowers, and other miscellaneous equipment	10,000
Total	$280,500

If Oakland College outsources maintenance, it will be able to sell equipment for $30,000, and the three gardeners will be laid off.

Required

a. Analyze the one-year financial impact of outsourcing grounds maintenance.

b. How will savings in the second year differ from year one?

c. Discuss qualitative factors that should be considered in the decision.

PROBLEM 7-3. Incremental Analysis of Outsourcing Decision Selzer & Hollinger, a legal services firm, is considering outsourcing their payroll function. They have received a bid from ABC Payroll Services, Inc., for $16,000 per year. ABC Payroll will provide all payroll processing, including employee checks and payroll tax reporting. Selzer & Hollinger's costs for payroll processing in-house over the past year were as follows:

Cost	**Amount**
Payroll clerk (part-time)	$ 8,000
Annual cost of payroll processing software updates	975
Human resources manager's salary	75,000
Depreciation of computers used in payroll processing	1,800
Annual payroll tax update seminar costs for one employee	1,000

The payroll clerk works only on payroll processing currently and will be laid off if payroll is outsourced. The human resources manager spends 25% of her time currently on payroll-related issues. The computers would remain and be used for other tasks if payroll is outsourced.

Required

a. What is the annual impact of outsourcing payroll? Will the company save money or spend extra money if payroll is outsourced?

b. What qualitative factors should be considered in this decision?

PROBLEM 7-4. Make-or-Buy Decision For most construction projects, Bradley Heating and Cooling buys sheet metal and forms the metal into heating/cooling ducts as needed. The company estimates the costs of making and installing ductwork for the Kerry Park shopping mall to be as follows:

Materials	$30,000
Labor to form ductwork	2,000
Labor to install ductwork	8,000
Misc. variable costs	1,000
Fixed costs allocated based on labor hrs	2,500
Total cost	$43,500

The fixed costs relate to the company's building, equipment, and office staff. The company plans on billing the Kerry Park developer $60,000 for services. Bradley is currently behind schedule on other projects and is paying a late penalty of $1,000 per day. Walt Bradley, the owner of Bradley Heating and Cooling, is considering ordering prefabricated ductwork for the Kerry Park job. The prefabricated ductwork will cost $34,000 (including the cost of sheet metal). If Walt buys the prefabricated ductwork, he'll be able to reassign workers to another project and avoid 5 days of late fees.

Required

Should Bradley make the ductwork or buy it prefabricated?

PROBLEM 7-5. Keep-or-Buy Decision, Sunk Costs Susan Crossing purchased a used Ford Focus for $7,400. Since purchasing the car, she has spent the following amounts on parts and labor:

New stereo system	$1,000
New paint job	2,000
New tires	500
New muffler	125
Total	$3,625

Unfortunately, the car needs a few major repairs now; among other things, the brake routers and pads must be replaced and the radiator has sprung a leak (a new radiator is needed). The repairs are estimated to cost $2,000.

Susan has looked around at other used cars and has found a used Honda Civic for $7,500 that is in very good condition and is approximately the same age as the Ford Focus. Susan can sell the Ford Focus "as is" for $6,000.

Required

1. In trying to decide whether to repair the Ford Focus or buy the Honda Civic, Susan is upset because she has already spent $11,025 on the Focus. The car seems like it costs too much to sell at such a large loss. How would you react to her dilemma?
2. Assuming that Susan would be equally happy with either the Ford Focus or the Honda Civic, should she buy the Civic or repair the Focus? Explain your answer.
3. Are there any qualitative factors that might enter into this decision? Explain.

PROBLEM 7-6. Make-or-Buy Decision Curtis Corporation is beginning to manufacture Mighty Mint, a new mouthwash in a small spray container. The product will be sold to wholesalers and large drugstore chains in packages of 30 containers for $18 per package. Management allocates $200,000 of fixed manufacturing overhead costs to Mighty Mint. The manufacturing cost per package of 30 containers for expected production of 100,000 packages is as follows:

Direct material	$ 6.50
Direct labor	3.50
Overhead (fixed and variable)	3.00
Total	$13.00

The company has contacted a number of packaging suppliers to determine whether it is better to buy or manufacture the spray containers. The lowest quote for the containers is \$1.75 per 30 units. It is estimated that purchasing the containers from a supplier will save 10 percent of direct materials, 20 percent of direct labor, and 15 percent of variable overhead. Curtis's manufacturing space is highly constrained. By purchasing the spray containers, the company will not have to lease additional manufacturing space that is estimated to cost \$15,000 per year. If the containers are purchased, one supervisory position can be eliminated. Salary plus benefits for this position are \$70,000 per year.

Required
Should Curtis make or buy the containers? What is the incremental cost (benefit) of buying the containers as opposed to making them?

PROBLEM 7-7. Additional Processing Decision and Qualitative Factors Mahulena Carpet produced 1,000 yards of its economy-grade carpet. In the coloring process, there was a pigment defect and the resulting color appeared to be faded. The carpet normally sells for \$10 per yard: \$5 of variable cost per yard and \$3 of fixed cost per yard have been assigned to the carpet.

The company realizes that it cannot sell the carpet for \$10 per yard, through its normal channels, unless the coloring process is repeated. The incremental cost of the process is \$2 per yard. However, Practical Home Solutions is willing to buy the carpet in its current faded condition for \$7 per yard.

Required

a. Should Mahulena repeat the coloring process or sell the carpet to Practical Home Solutions?

b. Suppose Practical Home Solutions is willing to buy the carpet for \$9 per yard if Mahulena's brand is associated with the carpet by means of a tag indicating the carpet was produced by Mahulena (a highly regarded producer). Would you accept Practical Home Solutions's offer if you were the president of Mahulena?

PROBLEM 7-8. Additional Processing Decision with a Production Constraint Mega Chemical Company produces ZylexA and a related product called ZylexB. ZylexB, which sells for \$16.00 per gallon, is made from a base of ZylexA plus additional ingredients. It takes 30 minutes to manufacture a gallon of ZylexA and an additional 15 minutes to manufacture a gallon of ZylexB. ZylexA sells for \$10.00 per gallon. The cost per gallon of manufacturing ZylexA and the additional costs to convert it into ZylexB are:

	ZylexA	Additional Cost to Convert ZylexA into ZylexB
Material	\$2.50	\$2.00
Labor	3.00	0.80
Variable overhead	2.75	1.30

Both products have been successful and demand for both products is strong and beyond the company's capacity. Since it takes additional time to manufacture ZylexB, the vice president of production is trying to determine whether ZylexB should be produced.

Required
Which product makes the largest contribution to company profit, given a capacity constraint measured in terms of production time?

PROBLEM 7-9. Dropping a Product Line Pantheon Gaming, a computer enhancement company, has three product lines: audio enhancers, video enhancers, and connection-speed accelerators. Common costs are allocated based on relative sales. A product line income statement follows:

Pantheon Gaming
Income Statement
for the Year Ended December 31, 2008

	Audio	Video	Accelerators	Total
Sales	$1,025,000	$2,125,000	$2,120,000	$5,270,000
Less cost of goods sold	563,750	1,168,750	1,908,000	3,640,500
Gross margin	461,250	956,250	212,000	1,629,500
Less other variable costs	50,000	65,000	21,000	136,000
Contribution margin	411,250	891,250	191,000	1,493,500
Less direct salaries	125,000	140,000	56,000	321,000
Less common fixed costs:				
Rent	11,669	24,194	24,137	60,000
Utilities	3,407	7,063	11,530	22,000
Depreciation	8,492	17,605	3,903	30,000
Other administrative costs	147,059	191,176	61,765	400,000
Net income	$ 115,623	$ 511,212	$ 33,665	$ 660,500

Since the profit for accelerators devices is relatively low, the company is considering dropping this product line.

Required

a. Determine the impact on profit of dropping accelerator products.

b. Discuss the potential qualitative effects of discontinuing the sale of accelerator products.

PROBLEM 7-10. Drop a Product/Opportunity Cost Midwestern Sod Company produces two products: fescue grass and Bermuda grass.

	Fescue Grass	Bermuda Grass
Selling price per square yard	$2.00	$2.85
Less variable cost per square yard (water, fertilizer, maintenance)	.55	1.15

The company has 120,000 square yards of growing space available. In the past year, the company dedicated 60,000 square yards to fescue and 60,000 square yards to Bermuda grass. Annual fixed costs are $120,000, which the company allocates to products based on relative growing space.

Martha Lopez, the chief financial officer of Midwestern Sod, has suggested that in the coming year, all 120,000 square yards should be devoted to Bermuda grass. The president vetoed her suggestion, saying, "I know that right now home construction is booming in our area, and we can sell all the grass we can produce, irrespective of what type. But, you know a lot of developers really like that fescue grass and I'd hate to disappoint them by not offering it."

Required

What is the opportunity cost of the president's decision to stick with both types of grass?

PROBLEM 7-11. Drop a Product Decision Lennon Fans manufactures three model fans for industrial use. The standard selling price and cost of each fan follow:

	Model 501	Model 541	Model 599
Selling price	$5,000	$10,000	$13,000
Unit cost:			
Material	1,050	4,500	6,000
Direct labor	500	2,000	4,000
Overhead	769	3,077	6,154
Unit profit (loss)	$2,681	$ 423	($3,154)

Essentially, all overhead costs are fixed. Some of the fixed overhead costs are direct costs to particular models and others are common fixed costs.

Estimated total overhead

	Model 501	Model 541	Model 599	Total
Direct fixed	$4,000,000	$1,500,000	$500,000	$ 6,000,000
Common fixed				4,000,000
Total				$10,000,000

Lennon allocates overhead costs to products using a single overhead rate developed as follows. Estimated total overhead is divided by estimated direct labor cost. This results in an overhead rate per labor dollar. This rate is used to assign standard overhead to products.

Below are estimates of sales and direct labor. These values imply an overhead rate of $1.5385 per labor dollar ($10,000,000 ÷ $6,500,000).

	Model 501	Model 541	Model 599	Total
Estimated unit sales	1,000	2,000	500	3,500
Estimated labor	$500,000	$4,000,000	$2,000,000	$6,500,000

Required

a. Because it is showing a loss, the controller of Lennon has asked you to analyze whether the Model 599 should be dropped. You should assume that direct fixed costs will be avoided if a model is dropped but common fixed costs will not be avoided if the model is dropped.

b. Explain why the method used to allocate costs at Lennon results in "unreasonably high" charges to the Model 599 pump.

PROBLEM 7-12. Cost Allocation Death Spiral Carpets Unlimited produces and sells three lines of carpet (economy, standard, and deluxe). Jeff Choi, the chief financial officer of the company, has prepared the following report on the profitability of the company in the past year. In the report, fixed costs are allocated based on yards of carpet.

	Economy	Standard	Deluxe	Total
Yards of Carpet	20,000	30,000	50,000	100,000
Sales	$200,000	$450,000	$1,000,000	$1,650,000
Less variable costs (Dye, yarn, labor, etc.)	100,000	270,000	600,000	970,000
Less fixed costs (Depreciation, supervisory salaries, etc.)	110,000	165,000	275,000	550,000
Profit (loss)	$ (10,000)	$ 15,000	$ 125,000	$ 130,000

Upon seeing the report, Matt Williams, the president of Carpets Unlimited, suggested that the company should consider dropping the Economy grade and concentrate on the two other lines. Jeff replied, however, that that would lead to the "cost allocation death spiral."

Required

a. Revise the report assuming the company drops the economy grade.

b. If either the standard or the deluxe grades is reporting a loss in part a, revise the report assuming that it is also dropped.

c. Explain what Jeff means by the "cost allocation death spiral."

PROBLEM 7-13. Joint Costs and Decision Making Sylvarboris Wood Products purchases alder logs for $80 per log. After stripping the bark, the log is spun on a veneer cutter, which peels thin layers of wood (referred to as veneer) that are sold to furniture manufacturers for $140 per 3′ × 30′ sheet of veneer. The peeled log (referred to as a peeler) is sold for $40 to companies that use the logs to construct outdoor play equipment. On average, each alder log yields one 3′ × 30′ sheet of veneer and (obviously) one peeled log. The cost of processing each log into a sheet of veneer and a peeled log is $20 in addition to the $80 cost of the alder log. On average, a peeled log weighs 60 pounds and an average 3′ × 30′ sheet of veneer weights 10 pounds.

Required

a. Suppose Sylvarboris were to allocate all joint costs based on the weight of the joint products. Calculate expected profit per sheet of veneer and per peeler.

b. The profit per peeler in part a is negative. Does this imply that the company should not sell them?

c. Suppose Sylvarboris were to allocate all joint costs based on the relative sales values of the joint products. Calculate expected profit per sheet of veneer and per peeler.

d. Briefly explain why the relative sales value approach is the preferred method for allocating joint costs.

PROBLEM 7-14. Joint Costs and Additional Processing Good Earth Products produces orange juice and candied orange peels. A 1,000-pound batch of oranges, costing $400, is transformed using labor of $40 into 100 pounds of orange peels and 300 pints of juice. The company has determined that the sales value of 100 pounds of peels at the split-off point is $300 and the value of a pint of juice (not pasteurized or bottled) is $0.30. Beyond the split-off point, the cost of sugar-coating and packaging the 100 pounds of peels is $50. The cost of pasteurizing and packaging the 300 pints of juice is $150. A 100 pound box of candied peels is sold to commercial baking companies for $500. Each pint of juice is sold for $1.

Required

a. Allocate joint costs using the relative sales values at the split-off point and calculate the profit per 100 pound box of sugar-coated peels and the profit per pint of juice.

b. What is the incremental benefit (cost) to the company of sugar-coating the peels rather than selling them in their condition at the split-off point?

c. What is the incremental benefit (cost) to the company of pasteurizing and packaging a pint of juice rather than selling the juice at the split-off point?

PROBLEM 7-15. Joint Costs Gavin West is a commercial fisherman and he has just returned from a trip off the coast of Maine. He has calculated the cost of his catch as follows:

Wages of deckhands	$25,000
Gavin's wage	14,000
Food, medical supplies, etc.	4,000
Depreciation of netting and other equip	4,500
Depreciation of boat	10,500
Fuel	14,000
Total	$72,000

Gavin's nets yielded a catch of 12,000 pounds of salmon, 18,000 pounds of halibut, and 20,000 pounds of flounder. Salmon sells for \$6 per pound, halibut for \$4 per pound, and flounder for \$2 per pound.

Required

a. Allocate joint costs based on weight. With these costs, what is the profit associated with each type of fish?

b. Allocate joint costs based on relative sales values. With these costs, what is the profit associated with each type of fish?

c. Gavin is considering turning the flounder into fish paste. The incremental cost of this operation is \$8,000. Each pound of flounder yields one half pound of paste, and the paste sells for \$4 per pound. Will Gavin be better off selling the flounder or turning it into paste? What role does the allocated joint cost play in this decision?

PROBLEM 7-16. Joint Costs Northwest Minerals operates a mine. During July, the company obtained 400 tons of ore, which yielded 100 pounds of gold and 50,000 pounds of copper. The joint cost related to the operation was \$400,000. Gold sells for \$270 per ounce and copper sells for \$0.68 per pound.

Required

a. Allocate the joint costs using relative weight. With these costs, what is the profit associated with each mineral? What is the drawback of this approach?

b. Allocate the joint costs using the relative sales values. With these costs, what is the profit associated with each mineral?

c. With the relative sales value approach to allocation, what is the smallest value of joint cost that would result in cooper showing a loss? What is the smallest value of joint cost that would result in gold showing a loss?

PROBLEM 7-17. (Appendix) Batch Size Decision and Constraints At Dalton Playground Equipment, the powder-coating process is a bottleneck. Typically, it takes approximately two hours to switch between jobs. The time is spent cleaning nozzles, and paint tanks, and recalibrating equipment. Currently, the company runs relatively small batch sizes through the process but is considering increasing them to reduce setup time.

With small batch sizes, powder coating can process approximately 2,500 units per 8-hour shift and products have an average contribution margin of \$40. With large batch sizes, powder coating can process approximately 3,000 units per 8-hour shift.

Required

a. Calculate the additional profit associated with running larger batch sizes through the powder coating process.

b. What potential problems are created by the larger batch sizes?

PROBLEM 7-18. (Appendix) Managing Constraints Reece Herbal Supplements purchases, in bulk, a variety of dietary supplements that the company bottles, packages, and ships to health-food stores and drugstores around the country. The company has a good reputation, and its products are in high demand. Last year, the company purchased mechanical packaging equipment for \$260,000 and reduced its shipping department by two people, eliminating an annual salary expense of \$100,000. When it works, the equipment packages product 10 percent faster than the previous manual system. Unfortunately, the equipment has broken down on many occasions for up to four hours. Normally (when the packaging equipment is working), the company packages 2,000 bottles per hour and the average contribution margin per bottle is \$0.50. The general manager of operations has suggested that the company rehire the two packaging workers as back up for the new packaging system. The company president doesn't think this is a good idea, since the workers will be "sitting around doing nothing for 30 hours per week!"

Required
Comment on the general manager's suggestion and the president's reaction. Support your answer with an estimate of the financial impact of rehiring the two workers.

CASES

7-1 PRIMUS CONSULTING GROUP

Primus is a firm of consultants that focuses on process reengineering and quality improvement initiatives. Northwood Industries has asked Primus to conduct a study aimed at improving on-time delivery. Normal practice for Primus is to bill for consultant time at standard rates plus actual travel costs and estimated overhead. However, Northwood has offered a flat $60,000 for the job. Currently, Primus has excess capacity so it can take on the Northwood job without turning down other business and without hiring additional staff. If normal practices were followed, the bill would be:

Classification	Hours	Rate	Amount
Partner	80	$250	$20,000
Senior consultant	110	$150	16,500
Staff consultant	145	$ 85	12,325
Travel costs			15,000
Overhead at $25 per nonpartner hour			6,375
Total			$70,200

Overhead (computer costs, rent, utilities, paper, copying, etc.) is determined at the start of the year by dividing estimated annual overhead costs ($2,000,000) by total estimated nonpartner hours (80,000 hours). Approximately 20 percent of the total amount is variable costs. All Primus employees receive a fixed wage (i.e., there is no compensation for overtime). Annual compensation in the previous year amounted to the following:

	Per Hour
Partner	$260
Senior consultant	$110
Staff consultant	$ 60

Required
What will be the effect on company profit related to accepting the Northwood Industries job? What qualitative factors should be considered in the decision whether or not to accept the job?

7-2 FIVE STAR TOOLS

(Note: This case relates to the appendix on the Theory of Constraints.)

Five Star Tools is a small family-owned firm that manufactures diamond-coated cutting tools (chisels and saws) used by jewelers. Production involves three major processes. First, steel "blanks" (tools without the diamond coating) are cut to size. Second, the blanks are sent to a chemical bath that prepares the tools for the coating process. In the third major process, the blanks are coated with diamond chips in a proprietary process that simultaneously coats and sharpens the blade of each tool. Following the coating process each tool is inspected and defects are repaired or scrapped.

In the past two years, the company has experienced significant growth and growing pains. The company is at capacity in the coating and sharpening process, which requires highly skilled workers and expensive equipment. Because of the bottleneck created by this operation, the company has missed deadlines on orders from several important customers.

Maxfield Turner the son of Frederick Turner, founder of Five Star Tools, is the president of the company. Over lunch he and Betty Spence, vice president of marketing, discussed the situation. "We've got to do something," Betty began. "If we don't think we can meet a customer's order deadline, we should turn down the business. We can't simply keep customers waiting for product or we'll develop a reputation as an unreliable supplier. You know as well as I do that this would be devastating to our business."

"I think there may be another approach, Betty," replied Max. "Some of our products are exceptionally profitable. Maybe we should concentrate on them and drop some of the less profitable ones. That would free up our production resources. Or, maybe we can figure out a way to run more product through the coating process. If we could just loosen that constraint, I know we could improve our response time and profitability. I'll tell you what I'll do. I'll get the accounting department to prepare an analysis of product profitability.

That should help us figure out which products to concentrate on. And, I'll get the production people thinking about how to free up some time in coating. We'll meet early next month and try to get a handle on how to deal with our production constraints."

Required

a. What steps can be taken to loosen the constraint in Coating and Sharpening?

b. Consider the Model C210 and the Model D400 chisels. Which product should be "emphasized" given the constraint in Coating and Sharpening cannot be loosened?

c. Focusing only on the Model C210 Chisel and the Model D400 Chisel, what would be the benefit to the firm of gaining one more hour of production time in Coating and Sharpening?

d. In Coating and Sharpening, the operator begins by inspecting items that have arrived from the Chemical Bath. If rough edges or blemishes are detected, the operator smoothes and/or buffs the items before actual coating or sharpening takes place. (Note that this process is in addition to the inspection that takes place at a separate inspection station following coating and sharpening.)

In order to save valuable time in Coating and Sharpening, management is considering forming a separate inspection station before the coating and sharpening process. The inspection station can utilize existing smoothing and buffing equipment, and it can be staffed on an as needed basis by an employee who normally works in the Chemical Bath area, which has excess capacity (so the employee will not be missed for brief periods). Management estimates that this action will free up 240 hours in Coating and Sharpening (an average of 5 minutes per hour × 8 hours per day 3 360 operating days per year). Management has calculated that the average contribution margin per unit for its products is $275. The average contribution margin per hour spent in Coating and Sharpening is $800.

Based on this information, estimate the incremental profit per year associated with adding the new inspection station.

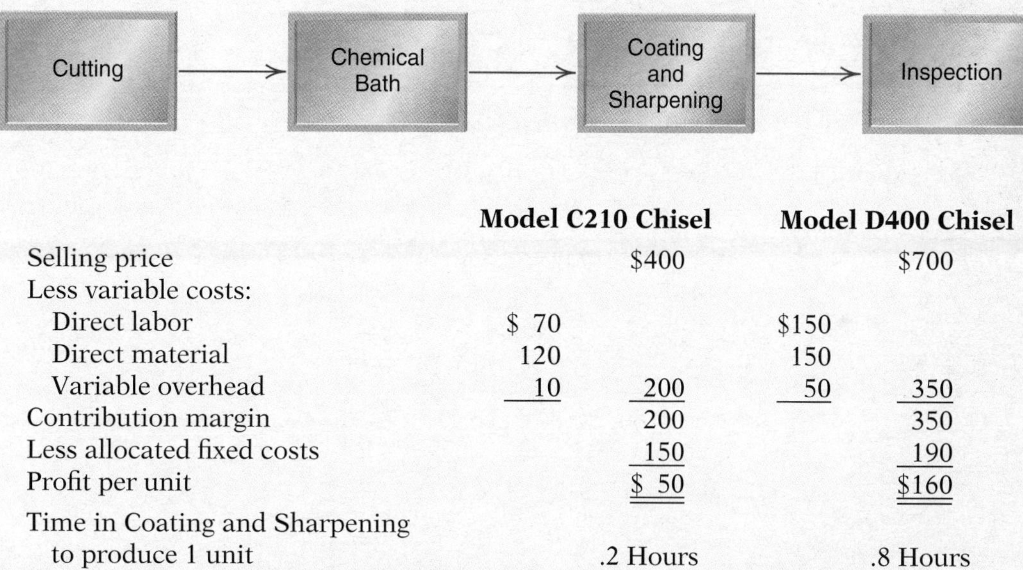

	Model C210 Chisel		Model D400 Chisel	
Selling price		$400		$700
Less variable costs:				
Direct labor	$ 70		$150	
Direct material	120		150	
Variable overhead	10	200	50	350
Contribution margin		200		350
Less allocated fixed costs		150		190
Profit per unit		$ 50		$160
Time in Coating and Sharpening to produce 1 unit		.2 Hours		.8 Hours

CHAPTER 8

LEARNING OBJECTIVES

1. Compute the profit maximizing price for a product or service.
2. Perform incremental analysis related to pricing a special order.
3. Explain the cost-plus approach to pricing and why it is inherently circular for manufacturing firms.
4. Explain the target costing process for a new product.
5. Analyze customer profitability.
6. Explain the activity-based pricing approach.

PRICING DECISIONS, ANALYZING CUSTOMER PROFITABILITY, AND ACTIVITY-BASED PRICING

Nancy Sanchez, vice president of marketing for Wholesale Office Products, recently attended a management training seminar where the instructor made the following point:

All customers are not the same—some are highly profitable and some are marginally profitable at best. To be successful, companies need to analyze the profitability of customers. Marginally profitable customers should be charged increased prices or their business should be dropped. The highly profitable customers—those are the ones you want to focus on. Direct your marketing campaigns towards them and you'll be on your way to achieving major increases in shareholder value!

Driving home from the seminar, Nancy thought about what she had learned and changes that needed to be made at Wholesale. In particular, she thought about her company's approach to pricing. Currently, the company charges all customers a 10 percent markup over the cost of products ordered. But some customers are much more difficult to deal with than others. In particular, some customers want frequent deliveries of relatively small orders. This means that relatively more time is spent picking and packing their orders, and delivery costs are higher. "What we need to do," Nancy decided, "is determine the profitability of our various customers and then come up with a more rational approach to pricing. First thing tomorrow, I'll set up a team with members from distribution, marketing, and accounting to work on customer profitability, measurement, and pricing."

Pricing decisions are often the most difficult decisions that managers face, and in this chapter we will examine them in some detail. We begin by discussing the profit maximizing price from the standpoint of economic theory. Then we discuss pricing special orders and prices set by marking up costs as well as determining the target cost for a new product. We will conclude the chapter with a discussion of measuring customer profitability and activity-based pricing—two topics that relate directly to the problem Nancy Sanchez is facing at Wholesale Office Supplies.

THE PROFIT MAXIMIZING PRICE

Compute the profit maximizing price for a product or service.

Economic theory suggests that the quantity demanded of a product or service is a function of the price that is charged and that generally, the higher the price, the lower the quantity demanded. If managers can estimate the quantity demanded at various prices (admittedly a difficult but not an impossible task), determining the optimal price is relatively straightforward. Simply subtract variable costs from price to obtain the contribution margin, multiply the contribution margin by the quantity demanded, subtract fixed costs, and estimate profit. The price with the highest profit should be selected. This is much simpler than it sounds. Consider the following example.

Next month, Test Technologies will begin to market a new electronic testing device called the Model TM20. The variable costs of producing and marketing the device are $1,500 per unit, and fixed costs are $7,000,000 per year. The market research team at Test Technologies estimate demand at various prices as indicated in Illustration 8-1. Note that with a price of $6,000 per unit, the quantity demanded is only 1,000 units whereas demand increases to 19,000 units if the price is dropped to $2,500 per unit. By subtracting the variable cost of $1,500 per unit from each price we obtain the contribution margin per unit, which we multiply by the quantity demanded to estimate the total contribution margin. From the total contribution margin, we subtract fixed costs of $7,000,000 to obtain a measure of profit. In this case, the optimal price would be $3,500 per unit, because this price yields the highest total profit ($17,000,000 per year).[1]

The most difficult part of determining the profit maximizing price is determining the demand function, which is the relation between price and the quantity

[1]The approach to pricing in Illustration 8-1 is equivalent to an approach you may have learned in economics; namely, select a price such that marginal revenue equals marginal cost.

Illustration 8-1
Estimating the profit maximizing price

A	B	C	D = A − C	E = B × D	F	G = E − F
Price per unit	Quantity demanded	Variable cost per unit	Contribution margin per unit	Total contribution margin	Fixed Costs	Profit
$6,000	1,000	$1,500	$4,500	$ 4,500,000	$7,000,000	$(2,500,000)
5,500	2,000	1,500	4,000	8,000,000	7,000,000	1,000,000
5,000	4,000	1,500	3,500	14,000,000	7,000,000	7,000,000
4,500	6,000	1,500	3,000	18,000,000	7,000,000	11,000,000
4,000	9,000	1,500	2,500	22,500,000	7,000,000	15,500,000
3,500	12,000	1,500	2,000	24,000,000	7,000,000	17,000,000
3,000	15,000	1,500	1,500	22,500,000	7,000,000	15,500,000
2,500	19,000	1,500	1,000	19,000,000	7,000,000	12,000,000

demanded. While this is as much art as science, a number of approaches can be used. For example, Test Technologies could ask sales managers in various regions to estimate the quantities they can sell at various prices and then sum their responses to estimate the total quantity demanded at various prices. Or the company could test-market the product with a number of potential customers and experiment with various prices. From this experience, the company would extrapolate to the entire market for the product. Still, it must be admitted that estimating the demand function is quite challenging and that's why some companies turn to a more simple approach—cost-plus pricing which we discuss later in the chapter. Now let's turn to the pricing of special orders and return to a concept we've stressed throughout the book—incremental analysis.

PRICING SPECIAL ORDERS

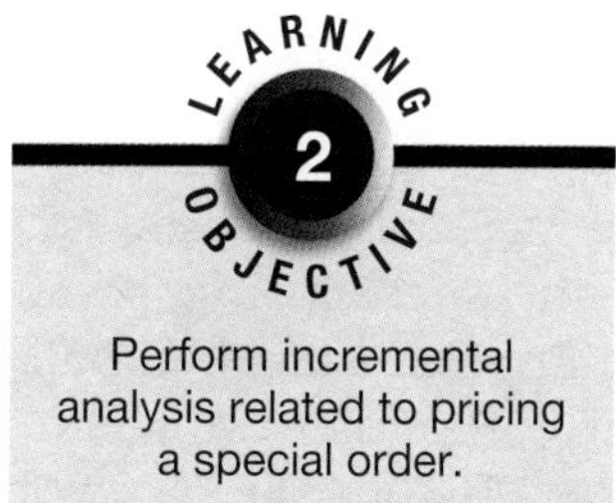

Perform incremental analysis related to pricing a special order.

In general, products are not sold for a price less than their full cost. In some circumstances, however, it may be beneficial to charge a lower price. This is often the case when companies are faced with special orders from customers. If granting a price below full cost for a special order will not affect demand for its other products, a company may actually be better off charging a price below full cost.

Decision Making/ Incremental Analysis

Consider a situation faced by Premier Lens Company, which manufactures camera lenses. Its lenses are sold through camera shops with a variety of mounting adapters to fit most popular 35-millimeter digital cameras. Recently, Blix Camera Company has asked Premier to produce 20,000 lenses for their compact 35-millimeter digital camera. The lens is identical to the Model A lens that Premier currently sells for $85. However, the model to be produced will substitute the Blix name for the Premier name stamped on the lens.

In the past year, Premier sold 280,000 units of the Model A. However, the company has been operating at only 75 percent of practical capacity and can easily accommodate production of the 20,000 additional units. The standard cost of producing the Model A is $75.

Illustration 8-2
Incremental analysis of special lens order

Incremental revenue (20,000 × $73)		$1,460,000
Less incremental costs:		
Direct material (20,000 × $30)	$600,000	
Direct labor (20,000 × $15)	300,000	
Variable overhead (20,000 × $10)	200,000	1,100,000
Net benefit of special order		$ 360,000

Blix Camera Company has offered to buy the 20,000 lenses for $73 each. Since the total standard cost is $75, it appears that the special order should be turned down. However, the incremental analysis presented in Illustration 8-2 indicates that the special order will make a substantial contribution to company income.

Model A Standard Unit Cost	
Direct material	$30.00
Direct labor	15.00
Variable overhead	10.00
Fixed overhead	20.00
Total	$75.00

The special-order decision presents two alternatives: accept or reject the special order. Since the income from the main business is the same under both alternatives, it is *not incremental* and need not be considered in the decision. The most obvious incremental item is the revenue associated with the special order. If Premier accepts the order, its revenue will increase by $1,460,000. In addition, direct material, direct labor, and variable overhead will increase by $1,100,000 if the special order is accepted. These costs are incremental, because they will be incurred if the special order is accepted and they will not be incurred if the special order is not accepted. Since incremental revenue exceeds incremental cost by $360,000, it appears to be quite beneficial to accept the special order.

Note that in the calculation of the net benefit of accepting the special order, none of the fixed costs of production are considered to be incremental costs. This is because these costs will be incurred whether or not the special order is accepted. This assumption seems reasonable given that the Premier Lens Company has excess capacity. However, suppose the management of Premier anticipates some increase in fixed costs if the special order is accepted. By how much could fixed costs increase before acceptance of the special order would be inadvisable? As long as fixed costs increase by less than $360,000, the excess of incremental revenue over incremental cost, acceptance of the special order will increase company income.

Explain the cost-plus approach to pricing and why it is inherently circular for manufacturing firms.

COST-PLUS PRICING

Perhaps in part because of the difficulty of estimating demand functions, many companies use so-called **cost-plus pricing**. With a cost-plus approach, the company starts with an estimate of cost and adds a markup to arrive at a price that allows for a reasonable level of profit. To illustrate cost-plus pricing, suppose the Chicago Pump Company produces a variety of pumps used in the mining industry. The company has recently introduced the Model L50 pump. To produce the pump, the company must incur $1,000,000 of annual fixed costs and variable costs of $200 per unit. The company estimates that it can sell 10,000 pumps annually and marks up cost by 30 percent. In this case, as indicated in the top section of Illustration 8-3, the price will be $390 per unit, which includes total cost of $300 and markup of $90.

The obvious advantage of a cost-plus pricing approach is that it is simple to apply. Also, if a sufficient quantity can be sold at the specified price, the company will earn a reasonable profit. However, the approach also has limitations.

An obvious difficulty is choosing what markup percent to use. Is 30 percent an appropriate markup or should 10 percent, 20 percent, or 40 percent be used? Determination of an appropriate markup requires considerable judgment, and experimentation with different markups may be necessary before a final decision is reached.

Another problem is that cost-plus pricing is inherently circular for manufacturing firms.[2] You must estimate demand to determine fixed manufacturing costs per unit so that you can mark up cost to obtain a price. However, the price affects the quantity demanded; the higher the price, the lower the quantity demanded for most products. What would happen if demand for the Model L50 pump produced by Chicago Pump actually turned out to be 9,000 units? In this case, the cost per pump, as indicated in the bottom half of Illustration 8-3, would increase (because fixed costs would be spread over fewer units) and the price would be increased to $404. But what will happen to the quantity demanded when the price is increased? That's right, fewer units will be purchased, the cost per unit will go up, and the cost-plus price will be increased, resulting in lower demand! This circular process (increased price, decreased

Illustration 8-3
Cost-plus pricing for Model L50 Pump

Estimated quantity demanded in units	10,000
Total fixed costs	$1,000,000
Fixed costs per unit ($1,000,000 ÷ 10,000)	$100
Variable costs per unit	200
Total cost per unit	300
Markup at 30%	90
Price	$390
Suppose the actual quantity demanded is less (say 9,000 units)	9,000
Total fixed costs	$1,000,000
Fixed costs per unit ($1,000,000 ÷ 9,000)	$111
Variable costs per unit	200
Total cost per unit	311
Markup at 30%	93
Price	$404

[2]Cost-plus pricing is not inherently circular for retail firms. Such firms typically mark-up the cost of merchandise from supplies which is a variable cost. They do not mark-up fixed cost per unit which would require an estimate of the quantity demanded *before* setting price.

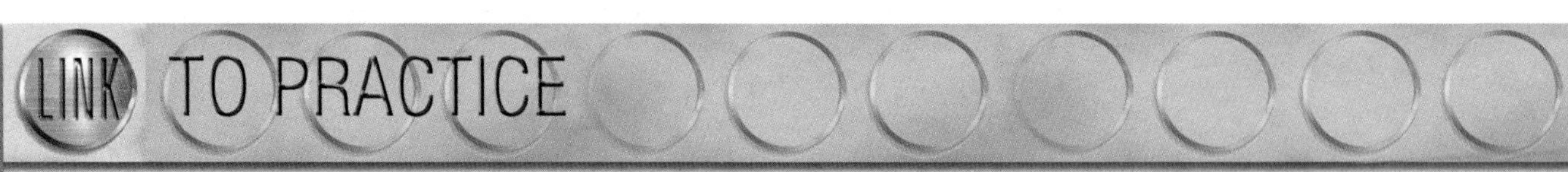

Insull's Most Radical Innovation Wasn't Technology—It Was Pricing!

Samuel Insull was Thomas Edison's right-hand business partner, taking care of financing, operations, hirings, firings and mergers. In 1892, he left Edison's employ and became the president of a small electricity producer. The problem for the company back then, as it is for many companies today, was the mismatch between capacity and spikes in demand during peak usage hours. Insull solved that problem by charging different rates to consumers to boost demand when it tended to be slow, primarily evenings when companies were shut down for the night. It was obvious that Insull was charging consumers less than the average cost per kilowatt hour. But Insull knew that he was building demand and that the fixed cost per hour would drop, making huge power stations feasible and profitable.

Sir Harold Evans, the author of *They Made America* (Little, Brown and Company, 2004), refers to this action as "the single most significant innovation in the single most important technological advance of the 20th century." By 1898 Insull had bought out all the power generators in downtown Chicago and 15 years later his company, by then known as Commonwealth Edison, had become the dominant energy company in the Midwest.

Source: Nicholas G. Carr, "Suits to the Rescue," *Strategy+Business* (Spring 2005), pp. 26–29.

demand, increased cost per unit, increased price) is obviously not a strategy used by successful companies!

Explain the target costing process for a new product.

TARGET COSTING

Manufacturing companies are always searching for ways to cut costs. Unfortunately, once a new product is designed (the product's features are specified, detailed engineering plans are made, and manufacturing of the product is ready to commence) it is very difficult to make changes that will reduce costs. In fact, it is commonly accepted that 80 percent of a product's costs cannot be reduced once it is designed. The primary reason for this state of affairs is that product features drive costs. Consider the case of KC Home Appliances. The company is bringing a new coffeemaker to market designed with an automatic burr grinder, a water filter, and a stainless steel carafe that keeps coffee warm for six hours. These features will largely determine the cost of manufacturing the coffee pot and it will be very difficult to reduce them once the coffee pot is being produced. Indeed, costs related to purchases of equipment to produce the grinders, the filters, and the carafes are sunk costs and cannot be changed.

To confront this difficulty, a number of companies have turned to **target costing**, which is an integrated approach to determining product features, product price, product cost, and product design that helps ensure a company will

Illustration 8-4
The target costing process

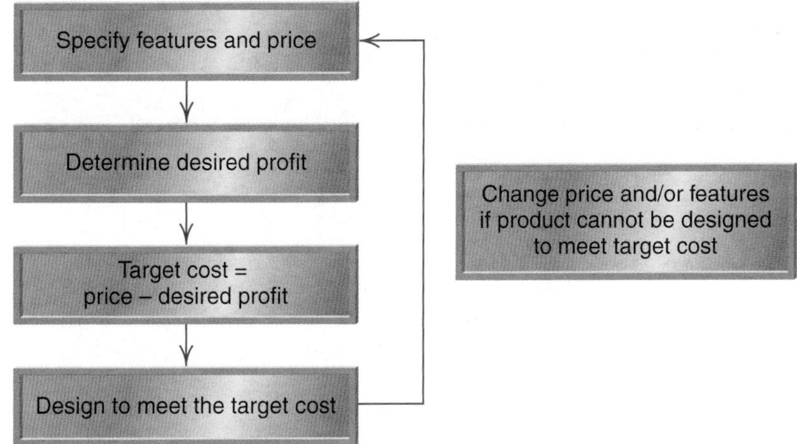

earn a reasonable profit on new products. The target costing process is presented in Illustration 8-4. The process begins with a careful analysis of competing products and customer needs and wants. This leads to a specification of product features and a price that the company believes will be attractive to customers given the product features. Suppose KC Home Appliances determines that, given the features of its new coffee maker, it can sell 50,000 units per year at $200 each. The second step in the target costing process is to specify a desired level of profit. Suppose that KC wants a profit margin of 30 percent or, alternatively, a profit of $60. The price and the desired profit determine the target cost, which is $140 (see Illustration 8-5). Finally, the product engineering department, working with substantial input from the cost accounting department, develops a detailed design for a product that can be produced for $140 or less. If

Target Costing Seminars Help Companies Join the Target Costing Bandwagon

A number of organizations help companies learn about cutting-edge techniques by sponsoring conferences. In 2004, The Management Roundtable sponsored a seminar titled "Lean By Design: Front End Techniques for Better, Faster, Cheaper Products." Interestingly, several of the sessions focused on Target Costing.

For example, Jay Mortensen, Director of Target Costing and Cost Engineering at Maytag, presented a case study on the tactics and techniques for applying Target Costing in the product development process. And Tami Caperauld, Leader of the Market-Driven Target Costing Implementation Group at Boeing Commercial Airplanes and Dr. Shahid Ansari, an accounting professor at California State Northridge, talked about best practices developed by the Consortium for Advanced Manufacturing—International (better known as CAM—I).

Illustration 8-5
Target cost of KC Home Appliance's new coffeemaker

Quantity demanded given features	50,000 units
Price given features	$200
Required profit margin per unit (30% × $200)	60
Target cost	$140

the product cannot be produced for $140 per unit, then the company will reconsider features and price. For example, the company may decide to slightly lower its price and go with a plastic carafe as opposed to a more expensive stainless steel carafe.

Companies using target costing often set up cross-functional product development teams, including staff from engineering, marketing, and cost accounting. This helps ensure good communication among the parties involved in the product development/pricing process.

Analyze customer profitability.

ANALYZING CUSTOMER PROFITABILITY: Revisiting the Wholesale Office Supply Case

Recall that in the chapter opener, Nancy Sanchez, vice president of Wholesale Office Supply, wanted to know the profitability of various customers as a basis for setting prices and targeting marketing campaigns. To accomplish her objective, she needs a **customer profitability measurement (CPM) system**. With a CPM system, the indirect costs of servicing customers (including the cost of processing orders, the cost of handling returns, the cost of shipments, etc.) are assigned to cost pools. Using cost drivers, these costs are then allocated to specific customers. Subtracting these costs and product costs from customer revenue yields a measure of customer profitability. A graphical presentation of CPM is presented in Illustration 8-6.

Illustration 8-6
Graphical presentation of customer profitability measurement

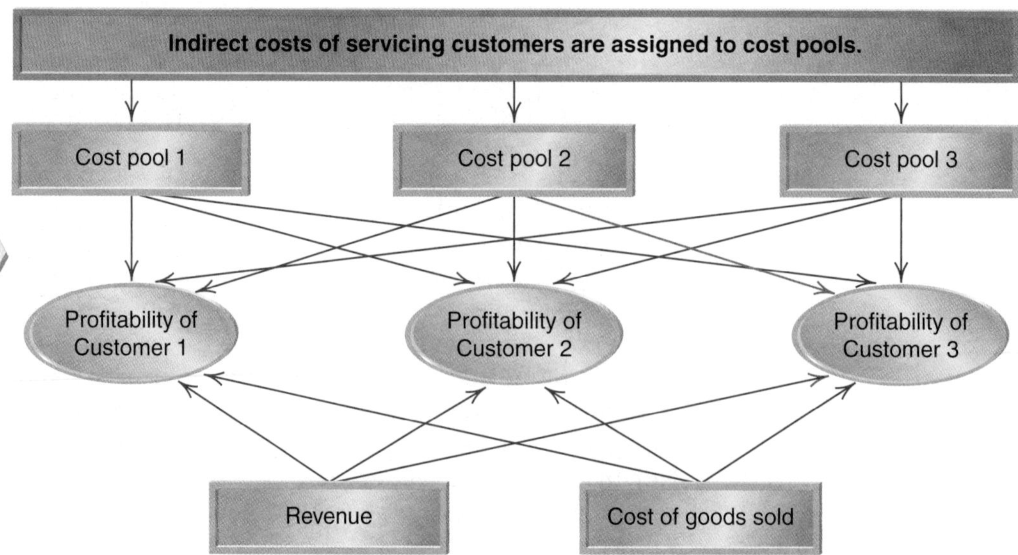

Illustration 8-7
Cost pools and drivers for indirect costs to service customers at Wholesale Office Supplies

Cost pools	Annual Cost	Cost driver	Annual driver quantity	Allocation rate
Cost pool related to processing Internet orders	$ 434,400	Number of Internet orders	362,000	$1.20
Cost pool related to processing orders received via phone, fax, or mail	576,000	Number of fax/phone/ mail orders	128,000	$4.50
Cost pool related to picking orders from stock in the warehouse	7,200,000	Number of line items in orders	8,000,000	$0.90
Cost pool related to shipping	720,000	Miles to customer location	2,000,000	$0.36
Cost pool related to packing orders	6,000,000	Weight of order	15,000,000	$0.40
Cost pool related to processing returns	52,000	Number of items returned	65,000	$0.80
	$14,982,400			

You probably notice a connection between activity-based costing (ABC) presented in Chapter 6 and CPM. In Chapter 6, we used ABC to allocate costs to products and services. In this section, we're going to use ABC to allocate costs to customers so that we can determine the full cost of serving them. To facilitate our discussion of customer profitability measurement, we will consider the situation facing Nancy Sanchez at Wholesale Office Supply. Assuming her company has a reasonably sophisticated computerized information system, it can easily trace sales revenue and cost of goods sold to individual customers. The challenging task will be to trace the indirect costs of serving customers to individual customers.[3]

Suppose the team that investigated CPM at Wholesale Office Supplies determined the cost pools and cost drivers indicated in Illustration 8-7. In total, indirect costs amount to $14,982,400 per year. The first two cost pools relate to the costs of processing Internet orders versus orders placed by phone, fax, or mail. Note that the cost per Internet order is substantially less ($1.20 per order versus $4.50 per order). The next cost pool relates to the costs incurred in picking orders from stock in the warehouse. More time is spent as the number of different items in the order increases since different items are stored in different locations in the warehouse, and each line on an order form relates to a specific item. Thus, the cost driver is the number of line items in an order. The final three cost pools relate to shipping and packing orders and processing returned merchandise.

---

[3]See L. Brem and V. G. Narayanan, "Owens and Minor (A) and (B)," *Harvard Business School Cases* (2000) for a description of customer profitability measurement at the company Owens and Minor. These cases also discuss an activity-based pricing system that we will cover at the end of this chapter.

Illustration 8-8
Customer profitability analysis for two customers

Customer 1		
Revenue		$740,000.00
Less cost of goods sold		666,000.00
Gross margin		74,000.00
Less indirect costs:		
165 Internet orders × $1.20	$ 198.00	
20 fax orders × $4.50	90.00	
2,500 line items × $0.90	2,250.00	
1,200 miles × $0.36	432.00	
900 pounds × $.40	360.00	
210 items returned × $0.80	168.00	3,498.00
Customer profit		$ 70,502.00
Profit as a percent of sales		9.53%
Customer 2		
Revenue		$735,000.00
Less cost of goods sold		661,500.00
Gross margin		73,500.00
Less indirect costs:		
0 Internet orders × $1.20	$ -0-	
320 fax orders × $4.50	1,440.00	
5,100 line items × $0.90	4,590.00	
3,300 miles × $0.36	1,188.00	
870 pounds × $0.40	348.00	
910 items returned × $0.80	728.00	8,294,00
Customer profit		$ 65,206.00
Profit as a percent of sales		8.87%

The next step in the customer profitability analysis is to apply the indirect costs to specific customers. Consider the two customers analyzed in Illustration 8-8. Although Customers 1 and 2 have about the same level of sales, Customer 2 imposes more than twice as much indirect costs on Wholesale Office Supplies ($8,658 for Customer 2 versus $3,498 for Customer 1). This results because Customer 2 places more orders and uses the more costly fax method rather than the Internet. Customer 2 also orders a greater variety of items (indicated by its 5,100 line items), which leads to higher order-picking costs. Finally, more miles are traveled to deliver orders for Customer 2, and Customer 2 returns more merchandise.

Wholesale Office Supplies could perform the same analysis for all of its customers and then sort them into groups based on their relative profitability. The most profitable customers may receive special treatment (e.g., occasional calls/visits from the president of Wholesale Office Supplies, special discounts or promotions, etc.) to ensure their continued business. The company may also study the characteristics of the most profitable companies in an effort to gain a better understanding of how to expand business to similar customers. With respect to the least profitable customers, the company may increase prices, try to move them to less costly service (e.g., require that they place orders over the Internet ordering system), or even drop them.

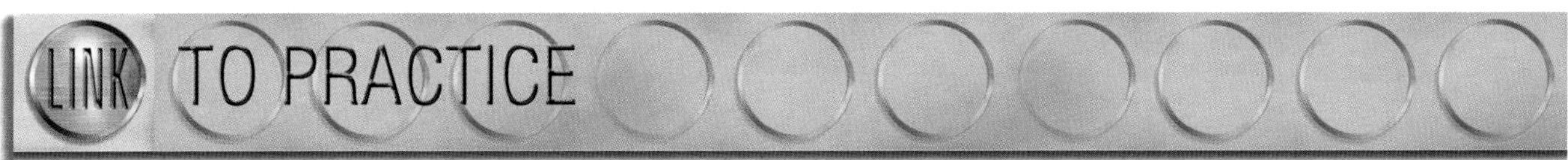

Customers Requiring "Display-Ready" Pallets Can Hurt Profitability

Some manufacturers have begun providing retail customers with goods already packed in display cases that are stacked on custom tiered pallets with special custom promotional signage. This is obviously desirable from the retailer's standpoint if the service doesn't lead to additional charges, since it shifts costs previously incurred by the retailer to the manufacturer. From the manufacturer's standpoint, the service requires additional labor and materials and may turn once profitable customers into customers who are a drag on profit. A specific problem is that some manufacturers are shipping almost all pallets as display-ready when only 20-40 percent end up being used by the retailer as configured.

One company that was delivering branded food products found, through customer profitability analysis, that it was losing over $1.1 million per year from just one customer because it was providing the customer with display-ready shipments 100 percent of the time. The customer, however, used the cases only 30 percent of the time. The company solved the problem by convincing the company to order display-ready on an as-needed basis.

Source: Marc Shingles, "How to Find—and Take Advantage of—Your Profitable Customers," *Darwin* (July 2003). www.darwinmag.com.

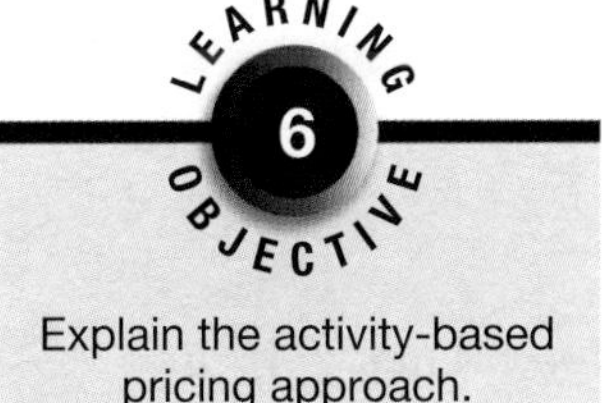

Explain the activity-based pricing approach.

ACTIVITY-BASED PRICING

The same type of information used to analyze customer profitability can form the basis for an activity-based pricing system. Essentially, **activity-based pricing** is an approach to pricing in which customers are presented with separate prices for services they request in addition to the cost of goods they purchase. This causes customers to carefully consider the services they request and may lead them to impose less cost on their suppliers. Some companies refer to activity-based pricing as menu-based pricing since customers are presented with a menu of prices related to the various services they request in addition to the products they purchase.

Let's see how an activity-based pricing system might work at Wholesale Office Supplies. Suppose that, based on the study of indirect costs presented in Illustration 8-7, the company set the prices for services indicated in Illustration 8-9. As

Illustration 8-9
Activity-based pricing for indirect cost at Wholesale Office Supplies

Charge for Internet orders	$1.25
Charge for phone, fax, or mail orders	$4.75
Charge per line item in an order	$1.00
Delivery charge per mile	$0.40
Packing charge per pound	$0.50
Per item restocking charge for returned merchandise	$1.00

you can see, the company proposes to charge customers $1.25 for every order placed via the Internet whereas phone, fax, or mail orders are priced at $4.75 per order. Each line item in an order is associated with picking an item from the warehouse and the company charges $1 for this activity. Delivery charges are $0.40 per mile ($0.04 higher than cost), packing is $0.50 per pound ($0.10 higher than cost), and the company charges $1 to restock a returned item ($0.20 higher than cost).

Some customers might object to this pricing scheme by arguing that the price they pay for the goods they purchase should cover these costs. There are a number of ways to deal with this resistance. The company could lower its prices for goods (at least slightly) and then encourage customers to make fewer but larger purchases to reduce their overall costs. Customers could also be encouraged to limit the variety of goods they purchase, since variety leads to separate line items on order forms and higher cost (e.g., does the customer really need 10 different pens in four different colors?). Alternatively, the company might decide to just use the activity-based pricing approach for its less profitable customers. Then, the most profitable customers, who are still paying just for the goods they purchase, will perceive that they are getting a "break" because they are valued customers. And the least profitable customers will be paying for the extra costs they impose on the company.

MAKING BUSINESS DECISIONS

When making a pricing decision, don't get overly focused on the current cost per unit. The quantity demanded is affected by the price and this quantity changes the cost per unit because fixed costs are spread out over more or less units.

Ideally, you want to determine the price that maximizes profit. The profit maximizing approach we learned in this chapter can be difficult to implement because of difficulty in estimating the relation between the quantity demanded and price. However, at a minimum, it provides a useful framework for thinking about pricing decisions since it takes into account price, demand, variable costs, and fixed costs.

KNOWLEDGE AND SKILLS (K/S) CHECKLIST

Knowledge and skills are needed to make good business decisions. Check off the knowledge and skills you've acquired from reading this chapter.

- ❐ K/S 1. You have an expanded business vocabulary (see key terms).
- ❐ K/S 2. You can compute the profit maximizing price for a product or service.
- ❐ K/S 3. You can explain the target costing process.
- ❐ K/S 4. You can perform customer profitability measurement.
- ❐ K/S 5. You can explain how activity-based pricing will impact the costs customers impose on suppliers.

SUMMARY OF LEARNING OBJECTIVES

1 ***Compute the profit maximizing price for a product or service.*** The first step in computing the profit maximizing price is to estimate the quantity demanded at various prices. Then, variable costs are subtracted from price to determine the contribution margin per unit. From the total contribution margin, subtract fixed costs to determine profit. The price that yields the highest profit is the profit maximizing price.

2 ***Perform incremental analysis related to pricing a special order.*** Special orders will yield an incremental profit as long as the selling price exceeds the incremental cost of filling the order. Fixed costs that are not affected by the special order are irrelevant to the decision as to whether the order should be taken.

3 ***Explain the cost-plus approach to pricing and why it is inherently circular for manufacturing firms.*** In cost-plus pricing, the full cost per unit is determined and price is set by adding a prespecified markup to the cost. This process is circular for manufacturing firms in that the quantity demanded, which is needed to estimate full cost per unit, is determined prior to setting the price, which has a major impact on the quantity demanded.

4 ***Explain the target costing process for a new product.*** Using target costing, companies analyze the marketplace and decide on a set of features and a price point for their product. They subtract a desired profit level from the price to solve for the target cost. The product is then designed to meet the target cost when it is produced. If the target cost cannot be achieved, the company may reconsider the set of features and the price or decide not to go ahead with the product.

5 ***Analyze customer profitability.*** The profitability of a customer depends not just on what is purchased, but also on the set of services provided to the customer (e.g., order processing, shipping, handling returns, etc.). To analyze the profitability of a customer, the cost of such services must be subtracted from the customer's gross margin. This requires that service costs be grouped into cost pools and related cost drivers must be identified so that the cost per unit of service can be allocated to specific customers.

6 ***Explain the activity-based pricing approach.*** In activity-based pricing, customers are presented with a menu of prices and are charged for *services* provided to them (in addition to being charged for the goods they purchase). The charge for such services is usually determined based on an analysis of their cost. Since they are charged for specific services, customers will carefully consider the services they request and may end up imposing less cost on suppliers.

REVIEW PROBLEM

Heartland Tools is a large Midwest company that designs and manufactures dies, jigs, fixtures, roll-form tooling, and special machines. Equipment used by the company includes milling machines, HeliArc welders, drill presses, hydraulic presses, and heat treatment ovens. Due to intense competition from foreign companies, the firm currently has substantial excess capacity, and in the prior year, the company laid off 545 employees.

To price its product, the company estimates design and product costs and marks the total up by 40 percent to cover administrative and marketing costs and to earn a profit. Product costs include material, labor, depreciation of equipment, and other overhead. The costs in the "other overhead" cost pool are primarily fixed costs.

Costs are estimated as follows:

1. Design costs	Based on estimated engineering hours times a rate of $40 per hour.
2. Material	Estimate of the actual cost of materials.
3. Labor	Estimate of actual direct labor costs (estimate of actual hours multiplied by the wage rate of employees likely to be assigned to the job).
4. Depreciation of manufacturing equipment	Based on predetermined overhead rates for each type of equipment. For each type of equipment, the company divides estimated annual depreciation by estimated annual hours of use.

Equipment type	Annual depreciation	Annual hours of use
Milling	$6,000,000	4,000
Welding	$2,000,000	8,000
Drill press	$1,000,000	5,000
Hydraulic press	$4,000,000	4,000
Heat treatment	$5,000,000	4,000

5. Other manufacturing overhead (i.e., other than depreciation) — Estimated as $50 per direct labor hour.

The company is currently pricing a job for Preston Manufacturing. A preliminary bid form indicates the following:

Preliminary/incomplete cost estimate and bid for Preston Manufacturing

Material		$25,000
Direct labor	28 hours × $25	$ 700
	15 hours × $18	$ 270
	25 hours × $30	$ 750
Design time	18 hours	
Milling time	9.0 hours	
Welding time	5.0 hour	
Drill press time	7.0 hours	
Hydraulic press time	6.5 hours	
Heat treat time	2.0 hours	
Other overhead		______
Estimated total cost		______
Mark up at 40%		______
Bid		______

Required

a. Estimate total cost and the bid price with the 40 percent mark up.
b. Preston has told Heartland that it will use another supplier if Heartland's bid is over $50,000. Heartland's CFO strongly objects to a $50,000 price since it will not even cover full costs. Evaluate the CFO's position. Should the company price the job at $50,000?

Answer

a. **Cost-Plus Price for Preston Manufacturing**

Material			$25,000
Direct labor	28 hours × $25	$ 700	
	15 hours × $18	270	
	25 hours × $30	750	1,720
Design time	18 hours × $40		720
Milling time	9.0 hours × $1,500	13,500	
Welding time	5.0 hour × $250	1,250	
Drill press time	7.0 hours × $200	1,400	
Hydraulic press time	6.5 hours × $1,000	6,500	
Heat treatment time	2.0 hours × $1,250	2,500	25,150
Other overhead	68 direct labor hours × $50		3,400
Estimated total cost			$55,990
Mark up at 40%			22,396
Bid			$78,386

Equipment type	Annual depreciation	Annual hours of use	Overhead rate
Milling	$6,000,000	4,000	$1,500
Welding	$2,000,000	8,000	$ 250
Drill press	$1,000,000	5,000	$ 200
Hydraulic press	$4,000,000	4,000	$1,000
Heat treatment	$5,000,000	4,000	$1,250

b. It appears that the only costs that are likely to be incremental are those related to design, material, and labor. Assuming this is the case, the company will generate an incremental profit of $22,560 at a price of $50,000. Given the company is operating below capacity (and assuming this "low" price does not negatively impact future prices to Preston or other customers), charging $50,000 for the job is a good decision.

Incremental revenue		$50,000
Incremental costs		
Design costs	$ 720	
Material	25,000	
Labor	1,720	27,440
Incremental profit		$22,560

KEY TERMS

Activity-based pricing (311)
Cost-plus pricing (304)
Customer profitability measurement (CPM) system (308)
Target costing (306)

SELF ASSESSMENT *(Answers Below)*

1. To determine the profit-maximizing price, a manager must:
   a. Estimate the quantity demanded for various prices.
   b. Estimate variable costs.
   c. Both a and b are correct.
   d. None of the above is correct.

2. Cost-plus pricing:
   a. Leads to profit maximization.
   b. Is inherently circular for manufacturing firms.
   c. Is difficult to perform.
   d. None of the above is correct.

3. Target costing:
   a. Requires specification of desired level of profit.
   b. Targets specific costs for reduction.
   c. Is used primarily with products that are already in production.
   d. Leads to profit maximization.

4. Customer profitability is measured as:
   a. Revenue − cost of goods sold.
   b. Revenue − indirect manufacturing costs.
   c. Revenue − cost of goods sold − indirect service costs.
   d. Revenue − cost of goods sold − indirect manufacturing costs.

5. With activity-based pricing:
   a. Customers face a menu of prices for various services.
   b. Customers are encouraged to consider the costs they impose on a supplier.
   c. Customers may be charged less if they request less product variety in their orders.
   d. All of the above are correct.

6. The formula for target cost is:
   a. Price − desired profit.
   b. Desired profit ÷ price.

c. Absorption cost × profit percentage.
d. Desired profit − absorption cost.

7. Typically, which departments are involved in setting target costs?
a. Engineering.
b. Marketing.
c. Cost accounting.
d. All of the above.

8. Which of the following is an advantage of cost-plus pricing?
a. The selection of a markup percent is easily done.
b. The method is simple to apply.
c. The cost-plus pricing method is inherently circular.
d. All of the above are advantages to the cost-plus pricing method.

9. When is it beneficial for companies to accept an order that is priced at less than the product's full cost?
a. When the company is operating at capacity.
b. When incremental revenue exceeds more incremental cost.
c. It is always advantageous to have higher sales.
d. It is never beneficial to accept an order that is priced below full cost.

10. "Cost-plus" pricing includes which of the following costs?
a. Manufacturing costs.
b. Selling costs.
c. Administrative costs.
d. All of the above costs are included in cost-plus pricing.

Answers to Self Assessment

1. c; **2.** b; **3.** a; **4.** c; **5.** d.; **6.** a.; **7.** d.; **8.** b.; **9.** b.; **10.** a.

INTERACTIVE LEARNING

Enhance and test your knowledge of Chapter 8 using Wiley's online resources.

1. Learning Objectives
2. Multiple Choice
3. Language of Business—Matching of Key Terms
4. Critical Thinking
5. Demonstration—Target costing
6. Case—*Nelson Plumbing Products*; Determine the profit maximizing price

Go to our dynamic Web site for more self-assessment, Web links, and additional information.

QUESTIONS

1. According to economic theory, how would a manager determine the profit-maximizing price for a product or service?
2. Why is cost-plus pricing inherently circular for a manufacturing firm?
3. To implement target costing for a new product, companies often set up a cross-functional team with members from engineering, marketing, and cost accounting. Why is a cross-functional team desirable when implementing the target costing approach?
4. How is cost allocation used in customer profitability analysis?
5. Explain why less profitable customers may become more profitable if a supplier switches to activity-based pricing.
6. Explain the target costing process. How is it calculated?
7. Explain how the profit-maximizing price is calculated. Why is the profit-maximizing price extremely difficult to calculate for an actual product?

8. What is a "special order"? What does whether a company is operating at capacity or has excess capacity matter in deciding whether to accept the special order or not?

9. What are the disadvantages of the cost-plus approach to pricing?

10. What is the lowest per-unit price on a special order that a company could accept and still not show a loss from the special order?

EXERCISES

EXERCISE 8-1. Group Assignment Consider a company that manufactures and sells personal computers (let's call the company Bell Computers). Recently the company lowered its prices dramatically. The company is very efficient and needs only five days of inventory, collects its receivables within 30 days, and has suppliers who are willing to wait 59 days for payment. A competitor commenting on the aggressive pricing stated that "We're in a commodity business and a price war in a commodity business is really dumb."

Required
Discuss the competitor's comment that lowering prices is a dumb move by Bell Computers.

EXERCISE 8-2. Writing Assignment Brindle Corporation is considering an initiative to assess customer profitability. The company's CFO, John Bradley, stated his position as follows: "I strongly suspect that some of our customers are losers—in other words, they're not covering product costs and service costs. Think about our Weston account. Weston places a ton of small orders and they're always asking us to expedite them. Then our accounting department has to follow up because Weston misplaces billing records, which really slows down their payments. We're going to make a $1,000,000 investment in CRM (customer relationship management) software to help us assess customer profitability, but I'm confident that the investment will really pay off when it helps us identify this type of loser customer."

The position of the company's marketing vice president, Jerry Brown, is quite different. "This $1,000,000 investment is a waste of money. We'll go through the exercise and find out that some customers are more profitable than others, but we're not going to change a thing. Even the less profitable customers make a contribution to covering overhead and we're not going to drop a single one."

Required
Write one or two paragraphs elaborating on the arguments of the CFO and the marketing vice president. In your discussion, consider the fact that the bonus compensation of the marketing VP is based on sales volume. Could this be influencing Jerry's position?

EXERCISE 8-3. Internet Assignment Go to the Web and search for information on how customer relationship management (CRM) software is used to assess customer profitability. What is the relationship between the process used in profitability assessment and activity-based costing?

EXERCISE 8-4. Profit-maximizing price The editor of *Spunk Magazine* is considering three alternative prices for her new monthly periodical. Her estimate of price and quantity demanded are:

Price	Quantity Demanded
$6.95	20,000
$5.95	25,000
$4.95	32,000

Monthly costs of producing and delivering the magazine include $80,000 of fixed costs and variable costs of $1.50 per issue.

Required
Which price will yield the largest monthly profit?

EXERCISE 8-5. Profit-maximizing price Erin Hamill is the owner/operator of a tanning salon. She is considering four price levels for a weekly tanning pass. Her estimate of price and quantity demanded are:

Price	Quantity Demanded
$11.00	320
$10.00	365
$ 9.00	385
$ 8.00	420

Monthly costs of providing the tanning service include $1,200 of fixed costs and variable costs of $2.00 per service.

Required
Which price will yield the largest monthly profit?

EXERCISE 8-6. Analyzing a Special Order PowerDrive, Inc. produces a hard disk drive that sells for $140 per unit. The cost of producing 20,000 drives in the prior year was:

Direct material	$ 500,000
Direct labor	300,000
Variable overhead	100,000
Fixed overhead	1,200,000
Total cost	$2,100,000

At the start of the current year, the company received an order for 2,000 drives from a computer company in China. Management of PowerDrive has mixed feelings about the order. On the one hand they welcome the order because they currently have excess capacity. Also, this is the company's first international order. On the other hand, the company in China is only willing to pay $100 per unit.

Required
What will be the effect on profit of accepting the order?

EXERCISE 8-7. Analyzing a Special Order Budget Tax Service, Inc., prepares tax returns for small businesses. The cost of preparing 725 tax returns in the prior year was:

Direct labor	$326,250
Variable overhead	271,875
Fixed overhead	275,000
Total cost	$873,125

At the start of the current year, the company received an offer from Advantage Business, a firm that provides bundled services to businesses. Advantage wants Budget Tax Service to prepare tax returns for its 120 small business clients. Budget Tax Service has the capacity to prepare up to 900 returns in a given year, so this special order would not take away revenue from any of Budget Tax Service's current clients. Advantage is willing to pay $925 per tax return.

Required
What will be the effect on Budget Tax Service's profit if they agree to prepare returns for the 120 clients of Advantage Business?

EXERCISE 8-8. Analyzing a Special Order; Service Company Flamingos To Go is a service company owned by Irvin Vonnet that will "plant" plastic flamingos on a special day in people's yards to help celebrate and advertise birthdays, births, anniversaries and other important milestones. The average delivery is priced at $60. The costs of providing 785 deliveries in the past year were:

Direct labor	$11,775
Variable overhead	7,850
Fixed overhead (advertising costs, phone service, insurance)	16,000
Total cost	$35,625

At the start of the current year, Irv received a phone call from the local rotary club. The club would like to contract with Flamingos To Go to have flamingos delivered to the yards of each of their members in the upcoming year; this contract would provide an additional 120 deliveries for Flamingos To Go. However, the Rotary club wants a special price since they are ordering a large number of deliveries; they have told Irv that they would like a price of $50 per delivery. Flamingos To Go can make up to 1,000 deliveries per year without incurring additional fixed costs.

Required

What will be the affect on profit if Irv accepts the special order?

EXERCISE 8-9. Cost-Plus Pricing World View is considering production of a lighted world globe that the company would price at a markup of 20 percent above full cost. Management estimates that the variable cost of the globe will be $50 per unit and fixed costs per year will be $100,000.

Required

a. Assuming sales of 1,000 units, what is the full cost of a globe and what is the price with a 20 percent markup?

b. Assume that the quantity demanded at the price calculated in part a is only 500 units. What is the full cost of the globe and what is the price with a 20 percent markup?

c. Is the company likely to sell 500 units at the price calculated in part b?

EXERCISE 8-10. Cost-Plus Pricing The chief engineer at Future Tech has proposed production of a high-tech portable electronic storage device to be sold at a 40 percent markup above its full cost. Management estimates that the fixed costs per year will be $240,000 and the variable cost of the storage device will be $12 per unit.

Required

a. Assuming sales of 50,000 units, what is the full cost of a storage device and what is the price with a 40 percent markup?

b. Assume that the quantity demanded at the price calculated in part a is only 30,000 units. What is the full cost of the storage device and what is the price with a 40 percent markup?

c. Compare the selling prices computed in parts a and b above; does the selling price increase, decrease, or stay the same when the number of units produced and sold decreases? Why does this change occur?

EXERCISE 8-11. Target costing Go to the Web and search for information on how companies are implementing target costing. Find an example of how target costing has actually been used at a company and summarize that company's experience in a few paragraphs.

EXERCISE 8-12. Target costing A cross-functional team at Mazzor Systems is developing a new product using the target costing methodology. Product features in comparison to competing products suggest a price of $2,000 per unit. The company requires a profit of 20 percent of selling price.

Required

a. What is the target cost per unit?

b. Suppose the engineering and cost accounting members of the team determine that the product cannot be produced for the cost calculated in part a. What is the next step in the target costing process?

EXERCISE 8-13. Target costing A new product is being designed by an engineering team at Odin Security. Several managers and employees from the cost accounting department and the marketing department are also on the team to evaluate the product and determine the cost using a target costing methodology. An analysis of similar products on the market suggests a price of $150 per unit. The company requires a profit of 40 percent of selling price.

Required

a. What is the target cost per unit?

b. The members of the team subsequently determine that the product cannot be produced for the cost calculated in Part a. What is the next step in the target costing process? Does the new product get eliminated from consideration now?

EXERCISE 8-14. Target costing The product design team at New Time Products is in the process of designing a new clock using target costing. Product features in comparison to competing products suggest a price of $27 per unit. The company requires a profit of 25 percent of selling price.

Required

a. What is the target cost per clock?

b. Suppose it appears that the clocks cannot be manufactured for the target cost. What are some of the options that the company should consider?

EXERCISE 8-15. Customer Profitability Analysis Delta Products has determined the following costs:

Order processing (per order)	$ 5.00
Additional handling costs if order marked rush (per order)	8.50
Customer service calls (per call)	10.00
Relationship management costs (per customer per year)	$2,000.00

In addition to these costs, product costs amount to 90 percent of sales.
In the prior year, Delta had the following experience with one of its customers, Johnson Brands:

Sales	$53,800
Number of orders	200
Percent of orders marked rush	60
Calls to customer service	140

Required
Calculate the profitability of the Johnson Brands account.

EXERCISE 8-16. Activity-Based Pricing Refer to the information in Exercise 15. For the coming year, Delta Products has told Johnson Brands that it will be switched to an activity-based pricing system or it will be dropped as a customer. In addition to regular prices, Johnson will be required to pay:

Order processing (per order)	$ 6
Additional handling costs if order marked rush (per order)	10
Customer service calls (per call)	15

Required

a. Calculate the profitability of the Johnson Brands account if activity is the same as in the prior year.

b. Assume that Johnson Brands decides to accept the activity-based pricing system offered by Delta Products. What changes will likely be made by Johnson?

EXERCISE 8-17. Customer Profitability Analysis Triumph Corporation has analyzed their customer and order handling data for the past year and has determined the following costs:

Order processing cost per order	$ 7
Additional costs if order must be expedited (rushed)	$ 8
Customer technical support calls (per call)	$ 12
Relationship management costs (per customer per year)	$1,200

In addition to these costs, product costs amount to 75 percent of sales.
In the prior year, Triumph had the following experience with one of its customers, Julius Company:

Sales	$15,000
Number of orders	160
Percent of orders marked rush	70
Calls to technical support	80

Required
Calculate the profitability of the Julius Company account.

EXERCISE 8-18. Activity-Based Pricing Refer to the information in Exercise 17. For the coming year, Triumph Corporation has told Julius Company that it will be switched to an activity-based pricing system or it will be dropped as a customer. In addition to regular prices, Julius will be required to pay:

Order processing (per order)	$10
Additional handling costs if order marked rush (per order)	$18
Technical support calls (per call)	$20

Required

a. Calculate the profitability of the Julius Company account if activity is the same as in the prior year.

b. Is it realistic to expect Julius Company's activity to be the same this year as the previous year if activity-based pricing is instituted? How might Julius Company react to the new pricing scheme? How might their order behavior change as a result of the new fees?

PROBLEMS

PROBLEM 8-1. Determining the Profit-Maximizing Price Spencer Electronics has just developed a low-end electronic calendar that it plans on selling via a cable channel marketing program. The cable program's fee for selling the item is 15 percent of revenue. For this fee, the program will sell the calendar over six 10-minute segments in September.

Spencer's fixed costs of producing the calendar are $120,000 per production run. The company plans to wait for all orders to come in, and then it will produce exactly the number of units ordered. Production time will be less than three weeks. Variable production costs are $20 per unit. In addition, it will cost approximately $6 per unit to ship the calendars to customers.

Marsha Andersen, a product manager at Spencer, is charged with recommending a price for the item. Based on her experience with similar items, focus group responses, and survey information, she has estimated the number of units that can be sold at various prices:

Price	Quantity
\$69.99	10,000
\$59.99	15,000
\$49.99	25,000
\$39.99	40,000
\$29.99	60,000

Required

a. Calculate expected profit for each price.

b. Which price maximizes company profit?

PROBLEM 8-2. Determining the Profit Maximizing Price Elite Kitchenware has come out with a new line of dishes that it plans to test market through a series of demonstrations at the local mall throughout the month of August. If the demonstrations result in enough sales, then the program will be expanded to other malls in the region. The cost of the demonstrations is a flat fee of \$1,000 to the mall owner/operator and a commission of 25 percent of revenue to the person giving the demonstrations (the demonstrator will not receive any salary beyond this commission).

Elite Kitchenware's fixed costs of producing the dishes are \$5,000 per production run. The company plans to wait for all orders to come in, and then it will produce exactly the number of units ordered (there will be no beginning or ending inventory). Variable production costs are \$15 per set of dishes. In addition, it will cost approximately \$10 per set to ship the dishes to customers.

Beverly Slater, a product manager at Elite Kitchenware, is charged with recommending a price for the item. Based on her experience with similar items, focus group responses, and survey information, she has estimated the number of units that can be sold at various prices:

Price	Quantity
\$69.99	300
\$59.99	500
\$49.99	650
\$39.99	800
\$29.99	1,000

Required

a. Calculate expected profit for each price.

b. Which price maximizes company profit?

PROBLEM 8-3. Ethics and Pricing Decisions LowCostDrugs.com is an online drugstore. Recently, the company used a computer program to analyze the purchase behavior of customers sorted by zip code and found that customers in some zip codes are, on average, less price-sensitive than customers in other zip codes. Accordingly, the company has raised prices by three percent for the customers in the less price-sensitive zip codes. Note that zip code is automatically identified when a customer comes to the company Web site.

Required

Is it ethical for LowCostDrugs.com to charge some customers a higher price based on their analysis of prior purchasing behavior?

PROBLEM 8-4. Determining the Profit Maximizing Price RoverPlus, a pet product superstore, is considering pricing a new RoverPlus labeled dog food. The company will buy the premium dog food from a company in Indiana that packs the product with a RoverPlus label. Rover pays $6 for a 50-pound bag delivered to its store.

The company also sells Royal Dog Food (under the Royal Dog Food label), which it purchases for $9 per 50-pound bag and sells for $16.99. The company currently sells 25,000 bags of Royal Dog Food per month, but that is expected to change when the RoverPlus brand is introduced.

The company will continue to price the Royal Dog Food brand at $16.99. The quantity of RoverPlus and the quantity of Royal Dog Food that will be sold at various prices for Royal are estimated as:

Price of RoverPlus	Quantity RoverPlus	Quantity Royal
$ 8.99	35,000	11,000
$ 9.99	34,500	11,300
$10.99	34,000	11,500
$11.99	33,000	12,000
$12.99	30,000	13,000
$13.99	25,000	14,000
$14.99	15,000	15,000
$15.99	10,000	19,000
$16.99	5,000	21,000

For example, if RoverPlus is priced at $8.99, the company will sell 35,000 bags of RoverPlus and 11,000 bags of Royal at $16.99. On the other hand, if the company prices RoverPlus at $16.99, it will sell 5,000 bags of RoverPlus and 21,000 bags of Royal at $16.99. This is 4,000 fewer bags of Royal than is currently being sold.

Required

a. Calculate the profit-maximizing price for the RoverPlus brand taking into account the effect of the sales of RoverPlus on sales of the Royal Dog Food brand.

b. At the price calculated in Part a, what is the incremental profit over the profit earned before the introduction of the RoverPlus branded dog food?

PROBLEM 8-5. Determining the Profit-Maximizing Price Adagio Music Publishing is a large company that publishes and prints sheet music for composers and also records and sells CDs of their compositions. Adagio is considering purchasing a line of CDs from a well-regarded composer, Jacques Elles, from another company, to be sold under the Adagio Music label. Adagio pays $6 for a CD to be delivered to its store.

The company also sells CDs of the composer Julian West, which it purchases for $8 per CD and sells for $17. The company currently sells 900 Julian West CDs per month, but that is expected to change when the Elles CD is introduced.

The company will continue to price the Julian West CD at $17. The quantity of Elles CDs and the quantity of West CDs that will be sold at various prices for Elles is estimated as:

Price of Elles CD	Quantity Elles CD	Quantity West CD
$ 9	1,000	225
$10	950	300
$11	875	375
$12	775	420
$13	600	500
$14	500	550
$15	350	600
$16	250	650
$17	175	700

For example, if the Elles CD is priced at $9, the company will sell 1,000 CDs by Elles and 225 CDs by West at $17. On the other hand, if the company prices the Elles CD at $17, it will sell 175 CDs by Elles and 700 CDs by West at $17. This is 25 fewer West CDs than is currently being sold.

Required

a. Calculate the profit-maximizing price for the Jacques Elles CD taking into account the effect of the sales of the Elles CD on sales of the Julian West CD.

b. At the price calculated in Part a, what is the incremental profit over the profit earned before the introduction of the Jacques Elles CD?

PROBLEM 8-6. Cost-Plus Pricing Wendel Stove Company is developing a "professional" model stove aimed at the home market. The company estimates that variable costs will be $2,000 per unit and fixed costs will be $10,000,000 per year.

Required

a. Suppose the company wants to set its price equal to full cost plus 30 percent. To determine cost, the company must estimate the number of units it will produce and sell in a year. Suppose the company estimates that it can sell 5,000 units. What price will the company set?

b. What is "odd" about setting the price based on an estimate of how many units will be sold?

c. Suppose the company sets a price as in part a, but the number of units demanded at that price turns out to be 4,000. Revise the price in light of demand for 4,000 units.

d. What will happen to the number of units that will be sold if the price is raised to the one you calculated in part c?

e. Explain why setting price by marking up cost is inherently circular for a manufacturing firm.

PROBLEM 8-7. Cost-Plus Pricing The product design team of Cervantes Vehicle Company is in the process of designing a new model of golf cart. The company estimates that variable costs will be $25 per unit and fixed costs will be $750,000 per year.

Required

a. Suppose the company wants to set its price equal to full cost plus 40 percent. To determine cost, the company must estimate the number of units it will produce and sell in a year. Suppose the company estimates that it can sell 7,500 units. What price will the company set?

b. Suppose the company sets a price as in Part a, but the number of units demanded at that price turns out to be 5,000. Revise the price in light of demand for 5,000 units.

c. Compare the two prices you calculated above; why are the prices different? What is likely to happen to the quantity demanded if the company is forced to raise its price to the price calculated in part b?

PROBLEM 8-8. Cost-Plus Pricing Emerson Ventures is considering producing a new line of hang gliders. The company estimates that variable costs will be $325 per unit and fixed costs will be $330,000 per year.

Required

a. Emerson has a pricing policy that dictates that a product's price must be equal to full cost plus 60 percent. To calculate full cost, Emerson must estimate the number of units it will produce and sell in a year. Emerson estimates at the beginning of the year that they will sell 1,500 gliders and sets their price according to that sales and production volume. What is the price?

b. Right after the beginning of the year, the economy takes a dive and Emerson finds that demand for their gliders has fallen drastically; Emerson revises its sales and production estimate to just 1,000 gliders for the year. According to company policy, what price must they now set?

c. What is likely to happen to the number of gliders sold if Emerson follows company policy and raises the glider price to that calculated in part b?

d. Why is setting price by marking up cost inherently circular for a manufacturing firm?

PROBLEM 8-9. Target Costing Baker Plumbing Fixtures is developing a pre-plumbed, acrylic shower unit. The team developing the product includes representatives from marketing, engineering, and cost accounting. To date, the team has developed a set of features that it plans on incorporating in the unit including a seat, two shower heads, four body sprays, and a steam unit. With this set of features, the team believes that a price of $3,500 will be attractive in the marketplace. Baker seeks to earn a per unit profit of 25 percent of selling price.

Required

a. Calculate the target cost per unit.

b. The team has estimated that the fixed production costs associated with the product will be $1,500,000 and variable costs to produce and sell the item will be $2,000 per unit. In light of this, how many units must be produced and sold to meet the target cost per unit?

c. Suppose the company decides that only 1,800 units can be sold at a price of $3,500 and, therefore, the target cost cannot be reached. The company is considering dropping the steam feature, which adds $600 of variable cost per unit. With this feature dropped, the company believes it can sell 2,500 units at $3,000 per unit. Will Baker be able to produce the item at the new target cost or less?

PROBLEM 8-10. Target Costing Symphony Sound, is designing a portable recording studio to be sold to consumers. The team developing the product includes representatives from marketing, engineering, and cost accounting. The recording studio set will include sound-canceling monitor headphones, audio recording and enhancement software, several instrumental and vocal microphones, and portable folding acoustic panels. With this set of features, the team believes that a price of $4,000 will be attractive in the marketplace. Symphony Sound seeks to earn a per unit profit of 20 percent of selling price.

Required

a. Calculate the target cost per unit.

b. The team has estimated that the fixed production costs associated with the product will be $1,860,000 and variable costs to produce and sell the item will be $2,500 per unit. In light of this, how many units must be produced and sold to meet the target cost per unit?

c. Suppose the company decides that only 2,000 units can be sold at a price of $4,000 and, therefore, the target cost cannot be reached. The company is considering dropping the folding acoustic panels, which add $750 of variable cost per unit. With this feature dropped, the company believes it can sell 2,700 units at $3,200 per unit. Will Symphony Sound be able to produce the item at the new target cost or less?

PROBLEM 8-11. Analyzing Customer Profitability Lauden Conference Solutions specializes in the design and installation of meeting and conference centers for large corporations. When bidding on jobs, the company estimates product cost and direct labor for installers and marks the total cost up by 30 percent. On a recent job for Orvieto Industries, the company set its price as follows:

Product costs including podiums, seating, lighting, etc.	$140,000
Installer salaries	20,000
Total	160,000
Markup at 30 percent	48,000
Bid price	$208,000

The job turned out to be a big hassle. Orvieto requested 20 change orders, although the dollar value of the products they requested changed very little. The company also returned 25 items that had extremely minor flaws (scratches that were barely visible and would be expected in normal shipping). Orvieto also requested six meetings with designers taking 30 hours before its plan was finalized. Normally, only two or three meetings are necessary.

Nancy Jackson, controller for Lauden, decided to conduct a customer profitability analysis to determine the profitability of Orvieto. She grouped support costs into three categories with the following drivers:

Driver	Annual value of driver	Annual cost
Change orders	700 change orders	$175,000
Number of returns	850 product returns	63,750
Design meeting hours	1,200 meeting hours	60,000

Required

a. Calculate the indirect service costs related to the job performed for Orvieto Industries.

b. Assuming that Orvieto Industries causes a disproportionate amount of indirect service costs, how should Lauden deal with this situation?

PROBLEM 8-12. Activity-Based Pricing Consider the information in Problem 8-11. Lauden Conference Solutions has decided to adopt an activity-based pricing scheme. On future jobs, the company will charge a 30 percent markup on the sum of product costs plus installer salaries. In addition, the company will charge $300 per change order, $100 per product return for products that are in excellent condition, and $75 per meeting hour with a Lauden conference room designer.

Required

a. What would the profit be on the order from Orvieto in Problem 8-11?

b. Identify pros and cons of adopting the activity-based pricing scheme.

CASES

8-1 PRESTON CONCRETE

Preston Concrete is a major supplier of concrete to residential and commercial builders in the Pacific Northwest. The company's policy is to price deliveries at 20 percent over full cost per cubic yard (including an allowance for administrative costs). At the start of 2005, the company estimated costs as follows:

Material costs = $60 per cubic yard

Delivery costs = $200,000 per year + $8 (mile) + $40 (truck hour)

Yard operation costs = $200,000 per year + $10 per cubic yard

Administrative costs =$1,000,000 per year

Delivery costs include a rate per mile, recognizing that more miles result in more gas and maintenance costs, and a rate per truck hour since, even if a delivery truck is kept waiting at a job site, the truck must be kept running (so the concrete mix will not solidify) and the driver must be paid. At the start of 2005, the company estimated that it would deliver 400,000 cubic yards.

Required

a. On October 28, Fairview Construction Company asked Preston to deliver 5,000 cubic yards of concrete. The job will require driving 7,000 miles and 250 truck hours. What will the price be if Preston follows its normal pricing policy?

b. A sharp increase in interest rates has reduced housing starts and the demand for concrete. Fairview has indicated that it will sign a firm order agreement only if the price is $86 per cubic yard. Should Pearson accept the order? Briefly indicate factors that, while hard to quantify, should be taken into account in this decision.

8-2 GALLOWAY UNIVERSITY MEDICAL CENTER PHARMACY

Galloway University Medical Center (GUMC) has a top-rated medical facility that draws patients from a three state area. On the day of discharge from the GUMC hospital, most patients fill their prescriptions from the GUMC pharmacy. However, when it comes time to renew them, they turn to a local pharmacy because that is more convenient than driving back to the GUMC pharmacy. To encourage prescription renewals, GUMC is considering offering either free overnight delivery or reduced prices on renewal orders.

Currently, the GUMC pharmacy has revenue of $50,816,000 per year on 794,000 orders. The gross margin (price minus cost of drugs) is approximately 20 percent. Free overnight delivery is expected to cost $7 per order and result in 110,000 renewal orders per year. To deal with the increased volume, the pharmacy will need to hire two pharmacists at $85,000 each per year and an additional staff person (to handle shipping) at $45,000 per year.

Alternatively, the pharmacy can generate 110,000 renewal orders per year by offering 15 percent off on the prices of renewal orders. With this option, two pharmacists must be hired, but no additional staff person will be needed.

Required

Estimate the impact on annual pharmacy profit of free delivery and "15 percent off on renewals." Which option should be selected?